C000218574

The SERPENT *and the* CROSS

The SERPENT *and the* CROSS

Religious Corruption in an Evil Age

Alan Morrison

British Library Cataloguing in Publication Data
A catalogue record for this book is available from the British Library.

Copyright © 1994 by Alan Morrison

All rights reserved. No part of this work may be reproduced, stored or introduced into a retrieval system, or transmitted, in any form or by any means (electronic, mechanical, photocopying, recording or otherwise), except for brief quotations embodied in articles or reviews, without the prior written permission of both the copyright owner and the publisher of this book.

The Scripture quotations in this publication, unless otherwise stated, are from the New King James Version, copyright © 1979, 1980, 1982, by permission of Thomas Nelson, Inc., Nashville, Tennessee, U.S.A.

First published in 1994 by K & M Books
47 Elvetham Road, Birmingham B15 2LY

Cover design by John Shakespeare.
Designed and typeset by Diakrisis, Crich, Derbyshire.
Set in 10/12 pt Times New Roman.

Printed and bound in Great Britain by
Butler & Tanner Ltd., Frome and London.

ISBN 0 9523041 0 4

Dedicated to the memory of
Irenaeus (*c.* A.D. 130 – *c.* 200),
Bishop of Lyons,
Apologist for Christian Truth
against
forbidden knowledge

TABLE OF CONTENTS

ACKNOWLEDGEMENTS

The number of people who have contributed, in some small way, to the making of this book is so extensive that to list them all in full would take many pages. But there are certain groups and individuals who stand out as being worthy of special mention.

First, I want to thank the one hundred and twenty people who generously sponsored this project so that I could be engaged in full-time writing over an eight-month period in 1992-1993. As a result of their help and determination that this project should succeed, I was able to carry out an intensive level of research which would not otherwise have been possible.

I am also indebted to the small army of proof-readers and critics who, over the years, have pored their way through a continuously developing and expanding manuscript, and who have each provided the feedback necessary to bring this work to maturity. Especially deserving of a mention are David Blunt and John Shakespeare, whose eagle eyes picked out the nits and prevented my blunders from making it into print. Their forthright suggestions and constructive criticisms have made a vital contribution to the finished product.

There are two other men who have played a particularly vital role in bringing this work to its completion. First, heartfelt thanks are due to my good friend Peter Watson, who has, from the outset, encouraged me to complete this project at times when I was ready to give it up. Always there with his indomitable, lightning humour, he has shared in all my troughs and summits over the years. Second, I am also deeply indebted to my friend and publisher, Michael Kimmitt, for having the courage to publish this book and for gently prodding me towards its completion.

This entire project would never have happened without the continual support and encouragement of my dear wife (and best critic), Catherine. The long daytime hours in libraries and long nights huddled over a computer might have driven lesser mortals to despair. But, as one who had herself spent many years exploring a maze of spiritual deceptions before discovering the truth which can only be found in Jesus Christ, she knew the grave necessity of this book in the present times. Her timely suggestions, infinite patience, and judicious advice have made an immeasurable contribution to the work you now have in your hands.

Finally, these acknowledgements would be incomplete without the open recognition that behind all the above support lies the hand of a hidden Helper. This book is a hymn of gratitude to Him for plucking me out of the fire and revealing to me the enormity of the conflagration. His sovereign power has pitted me against some seemingly impossible odds and brought me through them all — not without cost, but always, I hope, wiser and with a strengthened faith. Truly, without Him, I could have done nothing.

PREFACE

This book has been more than eight years in the making. That is how long it has taken from its original conception in 1985 to the form in which it now appears. In its earliest draft in 1987, with the title 'The New Babel', it was an idea before its time, exposing trends which most believers had never experienced and many had never even heard about. At that time, the New Age Movement was hardly known this side of the Atlantic, and such a dark view of the world and of today's churches would not have been readily accepted in many Christian circles. Having been dissuaded from pursuing the project any further, I embarked on four years of intensive study at theological college. However, there was a wise providence in this delay; for I had a great deal more to learn and discover before the time would be ripe for publication.

It was my personal experience in two particular areas during the ensuing years which made me realise the need to revive this work. First, during my time at college and as a result of being involved with a number of churches, I became convinced that there was the need for far greater understanding and discernment concerning the meaning of the term 'occult'. In many Christian circles, the occult is perceived as consisting exclusively in ouija-boards, séances, Hallowe'en and open worship of the devil. Dangerous as these activities are, I propose to show that they act as 'smoke-screens' to obscure the **real** occult — the true extent of which most Christians seem to be completely unaware. The second impulse to revive the book was the discovery that so many satanic influences which I had renounced on becoming a Christian were gaining increasing popularity within the Church and were upheld as valid Christian experience. When people start running into a building which is on fire and filled with explosives, the knowing onlooker can do only one thing: sound a clear alarm. This book is that alarm.

A cosy, 'chocolate-box' Christianity has been propagated by the mainline churches for long enough, with its associated illusion that the Church can cooperate with the world in order to bring about an age of 'peace and justice'. People have forgotten what true discipleship really involves, and from what it is that believers have been rescued (see Col.1:13). There is a ministry of discernment necessary today which involves the methodical undeceiving of the sheep from this stultifying mindset. In this way, the Church will be equipped to stand its ground and continue to fulfil the Great Commission commanded by the Lord Jesus Christ (Mt.28:18-20). Paul the Apostle would not have believers ignorant of Satan's devices (2 Cor.2:11), and this book seeks to conform to that noble desire.

As soon as one begins to cut through the surface of human movements and world events, one discovers that they are not how they appear to the undiscerning eye. The word 'occult' means hidden. Behind the facade of many developments one will discover the evil designs of fallen angels headed up by Satan, that arch-enemy of all that is good and godly. So when the Holy Scriptures tell us that *'we do not wrestle against flesh and blood, but against principalities, against powers, against the rulers of the darkness of this age, against spiritual hosts of wickedness in the heavenly places'* (Eph.6:12), this is not merely an admonition about the struggle with temptation to personal sin. It is a clear-sighted overview, through the medium of Divine revelation, of the cosmic backcloth to a titanic struggle which has continued since the beginnings of human history. This struggle began with the murderous lies of a serpent and climaxed in the life-giving Truth on a Cross. It was a movement from human catastrophe to Divine victory.

Although the means have taken many forms, the aims of the satanic realm have remained constant from the outset. Old heresies simply reassert themselves in different guises. More than eighteen hundred years ago, Irenaeus of Lyons sought to expose the Gnosticism of his era in his book, 'The Refutation of Knowledge Falsely So-Called'. In the introductory note to a modern translation of this work, A. Cleveland Coxe states that Irenaeus's principal task was twofold: *'To render it impossible for anyone to confound Gnosticism with Christianity, and to make it impossible for such a monstrous system to survive, or ever to rise again'.*†

Although he certainly succeeded in his first aim, the sad fact is that the monstrous system of Gnosticism has never been laid to rest. Instead, it went underground and lay deceptively dormant for many centuries; and during the past one hundred and thirty years it has resurfaced in modern clothing with a vengeance. For just as the Gnostic movement of the first and second centuries burst upon the Church with singular ferocity as an expression of the rage and malice of Satan after his defeat by the Lord Jesus Christ, so we are witnessing in our own day the resurgence of this rage as a backlash against the mighty progress of the Gospel during the four hundred years since the European Reformation.

This present work, therefore, sets out to show that — contrary to the fashionable thinking of many in the churches today — the development that people call the New Age Movement is not just a cult which has suddenly blossomed at the end of the twentieth century. Neither is it confined to a small number of naïve idealists in search of a spiritual utopia. For it has pervaded a great many areas of cultural life today — science, the arts, the media, medicine, education, churches, business and world government — and is ardently promoted by the Princes, Presidents and Prime Ministers of many lands. The entire concept of a 'New Age', with its political counterpart the 'New World Order', fulfils every ambition of Satan in his long war against God and in his futile kingdom-building on earth.

Unless these modern religious developments can be seen in their historical (as well as their biblical) context, we will not grasp the true significance of their purpose in the world today. In so many of the current, modern antichristian influences — including those of the New Age Movement — we can see all the

† A. Cleveland Coxe, 'Introductory Note to Irenaeus Against Heresies' in Alexander Roberts and James Donaldson (eds.) *The Ante-Nicene Fathers: Translations of the Writings of the Fathers down to A.D. 325* (Eerdmans, 1977), Vol.1, p.310.

hallmarks of the ancient heresy of Gnosticism. Indeed, after studying the extent to which these influences have pervaded society today, one can only conclude that we are living in a Gnostic world. We are now living in a culture which scoffs at the devil, demons, angels, miracles and Messiah of the Bible, yet which earnestly embraces the concepts of ETs, UFOs, spirit-guides, earth mysteries, cosmic consciousness, mind-control, magic, witchcraft, self-hypnosis, spiritism, astrology, parapsychology, and a quantum leap in human 'evolution' leading to a Golden Age on earth. *The Serpent and the Cross* is an encyclopaedic exposé of the historical development and vast modern growth of this 'New Gnosticism', in both the secular world and the professing Church.

The description of this present age as being 'evil', as in the subtitle of the book, may appear somewhat pessimistic to many people; but this is the specific label given to it in the New Testament (Gal.1:4), to say nothing of the general remarks of both the Lord Jesus Christ and His Apostles (e.g., Mt.24:37; Jn.15:18-19; Eph.6:12; 1 Jn.5:19). As this evil age draws to its inevitable climax — the crisis-point of cosmic history — this book has been written in the prayerful hope that it will fulfil three purposes:

First, my heart's desire is for the equipping of the saints that they may be wise, discerning and knowledgeable apologists who will not be dumbstruck by the widespread doctrinal delusions disseminated in the world and among the churches today. Every believer should feel great optimism concerning God's saving work in the world, and an undergirding confidence that the victory is (and always has been) His alone. Second, I see a great need to dispel the rife but erroneous notion that the world is building up to a glorious era of 'peace and justice' on earth. To cling to that illusion will only bring heartache and bewilderment as the harrowing events of the coming years inevitably unfold. Third, and above all other aims, I want to give supreme glory to our great God and Saviour at a time in earth history when His holy name has been horridly eclipsed by a defiant and blasphemous quasi-religious humanism. This book could never have been accomplished without His continual encouragement — sometimes through the most unexpected of human instruments. Neither could its completion have been achieved without His invincible protection from the dark forces which have so often, like Bunyan's Appolyon, stood menacingly in the way of my labours.

A good deal of prayerful consideration has gone into the making of this book, and it is with the greatest trepidation that I send these words out into the world (Mt.12:36-37). If you find that there is anything of value in them, account it to the work of my Master. All the rest — the ramblings, ruminations and inevitable wrongnesses — are mine alone, and for these I ask your forbearance.

Alan Morrison
The Manse
Crich
DE4 5DD

February 1994

PART ONE

THE MYSTERY OF LAWLESSNESS

The History and Foundations of Religious Corruption

'Truly, this only have I found: that God made man upright, but they have sought out many schemes'
(Ecclesiastes 7:29)

Chapter One

FATHERING THE LIE

The Fount of False Religion

'He feeds on ashes; a deceived heart has turned him aside; and he cannot deliver his soul, nor say, "Is there not a lie in my right hand?"'
(Isaiah 44:20)

At the heart of the Holy Bible lies a unique revelation: That the world in general, and the Church in particular, is involved in a spiritual battle of cosmic proportions. Behind this warfare lies an evil power beyond our conception in its depth and scope, and which — left to our own devices — we are unable to overcome. But where does this power of evil originate? How has such a situation come into being? The answer can be found in the first three chapters of the Book of Genesis. Within those pages, we have the seeds of the entire history of the cosmos — timeless truths, more astounding than the greatest science-fiction story — which provide us with the framework for a perfect understanding of every situation which now befalls the human race. Every hurt, every tragedy, all the evil, corruption, confusion, crime, violence, even death itself, can be understood through a proper grasp of the awesome truths contained in these first three chapters of the Bible.

In the beginning, there was no corruption in the world (Gen.1:31). The first human beings were created wholly sinless (Gen.1:26-27). Therefore, any form of corruption could occur only through the intervention of an outside agency. The Bible teaches that this was undertaken by a personal spirit-entity, an angel of massive power who had originally been created by God and who would later be known as Satan or the devil.[1] In the popular mind, the devil is a ridiculous anachronistic fantasy-figure, and a belief in his existence today is generally regarded with contempt, not only in the secular world but in many sections of the professing Church. One leading family encyclopaedia states under the entry for 'Devil':

> 'Contrary to popular opinion the Devil has a very minor role in the biblical writings... Strictly Jewish and Christian monotheism seems to offer no place for a Devil except as a subordinate of God, and perhaps he is best regarded as a valuable but mythological expression of the reality of evil'.[2]

---

1 The name *Satan* is derived from the Hebrew for 'adversary' or 'opponent'.

2 Christopher Cook (ed.), *Pears Family Encyclopaedia* (Pelham Books, 1985), 94th Edition.

The devil is certainly a subordinate of God, but to say that he has a very minor role in the Bible is a profoundly ignorant statement. Furthermore, as we shall come to appreciate, the destruction of his evil work in the world is at the very heart of the biblical narrative. For this reason, the devil is specifically mentioned in the Bible with great purpose, more than one hundred and forty times, under an astonishing variety of names such as Abaddon, Accuser, Adversary, Angel of the Bottomless Pit, Angel of Light, Apollyon, Belial, Beelzebub, Devil, Dragon, Evil One, Father of Lies, god of this world or age, Murderer, Ruler of Demons, Ruler of the Power of the Air, Ruler of this World, Ruler of Darkness, Satan, Serpent, Tempter and Wicked One. There are also three primary Old Testament passages which identify Satan as an angelic being (1 Chr.21:1; Job 1–2, and Zec.3:1).

The spirit-being that we know as the devil or Satan was created an angel of extremely noble rank.[3] However, at some point in the early history of the cosmos, a rebellion took place among the angels which was led by this Satan (Mt.25:41; cf. Job 4:18), resulting in the 'fall' of a vast quantity (but not the majority) of apostate angels (Rev.12:4a). There are a couple of Old Testament texts which make an oblique reference to the nature of Satan's original designation as an angel of God and to his subsequent rebellion. Although Isaiah 14:12-17 and Ezekiel 28:12-19 are, on the surface, directed respectively at the Kings of Babylon and Tyre, they far transcend the simple application to these earthly characters. Surely, there is also a figurative reference to the spirit-entity, Satan, who is behind any human activity which sets itself up against God, and who is allotted in Scripture a role as the instigator of all evil government in world-history (e.g., Dan.10:13; Jn.7:7; Rev.13:8), of which Babylon and Tyre were the chief forerunners. As Professor H.C. Leupold says, in his comment on Isa.14:12:

> 'Much to the point is Delitzsch's remark that a measure of "self-deification after the manner of the Devil and as a forerunner of the Antichrist" are to be found here (cf. Dan.11:36 and 2 Th.2:4)...Also Ezk.28:13ff. and Ps.48:2 may be compared'.[4]

Similarly, when it is stated that the king of Babylon *'shall be brought down to Sheol, to the lowest depths of the pit'* (Isa.14:15), there is surely an echo here of the fate of Satan himself. As Professor J. Ridderbos puts it, *'[the King of Babylon's] humiliation also is an example of Satan's fall from the position of power that he has usurped (cf. Luke 10:18; Rev.12:9)'*.[5] This is the root of the cardinal sin of pride. It would seem that to fall into this sin is in the capacity of the rational creature, if left to his own devices in the exercise of his freewill.[6] Tracing

---

3 That there is such rank among the angels cannot be denied in the face of the Scripture evidence; although we do not endorse the fanciful hierarchies which have been suggested in some quarters. For discussion on this, see F.S. Leahy, *Satan Cast Out: A Study in Biblical Demonology* (Banner of Truth, 1975), pp.14ff.

4 H.C. Leupold, *Exposition of Isaiah* (Baker Book House, 1976), p.260.

5 J. Ridderbos, *Isaiah* (Zondervan, 1985), p.142.

6 The fact that the majority of the angels did not fall with Satan was due to the fact that they were 'elect' (cf. 1 Tim.5:21), i.e., chosen by God and enabled to stand with Him in

things back to the earliest origins of evil, when we come to the fall of the angel, Satan, we appear to reach a dead end — a seeming moral impasse.[7] We know of no external temptation of Satan, yet this initially-pure created being led a rebellion of angels against his Creator. Here the question must be asked: *what could conceivably have led to the fall of this once glorious angelic being?*

One hesitates to speculate at this point, but three possibilities spring to mind: the first is that he had come to the conclusion that God was just as much a creature as he was, and that He was merely setting Himself up as the Creator — in which case he could just battle it out with Him in order to gain the upper hand. A second possibility is that he began to believe that there was never any creation of Divine origin, but that everything — including God Himself — had simply 'evolved' out of a 'cosmic soup'. A third possible reason for the fall of Satan is that he objected to being required to be a servant of God's human creatures, who were made *'a little lower than the angels'* (Ps.8:5). The Letter to the Hebrews describes angels as being *'ministering spirits sent forth to minister for those who will inherit salvation'* (Heb.1:14). Knowing that pride has been the devil's big problem (1 Tim.3:6), it is more than likely that it was this factor which prevented him from entertaining the idea of such service to those he would regard as lower than himself. The analogy to all this is that Jesus Christ — God manifest in the flesh — willingly humbled Himself (Phil.2:5-8), being made a little lower than the angels (Heb.2:9), in order to serve and save human beings; and through that humiliation He brought about the defeat of the one whose pride prevented him from being a servant.

This is not just worthless speculation. For it is clear that the very nub of the problem of evil in the universe is the *hubris* by which the rational creature (human or angelic) judges for himself, according to his own values, whether a thing is right or wrong. In just the same way that when *'there was no King in Israel, every man did that which was right in his own eyes'* (Jdg.21:25), so, when the creature begins to doubt that there is a King in heaven, he will build a world based on situation ethics — a world which ultimately issues in disorder, lawlessness and chaos, as we shall later show.

In spite of the goodness of the original creation, in Gen.2:15 there is a hint that there was something of which the newly created man needed to beware. When we are told that *'the LORD God took the man and put him in the garden of Eden to tend and keep it'*, the Hebrew word which is here translated as 'keep' actually means *'to guard, to protect, to hedge about (as with thorns)'*.[8] One does not build a thorn hedge around something unless one intends to keep something, or someone, out. (Today we would use barbed wire!). So there is possible confirmation here that something did indeed exist which man needed to guard against; and,

---

the event of an apostasy by the other angels. Like the divine election of humans, this is a mystery which has only been partially revealed in Scripture.

[7] It is worth noting here that his name has not always been Satan, which is the Hebrew word for 'adversary' or 'opponent', and obviously only came to be applied after his fall.

[8] *Strong's Exhaustive Concordance of the Bible*, Index No.8104.

since this warning was immediately followed — in the same breath, as it were — by the further exhortation not to partake of the fruit of the Tree of Knowledge, it would not be unreasonable to assume that they are somehow connected. In the third chapter of the Book of Genesis we will discover that connection.

The warning to 'guard the garden' turned out to be sound advice indeed — the advice of a Father to His children. For immediately after this warning, the Bible tells us that a serpent *'more cunning than any beast of the field which the LORD God had made'* (Gen.3:1) came to the first woman in creation and posed one question and made one proposition which were to change the entire course of human history. Although it is not specifically identified as such in this passage, the testimony of other Scriptures elsewhere in the Bible leave us in no doubt that this creature was an embodiment of the fallen angel, Satan (2 Cor.11:3; Rev.12:9; 20:2). We shall now see just how he set out, for the first time, in his attempt to usurp God's dominion; for within this strategy lies a simple blueprint which contains the key to all forms of human (and especially religious) corruption.

I. THE 'SATANIC INITIATION'

It is of paramount importance for us to realise that the Fall of our first parents in Eden did not only involve a flagrant act of disobedience — a clear breach of God's law which would be punishable by death. If we see the Fall *solely* in such forensic terms, we will overlook some vital elements in the subsequent religious developments of the human race. What needs to be understood is that one of the most significant primordial constituents of the Fall was the involvement of the human race in what we can call a 'Satanic Initiation' — the forging of what amounted to a compact with the devil which led directly to a descent into amorality, witchcraft, sorcery, idolatry, and every other aspect of false religious endeavour.

The use of the term 'Satanic Initiation' is a most fitting way to describe the relationship which came into being when the devil made his earliest appearance in the lives of our first parents. For through their response to this fallen angel, they were *initiated* into a relationship with him which provided a prototype for his relationship with every human being subsequently born into this world. This 'Satanic Initiation' involved three major elements: first, an enduring question; second, a threefold lie; third, a pseudo-remedy. We shall now examine these in more detail.

1. Satan's Enduring Question

Satan's first line of attack was to question the very words of God: *'Has God indeed said...?'* (Gen.3:1). In doing this, he used a strategy which would form the basis of every future attempt to undermine the unique authority of Jehovah. Since the canon of Scripture was completed — the written 'words of God', His final revelation to mankind — that same question, *'Has God indeed said...?'*, still lies behind the vast majority of the attacks on the history, theology and integrity of the Bible which have dogged the Church in the last few centuries.

2. Satan's Threefold Lie

Alongside that enduring question in satanic strategy came a threefold lie. This 'lie' is at the very heart of all that is awry in the cosmos, and is referred to by biblical writers as such — for it has continually been *'exchanged'* for the truth of God (Rom.1:25; 2 Th.2:11; cf. Rev.21:27; 22:15). It is the root of falsehood in every form and was brought into being by Satan, as is evidenced by the fact that Jesus told the Pharisees that the devil was the 'father of the lie' (Jn.8:44). This original 'lie' has three essential components which have great significance for our study into religious corruption. We shall examine these separately.

i. The Illusion of Personal Divinity

The first part of Satan's threefold lie involved the promise that our first parents would *'be like God [or gods]'* if they partook in the fruit of the tree of knowledge of good and evil (Gen.3:5). This could be referred to as the cardinal sin in the cosmos. It was the beginning of an endemic sinful process in which human beings 'strive against their Maker', imagining themselves to be unbegotten (cf. Isa.45:9-10), in the belief that there is no Transcendent Creator God and that it is human beings alone who determine their own destiny.

The significance of this aspect of the Satanic Lie for the subsequent religious development of the world is cataclysmic; for it has led to the idea that Man can become God. This has been manifested, firstly, in the practice of spiritual techniques and systems which will lead to a personal experience of the divine and even to actual 'deification' — which, as we shall discover, is an integral component in the world's religions. Secondly, it has materialised in the substitution of the creature for the Creator as the object of worship and the focus of religious power (cf. Rom.1:25), so that people worship anything **but** the true God, whether it is an image of an animal or a human being, or even themselves.

Here we see the heinous nature of idolatry. It is not merely a matter of the created being raising *his own self* up above the Creator; it is also the created being raising up *any created thing* above the Creator — to whom alone worship is due (Rev.4:11). Just take time to read the forty-fifth chapter of Isaiah. There you will find the most flesh-withering statement in the entire Bible concerning the Lord's declaration of His Creatorship over and above the creature. It is a complete denunciation of the primal sin of creature-pride, its centrepiece being the statement: *'Woe to him who strives with his Maker!'* (Isa.45:9). It is this 'striving with his Maker' which is at the heart of all the problems in the universe from the fall of Satan to the sound of the final trumpet. As Isaiah puts it elsewhere:

> 'Shall the potter be esteemed as the clay; for shall the thing made say of him who made it, "He did not make me"? Or shall the thing formed say of him who formed it, "He has no understanding"?' (Isa.29:16; cf. Rom.9:21).

The elevation of the creature above the Creator: This is the wellspring of all evil and human travail. It is surely not insignificant that the very first of the Ten Commandments states: *'You shall have no other gods before Me'* (Ex.20:3), and that the Apostle John abruptly concludes his First Letter to leave the stark warning resounding in the minds of his readers: *'Little children, keep yourselves from idols'* (1 Jn.5:21). The elevation of the creature above the Creator: the making of the creature into God. This violation of God's law is at the heart of all human civilisation throughout every age of Man. It has climaxed and expressed itself (and will again) with great vividness at certain points in history (e.g., Gen.3:6-7; 6:5,11-12; 11:4; Isa.47:10; Lk.22:52; Acts 12:21-22; 2 Th.2:4). But ripeness for the fullness of judgement on this sin will not be reached until the return of the Lord Jesus Christ, when the world-system which is under the rulership of Satan (known spiritually as 'Mystery Babylon') will finally be destroyed (Rev.18:21).

A further religious outworking of this aspect of Satan's threefold lie (*'you will be like God'*) — one which we shall be developing in some detail in the course of this book — involves the universal development of sorcery and magic, which has been defined as *'a system of beliefs and practices by which it is believed that man may control the natural and supernatural forces that affect his life'*.[9] Notice that it is said *'that **man** may control... '*, rather than God. This is yet another facet of the operation of self-divinity, the setting-up of oneself over and against the Creator. Such is the context in which the prophet Samuel spoke of rebellion and the sin of witchcraft as being directly akin to one another (1 Sam.15:23).

ii. The Attainment of Unconditional Eternal Life

A primary object of Satan's enduring question was to persuade our first parents that in following him they would *'certainly not die'* (Gen.3:4), as the Lord had originally said they would if they disobeyed Him (Gen.2:16-17). In effect, Satan was promising them unconditional eternal life. This forms the second component in his threefold lie. However, the complete reverse of what he promised actually came to pass. Because our first parents were beguiled by Satan's questioning of God's statement that they would die if they disobeyed His commandment, death then came into the world, just as the Lord has spoken (Rom.5:12). This is why Jesus said that Satan *'was a murderer from the beginning'* as well as the father of the lie (Jn.8:44). Satan promised life and instead brought death to humanity.

In terms of the outworking of religious corruption across the globe, this aspect of the lie has manifested itself in the many doctrines and philosophies which support the notion of unconditional eternal life, such as reincarnation, spiritualism, and the undergoing of out-of-the-body experiences (known as 'obes') and alleged after-death states of bliss, etc. In short, initiation into this lie has led to the ready acceptance of any religious experience which Satan can use to convince people that God does not punish sin and that everyone goes to heaven unconditionally.

iii. The Acquisition of Forbidden Wisdom

The third part of Satan's threefold lie was to persuade our first parents that they could acquire a level of wisdom over and above that with which they had been endowed by their Creator: *'And when she saw that it was a tree desirable to make one wise... '* (Gen.3:6). The clear implication in Satan's strategy here was that

[9] *Macmillan Encyclopedia* (Macmillan, 1986), p.759.

there was some special, esoteric knowledge which God was concealing from His human creation, the acquisition of which would enhance their lives. In fact, Satan's suggestion was that God was being a 'dog-in-the-manger' by denying our first parents the possibility of having their eyes opened and being like Him (see Gen.3:5). In other words, the fallen angel was suggesting that God was wrongfully making an exclusive claim to the attribute of divine wisdom which could, in reality, be acquired by anyone. The outworking of this strategy, in terms of subsequent religious corruption, has been centred on the fascination with esoteric teachings as found in occult-mystical belief systems and the mystery religions. In common with the majority of the world's religions, they hold to the idea that one can be initiated into a body of 'higher-wisdom-teachings' which will bring about supernatural change and even deification.[10]

3. Satan's Pseudo-Remedy

Once our first parents had rejected the commandment of their Creator and received an initiation into Satan's ways, they also became aware of their state of separation from God and of the disruption of the Edenic accord through their disobedience: *'Then the eyes of both of them were opened, and they knew that they were naked'* (Gen.3:7). It must have been a devastating experience, in the wake of what was, in effect, a spiritual suicide and parricide.

Immediately, this guilty couple set about trying to redeem their situation through their own efforts: *'and they sewed fig leaves together and made themselves coverings'* (Gen.3:7). In order to counteract the devastating nature of their predicament, our first parents originated the first attempt at self-reformation in the history of the world.[11] Here was the prototype for all humanistic philosophies, ideologies and actions: The illusion that we can put things to rights without coming in submission to God — what we can call the 'Law of Godless Reformation'. Jesus Himself described the folly of the kind of reformation which is not inspired by the Holy Spirit in His vivid story of the banished unclean spirit returning to the empty house, swept clean, with *'seven other spirits more wicked than himself'* (Mt.12:43-45; Lk.11:24-26; cf. Job 31:33; Pro.28:13). Who can forget the Lord's solemn warning that *'the last state of that man is worse than the first'* (Mt.12:45), with its clear implication that all forms of Spirit-less reformation will result in even greater evil than that from which people originally sought to be delivered?

In this 'Satanic Initiation' received by our first parents — his enduring question, threefold lie and pseudo-remedy — we now have a complete model for all subsequent development of the human race. It is of vital importance for us to grasp the supernatural significance of the events recorded in these verses of Scripture and the cataclysmic effect they have had on the world-system and are still having on our lives today. As a judgement on the ready response of the first human pair to the suggestions of the devil, the whole world-system became distorted

---

[10] Even in those religions which do not profess such 'higher-wisdom-teachings', one will find sects which do. An example of this is the Sufi sect of Islam.

[11] The offerings of Cain, who belonged to Satan (1 Jn.3:12), provide another early illustration of the religious pseudo-remedy (Gen.4:3-7).

— shot through with imperfection. Until the human acceptance of Satan's lies there was no such thing as death; and, even though the Lord's human creation had been entrusted with the responsibility of work (Gen.2:15), this was to have been a wholly rewarding activity, complete in its perfection, under the blessing of its Creator (Gen.1:28-31). The Edenic accord was, however, shattered and the Lord pronounced a just judgement on His creation.

For the woman, there would be a multiplying of conception, which would become a painful event. Her motherhood would be fraught with sorrow, and in her marital relations she would become subjugated to her husband (Gen.3:16). For the man, his working conditions were to be affected; the ground would be cursed and bring forth weeds alongside the fieldcrop, which would be harvested amidst great toil (Gen.3:17-18). These would become the universal conditions of men and women from that time henceforth. Physical death, too, was to become a part of life (having not been built into the original creation, Gen.3:19), in fulfilment of the Lord's earlier promise (Gen.2:17). As Paul the Apostle was later to say: *'Through one man sin entered the world, and death through sin, and thus death spread to all men, because all sinned'* (Rom.5:12). Adam's sin was the sin of us all. Original sin. His guilt is ours also. It is for this reason that we can all cry out with the psalmist: *'Behold, I was brought forth in iniquity, and in sin my mother conceived me'* (Ps.51:5; cf. Mk.7:21-23).

Today we can see the results of the combination of our ancestral sin and this life-distorting curse working through such things as poverty, famine, warfare, terrorism, earthquakes, marital discord, adolescent rebellion, poor labour relations, addictions, criminality, sexual immorality, anarchism, cruelty, narcissism, disease, disasters, bereavement and every human heartache imaginable. The fact that a lengthy but indeterminable time has passed between the events of early Genesis and our own century is irrelevant. We are still busily, though largely ignorantly, working out the effects of the Fall at the end of the twentieth century.

Before moving through history as we trace the subsequent development of religious corruption in the world and among the people of God, let us focus on a highly relevant aspect of the Fall which provides the background to all forms of corruption — whether religious or ethical: the original satanic *gnosis*, the deadly knowledge into which Satan initiates all his subjects.

II. THE SATANIC GNOSIS

A radical part of the 'Satanic Initiation' — into which all the descendants of Adam have been plunged (Rom.5:12) — was the receiving of the fruit of the Tree of the Knowledge of Good and Evil. The question arises here: What exactly is this *'knowledge of good and evil'* which is associated with the disobedience to the Lord's command? We know that it cannot be the simple human knowledge to discern the difference between what is right and what is wrong. Our first parents already had such a *human* knowledge of good and evil. For we can deduce from other places in Scripture that the Law of God was 'written on their hearts' (cf. Rom.2:14-15); and if they had not understood the difference between good and evil, the Lord would not have given them a commandment not to eat of the tree in the midst of the Garden of Eden. So the knowledge of good and evil referred to here is no ordinary knowledge of right and wrong. Instead, when the Scripture here speaks of the ability to 'know good and evil', it is stressing that this knowledge is a knowledge *comparable to that of God.* This is clear from the context in Genesis 3, and is explicitly stated in vv.5 and 22a. Clearly the text is referring to something which is the prerogative of God and God alone: namely, that knowledge which enables one to *determine for oneself* what is good and what is evil. But only God can really *know* good and evil in such a manner.

So, this promise of Satan does not refer to any natural, human knowledge of good and evil; it refers rather to the *usurpation of God's exclusive knowledge and dispensing of these matters*, which is so vast in comparison to our puny comprehension that He can work all things (even evil things) together for the higher good (see, e.g., Gen.50:20; cf. Rom.8:28). Man can never really do that, even though he may convince himself that he can. What has therefore happened in the wake of the Fall is that Man has set himself up as the sole arbiter of what is good and what is evil for the world and for his future, thus 'dethroning God' — under His warrant and permission — from what is, by rightful order, His unshared privilege. In other words, Man, who was not satisfied to be simply the *image* of God, determined to make himself into an actual 'god'. This was the satanic *gnosis*; and it was a principal consequence of the Fall.

How has this self-imposed condition of man as the sole determiner of what is good and evil worked itself out in the development of the human race? There are two principal areas in which we can see the corrupt post-Fall outworkings of human beings setting themselves up as their own gods — as doing that which is right in their own eyes (cf. Dt.12:8; Jdg.21:25; Pro.3:7; 12:15; 21:2; 30:12; Isa.5:21). The first of these is that of *morality* (cf. Rom.1:24-32), while the second is that of *religion* (cf. Rom.1:18-23). Remember that the Fall of Man in Eden did not *merely* involve disobedience to the Creator; it actually embodied a total seduction — moral and spiritual — into the ways of Satan, which has reverberated down the corridors of time with disastrous results.

In the area of *morality*, this self-determination manifests itself in an almost infinite variety of ways: Situation ethics, the lust for power, naked greed and unholy ambition, marital infidelity, contraceptive abortion, homosexuality, fornication, — human beings determining what is right for themselves, without any reference to God's revelation and His will for His creation. This moral degeneration affects all applications of human knowledge (i.e., *gnosis*, science) to a greater or lesser degree. It is the epitome of that *'knowledge falsely so-called'* (1 Tim.6:20) which opposes God's truth. As far as *religion* is concerned, some of the ways that this self-determination has repeatedly manifested itself are in idolatry, apostasy, syncretism, sorcery, mysticism, magic, witchcraft and occultism. Man become 'God', determining what is best for himself without any reference to the One who is the fount of all life and creation.

As we will come to appreciate during the course of this book, all corrupt religious endeavours and enterprises have their source in the relationship which our first parents contracted with the devil, in which he questioned the truth of God's words (*'Has God indeed said...?'*, Gen.3:1), promised unconditional eternal life (*'You will not surely die'*, Gen.3:4), pledged the experience of personal 'divinity' (*'You will be like God'*, Gen.3:5), and fostered the desire for wisdom beyond that which God had originally bestowed on His human creation (Genesis 3:6). Added to this was the self-help approach to spirituality: the attempt at salvation solely through their own efforts (*'and they sewed fig leaves together and made themselves coverings'*, Gen.3:7). This merely signifies the desperate *humanistic* attempts which have been made to try and rectify the tragedy of the post-Fall human condition: that of alienation from God. What this has come to mean is that any form of political or personal reformation in a Godless society, although often having an appearance of humanitarian benefit, actually leads in the long term to increased evil: The Law of Godless Reformation.

We have now gathered together all the elements of the Fall which would be pertinent to the future development of humanity. Let us now examine these corrupt outworkings in greater detail — especially in their application to the progress of world religion and the global political structures of the nations.

III. THE SATANIC WORLD-SYSTEM

So often, professing Christians seem to forget that the devil, from the very beginning, has not only been a liar and a murderer, but has also been hell-bent on setting up his kingdom on earth as a demonstration of his imagined superiority to Jehovah, his God and Creator, and in gross, earthly imitation of the spiritual Kingdom of God which the Lord is effecting.

So we have a double kingdom conflict: The kingdom of God, which is built on reality, invisible to the eye yet everlasting; and the kingdom of Satan, which is an illusion, founded in the world and temporary. This conflict shapes all of world history from the Fall to the Final Trump, and was ordained to be that way by God Himself (Gen.3:15). Jesus endorsed this same conflict when He said: *'Do not think that I came to bring peace on earth. I did not come to bring peace but a sword'* (Mt.10:34). And again: *'Do you suppose that I came to give peace on earth? I tell you, not at all, but rather division'* (Lk.12:51). The division occurs naturally. The one group ('the sheep') hears Christ's voice and goes into the spiritual kingdom of God; the other group ('the goats') rejects the claims of Christ and remains in Satan's earthly kingdom (Jn.10:1-5; 2 Cor.2:14-16; Mt.25:31ff.). The setting-up of his kingdom on earth has been Satan's aim from the commencement of human history. It is interesting to discover that the Greek word *antichristos,* antichrist, can be translated as '*instead of* Christ' as well as '*against* Christ'.[12] Hence, Satan's great cause in these last days is the final establishment of his kingdom on earth in crass counterfeit of the spiritual kingdom of Christ.

From the moment that the Fall had been enacted in human history, a whole new *'world'* came into being — a world which had the devil firmly at its helm

---

[12] The Greek prefix, *anti-*, can mean both 'against' and 'in the place of'.

(although under the permissive will of God). It is precisely this 'world-system', under the dominion of Satan, which was being referred to by the Lord Jesus Christ when He described Satan as *'the ruler of this world'* whom He had come to *'cast out'* (Jn.12:31). From the time that our first parents turned away from their Creator, a whole new *'world'* came into being — a world based on sin, which is enmity towards God and the lawless abandonment of His commandments — a world which was to last throughout history, until the return of the Lord Jesus Christ and His subsequent judgement of it. This 'world' over which Satan has dominion refers, therefore, to that imperfect society of man which has set itself up in opposition to God, and which has been in total conflict with God and the kingdom He has been building since the time of the Fall. This ages-long 'kingdom-conflict' became an intrinsic element in world history, not through the will of Satan, but by the judgement of God. As the Lord cursed the serpent, that embodiment of the devil (Gen.3:14), He also foretold to Satan what would be the outcome of his actions in subverting God's innocent creation:

> 'And I will put enmity between you and the woman, and between your seed and her Seed; He shall bruise your head, and you shall bruise His heel' (Gen.3:15).

We should carefully examine these words. Not only are they multi-layered in meaning but they have supreme significance for an understanding of all subsequent developments in the course of world history. The phrase *'enmity between...your seed and her Seed'* is a prefiguration of the spiritual battle which lies at the heart of the biblical message. On a general level this battle is between, on the one hand, every regenerated human being from the Old and New Covenant eras (the seed of Eve), and on the other hand, Satan's fallen angelic accomplices, together with those influenced by them on earth (cf. Jn.8:44, *'offspring of vipers'*, Mt.3:7; 12:34; 23:33). Theologians refer to this as the 'Antithesis' — a spiritual battle of cosmic proportions which was set to last until the return of the Lord Jesus Christ at the Last Day. The Bible is the revelation both of this spiritual battle and the God-given antidote to the evil engendered by the Fall.

It is in this last respect that there is yet another dimension to this Gen.3:15 passage, in that 'the seed of the woman' refers to Jesus Christ Himself (who was descended, via Abraham and David, from Eve, cf. Lk.3:23-38) and was also, literally, born of a woman (the virgin Mary) rather than both man and woman (Gal.4:4). This verse has been called the 'Protevangelium', the first glimmering proclamation of the Gospel and announcement of the coming of Christ. Indeed, the Incarnation of Christ certainly dealt a death-blow to Satan, as foretold in the phrase *'He shall bruise your head'*. There is a sense also in which the New Testament Church actually participates in this crushing of Satan (Rom.16:20a) as *'joint heirs with Christ'* and co-conquerors (Rom.8:17, 37), through *'the word of their testimony'* and the yielding of their will to God (Rev.12:11; cf. Lk.14:26). The Lord's prediction that Satan would bruise the *heel* of the woman's seed refers to both the general oppression of the Lord's people by Satan, as well as the more particular affliction of Christ at His crucifixion — a fact which finds an echo in the Book of Isaiah in his prophecy of the coming Christ: *'He was wounded for our transgressions, He was bruised for our iniquities'* (Isa.53:5).

Now Satan had heard it from God, in this saying in Gen.3:15, that there was One coming who would devastate him; and the Old Testament reveals successive attempts by the would-be ruler of the world to destroy the Seed of the Woman whom he knew was the only one who could take his usurped rulership from him. Before we go further into this, it is worth noting that after the Fall had occurred, the Lord, to fulfil His own purposes, permitted Satan to continue to have access to heaven, acting as *'accuser'* — a powerful cosmic role in which the fallen angel has been used by God for the refining of the saints. In the same way that sin mysteriously hardens the hearts of humans, making them progressively insensitive to the sinful nature of their behaviour (Heb.3:12-13; Ex.9:12; Jos.11:20; Isa.63:17; cf. 2 Th.2:11-12), so Satan has, in some equally mysterious manner, been hardened to his own sin, believing his own lies and feeling no contrition before the Lord (Isa.44:20). In his role as 'accuser', Satan was permitted to come before the throne of God and point out the sins, faults and weaknesses of God's chosen ones (e.g., Job 1:6-12; 2:1-10; Zec.3:1-2; cf. 1 Kgs.22:19-23).

Coupled with this, Satan was also permitted to exercise a far-reaching power over the nations as conglomerate entities. This was especially obvious in the demeanour of those surrounding, opposing and subverting the developing chosen nation, Israel. In this way, he came to have control over the religious affairs (e.g., Dt.32:17), politics, morality and war plans (Lev.18:1-24; 20:1-23; Dan.10:13,20) of the nations, as well as over the lives of individuals through indiscriminate demonic possession and affliction, which had reached a crisis point by the time of our Lord's ministry on earth, when He was confronted by a great many unclean spirits (e.g., Mk.1:34; 6:13; 16:9).[13] But exactly how far did Satan's dominion extend prior to the coming of the Lord Jesus Christ?

When Satan showed Jesus *'all the kingdoms of the world'* (Lk.4:5) — believing himself to be their ruler and owner — he was referring to the kingdoms of the biblical world. Human kingdoms in Scripture have consistently proven themselves to bear the satanic hallmark: they are invariably an attempt by humanity to create a grand, collective powerbase, independent of God (cf. Ps.2:1). Among these monolithic, humanistic empires have been the Babylonian (*c*.3500 – 538 B.C.), Egyptian (*c*.3000 – 332 B.C.), Assyrian (*c*.2250 – 612 B.C.), Medo-Persian (538 – 332 B.C.), Graeco-Macedonian (333 – *c*.200 B.C.), and the Roman (*c*.200 B.C. – A.D. 476). From any high mountain near the Jordan it would be possible to see some part of each of these historical empires, of which the most significant and powerful by far was ancient Babylon.

In the post-diluvian world, Babylon, whose later dynasties are recorded in the Bible, is directly derived from the Sumero-Mesopotamian kingdom initiated by

---

[13] Although Satan has controlled these affairs of the nations, the Bible always makes it clear that it is God who is in ultimate control of the nations which He alone ordained should come into being after His judgement at Babel (see Gen.11:9; Acts 17:26; 2 Chr.20:6; Ps.22:28; Rev.12:5).

Nimrod at Shinar (Gen.10:10), the most ancient 'cradle of human civilisation' and seedbed of the mystery-religions, occultism and idolatry — of **all** that which attempts to set itself up against God. The culture, government and religion of Babylon recorded throughout Scripture are a cumulative human representation of the satanic endeavour to 'outgod God', to *'be like the Most High'* (Isa.14:14). On a spiritual level, Babylon is the means (as a counterfeit of God's plan) through which, from the earliest human history, Satan's evil philosophy (his 'Initiation' strategy) worms its way into the religious developments of the world. The ultimate purpose of this has been the creation of an anti-Jehovah world-system — known in Scripture as *'Mystery Babylon'* — which would set itself up against the redemptive plan of God, but which will surely be destroyed when the Lord Jesus returns at the end of this present evil age (Rev.17:1 – 18:24).

The satanic world-system and religion was introduced for the first time on the planet earth at the beginning of human history in Eden, when the invitation to *'be like God'* was compounded with the knowledge and wisdom which Satan, posing as the 'Bringer of Light' (Lucifer), imparted to our first parents. After the Fall, the ungodly progeny fathered by Cain carried the 'Satanic Initiation' through to the time of the Flood. The wickedness at that time became so great that the Lord had to intervene with the judgement of a universal Flood (Gen.6–9). During the following period of renewed human development in the post-diluvian world, this 'Satanic Initiation' worked especially through the line of Ham (Genesis 10:6-10), culminating in the episode at Babel in Sumero-Mesopotamia, the cradle of ancient cultures and religions.

In order to trace the biblical root of Babylon, we must go back to the time when *'the whole earth had one language and one speech'* (Gen.11:1). Previous civilisation had been wiped out by the Flood, and Noah's great-grandchild, a man called Nimrod, started a kingdom which was centred in a part of Mesopotamia known as Shinar. Within this kingdom lay the city which came to be known as Babel.[14] This Nimrod is referred to as being *'a mighty one on the earth'* and *'a mighty hunter before the LORD'* (Gen.10:8-9). The phrase *'before the LORD'* carries the significance of being *'in the face of the LORD'*, in the sense of setting himself up as something special in front of God — as in our phrase 'to fly in the face of...'. When we learn that the name Nimrod comes from the Hebrew verb-form *nimrodh*, 'let us revolt or rebel',[15] we have here an image of a potentate setting himself up against God and building an earthly kingdom *'in his own strength'*. Thus, not only is this Nimrod in the image of his father Satan, but he is also a type of the ultimate rebel, the *'man of lawlessness'*, prophesied by the Apostle Paul as heading up the spiritual Babel of the End-time (2 Th.2:2-12).

It had not taken very long since the time of the Flood for the evil, self-seeking heart of humanity to reassert itself. The Babel of Nimrod's kingdom was set up in direct contravention of God's earlier covenant with Noah, which stipulated that all his descendants, in the wake of the Flood, should *'Be fruitful and multiply, and*

---

[14] Babylon is the Greek rendering of the Hebrew word *babel*.

[15] H.C. Leupold, *Exposition of Genesis* (Wartburg Press, 1942), p.366.

fill the earth' (Gen.9:1). Instead of obeying this edict, the entire peoples of that time had gathered themselves together in one place, *'in the land of Shinar, and they dwelt there'* (Gen.11:2). With flagrant wilfulness, these people had said:

> 'Come, let us build ourselves a city, and a tower whose top is in the heavens; let us make a name for ourselves, lest we be scattered abroad over the face of the whole earth' (Gen.11:4).

In other words, they were collectively setting up the first one-world, ecumenical, autonomous, political and religious state-system. This is the epitome of spiritual pride and a sure pointer to the satanic origins of this human endeavour. Notice the striking similarity between the above statement and that of the king of Babylon as a type of Antichrist and echo of Satan: *'I will ascend into heaven, I will exalt my throne above the stars of God'* (Isa.14:13). The so-called Tower of Babel (Gen.11:1-9),[16] the ultimate monument to human ambition, pride and rebellion against God, was probably the first recorded instance of what later came to be known as 'ziggurats' — huge pyramid-like structures with seven levels, of which the highest (*'whose top is in the heavens'*) was reserved for the gods to come down and have sexual intercourse with a chosen woman of the city, in the magical belief that this would result in increased fertility of the land.[17] This was the climax of human 'civilisation': The epitome of man striving against his Maker.

IV. THE SATANIC ROOTS OF WORLD RELIGION

The result of this episode in human history was a judgement from God which was to have a momentous effect on the religious practices of the biblical world and of all later civilisation. The cult of this early Sumerian civilisation involved a highly organised system of deities, divination, myths, magical spells and incantations,[18] so the divine decision to confound the language of these people (Gen.11:7) not only ensured that their project came to an end but, because the Lord *'scattered them abroad from there over the face of all the earth'* (Gen.11:8), this also contributed towards the worldwide transmission of these religious practices. This must surely account for the extraordinary similarity of the myths, sorceries and deities of so many subsequent pagan traditions,[19] with each tradition developing

---

[16] The word *babel* is derived from the Assyrian *bab-ili*, meaning 'gate of god', which is how the self-exalting Babylonians viewed their *ziggurats*. The use of the word here in Genesis is a deliberate play on the Hebrew word *babil*, meaning 'to mix up' or 'confound'. Our English word 'babble' is probably derived from this.

[17] This was not the first biblically-recorded instance of the folly of trying to be a somebody — a person of consequence, who desires to make a name for himself in this way. Many years earlier, the ungodly murderer Cain had *'built a city, and called the name of the city after the name of his son'* (Gen.4:17), an act of vanity later to be derided by the psalmist as *'the way of those who are foolish'* (Ps.49:11-13).

[18] See Kurt Seligman, *Magic, Supernaturalism and Religion* (Granada, 1975), pp.27–40.

[19] There are two points worth noting here in support of this: **1)** That antiquities of indisputable Sumero-Mesopotamian origin have inexplicably been found in archaeological excavations sixteen-hundred miles away in the Indus Valley region (*Chambers's*

idiosyncratically according to the culture in which it was to unfold.[20] Yet, how had all these pagan practices arisen in the first instance, prior even to the atrocity on a plain in Shinar? The Bible shows that at the outset of human history God had clearly revealed Himself to all in the world. As the prophecy of Isaiah states:

> 'Have you not known? Have you not heard? Has it not been told you from the beginning? Have you not understood from the foundations of the earth? It is He who sits above the circle of the earth, and its inhabitants are like grasshoppers, who stretches out the heavens like a curtain, and spreads them out like a tent to dwell in. He brings the princes to nothing; he makes the judges of the earth useless' (Isa.40:21-23).

So, the principal revelation of the Lord was through the works of creation in nature: *'The heavens declare the glory of God; and the firmament shows His handiwork'* (Ps.19:1). Whatever the moral or spiritual state of humanity, the Lord has always been in evidence through this medium and He has never left Himself without a witness (Acts 14:17). Therefore, in God's eyes, the denial of His existence or the worshipping of other gods (which are *'not gods, but the work of men's hands, wood and stone'*, Isa.37:19) is an abomination to Him (Dt.7:25-26) and thoroughly inexcusable. The Apostle Paul demonstrates this when he says:

> 'For the wrath of God is revealed from heaven against all ungodliness and unrighteousness of men, who suppress the truth in unrighteousness, because what may be known of God is manifest in them, for God has shown it to them. For since the creation of the world His invisible attributes are clearly seen, being understood by the things that are made, even His eternal power and Godhead, so that they are without excuse' (Rom.1:18-20).

Yet, because of our fallen nature, this general revelation of God has not proved to be sufficient for our faithfulness to Him. The satanic lie that human beings can build up this world independent from the design of its Creator has turned people from the simplicity of obedience towards Him, resulting in the invention of other

---

Encyclopaedia, Vol.VII, p.457), and **2)** In spite of the fact that many facets of Sumerian religion and culture can be identified in many other cultures, no trace of the Sumerian language — that spoken by the builders of the biblical Babel — can be found in any other language of the world, living or dead (*Chambers's Encyclopaedia*, Vol.XIII, p.279). Both of these factors lend considerable external evidence to the biblical affirmation in Genesis 11 of a confounded universal language and scattered culture.

[20] This does not mean that *every* religion and cult of today has its *direct* historical roots in Babel. There are really two classes of false (i.e., Satan-fathered) religion: first, those which have their roots directly in the ancient occultic religion of Babel; second, those which have arisen since that time as a result of the oracular revelation of a multitude of demonically-inspired men and women. The demonstrably ancient religions (e.g., Shamanism and Hinduism) fall into the first category; while cults such as Baha'ism, Buddhism, Lamism, Taoism, Mormonism, Jehovah's Witnesses, Islam, Christian Science, etc., belong to the second category, having been founded by various people who claim to have received direct revelation from the 'spiritual realm'.

gods *in our image* or of other creatures which can be manipulated for the enhancement of a godless world-system. As Paul continued in his exposé of the origins of false religion, although people knew God,

> ' they did not glorify Him as God, nor were thankful, but became futile in their thoughts, and their foolish hearts were darkened. Professing to be wise, they became fools, and changed the glory of the incorruptible God into an image made like corruptible man — and birds and four-footed beasts and creeping things' (Rom.1:21-23).

This was the state, first, of the ante-diluvian world, necessitating judgement (Gen.6:12), and again on a plain in Shinar when the mighty tower was built (Gen.11:1-9). However, God had been revealed both *outwardly*, through nature, and *inwardly* through conscience. Regardless of the depravity of human nature brought into being by the Fall, human beings have always retained what Benjamin Warfield refers to as a *notitia Dei insita* (a natural knowledge of God) and what John Calvin refers to as a *Divinitatis sensum* (awareness of divinity) and a *semen religionis* (seed of religion) in their hearts.[21] As Calvin puts it: *'There are two principal parts of the light which still remains in corrupt nature: first, the seed of religion is planted in all men; next, the distinction between good and evil is engraved on their consciences'*.[22] All this provides an inner witness which should convict us of our guilt before God (Rom.2:14-15; cf. Acts 24:25).

However, in spite of this, the bulk of humanity has generally opted for whatever seemed right in its own eyes. Our Creator has waited patiently for His people to seek Him, *'in the hope that they might grope for Him and find Him'* (Acts 17:27), for He is always near and ready to respond. Yet, tragically, human history shows that this world has consistently *'exchanged the truth of God for the lie, and worshipped and served the creature rather than the Creator'* (Rom.1:25). Although this has arisen principally through the actions of our sinful nature, there is also interaction with the demonic realm, which seeks to interfere with our spiritual relationship with God. This was the legacy of the Fall: universal strife, hardness of heart and worldwide religious corruption — with every human child born on this planet being open to interference from the satanic powers. Hence, John can describe the whole world as lying *'under the sway of the wicked one'* (1 Jn.5:19), while Paul warns us that *'we do not wrestle against flesh and blood, but against principalities, against powers, against the rulers of the darkness of this age, against spiritual hosts of wickedness in the heavenly places'* (Eph.6:12).

It is clear from Scripture that the whole of human history is built around a battle involving these *'rulers of the darkness of this age'*, a vast pantheon of wicked spirit-entities of varying rank and ability, under the rulership of a once-mighty, but now fallen, angelic being (Eph.2:2; 6:10-18). These evil entities have invaded the life of humanity at every level — much of which we just take for granted —

---

21 Benjamin B. Warfield, *Biblical and Theological Studies* (P. & R., 1968), p.567. See also F.L. Battles (trans.), *John Calvin: Institutes of the Christian Religion*, Book I, Chapter iii, §1, (Westminster Press, 1960), Vol.I, pp.43-44.

22 F.L. Battles, op. cit., Vol.I, p.43n.

tempting, perverting, twisting and deceiving, posing as angels of light in order to bring to fruition the aims of this evil age. This has especially been the case in relation to the desire of Satan to destroy the 'seed of the woman' — the promised Redeemer — which he had heard promised by God, as recorded in Gen.3:15. Many times throughout history Satan tried to flush out this Redeemer; but because the devil is not omniscient, it was just a matter of hit-and-miss down the ages.

First, he sought to destroy Abel through his envoy, Cain (Gen.4:8; 1 Jn.3:12); but God raised up Seth in his place (Gen.4:25). Then he tried to pollute the godly line of Seth with an unprecedented outburst of demonic evil (Gen.6:1-2); but God raised up Noah with his immediate family and drowned the rest of the world's population (Gen.6:8). The old serpent subsequently tried to have every male child in Israel killed at birth by the midwives; but God made provision to ensure that this would not succeed (Ex.1:15-22). Later, he stirred up Queen Athaliah to murder all the royal heirs of Judah (from which ancestral line the Lord Jesus would come); but Jehosheba hid little Joash — the last royal heir in line — in the recesses of the temple for six years (2 Kgs.11:1-3). Satan then stirred up Haman to destroy all the Jews (Est.3:6); but they were miraculously delivered at the expense of their Gentile enemies (Est.9:1-17). In the fullness of time, when the Lord Jesus was born, Satan used his servant Herod to issue an edict that all the male babies under two years of age in Bethlehem and its environs should be killed (Mt.2:16-18); but that too was an abortive measure. Finally, he attempted to destroy the Lord Jesus Himself by inciting his earthly agents to crucify Him (e.g., Lk.4:28-30; Jn.11:53; Luke 23:8-12; cf. Acts 4:27-28). But it is a singular fact that *every* act of Satan in history has been an abject failure, rebounding ultimately on himself, leading to his own eventual judgement (Rev.20:10).

The world-system under the rulership of Satan has always sought to kill God and His Christ. This is the secret desire of every unregenerate man and woman in the cosmos; and the spiritual battle initiated by Satan in Eden came to its climax in the attempted "killing off" of God in Christ by the rulers of the world (see Psalm 2). The political, philosophical and religious systems of the mighty kingdoms and empires of this fallen world have always belonged to Lucifer, inasmuch as he has been the driving force behind that incongruous mixture of wisdom and tyranny, science and sorcery, cultural achievement and despotism, social sophistry and violence, great art and idolatry — all matching the character of Lucifer the Lightbearer: outstandingly brilliant, extremely knowledgeable, unfathomably mystical — yet all ultimately in the service of self, degenerating into hypocrisy and hedonism, autocracy and base magic. As Solomon knew only too well: *'Pride goes before destruction, and a haughty spirit before a fall'* (Pro.16:18).

The whole world, therefore, since the time of the Fall in Eden, has been engaged in constant conflict with the powers of darkness — those invisible spiritual entities who dwell in another dimension, seeking to tyrannise human affairs at both individual and global levels, and attempting to undermine God's plan of redemption. However, Jesus Christ, *'the Son of God was manifested, that He might destroy the works of the devil'* (1 Jn.3:8; cf. Heb.2:14-15) and draw a redeemed people to Himself (Jn.6:35-40,44; 10:14-16; Tit.2:13-14). This is the primary purpose of the thread of redemption running through the Scriptures: the ultimate reversal of the degenerative, cosmos-changing effects of the Fall (Heb.2:14-15).

However, until such time as the Lord Jesus returns to the earth to judge the world, gather His people, and bring in the New Heavens and New Earth, the process of degeneration will continue to spread into every area of human existence. Even the Church is not exempt from this process. Although it is true that the body of Christ — the Church spiritually-discerned — is forensically pure and spotless on the basis of the finished work of the Lord Jesus Christ (Eph.5:25-27; 1 Pet.1:14-20), the sad fact is that the institutions of the Church as manifested in this present world have always tended towards corruption to a greater or lesser degree, and will continue to do so until the end of the present Age. This theme will form the focus of a major part of this book. The following section provides an introduction to this process, while bringing the present chapter to its conclusion.

V. THE SATANIC CORRUPTION OF THE CHURCH

> 'Beware lest anyone cheat you through philosophy and empty deceit, according to the tradition of men, according to the basic principles of the world, and not according to Christ' (Col.2:8).

So said the Apostle Paul, warning the church at Colossae of spiritual atrophy and compromise. From time immemorial and until the first coming of the Lord Jesus Christ, the satanic forms of religion had held all the nations of the world in spiritual bondage. This is why students and practitioners of the occult refer to their craft as the 'Ancient Religion' or 'Ancient Wisdom Tradition'. The occultists of today hark back, with great approval, to the times when this religion was internationally practised under a variety of guises such as fertility cults, shamanism, tribal witchcraft, Druidism, the 'mystery' religions, and so on. The Old Testament nation of Israel came into being within the context of a proliferation of such satanic influences among the nations of the world. The Lord was purifying a people for Himself, a *'special treasure'* (Ex.19:5-6), from the midst of this spiritual debauchery. The Old Testament faithfully records the spiritual battle between this new holy nation which was called to practise obedience to God's law, and the surrounding nations which practised the satanic religion in the form of false god and goddess worship, demon and spirit invocation, ecstatic trance-states, temple prostitution, sex magic, witchcraft, idolatry, divination, etc.

However, the spirituality of the Lord's chosen nation, Israel, repeatedly degenerated as time went by, thus demonstrating two great principles of spiritual life which the Lord wishes us to know. First, that an adherence to the Old Covenant law can only serve, at best, to make those who so strive painfully aware of their essential defects and the collective fallen nature of humanity (Rom.3:19-20), while at the same time exposing the intrinsic inadequacy of that law to truly sanctify us (Heb.10:1). Second, that through an understanding of this inadequacy we are brought to the realisation that we need a Divine Mediator (Gal.3:19-20), without whom we can do nothing.

By the time of Jesus' earthly ministry, religious practice among the Lord's people had become so corrupted that the spiritual truth which was originally delivered to the nation Israel had become unrecognisable in the hands of the various sects and factions which had abounded during the inter-Testamental period. When we examine the condition of Israel which confronted the Lord Jesus, we find that there were three main deceiving faces of false religion, providing us with a perfect paradigm for the corruption of true spirituality among the Lord's people in all eras — especially applicable to developments within the New Testament Church. The Jewish historian, Flavius Josephus, when explaining Judaism to the Greek-speaking world, referred to these three particular philosophical groups, which he identified as the Pharisees, the Sadducees and the Essenes.[23] However, most important for the present work is the fact that these three tendencies are not merely confined to the inter-Testamental errors of the Jews. For each one represents a different aspect of religious corruption, the three great religious traps which have been the earthly expression of satanic spirituality for aeons: liberal-humanism, legalism, and occult-mysticism. Let us now examine these in more detail.

1. The Sadducees: Model of Liberal-Humanism

The Sadducees were a Jewish aristocratic elite who tended to regard Judaism as *'a temple-centred religion rather than a law-centred way of life'*.[24] They did not believe in resurrection, spirits or angels (cf. Mk.12:18; Lk.20:27; Acts 23:8), tending rather to busy themselves with temple administration and ritual, whilst appeasing their political rulers in Rome through diplomacy and sycophancy.

These Sadducees were essentially a humanistic grouping who, although believing in God, denied that He has ever intervened in the course of human history; therefore, there is no foreordination, no divine co-operation in human action, while good and evil depend purely on human free-will and self-determinism. They are well-described as *'a loose confederation of wealthy and powerful men...who took a secular-pragmatic, rather than a religious-ideological stance with regard to the nation and its laws'*.[25] These descriptions of the Sadducees find a fine parallel with many of the leaders in the mainstream churches of today. These are the 'gentlemen of the broad swallow', the Latitudinarians, those who do not affirm a belief in the resurrection and the divine, miraculous intervention of God in history; those who play at politics and who busy themselves with the upkeep of 'temple administration' and ritual rather than the preaching of the Word. They are essentially secular-pragmatists carving out a niche for themselves in a role of respectability in theological colleges and denominational high-office. These are the liberals, the false professors, the ones who are peddling the

---

23 Flavius Josephus, *Antiquities*, Book XIII, Chapter 9. It is not beyond the bounds of possibility that these three Jewish sects were the *'three false shepherds'* which Zechariah prophesied would be *'cut off'* by Messiah (see Zec.11:8 in its context), who was *'the Good Shepherd'* (Jn.10:11).

24 Walter Elwell (ed.), *Evangelical Dictionary of Theology* (Marshall Pickering, 1984), p.966.

25 Ibid.

'elementary principles of this world' rather than the fundamental truths of the Scriptures — yet who are dishonest enough to do it behind a clerical collar, a cassock, a churchified title. They are the ones who are contemptuous about the phrase 'born again', and who sneer at those who are willing to stand up for the true faith. They are the modern 'slaughterers of the flock' (cf. Zec.11:4-7).

Such are the characteristics of liberal-humanist religion, as it manifests itself in the Christian scene. It is the first of the three major forms of religious corruption which have plagued the Church from the earliest era.

2. The Pharisees: Model of Legalism

Legalism has been defined as *'the tendency to observe letter or form rather than spirit'*.[26] Highlighting this approach to religion, Jesus said to the Pharisees:

> 'Woe to you, scribes and Pharisees, hypocrites! For you pay tithe of mint and anise and cummin, and have neglected the weightier matters of the law: justice, mercy and faith. These you ought to have done, without leaving the others undone' (Mt.23:23).

The Pharisees were surely the greatest legalists of all time. Adhering to the Mosaic Law by the letter, rather than seeing it as a humble gateway to sanctification, they used it as a club with which to batter the common people. Not only this, but they also added many new regulations to those ordained by God and constrained others to keep to them (Mt.23:1-4). However, unlike the Sadducees, they did believe in the resurrection from the dead, and in spirits and angels.

There is always a tendency in religious affairs, when they are not the outcome of true regeneration, for spiritual expression to be reduced to a mere outward ceremony and profession. This is as true today as it was in the time of Jesus. For the Pharisee has been a common occurrence throughout the history of the Church. They are the churchgoers who are more concerned with the neglected shine of another person's shoes than with the obdurate state of their own hearts. They are the ones who live in the Town of Morality rather than in the Valley of Grace. In such circles, formalism and ritualism are substituted for genuine worship and spirituality. Such folk will often expect you to pledge unswerving loyalty to the constitution of their church rather than to the Word of God. They are the ones who practise what they do because it makes them feel secure rather than because it is what the Lord requires of them. They are the ones who want to make you more like them than like Christ. They are the ones who are inwardly lukewarm and complacent in their spirituality but tend to say 'Amen' the loudest. They are the ones whose rules have been constructed on the doctrines of men rather than on the commandments of God. They will often emphasise the wrath of God and display little of His love in their lives. Theirs is an orthodox religion of the head rather than a spirituality of the heart; and their emphasis will often be on the acquisition of doctrinal knowledge at the expense of the fostering of spiritual growth. Legalism is the clinical practice of preserving religion on an intellectual life-support system when it is technically soul-dead.

---

[26] *Chambers English Dictionary* (Chambers, 1988), p.816.

For the diligent but unsuspecting Christian, legalism (or neo-nomianism, as it is also known) can create great problems in his or her spiritual progress. As one writer puts it: *'Legalism inevitably undermines Christian assurance and joy and tends to create a self-centred, excessively introspective piety'*.[27] Such a mindset is the second major form of religious corruption into which many professing Christians have fallen, and still continue to fall.

3. The Essenes: Model of Occult-Mysticism

The third example of religious corruption into which Israel had fallen by the time of the Messiah is represented by the Essenes. It is significant that this sect is never directly mentioned in the New Testament — unlike the Pharisees and Sadducees who feature so prominently in the four Gospels. Perhaps this is typical of the mystery surrounding mysticism; most likely it is because they never attempted to confront Jesus directly and tended to live in secluded, secretive circumstances. However, there are many indirect references which are most instructive.

The word *essene* is derived from the East Aramaic, *hasen*, meaning 'the pious ones' (from which the name of the orthodox Jewish *Hasidim* is derived). The Essene sect (2nd century B.C. to 2nd century A.D.) was an ascetic, commune-based, Jewish monastic order which regarded itself as the true Israel. In some ways they resembled the Pharisees in terms of such elements as ritual purity and legal observances; indeed, in this respect they often out-Phariseed the Pharisees! But their rigid adherence to the Levitical code was augmented by many additional works and practices which were, at best, in transgression of Pentateuchal Law and, at worst, downright sorcery and superstition. For example, they adored the sun and earnestly prayed to it before it rose,[28] they used a variety of magical and esoteric books, they practised divination and developed a highly elaborate angelology and cosmogony which went far beyond the biblical teachings of Moses.[29] Their teaching on angels was, in fact, *'derived from the Magi'*,[30] and in many ways they *'became the forerunners of the Gnostics and of the Jewish Cabbalists'*.[31] This knowledge that the angelology of the Essenes was derived from the Magi takes on an important significance when we are informed that among these Magi *'there was a strong tradition which favoured the exercise of sacerdotal and occult powers'*.[32] Even more significant, these Magi *'were in communication with evil spirits, and...they were well acquainted with Mesmerism and every practice of*

---

[27] S. Ferguson, D.F. Wright, J.I. Packer, *The New Dictionary of Theology* (IVP, 1988), p.379.

[28] J. Hastings (ed.), *Dictionary of the Bible* (T. & T. Clark, 1898), Vol.I., p.769.

[29] J. Hastings (ed.), *Dictionary of the Apostolic Church* (T. & T. Clark, 1915), p.368.

[30] *Chambers's Encyclopaedia* (George Newnes, 1963), Vol.V, p.395.

[31] Ibid. The Cabbalah is *'the ancient esoteric Jewish mystical tradition of philosophy containing strong elements of pantheism and is akin to Neo-Platonism'* (Hutchinson Encyclopedia, 1991, p.453). It is a *'theosophical system'* which *'has strong connections with gnosticism and also with magical practices'* (Macmillan Encyclopedia, 1986, p.659).

[32] Merrill C. Tenney, *The Zondervan Encyclopedia of the Bible*, 1975, Vol.IV, p.31.

modern Spiritualism'.[33] So the influences on the Essenes were decidedly occult.

However, it has been suggested by those with a vested interest in syncretism and the promotion of New Age religion — that Christianity was either influenced by, or developed from, Essenism. They point to some apparent similarities between Jesus' teaching and that of the Essenes, such as their piety, holiness and love of justice and righteousness, citing also as significant the fact that there is no recorded direct criticism of them by Jesus (unlike His scathing treatment of both the Sadducees and Pharisees). In truth, there are far more similarities between Essenism and the later Gnosticism than with true Christianity. As one authoritative source puts it: *'The suggestions, occasionally made, that St. John the Baptist and even Christ Himself had Essene connections, are most improbable'*.[34] Let us list some of the glaring contrasts between Essenism and Christianity.

Unlike the Essenes, Jesus did not withdraw, nor advocate withdrawal from the world (cf. Jn.17:15,18); neither did He reject the aged and the physically handicapped (cf. Mt.12:9-13; 15:30) nor advocate hatred of His enemies, as did the Essenes. He never purified Himself before eating with sinners (Mt.9:10-13); He did not advocate or practise vegetarianism (Mt.14:19), and did not believe that defilement and uncleanness comes from unpurified food, clothing and people (Mt.15:11) — all of which were part and parcel of being an Essene. So deep was their bondage to the laws of purification that if one of their members was expelled from the community for sins committed, he would find himself unable to eat the unpurified food of the outside world and die of starvation.[35] The Essenes also had such a highly developed system of elitism within their sect that the more 'advanced' members believed that they became spiritually polluted if they came into physical contact with, or ate food prepared by, novitiates.[36] It is also quite probable that Jesus was referring to the Essenes when He made the enigmatic statement: *'You have heard that it was said, "You shall love your neighbour and hate your enemy"'* (Mt.5:43). Nowhere is the idea of hating one's enemy advocated as such by the Law in the Old Testament (cf. Lev.19:17-18). There are, however, a number of such references in the Essenic documents found at Qumran in 1948.[37]

The mysticism, asceticism, esotericism and magical practice of the Essenes represents the third and most significant form of religious degeneration into which human beings have been plunged by dint of their own warped natures, aided and abetted by Satan. Jesus explicitly warned of those who try to convince people that the true Christ is to be found in ascetic sects or secret groups of initiates with their esoteric codes — a phenomenon especially to be expected at the end of the Age (Mt.24:23-26). Those who make their spiritual homes *'in the desert'* (both

---

[33] G.H. Pember, *Earth's Earliest Ages and their Connection with Modern Spiritualism, Theosophy, and Buddhism* (G.H. Lang, n.d., first published in 1876), p.162.

[34] F.L. Cross & E.A. Livingstone, *The Oxford Dictionary of the Christian Church* (O.U.P., 1983), p.471.

[35] J. Hastings (ed.), *Dictionary of the Bible* (T. & T. Clark, 1898), Vol.I, p.769.

[36] Ibid. One is here reminded of the caste system in India.

[37] G. Vermes, *The Dead Sea Scrolls in English* (Penguin Books, 1975), pp.72-73, 91.

literally, as with many of the Essene communes, and symbolically, referring to all ascetic withdrawal from the world) or who meet secretively in *'inner rooms'* (as in esoteric coteries or cabals), in order to discover occult 'truths', are not the true servants of Christ.

* * * * * * *

The above 'three false shepherds', manifested in Jesus' time as the Sadducees, Pharisees and Essenes, symbolise historically the religious bottlenecks into which Satan has tried to force all the spiritual aspirations and movements within humanity. Within the Church this has been a particularly destructive affair, in which those claiming to have an allegiance to Christ advocate philosophies which are imitative of the world, inaugurate Spirit-void, rule-bound tyrannies, and even initiation into mysticism and sorcery — as we shall document throughout this book.

History shows that the visible manifestation of God's people on earth has a tendency to fall into one or more of the above three degenerative states in the process of time. Although the satanic stream of Liberal-Humanism still holds great sway in the religious scene, it is largely confined to the seminaries, universities and mainstream denominational churches. Fortunately, it is today quite recognisable for what it is and now hardly constitutes a 'deception' so much as a glaring error! In any case, as we shall later learn, its most pervasive work was done in the last century as a preparation for the more catastrophic religious developments of the present time. One of the greatest polemics against 'Christian' liberalism, by J. Gresham Machen, first appeared in 1923; and it needs nothing further adding to it today.[38] Legalism, as a form of religious degeneration, can be very subtle indeed; and, ironically, it most easily penetrates those Christian circles which set great store on a dogmatically-applied adherence to biblical orthodoxy. But compared with the third form of religious degeneration — occult-mysticism — such legalism is not so much a deadly threat as an unfortunate menace. Fortunately, there are a great many books which have been written concerning the need for heart-spirituality and inner holiness in the life of the Christian, all of which will adequately counteract the proponents of externalised religion and formalism.

However, although there has been a great deal of material polemicising against liberalism and legalism, there has been very little which systematically catalogues the interaction between occult-mysticism and the Christian Church in the course of history. For this reason, the principal subject of this present book will be a study of the history and development of forms of religious degeneration similar to that which was manifested in the Essenes: occult-mysticism — the idea that there is a secret mystical doctrine into which a person can be initiated and by which he can reach up to God, and even become God himself. For it is this aspect of world religion which has its roots clearly grounded in the Fall in Eden and in the 'Initiation' which was introduced there by the fallen angelic hosts. It also forms the impulse for that essence of all false religion: the divinisation of man — the usurping by man of what is essentially divine, the realisation of the Lie.

[38] J. Gresham Machen, *Christianity and Liberalism* (Eerdmans, 1985).

EPILOGUE

The satanic religion is just as powerfully at work today as it was in Eden — desperately subtle, concentrating on clever argument, philosophies and ideologies to eclipse the Word of God: subtle enough, in fact, to deceive even the elect, if such a thing was possible. On the spiritual front at this present time, in both the Church and the secular world, we have the growing popularity of occult-mysticism and sorcery — having worked secretively and deceptively for the last couple of millennia. The secular world combines these with the dispassionate disciplines of science and sophistry, now working flat-out to disprove the existence of the one true God of the Bible. Within the worldwide visible Church, alongside the twin-influences of mysticism and sorcery, are the further stagnant waters of worldliness, liberalism and legalism — all designed to encourage the illusion that we are not complete in Christ.

In the following chapters, we will explore these developments from many different angles: the growth of Gnosticism and its transformation into new forms, the development of mysticism ancient and modern, the vagaries of scientific research, the fulminations of feminism, the manifold works of magic and sorcery, the mental and emotional fascism of the mind-sciences, the presence of the New Age Movement in the world and in the Church, and the global process towards a Christ-defying syncretism. We will then come to appreciate that today there is little difference between the professing Church and the unbelieving world in so many areas of life and work.

We will also learn the wisdom of Solomon when he made his terse observation that there is nothing new under the sun.

Chapter Two

IN THE WAKE OF THE CROSS

Spiritual Subterfuge Anno Domini

'And I saw an angel come down from heaven, having the key of the bottomless pit and a great chain in his hand. And he laid hold on the dragon, that old serpent, which is the Devil, and Satan, and bound him a thousand years, and cast him into the bottomless pit, and shut him up, and set a seal upon him, that he should deceive the nations no more, till the thousand years be fulfilled: and after that he must be loosed for a little season' (Rev.20:1-3).

Before we can come to a full understanding of the present-day religious corruption in the world and in the Church, we must first examine the historical and spiritual background out of which it has developed. In the previous chapter, we gave a detailed exposition of the primordial inception and subsequent outworking of Satan's ancient war with God among the nations, and in opposition to the Lord's ancient covenant people, Israel. This warfare, although retaining the same essential elements throughout history, has taken many tactical forms, according to the needs of the times and the permitted powers of the demonic realm. In the present chapter, before examining certain doctrinal developments in the early Church, we will demonstrate that the coming of the Lord Jesus Christ brought about a sweeping change in the manner in which the powers of darkness have carried out their warfare against the Church. For this purpose, we will first examine what the Scriptures have to say on the matter; then we will be in a position to determine how this has worked out in history.

I. THE DEFEAT OF SATAN

Until the life, passion and death of Jesus Christ on the cross, Satan had access to the throne of God (Job 1:6-12; 2:1-7) and fulfilled the role of 'accuser' (e.g., Zec.3:1-2). However, after the ascension of the Lord Jesus, Satan was cast out of heaven (Rev.12:10), while Christ continued his work as the *'one Mediator between God and men'* (1 Tim.2:5) interceding on behalf of His people, pleading for us on the basis of His holy sacrifice, thus eliminating Satan's accusatory role (Rom.8:33-34,38-39). This victory of Christ over Satan was not a partial, incomplete affair — it was final and absolute.

When those people whom Satan had 'fathered' (Jn.8:44, cf. Jesus' naming of the Pharisees as *'Serpents, brood of vipers'*, Mt.23:33) conspired to destroy the

Son of God, they made a fatal misjudgement. In thinking that they could destroy God's plan by having Jesus put to death, they revealed their profound ignorance of spiritual truth. For, at the heart of Jesus' death and atonement, there was

> 'a mystery, the hidden wisdom which God ordained before the ages for our glory, which none of the rulers of this age knew; for had they known, they would not have crucified the Lord of glory' (1 Cor.2:7-8).

This concealment of the true significance of Jesus' spiritual mission from what Paul here calls *'the rulers of this age [Greek: aeon]'* must surely apply not only to Satan's *human* collaborators but also to the entire demonic realm, as Scripture reveals them to be *'the rulers of the **darkness** of this age'* (Eph.6:12) and Satan himself to be *'the god of this age'* (2 Cor.4:4). In other words, the satanic powers had no foreknowledge that Jesus' death and atonement would signal the destruction of their world-system. There is an interesting corroborative statement to this effect in Ignatius of Antioch's letter to the Ephesians written only seventy-five years after the death of Christ:

> 'Now the virginity of Mary, and He who was born of her, were kept in secret from the ruler of this world [Satan]; as was also the death of our Lord; three of the mysteries the most spoken of throughout the world, yet done in secret by God'.[1]

Something of the nature of this secrecy can be seen in the fact that King Herod, as a human agent of Satan, was forced to carry out a mass slaughter of innocent babes in the vain hope of flushing out the Messiah (Mt.2:3-18). The devil is certainly not omniscient!

Thus Jesus completely vanquished Satan and all his works of darkness (Jn.12:31; Gal.1:4; Heb.2:14; Rev.12:10-11) through His obedience to the will of His Father (Lk.22:42; Jn.4:34; 6:39-40), coupled with His successful resistance to satanic temptation in the wilderness (Mt.4:10-11) and throughout the whole of His life (Jn.14:30). As Paul puts it, *'Having disarmed principalities and powers, He made a public spectacle of them, triumphing over them in it [i.e., the cross]'* (Col.2:15). The world-system had indeed been under the (usurped) rulership of Satan for a time, but Jesus overcame this 'world' (Jn.16:33) when His blood was shed on the cross. As a result, He could comfort His disciples after the Resurrection with the assurance that *'all authority has been given to Me in heaven and on earth'* (Mt.28:18).

The far-reaching cosmic significance of this mighty victory cannot be over-emphasised. It had been anticipated by Jesus when, after the return of the seventy disciples from a successful mission in which even the demons were subject to His authority, He said, *'I saw Satan fall like lightning from heaven'* (Lk.10:17-18). This complete authority of Jesus over the demonic realm in the wake of His death, resurrection and ascension was prophesied by David when he

---

[1] *The Ancient and Modern Library of Theological Literature: The Apostolic Fathers*, Part II, 'The Epistles of St. Ignatius and St. Polycarp' (Griffith, Farran, Okeden & Welsh, 1889), p.78.

said, *'You have ascended on high, You have led captivity captive'* (Ps.68:18; cf. Eph.4:7-10). This is a wonderful reference to the triumphant spectacle of Jesus taking the sting out of demonic power as He ascended to heaven, prompting Paul to declare jubilantly to all believers that

> 'He has delivered us from the power of darkness and translated us into the kingdom of the Son of His love, in whom we have redemption through His blood, the forgiveness of sins' (Col.1:13-14).

From this point on, the whole of the created order was disturbed as Christ's great victory set in motion the antidote to the evil effects of the Fall which was both prospective and retrospective.[2] The satanic realm was then 'cast down to the earth' from heaven (Rev.12:7-9), exactly as Jesus had foreseen and foretold (Lk.10:18; Jn.12:31). From this point on, Satan's domain would be restricted to the realms of 'the earth', and his forces condemned to operate from a habitation which Paul calls *'the air'*, over which Satan wields his authority as *'prince of the power of the air'* (Eph.2:2). What could the Apostle have meant by this word 'air'? Athanasius of Alexandria, writing in about AD 300, also spoke of Satan as *'having fallen from heaven and wandering about our lower atmosphere, there bearing rule over his fellow spirits'*.[3] Although the Greek word used in Eph.2:2, *aeros*, is used to refer to the lower atmosphere, we learn elsewhere in the Ephesian letter that these demonic powers operate *'in the heavenly places'* (Eph.6:12). Furthermore, demons or spirits were referred to in Greek magical texts and other literature as having their spiritual abode 'in the air'.[4] However, we do know that these demons are spirit beings who do not have a physical body — so 'the air' here cannot be referring simply to the air which we breathe.

It would seem, therefore, that the satanic realm, although not being *materially* manifested on the earth, has access to human affairs from an other-dimensional 'etheric envelope' which corresponds to the environs of our earth. It is this *spiritual* abode which is the current dwelling-place of Satan and his fellow evil spirits. In the ensuing chapters, we will often refer back to this information in order to appreciate its significance for a number of present-day demonic developments — including numerous manifestations of spirit-entities, discarnate beings and the increasing phenomenon of UFOs and apparitions of alleged alien beings.

II. THE MYSTERIOUS 'DELAY' OF THE KINGDOM

In spite of the fact that Satan was defeated at the cross, judged, cast out and overcome, this does not mean that evil is over and done with in its outworkings. The fact that there was a 'legal' victory did not mean that the war was completely over. There still remained the need for a lengthy, spiritual 'mopping-up'

---

[2] Jesus' atonement can be said to be retrospective in the sense that its saving effects covered even those who were saved before His incarnation.

[3] Athanasius, *De Incarnatione*, quoted in J. Hastings (ed.), *Dictionary of the Apostolic Church* (T. & T. Clark, 1915), Vol.I, p.47.

[4] W.F. Arndt & F.W. Gingrich, *A Greek-English Lexicon of the New Testament and Other Early Christian Literature* (University of Chicago Press, 1979), p.20.

operation to bring things to their full completion. Although it is true that Jesus came into the world to *'destroy the works of the devil'* (Jn.3:8), and to found the Kingdom of God through the preaching of the Gospel, the Bible makes it clear that the total object of His mission was not perfectly fulfilled during His earthly life. Apart from the fact that the forces of evil had yet to manifest the fullness of their iniquity in this present evil age, the death and atonement of Jesus — although securing complete and instantaneous victory over the satanic realm — did not bring about its immediate destruction, because there remained yet to be fulfilled a most important aspect of the Divine Plan.

This suspension of the final enactment of judgement on the world is the reason that unbelievers will scoff at the very idea that Jesus Christ will return to carry out this task (2 Pet.3:3-4). However, many *believers* have also been bewildered by this postponement of the public display of God's victory over Satan, in which there has been an abeyance of Christ openly taking His place as King of the world and 'making all things new'. It is not surprising that the Lord's people should be perplexed at this 'delay' — especially those who were alive during Jesus' post-resurrection ministry on earth. For example, shortly before Jesus' ascension, His disciples asked Him, *'Lord, will You at this time restore the kingdom to Israel?'* (Acts 1:6). But they were ignorant of a vast 'mystery' which is absolutely central to God's plan, in His suspension of the final fulfillment of Christ's victory. They did not know about *'the mystery of Christ...that the Gentiles should be fellow heirs, of the same body, and partakers of His promise in Christ through the gospel'* (Eph.3:4-6), although they must have known the words of the prophets which spoke of it (e.g., Isa.11:10; 60:1-14). Even the Song of Moses found a place for the Gentiles to rejoice with the Lord's people at the prospect of God avenging the spilled blood of His servants (Dt.32:43). But these disciples were ignorant of the mystery which revealed *'that hardening in part has happened to Israel until the fullness of the Gentiles has come in'* (Rom.11:25). It had not yet been revealed to them, as it was later to the *'holy apostles and prophets'* (Eph.3:5), that there was a *'mystery of godliness'* which meant that not only would God be *'manifested in the flesh, justified in the Spirit'* and *'seen by angels'*, but that He must also be *'preached among the Gentiles'* and *'believed on in the world'* (1 Tim.3:16).

It is to this same 'mystery' that the Apostle John refers when he speaks of the *'delay'* in the final ratification of Christ's victory as *'the mystery of God'*, which would not be fulfilled until the seventh trumpet, at which time the kingdoms of this world would openly become the kingdoms of the Lord Jesus Christ (Rev.10:5-7; 11:15-19). Before that climax could come, there was to be a time lapse of undisclosed duration, a *'delay'* (Greek, *chronos*, 'time', Rev.10:6), when there would be a testimony of the Gospel through the true Church (symbolised by the *'two witnesses'* in Rev.11:1-6) — what we may call the Gospel Age — after which Christ would return to earth *'coming on the clouds of heaven with power and great glory'* (Mt.24:30) to complete the work which He had begun, judging the world and gathering in believers from all ages. For this reason, when those who have been persecuted cry out: *'How long, O Lord, holy and true, until You judge and avenge our blood on those who dwell on the earth?'*, they are given a white robe and told to *'rest a little while longer'* until the building of the Church is complete at the end of this present Age (Rev.6:9-11). This lengthy time of 'mystery' between Christ's victory and the open manifestation of His Kingdom is a time when the Lord's people do need great faith and perseverance in order to remain confident in the Lord and not be intimidated by those scoffers who say: *'Where is the promise of His coming?'* (2 Pet.3:3-4) or by the persecutions which may come their way. This 'mystery time of delay' is what John refers to as *'the kingdom and patience of Jesus Christ'* (Rev.1:9). It is a time which involves, to the uttermost, *'the perseverance and faith of the saints'* (Rev.13:10; 14:12). But that faith is greatly helped by the fact that the Lord's people (those who have been given 'ears to hear') have had it revealed to them that Satan and his followers will one day themselves reap their punishment. This is what is meant in the word:

> 'If anyone has an ear, let him hear. He who leads into captivity shall go into captivity; he who kills with the sword must be killed with the sword' (Rev.13:9-10).

The fulfillment of this two-part prophecy is foretold in Rev.19:20-21: *'Then the beast was captured, and with him the false prophet...and the rest were killed with the sword'* (cf. Rev.19:15). Because we know this, we can rest in supreme confidence. For a little while, we have to accept the fact that the knowledge of the cosmic work of redemption (the Gospel), which Jesus' life and death had irrevocably introduced into the heart of the satanic world-system, had first to be spread across the whole earth to all nations (Mt.28:19; Lk.24:47; Acts 1:8), before the Kingdom of God would be fully established and the works of the devil finally destroyed at His second coming. In the words of William Perkins (1558-1602), *'the Kingdom of God has come in grace, but not yet in glory'*. The disciples who were alive during Jesus' post-resurrection ministry did not have the benefit of all this revelation. But we are most privileged to have this knowledge at our disposal. These important assurances given in His word will prevent the Lord's people from being tempted to walk by sight rather than by faith.

So, we have this 'Mystery of God' operating throughout the Gospel Age, with the full renewal of the cosmos and Final Judgement awaiting the full number of Gentiles and Jews being brought into the Church. However, alongside this *'Mystery of God'* runs another mystery which is a dark mirror of it: the *'Mystery of Iniquity'* or *'Lawlessness'* (2 Th.2:7) — the extraordinary fact that alongside the sowing of the seed of the Gospel, there is to be a sowing of tares among the wheat: a unique work of Satan which will not be rectified until the harvest at the end of the age (Mt.13:24-30,37-43).

This leads to the raising of a number of important questions. Just how has Satan operated throughout the Gospel Age, as he awaits that necessarily-delayed, impending judgement on his work and person? What powers remain to the demonic realm in the wake of their defeat by the Lord Jesus Christ on the Cross? If we can uncover the answers to these questions, this will aid us in our understanding of the present-day situation in the Church and in the wider world.

III. THE BINDING OF THE 'STRONG MAN'

Although the evil effects of the Fall are still very much with us throughout the Gospel Age, the powers of the satanic realm and its ability to influence human affairs in the wake of Christ's absolute victory have been greatly transformed. Throughout the Gospel Age, Satan has carried on his God-permitted warfare with humanity from his stronghold in 'the air'; but this has been severely restricted in comparison with his dominion of 'the nations' prior to the triumphant Ascension of Christ. Although it is true that Satan is still highly active in the affairs of men (and especially those of the Church, 1 Pet.5:8; Eph.4:27; cf. Eph.6:11; Jas.4:7), there are a number of significant Scriptures which reveal that he has been *'bound'* or restrained in the wake of Christ's victory. Let us examine these texts.

For example, Jesus said to the Pharisees, *'How can one enter a strong man's house and plunder his goods, unless he first binds the strong man? And then he will plunder his house'* (Mt.12:29). As is clear from the context (cf. Mt.12:22-29), Jesus was here describing the victorious aim of His earthly mission, which was set in motion at the scene of the Temptation in the wilderness (Lk.4:1-13), consolidated through the mission work of Jesus and the disciples, and finally fulfilled at Calvary. He came to bind the 'strong man', Satan, so that the privileges of despotic power over humanity, previously held by Satan and his fallen angelic helpers, would be confiscated and transferred to the new King of Kings, and subsequently to His labourers who would preach the Gospel with great success following the Ascension (Mt.16:18-19; Eph.5:2; Gal.1:4; Heb.2:14; Ps.68:18; Isa.53:12a; Eph.4:7-16). In this way, Satan's 'house', or domain, has been well and truly plundered as souls among the nations (Gentiles) began to be delivered from the power of darkness and transferred into the kingdom of Christ (Col.1:13). Spiritual supremacy over this planet was now in the hands of the Lord Jesus Christ (Mt.28:18-20).

In Jerusalem, shortly before His arrest, Jesus predicted His death on the Cross and said, *'But for this purpose I came to this hour'* (Jn.12:27). To what purpose was He referring? Four verses later He tells us: *'Now is the judgement of this world; now the ruler of this world will be cast out'* (Jn.12:31). The term 'cast out' is most appropriate. In the same way that Jesus 'cast out' demons from individual people during His earthly walk, so He also banished the Prince of Demons from his then-current sphere of activity as the *'ruler of this world'*. From the moment that Jesus' mission on earth was fulfilled, Satan legally ceased to be its ruler. The end of the last Gospel record is the final time that he is referred to as such (Jn.14:30). Throughout the rest of the New Testament, Satan is never once referred to as being the 'ruler of the world'; instead, he assumes the title of *'prince of the power of the air'* (Eph.2:2), having been cast out of heaven in the wake of the Cross (Rev.12:10; Jn.12:31). Another of Satan's titles in the wake of the Cross is *'the god of this age/world'* (2 Cor.4:4), which does not mean that he is an actual god, but is a reference to the fact that the heathen world in this evil age (from which Christians have been *spiritually* delivered, Gal.1:4), deifies him through its allegiance to the Lie that he planted in world history in Eden. And when John says that *'the whole world lies under the sway of the wicked one'* (1 Jn.5:19), the imagery does not imply *legitimate* rulership but, rather, the ongoing mesmerisation of the world with the elemental principles of the Lie. Satan is still a powerful force in the world, but he is not its legitimate Prince; and because he knows that his time is limited, he is filled with a rage which he vents on the Church (Rev.12:12-17). In other words, Satan is a dethroned vagrant without a kingdom, wandering about in a state of vindictive perplexity, with strictly limited powers as he awaits the inevitable coming judgement.

A number of other Scriptures make reference to this 'binding' or restraining of Satan which our Lord promised would be fulfilled in the wake of His victory on the Cross. In his second letter to the Thessalonians, Paul reveals that the return of Christ will not happen until two events have taken place in history: first, the final great apostasy, followed by the revealing of the 'Man of Sin' (2 Th.2:3) — a personal figure agreed by discerning Bible expositors to be the final and ultimate manifestation of Antichrist (cf. 1 Jn.2:18). A few verses later, Paul speaks of a powerful restraining factor which prevents this ultimate event from taking place before its appointed time (2 Th.2:6). The restraint here involves the Divinely-appointed holding back of the full exercise of demonic *'power, signs, and lying wonders'* by the Satan-inspired Man of Sin, coupled with a universal belief in the Satanic Lie (2 Th.2:9-11) — all of which will be released from that restraint at a certain point in history. The context clearly implies that this release of the demonic powers from their former restriction will take place shortly before the Second Coming of Christ (2 Th.2:8). There is a remarkable correlation of these verses in Paul's second letter to the Thessalonians with the first ten verses of the Book of Revelation, Chapter 20, in which the threefold sequence of events follows the same pattern:

1. There is a lengthy period of Divine restraint upon the powers of darkness preventing them from gathering the nations into one conglomerate Church-destroying, Christ-hating entity.
2. This is followed by a short period (*'a little season'*, A.V.) during which the restraint will be taken away and Satan permitted to achieve his goal.
3. This short period of demonic mayhem is immediately succeeded by the Second Coming of Christ, who will effect the resurrection, judge the world, and bring in a completely reconstituted universe.

It may be objected by some that the verses in Rev.20:1-3 which speak of the binding of Satan cannot possibly refer to the Gospel Age because Satan has very obviously been able to wreak havoc in both the Church and the world during the last two thousand years and therefore cannot have been 'bound'. We would certainly not dispute that there has been a considerable amount of Satan-induced havoc throughout the Gospel Age. However, we are not claiming that these verses say that *all* satanic activity has been *wholly* bridled, for they refer only to a *particular historical situation* which is being held back from fulfilment until the time is ripe in God's cosmic plan. The specific historical situation which Satan is restrained from fulfilling throughout the Gospel Age involves the coercing of the gathered nations into an all-out global declaration of war against the true Church and her Master, Jesus Christ. This is why the text states that when the restraint has been loosed, Satan *'will go out to deceive the nations which are in the four corners of the earth, Gog and Magog, to gather them together to battle'* (Rev.20:3,7-9; cf. 17:13-14). That has been his object throughout history, and its constraint in this present age has enabled the Gospel to be spread throughout the nations by a postponement of the time of the end — that 'delay' which is called the *'mystery of God'* (cf. Rev.10:5-7).

When the Apostle prophesies that the Satan-inspired nations *'surrounded the camp of the saints and the beloved city'* (Rev.20:9) after the Old Serpent has been released from being bound, we know that it was from fulfilling this particular event that the demonic realm had been restrained during the Gospel Age. The phrase *'the camp of the saints'* is not referring to the present-day capital of the modern secular state of Israel, because in the New Testament it is the Church (composed of both converted Jews and Gentiles) which is known as both 'Israel' and 'Jerusalem' (cf. Gal.6:16; Heb.12:22-23; Rom.11:26a). In the time of the Lord's Old Covenant people, the children of Israel, Satan worked perpetually through the heathen nations to effect the destruction of the nation chosen by God. Now that the Lord's people in the Gospel Age is represented by a spiritually-gathered, trans-national body, the devil's attentions are focused on the destruction of the Church, its doctrines, institutions, and the faith of individual believers. Such a mustering of the nations of the world-system into a global anti-Jehovah confederacy has been Satan's aim since the dawn of history. He almost succeeded at Babel on the plain of Shinar, but the time was not yet ripe and God intervened to confound his designs (Gen.11:1-9). When he finally achieves his aim at the end of history — referred to mystically in the Bible as 'Armageddon' (Rev.16:16) — although it may at first appear to be Satan's victory, it is really his defeat. For all along it was God Himself who *'has put it into [the nations'] hearts to fulfil His purpose, to be of one mind, and to give their kingdom to the beast, until the words of God are fulfilled'* (Rev.17:17). It is this assurance of divine sovereignty which enables the Lord's people to maintain *'patience and the faith'* during these difficult times (Rev.13:10).

We must not imagine that this term 'Armageddon', occurring in the highly symbolic Book of Revelation, refers to a literal battle with material weapons on a war zone in the modern state of Israel. It is, rather, the climax of the ancient, perennial spiritual warfare by which Satan has attempted to destroy the testimony of God and of His people through the mass seduction of the unbelieving nations. Throughout the existence of ancient Israel, Satan continually energised the nations into enmity and warfare against the people of God. Many of the earthly principles in the Old Covenant were types and shadows of spiritual realities in the New. So, whereas the earthly nation, Israel, did battle with *material* weapons against the surrounding nations, in the strength of the Lord, to maintain national purity, the trans-national Body of Christ fights with *spiritual* weapons against spiritual enemies — both earthly and discarnate — in the strength of the Lord, as part of a lifelong personal sanctification process. As Paul puts it: *'For the weapons of our warfare are not carnal but mighty in God for pulling down strongholds'* (2 Cor.10:4). Elsewhere, he reveals that Christians *'do not wrestle against flesh and blood, but against principalities, against powers, against the rulers of the darkness of this age, against spiritual hosts of wickedness in the heavenly places'* (Eph.6:12). In just the same way that the Lord saw fit in O.T. times to leave some of the surrounding nations unconquered, *"that He might test Israel by them"*, even after Israel had been brought into the promised land (Jdg.3:1), so He has left the demonic realm today with a measure of power to test the Church — even in the wake of Christ's victory on the Cross.

The evidence of history itself bears out this 'binding' or restraining of Satan throughout the Gospel Age in this manner. One has only to compare pre-Christian civilisations with those of the last two millennia to see the extraordinary difference between the two eras. Although there have been empires of a sort since the Ascension of Christ, they have been on a much smaller scale than their counterparts of the pre-Christian era; and those which have threatened to become vast, monolithic, international empires (e.g., Napoleon, Hitler, etc.) have been constrained before they could properly exercise their full-blown global ambitions. Throughout the present Gospel Age, there have been many restraints which have prevented Satan from achieving his aim of gathering the nations into a global confederacy: The shifting interests of narrow national causes and the divisions of language ordained by God as an outworking of His original judgement at Babel, coupled with an international Gospel ministry, have (until recently) all worked against creating the conditions for the global confederacy sought by the satanic realm. Although Satan still has enormous power amongst the nations of the world, the exercise of that power has been forced to operate within the confines of this Gospel Age. This is because something has been restraining the ability of Satan to *'deceive the nations'* (Rev.20:3) in the manner in which his unbridled lusts would have it — a matter which is hardly surprising in view of the fact that *'all authority in heaven and on earth'* has been given to Jesus in the wake of the Cross (Mt.28:18), after which Satan was *cast out* from his usurped rulership of the world (Jn.12:31).

To sum up, in the wake of the Cross, Satan ceased to be the *'ruler of the world'*, and it is in this sense that he is said to be bound. Prior to Christ's incarnation (i.e., B.C.), the nations were living in sheer spiritual darkness as the Lord's grace was confined almost exclusively to His chosen people, Israel. But since Jesus' Ascension, Satan has been unable to wield the same international power and influence, as spiritual priority has been given to the worldwide spread of the Gospel to all nations. However, he has not been slow in devising a strategy to compensate for that loss of authority which he originally wielded as ruler of the world. For in the wake of his restriction, Satan has been operating through the leavening factor of the politico-economic and religious systems of the world, as symbolised by the two beasts in the Book of Revelation, chapter 13. For the Scripture expressly states concerning Satan that, in the Gospel Age, *'his power, his throne, and great authority'* was given to the beast which rose out of the sea (symbol of the restless political tumult of the nations, Rev.13:2b; cf. 13:12). In other words, while Satan has been bound, restricted and under restraint, he has been working covertly through the world government of the nations, which, in turn, provide the power and authority behind the development of antichristian world religion, symbolised by the second beast (Rev.13:11-12).

This condition will prevail until the approach of the close of the age, at which time Satan and his fellow demons will, in the providence of God, be *'released for a little while'* from their restraint (Rev.20:3,7-10), so as to galvanise the final manifestation of Antichrist (2 Th.2:3-12; 1 Jn.2:18). This evil horde will capitalise on the well-prepared, universal, religious movement (Rev.13:11ff.) and global political confederacy (Rev.13:1-8; 17:12-18), so that the previously-restrained *'mystery of lawlessness'* can come to its fullness and ripeness for judgement (Rev.18; 20:7-10). In other words, once the testimony of the Church has been completed and the full number of the elect has been saved, the *'rulers of the darkness of this age'*, under their leader Satan, will be unleashed from their restraint and permitted to achieve their ambition. As John puts it:

> 'Now when they [i.e., the two witnesses, symbol for the Gospel message of the Church] finish their testimony, the beast that ascends out of the bottomless pit will make war against them, overcome them, and kill them' (Rev.11:7).

This eventual apparent 'overcoming' of the saints is a necessary and inevitable development which needs to be clearly understood by the people of God, lest they feel they have been abandoned by God and begin to walk by sight rather than by faith. It is for this reason that we have been given some great and precious promises in the Scriptures. To this, we will now turn.

IV. THE 'SHATTERING' OF THE HOLY PEOPLE

Contrary to the belief of many Christians, the Bible does not present any evidence that the return of the Lord will be preceded by a Golden Age of global revival or a largely 'Christianised' world — a fantasy which has sometimes been called the 'latter-day glory of the saints'. It is most important that we understand this from a biblical perspective rather than from the systems and traditions of men, because the entire concept of a future *earthly* Golden Age, as we shall later show, is fundamental to Jewish and Gnostic belief-systems rather than to the Word of God. Many believers claim that the Scripture which says that *'the earth shall be full of the knowledge of the Lord as the waters cover the sea'* (Isa.11:9; cf. Hab.2:14) refers to a future Christianised world prior to the Second Coming of the Lord Jesus Christ and Final Judgement. But this is to pluck a verse out of its context, where it clearly refers primarily to the conditions which will prevail in a wholly renewed creation, *after* the Lord's return. As Professor E.J. Young comments on these verses:

> 'When the Messiah has completed His Messianic work, peace is introduced into the hearts of men, and insofar as men are true to the principles of peace which they have received from the Messiah, so far do the blessings depicted herein obtain. In its fullness, however, this condition will not be realized until the earth is covered with the knowledge of the Lord, and that condition will only obtain in the new heavens and the new earth wherein dwelleth righteousness'.[5]

So, let us again emphasise this point: The concept of the world being wholly (or almost wholly) Christianised *before* the return of the Lord Jesus Christ has no basis in Scripture and holds out a false hope by which many saints will either become downcast or cherish dreams which cannot find fulfilment. In contrast to the prophetic systems devised by men, the Word of God tells a very different story; for there are many places, in both Old and New Testaments which speak of the saints being 'overcome' by the powers of evil on the earth. The prophet, Daniel, tells us of the time at the end of history, which corresponds to Satan's *'little season'* (Rev.20:3), as being one in which war will be made by a God-hating tyrant (surely, the Antichrist)

> 'against the saints, and *prevailing against them,* until the Ancient of Days came, and a judgement was made in favour of the saints of the Most High, and the time came for the saints to possess the kingdom' (Dan.7:21-22).

Although such persecution has happened on many occasions in the Church Age, the situation here is particularly associated with the activities of the final manifestation of Antichrist. Here, the adversary of Jehovah-Christ is said to be *'prevailing against'* the people of God in the days before the return of the Lord Jesus — a reference which clearly militates against any idea of a world in the throes of a global revival. Just to emphasise this point, we should note that Daniel then adds that the Antichrist

> 'shall speak pompous words against the Most High, *shall persecute the saints of the Most High*, and shall intend to change times and law. Then *the saints shall be given into his hand* for a time and times and half a time. ' (Dan.7:25) [emphasis added]

Then, in the following chapter, this period immediately prior to the Lord's return is described as one in which the Antichrist *'shall destroy...the holy people'* (Dan.8:24), and will *'even rise against the Prince of princes'*, i.e., the Lord Jesus Christ. But this tyrannical world-system will be miraculously destroyed by the Lord — as the text so beautifully puts it, *'broken without human means'* (Dan.8:25; cf. 2 Th.2:8). This is an echo of the way in which the mighty Goliath (a type of Antichrist) was miraculously destroyed by little David (a type of Christ), in whose hand *'there was no sword'* (1 Sam.17:50). In the final chapter of the Book of Daniel, far from being told that the Church will bring about a

---

[5] Edward J. Young, *The Book of Isaiah* (Eerdmans, 1965), Vol.1, p.391.

Christianised world, the prophet is informed by an angel that it is only *'when the power of the holy people has been completely shattered'* that the end of the age will come (Dan.12:7). Similarly, this same pattern is borne out repeatedly in the prophecy of the Book of Revelation, which shows that there will come a moment when the witness of the Church in the Gospel Age will be completed and Satan will be entirely unbound from his former restriction and *'will make war against [the saints], overcome them, and kill them'*, to the great rejoicing of the unbelieving world (Rev.11:7). Elsewhere, when the Apostle is describing the culmination of the satanic world-system in the rule of the Antichrist, he speaks of the fact that it will be *'granted to him to make war with the saints and to overcome them'* (Rev.13:7).

It is clear that this 'war with the saints' is really a war against the Lord — against the transcendent Jehovah of the Bible and the Lord Jesus Christ. And when the antichristian world-system embarks on its 'little season' under its ruler, Satan, waging war against the Lamb of God, the Lord *'will overcome them, for He is Lord of lords and King of kings; and those who are with Him are called, chosen, and faithful'* (see Rev.17:12-14). In the moment that Satan will appear to have achieved his much desired suppression of the saints and dominion over the kingdoms of the world, in fact just the opposite will be true. This is always the Lord's way of working: He permits evil to appear to be in the ascendency but then shows His supremacy by overturning it to His glory. When Satan appeared to have destroyed the Saviour of the world through His execution on the Cross, this was in fact God's supreme victory as Jesus' death on the Cross and His subsequent resurrection secured salvation and eternal life for all those who repent and believe in Him. This will also be the case at the time of the end. When Satan and his followers will suppose that they have finally achieved their sought-after dominion over the world, loud voices will be heard in heaven, saying, *'The kingdoms of this world have become the kingdoms of our Lord and of His Christ, and He shall reign forever and ever'* (Rev.11:15).

The great 'Mystery of God' is that, all along, every nook and cranny of history — no matter how dark or evil — is leading to the moment when the Lord God Almighty will take His great power and reign (Rev.11:17). This visibility of the divine victory could have been executed at any moment in time, if He had so chosen it; but that has not been God's manner of working. In just the same way that Jesus forewent calling down twelve legions of angels to assist Him in avoiding arrest in the Garden of Gethsemane (Mt.26:53), so the Sovereign Creator has put in abeyance the moment when He could so easily have wiped out Satan and taken His great power and reigned. The power of evil has first to come to its fullness, to be ripe for judgement — then the end will come and there will *'be delay no longer'* (Rev.10:6-7). But until that moment, the saints will suffer, especially as the time of the end draws near.

Let it again be said: the Bible does not present a picture of a Christianised world prior to Jesus' Second Coming. On the contrary, according to the Lord Jesus Himself, when He returns to wind up this present evil age, the overall state of the planet will be very similar to the time of Noah just prior to the Flood (Lk.17:26-27), and the time of Sodom just prior to the cataclysm which destroyed that city (Lk.17:28-30). How were things in the time of Noah? Read Gen.6:5,11-12 to find out. How were things in the city of Sodom? Read Gen.18:20-21. The picture here, in both illustrations, is of a wholly sinful, unconcerned world, carrying on its business without a care to know spiritual Truth. With great relevance, Prof. R.C.H. Lenski makes the following astute observation in his comment on Rev.12:6:

> 'The old Jewish dream of a grand Jewish dominion over all the nations of the world — a dream that is constantly being revived to this day in the minds of all those who work to make the kingdom of God an outward world power and dominion — is just about the opposite of what John is here given to see in regard to the church. Ever, here on earth, she is not on the throne but in a place in the wilderness, a little flock under the cross. But the day of her final... *"ransoming"*, *"redemption"* (Lk.21:28; Rom.8:23; Eph.1:13-14), is fast drawing nigh'.[6]

It is most important that the saints grasp these truths, otherwise they will become greatly downcast when they suffer at the hands of the world. However, the stark truth of an oppressed Church *on earth* is always displayed in Scripture in the context of *spiritual* supremacy and *heavenly* glory. In the eyes of the world, the church is a weakling; but with the spiritual eyesight (insight) of the believer and in the eyes of God she is beautiful, powerful, and ultimately triumphant (cf. Isa.43:1-7). If we fool the Lord's people into believing that the history of this planet is leading to a largely-converted world which will usher in the return of the Lord Jesus Christ, then we are inculcating a grave deception which will serve only to create a false sense of worldly security and complacency. So, let us be quite clear on this; rather than advocating the appearance of any Golden Age for the Church immediately before Christ returns, the Scriptures show an outwardly ruinous phase of apostasy, false religion, pseudo-prophets and teachers, increased demonic activity and intensified persecution of faithful believers. Prof. H.C. Leupold writes, in his comment on Dan.12:7, concerning the naked reality of this complete 'shattering of the power' of the Church before Christ returns:

> 'Hard though this seems, it is merely one of those necessities to which human pride and self-will put the grace of God before God's gracious purposes can be accomplished. Strangely, man is so set on trusting in himself and depending on his own power that, unless that power is reduced to a helpless minimum, he will refuse to put his confidence wholly in the good Lord. Only after we have been rendered weak are we capable of becoming truly strong. Israel of O.T. days had to be reduced to the impotence of the last times before the Saviour could come. So her trust in self will have to be broken again before the Christ can return. It is far more important to know that than to be able to foretell

---

[6] R.C.H. Lenski, *Interpretation of Revelation* (Augsburg, 1963), pp.370-371.

in exact terms of years how long this old world order is still to continue'.[7]

The profound truth which lies at the heart of all these verses in Daniel and Revelation is echoed in that great saying of the Apostle that *'we walk by faith, not by sight'* (2 Cor.5:7). Scripture reveals — no matter how events may appear to the contrary — that the oppressed saints throughout this age are blessed *'with every spiritual blessing in the heavenly places in Christ'* (Eph.1:3; 2:6). Take note that the Scripture says *'in the heavenly places'*; for it is not in earthly terms that the saints receive their primary blessings. Unless one has a simple grasp of these facts, one will live either in dreams or in misery, rather than in biblical reality — especially as we work our way through the facts given in this present book. The 'crown of life' is worn by simple faith and trust rather than by the evidence of our eyes, until we come into glory (see Rev.2:10). Although in the world we will indeed have tribulation, we can *'be of good cheer'* because the Lord Jesus Christ assures us that He has *'overcome the world'* (Jn.16:33). The saints of the first two centuries were painfully and exquisitely aware of all this; and as the end of this Age draws to a close, believers will again have to muster that strength in the Lord in the face of the widespread persecution which will inevitably develop.

This pattern of the restraining of Satan during the Gospel Age and his subsequent release for a short time prior to Jesus' return is clearly set out in some words of John when he reveals that the satanic manifestation of power ruling over the nations *'was, and is not, and will ascend out of the bottomless pit and go to perdition'* (Rev.17:8). The *'was'* refers to the time before Christ's victory, when Satan had a massive hold over all aspects of life and people on earth as the ruler of it. The *'is not'* speaks of the time in which John was writing, the Gospel Age, referring to the devil as having been defeated, disarmed, disgraced, 'bound' and cast out from his rulership of the world. It is for this reason that the Church in the Gospel Age can be described as being *'nourished'* away from *'the presence of the serpent'* (Rev.12:14). The ascent of Satan *'out of the bottomless pit'* refers to the time at the end of the Age when he will be loosed from his restraint and allowed once more to assert the same dominion over the nations that he exercised before the Incarnation of Christ (Rev.20:1-3). However, because there is now instant global communication and travel, coupled with all the preparatory work throughout the Gospel Age, his attempted kingdom on earth will be so much easier to implement than it once was .

This entire satanic sequence of *'was...is not...will ascend'* is an uncanny counterfeit of the true Christ who lived, died, rose from the dead and will come again in glory. Satan is also going to 'rise again' from the death-blow which our Lord dealt him at the Cross and attempt to make a glorious comeback — a counterfeit 'resurrection from the dead'. At the outset of the Book of Revelation, Jesus Christ — in contradistinction to Satan — is described as *'the Alpha and the Omega, the Beginning and the End...who is and who was and who is to come'* (Rev.1:8). Here the Lord Jesus is described as being constantly alive — *'the same yesterday,*

[7] H.C. Leupold, *Exposition of Daniel* (Baker Book House, 1969), p.541.

today, and forever' (Heb.13:8) — whereas the current state of Satan in Rev.17:8 is very definitely described as one who *'is not'*. The point of all this is to comfort us, during this Gospel Age, with the truth that the Spirit and redemptive power of the risen Christ are very much with us, whereas the original universal power of the satanic realm has been held in check by the sovereignty of God for this period to enable the Gospel message to be carried throughout the world.

The demons themselves, during Christ's earthly walk, were actually aware of this power of the Son of God to place them under restraint, although they were ignorant of the manner and timing of when it would happen. They did know that once Jesus had cast them out — whether it was individually during His earthly ministry, or collectively after His victory on the Cross — they would be put under restraint by the Lord of all. This is clearly demonstrated in the account of the demon-possessed man of Gadara. As Jesus approached him, the demons cried out, *'What have we to do with You, Jesus, You Son of God? Have you come here to torment us **before the time**?'* (Mt.8:29). Luke, in his record, adds the fact that the demons *'begged Him that He would not command them to go out **into the abyss**'*, pleading instead to be allowed to take possession of a herd of swine (Lk.8:31-32). So these demons were well aware that their freedom to possess all manner of persons was one day coming to a close — that there would come *'the time'* when they would be cast out into *'into the abyss'* — the title given by Scripture to the other-dimensional condition of restraint. All this came to pass after Jesus had ascended to sit down at the right hand of God, leaving the Holy Spirit to continue the distribution of the benefits of His victory, plundering the spoils of Satan (Ps.68:18; Eph.4:8) and equipping believers to withstand the ravages of the dethroned devil, of which they would be the special recipients.

Satan still remains *'the adversary'* of the Lord's cause during the Gospel Age (1 Tim.5:14; 1 Pet.5:8), and *'the spirit who now works in the sons of disobedience'* (Eph.2:2). However, although he wanders about *'like a roaring lion'* he is all roar and no bite for those who are *'steadfast in the faith'* and who *'resist him'* in submission to God (1 Pet.5:9; Jas.4:7). The true Church, of course, is the particular object of Satan's anger. Having failed in his attempt to destroy the Lord's Anointed One during His earthly pilgrimage, Satan transferred his spiritual warfare to be directed against the Lord's Church on earth (Rev.12:13-17). Although the satanic realm has been 'bound' throughout the Gospel Age — insofar as mustering the nations and religions of the world into an all-out climax against the Lord and His Church is concerned — it has still been most active in pursuit of its vicious aims. Indeed, when one considers the significance and extent of the activities which we will be cataloguing throughout this book, one may well wonder whether Satan's *'little season'* is upon us, so far-reaching has his work been in preparation for the final showdown with his divine Adversary.

As we have shown, the profound setback which Satan received after the building of Babel did not deter him from continuing in his vain attempts to achieve his aim in history — a fact which we can see enshrined in the vast humanistic designs of the pre-Christian Babylonian, Assyrian and Graeco-Roman empires. Similarly, the complete defeat at the time of Calvary did not deter him from continuing to wage war against God and His people. On the contrary his anger was unbounded and especially obvious in the violent persecutions which took place in the early years of Church history. However, because of the Divinely-appointed restriction upon the achievement of his goal in the Gospel Age, even his most ferocious fury was unable to bring his ultimate goal to fruition. Despite the fact that the overt sorcery and utopian ideals of the empire-nations in the pre-Christian era were still operative in the early Church years, the power of the Gospel became overwhelming for the satanic realm, especially in terms of the development of the so-called 'Christian' nations. Thus, if Satan's strategy was to be at all effective, it had to operate in a completely different manner. And this is where the stream of thought which we call the 'Occult' began to manifest itself in world history.

V. THE BEGINNINGS OF OCCULTISM IN SATANIC STRATEGY

As a result of his restrictive binding, Satan began to mastermind his attempted destruction of the Church of Christ from his other-dimensional abode around the earth (cf. Eph.2:2). First came wave-after-wave of terrible persecutions; but these had entirely the reverse effect to that which he desired. For the faith of the saints in these perilous circumstances was evident for all to see, and this attracted many unbelievers to the truths of the Gospel. Because of the abject failure of these persecutions, Satan was forced to change tack, as it were, in his orgy of outrage; and he thus brought into being an occultic plan of global proportions. This has entailed working in a covert fashion as he gradually weaves his tangled web of deceit in every corner of the world, in preparation for his *'little season'*, when he will imagine that he has at last built his 'kingdom of heaven' on earth. When this time finally comes, God will permit all his beguiling intrigues and cabals, together with the complete extent of man's depravity, to come to fruition in an open fullness, as a precursor to Satan's final judgement. As we shall come to see, this strategy would involve a satanic 'gospel' of great seductive power which would work secretly as it gathered impetus, but which would be more clearly revealed in the fulness of time. This is the true place and purpose of 'occultism'.

Before examining this secret work of Satan throughout the Gospel Age, it would be in our interests to discuss the precise meaning of the word 'occult' and the context in which it is being used in this book. In the first place, we should not make the mistake of thinking of the term 'occultism' in its conventional, misunderstood sense, i.e., as a mere reference to overtly unsavoury pseudo-spiritual practices such as black magic, divination, psychic exploration, witchcraft, devil worship, etc. Although such practices could be put under a broad heading of 'occult', to restrict its application to these things alone would be a great boon to the strategy of the satanic realm. *For the true breadth of occultism actually concerns the entire spectrum of Satan's secret work in the world and among the churches.*

This true meaning of occultism, as encompassing *all* the secret work of Satan, is one which has been widely ignored or completely misunderstood. In many Christian circles, the 'occult' is perceived as consisting exclusively in the use of

Ouija Boards, attendance at séances, the celebration of Hallowe'en and ritual devil worship. However, although these activities are certainly part of the highly unsavoury work of the devil, they are in effect 'smoke-screens' thrown up by Satan to obscure the *real* occult, of which many Christians seem to be completely unaware. The word 'occult' is derived from the Latin *occultus* meaning 'hidden' or 'secret', and if we are to come to a correct understanding of the true work of the satanic realm, we must not be fooled into thinking that it is manifest only in what is *obviously* evil. In fact, as we will show, the vast majority of the activities of the satanic realm in the world today are manifested in systems, practices and philosophies which have a purportedly 'humanitarian' or spiritually-beneficient function, and an outwardly appealing veneer. This should not surprise us in view of Paul's sombre warning that *'Satan himself transforms himself into an angel of light. Therefore it is no great thing if his ministers also transform themselves into ministers of righteousness'* (2 Cor.11:14-15).

Many seem to forget that the world, under its usurper Satan, is at war with the true Church; and after the failure of the persecutions, satanic warfare in the Gospel Age involved the *'spewing out'* of a huge flood of ideologies, philosophies, scientific theories, popular movements and spiritual deceptions, with which to carry away the Church of Jesus Christ (Rev.12:15-16; cf. 2 Tim.4:3-4).[8] The true Church, however, is able to withstand this flood of abominations, which only enrages the restrained satanic realm even further (Rev.12:17). Throughout the Gospel Age, because of the restrictions imposed on Satan in the wake of the Cross (coupled with other causes which we shall uncover shortly), he has been forced to work in a great measure on an 'underground' basis. This has meant that various mystery religions, secret coteries, and esoteric cults were to be the vehicles for the dissemination of the satanic Lie. This is the true basis of all occultism.

Although the open sorcery of the more primitive cultures has continued more or less unabated from ancient times, the Western nations have never been open to the practice of such overt perversions. For this reason, the essential magic at the heart of that sorcery was held in the Western nations by secret groups and organisations, until such time as the world was ripe for its wider distribution. And here there is a counterfeit involved; just as the Lord God has always preserved His teachings in the form of the Holy Scriptures and by his singular care and providence kept them pure in all ages, so Satan has sought to do the same with his dogmas. But, whereas the Lord's Truth has been preserved openly and without subterfuge — at one time, in this land, on the tabletops of the majority of homes — Satan's lies have been preserved in the form of secret writings or by oral traditions held by select occult groupings throughout the world. One does not need to be a great researcher or historian to discover these things.

In the East, these secrets have been openly practised for millennia through a

---

[8] Floods, rivers and waves of the sea are often used in Scripture to depict the collective work of the ungodly against the godly — the working of humanistic movements which set themselves up in opposition to the One True God (2 Sam.22:5; Ps.18:4,16; 69:1-2,14-15; Jer.46:7-8; 47:2; 51:55; Lam.3:52-54; Jude 13; cf. Jas.1:6).

wide variety of ancient mystical teachings. However, Satan has pursued a policy of the 'Westernising' of this Eastern knowledge through the occult doctrine of groups such as the Gnostics, Hermeticists, Templars, Cathars, Rosicrucians, Illuminati, Freemasons, Theosophists, Anthroposophists and others. It is worth noting here that, when speaking of the fact that the end of the Age would be characterised by false christs and false prophets who would attempt to deceive the elect, the Lord Jesus Christ warned that the truth about His second coming is not to be found in eremitic or occultic circumstances:

> 'Then if anyone says to you, *"Look, here is the Christ!"* or *"There!"* do not believe it. For false christs and false prophets will arise and show great signs and wonders, so as to deceive, if possible, even the elect. See, I have told you beforehand. Therefore if they say to you, *"Look, He is in the desert!"* do not go out; or *"Look, He is in the inner rooms!"* do not believe it. For as the lightning comes from the east and flashes to the west, so also will the coming of the Son of Man be"
>
> (Mt.24:23-26).

This warning about the 'desert' and the 'inner rooms' is a categorical rejection of all ascetic and esoteric coteries which lay claim to Messianic truth. The open heart of Christian Truth is that it *'was not done in a corner'* (Acts 26:26). In fact the entire Gospel message is the very opposite of 'occult' teaching. As the Lord Jesus Himself said, *'I spoke openly to the world...and in secret I have said nothing'* (Jn.18:20; cf. Isa.48:16). But Satan has been working secretly — both politically and spiritually — on a vast scale throughout the Gospel Age. Alongside of this subterfuge, he has mounted a constant onslaught, intensifying periodically, of false teaching against the true Church of Christ. This important truth was foreseen and predicted by both the Lord Jesus Christ and His apostles, as one can see from the many prophetic references which relate not only to the spread of false doctrine in the world at large (Mt.24:5,11; 2 Th.2:4; 1 Tim.4:1; 2 Tim.3:1-9; 2 Pet.3:1-4; 1 Jn.2:18,19; 4:1-3) but also to the fact that people who do not inwardly serve the cause of Christ would creep into the churches with the express purpose of deceiving all those who have been saved by the Lord (Acts 20:28-31; Rom.16:17,18; 2 Cor.2:17; Gal.1:6,7; 2 Pet.2:1-3).

In terms of the Gospel Age, one can say that the true depths of satanic occultism are represented by the *'mystery of lawlessness'* which was already at work when Paul was alive (2 Th.2:7). Similarly, the Apostle John refers to *'the spirit of the Antichrist, which you have heard was coming, and is now already in the world'* (1 Jn.4:3). In other words, the preconditions which will eventually issue in the revealing of the Antichrist at the end of the Age were already at work in the first century of the Church. A 'mystery' in Scripture always refers to something which was formerly hidden but is now revealed to those who are the children of God. The secret work of Satan is clearly unfolded to us in the Word of God, especially in the Book of Revelation and other specific texts in the New Testament (e.g., Eph.6:10ff.; 2 Th.2:3-12, etc.). The background to religious corruption in the Gospel Age can be found in a huge build-up, over many centuries, of numerous occult groupings — a 'mystery of lawlessness' on a vast scale — which have helped to disseminate the teachings of Satan in the wake of the Cross.

All the occult work of Satan in the past two thousand years is now culminating in the growth of a spiritual development known today as the 'New Age Movement', and in its politico-economic sister: the 'New World Order'.[9] One of the central claims of this book is that the New Age Movement is *not* just another strange sect or cult of the modern era like Jehovah Witnesses, Mormons or Christian Scientists. Unless we have a proper grasp of this, there will be a fundamental misunderstanding of all the spiritual developments which are taking place in the modern world. For what we today call the 'New Age Movement' or the 'New Consciousness' is not *new* at all; it is actually the culmination of years of careful occult preparation. It is at least as old as the hills and could well prove to be the climax of every ambition of Satan in his long war against God. The New Age Movement (in conjunction with the moves to create a New World Order) has a far-reaching eschatological dimension and exhibits all the signs of being a major vehicle for the final manifestation of Satan's attempted kingdom-building project on earth — a project which has passed through many phases down the millennia. The New Age vision for the future of human civilisation is entirely in harmony with the biblical data concerning the approach of the end of this evil age, when man will finally begin to believe that he has subdued the world, brought down the Church and removed the need for belief in the transcendent God of the Bible. Never before in history have all the conditions been so advantageous to the fulfilment of this fundamental aim of Satan and his demonic realm.

As we progress through this book, we will see the numerous twists and turns of historical development which have made possible the prevailing conditions of the present day. We will come to see that the influence of the New Age Movement is sweeping through the formative institutions of Western culture — especially the intelligentsia, the 'caring' professions (social work, nursing, etc.), medicine,

[9] The connection between the New Age Movement and the New World Order is not a fanciful one. The term 'New World Order' first appeared, in connection with the New Age, in the writings of the occultist, Alice B. Bailey, whose husband, Foster Bailey, was a prolific writer and expert on Freemasonry. Furthermore, it is no coincidence that the U.S. one-dollar banknote shows an Egyptian pyramid with an occultic 'All-Seeing Eye' atop — a Masonic representation of the 'Great Architect of the Universe' — under which is the inscription *Novus Ordo Seclorum*, Latin for 'New World Order'. This design was brought into circulation in 1935 by order of Franklin D. Roosevelt, President of the United States of America and a 32nd degree Freemason. The rich vein of Masonic symbolism in the artwork of the one-dollar banknote (and in the Great Seal of the United States of America) is really quite astonishing and should be studied by all readers who desire to comprehend the powers of darkness which have propagated the 'mystery of iniquity' in this present evil age. See the chapter 'The Great Seal' in A. Ralph Epperson, *The New World Order* (Publius Press, 1992), available from 3100, Sth. Philamena Place, Tucson, Arizona 85730, USA. Historic Freemasonry, when properly understood, is the culmination of thousands of years of occult development and is intimately connected with the forces which have propagated the New Age Movement, as we shall be showing later in this book.

psychology, psychotherapy, multi-national industry, the major religious faiths, global agencies and world government organisations. There is no area of life which is now devoid of this New Age activity. Strangely, there is a reluctance among many groups of believers to face up to the fact that there is a cosmic malevolence of global proportions in these developments. Until Christians wake up to these facts, they will continue to hold an entirely inadequate view of this movement and will fail to measure up to it apologetically. Satanic activity during the past two thousand years has not been confined merely to the tempting of people to sin, as some appear to believe. For Satan has continued to mastermind a grandiose world-plan from his beleaguered stronghold in 'the air'; and what we call the 'New Age Movement' is the net result of that activity.

Even secular observers of New Age developments have not been slow to grasp the fact that they are not 'new' phenomena. As one scholarly publication puts it:

> 'Despite its relatively recent appearance, the [New Age] movement should not be viewed as a startlingly new phenomenon in Western culture. Rather, it is more adequately seen as *the latest phase in occult-metaphysical religion,* a persistent tradition that has been the constant companion of Christianity through the centuries and has blossomed heartily as a product of eighteenth-century scientific enlightenment'.[10] [emphasis added]

This is an uncommonly accurate summation of what the New Age Movement is: the latest phase in *'occult-metaphysical religion'*. However, rather than being a mere constant *companion* of Christianity through the centuries, it would be more accurate to say that this occult-metaphysical religion has been a constant *combatant* of Christianity. In fact, this occult-metaphysical tradition — of which the New Age Movement is merely the latest phase — is really a continuation of the ancient heresy of 'Gnosticism' which has plagued the Church since the very beginning of her history. We believe, therefore, that it would be far more consistent with Christian analysis to speak of the 'New Gnosticism' rather than the New Age Movement or the New Consciousness; and this is the convention we shall adopt throughout the rest of this book.

In the following section, we will examine the rise of ancient Gnosticism in the Church. A sound knowledge of these early Church developments in the wake of the Cross will give us a greater understanding of later developments in satanic strategy during the Gospel Age.

VI. GNOSTICISM: THE ANTITHESIS OF CHRISTIAN TRUTH

Earlier in this chapter we examined the effect that the sinless life, sacrificial death and victorious ascension of the Lord Jesus Christ had on the work of Satan in the world. We came to see that the devil has been put under severe restriction from being able to achieve his ultimate goal of complete anti-Jehovah dominion over the kingdoms of the world. However, although the binding of Satan ensured

---

[10] J. Gordon Melton, *New Age Encyclopedia*, Gale Research, 1990, p.xxii.

that there could not be a premature eclipse of the work of the Gospel in the world, we should not underestimate the influence which the demonic realm has been able to exert on the affairs of human history during the past two thousand years. Satan's aim in history is to have a collective power-base among the nations of the world and, ultimately, to destroy the Church. The very existence of the Church is a torment to Satan and his followers, which must be obliterated (cf. Rev.11:7-10).

During the first three centuries after the victory of Christ, Satan certainly stirred up a great degree of persecution of the Church through the governing authorities. However, because of the severe restriction on his activities in the present age, this had exactly the opposite effect to that which he intended. One of the great facts in Church history is that the more the Church has been persecuted, the more it has thrived. Unbelieving people who lived during the first three centuries of the Church saw the faith exercised by the saints in the face of persecution and liquidation, and this moved them to embrace that faith for themselves. Not only did such persecution lead to the enlargement of the Church, but the Scripture shows that it actually worked to the eternal benefit of the Lord's people (Rev.2:10). As John Calvin has put it: *'Whatever poison Satan produces, God turns it into medicine for his elect'*.

Alongside this phase of persecution during these early centuries of Church history, Satan also brought into being a form of counterfeit Christianity, known as Gnosticism, which threatened to destroy the true witness of the Church. This was Satan's first mighty assault on Christian doctrine, the primal hammer-blow in a theological battle which has never abated. The word 'gnostic' is derived from the Greek word *gnostikos*, meaning 'knowing one', from the noun *gnosis*, 'knowledge'. The term has come to be applied to a widely-based religious movement which posed a major threat to the purity of the Truth in the period of the early Church. Although there was an incipient Gnosticism around during the first century, the stream of *gnosis* did not become properly established until the second century, by which time Gnosticism had become the first and foremost heresy in the Christian Church. The most clearly organised systems were those of Basilides (A.D.130), who claimed that his doctrine came from Peter, and Valentinus (A.D.150), who claimed to have received Pauline teaching via a man named Theudas. Needless to say, their claims were totally unfounded.

A Gnostic is a person who claims to have received esoteric knowledge (*gnosis*) given by special revelation — either through direct experience or by initiation into an occult tradition — which can then be transmitted to others, through personal teaching and training, or in doctrines handed down through the workings of an initiated group or organisation. Gnosticism, as it has flowered in the Gospel Age, has been well defined as *'Christianity perverted by learning and speculation'*.[11] As one heresiologist has put it:

> 'The gnostic position was a response to the widespread desire to understand the mystery of being: it offered detailed secret knowledge of the whole order of reality, claiming to know and to be able to explain

[11] H.M. Gwatkin, *Early Church History* (Macmillan, 1909), Vol.II, p.73.

> things of which ordinary simple Christian faith was entirely ignorant. It divided mankind into various classes, and reserved its secret wisdom for those who were recognized as belonging to the highest, most spiritual call, a religious elite. Thus, it naturally appealed to many who felt that they were above mingling with the common herd of ordinary Christians who were content with the simple Gospel'.[12]

There is, however, a vast gulf between Christian Truth and Gnostic knowledge. The gnostically-inclined person will always desire a 'higher' form of knowledge which will tune him or her into the world of spirit. Such a person will look down his nose at the *'simplicity that is in Christ'* (2 Cor.11:3) and the truth of the Gospel, believing that authentic truth could not possibly be so naive and so widely attainable. The Christian Gospel is freely proclaimed to all — regardless of their class, education, intelligence quotient, financial status, and psychological condition — whereas Gnosticism always develops an elitist system. The Gnostic views the 'ordinary' Christian believer as one who has merely received the outer husk of Christianity, whereas he regards the one with *gnosis* as having been endowed with something far deeper and more meaningful. Spiritual pride and elitism will always rear their ugly heads when the human being seeks spiritual knowledge and enlightenment outside of the context in which it has been ordained by God. We are reminded here of the desire of the woman in Eden for wisdom beyond that with which she had been endowed by the Lord (Gen.3:6).

There are a number of indications that Paul the Apostle was well aware of the religious tendency to Gnosticism, about which he warned the recipients of his letters. In his epistles to the Corinthians, he was especially careful to highlight the difference between forbidden *gnosis* and genuinely-Christian *knowledge*. When he tells the believers at Corinth that *'Knowledge [*Greek: *gnosis] puffs up, but love [*Greek: *agape] edifies'* (1 Cor.8:1), it is obvious that he is not referring to *all* knowledge. In fact, in another letter he makes it clear what kind of knowledge it is that should be avoided by those who would embrace true religion. Concluding his first letter to Timothy, the Apostle writes:

> 'O, Timothy, guard the deposit, having turned away from the profane empty babblings and opposing theories of the *falsely named knowledge* (Gk., *pseudonumos gnoseos*), which some having asserted have missed the mark concerning the faith' (1 Tim.6:20-21, author's translation).

For Paul to speak of those asserting the falsely-named knowledge as having 'missed the mark' is most appropriate. The actual words 'pseudonymous gnosis' formed the basis of the title for a massive work by Irenaeus of Lyons (*c.* A.D.130-200) called 'Against Heresies or A Refutation and Overthrow of Falsely Named Knowledge', in which he exposed the deception of the many Gnostic schools of his time.[13] There are other New Testament Scriptures which

---

[12] Harold O.J. Brown, *Heresies: The Image of Christ in the Mirror of Heresy and Orthodoxy from the Apostles to the Present* (Baker Book House, 1984), pp.39-40.

[13] This work is well worth obtaining as it constitutes an exhaustive first-hand exposé of

appear to take issue with incipient Gnostic teachings. In his letter to the Colossians, Paul warns against being taken in by those who have an interest in speculative and esoteric matters, who have an appearance of spirituality, but who worship angelic beings and practise asceticism (Col.2:18-23). In his second letter to Timothy, he speaks of a time coming when people

> 'will not endure sound doctrine, but according to their own desires, because they have itching ears, they will heap up for themselves teachers; and they will turn their ears away from the truth, and be turned aside to fables' (2 Tim.4:3-4).

The Greek word here translated as 'fables' is *muthos*, from which we derive our word 'myths'. When one examines the theological systems of the Gnostics, one is certainly confronted with myths on a vast scale. Other Scriptures also appear to refer to the incipient Gnosticism of the second half of the first century. In John's first letter, the Apostle identifies the spirit of Antichrist as disbelief in the fact that Jesus is the Christ and that He was a real man of flesh (1 Jn.2:22; 4:1-3; 5:1). This suggests that John was well aware of Gnostic-type doctrine when he wrote these words. Many Gnostic sects were 'Docetic' (from the Greek *dokeo*, to seem), that is, they believed that Jesus was not a real man but was a kind of spirit-being who only *appeared* to be a man. Because they believed that matter was inherently evil, they could not accept that Jesus would partake of it. It is highly significant that the Apostle actually makes the rejection of this view a litmus test of true Christianity (1 Jn.4:2-3; 2:22-23). In their opposition to these Gnostic beliefs, the faithful of the early Church were laying down perennial principles for us to follow. As the ultimate snub to the Gnostic mindset, Paul said that even if people claim to understand *'all mysteries and all knowledge'* (Greek: *gnosis*), this experience in itself is worthless (1 Cor.13:2).

At this point, let us discover what sort of 'knowledge' it is that the Gnostic is seeking. What exactly is the *gnosis* which forms the basis of his spiritual ambition? Occult researcher, James Webb, states that

> 'The Gnosis, the knowledge which ensures salvation, is the realization by man that he contains a spark of God, and of the necessity of awakening from the half-life he leads on earth — described variously as "numbness", "sleep", or "intoxication" — to a full consciousness of his divinity and of how it has been ensnared in matter'.[14]

The Gnostic is, therefore, seeking a special knowledge which will bring him into an awareness of himself as God. In short, he is seeking to attain personal divinity. This is a phenomenon which will confront us again and again in this book, as it constitutes one of the major components of all corrupt religious enterprise. For this is the same 'knowledge' which our first parents saw as having the potential to make them at least as wise as their Creator, and certainly wiser than He had originally intended (Gen.3:4-6). In other words, having the *gnosis* is just

---

the second century equivalent of today's New Age Movement.

[14] James Webb, *The Occult Underground* (Open Court, 1974), p.199.

another form of the Initiation which our first parents received from Satan at the dawn of history. It is in Eden that the *gnosis*, the satanic antithesis of true knowledge, made its first entrance on the world stage, and it has haunted God's people ever since. The Hebrew word for 'wizard' is *yiddeoni*, which means 'knowing one', that is, one who has secret knowledge (*gnosis*). The Children of Israel were commanded to avoid the *yiddeoni* (Dt.18:10-12), just as the Christian is counselled to turn away from the Gnosis which is *'falsely so-called'* (1 Tim.6:20-21).

In support of their concept of *gnosis*, Gnostics will often quote Jesus as saying: *'You shall* ***know*** (Greek: *ginosko*) *the truth, and the truth shall make you free'* (Jn.8:32). But this is to remove these words from their context. The full quotation is prefixed by the statement *'If you abide in My word, you are My disciples indeed'*, and suffixed by Jesus showing that the bondage from which the Christian is removed has nothing to do with being *'ensnared in matter'* but is a reversal of his or her *enslavement to sin* (see Jn.8:30-35). Christian freedom is about obedience to the words of Christ and liberation from the lawlessness and lies (which include the *gnosis*) which Satan introduced into world history at the beginning. Christian freedom is not about techniques of consciousness-raising in order to achieve divinity but is about a relationship with a Person. When Jesus prayed, concerning His disciples, *'And this is eternal life, that they may* ***know*** *You, the only true God, and Jesus Christ whom You have sent'* (Jn.17:3), He was proclaiming a personal knowledge of the Living God in the Man, Christ Jesus. Surely, that is the greatest 'gnosis' one could receive — and it requires no technique, system or practices in order to achieve it, but faith alone.

What made the Gnostic heresy so different from other false teachings was that to the gullible and undiscerning believer, it could appear to carry even more spiritual weight than the teaching of the Church of the Living God, which is *'the pillar and ground of the truth'* (1 Tim.3:15). However, it is most important for the development of our Christian discernment to realise that Satan, rather than substituting outright falsehood for truth, has generally sought to mingle the two together in deceptive harmony. As Irenaeus of Lyons has put it:

> 'For no false teaching desires to offer itself to our view openly, lest such exposure should lead to conviction; but, craftily putting on a plausible dress, makes itself by its outward form appear to the simpler sort to be truer than Truth itself '.[15]

One of the great claims of the perpetrators of early Gnosticism was that their religion was actually the true kernel of Christianity — that Jesus and the Apostles were Gnostics upholding Gnostic ideals but whose teaching was distorted into mere religious forms, a lifeless husk, by those who came after them. But this claim just does not stand up at a number of crucial points. Jesus predicted that the Apostles would be persecuted (Mt.24:9; Jn.15:18-21), as indeed they and many others in the first two centuries were, by the Roman Empire. But if it is true that

---

[15] Irenaeus of Lyons, *'Against Heresies'* or *'A Refutation and Overthrow of Knowledge Falsely So-Called'*, Introduction §2.

they had been Gnostics, they would have suffered no persecution at the hands of the Rome of that period, for it was a syncretistic dustbin for every cult with which the empire came in contact. It was precisely because Christianity was entirely new and offered something radically different from any other form of spiritual expression in the world (which Gnosticism did not) that it was subject to so much persecuting zeal by the Roman authorities. If Christianity had been another Gnostic-style cult, it would simply have been swallowed up into the morass of syncretic religion along with Valentinism and the teaching of Cerinthus and would never have been preserved through the ages. Moreover, if Jesus and the Apostles had been preaching a Gnostic gospel such as, *'Tune into your divine consciousness'*, or *'Don't just worship Christ, be one!'*, or *'The Jehovah-God of the Old Testament is not the Supreme Being'*, they would have been most acceptable to the religious thought of the time, and would never have been subject to persecution. In fact, it would be no exaggeration to say that the early Christians were persecuted precisely because they were *not* Gnostics!

The claim that Jesus was a Gnostic-style teacher is not only held by advocates of Gnosticism today, but it is also the view of many in the field of comparative religion who contend that Jesus was associated with the incipient Gnostic sect and ascetic fraternity called the *Essenes*, who did not mix with those outside their communities.[16] However, as Nesta Webster points out in her informative work on secret societies,

> 'Christ did not live in a fraternity but...associated with publicans and sinners. The Essenes did not frequent the Temple [but] Christ was there frequently. The Essenes disapproved of wine and marriage, whilst Christ sanctioned marriage by His presence at the wedding of Cana in Galilee and there turned water into wine... One of the principal traits of the Essenes which distinguished them from the other Jewish sects of their day was their disapproval of ointment, which they regarded as defiling, whilst Christ...commended the woman who brought the precious jar of ointment'.[17]

It is not only the scholars and comparative religionists who want to fashion the Lord Jesus into a Gnostic and Christianity into Gnosticism. Even the rock musician and Neo-Gnostic John Lennon, wearing his writer's hat, summed up this concept in a chapter entitled 'The Mysterious Smell of Roses' in his surrealist anthology, *Skywriting by Word of Mouth*:

> 'It seems to me that the only true Christians were (are?) the Gnostics, who believe in self-knowledge, i.e., becoming Christ themselves, reaching the Christ within'.[18]

---

[16] The worldview of the Essenes and its comparison with the doctrine of Christ has already been dealt with in some detail in Chapter 1.

[17] Nesta Webster, *Secret Societies and Subversive Movements* (Bloomfield Books, f.p. 1924), p.24.

[18] John Lennon, *Skywriting by Word of Mouth* (Harper & Row, 1986), p.35.

In saying this, Lennon — who, in 1966, had claimed that the Beatles *'were bigger than Jesus'* — was simply echoing the ancient gnostic scripture known as the 'Gospel According to Philip', which includes within its pages the claim that the person who achieves 'gnosis' is *'no longer a Christian, but a Christ'*.[19] This is a classic Gnostic statement, suggesting that the person who has simple faith in Christ is only a Christian; whereas the one who realises his Christ-consciousness through *gnosis* is in an altogether-higher class of spirituality. That has always been the appeal of Gnosticism — especially to those too sophisticated to accept the simplicity (childlikeness) of Christian faith.

Throughout the first few centuries of the life of the Church, many Gnostic writings began to appear with titles which were very similar to those which had been written by Divine revelation. Works with names such as the Gospel of Thomas, the Gospel of Philip, the Epistle of Peter to Philip, the Acts of Peter, the Apocalypse of Paul, and so on, were a great confusion of the time and must have seduced many into a syncretic mix of Gnosticism and Christianity. Indeed, their proliferation was a major influence encouraging the Church to finalise an authoritative 'canon' of New Testament scriptures. Some of these Gnostic writings were discovered in Egypt in 1945. Known as the Nag Hammadi Texts, they have set the comparative religion scene alight with the promise of showing that the teaching of Jesus and much of early Christianity was really a Gnostic phenomenon. In 1990, a series of programmes called 'The Gnostics' was made for Channel Four television by the Gnostic sympathiser Tobias Churton. On the back cover of the accompanying book is written:

> 'The Gnostic Gospels were discovered in the sands of Upper Egypt in 1945. They comprise a golden string of secret teachings — an alternative tradition to conventional Christianity'.[20]

This parading of Gnosticism as being a viable 'alternative tradition to conventional Christianity' represents the heart-dream of the vast majority of teachers and academics in the comparative religion scene today. For such people, these writings appear to show that the Church can no longer lay any claim to exclusivity. The threat to the original purity of Christian doctrine by these writings was not lost on the fathers of the Church. For example, Athanasius, Bishop of Alexandria in N. Egypt, specifically warned about bogus writings in his 39th Festal Letter to Theodore, head of the monastery at Tabinnisi, which was not too far from where the Nag Hammadi texts were found. Athanasius had himself lived among the monastic communities which were being suffused with false scriptures, and he wrote:

> 'I fear lest, as Paul wrote to the Corinthians, some few of the simple should be beguiled from their simplicity and purity, by the subtlety of certain men, and should afterwards read other books — those called apochryphal — led astray by the similarity of their names with the true

---

[19] R.McL. Wilson, (ed.), *The Gospel of Philip*, (Mowbrays, 1962), 67:26-27, p.43.

[20] Tobias Churton, *The Gnostics* (Channel 4 with Weidenfeld & Nicholson), 1990, back cover.

> books... Forasmuch as some have taken in hand, to reduce into order for themselves the books termed apochryphal, and to mix them up with the divinely inspired Scripture, concerning which we have been fully persuaded, as they who from the beginning were eyewitnesses and ministers of the word, delivered to the fathers'.[21]

It is certainly no coincidence that these Gnostic works have been found in Egypt at this particular stage of world history. Such a discovery could not have occurred at a more opportune moment in the unfolding of Satan's assault on the Church. In his introduction to Irenaeus' work, *Against Heresies*, A. Cleveland Coxe stated that the principal task of Irenaeus in this great work was two-fold:

> '1) To render it impossible for anyone to confound Gnosticism with Christianity, and 2) to make is impossible for such a monstrous system to surface, or ever to rise again'.[22]

However, although Irenaeus' work was a valiant effort which could not have been bettered at the time, it is a demonstration of the hardiness of satanic doctrine and the inherent evil of this present age that the Church has never been able to finally overthrow the Gnostic stream of religion. There are two primary reasons for this: first, the ever-ready willingness of the world to receive such doctrine; and second, its chameleon-like nature. This ability of Gnosticism to reproduce itself in an ever-multiplying array of variations has been a major key to its survival, manifesting itself according to the situation in which it flowered. This is shown in the following statement from a heresiologist of the last century:

> 'Two elements thus combined towards the development of the Gnostic; *first*, a desire to form a philosophy of Christianity; and *secondly*, the craving after a philosophy of religion to which Christianity and the old faiths of the world should each contribute their share of truth and theory. Hence arose three principal types of intellectual speculation, the Judaizing, the Oriental, and the Greek. All three had the common feature of eclecticism, but the eclecticism of each was influenced by local colouring; and hence the general speculative tendency which produced Gnosticism produced a Cabbalistic, a Zoroastrian, or a mythological Gnostic, according to his antecedent habits of thought and the intellectual atmosphere in which he lived'.[23]

Even in the second century, Irenæus of Lyons could claim that *'every day every one of them invents something new'*.[24] In common with so many other man-made

---

[21] Ibid., p.5.

[22] A. Cleveland Coxe, 'Introductory Note to Irenaeus' *Against Heresies*' in Alexander Roberts and James Donaldson (eds.) *The Ante-Nicene Fathers: Translations of the Writings of the Fathers down to A.D. 325* (Eerdmans, 1977), Vol.I, p.310.

[23] John Henry Blunt, *Dictionary of Sects, Heresies, Ecclesiastical Parties, and Schools of Religious Thought* (Rivingtons, 1874), pp.176-177.

[24] Irenaeus of Lyons, *Against Heresies* or *'A Refutation and Overthrow of Knowledge Falsely So-Called*, I.18.1.

religious beliefs, Gnosticism was (and still is) a wax nose which can point in any direction. For this reason, it has never been a single identifiable religion as such — although there are certain essential features which tend to repeat themselves in whatever situation it occurs, as we will later show.

In addition to the individual variations, Gnosticism has always been the product of wave after wave of syncretism. It is a well-documented fact that the first Gnostic sects which arose in the post-Christian Roman Empire had, as their doctrines, *'an admixture of Indian, Egyptian, Babylonian, and Christian creeds, astrology and magic, with much of the Jewish Kabbala also'*.[25] Another writer sums up this endemic syncretism by concurring that

> 'the Gnostic systems compounded everything — oriental mythologies, astrological doctrines, Iranian theology, elements of Jewish tradition (whether biblical, rabbinical or occult), Christian-salvation eschatology, Platonic terms and concepts...'.[26]

This admixture of many varieties of the ancient satanic religion was the driving force behind the Gnostic stream at the commencement of the Gospel Age. It is as if the Gnostic movement of the first and second centuries burst upon the Church as an expression of the rage of the defeated and thwarted Satan (Rev.12:17). This was so marked that Church historian A.M. Renwick has noted that

> 'by the beginning of the third century A.D. most of the intellectual Christian congregations throughout the Roman empire were to some degree affected by it'.[27]

If one wishes to look for a doctrine which could *'seduce the elect'*, one need look no further than Gnosticism. Its fundamental tenets have never had any difficulty seducing the vast numbers of professing Christians who, because of an over-reliance on human wisdom, find themselves unable to rest in the simplicity of the Gospel. As Robert Law puts it:

> 'Of all the forces with which Christianity had to do battle for its career as the universal religion — Jewish legalism, pagan superstition, Greek speculation, Roman imperialism — none, perhaps, placed it in sharper hazard than Gnosticism, that strange, obscure movement, partly intellectual, partly fanatical, which, in the second century, spread with the swiftness of an epidemic over the Church from Syria to Gaul'.[28]

This veil of *gnosis* over the global churches of the first two or three centuries A.D. should not be underestimated. As the German scholar, Professor Kurt Rudolph, notes in his authoritative study:

---

[25] Leslie A. Shepard (ed.), *Encyclopedia of Occultism and Parapsychology* (Gale Research Co., 1979), Vol.1, p.378.

[26] Hans Jonas, *The Gnostic Religion* (Beacon Press, 1963), p.25.

[27] G.W. Bromiley (ed.), *The International Standard Bible Encyclopedia* (Eerdmans, 1982), Vol.2, p.484.

[28] Robert Law, *The Tests of Life: A Study of the First Epistle of St. John* (T. & T. Clark, 1909), p.26.

> 'The gnostic trauma of the first post-Christian centuries goes deeper that that of the bloody persecutions. One can almost say that Gnosis followed the Church like a shadow; the Church could never overcome it, its influence had gone too deep. By reason of their common history they remain two – hostile – sisters'.[29]

As this book progresses, we will come to see that the threat of Gnosticism to the purity of the Church and its epidemic proportions, are no less serious today than they were eighteen hundred years ago. However, there came a point in history when the Gnostic schools which had so widely plagued the Church in the first three centuries mysteriously disappeared from view. Concerning this phenomenon, Professor Rudolph states that

> 'the beginning and end of Gnosis in late antiquity cannot be pinpointed exactly. It makes its appearance at the beginning of the Christian era and disappears again at the latest in the sixth century'.[30]

In fact, the bulk of these groups had disappeared between 300-400 AD, although a further two hundred years were to pass before they had died away entirely. Humanly speaking, one of the primary reasons that Gnosticism disappeared from view at this time was the fact that once the Church had become intertwined with the secular ruling powers, the legal enforcement of Christianity came into being. This occurred with the professed conversion of the Roman Emperor Constantine in 312 A.D. Within a few years, decrees were issued prohibiting magic and divination (318 and 320), and after 330, Neoplatonism fell under the same condemnation. In the Eastern Empire in 380-381, all non-Christian religions were outlawed by Emperor Theodosius and it was declared illegal to depart from the Nicene Creed. This trend was soon followed in the West a couple of years later with the invasion of Italy.

With the Christian profession of Emperor Constantine, the monolithic State-Church had come into being, using every means at its disposal to repress those who would not conform to the new religious regime. However repugnant we may find such crude repression, and whether we agree or not with the 'Constantine Factor' as a valid manifestation in the life of the Church in the New Covenant, the fact remains that the prevention, by the Roman authorities, of the Gnostic stream (in whatever form) from spreading across the globe gained for the Church an extra twelve hundred years during which the divinely-inspired Scriptures (and the true Gospel) could be preserved. Perhaps this intervention of the Emperor Constantine and other national leaders is what is being prophesied by the Apostle John when he tells us that

> 'the earth helped the woman [i.e., the Church], and the earth opened its mouth and swallowed up the flood [i.e., false teachings] which the dragon had spewed out of his mouth' (Rev.12:16).

---

[29] Kurt Rudolph, *Gnosis: The Nature and History of Gnosticism* (Harper & Row, 1987), p.368.

[30] Ibid., p.367.

Until the time of Constantine's profession of Christianity, vicious persecution and doctrinal perversions of the faith had indeed been the experience of believers throughout the empire. Suddenly all this was changed and, although there would come an increasing institutionalisation and ritualisation of Christianity, the contents of the true Scriptures could be spread throughout the world as exploration and travel opened up. Let us always remember that whatever conceits man dreams up, the Lord always turns such evil to work for the good of His people and to the glory of His holy name. It is a marvellous thing that in spite of the crass and often perverted forms in which the Bible and its Christian teachings have been introduced into many places in the world, somehow the Truth has been preserved for those who have the God-given discernment to cut through the veil to the Light behind it.

However, the fading from sight of the Gnostic schools between the fourth and sixth centuries was by no means the end of the story. Although the binding of Satan meant that the major lines of his opposition to the progress of the Gospel (e.g., Gnosticism and repressive persecution by the Roman authorities) had been severely restricted, this merely heralded the beginning of a fresh initiative on Satan's part. In the following chapters, we will show that the collapse of ancient Gnosticism in the third century and its apparent disappearance for the ensuing twelve hundred years was merely to be a lengthy hiatus while it gathered strength for a major onslaught which first emerged into the light of day in the seventeenth century, began to flower in the late eighteenth century, and eventually came to fruition during the last four decades of the twentieth.

As we shall come to appreciate by the conclusion of this present work, the concepts which lie at the heart of Gnosticism in all its forms — if they can be inculcated far and wide enough throughout the world — will easily fulfil all the despotic earthly ambitions of *' the rulers of the darkness of this age...spiritual hosts of wickedness'* (Eph.6:12). One of the primary theses of this book — and one which we will repeatedly demonstrate — is that although the outward schools of the Gnostics died away between the third and sixth centuries, their doctrine was preserved by a great many individuals and monastic communities in the Middle East before being disseminated in a westward direction through various mystics and the secret teachings of a number of occult organisations — including the Jewish Kabbalah which thrived in South-Western Europe in the Middle Ages. As one researcher of occult history puts it:

> 'Gnosticism did not survive as organised opposition to Christianity: but Gnostic tenets were to prove among the hardest to eradicate from the ranks of heresy. Similarly, the mass of magical and debased Neo-Platonic literature like the *Hermetica* could be excluded from the sphere of influence of the Christian Church, but not destroyed. Among the Arabs, such traditions of thought lingered on, and were gradually re-introduced into Europe'.[31]

---

[31] James Webb, *The Occult Underground* (Open Court, 1974), p.201.

Today, a New Gnosticism is thriving in a multitude of ways, of which most people — especially those professing Christianity — are entirely unaware. As we come to the close of the twentieth century after the coming of the Lord Jesus Christ, we find ourselves living in the midst of a world-culture which is essentially Gnostic in its aims and concepts. In the following three chapters, we will be uncovering this phenomenon and tracing it back through its forebears. In doing so, we will begin to understand the significance and purpose of the spiritual battle in which every man, woman and child on this planet is involved.

PART TWO

THE GODS OF THE NATIONS

Religious Corruption in the World-System Today

'And war broke out in heaven: Michael and his angels fought against the dragon; and the dragon and his angels fought, but they did not prevail, nor was a place found for them in heaven any longer. So the great dragon was cast out, that serpent of old, called the Devil and Satan, who deceives the whole world; he was cast to the earth, and his angels were cast out with him... Woe to the inhabitants of the earth and the sea! For the devil has come down to you, having great wrath, because he knows that he has a short time' (Revelation 12:7-9,12).

Chapter Three

THE FOUNDING OF THE NEW GNOSTICISM

(1) The Seeds of Corruption

'There is nothing new under the sun. Is there anything of which it may be said, "See, this is new"? It has already been in ancient times before us' (Ecclesiastes 1:9-10)

In the last chapter, we established the biblical evidence that Satan has been under restriction during the Gospel Age, being unable to work in the nations to the extent that he could prior to Christ's victorious life, death, resurrection and ascension, and therefore constrained from being able to bring these nations into full and open revolt against Jehovah-Christ and His Church. We also examined the true meaning of occultism and charted the way in which the Gnostic heresy became a powerful antichristian force during the first three centuries of the Church, before disappearing almost entirely from view. However, as we also noted, this did not spell the end of *gnosis* and its work in the world. This is even recognised by scholars of Gnosticism. For example, Professor Kurt Rudolph of Philipp's University in Marburg, Germany, in his authoritative study on Gnosticism, acknowledges that there have been *'after-effects of Gnosis beyond its concrete historical existence'*, which can be seen in *'the reception of gnostic ideas and fragments of systems in modern syncretistic-theosophic sects'*.[1] Our business in this chapter is to show that there is a clear bridge between the modern 'syncretistic-theosophic' sects and the ancient stream of Gnosticism.

When broken down into its fundamentals, Gnosticism can be seen to exist within certain perpetual parameters. It has hallmarks which can be seen repeatedly, regardless of the manner in which it manifests itself. One writer asserts:

> '(a) It is rationalistic. It is seeking to answer questions outside the scope of the O.T. and the Apostolic witness, and to do so on wholly non-biblical assumptions. (b) It is mystical, in the sense of seeking identification with and absorption in the divine...(c) It is mythological, employing a system of mythology to express truth, as an essential supplement to (or in some cases substitute for) the biblical tradition'.[2]

---

1 Kurt Rudolph, *Gnosis: The Nature and History of Gnosticism* (Harper & Row, 1987), p.368.

2 Merrill C. Tenney (ed.), *The Pictorial Encyclopedia of the Bible* (Zondervan, 1975), Vol.2, p.737.

Extra-biblical rationalism, mysticism and mythology — these are some of the perennial features of Gnosticism. There are others which we can add to these:

- The idea of an ancient, 'secret wisdom tradition' to be passed within a group of initiates, a 'gnosis' which will bring liberation from the confines of the world of matter.
- The belief in an 'Inner Christ', that everyone possesses a spark of divinity within, which can be rekindled through the activation of various techniques.
- The concept of reincarnation or the pre-existence of souls (metempsychosis) crops up in many of the early Gnostic sects. This we will have cause to examine later in relation to the more recent manifestations of Gnosticism.

When we examine these various features, we will see that there is a clear stream of Gnostic religion which runs from the early Church era to the present day. In this historical passage of Gnosticism, there has been an identifiable movement of ideas from East to West. Professor John Mosheim has rightly noted that *'it was from oriental philosophy...that the Christian Gnostics derived their origin'*.[3] In fact, it would be fair to say that the ancient stream of Gnosticism represented the Christianising of the 'wisdom traditions' of the Orient — the 'Satanic Initiation' made palatable for the intellectual Christian mind. However, the oriental 'wisdom tradition' has not only undergone a *Christianising* of its content into the Gnosticism of the early Church; it has also experienced a centuries-long process of *Westernising*, leading to the eventual appearance of a New Gnosticism.

After the disappearance of ancient Gnosticism between the third and sixth centuries, a number of quasi-Christian sects holding Gnostic ideas had bubbled to the surface at various times. In the eighth century, a Balkan cult, which had its roots in the third century Gnostic sect of the Manichees, was founded by a man called Bogomil (Bulgarian for 'beloved of God'). Although Bogomilism made remarkable headway across Eastern Europe for a few centuries, it eventually died out because

> 'when the Turkish conquered Bosnia in 1463 and Herzegovina in 1482, large numbers of the people adopted Mohammedanism, which was found to have many affinities with Bogomilism'.[4]

The eleventh to thirteenth centuries also saw the rise of a number of Gnostic-style sects such as the Cathars, the Albigenses and the Templars, all of which were claimed by later occult organisations as being ancestral to their own. Although these groups were eventually purged by the Church of Rome, the secret doctrine which they represented was by no means dissolved; and in the early seventeenth century, a development was to take place which would set Europe on fire and provide a vital bridge between ancient Gnosticism and the New Gnosis in the historical outworking of satanic strategy.

---

[3] J.L. Mosheim, *An Ecclesiastical History, Ancient & Modern, from the Birth of Christ to the Beginning of the Eighteenth Century* (Blackie, Fullarton & Co., 1827), Vol.I, p.38.

[4] F.L. Cross & E.A. Livingstone (eds.), *The Oxford Dictionary of the Christian Church* (OUP, 1983), p.184.

Because each of the last four centuries has made its own contribution to the cumulative thrust of the New Gnosticism which dominates the modern world's religious aspirations, psychological theories, politics and philosophy, we will examine them in turn.

I. 17th & 18th CENTURY SEEDS OF CORRUPTION

The seventeenth century provided a particularly ripe opportunity for the appearance of certain developments which would seed the New Gnosticism. The earthly dominion of the Roman Catholic Church, which had successfully suppressed so many heresies and antichristian movements, had itself been dealt a massive blow by the Protestant Reformation. Although this paved the way for forms of Christianity in which the corruptions of the Vatican would be considerably lessened, if not totally absent, the Reformation also created openings for new movements in science and other disciplines, which would develop under the more tolerant eye of Protestantism, which had fixed its sights on its major enemy: the Papacy.

One of the prime contenders for this opportunity was the occult Order of the Rosy Cross, otherwise known as the Rosicrucians. The development of this esoteric order was to have a key role in the transition period from the Old Gnosticism to the New, adding to the speculative philosophy of the ancient Gnostics a form of millenarianism which would become central to Satan's strategy. To these progressions we will now turn our attention.

1. The Mysterious Order of the Rosy Cross

The Order of the Rosy Cross (or Rosicrucians) was an esoteric movement which had its inception in Germany in the early seventeenth century with the publication of two highly influential manifestos: The first was published at Kassel in Hesse in 1614, entitled the *'Fama Fraternitatis, dess Löblichen Ordens des Rosenkreutzes'* ('The Discovery of the Fraternity of the Most Noble Order of the Rosy Cross'). This included an additional work entitled *'Allgemeine und General Reformation, der gantzen weiten Welt'* ('The General Reformation of the Whole Wide World'). The second manifesto was the *'Confessione Fraternitatis, dess Löblichen Ordens des Rosenkreutzes, ad Eruditos Europae'* ('The Confession of the Fraternity of the Most Noble Order of the Rosy Cross, to all the Learned of Europe') which was published a year later. The *Fama Fraternitatis* recounted the life and work of one Christian Rosenkreutz who purportedly lived from 1378-1484. Of this man it is said that

> 'In his quest for wisdom, [he] had travelled to the Holy Land, Egypt, Morocco and Spain; his teachings reflected the influences of alchemy, Alexandrian Hermetism, Christian Gnosticism, Jewish mysticism (Qabbalah), and the Paracelsian medical tradition'.[5]

In 1604 it was reported that some members of the secret Order of the Rosy Cross discovered where the remains of Christian Rosenkreutz (German for 'Rosy Cross') lay, along with certain books and parchments and his uncorrupted body.

---

[5] Mircea Eliade (ed.), *Encyclopedia of Religion* (Macmillan, 1987), Vol.12, p.476.

However, the bulk of historical evidence would appear to show that this man was an invention of the author of the *Fama*, and that it was an elaborate ruse by occultists to galvanise the world at large (and Europe in particular) into developing a Gnostic outlook. One should be aware of the historico-spiritual context here in order to appreciate Satan's hand in these events: All this activity was happening in the shadow of the European Reformation — a crucial point in Church history.

By the start of the seventeenth century, Roman Catholicism, having deceived millions with its pseudo-Christianity for hundreds of years, had been shown to be a sham. Hundreds of thousands of people throughout Europe were imbued with a renewed sense of the divine inspiration of the Bible and the need to be 'born again' by the power of the Holy Spirit in order to qualify for entrance into the kingdom of heaven. Satan's anger at this historical development must have been intense; and as the Counter-Reformation gathered steam, it was not merely confined to Roman Catholic sects such as the Jesuits. In fact, the entire occult brotherhood across Europe was mobilised into action, and Rosicrucianism was born.

It would also seem that the Order of the Rosy Cross was attempting to pass itself off as a new Protestant brotherhood. There were references in its literature to the Pope as the Antichrist, together with the use of certain Christian catchphrases and aspirations — not to mention the fact that the *Fama* claimed a pedigree for its teachings going right back through Solomon, Moses and Adam after the Fall.[6] This counterfeiting of Christian traits is most characteristic of Gnostic religion.

It is also surely of some significance here that Martin Luther's personal insignia was a rose and cross, suggesting that the brotherhood was attempting to pass itself off as a kind of Lutheran sect. From an esoteric standpoint, however, the 'Rosenkreutz' of the Rosicrucians did not really signify a Rosy Cross at all, but instead, stood for two secret Alchemical symbols. Professor J.L. Mosheim, writing about Rosicrucianism in his superlative *Ecclesiastical History* in 1755, states that the Order of the Rosy Cross

> 'is drawn from the science of [alchemy]; and they only who are acquainted with the peculiar language of the [alchemists] can understand its true signification and energy. It is not compounded, as many imagine, of the two words *rosa* and *crux*, which signify *rose* and *cross*, but of the latter of these words [*crux*], and the Latin word *ros* which signifies *dew*... The *cross*, in the [alchemical] style, is equivalent to *light*; because the figure of the cross X exhibits, at the same time, the three letters of which the word *lux*, i.e. *light* is compounded. Now *lux* is called by this sect the *seed* or *menstruum of the red dragon*; or, in other words, that gross and corporeal light, which when properly ingested and modified, produces gold. From all this it follows that a *Rosecrucian* philosopher is one who, by the intervention and assistance of the dew, seeks for light, or, in other words, the substance called *the Philosopher's Stone*.[7] [emphasis in original]

---

6 See the translation of the *Fama Fraternitatis* in Frances Yates, *The Rosicrucian Enlightenment* (Routledge & Kegan Paul, 1978), pp.249-250.

The 'Philosopher's Stone' is the Alchemist's equivalent of *gnosis* — the secret substance or energy which would bring the desired change in matter or consciousness. The occultic art of alchemy involves the use of forbidden knowledge in order to tamper with the structure of matter and consciousness, thus usurping what is God's own domain. The two fundamental ideas of alchemy are: **1)** The unity of all matter; and **2)** The existence of a potent transmuting agent. These ideas have their roots firmly planted in the magical practices of Babylonia, Egypt, India and China, coupled with influences from the later Greek Pythagorean and Platonic Schools.[8] What all this means is that the myth of Christian Rosenkreutz was invented by some seventeenth-century Hermetic-Alchemists as a cover for the dissemination of occult teachings: and it certainly worked.

The whole of Europe became fired-up with enthusiasm for the 'Reformation of the Whole Wide World' propounded in the Order's manifestos, whether or not the enthusiasts were aware of the origin of the impulse. The fact that this Christian Rosenkreutz might not have existed is entirely irrelevant to the Gnostic mindset. In the words of one of the growing band of Neo-Gnostic scientists of today: *'When a myth is shared by large numbers of people, it becomes a reality'*.[9] And so, Rosicrucianism — the first pan-European Gnostic philosophy — was born.

Many different spiritual and philosophical streams had prepared the way for the coming of this new/old religion. According to Tobias Churton, who made a film on Gnosticism for Channel Four television, Rosicrucianism

> 'represents the confluence of four significant streams which had flowed through the Europe of the sixteenth century. Sometimes these streams flowed in the surface, sometimes underground'.[10]

These four streams are identified by Churton as:

1. Medieval mystics such as Ramon Lull (c.1232-1315), Meister Eckhart (c.1260-1327), Johann Tauler (c.1300-1361), and Heinrich Suso (c.1295-1366).

2. Renaissance science and philosophy such as the Kabbalah, magic and astrology, as represented in Giordano Bruno (1548-1600), John Dee (1527-1608), and the Hermetic tradition.

3. Certain of the Radical Reformers, such as Kaspar von Schwenkfeld (c.1490-1561) and Sebastian Frank (1499-1542).

4. Unadulterated occultism.[11]

Perhaps we are beginning to appreciate the way that, in the satanic strategy, a myriad of different influences sown in the world-system converge at key points in history to create the necessary development in world culture which is most helpful to Satan's long-term ambitions. Alongside these streams of thought converging in

---

7 J.L. Mosheim, op. cit., Vol.II, pp.164-165.

8 *Chambers's Encyclopaedia*, Vol.I, (George Newnes, 1963), p.229.

9 Quoted in Lyall Watson, *Lifetide* (Hodder & Stoughton, 1979), p.158.

10 Tobias Churton, op. cit., p.151.

11 Ibid.

European culture, there was another important seed sown in seventeenth and eighteenth century thought which made a vital contribution to the cumulative development of the New Gnosticism. That seed involved the concept of a future Golden Age on earth.

In this future Golden Age idea, or the making of the 'kingdom of heaven on earth' (as it is sometimes called), one can see an incipient idea of the New Age Movement which arose in the twentieth century through the theosophist Alice B. Bailey (about which more later). In fact, the entire concept of a future Golden Age or 'brotherhood of peace on earth' is a peculiarly Gnostic and occultic doctrine, rooting the eschatological fulfillment of history within the bounds of present earth history, before the cosmos has been renewed, transformed and purified into the New Heavens and the New Earth (Rev.21:1-5). Cerinthus, one of the most infamous of the ancient Gnostics, actually devised an entire eschatological system which had Christ returning to earth and reigning with His people in Israel for a thousand years.[12] Setting-up the kingdom of God on earth is actually a key Neo-Gnostic concept, which has its wellspring in the Rosicrucian influences of the seventeenth century. Frances Yates, former Reader in the History of the Renaissance at the University of London, believed that the 'general reformation of the whole wide world' which was presented in the original Rosicrucian manifestos has

> 'millenarian overtones; it will bring the world back to the state in which Adam found it, which was also Saturn's golden age. So, in the *Confessio*, the second Rosicrucian manifesto, the general reformation is said to presage "a great influx of truth and light" such as surrounded Adam in Paradise, and which God will allow before the end of the world. And...this millennium, this return to the golden age of Adam and Saturn, is said to be assisted by "the high society of the Rosicrucians" who wish to turn all the mountains into gold'.[13]

Thus, the fundamental principles of Gnosticism which we have already recorded came to have a further principle added to them: the idea that human beings can together form a global Brotherhood of Man and create heaven right here on earth. The concept of a future Golden Age on earth was, therefore, one of the most significant contributions to the modern revival of ancient Gnosticism on the part of the mysterious Order of the Rosy Cross. Indeed, one can go on to say that the blending of millenarian Rosicrucianism with its more secular counterpart Freemasonry in the eighteenth century, formed the primary precursor of what we call the New Age Movement today. One of the leading modern New Age gurus, Peter Lemesurier of the Findhorn Foundation in Scotland, has written a complete book on this idea of the creation of heaven on this earth; and he upholds the seminal importance of this convergence of Rosicrucianism and Freemasonry when he writes:

---

[12] It should be said that there are a large number of Christians today who unwittingly hold to an eschatology somewhat akin to that of the Gnostic, Cerinthus!

[13] Frances Yates, *The Rosicrucian Enlightenment* (Routledge & Kegan Paul, 1972), p.57.

> 'In due course the two streams of idealism — the one extravagantly occult [Rosicrucianism], the other more urbanely idealistic [Freemasonry]— were to come together once again in response to an unfulfilled need deep within the human psyche. And the eventual child of the union was to be the modern New Age Movement'.[14]

One therefore cannot ignore the role played by the Order of the Rosy Cross in creating the historical conditions necessary for the belittlement of biblical Christianity and the extolling of occult ideals in its place. After having remained out of view for so many centuries, the Ancient Religion was now to burst out of hiding with a vengeance, as it provided the basis for the next era of satanic strategy.

2. The Coming of Age of Human Reason

The effect that Rosicrucianism had on many aspects of European culture were crucial in terms of the progression of Satan's dark work during the Gospel Age. For it loosened the hold of the Church and Christianity on the minds of many who would be influential on the coming generation. The scholar of Rosicrucianism, Christopher McIntosh, has written about the magnitude of this development:

> 'The denial of the dogmatically rigid restrictions and regimentation of the church, the passionate belief in natural science as the way to all-round progress, the possession of an open world view and the yearning for religious unity and mutuality, the...striving for the harmony of religion and science and above all the call for a general reformation of "the whole wide world" — all of these are integral parts of the secret fraternity of the Rosicrucians. Thus Rosicrucianism, as a transition between the Renaissance and the scientific societies of the seventeenth century, forms a point of crystallisation. In its mode of thinking, one can discern an early form of the Aufklärung which in many respects was seminal to the further development of European science and culture'.[15]

This *Aufklärung* refers to the so-called 'Enlightenment' or 'Age of Reason', a seventeenth and eighteenth-century movement involving philosophers and scientists such as René Descartes (1596-1650), John Locke (1632-1704), Isaac Newton (1642-1727), François Voltaire (1694-1778), Denis Diderot (1713-1784), Jean Rousseau (1712-1778), and Immanuel Kant (1724-1804). Each of these men made their own contribution to a movement which was deistic, rationalistic and ultimately antichristian in its thrust, with a belief in the innate goodness of human nature, the supremacy of science over biblical authority, the substitution of human reason for Christian faith, the questioning of tradition and authority (both human and divine), and the relentless upward strides of human progress. The intense

---

[14] Peter Lemesurier, *This New Age Business: The Story of the Ancient and Continuing Quest to Bring Down Heaven to Earth* (Findhorn Press, 1990), p.178.

[15] Christopher McIntosh, *The Rosecross and the Age of Reason: 18th century Rosicrucianism in Central Europe and its Relationship to the Enlightenment* (E.J. Brill, 1992), pp.34-35.

kindling of Rosicrucianism across Europe had prepared the way for the subsequent 'Age of Enlightenment' because it dared to assert that there was an alternative way of salvation to that of 'conventional' Christianity, that the Bible was not the final authority in terms of life and doctrine, and that the 'Brotherhood of Man' could work together to bring a Golden Age of peace and justice on earth. The nature of this 'preparationism' for the later 'Enlightenment' is shown in the following statement from the Oxford historian Frances Yates:

> 'The most striking aspect of the Rosicrucian movement is...its insistence on a coming Enlightenment. The world, nearing its end, is to receive a new illumination in which the advances in knowledge made in the preceding age of the Renaissance will be immensely expanded. New discoveries are at hand, a new age is dawning. And this illumination shines inward as well as outward; it is an inward spiritual illumination revealing to man new possibilities in himself, teaching him to understand his own dignity and worth and the part he is called upon to play in the divine scheme'.[16]

Here we can see the significant link between the covert Rosicrucian 'enlightenment' and the overt historical 'Enlightenment' which was to follow in its wake. That link was 'illuminism'. As Frances Yates concurs:

> 'the Rosicrucian Enlightenment was indeed...an enlightenment, putting forward within its own strange frame of reference of magical and angelic agencies, of prophecy and apocalypse, a movement most of the aspects of which can only be described as enlightened. Though the Enlightenment proper, the *Aufklärung*, seems to introduce a very different atmosphere, yet its rationalism was tinged with illuminism'.[17]

This word 'illuminism', as cross-fertilising both Rosicrucianism and the Age of Enlightenment, gives us some important information here. For it is simply an alternative word for the *gnosis*. An 'illuminist' (essentially, a Gnostic) can be defined as one who *'claims to have special enlightenment, especially in philosophical or religious matters'*.[18] Groups which boast such 'enlightenment' or *gnosis* have been called *Illuminati*. Therefore, in spite of the rationalism of the European Enlightenment, the thrust behind both this Age of Reason and the Order of the Rosy Cross is essentially Gnostic. Both sought to find enlightenment outside of the scope of the Divine revelation given in the Old and New Testaments. Both glorified the mind of man rather than the Word of God. Both believed in the possibility of a man-made Golden Age on earth. Both made man into a little god. The significance of this 'Enlightenment' in terms of satanic strategy is very well summed up in the words of Colin Brown:

> 'In 1784 Immanuel Kant wrote an article in answer to the question "What is enlightenment?" He replied that enlightenment was man's

---

[16] Frances A. Yates, ibid., p.232.

[17] Ibid., p.233.

[18] *Chambers English Dictionary*, (Chambers, 1988), p.710.

> coming of age. It was man's emergence from the immaturity which caused him to rely on such external authorities as the Bible, the church, and the state to tell him what to think and to do... The motto of enlightenment was *Sapere aude* — "Have courage to use your own understanding"'.[19]

This motto is in complete contradiction to the Word of God which says, *'Trust in the LORD with all your heart, and lean not on your own understanding'* (Pro.3:5). Our Creator knows only too well that *'he who trusts in his own heart is a fool'* (Pro.28:26). In many ways, this 'Enlightenment' was the first stage of the 'General Reformation of the Whole Wide World' called for in the manifestos of the Order of the Rosy Cross in 1614. The rise of Rosicrucianism had paved the way for these European scientific, political, intellectual and religious developments and thus formed a vital bridge between the Old Gnosticism and the New, adding its own distinctive emphases along the way. As Christopher McIntosh puts it:

> 'Rosicrucian vision was therefore both traditional and radical, both theological and scientific... It looked forward to an age when religion and science would work hand in hand'.[20]

One can see clearly the unique stamp of Satan in all these developments, as the evil angel struggled to reassert the hold over the nations of the world which he had enjoyed before Christ came as its Saviour. For these European developments of the seventeenth and eighteenth centuries led to a huge upsurge of antichristian endeavour which — as we shall more fully appreciate by the conclusion of this book — could well be set to climax in the present generation. Especially was this the case in terms of the subordination of Christian doctrine to the findings of scientific endeavour. As a leading historian who specialises in seventeenth century affairs has noted:

> 'Towards the close of the seventeenth century the prestige of Scripture, though outwardly unchanged, had actually diminished appreciably'.[21]

The job had been done. The Rosicrucian 'Enlightenment' had served its purpose. Now the counter-Reformation satanic strategy could move forward at a great pace. In Rosicrucian-inspired Europe, in the seventeenth and eighteenth centuries, the soil was now prepared for the planting of seeds which would precipitate a vast occult revival in the nineteenth century, and the most widespread movement of antichristian activity during the past two thousand years. It is to that period that we now turn.

---

[19] Walter A. Elwell (ed.), *Evangelical Dictionary of Theology* (Marshall Pickering, 1984), p.355.

[20] Christopher McIntosh, *The Rosecross and the Age of Reason: 18th century Rosicrucianism in Central Europe and its Relationship to the Enlightenment* (E.J. Brill, 1992), p.26.

[21] Basil Willey, *The Seventeenth Century Background: Studies in the Thought of the Age in Relation to Poetry and Religion* (Routledge & Kegan Paul, 1986), p.73.

II. 19th CENTURY SEEDS OF CORRUPTION

After centuries of secret workings, and having initiated the development of Rosicrucianism in the seventeenth century and the 'Enlightenment' which followed it, Satan had finally succeeded in laying the ground for a number of seeds which would be sown with ease during the last half of the nineteenth century. These were given in the form of certain philosophies, organisations and individuals which would serve the secret plan of the satanic realm in the build-up to its planned Golden Age on earth. The prime contenders in this were the Theory of Evolution, Theological Liberalism, Socio-Political Utopianism, the 'Mind-Sciences', Comparative Religion and the Theosophical Society. These six seeds of corruption received almost immediate worldwide acceptance during the ensuing hundred years or so, coming to full bloom towards the close of the twentieth century. Although they may appear to be unrelated developments, not only were they inseparably linked in ways which shall be revealed but they also were to become the harbingers of many other antichristian offshoots. Discerning research brings one to the inescapable conclusion that they were implanted by Satan in world culture in order to undermine the true Gospel and bring the swell of lawlessness to its approaching tidal-wave proportions.

Although during the course of this book, we will be exposing the outworking of these six seeds in many different fields, within the special context of this present chapter we will show briefly the unique contribution they have made to the founding of the New Gnosticism.

1. From Slime-Pit to 'Civilisation': The Cult of Darwinism

By far the most far-reaching seed of corruption to be sown by Satan in the nineteenth century was the *Theory of Evolution* — the claim that primitive organisms have gradually developed over billions of years into the variety of species known to us today. Although it was first sounded in 1809 by Jean Lamarck (1744-1829), it was not until Charles Darwin (1809-1882) and Alfred R. Wallace (1823-1913) put forward their theory in 1858 that it began to receive wide acceptance. One of Darwin's biographers notes that *'more than any modern thinker — even Freud or Marx — that affable old-world naturalist from the minor Shropshire gentry has transformed the way we see ourselves on the planet'*.[22] The significance of this theory to the progress of Satan's earthly ambitions and his strategy during the Gospel Age cannot be over-emphasised. As one writer puts it: *'Every attack on the Christian Faith made today has, as its basis, the doctrine of evolution'*.[23]

Darwin's family background was steeped in Unitarianism — which has been neatly termed as *'a feather-bed for falling Christians'*. It could well be that the motives behind his work lay in his own internal struggles with religion in general and Christianity in particular. In 1851, just eight years before the publication of 'The Origin of Species', his little daughter Annie had died tragically of a sudden disease. This catastrophe shattered the man emotionally, and certainly played

---

[22] Adrian Desmond & James Moore, *Darwin* (Michael Joseph, 1991), p.xxi.

[23] Wallace Johnson, *Evolution?* (TAN Books, 1992), p.114.

havoc with him spiritually. In the most recent biography of Darwin, it is noted:

> 'Annie's cruel death destroyed Charles's tatters of belief in a moral, just universe. Later he would say that this period chimed the final death-knell for his Christianity... Charles now took his stand as an unbeliever'.[24]

This man, armed with his root of bitterness — Satan's favourite foothold — and his scientific theories, appeared in world history at a most opportune moment from the standpoint of the demonic realm. The Rosicrucian-inspired 'Enlightenment' of the seventeenth and eighteenth centuries had given rise to a massive interest in scientific research and thinking, all of which culminated in the development of the Theory of Evolution. From the standpoint of satanic strategy, here was a theory that was just waiting to be formulated. Indeed, it is generally marked by Neo-Gnostics as being fundamental to the increasing popularity of their teachings in the late nineteenth and ensuing twentieth centuries. Here was a theory which could buttress that ancient ambition of the nations: to jettison the necessity for a sovereign Creator. And in terms of the infiltration of Gnostic ideology into science, which had been initiated by the Rosicrucian enlightenment some two hundred and fifty years earlier, the Theory of Evolution represented the perfect fulfilment of a dream. The physicist and mathematics Professor of Oregon State University, Dr. Wolfgang Smith, expresses this superbly when he writes:

> 'As a scientific theory, Darwinism would have been jettisoned long ago. The point, however, is that the doctrine of evolution has swept the world, not on the strength of its scientific merits, but precisely in its capacity as a Gnostic myth. It affirms, in effect, that living beings create themselves, which is in essence a *metaphysical* claim... Thus, in the final analysis, evolutionism is in truth a metaphysical doctrine decked out in scientific garb. In other words, it is a scientistic myth. And the myth is Gnostic, because it implicitly denies the transcendent origin of being; for indeed, only after the living creature has been speculatively reduced to an aggregate of particles does Darwinist transformism become conceivable. Darwinism, therefore, continues the ancient Gnostic practice of depreciating "God, the Father Almighty, Creator of Heaven and earth". It perpetuates, if you will, the venerable Gnostic tradition of "Jehovah bashing". And while this in itself may gladden Gnostic hearts, one should not fail to observe that the doctrine plays a vital role in the economy of Neo-Gnostic thought, for only under the auspices of Darwinist "self-creation" does the Good News of "self-*salvation*" acquire a semblance of sense'.[25]

---

[24] Ibid., p.387.

[25] Wolfgang Smith, *Teilhardism and the New Religion: A Thorough Analysis of the Teachings of Pierre Teilhard de Chardin*, (TAN books, 1988), pp.242-243. This book cannot be recommended highly enough. It is a devastating critique of one of the main perpetrators of Neo-Gnostic philosophy, and a masterful debunking of Evolution Theory.

The most pervasive aspect of Evolution Theory was not so much the theory itself as a biological statement, but the subsequent application of it to numerous aspects of life, culture, politics, psychology and, above all, religion. The humanist and atheist, Sir Julian Huxley (1887-1975), writing in the mid-1950s, states that

> 'The concept of evolution was soon extended into other than biological fields. Inorganic subjects such as the life-history of stars and the formation of the chemical elements on the one hand, and on the other hand subjects like linguistics, social anthropology, and comparative law and religion, began to be studied from an evolutionary angle, until today we are enabled to see evolution as a universal and all-pervading process'.[26]

Herbert Spencer (1820-1903), who had propounded his own version of Evolution Theory in his 'Principles of Psychology' (1855) four years before Darwin's 'Origin of Species', had also rigorously applied this theory to the whole field of social ethics. By 1884, he was frankly suggesting that *'the principle of survival of the fittest implies that people who are burdens on society should be allowed to die rather than be helped by society'*.[27] This should not surprise us. Time and again, during the course of this book, we will see the stark antichristian outworkings of Evolution Theory. Especially is this the case in regard to its religious repercussions. For the real heart of Evolutionism is its implication that the Bible is not a trustworthy record of Divine creative action, coupled with the plainly God-denying thesis that the cosmos is self-generating, self-sustaining and improving ever-onward and upward. Julian Huxley supports this idea when he says: *'Evolution, if consistently accepted, makes it impossible to believe in the Bible'*.[28]

Because it came to be perceived that Evolution had taken the bottom out of Christian theology, there arose the need for new religious initiatives. The rise of Darwinism had dealt such a blow to conventional religion in the West that a number of satanic elements sprang into the breach, and it would prove to be the harbinger of a great many Neo-Gnostic developments during this present century. Peter Lemesurier, the director and guru of the New Age centre at Findhorn in Scotland cites a vast number of religious developments which filled the perceived vacuum left in the wake of Evolution Theory. Among these are the transcendental magic of Roman Catholic priest turned occultist, Eliphas Lévi (1810-1875); the much fêted *Zanoni* novels of the Tory politician Lord Edward Bulwer-Lytton (1803-1873), which revealed Rosicrucian secrets to the masses; the popularisation of the concepts of Reincarnation and *Karma* via Oxford Professor Max Müller's translations of the Hindu scriptures (1900); the syncretistic philosophy of Arthur Schopenhauer (1788-1860); the Theosophical Society (1875); the early twentieth century political developments in India (both Gandhi and Nehru had passed

---

[26] Julian Huxley, 'Evolution and Genetics', quoted in J.R. Newman (ed.), *What is Science?* (Simon & Schuster, 1955), p.272.

[27] A. Hellemans & B. Bunch, *The Timetables of Science* (Simon & Schuster, 1988), p.362.

[28] Quoted in *The Unseen Hand: An Introduction to the Conspiratorial View of History* (Publius Press, 1985), p.362.

through the echelons of the Theosophical Society); the magical Order of the Golden Dawn (1887), which had so captivated such artistic worthies as W.B. Yeats; the Anthroposophical Society (1913); the Arcane School and Lucis Trust of Alice Bailey (1922); the sex-magic cult of the 'Order of the Templars of the Orient' (1920s), as patronised by such occultists as Rudolf Steiner (1861-1925) and Aleister Crowley (1875-1947); the White Eagle Lodge (1937); and the Nazi Party's occult group 'Die Thulle-Gesellschaft'.[29]

Many more developments could be given here which came to fill the perceived spiritual vacuum left by the satanic seed of Evolution Theory. In the ensuing sections of this chapter, we will be looking into a good number of them. Further comments outlining the untenable nature of the Theory of Evolution itself will be reserved for a later chapter on the role of science in the unfolding of the New Gnosticism. Our purpose in raising it here is to demonstrate its unique function as one of six fundamental seeds sown by Satan in the late nineteenth century as an outworking of earlier, preparatory, Gnostic and occult activity, and as a radical harbinger of the subsequent Neo-Gnostic revival.

2. The Axe in the Tree: Theological Liberalism

A further seed of corruption sown by Satan in nineteenth century culture was that of *theological liberalism.* This phenomenon first developed in Germany in the nineteenth century, although a number of different streams of thought had prepared the way — not least of which was the so-called Enlightenment of the seventeenth and eighteenth centuries, with its declared ambition to lessen the influence of the Bible and the Church. The first real manifestation of theological liberalism was at the University in Tübingen. Here, a theologian named Ferdinand Baur (1792-1860) had formed a school of theology which would raise questions about the Christian faith designed to undermine its status as the exclusive fount of Truth. Among the areas which came under scrutiny were the Person of Christ, the nature of sin and human depravity, the authority of the Bible, the way of spiritual salvation and the doctrine of the Church. But by far the most important and far-reaching of the liberal incursions into Divine truth was the assertion of the immanence of God (His omnipresence) at the expense of His transcendence (His 'otherness' from His creation), so that the Creator becomes styled simply as 'an expression of the cosmic process in all its manifestations'. The central importance of this aspect of theological liberalism to Christian doctrine is shown by J. Gresham Machen when he writes:

> 'The truth is that liberalism has lost sight of the very centre and core of the Christian teaching. In the Christian view of God as set forth in the Bible, there are many elements. But one attribute of God is absolutely

[29] Peter Lemesurier, *This New Age Business: The Story of the Ancient and Continuing Quest to Bring Down Heaven on Earth* (Findhorn Press, 1990), pp.183-195. Notice the title of this book — that 'bringing down of heaven onto the earth' again. We will also later come to appreciate that Adolf Hitler was just as avid a Neo-Gnostic as Mr. Lemesurier.

> fundamental in the Bible; one attribute is absolutely necessary in order to render intelligible all the rest. That attribute is the awful transcendence of God. From beginning to end the Bible is concerned to set forth the awful gulf that separates the creature from the Creator. It is true, indeed, that according to the Bible God is immanent in the world. Not a sparrow falls to the ground without Him. But He is immanent in the world not because He is identified with the world, but because He is the free Creator and upholder of it. Between the creature and the Creator a great gulf is fixed'.[30]

This obsession of theological liberalism with upholding the 'immanence' of God to the exclusion of His transcendence — which is the Western theological expression of ancient pantheism — has great significance to our charting of the transition from the old Gnosticism to the new. For the approach to the Scriptures inaugurated at Tübingen owed much to the philosophy of Georg Hegel (1770-1831); and this provides an important link with the past. According to Professor Kurt Rudolph, Ferdinand Baur, in his monograph *Die Christliche Gnosis Oder Die Christliche Religions-Philosophie* (1835), maintained that Jakob Boehme (1575-1624), Friedrich Schelling (1775-1854), Friedrich Schleiermacher (1768-1834) and Hegel were the philosophical heirs of the ancient *gnosis*.[31] This is supported by another scholar who also claims that Hegel's early writings were very much influenced by Christoph Oetinger (1702-1782), the gnostic Kabbalist and disciple of both Jakob Boehme and Emanuel Swedenborg (1688-1722).[32] Once again, we discover that there is nothing that is new under the sun. In the theological liberalism of the nineteenth century, we have yet another manifestation of the ancient war between the 'cult of man' and the 'power of God'.

This period also marked the appearance of the sister-discipline of Theological Liberalism, 'Higher Criticism', which questioned the authorship and dating of individual books of the Bible. The innocuous enquiry into such matters by the faithful believer is not intrinsically wrong; but when it is undertaken at the hands of men who are plainly seeking to undermine the claims of Scripture and who are using secular yardsticks in their researches, such study is bound to issue in unreliability, at the very least. Such unsanctified exploration naturally led to an enquiry into the identity of the historical Jesus — typified in the anti-supernaturalistic book *The Life of Jesus*, written in 1835 by Baur's pupil, D.F. Strauss (1808-1874). Coupled with this, liberal theologians eagerly responded to the contemporary findings of science, especially when they could be brought to bear on the downgrading of evangelical faith. The scientistic theory of evolution dovetailed neatly with the

---

[30] J. Gresham Machen, *Christianity and Liberalism* (Eerdmans, 1923), pp.62-63. This is one of the most thorough refutations of theological liberalism, showing that it and Christianity are really two entirely different religions.

[31] Kurt Rudolph, *Gnosis: The Nature and History of Gnosticism* (Harper & Row, 1987), p.368.

[32] Mircea Eliade (ed.), *The Encyclopedia of Religion* (Macmillan, 1987), Vol.5, p.576. See also *Chambers Biographical Dictionary*, p.1099.

teaching of the theological liberals, who had already posited an 'evolutionary' development of religion throughout the millennia (based on Hegel's idea of historical evolution), culminating in Christianity, which they portrayed as a hybrid religion of the Near East. All these developments served to loosen the hold of the Bible and the Christian faith, and when Charles Darwin arrived on the scientific scene mid-century, the intelligentsia of Europe were more than ready to embrace the findings of theological liberalism and jettison biblical teaching.

Eventually, the individual findings of the Tübingen School were discredited as archeological evidence began to be discovered; but the damage had been done and the seal was set on a critical, rationalistic and sceptical approach to the Bible becoming the dominant approach in German theological circles. Many teachers and ministers were attracted to study in Germany at this time; and by the close of the nineteenth century, the majority of theologians around the world had imbibed the apostate principles of German Higher Criticism and Darwinian evolution. When that leaven in the theological scene was commingled with the indigenous theological liberalism in Great Britain (Latitudinarianism: the 'Broad Church' movement) and in the United States of America (born out of Unitarianism), the scene was set for a steady global decline among both churches and institutions of theological learning. Indeed, it was not long before those involved in these international religious developments began to give priority to the building of a kingdom of God on earth, which manifested itself as the 'Social Gospel'. In this kingdom, the 'brotherhood of man' could come to live in peace, justice and harmony in the world. That all this was a part of Satan's plan is clear for all to see. For in preference to the application of salvation to the souls of individuals, the church began to cultivate a concern for social action and an interest in the kind of socio-political utopianism to which we will be referring in a later section.

By the time that Neo-Gnosticism began its ascendency in the 1960s, professing Christian theologians were already declaring boldly that *'God is dead'*. A lethal combination of human philosophy and scientistic speculation had finally begun to achieve its goal of absolute Deicide: the killing off of the Transcendent Personal God of the Bible — a satanic ambition realised. Just as Evolution Theory had been applied to many other aspects of life, including the Bible and Christian faith, so other scientific 'discoveries' were brought to bear on the same areas. That a key revelation in the scientific community — the Theory of Relativity — had been superimposed on Christian truth can be seen in the following statement of a well-known churchman in the magazine *Playboy*, which regularly featured interviews with 'death-of-God' theologians in order to justify its own role in the 'sexual revolution' which had begun in the 'swinging' 1960s:

> 'We death-of-God theologians, along with a good many others today, accept without reservation the relativistic intellectual and spiritual climate of our time... We have given up believing that there is something about Christians that makes our views inevitable or necessary or (by definition) better than alternatives. We merely represent one of the possible intellectual options today'.[33]

This utterance represents the thinking of a great many professing Christian theologians, Archbishops, Bishops, and ministers of the Church today. In this, we can see that the satanic seed planted in the mid-1800s in Tübingen — which was itself the result of Gnostic-inspired Hegelian philosophy and science (falsely so-called) — has finally come to flower in our own time. That these people continue to remain within the auspices of the Church is one of the more bizarre anomalies of this present age. Truly, *'the court which is outside the temple [of God]...has been given over to the Gentiles'* to be trampled by them underfoot (Rev.11:1-2). But it will not always be so. When the witness of the Gospel has come to an end, the most intense persecution of the Church yet will begin to take place a short season before the return of the Lord (Rev.11:7ff). When that time comes, there will be a sifting of the wheat from the chaff — the true believers from the false — and the true nature of the satanic stream of theological liberalism and all that it has spawned will be revealed for all to see (Rev.13:7-10).

3. The Many-Named God of Comparative Religion

One of the most galling aspects of Christianity, so far as the satanic powers are concerned, is its claim to exclusivity — that there is eternal salvation *only* through faith in Jesus Christ. It is, therefore, hardly surprising to discover that one of the most far-reaching of all the seeds sown by Satan in world-culture in the nineteenth century strikes at the very heart of this particularity of the Christian Gospel. We refer to the academic discipline known as 'Comparative Religion', which can be defined as

> 'The branch of study which investigates by scientific and historical methods the religions of the world in their mutual relations'.[34]

It would be most significant to our study to enquire by what 'scientific methods' Comparative Religionists arrive at their conclusions. The answer is provided when we are told that the term, 'Comparative Religion', *'originated in the last quarter of the nineteenth century to denote one of the sciences based on the evolutionary theories of Darwin and Spencer'*.[35] Here again, we discover the capacity of Darwinistic Evolution Theory to father so many other developments. Under the influence of evolution theory, and with the added impetus of a gathering quantity of anthropological discoveries, a number of scholars found what they believed to be evolutionary links between various religious traditions. Chief among these were F. Max Müller (1823-1900), the Oxford professor who translated the Hindu Scriptures into English, and Cambridge professor J.G. Fraser (1854-1941), who wrote a highly fanciful 12-volume work entitled 'The Golden Bough'.

The essential claim of Comparative Religion is that *'behind all these religions there are common principles and spiritual realities'*.[36] In this way, all the world's

---

[33] Rev. (sic) William Hamilton writing in *Playboy*, August 1966, p.84.

[34] *The Oxford Dictionary of the Christian Church*, op.cit., p.324.

[35] J.D. Douglas (ed.), *New International Dictionary of the Christian Church* (Zondervan, 1974), p.249.

[36] *Chambers's Encyclopaedia* (George Newnes, 1963 edition), Vol.III, p.808.

religions are reduced to different expressions of the same cosmic and divine principles. The moral codes of Judaism, Islam, Buddhism, Hinduism and Christianity — the so-called 'living religions' — are merely diverse aspects of the same fundamental 'Golden Rule', while their gods and goddesses are merely different facets of the same underlying Deity. Religions are, therefore, to be seen as products of their cultural and historical circumstances. Through this reasoning, Christianity is shown to have arisen merely as an offshoot of monotheistic Judaism while gathering a few other sectarian influences along the way. It is comparative religionism which has given rise to the present age being referred to as C.E., the Common Era, rather than A.D., in the year of Our Lord. World religion, for these people, has merely been the product of a succession of anthropological eras in which certain forms of religion prevailed — polytheistic, monotheistic, Christian, etc. — all of which will evolve (true to Darwinistic thinking) and culminate ultimately in some vast world religion rooted in mystical, utopian, universalist, ethical ideals.

When the Enlightenment Deists had embarked on a search for the principles common to all religions in the seventeenth and eighteenth centuries, the fertile ground was laid in which an over-arching philosophy of religion could flourish. This came about primarily through the work of Georg Hegel, who *'saw all forms of religion as manifestations of the absolute religion in the process of becoming'*.[37] Now the foundations of Comparative Religion could be established. It is a singular fact that the protagonists of unsanctified learning will always fail to discern the truth in any form of exploration which they undertake. Although it is certainly true that great similarities can be discerned between the various religions of the world — and there are certain aspects of Christian doctrine which we can see echoed in some of these religions — it does not at all prove that Christianity is merely derivative of those religions, or that it shares the same bedrock. The true facts behind the existence of the world's religions are clearly outlined in the Bible. There is a 'seed of religion' resident within human beings, even in the wake of the Fall. But that seed, whenever it sprouts among those *'who do not know God, and...who do not obey the gospel of our Lord Jesus Christ'* (2 Th.1:8), always transmutes into idolatry, sorcery or mysticism. This is because unbelievers perpetually *'suppress the truth in unrighteousness'* (Rom.1:18). For this same reason, human beings across the globe will always desire to worship something — anything — but such worship, when it occurs in the mind of one who has not been regenerated by the Holy Spirit, will always be directed, at best, towards a hunk of wood, metal, stone, or, at worst, towards himself !

In terms of satanic strategy, it is clear that Comparative Religion — a bi-product of Darwinian Evolution — has been designed to undermine the concept of the exclusiveness of Christianity as Divine revelation. If the devil can stimulate heathen academics to encourage the idea that one religion is as worthy as another, then the Christian claims about eternal salvation will be negated and seen to be negative, sectarian assertions. For this reason, it is necessary for believers today

---

[37] J.D. Douglas (ed.), *The New International Dictionary of the Christian Church* (Zondervan, 1974), p.777.

to stress the fact that Christianity is *not* a religion. We can be certain that the Lord Jesus Christ — who was crucified by very religious people — never intended that His message should become one more religion of the world. Instead, He declared that His Gospel is *the* incomparable Way of truth and life, without which no man or woman can ever come to God.

4. The Myth of Human Progress: Socio-Political Utopianism

A further major seed to be implanted by Satan in world culture in the nineteenth century was what we can call Socio-Political Utopianism. The essential concept has always been around in one form or another, but it was not until the appearance of the nineteenth century writings and dogma of Karl Marx (1818-1883) that it became a political force of potentially global proportions. It is for this reason that we term it as a nineteenth century seed of corruption.

Although it is not generally realised among believers today, many of the catchwords of human aspiration — 'progress', 'civilisation', 'brotherhood of man', 'new society', 'New World Order', and so forth — are rooted in a worldview which puts man on the pedestal in place of God as the pinnacle of cosmic existence. In tandem with this goes the concept of human 'liberation' in all its forms, but especially as exemplified in the many liberation movements which have sprung up in the past century. In many ways, the idea of human progress towards a problem-free planet, coupled with the romanticism of liberation movements, is an extension of the Rosicrucian idea of the future Golden Age on earth. However, there are differences between the Rosicrucian ideal and its secular counterpart: Whereas the Rosicrucian concept envisioned in the document 'The General Reformation of the Whole Wide World' was rooted in occult aspirations, the political liberation movements of history in the past three hundred years have been predominantly secular-political in their ideals. This does not mean that there has been no spiritual or religious input into revolutionary politics. In fact, it can be shown that the major national revolutions and upheavals of the past three centuries have been thoroughly rooted in the millennial and spiritual aspirations which were prefigured in the Rosicrucian Enlightenment. Let us just expand this theme.

The principal mass political upheavals and revolutions of the past three centuries in Europe have been those of France, Russia and Nazi Germany. The rise of the millennial Nazi Party in Germany in the 1930s had its ancestry firmly in the European occult. We have already mentioned the Nazi Party's occult group 'Die Thulle-Gesellschaft'. Indeed, the entire concept of Nazism was founded on the essential principles of an occult sect known as Ariosophy. As a leading scholar has noted, Ariosophical doctrines

> 'advocated the rule of gnostic elites and orders, the stratification of society according to racial purity and occult initiation, the ruthless subjugation and ultimate destruction of non-German inferiors, and the foundation of a pan-German world-empire. Such fantasies were actualized with terrifying consequences in the Third Reich: Auschwitz, Sobibor and Treblinka are the hellish museums of Nazi apocalyptic, the

roots of which lay in the millennial visions of Ariosophy'.[38]

The Nazis held to the basic idea of a one thousand year Reich (kingdom) which, ironically, was a perverted version of ancient Jewish millennialism. Many characteristics of the Nazi Reich teachings were borrowed from Theosophical Society founder Helena Blavatsky's *magnum opus* 'The Secret Doctrine', in which was found the concept of a super-race of Aryans, as well as details of the ancient occult-influenced civilisations of Atlantis and Lemuria. Heinrich Himmler's Nazi S.S. was modelled on Ignatius of Loyola's Society of Jesus (Jesuits), and he believed it had a special mission to fulfil in the establishment of the Aryan Race in all its purity. On this, Nigel Pennick writes:

> 'Ignatius Loyola was a Basque...Some German occultists had claimed that the Basque people was the last remnant of the Atlantean race... Himmler believed that [Loyola's Spiritual Exercises] had been handed down from the Masters of Atlantis, and that now he was the man chosen by the "higher powers" to use them in the reactivation of Vril for the dominance of the Teutonic race over all others'.[39]

Admittedly, the Nazi millenarian vision was something of a distortion of the original Rosicrucian manifestos; but it was still a classic case of occult-inspired Political Utopianism, only it was to be maintained with a rule of terror by a despotic hierarchy rather than merely being propagated through initiation into esoteric principles. Similarly, although the revolutionary upheavals in France and Russia began life ostensibly as popular revolutions, they were still rooted in European Gnostic doctrine. The French Revolution has been shown in many authoritative publications to be the outcome of a welter of European occult activity, culminating in a group called the Illuminati which made a point of working through Freemasonry — the effects of which are still operating in the world today. As the historian Nesta Webster disclosed in 1924:

> 'In the opinion of the Grandmaster of German Freemasonry, a secret sect working within Freemasonry had brought about the French Revolution and would be the cause of all future revolutions'.[40]

Similarly, the Russian Revolution was brought about through the underground activities of occult organisations (coupled with the contrivances of international financiers). Indeed, not only were the actions of this Revolution motivated by occult concerns, but the very ideological foundations had their roots in Gnosticism. We have already shown how Hegel has been regarded as a philosophical heir of ancient Gnosticism. This must surely implicate Karl Marx, who owed the entire foundation of his ideas to the philosopher. Indeed, one prominent religious

---

[38] Nicolas Goodrick-Clarke, *The Occult Roots of Nazism: The Ariosophists of Austria and Germany, 1890-1935* (Aquarian Press, 1985), note on dust jacket.

[39] Nigel Pennick, *Hitler's Secret Sciences: His Quest for the Hidden Knowledge of the Ancients* (Neville Spearman, 1981), pp.104-5.

[40] Nesta H. Webster, *Secret Societies and Subvervsive Movements* (Christian Book Club of America, fp.1924), p.254.

publication has claimed that *'both Hegel and his materialist disciple Marx might be considered direct descendants of gnosticism'*.[41] In conjunction with this comes the revelation that *'Communism was handed down in the dark through the secret societies of the nineteenth century'*.[42] Whether one believes in conspiracy theories or not (and, given the evidence, it would be foolish not to do so), the fact remains that it can be clearly shown that all the revolutionary developments between the eighteenth and twentieth centuries were the result of considerable occult activity behind the scenes, as various cliques and coteries attempted to work towards their desired Utopia.[43]

The main feature of the French and Russian revolutions was that, no matter how they turned out in the end, they were humanist-motivated revolutions inspired by essential Gnostic principles. Most importantly, what had happened in each case was that the biblical notion that rulers are appointed by God (under commandment to serve Jesus Christ, whether they realise it or not, Ps.2:10-12) had been eclipsed by the popular concept of 'people power', through which governments are believed to be the product of the choice of the people. Today, this notion of 'social democracy', because it is usually contrasted with the worst of dictatorships, is reckoned to be the best form of governmental authority; but this is to misunderstand the purpose of government in the Divine Plan. Both evil despotism *and* social democracy are unbiblical distortions of God's way of government.

The Bible clearly shows that earthly leaders are required to administer justice (including the death penalty for murder) and to promote the general welfare of the people — all to prevent a world in rebellion from drifting into chaos (Rom.13:1-7). The state was ordained *'for the punishment of evildoers and for the praise of those who do good'* (1 Pet.2:13-14), *'to execute wrath on him who practices evil'* (Rom.13:4), and *'that we may lead a quiet and peaceable life'* (1 Tim.2:2). This is part of what John Calvin called the *'generalem Dei gratiam'* (general grace of God), through which the post-diluvian world is preserved from chaos in order that His eternal plan of redemption can be effected. The fact that the unbelieving world has often moulded the state into many additional functions which God did not indicate (e.g. state ownership of the means of production, persecution of dissidents, overburdensome taxes, etc.) does not detract from the propriety of that original function of *preserving order and promoting welfare in a fallen world.*

The Bible does not sanction cruel and rapacious government (e.g., Isa.14:4-20; Jer.5:28-29; Ezk.34:2-10), although, in the providence of God, such government may come to pass as a chastisement upon a rebellious people. But neither does the

---

[41] Mircea Eliade (ed.), *The Encyclopedia of Religion* (Macmillan, 1987), Vol.5, p.576.

[42] Nesta H. Webster, *Secret Societies*, op. cit., p.268. For further information, read Nesta Webster's other books, *The Socialist Network* (Bloomfield Books, fp.1926), and *World Revolution* (Bloomfield Books, fp.1921).

[43] For a thorough introduction to this vast subject area, see A. Ralph Epperson, *The Unseen Hand: An Introduction to the Conspiratorial View of History* (Publius Press, 1985), 488pp.

Word of God endorse the concept of a majority of the people choosing the rulers who best suit their own whimsical desires.[44] Both despotism and democracy have been designed by the devil and his earthly agents to promote his global strategy in the Gospel Age. The word 'democracy' comes from two Greek words, *demos* meaning 'the people', and *kratos* meaning 'power'. Democracy is basically 'people-power'. But where do we find such a governmental idea represented in the Bible? Just as people will heap up for themselves religious teachers who will serve up what their itching ears want to hear (2 Tim.4:3-4), so they will also heap up for themselves political leaders who tickle their desires in the same way. It is of interest to learn that 'people power' as a political force has its earthly origins in the Rosicrucian-inspired European 'Enlightenment'. As one Christian writer has put it:

> 'Throughout history, it has been believed that kings, good or bad, were set up by divine appointment. The belief extends far beyond the Judeo-Christian West... Nevertheless, man's natural inclination is to rebel against divine rulership for whatever cause, and the first successful confrontation of this age took place in England, in 1215, with the signing of the *Magna Carta*. Here, the monarch of the day was made subject to the law of the land instead of remaining placed above the law. In France, however, the kings still exercised their divine rights until the French Revolution, which began in 1789. Rousseau's *Social Contract*, published in 1762, put forward a radical and secular theory of government based on a general will of the people rather than on laws appointed by God, paving the way for the French Revolution and, incidentally, for the American Revolution, announced by the Declaration of Independence thirteen years earlier. By removing God from human affairs and declaring man to be inherently good, Rousseau had set the stage for secular humanism'.[45]

In support of this writer's claim, this 'God-removing' pattern of historical events is not lost on the Neo-Gnostics themselves. For example, the occult college known as the 'School for Esoteric Studies', founded by the occultist Alice B. Bailey in New York, has put out a pamphlet which recognises only too well that the foremost historical event which has paved the way for their occult schedule was

> 'the signing of the Magna Carta. This document was signed at Runnymede, during the reign of King John on June 15, 1215 A.D. Here the idea of liberation from authority was presented with the emphasis upon the personal liberty and rights of the individual. The growth and

[44] For an instructive example of God's disapproval of people-power, see 1 Sam.8:4-22. There, the people decided that God's way of government was not good enough and that they wanted a human ruler of their own making. It is highly significant that it was not their rejection of their original Divinely-appointed ruler, Samuel, for which the Lord upbraided them, but rather their implicit rejection of God Himself.

[45] Ian T. Taylor, *In the Minds of Men: Darwin and the New World Order* (TFE Publishing, 1987), pp.31-32.

> development of this basic idea repeated itself in other major events: The founding of the French Republic with its emphasis on human liberty... The Declaration of Independence and the Bill of Rights (in the U.S.) determining national policy... The Universal Declaration of Human Rights, bringing the whole question into the international field, and in principle *guaranteeing to men and women everywhere in the world liberty and freedom to develop the divine reality within themselves*'.[46] [emphasis added]

It is vitally important to understand this fact: The political, social and religious freedom which is sought by unregenerate human beings — regardless of any high-sounding altruistic aims — will always be used ultimately *'to develop the divine reality within themselves'*, that is, to lift themselves up as gods. It is a sad fact that many Christians believe that the humanistic form of government we call 'social democracy' somehow has God's endorsement, and that through the process of 'common grace' the pinnacle of 'civilisation' will be reached as believer and unbeliever work together for the good of all. But that is not at all the prospect for the future shown by the Bible, as we have already demonstrated in the previous chapter. One of Satan's neatest strategies in recent times has been to dupe so many believers into imagining that there is such a thing as 'civilisation', upward human progress, and that unregenerate men and women are somehow not really so bad after all. Never has there been such a need for a powerful restatement of the doctrine of human depravity. It is not any innate goodness in humanity which makes people dream up democratic institutions and inalienable human rights, but the desire to be free from Divine authority.

What we today call 'democracy' had always been the highest ideal of the secret societies and occult sects in the heart of Europe in the seventeenth and eighteenth centuries. Accordingly, the Illuminati, an occult brotherhood founded by Adam Weishaupt in Bavaria in 1776, has been described as *'A secret society devoted to anti-priestly and **democratic** ideals'*.[47] Because of their belief in the innate goodness of humanity and their desire to give full rein to human creative powers, it has always been the aim of the occultists to gain as much freedom for humans as possible — the *'liberty and freedom to develop the divine reality within themselves'*, as the above-mentioned 'School for Esoteric Studies' phrased it.

It is a sad fact that Christian believers have been lulled into a false sense of security in terms of the aims and ethics of unbelievers. They have failed to hold before them the fact that the human heart *'is deceitful above all things, and incurably sick'* (the literal Hebrew translation of Jer.17:9). They have chosen to turn away from the Christian view of man, which asserts that

> 'the mind of man has been so completely estranged from God's righteousness that it conceives, desires, and undertakes, only that which is

[46] Jan van der Linden, *The Inner Life of the United Nations* (School for Esoteric Studies Inc., n.d.), pp.3-4. This occult college is an offshoot of theosophist Alice Bailey's Lucis Trust (formerly the Lucifer Trust), about which more later.

[47] John R. Hinnells (ed.), *The Penguin Dictionary of Religions* (Penguin, 1984), p.161.

> impious, perverted, foul, impure, and infamous. The heart is so steeped in the poison of sin, that it can breathe out nothing but a loathsome stench. But if some men occasionally make a show of good, their minds nevertheless ever remain enveloped in hypocrisy and deceitful craft, and their hearts bound by inner perversity'.[48]

This is not a pessimistic view of human nature: it is the view of biblical realism (Rom.3:9-18). This is not to say that unbelievers never do anything of any civic worth; but the biblical view is that it is *the Divine restraint of their evil natures* which enables them to do *apparently* good works and prevents them from showing the true depths of evil which lie behind the mask. As William Perkins (1560-1602) puts it:

> 'If God did not thus moderate and restrain the natures of men, but suffer them to break out to the full, all societies and commonwealths would be turned upside-down, because every man by the universal corruption of his nature, would break out into every sin'.[49]

One day, that restraint will be removed and the full nature of man's depravity will be exposed (Rev.9). There have been many occasions in history when that depravity has peaked in the actions of some unreservedly-wicked people. These are just a taste of things to come; and it is of great comfort to the believer to know that when the power of darkness will be at its zenith, the Lord will intervene to fully establish His kingdom (2 Th.2:8; Rev.19:19-21). Just as the Man of Sin cannot appear in history because there is a Divine restraint (2 Th.2:3-8), so the full sinfulness of man in general will not reach its climax until a similar restraint on his behaviour is removed. There has only ever been God's Way (under the guidance of the Holy Spirit) or Man's Way (under the dominion of Satan), although the latter has manifested itself in numerous, superficially-differing schemes. The truth which believers need to grasp is that what we today call 'secular humanism' is not merely a materialistic philosophy which is devoid of any religious or spiritual input. It is actually a natural outworking of the Gnostic mindset, which has always sought to put Man on the throne in place of God. As James Webb states:

> 'In this century, with the presentation of traditional religious positions in secular form, there has emerged a secular Gnosticism beside the other great secular religions — the mystical union of Fascism, the apocalypse of Marxist dialectic, the Earthly City of social democracy. The secular Gnosticism is almost never recognized for what it is, and it can exist alongside other convictions almost unperceived'.[50]

Fascism, Marxism, Liberation Movements and Social Democracy — although they appear to be very different — all drink from the same poisoned trough. Each

---

48 F.L. Battles (trans.), *John Calvin: Institutes of the Christian Religion*, Book II, chapter v, §19, (Westminster Press, 1960), Vol.I, p.340.

49 William Perkins, 'An Exhortation to Repentance: Sermon on Zephaniah 2:1-2', in *Perkins' Workes*, 1604, Vol.III, p.416.

50 James Webb, *The Occult Establishment* (Open Court, 1976), p.418.

of these 'secular religions' represents a different aspect of man's usurpation of Divine authority in human government, an outworking of the satanic Lie which rests at the heart of the temptation of our first parents, *'You will be like gods'* (Gen.3:5). The *'secular Gnosticism'* which *'is almost never recognised for what it is'*, is that urge for earthly liberation which manifests itself in so much political ideology. The Christian knows that true personal liberation comes only through a personal relationship with the Man Christ Jesus, and that there will be peace only when He has transformed the cosmos after His return. The very idea that human beings can be liberated on this present earth, through human effort, from the problems of this fallen world is utterly Gnostic in its foundations. This lack of recognition of the advance of secular Gnosticism in political activity has enabled it to thrive as a viable ideal in the minds of men and women — and especially in those Christian circles where it is believed that the Church can work together with the state in order to create an era of peace and prosperity. What many Christians appear to have overlooked is that they have become partakers in a huge ideological shift away from the biblical view of Government and authority to one which has been masterminded by Satan as part of his strategy among the nations in the time of the end of the Age. All of these developments in the political sphere, as the Neo-Gnostics well recognise, have been 'loosening things up' in preparation for the climax of all history. The stark truth is that although 'Liberty, Equality and Fraternity' may sound like very noble and desirable ideals, they can never succeed when they are enacted in a community of individuals whose every deed takes place under the sway of Satan.

So, the concept of an occult-inspired coming New Age on earth is no new idea. In fact, the very concept of a future Golden Age is a vital part of Satan's plan, having been spawned by the Old Serpent in world-history as a counterfeit of the true New Age which will happen in a totally-reconstituted cosmos as prophesied in the Old Testament Book of Isaiah (Isa.65:17; 66:22) and vividly portrayed in the Book of Revelation (Rev.21:1ff.). The devil, as a diligent student of Scripture, knows full well that his future doom, and that of all his followers, is openly marked out within its pages (Gen.3:15; Isa.27:1; Rev.12:12; 20:10). His aim, therefore, in proposing an alternative 'heaven on earth', is to lull unbelievers into a false sense of security so that they will not realise that there is a *'wrath to come'* from which they must flee. As he has no real kingdom of his own to offer, the best he can do is to attempt to prevent as many souls as possible from entering the kingdom of heaven. Thus, he holds out to them the hope of a coming 'heaven on earth' which he hopes will prove a more attractive proposition than the eternal life proclaimed in the Christian Gospel. In keeping with this 'dog-in-the-manger' aim, Neo-Gnostic writers have taken the interpretation of biblical prophecy on board in a big way, especially that which relates to their projected earthly millennium. The Book of Revelation is especially susceptible to this treatment, only it is subjected to the most atrocious allegorisation. For example, in a typical Neo-Gnostic interpretation of the Apocalypse, the New Age biologist Peter Russell writes:

'If the Revelation of St. John were to be considered metaphorically as well as literally, "Christ" would symbolise this inner source of wisdom. The dependent and conditioned mode of thought — the ego-mind — would then be symbolized by the "Antichrist". It is that aspect of ourselves that stands against our inner knowing — it is anti-"the Christ within"... The good news is that St. John foresees the battle of Armageddon being won by Christ — suggesting that our higher knowing will eventually defeat the Antichrist within. Then Christ's kingdom reigns. This we might interpret as a world freed from the dictates of our ego-mind, a world in which a liberated mind is the norm rather than the exception... There will, at last, be peace on earth — the inner peace we have been seeking all along".[51]

In squeezing his psychologized pathway to a Golden Age on earth out of the Book of Revelation, Peter Russell has rendered an interpretation which may be compatible with the mindset of a graduate in philosophy, psychology and comparative religion but one which would have been completely lost on the persecuted Christians of the late first century — or, indeed, of any era of the Church. The Apostle John was writing not because of any desire to be 'free of the dictates of the ego-mind' in order to tap into an 'inner source of wisdom', but as a *'companion in tribulation'* (Rev.1:9) for the comfort of all those believers who suffer persecution because of their willingness to openly proclaim the Gospel of Jesus Christ. This highly cavalier approach to the Scriptures is yet another perennial hallmark of Gnosticism. When referring to the ancient Gnostics' approach to the New Testament, J.L. Mosheim points out that they:

'not only interpreted these sacred books most absurdly, by neglecting the true spirit of the words and the intention of the writers, but also corrupted them in the most perfidious manner, by curtailing and adding, in order to remove what was unfavourable, or to produce something conformable to their pernicious and extravagant system'.[52]

One of the main reasons why this Golden Age on earth has always grabbed so many people's attention is because it represents 'hope' in an apparently hopeless and futile world of existential despair (what Albert Camus and Jean-Paul Sartre would have called 'Le Théâtre de l'Absurde'). As this book progresses, we will see this Golden Age theme repeated in numerous guises. For the concept of a Golden Age on earth has a compelling universal attraction to Everyman of whatever religion or none. However, is it not somewhat ironic that in spite of the Gnostic view of matter as an intrinsically evil product of the Fall, the promoters of the New Age should seek to anchor their 'heaven' within the confines of the universe as it is now constituted? Contradictory as it is, Gnostics will always seek to 'bring down heaven on earth'. As Professor Wolfgang Smith puts it:

---

[51] Peter Russell, *The White Hole in Time: Our Future Evolution and the Meaning of Now* (Aquarian Press, 1992), p.178.

[52] J.L. Mosheim, op. cit., Vol.I, p.39.

> 'In place of an Eschaton which ontologically transcends the confines of this world, the modern Gnostic envisions an End *within history*, an Eschaton, therefore, which is to be realized *within the ontological plane of this visible universe*'.[53] [emphasis added]

Why should this be? Why is it that the Gnostic — in spite of his belief that man is entrapped in coarse matter — will always seek to create heaven *here on earth*? Surely, the reason is because it is the earth which is the sole domain of his master, Satan. Since the devil's defeat by the Lord Jesus Christ, he no longer has any access to heaven and his sphere of activity has been limited to the earth and its immediate environs (see Rev.12:7-9). The Old Serpent, for all his self-styled ingenuity, can never promise a heaven in any other location than on the earth as it is presently constituted! That is the best he can ever offer, although it seems to be enough for all those who are duped by his wiles. This is also the reason for the current Neo-Gnostic obsession with the Earth as 'The Great Mother'. Today, the 'Greens' and ecologists have revived the ancient pantheistic concept of the planet as *'Gaia'* — the Greek goddess and name for Mother Earth,[54] often referred to by polytheists as *'the oldest of divinities'*.[55] This divinisation of the earth is a classic Gnostic stamping-ground. As the gnostic psychologist C.G. Jung has written:

> 'According to [the alchemist] Basilius Valentinus, the earth (as *prima materia*) is not a dead body, but is inhabited by a spirit that is its life and soul. All created things, minerals included, draw their strength from this earth-spirit. This spirit is life...and it gives nourishment to all the living things it shelters in its womb'.[56]

Earth magic, leylines, power points, nature spirits, the current obsession with the earth and its eco-system — all these fetishes and sacred cows of the Neo-Gnostic are intimately connected with the fact that the sole focus of Satan's activity is the earth. Although a healthy concern for the environment and its wildlife is a worthy one (and even a biblical one, Genesis 1:26-31; 2:15; Proverbs 12:10; Deuteronomy 25:4), the Christian could never make a god or goddess out of the planet, having been exhorted to set his affections on the things which are above (Col.3:1-3). The grand irony is that in spite of the fact that the Gnostic believes in the inherent evil of matter and his great need to be liberated from entrapment in it, he is forever earthbound until he is released from his bondage to Satan, who is the god of this very world (2 Cor.4:3-4). The earth is the full extent of Satan's haunt, and he makes the most of it, offering there perfection, peace and a Golden Age, if only people will follow him. However, just as he could not fulfil his promise to our first parents of 'no death' if they succumbed to his temptation in Eden (Gen.3:4-6), so he cannot even deliver a 'heaven on earth' (as history will finally

---

[53] Wolfgang Smith, *Teilhardism and the New Religion* (TAN Books, 1988), p.238.

[54] See, for example, J.E. Lovelock, *Gaia* (Oxford University Press, 1979).

[55] Barbara G. Walker (ed.), *The Woman's Encyclopedia of Myths and Secrets* (Harper & Row, 1983), p.332.

[56] C.G. Jung, *Psychology and Alchemy* (Routledge & Kegan Paul, 1957), p.329.

prove, Rev.18:21). The promise of a future Golden Age on earth offered by Satan and his associates — whether it be Rosicrucian, political-liberationist, New Age advocate or otherwise — will always be a huge confidence trick; for it can only ever be, at best, the cosmic equivalent of a houseparty on a sinking ship.

Throughout this present Age, human beings are being gathered into two great bodies: One is the body of Christ (Eph.1:22-23), the other is the body of Antichrist (Rev.13:4,8,12). One is an organism of quickened souls, the other an organisation of dying rebels. The body being gathered by Antichrist is a counterfeit of the body being brought in by Christ. Thus, these two bodies are being prepared in entirely different ways and are working with entirely different material. The former is being gathered by the Holy Spirit, enabling all believers to be *'baptized into one body'* (1 Cor.12:13), whereas the latter is being unified and confederated by *'the spirit of the Antichrist'* (1 Jn.4:3), which is *'the spirit who now works in the sons of disobedience'* (Eph.2:2). The body of Christ is being prepared out of *living* material (1 Pet.2:4-5), having been *'raised from the dead...[to] newness of life'* (Rom.6:4; cf. Col.2:12); whereas the body of Antichrist is being built up with dying matter. Regardless of the aims of politicians or ideological visionaries to create a 'New World Order', a 'Brotherhood of Man', or a 'Great Society', they can only ever construct their dreams on the foundations of decay. As one writer expresses it:

> 'Satan cannot create an *organism*; he can only form an *organisation*. Hence, he is drawing unquickened human beings together around the unifying idea of "fraternity", or "co-operation", or "society", and is diligently propagating the belief that, when that great organisation takes shape, the permanent advantage of all mankind will be secured. When this body is formed (as it surely will be), then the expected leader or head will be brought forth, that "man of destiny", "whose coming is according to the *working of Satan*, with all power and signs and wonders of falsehood, and in every deceit of unrighteousness in them that perish"'.[57]

Since the time of the Fall of Adam, the godless world has been an orphaned family without an earthly head. Having also rejected the One who came in His Father's Name, when the time comes that their master comes in his *own* name, him they will receive (Jn.5:43). Whereas the mass of people rejected the true Christ and put Him to death when He came among them with His faithful promises, they will welcome the advent of the Antichrist with his lying designs and hail him as their saviour. Socio-Political Utopianism is a supreme illusion which can only ever give crumbs of false comfort before the inevitable collapse of human history. There can be no Golden Age until every vestige of evil, which is the leading principle of this present age (Gal.1:4), has been wholly eradicated from the Cosmos (Rev.20:9-21:5).

---

[57] Philip Mauro, *The Number of Man: The Climax of Civilisation* (Morgan & Scott, 1910), p.53.

5. Manipulation of the 'Mind-Sciences'

Another nineteenth-century satanic seed which was to have a global impact was the institutionalisation of what we can call the 'mind-sciences'. Under this heading we place all those developments which would concern themselves with the therapeutic and non-therapeutic causation of change in human consciousness and deep manipulation of the minds of men and women. The use of trance, hypnosis, psychotherapy, visualisation techniques, and other systems for the exploitation of 'mind-power' all have their immediate roots in the psychic explorations and extensive writings of the Viennese School of Sigmund Freud (1856-1939) and those of his pupils Wilhelm Reich (1897-1957) and Carl Gustav Jung (1875-1961). Various other occultists such as Franz Anton Mesmer (1734-1815) and Gustav Fechner (1801-1887) had earlier created the climate which would be conducive to the development of the mind-sciences in the nineteenth century, which, in turn, has been a leading influence in the development of the New Gnosticism.

It can also be shown that the mind-sciences developed by psychologists and psychotherapists during the past two centuries have their roots in occult techniques going right back to ancient times. However, as we will be dealing with the mind-sciences in considerably more detail in Chapters 7 and 11, we will reserve further comment until then.

6. The 'God-Wisdom' of Theosophy

Although the previous five nineteenth-century satanic seeds have been movements and influences, the sixth seed which was destined to have the most profound effect on the growth of Neo-Gnosticism in the twentieth century is an actual organisation. The Theosophical Society was founded in New York on November 17th, 1875, by the Russian medium and adventuress Helena Petrovana Blavatsky and Col. Henry Steel Olcott (an associate of Mary Baker Eddy, founder of Christian Science). After Blavatsky's death, the development of the Theosophical Society in Britain as well as on the international front was taken up in 1891 by former Anglican clergyman's wife and champion of socialism, Annie Besant, together with erstwhile Anglican vicar and paedophile C.W. Leadbeater. The main stated objectives of the society were:

1. To form a nucleus of the Universal Brotherhood of Humanity without distinction of race, creed, sex, caste, or colour.

2. To encourage the study of Comparative Religion, Philosophy and Science.

3. To investigate the unexplained laws of Nature and the powers latent in man.

These objectives were entirely compatible with the goals of countless esoteric organisations which had existed in the centuries beforehand. However, there was a crucial difference: The Theosophical Society was not operating as a clandestine group but was publicly seeking proselytes across the globe. It represented the beginnings of the *open* embodiment and fulfilment of all that Rosicrucianism and Freemasonry had developed in secret groups for centuries. The occult had finally 'come out' into the open.

The core of the Blavatsky theosophical teaching is rooted in a syncretism which pulls together strains from Hinduism, Buddhism, Zoroastrianism and gnostic Christianity — all of which deny the Transcendent Creator God and use practices to bring about the 'divinisation' of the individual. One of the main hallmarks of the Theosophical Society was its claim to have been set up under the direct guidance of a group of spirit-entities known variously as the 'Brotherhood of Luxor', the 'Mahatmas', the 'Overlighting Ones' or the 'Ascended Masters'. These beings were credited with masterminding the cosmic plan of which the earth is a part. As we work through this book, we will repeatedly have cause to refer to this phenomenon. It is one of the extraordinary foundations upon which the New Gnosticism has developed. (We will deal with the work of this alleged 'brotherhood' in more detail in the following chapter).

One of the major contributions of the Theosophical Society to the New Gnosticism was the concept of 'spiritual evolution', developed in Blavatsky's massive work *The Secret Doctrine*. Once Darwin's theory had come into vogue, it was but a short step to extend that concept further. Just as man had already evolved from lower life forms, so he will continue to evolve into a mighty cosmic organism — with each individual being reincarnated many thousands of times until he reaches perfection. However, she was not alone in positing a spiritualised evolution-theory. As one writer notes:

> 'It has been made since Madame Blavatsky's time by Teilhard de Chardin and, in her own century, was expressed in different forms by both Bergson and Nietzsche'.[58]

But in the late nineteenth century it was Blavatsky's unique conception which so captivated the hearts of the people. That vacuum left by the undermining of Christian faith had led to the need for a new religious aspiration. And in this respect, *'It was the genius of H.P. [Blavatsky] to apply Darwin's theory to produce a hopeful resolution of the human condition'*.[59] Rather than basing her spiritualised evolution on natural selection or chance development, she offered people hope by declaring that there was a plan to the evolving universe and that the next leap in evolution into a Golden Age was not far away. This would be preceded, she claimed, by the advent of a World Teacher, who would lead the planet into a time of unprecedented peace and harmony. In the early part of the twentieth century, Theosophists Annie Besant and C.W. Leadbeater tried to establish Jiddu Krishnamurti as this teacher, but he pulled out of the enterprise.[60] That role still remains to be filled, as we shall see shortly when we examine the claims of one of the many organisations which grew out of the Theosophical Society.

Although the word 'theosophy' had been in use on occasion in previous centuries, this was the first time it had been applied to a specific organisation. It is

---

[58] James Webb, *The Occult Underground* (Open Court, 1974), p.91.

[59] James Webb, *The Flight from Reason* (Macdonald, 1971), p.52.

[60] Krishnamurti continued to disseminate his personal philosophy in large tent-meetings held every year at boarding schools which he founded in Hampshire, U.K., India and the U.S., until his death in 1987.

derived from a combination of the Greek words *theos,* god, and *sophos*, meaning wise. It therefore means 'wise in the things of God' or simply 'divine wisdom'. Generally speaking, theosophy can be defined as

> 'Any system of thought concerned with the relationship between God and the creation, especially one intended to help man achieve *direct experience of the divine.* The word can describe any articulate mystical system; it has been applied especially to Kabbalah, [and] Neoplatonism'.[61] [emphasis added]

Standing firmly in this tradition, the Theosophical Society thus provided the consummate bridge between the Old Gnosticism and the New. Indeed, the fact that we are dealing with a modern manifestation of ancient Gnosticism is fully understood by Theosophists themselves. The Jungian psychologist and theosophist, Stephan Hoeller, discloses that

> 'in such works as *The Undiscovered Self* and *Civilisation in Transition* Jung clearly recognized modern Theosophy as an important contemporary manifestation of Gnosticism, and he likened it to a submarine mountain range spreading beneath the waves of the mainstream culture, with only the projecting mountain peaks becoming visible from time to time through the attention received by Mme. Blavatsky, Annie Besant, Krishnamurti and others'.[62]

The Theosophical Society has been estimated to have passed the occult tradition to more than one hundred separate organisations in the U.S. and many more in Europe.[63] As one researcher has put it: *'No single organisation or movement has contributed so many components to the New Age Movement as the Theosophical Society'.*[64] Among the many occult and Oriental ideas which the Theosophical Society has spawned, developed, and popularised in the West are reincarnation, spirit-entities directing earth history, astrology, the 'channelling' of instructional material from the spirit world, the existence of the ancient civilisations of Atlantis and Lemuria, and the disciplines of yoga and meditation. In much the same way that the 'respectability' of Comparative Religion led to the denial of the exclusive claims of Christian salvation, so the acceptability of contact with spirit-entities which was encouraged by the Theosophical Society has led to a denial of Christian claims about heaven, hell and the after-death experience.

If readers are in any doubt as to the spiritual pedigree of this organisation, in 1887 it was responsible for publishing a magazine called *Lucifer*, designed *'to bring to light the hidden things of darkness'.*[65] Furthermore, the logo of the Theosophical Publishing House today still depicts a serpent entwined around a large

---

[61] John R. Hinnells (ed.), *Dictionary of Religions* (Penguin, 1984), p.329.

[62] Stephan A. Hoeller, *The Gnostic Jung and the Seven Sermons to the Dead* (Quest Books, 1982), p.26.

[63] J. Gordon Melton, *New Age Almanac* (Visible Ink, 1991), p.32.

[64] Ibid.

[65] From the Preface to H.P. Blavatsky, *The Secret Doctrine* (Quest Books, 1966), p.xvii.

'T'. One would have to be extremely naive to fail to recognise the many clues to the origin of the Theosophical Society.[66] Although its power as an individual organisation has waned over the years, the original Theosophical Society, having served its purpose, has nevertheless spawned an enormous number of expanding esoteric societies and organisations in the twentieth century which are drawing many people of all ages into their ranks. In the next section, we will give brief details of some of the most significant of these offspring.

III. 20th CENTURY SEEDS OF CORRUPTION

The Theosophical Society was really the beginning of Satan's occult plan coming into full view for the first time since the years of the early church. The Gnostic teachings which had been shrouded in occult societies for centuries had finally 'come out' (to use a phrase borrowed from the homosexual movements of today). Thus, with the advent of the Theosophical Society, occultism became respectable. It was towards this rendering of occult knowledge as respectable that Satan had been working since the time of the Cross. Here, at last, was the 'designer religion' for atheists, agnostics and mini-antichrists. The significance of this historical development is well-understood by the Neo-Gnostics themselves. In his definition of the New Age Movement, Peter Lemesurier of the Scots-based, Neo-Gnostic, Findhorn Foundation writes:

> 'Typically it could be said to refer to the whole family of movements, groupings, communities and networks of non-conventional millenarian idealists that have grown up out of the Theosophical initiatives and associated splinter-groups during our own century, and particularly since about the 1950s'.[67]

Similarly, when commenting on the widespread dissemination of occultism in the wake of the nineteenth century Theosophical Society, David Spangler — a former student of the occultist Alice B. Bailey and guru of the Findhorn Community in Scotland — reveals that

> 'throughout the last century there has been the release of information and concepts held confidential for centuries within select occult groups'.[68]

According to David Spangler, this release of information is being diffused through such groups as the Theosophical Society, the Anthroposophical Society (Rudolph Steiner Schools/Camphill Trust Villages), the Lucis Trust, New Thought Movements (e.g., Christian Science, Visualisation techniques, the power of Positive Thinking, Prosperity Consciousness, Possibility Thinking, and other

---

[66] It is interesting that Satan and his followers so often leave such obvious clues to their true identity scattered like confetti around their concerns. It is almost as if the Old Serpent is confidently goading people into a paper chase on the trail to uncovering his evil designs.

[67] Peter Lemesurier, op. cit., p.183.

[68] David Spangler, *Revelation: The Birth of a New Age* (Findhorn Press, 1971), p.124.

uses of 'mind-power'), the writings of Teilhard de Chardin, coupled with the now-widespread late twentieth century blending of the cultures and beliefs of East and West.[69] These constitute some of the prime foundation-laying influences of the New Gnosticism. Many of these influences have their actual roots in the *avant-garde* initiatives of the Theosophical Society which was established in 1875; whereas others — such as the writings of Teilhard de Chardin — must surely have had the reception for their ideas greatly enhanced as a direct result of the work of the Theosophical Society in opening up the debate on 'spiritual' evolution and in pioneering the revolutionary concept of 'comparative religion'.

In the remainder of this section, we will give brief details of the groups mentioned by David Spangler which have a bearing on the present analysis of the historical movement from the Old Gnosticism to the New. This will not only show their place in the historical development of satanic strategy but will also give working examples of how this strategy operates. Although some or all of these groups may be little known by the majority of readers, their cumulative and collective influence has been enormous. Here we are concerned with the harbingers of the twentieth century which have prepared the way, thus enabling the thriving of a New Gnosis which would come in their wake.

1. In Trust to Lucifer : The Alice Bailey Inheritance

One of the most important of all the offshoots from the Theosophical Society was the Lucis Trust. Known initially as the Lucifer Trust, this group was founded by ex-Theosophist Alice LaTrobe Bateman Bailey in 1922, and has come to wield more influence in 'respectable' institutions than any other post-Theosophical Society grouping. Born into a wealthy family in Manchester, England in 1880, she was raised in the Anglican Church. When she was fifteen, she allegedly received a visit from a mysterious turbaned stranger, whom she presumed to be Jesus Christ, who informed her that she had to prepare herself for her life mission.

For a time she worked for the Y.W.C.A., where she met her future husband, a theological student training for ministry in the Episcopal Church in the U.S. After eight years of marriage, Bailey left her husband because of his violent temperament, and it was shortly after this that she came in contact with the Theosophical Society in California. At one of the meetings she noticed a portrait on the wall and recognised it as the mysterious visitor she received as a young girl. This was a picture of one of the so-called 'Ascended Masters', known as Kuthumi, who had worked through H.P. Blavatsky. Three years later she was contacted telepathically by another of these Masters, Djwal Khul (Master D.K.), and this was the beginning of a psychic relationship through which some twenty books would be 'channelled' from the world of spirits during the following thirty years. This led to some resentment in the Theosophical Society, many of whose adherents believed that messages from the Masters could only come through their founder,

[69] Ibid. The blending of the cultures and beliefs of East and West will be discussed in Chapter 9 on the subject of mysticism. 'New Thought' techniques will be examined in Chapter 11 under the 'mind-sciences'.

H.P. Blavatsky. Eventually Bailey was forced out of the T.S. by Annie Besant, who was in the process of taking over the organisation. With her would also go the man who was to be her next husband, Foster Bailey — a 33rd degree Freemason and writer on Masonic teachings — and together they set up the Lucis Trust.

The Trust was founded on the theosophical concepts of a coming world religious confederacy that would unite East and West and of a future World Teacher that would usher in a Golden Age on earth. In fact, Alice Bailey was the originator of the term 'New Age', which has been adopted by the modern movement of Neo-Gnostics as an embodiment of many earlier occult, Rosicrucian, Theosophical and alchemical ideals. Her massive two-volume work, 'Discipleship in the New Age' (1944 and 1955), provides state-of-the-art 'prophetic revelation' on the world conditions and spiritual forces which were to initiate the New Age some decades later.

As a highly-organised esoteric group committed to the developing of a global Neo-Gnostic philosophy, the Trust also functions as an official Non-Governmental Organisation within the United Nations, known as 'World Goodwill', and has its international headquarters in the United Nations Plaza in New York,[70] coupled with other offices in Geneva and London. In 1923, the Trust had formed an occult society called the Arcane School, and, later, an educational establishment called the School for Esoteric Studies, which is situated in New York.[71]

Alice Bailey's official biography,[72] was written by Sir John Sinclair, who was British director of the Lucis Trust from 1957-1961. After her death in 1949, the Trust continued to be headed by her second husband, Foster Bailey, who died in 1977. Today, the Trust is still the most highly admired and mature of all the esoteric societies, while the thirty 'channelled' Lucis books encased in their familiar dark blue covers remain best-sellers throughout the Neo-Gnostic world-scene.

2. The Occult Science of Rudolph Steiner

An organisation calling itself the Anthroposophical Society (from the Greek words: *anthropos*, man, *sophos*, wisdom) was founded in Berlin in 1913 by the former head of the German Theosophical Society, Rudolph Steiner. Like Alice Bailey, Steiner had come in touch with an occult 'Master' at a tender age, and this encouraged him to develop his powers and delve deeper into occultic matters.[73] He had also spent some time as an initiate in the 'Order of the Templars of the Orient', a society which advocated Tantric sex-magic and which boasted among its membership Aleister Crowley.[74]

---

[70] The full address, for those who may wish to verify this, is 866, United Nations Plaza, Suite 566-7, New York 10017-1888, U.S.A.

[71] The School for Esoteric Studies, Suite 1903, 425, Madison Avenue, New York, NY 10017, U.S.A.

[72] John Sinclair, *The Alice Bailey Inheritance* (Turnstone Press, 1984).

[73] Colin Wilson, *Rudolf Steiner: The Man and his Vision* (Aquarian Press, 1985), pp.43-44.

[74] For details of Steiner's involvement in the Order of the Templars of the Orient, see James Webb, *The Occult Establishment* (Open Court, 1978), p.489.

Steiner broke away from the Theosophical Society because he felt it was too biased towards the Eastern mystical tradition; he favoured the teachings of the Essenes, Gnostics and Rosicrucians, on which his work is largely based. Holding to the Neo-Gnostic belief that *'the Essenes are the bridge from the Mysteries to Christianity'*,[75] his books 'Occult Science', 'Knowledge of the Higher Worlds', and 'From the Buddha to Christ' are classics of the esoteric literature, elaborating on the cosmic histories of Helena Blavatsky's 'Secret Doctrine', and encouraging contact with discarnate entities through the use of strange forms of meditation, art, movement (known as Eurhythmics) and nature forms.

In 1904, Steiner published a magazine called 'Lucifer-Gnosis',[76] and his interpretation of the Gospels (on which he wrote many books) is based on the same esoteric Gnosticism which so plagued the early Church. As any faithful Anthroposophist will reveal, Steiner claimed that his main purpose was to introduce the West to the concept of reincarnation. Today, his occult legacy is subtly permeated throughout society by the many award-winning and prestigious international 'Waldorf' schools (over 25 in the U.K.) and the 'Camphill Trust' communities for the handicapped. Behind its renowned and lauded educational activities lies an esoteric programme of instruction in Steiner's occult philosophy which claims its roots in the mystery religions of ancient Greece and Persia. All members of staff in anthroposophical institutions — many of whom are sincere and hardworking carers — are required to undergo such occult instruction in a specially-designed 'Induction Course'. In some of these institutions, astrological charts and other means of occult divining are used to compile reports and assessments on pupils.[77]

In regard to the infiltration of occultism into the educational scene, the Steiner schools fit perfectly into Satan's end-time New Age philosophy.[78] They are model Neo-Gnostic schools — a fact which is all the more surprising when one considers the number of professing Christians, duped by Steiner's use of quasi-Christian vocabulary, who persist in sending their children to these institutions.

3. The Liberal Catholic Church and New Age Ritualism

The Liberal Catholic Church was founded by Anglican priest James Ingall Wedgewood in London in 1916. A powerful leader in this sect was C.W. Leadbeater, co-runner of the Theosophical Society with Annie Besant. Although many people will be unaware of the existence of this denomination, it has been instrumental in the syncretising of Christianity with New Age ideas and rituals. As with so many of these little-known groups, its true significance rests in the fact that it has spawned many individuals who have gone on to head up other organisations which have been influential in the more recent development of New Age

---

[75] Frederick Hiebel, *Treasures of Biblical Research and the Conscience of the Times* (Anthroposophic Press, 1970), p.9.

[76] Robert A. McDermott (ed.), *The Essential Steiner* (Harper & Row, 1984), p.27-28.

[77] The present author's wife, before she became a follower of Jesus Christ, worked as a music teacher in the Rudolf Steiner School in York, where astrological information was used in this way.

[78] Even the Findhorn Community contains a Rudolf Steiner School.

ideology and activity.

The Liberal Catholic Church was developed in order to provide sacred rituals which would be in line with Theosophical concepts such as the 'Ascended Masters', auras and colours. Details of their rituals are given in in C.W. Leadbeater's book *The Science of the Sacraments* (Theosophical Publishing House, 1929). As one researcher has written: *'The rituals are said to invoke powerful psychic forces'.*[79] At present, there are three Liberal Catholic branches in the U.S. with about 1500 members. There are also branches in Britain, Canada and Holland. In all there are about 10,000 members worldwide.

4. White Eagle Lodge: Precursor of the New Age Movement

The White Eagle Lodge is a group that emerged in 1934, and which has been most inspirational in providing the impetus for the Neo-Gnostic movement of today. It was founded by Grace Cooke (d.1979), a London spiritualist of some years' standing. She had been 'contacted' by a member of a group of spirits called the Polaire Brotherhood and was asked to train people up on their behalf for the coming 'Golden Age' on earth. The reason that this Lodge is entitled 'White Eagle' is because it was set up at the behest of a spirit-entity named White Eagle, who, it was claimed, was identified as John the Apostle and author of the Fourth Gospel. (John has often been claimed by the Gnostics of all eras as one of their own number, and his writings are reckoned by them as gnostic writings).

The U.K. headquarters of White Eagle Lodge is in Liss, Hampshire, where their specially-designed Temple is a landmark clearly visible from the main road. Their 'Sunday School' services for children are highly regarded by members. In the U.S., the headquarters is near Montgomery in Texas. Among the many beliefs and practices which have been of worldwide influence in religious developments during the past couple of decades are the acknowledgement of God as Father *and* Mother; the concept of the Cosmic Christ who shines in the human heart; the practice of Astrology; the exercise of psychic 'channelling' — through which one contacts spirits — and what they refer to as the 'Five Cosmic Laws' of Reincarnation, Karma, Opportunity, Correspondence and Compensation.

As with so many of these groups, the fact that it is little known and has not boasted millions of members does not at all inhibit its influence. One scholar of religious movements has said: *'[As] a precursor of the New Age Movement, the White Eagle Lodge remains a vital part of it'.*[80] These 'spawning' groups do not have to be large in themselves, but they are effective because they have groomed, to a high degree, the cream of New Age initiates, many of whom have gone on to found other similar, better-known groupings.

5. The Saint-Germain Foundation: New Age Building-Block

Another of the most important harbingers of the New Gnosticism is the Saint Germain Foundation established by Guy Warren Ballard (1878-1939). After

---

[79] Leslie Shepard (ed.), *Encyclopedia of Occultism and Parapsychology* (Gale Research, 1978), Vol.1, pp.526-527.

[80] J. Gordon Melton, *New Age Encyclopedia* (Gale Research, 1990), p.493.

becoming interested in the Theosophical Society, Ballard claimed to have met a mysterious individual in 1930 at the foot of Mount Shasta in California — a 'power centre' much visited by New Age explorers. This character identified himself as the Count of Saint Germain, an eighteenth century European nobleman who has been lauded in the occult community for his alchemical exploits and his more recent status as one of the 'Ascended Masters' known as Prince Rakocki. In one Neo-Gnostic publication, Saint Germain is referred to as

> 'the Wonderman of Europe, Lord of the Seventh Ray of Freedom, Hierarch of the Aquarian Age, Sponsor of the United States of America, Initiator of Souls in the Science and Ritual of Transmutation'.[81]

Ballard claims he was told by this phantom on Mount Shasta *'that he had come to initiate the Seventh Golden Age, the permanent Age of Eternal Perfection on Earth'*, and that Ballard was the man for the job of getting it organised.[82] So the work went on, and the Saint Germain Foundation was born. The teachings of the 'Ascended Masters' through this foundation consisted primarily in the claim that

> 'you can pray, you can meditate, you can contact God. The God of very gods is within you. You can make contact if you will it so... Jesus is the open door to the individual Christ consciousness—the kingdom of God that is, even now, within you'.[83]

They taught that people can call on these 'Masters' for assistance in contacting 'the God within' — the 'I AM' presence — through what they called 'decrees' or affirmations. After Ballard's death in 1939, the work was continued by his widow Edna. By 1988, the organisaton had more than 300 centres in the U.S., and had spawned many other groups which would provide the basis for the New Gnosticism. The importance of the teachings of the Saint Germain Foundation to satanic strategy is demonstated by the claim that they

> 'moved into and became quite influential in the larger occult community. In the 1970s, they became one of the building blocks of the New Age Movement'.[84]

In the 1950s, Mark L. Prophet, a member of the Saint Germain Foundation, created the 'Bridge to Freedom' organisation (the New Age Church of Truth) and the 'Lighthouse of Freedom'. After his death in 1973, his wife, Elizabeth Clare Prophet (known as Guru Ma) continued to head up what had become the 'Church Universal and Triumphant', the Summit Lighthouse Press and the New Age education centre, the Summit University. She still controls these groups to this day.

Another group which was heavily influenced by Guy Ballard's foundation was the Aetherius Society, which believed that the 'Ascended Masters' were actually

---

[81] Elizabeth Clare Prophet, *Prayer and Meditation: Jesus and Kuthumi* (Summit Press, 1963), p.4, illustration.

[82] J. Gordon Melton, *New Age Encyclopedia* (Gale Research, 1990), p.58.

[83] Elizabeth Clare Prophet, op. cit., inside cover.

[84] J. Gordon Melton, *New Age Encyclopedia*, p.59.

'Space Brothers' from another solar system. Through them, the term 'channelling' — the technique of psychic contact with spirit-entities — came into vogue, about which we will have more to say in the next chapter. The influence of the original Saint Germain Foundation cannot be over-emphasised. The groups which came out of it

> 'gave the [New Age] Movement its orientation to the [Ascended] Masters, leading to the production of literally hundreds of books of channelled material in the 1980s'.[85]

The influence which these published works and various splinter groups have had on the development of diabolic doctrine is enormous. And it all derived from one man's contact with a spirit-being at the foot of a mountain in 1930.

6. Teilhard de Chardin: Prophet of the New Gnosticism

Having examined a number of the primary groups comprising the background to the New Gnosticism, our understanding would be incomplete without a brief survey of the contribution of the French Jesuit priest who has influenced so many individuals and organisations in the past few decades. We are not merely speaking of fringe organisations here: Even the leader of the Liberal Democrat Party in the U.K., Paddy Ashdown, gave a lengthy quote from Teilhard de Chardin as the peroration of his first speech as leader at the Party Conference. As we have already noted earlier in this chapter, the psychic, David Spangler, claimed that Teilhard de Chardin (1881-1955) was one of the instruments through which there has been the release of information and concepts which were originally held confidential for centuries within select occult groups. Not surprisingly, therefore, we discover in this man's work the coming together of many different streams of the New Gnosticism: Evolution Theory (both scientific and spiritualised), Socio-Political Utopianism, mysticism, syncretism, pantheism, monism and Universalism — often expressed in identifiable terms (such as 'noosphere', 'Point Omega', etc.,) which are unique to his own writings.

Early in the 1980s, a celebrated survey of New Age advocates was carried out in the U.S., in which the question was asked: *'Which are the individuals whose ideas have influenced you most?'* At the top of the list, immediately above Carl Gustav Jung, Abraham Maslow, Carl Rogers, Aldous Huxley, Roberto Assagioli and Jiddu Krishnamurti, came the name of Pierre Teilhard de Chardin.[86] In an essay entitled 'The Universal Christ and the Convergence of Religions', Teilhard gave the New Gnosticism its clarion call when he spoke of

> 'a general convergence of religions upon a universal Christ who fundamentally satisifies them all: that seems to me the only possible conversion of the world, and the only form in which a religion of the future can be conceived'.[87]

---

[85] Ibid.

[86] Marilyn Ferguson, *The Aquarian Conspiracy: Personal and Social Transformation in the 1980s* (Granada-Paladin, 1982), p.463. The contribution of these characters to the New Gnosticism will be examined in later chapters.

It was his own peculiar application of the Darwinist Theory of Evolution which powered his thinking. For he did not regard this theory as a mere scientific concept, but as one which could be spiritualised into a cosmic reality. Having once written that *'neither in its impetus or in its achievements can science go to its limits without becoming tinged with mysticism and charged with faith'*,[88] he proceeded to elaborate a pseudo-scientific theory of universal spiritual development which would culminate in what he termed 'Point Omega' — a Universalist conception of the consummation of human history. Darwinism had provided the Neo-Gnostics with the scientific foundations which appeared to refute the concept of a Transcendent Jehovah as Creator. Teilhard recognised that in the wake of these biological scientific revelations, *'a religion of the earth is being mobilised against the religion of heaven'*.[89] And here we could not have had a better description of the spiritual battle between Gnosticism and Christianity: *'A religion of the earth being mobilised against the religion of heaven'*. Just as Satan can only ever offer the cheap promise of a future 'heaven on earth', so he can only provide a pitiful *religion of the earth* in order to effect it. And it was to the global acceptance of this pathetic religion, based on the Theory of Evolution, that Teilhard de Chardin dedicated his life and work. As Professor Wolfgang Smith has well said: *'At Teilhard's hands the Darwinist theory has been transformed into a full-fledged religion: it has actually been turned into a cult'*.[90] On one occasion, Teilhard wrote a letter in which he clearly revealed his intentions in this area:

> 'As you already know, what dominates my interest and my preoccupations is the effort to establish in myself and to spread around a new religion (you may call it a better Christianity) in which the personal God ceases to be the great neolithic proprietor of former times, in order to become the soul of the world; our religious and cultural stage calls for this'.[91]

Again, we see here a classic hallmark of Gnosticism in that it claims to be a 'better Christianity' — a higher form of religion which has no need for a *personal* God, which is styled as the province of the spiritually immature. This 'new religion' which Teilhard de Chardin envisaged is now being realised in the present generation; and even in his own life, he began to see it come to fruition:

> 'Today, thanks to advances in our methods of observation and the development of our thinking, the Reality which the so-called pantheist mystics have always felt rising up in the heaven of souls, is beginning to win recognition even in the mass of mankind'.[92]

---

[87] Pierre Teilhard de Chardin, *Christianity and Evolution* (Collins, 1971), p.130.

[88] John Ferguson, *An Illustrated Encyclopaedia of Mysticism and the Mystery Religions* (Thames & Hudson, 1976), p.192.

[89] Pierre Teilhard de Chardin, *Science and Christ* (Collins, 1968), p.120.

[90] Wolfgang Smith, *Teilhardism and the New Religion* (TAN Books, 1988), p.219.

[91] Quoted in ibid., p.210.

[92] Pierre Teilhard de Chardin, *The Heart of the Matter* (Collins, 1978), p.211.

The mysticism which Teilhard embraced is universal, and won him admirers from many different cultures and religious affiliations. When staying in the Ordos Desert in Mongolia in the 1920s, he wrote his famous 'Mass on the World', based on a ritual in which the world is sacrificed to God in prayer. As an interesting and revealing commentary on the syncretic nature of this pagan mystic rite, Dr. Ursula King, founder of the Teilhard de Chardin Centre in London and lecturer in Theology at Leeds University, has written that

> 'the Tibetan Lama Anandagarika Govinda has pointed out that the Ordos Desert lies in an area which, for centuries, has been under the cultural influence of Tibetan Buddhism. For this reason he has explored similarities between his "Mass on the World" and the mystical meaning of the Tibetan Mantra *"Om mani padme hum"*, and also with certain ideas of the seventeenth century Buddhist poem *Bodhicharyavatara.* All those works place a similar emphasis on the spiritual transformation of matter, man and the world when offered up in an act of religious surrender'.[93]

The goal of the 'spiritual transformation of matter' is a fundamental Gnostic concept, and has been the preoccupation of the occult art of Alchemy for centuries. It seems that Teilhard had a special relationship with Tibetan Buddhism — a religion which has its roots firmly in the ancient occult tradition. When two Tibetan Lamas were interviewed in the Temple of the Great Jade Buddha in Shanghai in 1942, with Teilhard present, one of them said that *'Teilhard was a great "living Jesus" of the West. One day he would be famous and many people would be nourished by his message'.*[94]

However, in spite of all his religious charisma and mysticism, Teilhard was also impressed with such antichristian ideologies as Marxism (yet another 'religion of the earth'). He made repeated favourable references to it from as early as the 1920s after meeting a woman called Ida Treat, an active member of the French Communist Party who became his lifelong friend.[95] Here we note what will prove to be a repeated phenomenon during the build up to the climax of all history: an unholy alliance between two superficially-different developments (world government and world religion) with a mutual interest in the spirit of Antichrist (cf. the two beasts in Chapter 13 of the Book of Revelation). In support of this, in December 1966, under the heading, 'Atheism: two kinds of humanism', Time Magazine wrote:

> 'Many European Communist thinkers quote approvingly from the works of French Jesuit Pierre Teilhard de Chardin, whose [book] "The Phenomenon of Man" was recently published in Moscow'.[96]

---

[93] Ursula King, *Towards a New Mysticism* (Collins, 1980), p.61.

[94] C. Rivière, *Teilhard, Claudel et Mauriac* (Paris, 1963), quoted in Ursula King, op. cit., pp.83-84.

[95] Ursula King, op. cit., p.264, n.115.

[96] Quoted in John Cotter, *A Study in Syncretism: The Background and Apparatus of the*

In fact, the Moscow edition of this book was prefaced with an introduction by Roger Garaudy, who was chief theoretician of the French Communist Party — and who had also, interestingly, been invited to lecture at the Jesuit St. Louis University in December 1966.[97] Teilhard's relationship with China had also brought him into contact with the burgeoning development of Marxism there; and Ursula King discloses that

> 'Teilhard knew more about the rising forces of communism in China than one would generally suspect. He had for a long time been aware of the compelling attraction of Marxism and many of his essays refer to the inner strength and activating power of the Marxist belief in the development of man and the world'.[98]

Here again we see the Political Utopianism of the Neo-Gnostic in action. Both Teilhard and Marx were influenced by Evolution Theory, both of which held forth a past without a Fall into sin and lawlessness, while promising a future without Divine judgement. It is not without significance that the English edition of 'The Phenomenon of Man' contained an introduction by the atheist, scientist, founder of UNESCO, and evolution theory populariser Sir Julian Huxley, grandson of Sir Thomas Huxley. In this connection, it is worth mentioning that Teilhard himself was one of the key figures involved in the 'Piltdown Man' fraud of 1912, in which, through the discovery of bogus fossils, it was attempted to provide the so-called 'missing link' between apes and humans — a fraud which remained scandalously undetected until 1953. Malcolm Bowden, in his investigative book 'Ape Men: Fact or Fallacy?', clearly shows that the finger of suspicion points substantially, if not conclusively, at Teilhard as the chief perpetrator of this hoax.[99]

How significant it is to the subject of our study that the writings and philosophy of Pierre Teilhard de Chardin should have provided so much inspiration to mystics, evolutionists, socialist-utopians, Tibetan Buddhists, political leaders, New Agers, atheists and scientists alike. The widespread respectability and influence of the teachings of Teilhard de Chardin can be seen in the fact that even world leaders such as Mikhail Gorbachev (former president of the U.S.S.R. and now President of the International Green Cross/Green Crescent) use terminology unique to Teilhard's writings. In one international news report in 'Time' magazine, it was revealed that:

> 'Gorbachev may be the only world leader to use the word *noosphere* (a term that refers to human consciousness as it relates to the biosphere) in a major address'.[100]

Mikhail Gorbachev is far more than a political leader and self-styled international champion of the environment. He has been (and remains to this day) one of

---

Emerging One-World Church (Canadian Intelligence Publications, 1979), p.37.

[97] Ibid.

[98] Ursula King, op. cit., pp.82-83.

[99] Malcolm Bowden, *Ape Men: Fact or Fallacy?* (Sovereign Publications, 1977).

[100] *Time Magazine*, September 6th, 1993, p.50.

the major players in a global occultic web of intrigue which has as its aim the setting up of a 'New World Order' at the behest of a secret world government — which could well be the culmination of Satan's end-plan for this present evil age.

The real appeal of Teilhard de Chardin is that his teachings provide a philosophical groundplan for all those with Gnostic inclinations who are today seeking to develop a global religious, scientific and political climate which is conducive to the annihilation of the concept of the Transcendent, Judging, Sovereign God portrayed in the Bible and the establishment of a satanic reign of peace and justice on the earth.

7. Tuned-In and Turned-On: The Watershed of 1960s Drug Culture

Although we will be expanding on this subject in the next chapter, the present section on twentieth century seeds of satanic corruption would be incomplete without some final mention of the fundamental importance of the global developments which took place in the 1960s. At that time, a new counter-culture was formed which opened up the youth of that period to a massive infestation of demonic influence and extreme sinful behaviour. Central to this was the use of hallucinogenic and mind-altering drugs such as Marijuana, Cannabis resin, Lysergic Acid Dithylamide (LSD), di-Methyl Tryptamine (DMT), Mescaline, Peyote and other fungal concoctions.

The use of these substances on such a scale — which is still a vast growth industry to this day — brought millions of young and impressionable people under the sway of a number of influences which were to be of fundamental importance to satanic strategy at this point in history. First, it enabled people to alter their consciousness at will and thereby enter states in which they could more easily come into contact with evil spirits which masquerade as benign beings who have come to assist in the birthing of the New Age/New World Order (more on this in the next chapter). Second, the use of such drugs propagated the notion that 'ordinary' Christianity was of a lower order than the rich mystical experiences which were possible through such an alteration of consciousness. Eventually it was discovered that certain meditation practices could bring about the same effects as the drugs, which had merely paved the way for these 'deeper' religious experiences. Third, it compounded the concept of both Theosophy and Eastern religion, that one can tap into the 'God within' through such activity. Fourth, it brought about a realisation of people-power through encouraging rebellion against Biblically-rooted authority and morality, thus paving the way for the sexual revolution and such 'democratic human rights' as abortion on demand. Fifth, the 1960s drug culture perpetuated the notion that the long-desired Golden Age of peace and justice could be established on the earth — that it was possible, in the words of one psychologist who advocated such developments, *'to stay high forever and bring home the New Jerusalem, the Whole Earth'*.[101]

---

[101] John Heider, *'Catharsis in Human Potential Encounter'*, Journal of Humanistic Psychology, No.14, 1974. Quoted in John Rowan, *Ordinary Ecstasy: Humanistic Psychology in Action*, (Routledge & Kegan Paul, 1976), p.103.

Even at this time, the undercurrent feeling was that the movement was going to bring about a massive global change to usher in the New Age. 'Acid-Rock' (LSD influenced) groups such as the Grateful Dead, Country Joe and the Fish, Captain Beefheart and his Magic Band, Jefferson Airplane, and the Quicksilver Messenger Service all reflected this movement in their lyrics, exercising a vast influence over their audiences. The entire accent was on 'blowing your mind'. One chart-topping song of 1967, entitled 'San Francisco', made the claim that *'All across the nation, there's a new generation, such a strange vibration...'*. And 'strange vibration' it was.

Some readers may recall seeing news-footage of a huge utopian-based rock-music festival at Woodstock, in the U.S.A. in 1969, which brought the surrounding area to a complete standstill for tens of miles. At this gathering, more than a million people were swaying, trancelike, in the mists of marijuana, holding marathon encounter-therapy groups, reading each other's astrological birth charts and Tarot cards, listening to the hypnotic sounds of acid-rock music, and receiving instruction in the practice of Kundalini Yoga, Vippasana meditation and a host of other esoteric arts. The well-known haunting song 'Woodstock', written by the singer Joni Mitchell, was the anthem of this festival; and the Neo-Gnostic intent behind it is clearly portrayed in the lyrics:

> '...Gonna camp out on the land and set my soul free.
> We are stardust (billion year-old carbon)
> And we are golden (caught in the Devil's bargain)
> And we've got to get ourselves back to the Garden'.[102]

The 'Garden' here is the Garden of Eden, which the occultist, alchemist, magician and Gnostic will always seek to set up once more on the earth. Here we have the primary difference between the polluted way of the Gnostic and the sanctified Way of Christ. The Gnostic always tries to return to the conditions of Eden, to create heaven on earth through his own collective strength. But the Christian knows that a return to Eden would be a retrograde step, and so — in patience and faith — he awaits the making of all things new by the grace of his Creator.

The mystical and gnostic influences of the stoned-out 1960s moved from their initial confinement within 'fringe' groups and esoteric organisations to a burgeoning international respectability, and can today be observed in many areas of establishment life. As the 'flower-children' of that period grew up, they went on to take their place in society, spreading their doctrine as they went and thereby influencing the policies of their various professional occupations. For although they may have cut their hair and put on suits, they still continued to engage in the 'mind-expanding' practices which had played such a part in their formative years — a fact which has been well-documented in the book 'The Aquarian Conspiracy: Personal and Social Transformation in the 1980s', by the New Age researcher Marilyn Ferguson.[103] Not only that, but the children of the 1960s also went on to

---

[102] This song was also recorded by the rock group 'Matthew's Southern Comfort'.

[103] Marilyn Ferguson, *The Aquarian Conspiracy: Personal and Social Transformation in*

have families, and these children have also been reared on magic mushrooms, mandalas and meditation. So, not only are the dope-smoking, mind-expanding, acid-dropping flower people of the 1960s now positioned in places of power in government, medicine, psychiatry, computing, education and business; but their children are also now entering adulthood and taking their places in the world. Two generations of the children of the New Age have now come of age, the global effects of which we will discover in the following chapter. As the New Age physicist, Dr. Fritjof Capra of Berkeley University, has stated:

> 'The social movements of the 1960s and 1970s represent the rising culture, which is now ready for the passage to the solar age'.[104]

What is this 'solar age' into which we are now alleged to be moving? The Mexican-born Neo-Gnostic writer José Arguelles — who predicted there would be a global 'Harmonic Convergence' of psychic energy on August 16-17th 1987, based on an ancient Hopi Indian prophecy — claims that the New Age of Aquarius is a 'solar age' which replaces polluting forms of energy production with solar energy and an understanding of *'the common resonance of psychic and solar energy frequencies'*.[105] Essentially, the 'Solar Age' is a cleverly-coded Neo-Gnostic term used to refer to the New Age which is just dawning — the age in which the Sun-God, Lucifer, will be the dominant force. It is towards the fulfilment of this event which the occult influences of the 1960s were moving.

CONCLUSION

In this present chapter, we have charted the way in which certain human ideas, philosophies, movements and disciplines have been seeded by the powers of darkness in the midst of the Western nations — nations which previously adhered at least to a nominal Christianity. The effect of these developments was to loosen things up on a global scale in the scientific, theological, educational, medical, political and religious spheres, to prepare the way for the Neo-Gnosticism of today and for the cataclysmic events of the final quarter of the twentieth century. In the following chapter, we will undertake a detailed examination of the key strategies of this New Gnosticism together with its main hallmarks, in order that we may begin to appreciate the global magnitude of Satan's designs in this evil age.

---

the 1980s, (Granada/Paladin, 1982), 494pp.

[104] Fritjof Capra, *The Turning Point: Science, Society and the Rising Culture* (Flamingo, 1982), p.466.

[105] See José Arguelles, *The Transformative Vision: Reflections on the Nature and History of Human Expression* (Shambhala, 1975). Take careful note of the name of the publisher of this book. It will recur in a highly significant context in the following chapter.

Chapter Four

THE FOUNDING OF THE NEW GNOSTICISM

(2) The Leaven in the Loaf

'A little leaven leavens the whole lump' (Gal.5:9).

In the previous chapter, we looked at the primary ways in which Neo-Gnosticism has been seeded by Satan in world history. First, we saw how the manifestos of seventeenth-century Rosicrucianism acted as a bridge between the Old Gnosticism and the New in calling for a 'Reformation of the Whole Wide World' — a call which, to a great extent, found a response in the so-called 'Enlightenment' or 'Age of Reason' in the seventeenth and eighteenth centuries. This created the ideal environment in which Evolution Theory, Theological Liberalism, Socio-Political Utopianism, Comparative Religion and the 'Mind-Sciences' could flower. Then, into the spiritual vacuum left in the wake of these developments could flow the aspirations of the Theosophical Society, stimulating people to 'form a nucleus of the Universal Brotherhood of Humanity', to study comparative religion, and to develop psychic powers. We then exposed some crucial nineteenth-century developments which divulged secrets which had been held confidential for centuries within select occult groupings.

In the present chapter, we shall examine the manner in which all these influences have continued to be masterminded throughout the present century, leading to the creation of a worldwide, crusading, millenarian alliance which is rooted in Gnostic principles. Although this has recently been termed as the New Age Movement or New Consciousness, we prefer to put it under the title of the New Gnosticism because of its clear links with antichristian religious developments at the start of the Gospel Age. There are also certain key factors in our study of satanic strategy which we cannot reiterate often enough. First, that the New Gnosis is not 'new' at all and, second, that it is not just another cult. We are witnessing, in our time, the fast-growing acceptance at all levels of culture of a movement whose philosophy and practice is wholly opposed to Christianity. Unless believers relinquish their dreams of a wholly-Christianised world this side of the Day of Judgement, and wake up to the over-arching significance of the mass of deceptions in the world and in the professing Church, they are going to be overwhelmed by future events — not least of which will be the most furious persecution of faithful believers. In this second chapter on the founding of the New Gnosticism, we will undertake a substantial examination of some of the fundamental strategies being used to take over the minds and hearts of the world's population today.

I. MIND-GAMES: New Consciousness for Old

A primary tenet of Neo-Gnostic belief is that there is a need in each individual for an alteration of consciousness to occur before he or she can make any spiritual or 'evolutionary' progress. Breaking this belief down into its components, one influential New Ager sums up the teachings of the New Age Movement as follows:

> '1) The world, including the human race, constitutes an expression of a higher, more comprehensive Divine Nature; 2) Hidden within each human being is a higher divine self which is a manifestation of the higher, more comprehensive nature; 3) This higher nature can be *awakened* and can become the centre of the individual's everyday life; 4) This *awakening* is the reason for the existence of each individual life'.[1] [emphasis added]

This corresponds entirely with the world-view of the Gnostic, who holds the erroneous belief that

> 'man is a being with a divine spark, fallen into the world of matter, estranged and needing to be *awakened* by a divine call so as to be restored to his highest state.[2] [emphasis added]

In similar vein, another researcher has said that

> 'The Gnosis, the knowledge which ensures salvation, is the realization by man that he contains a spark of God, and of the necessity of *awakening* from the half-life he leads on earth — described variously as "numbness", "sleep", or "intoxication" — to a full consciousness of his divinity and of how it has been ensnared in matter'.[3] [emphasis added]

Notice how each of the above three quotes from entirely different sources uses the word *'awakening'* to express what is necessary in order to invoke the 'divine consciousness within'. One can see from these statements that there is a correspondence of sorts here with the Christian doctrine of redemption, in terms of the fact that man is indeed so estranged from God as a result of the Fall that there is the need for a 'call' from God so as to be restored into relationship with him. But the solution of the Gnostic to this problem does not lie in having faith in Christ or trusting in Him for a salvation which culminates in a future life of glory. Instead, when confronted by the fact of the Fall,

> 'the Gnostic responds by saying that a leap in consciousness will overcome the sense of conflict in the universe'.[4]

It is this concept of the necessity of a *'leap in consciousness'* in order to reach God — or, rather, to awaken one's 'God-consciousness' or the 'Christ within' —

---

1 Jeremy Tarcher, publisher of Marilyn Ferguson's *Aquarian Conspiracy*, quoted in Lowell D. Streiker, *New Age Comes to Main Street* (Abingdon, 1990), pp.26-27.

2 John Ferguson, *An Illustrated Encyclopaedia of Mysticism and the Mystery Religions* (Thames & Hudson, 1976), p.68.

3 James Webb, *The Occult Underground* (Open Court, 1974), p.199.

4 Tobias Churton, *The Gnostics* (Weidenfeld & Nicolson/Channel Four, 1990), p.128.

which lies at the heart of the New Age Movement today. It is for this reason that the New Age Movement is also referred to as the *'New Consciousness'*, although there is nothing new about it at all. The questions we will attempt to answer in this section are: Why is it that Gnostics Old and New advocate this 'leap in consciousness'? And what do they mean by saying that such a leap *'will overcome the sense of conflict in the universe'* ?

According to Gnostic teaching, the original Fall of Man was not a fall into sin or lawlessness, but was a descent into *self*-consciousness from *God*-consciousness — a plummeting into matter from spirit. To the Gnostic, gross matter is synonymous with evil. When Genesis 3:21 speaks of our first parents as having been clothed by God with *'tunics of skin'* in the wake of the Fall, Gnostics interpret this as referring symbolically to a change from a wholly ethereal body into a physical one made of gross matter. In the philosophy of the Neo-Gnostic, the forbidden fruit eaten by our first parents was symbolic of a descent into the predominant use of rational thought processes, which obscured the original 'God-Consciousness'. They believe that each person has a 'divine spark' within, but that this spark is obscured by the ego-consciousness which arises from being a person alienated from the divine through being 'ensnared in matter'. Entering into the spirit of the New Age means to seek ways of rekindling that spark of 'divinity'. Gnosticism teaches that this divine spark can be ignited through an alteration of consciousness. They claim that when humans first came into being, they were naturally in tune with the world of spirit and their own divinity, but when they lost that God-consciousness, means had to be devised to 'reconnect' with the spirit part of man — to awaken the divine spark. One of the touchstone tenets of Gnosticism states: *'Not sin or guilt, but unconsciousness is the cause of evil'.*[5] The Gnostic seeks to be awakened from his alleged human *un*consciousness into a full consciousness of his 'inner divinity'. Throughout history, certain individuals have been especially able to enter, at will, a state of 'higher consciousness': Shamans, Yogic masters, and, more latterly, the heroes of the Gnostic and Western esoteric traditions. These people acted as conduits, as it were, providing a hotline to the heavenlies, bringing essential teaching about a forgotten state which they claim can be re-attained by all those who will follow in their footsteps.

However, it should be stated here that there is a crucial difference between genuine Divine revelation and that which comes from the evil powers hell-bent on subjugating the world. Herein lies the difference between true Christianity and Gnosticism. The Creator of the universe has been most meticulous in the manner in which He has revealed Himself and His will to His human creation since the Fall. Fallen man has never been willing to accept this divinely-imposed limitation; and it is for this reason that magic, witchcraft and sorcery have proliferated to such an extent throughout human history. Fallen man always desires to develop his spirituality in his own way, by his own methods; and it is for this reason that there was a Fall in the first place. In other words, the Fall happened not merely because of wilful disobedience — although that was certainly a

[5] Mircea Eliade (ed.) *Encyclopedia of Religion* (Collins, 1987), Vol.5, p.567.

foundational part of it — but because of the creature's desire for a higher level of consciousness than that with which he had been endowed by his Creator. The woman saw that the tree of the knowledge of good and evil was *'a tree desirable to make one wise'* (Gen.3:6). In other words, *it was the desire for the gnosis which led to the Fall in the first place.* The Gnostic, far from providing a solution to this, merely recommends yet more of the same as a way out of the dilemma of being a fallen human being living in a fallen world. This is the essence of satanic religion, and has been so from time immemorial.

It is important for us to realise that the main interface between the demonic realm and humanity lies in the sphere of the imagination, through the use of mind-control. There is a thirst in the life-force of the demon for a control of human affairs, manifesting itself at its mildest level through simple manipulation of specific thought-patterns and behaviour; while at its most severe, it seeks to work through complete control of the life of the human creature. It is, therefore, necessary for appropriate opportunity to be provided in order that the unseen forces of evil can work at their most efficient in the human being. These footholds generally constitute such things as violent thoughts and actions, extreme anti-social behaviour, sexual immorality, compulsive drug-taking, sorcery, idolatry, and so on. This is precisely why the Apostle Paul advised that we should not give an 'opportunity' or 'foothold' (Greek: *topos,* 'place') to the devil through holding on to anger (Eph.4:26-27). It is through their curiosity about, and experience of, sinful phenomena that people become open to demonic interference, influence and affliction; this culminates in actual 'possession' in extreme cases, where a person deliberately and wilfully 'sells the soul' through yielding himself up to psychic forces which he is unable to handle, e.g., through ritual magic, psychic exploration, mediumship, repeated sexual depravity, extreme violence, and so on. We are referring here to the unbeliever, who is, by nature, in bondage to Satan (Acts 26:18; cf. Col.1:13). The Christian is indwelt by the Holy Spirit, and, although he can be sorely tested by Satan, he can never be in bondage to him (Rom.6:14; 1 Jn.3:8-9). On the other hand, the natural man's essential depravity makes him an easy and willing prey to the forces of darkness (Eph.2:2; 2 Cor.4:3-4).

Because the demonic realm exists in another 'dimension' from that of the human inhabitants of the earth — coupled with the fact that it is also under a degree of Divine restraint — it is necessary for certain conditions to prevail in order for its intentions to be carried out with maximum effectiveness. This limitation is openly recognised amongst those controlled by demonic forces. One 'spirit guide' frankly reported to the person through whom it was being 'channelled':

> 'We are unable to commune with humans whose vibrational fields are distorted by ego factors, emotional reactions, excessive conceptualisation, or past-future orientation'.[6]

What this means is that unless a person has begun to make some attempt to

---

[6] Ken Carey, *The Starseed Transmissions*, (Harper, 1982), p.35. There will be a good deal more discussion on this practice of 'channelling' later in this chapter.

dissolve their ego and open themselves up through consciousness-altering techniques, the demonic realm will be restricted in its ability to communicate with them. It is for this reason that one finds, in Neo-Gnostic circles, a tendency to stress the inferiority of the rational mind and conceptualisation, urging that it should be relinquished if one is to have truly effective communion with the spiritual realm. To this end, cunning methods of encouraging us to alter our normal level of consciousness and suspend our rationality have been devised by the forces of darkness — often in the interests of so-called 'self-improvement' — so that the person surrenders his or her mind to these forces without any awareness of the fact and what it entails. Many different techniques are recommended by the advocates of Neo-Gnosticism; however, they all fall under seven main headings:

- Meditation techniques, such as Kundalini, Vipassana, Tantrism, Zen, and various forms of guided imagery.
- Psychic exploration ('Channelling').
- Psychotherapies — especially the transpersonal and humanistic varieties, and those which involve hypnosis.
- Consciousness-altering drugs and other substances, such as Cannabis, LSD, and hallucinogenic fungi.
- Varieties of trance-inducing activities, such as Dervishism, visualisation, chanting of repetitive phrases (mantras) and choruses, and the hypnotic phenomenon known in certain professing Christian circles as being 'slain in the spirit'.
- Extreme asceticism, such as fasting, sleep-deprivation, etc.
- 'Close encounters' with a Guru or Master.

The combination of these influences constitutes the foundation of what is today called the New Consciousness — a term referring to the world-view which undergirds the many practices of the New Age Movement. In spite of the use of the word 'new' here, there is nothing new about them, for they are the fulfilment of the secret doctrine of the esoteric groups which Satan has preserved in the so-called civilised nations for centuries.

This manipulation of human consciousness can be observed in the worldwide resurgence of mysticism and occult gnosis through a wide variety of gurus and philosophies, which have attracted many millions of spiritually-experimenting people into Satan's occult plan. Although there have long been pockets of people around the world who advocated the alteration of consciousness, the manipulation of consciousness on a grand scale began in earnest in the mid-1960s with the advent of the hippie drug culture. Indeed, the 'psychedelic' 1960s proved to be a watershed in this development, as things began to move from being the sole province of the 'beard and caftan' set to that of the yuppie, businessman, politician and white-coated professional. It is necessary for good communication between the demonic realm and humanity that the 'inner life' or imaginal capacity of a person should be 'expanded' to its maximum, thus creating an openness to manipulation of the mind. This fact accounts for the huge growth in recent decades of the use of 'mind-expanding' drugs and all the other techniques which are being used to expand consciousness and create the illusion of realised divinity. As one Neo-Gnostic psychologist rightly claimed more than fifteen years ago that:

> 'the single major event forcing [the] development [of transpersonal psychology] has been the widespread use and abuse of psychedelic or mind-manifesting substances such as marijuana, LSD and mescaline... The psychedelic drugs gave incontrovertible proof that altered states of consciousness had reality and that paths toward transcendent experience existed...We were hunting for ways to stay high forever and bring home the New Jerusalem, the Whole Earth'.[7]

The 'psychedelic sixties' were, in fact, paving the way for the gathering wave of global demonic manipulation which would come in succeeding decades. That this was happening under the inspiration of demons we will show in a later section. At the same time, Eastern mysticism made a major assault on the West by cashing in on this new transcendentalism. Such practices have contributed to the manufacture of a 'New' Consciousness which is finely tuned to the promptings of the demonic realm. It is because of these developments today that there is the great need for a rational, discerning mind, together with the Christian concept of **objective reality** — all of which have become subject to much disparagement in the ethos of the New Gnosticism. Over twenty years ago, an international meeting attended by psychiatrists, psychologists, theologians, physicians, mathematicians, physicists and engineers, called 'The Interdisciplinary Conference on the Voluntary Control of Internal States of Consciousness', stated in its official invitation: *'We have reached the point in history at which the exploration of 'internal states' has become not only legitimate, but also a high-priority business of science'.*[8]

The 1960s and 1970s represented the grand harvest of the Neo-Gnostic revival which had begun almost one hundred years earlier with the inception of the Theosophical Society. During this time there was a global outburst of psychic activity which proved to be a watershed in the development of the New Gnosticism. A new age of eclecticism had dawned when every individual could pick and choose any components of any religious tradition or system and synthesise them into a hybrid of his own making. Irenaeus's observation of the ancient Gnosticism, that *'every day every one of them invents something new'*, is equally applicable to the New Gnosticism. Especially has this been the case with the phenomenon of meditation, which is probably the single most popular method of attaining a 'leap in consciousness'. As one observer writes:

> 'During the 1960s and 1970s, transpersonal psychologists examined a wide variety of meditation techniques...As a result of this approach, their work demonstrated that any given meditation practice could easily

---

[7] John Heider, *'Catharsis in Human Potential Encounter'*, Journal of Humanistic Psychology, No.14, 1974. Quoted in John Rowan, *Ordinary Ecstasy: Humanistic Psychology in Action*, (Routledge & Kegan Paul, 1976), p.103.

[8] William Johnston, *Silent Music: The Science of Meditation*, (Collins, 1974), p.23.

be lifted from its original religious context, or any religious context, and practised as a consciousness-altering technique in itself. This discovery has undergirded the sharing of meditation techniques across religious boundaries and has been an important factor in the emergence of such phenomena as a Christian Zen or the marketing of a form of Hindu Japa-Yoga as a 'non-religious' practice under the label Transcendental Meditation'.[9]

All these developments have been avidly encouraged in Departments of Religion throughout the world's institutions of higher education. In France, a country which boasts of having more than 10,000 clairvoyants, the prestigious Sorbonne in Paris has established a course in the subject of Astrology.[10] In 1984, a £½ million bequest by Arthur Koestler to the University of Edinburgh founded a Chair in Parapsychology which is making a significant contribution to research and development in the New Gnosticism. Over in the U.S.A., an authoritative source lists sixty-three different institutions of Higher Education which are offering fully-accredited degree and other graduate programmes in New Age-related topics.[11] In the Department of Religion at Concordia University in the U.S.A., one senior member of staff, a Roman Catholic priest, has written a three-volume tome entitled 'Toward the Recovery of the Primordial Tradition', in which he advocates developing powers of ESP and encouraging churches to rediscover what he claims to be the true origins of Christianity. In the second volume, entitled 'The Psychic Roots of Ancient Wisdom and Primitive Christian Gnosis', he writes

> 'It is this author's conviction that persons of spiritual vision and intellectual integrity, in East and West, might profitably begin to work together in a great global and transcultural effort towards a recovery of the sense of a "Primordial Tradition" of intuition and insight — leading to higher forms of consciousness in the human species and resulting ultimately in an expanded awareness in our culture of the Transcendental origins and destiny of the human species'.[12]

In keeping with this appeal, a multitude of organisations have been engaged in encouraging this 'expansion of consciousness' during the last couple of decades. Bhagwan Shree Rajneesh's Orange People, Maharaj Ji's Divine Light Mission, the Findhorn Foundation, the Church of Scientology, Unification Church, the School of Economic Science, Krishna Consciousness Society, the Baha'i faith, Tara Centres, the Aetherius Society, the Gatekeeper Trust, the Wrekin Trust, Centres of Transcendental Meditation, to name but a few, are among those which have made a major contribution to the growth of the New Gnosticism.

---

[9] J. Gordon Melton, *The New Age Almanac* (Visible Inc., 1991), p.69.

[10] From a BBC 'News Briefing' programme, Friday 11th February 1994, 0600 hrs GMT.

[11] J. Gordon Melton, *New Age Encyclopedia* (Gale Research Inc., 1990), pp.517-518.

[12] John Rossner, *Toward Recovery of the Primordial Tradition*, Vol.II, *'The Psychic Roots of Ancient Wisdom and Primitive Christian Gnosis'* (University Press of America, 1983), p.xi.

A number of scientists have also been conducting experiments in the field of consciousness-altering. In one series of experiments, Jean Houston and R.E.L. Masters used what is known as an 'Altered State of Consciousness Inducing Device' (an 'ASCID' — the pun is intentional) to bring on religious experiences in their subjects. After being exposed to this device, subjects quickly entered an altered state and experienced *'bliss, a mystical and oceanic ecstasy'* — experiences which were reported to be *'stunningly akin to the reports of classical mystical states'*.[13] One subject in the experiment reported his experience thus:

> 'There was a tremendous slow-motion kind of explosion and upsurge and outgo of energy all around and from the point where the light disappeared. It was incredible. Then the circle grew and grew to infinite proportions within me, and all the sound was white. It was a silent Beethoven symphony throbbing all over the place... I grew huge and transparent, filled and permeated with the light and the fire. And I thought: My God is a God of Love and he lives within me'.[14]

Such experiences are now being sought and experienced by many millions of people of all ages, as the use of consciousness-expanding practices has exploded across the globe. The influential Episcopalian priest Morton Kelsey — who, as an ardent advocate of Jungian psychology and shamanism, has been in the forefront of encouraging Neo-Gnosticism in the Church — highlights sixteen ways of *'encountering psychic reality'*, as he puts it, including dreams, sacramentalism, trance (in which he rightly includes the Charismatic experience of being 'slain in the spirit'), hypnosis, mediumship, oracles or divination, and mind-expanding drugs.[15] The New Age writer Marilyn Ferguson, who went on to write a book in 1983 called 'The Aquarian Conspiracy', which documented many of the manifestations of the New Age in the U.S. in the 1980s, had written a book some years earlier entitled 'The Brain Revolution: Frontiers of Mind Research'. In this work she asserted that, as the consciousness-altering community developed,

> 'we stand a chance of emerging from relative unconsciousness into fuller awareness prophesied by such multidimensional scientists and philosophers as William James, Carl Jung and Teilhard de Chardin'.[16]

One finds the same names cropping up repeatedly in Neo-Gnostic literature. After advocating LSD therapy for terminally ill patients, alcoholics, autistic children and psychopathic personalities, Marilyn Ferguson goes on to prophesy that

> 'the medical community will turn increasingly to biofeedback, acupuncture, and other healing tools now considered unorthodox... Meditation and similar relaxation techniques will become part of

---

[13] Marilyn Ferguson, *The Brain Revolution: Frontiers of Mind Research* (Davis-Poynter, 1974), pp.111-113.

[14] Ibid.

[15] Morton H. Kelsey, *Transcend* (Element Books, 1991), p.31.

[16] Marilyn Ferguson, *The Brain Revolution: Frontiers of Mind Research* (Davis-Poynter, 1974), pp.337-338.

> Western Folk knowledge... Psychic self-healing will become common, whether through meditation, autogenic training [hypnosis] or relaxation-visualization techniques'.[17]

Having been penned some twenty years ago, this prediction has now come to fulfilment. Today one can even read of such treatments being widely recommended in popular women's magazines on sale in the High Street (e.g., Vogue, Harper's Bazaar, Woman's Own, etc.). In a similar vein, when John Taylor, Professor of Physics at Southampton University in the 1970s, conjectures on the future of human society in his book 'The Shape of Minds to Come', he writes:

> 'It would use techniques of improving intelligence by an enriched early environment, together with brain grafts in infants and genetic engineering... It will also be necessary for a person to be made as aware of himself as possible by means of improvisional technique, and at a later age by means of drugs like DOET [an hallucinogen]... There would also be controlled drug sessions, where students would be guided in the expansion of sensory and emotional experience; self-hypnosis would also be taught... And, of course, the child would be caught young, even from before conception, as a part of genetic engineering'.[18]

When he asks: *'What about religion?'*, he answers that it will be eroded away

> 'by the mental revolution as having no relevance to modern problems, and be replaced by "metaphysics", where all experience is recognized as a manifestation of energy and "worshipped" as such'.[19]

This is pure Neo-Gnosticism: the worship of energy, the expansion of consciousness through drugs and psychotherapy, the teaching of self-hypnosis, the desire to tamper with genetic encoding to improve human characteristics. Professor Taylor is not just a lone voice; he is here speaking for a great many people in respectable and influential positions in our society today. The modern Christian lives in the midst of a Gnostic culture and is more often than not completely unaware of it. The same ideas were also voiced by that father of the New Age Movement and champion of Evolution Theory, Pierre Teilhard de Chardin, when he gleefully considered the many strongholds which science is besieging today. He eagerly looked forward to the time when there would be:

> 'the vitalization of matter by the creation of super-molecules. The remodeling of the human organism by means of hormones. Control of heredity and sex by manipulation of genes and chromosomes. The readjustment and internal liberation of our souls by direct action upon springs gradually brought to light by psychoanalysis. The arousing and harnessing of the unfathomable intellectual and effective powers still latent in the human mass'.[20]

---

[17] Ibid.

[18] John Taylor, *The Shape of Minds to Come* (Michael Joseph, 1971), pp.220-221.

[19] Ibid., p.239.

This is the Brave New Age of Neo-Gnosticism. A Golden Age of Humanism manufactured by men and women who have wilfully dispensed with the very God who created them. The enactment of all these things becomes perfectly possible when you believe, with biologist Elisabet Sahtouris, that the best definition of life you can find is, *'Something that creates itself continually'*.[21] When God has been pushed out of the picture and life has been reduced to a mere self-creating agency, every man can do whatever is right in his own eyes and in the imagination of his own heart. But, in spite of this atheistic approach to life and creation, the New Gnosticism still has its precious gods; and these come in the form of the many Gurus and Masters at whose feet the budding adepts sit and listen in raptured awe. One of the reasons that we cite having a Guru as one of the primary forms of consciousness-altering is that intimate contact with these Neo-Gnostic icons can have a totally transformative effect in the emotional and spiritual life of the seeker. In this description of what happened to one girl in the 'Darshan' meetings of the guru Mother Meera, who ministers in Germany, one can discern the sinister nature of the process involved:

> 'Darshan is silent. Mother Meera teaches in silence. Everyone in the room, taking their turn when they feel moved to, kneels before the Mother. She takes their head in her hands for a few minutes and then gazes into their eyes for a few more minutes. Her eyes are the most mysterious deep pools of light. That is all there is to it — but something amazing happens. There is amazing attention in the room'.[22]

Similarly, when one man vistited the Indian guru, Sai Baba, he said afterwards: *'The experience of being physically near Sai Baba daily at the ashram overwhelmed me again and again'*.[23] What is happening here is pure hypnotism — a 'mesmeric' experience with suggestions being implanted at a deep and fundamental level. The true role of these Gurus in the New Gnosticism is to act as purveyors of the 'Satanic Initiation'; for they are steeped in an occult power which is lethal to those who come under its control. The Hindu evangelist, Swami Vivekananda — one of the leading lights of the first Parliament of the World's Religions in 1893 — has disclosed some interesting information concerning the power of these 'enlightened ones'. He writes:

> 'What power on earth would not be his? He would be able to move the sun and stars out of their places, to control everything in the universe from the atoms to the biggest suns. This is the end and aim of *pranayama*. When the yogi becomes perfect there will be nothing in nature not under his control. If he orders the gods or the souls of the

---

[20] Pierre Teilhard de Chardin, *The Future of Mankind* (Harper & Row, 1964), p.149.

[21] Article by Elisabet Sahtouris in *One Earth: Magazine of the Findhorn Foundation*, Vol.8, Issue 4, Winter 1988.

[22] *Global Link Up*, Issue 52, Summer 1992, p.3. This is the leading New Age journal in the U.K.

[23] *One Earth*, Vol.6, Issue 6, Oct./Nov. 1986, p.18.

> departed to come, they will come at his bidding. All the forces of nature will obey him as slaves... He who has controlled prana has controlled his own mind and all the minds...and all the bodies that exist'.[24]

The controlling use of this power of the Guru can be clearly seen in the following statement of a devotee of the Guru Sai Baba who claims that *'for those who recognise Sai Baba as God manifest on Earth, the external form is the support that helps us toward the altar of our own divinity'.*[25] To come into relationship with one of these 'enlightened' gurus carries with it some highly-charged energy which affects the consciousness of the devotee to such an extent that he or she can ultimately undergo the illusion of becoming a Divine being. Intimate contact with a Guru or similar teacher is, therefore, one of the major sources for transmission of that leap in consciousness which is the essential Gnostic experience. It is effective, and it is efficient — often affecting hundreds of people at any one time.

There are so many more examples that we could give of the consciousness-altering achievements of all these techniques. But the question must here be asked: What is the hidden agenda behind all this consciousness-altering? What does Satan really achieve when he enables a person to undergo the illusion of Divine consciousness? Findhorn Community director, Peter Lemesurier sums it all up with the disclosure that

> 'you have only to achieve (or possibly re-achieve) a state of pure consciousness — and not merely the partial, distorted consciousness of dualistic thinking — for the Golden Age of ultimate, holistic reality to be restored on earth... In this state of pure consciousness, once attained, there is no thought, no judgement, no discrimination, no idea of imperfection, no regret, no suffering, no urge to reform the world'.[26]

Here we can see the significance of the alleged need for *'a leap in consciousness which will overcome the sense of conflict in the universe'*. Once achieved, the person ceases to be aware that there is anything fallen in the creation, he fails to perceive that there is a cosmic conflict and a deep antithesis between the Law of God and the ways of man. Most important to Satan's strategy, the person who attains a 'leap in consciousness' ceases to perceive the need for an objective salvation. Such a person will regard the Gospel as completely alien to his needs, for he will be under the illusion that they have already been met in his imagined achievement of 'pure consciousness'. But the Lord Jesus Christ did not say that those who have failed to 'raise their consciousness' will go to hell for eternity. Likewise, in order to enter heaven for eternity it is nowhere stated by the Head of the Church that there must be a 'rekindling of Divine Consciousness'. The only

---

[24] Nikhilananda, *Vivekananda: The Yogas and Other Works* (Ramakrishna-Vivekananda Center, 1953), pp.592-593, 598. *Pranayama* is a form of Yoga using breathing techniques.

[25] *One Earth*, Vol.6, Issue 6, Oct./Nov. 1986, p.17.

[26] Peter Lemesurier, *This New Age Business: The Story of the Ancient and Continuing Quest to Bring Down Heaven on Earth*, (Findhorn, 1990), pp.230-232.

requirement ordained by God for the avoidance of hell (eternal death) and entry into heaven (eternal life) is to believe in Jesus Christ and follow Him in obedience. The three thousand souls who were added to the Church (and who received the immediate gift of the Holy Spirit) a couple of months after Jesus' resurrection had not attended a consciousness-altering workshop or an esoteric meditation group. They had simply *'gladly received'* the word of the Gospel in their minds and hearts (Acts 2:38-41). The convoluted therapy and consciousness-altering techniques practised in the coteries of the New Gnosticism are infinitely surpassed by the *'simplicity that is in Christ'* (2 Cor.11:3).

Satan's last-ditch strategy throughout this Gospel Age is to take control of as many minds as possible as fully as he possibly can. The leap into the 'New Consciousness' takes place through the surrendering of one's mind to the occult plan of the demonic realm. All the many techniques and systems we have mentioned in this section — psychic exploration, meditation techniques, psychotherapy, consciousness-altering drugs, extreme asceticism, trance-inducement and subordination to a guru or master — are but a handful of a vast network of developments designed by the powers of darkness, in opposition to the kingdom of God, to deceive people into having a form of godliness appropriate to the ambitions of the devil. All this goes right back to ancient times. For it is the same Cosmic Lie which deceives the Neo-Gnostic today as that which deceived our first parents (Gen.3:4-6) and which corrupted them from the simple obedience required of them by their Creator. Those first human beings had also sought to achieve a 'leap in consciousness' — a knowledge (gnosis) which would make them wiser than their Creator had ordained — and the Initiation which they received has continued to be passed on through the shamans, yogins, Gnostics and 'knowing ones' of every era. Truly, there is nothing new under the sun.

II. CRITICAL MASS: The Hundredth Monkey Theory

Having devised so many different consciousness-altering techniques with which to ensnare people into his occult plan, Satan has had to find a way of encouraging as many people as possible across the globe to indulge in them. It is one thing to invent a system, but it is quite another to persuade people *en masse* to use it. In this section, we will show how this is being achieved.

Back in 1978, British biologist Lyall Watson referred to what he called 'Lifetides' — waves of change washing into the collective psyche of humanity at specific points in history. He cites Charles Darwin and Sigmund Freud as instigators of two of the primary waves in the latest 'lifetide' to wash over the human species — which is the equivalent of the New Age advocated by occultists. Indeed, Dr. Watson is an ardent advocate of occultism, proudly stating:

> 'I hold with Carl Gustav Jung that the only part of us in close touch with our roots is the unconscious, and that in normal people this manifests itself more clearly in so-called occult phenomena'.[27]

---

[27] Lyall Watson, *Lifetide* (Hodder & Stoughton, 1979), p.12. It should here be said that Hodder & Stoughton is **not** a Christian publisher, as some mistakenly believe. It is a

It is not too surprising that Dr. Watson should hold this view, as he lived for some time among a small community on a volcanic island in Indonesia *'where extra-sensory perception, psychic healing, precognition, power places and survival after death are taken for granted'*.[28] Repeatedly in the writings of the Neo-Gnostics, one finds a great admiration for the shamanistic religious traditions of primitive, aboriginal societies — a phenomenon which we will be examining in a later section. Dr. Watson believes that the 'Lifetide' influence which will this time push things over the edge into the 'Golden Age' is *'a general shift in awareness produced by deep undulations in the human spirit'*.[29] In order to support this belief, Dr. Watson has devised a theory which has become fundamental to the growth of the New Gnosticism in the last fifteen years. This theory, known as the 'Hundredth Monkey Concept', is based on observations of a colony of monkeys on an island near Japan in 1952. Dr. Watson records how these monkeys were given sweet potatoes by a group of researchers studying their feeding behaviour. Because the potatoes were covered in dirt, the monkeys were reluctant to eat them. One day, a juvenile called Imo washed her potato in a stream before eating it. This had never been done before. Six years later, the habit of washing food had spread through a great number of the tribe, with the adult members learning to do this from the juveniles. Now, so far, the story simply recounts the learning process among a group of monkeys. But he then proceeds to extrapolate out of these observed facts some wholly unwarranted and unsubstantiated conclusions. Like so many other Neo-Gnostic scientists today, Lyall Watson's writings are filled with a range of improvisations, conjecture, suppositions, leaps of faith, assumptions and 'what-ifs', all of which somehow become transmuted into fact. In respect of the monkey observations, he puts it like this:

> 'The details up to this point are clear, but one has to gather the rest of the story from *personal anecdotes* and *bits of folklore* amongst primate researchers, because most of them are still not quite sure what happened'.[30] [emphasis added]

If such was the case — that the rest of the story could only be gathered from *'personal anecdotes'* and *'bits of folklore'* — then there it should have been left. But Dr. Watson could not resist that Neo-Gnostic capacity for elaboration:

> 'So I am *forced to improvise* the details, but *as near as I can tell*, this is what *seems* to have happened'.[31] [emphasis added]

Notice the words of uncertainty emphasised in italics here. He then expands the anecdotalism to say:

> 'In the Autumn of that year an unspecified number of monkeys on

---

successful publisher of *religious* books, including those promoting the occult. Within its wide religious spectrum is a selection of purportedly Christian works.

[28] Lyall Watson, *Gifts of Unknown Things* (Sceptre, 1987), book cover.

[29] Lyall Watson, *Lifetide*, op. cit., p.13.

[30] Ibid., pp.156-158.

[31] Ibid.

> Koshima were washing sweet potatoes in the sea... *Let us say, for argument's sake* that the number was ninety-nine and that at eleven o'clock on a Tuesday morning, one further convert was added to the fold in the usual way. But the addition of the hundreth monkey apparently carried the number across some sort of threshold, pushing it through a kind of critical mass, because by that evening almost everyone in the colony was doing it'.[32] [emphasis added]

'Let us say, for argument's sake...'. Here he is drawing the conclusion that there is an optimum level of learning reached in a species which then results in the behaviour spreading very rapidly through the rest of the species. As if that projection was not already unwarranted enough, he then goes on to deduce that

> 'the relevance of this anecdote is that it *suggests there may* be mechanisms in evolution other than those governed by ordinary natural selection'.[33] [emphasis added]

'Suggests there may be...'. Notice yet again the words of uncertainty. But the purely hypothetical content of his evidence does not in the least restrain him from applying this 'discovery' in the most sweeping, presumptuous manner. In fact, it is no exaggeration to say that on this flimsy evidence rests one of the major suppositions of the New Age Movement today. For from this pseudo-observation of proliferation in behavioural learning development among a group of monkeys, Dr. Watson projects that there is a similar critical point at which there are massive leaps in global evolutionary development — a concept which can then be applied to the generation of the 'quantum leap' into the next stage of evolution today. In other words, if enough people can be made to engage in consciousness-raising activity, a critical point will be reached at which there will be a spontaneous, globally-consuming, psychic development in human consciousness.

Now, there may well be a grain of truth in the Hundredth Monkey idea, in terms of group learning and the rate at which knowledge is transmitted in any given community. But to apply that to some kind of psychic quantum leap in the evolution of humanity is pure conjecture. However, such uncertainty does not appear to matter too much in Neo-Gnostic circles, as reality is whatever each individual makes it out to be — a fact which is demonstrated by Lyall Watson when he quotes with approval another writer as saying, *'When a myth is shared by large numbers of people, it becomes a reality'*, to which he rejoins: *'I'll happily add my one to the number sharing that notion'.*[34] Such a cavalier approach to scientific and metaphysical matters is becoming endemic in these circles, where findings become based on pure conjecture, wishful thinking or sheer irrationality. According to the Professor of Mathematics at Oregon State University, Wolfgang Smith, such an approach to science illustrates the fact that there is an increasing inability to distinguish between genuine *'scientific knowledge'* and what he calls

---

[32] Ibid.

[33] Ibid.

[34] Quoted in Lyall Watson, *Lifetide* (Hodder & Stoughton, 1979), p.158.

'scientistic belief', which is based on pure conjecture.[35] We are now living in a world in which people will believe *anything*, regardless of whether or not it can be demonstrated as factual. In Neo-Gnostic circles, such an outlook has become so 'politically correct' that to question the shady conclusions of 'scientistic belief' will lead to accusations of being over-rationalistic or 'lacking in spirituality'. The cult of the irrational is fast becoming the soup-of-the-day. We will have cause to return on numerous occasions to this sinister phenomenon of the modern world.

Lyall Watson was by no means the first to develop a 'Hundreth Monkey Concept' of global spiritual evolution. The Russian occultist and mystic Georg Ivanovitch Gurdjieff (1873-1943) had also alluded to it in his writings. Back in the 1920s, occultist Alice B. Bailey, in her book, *The Reappearance of the Christ*, gave details of what she called the 'Day of Supplication', when all followers will come together in prayer at the same time and will thus be able to influence the course of the world by means of intense collective concentration.[36] Similarly, the Jesuit priest Pierre Teilhard de Chardin had also unfolded this concept in his writings when he said

> 'It would seem that a single ray of such light falling like a spark, no matter where, on the Noosphere, would be bound to produce an explosion of such violence that it would almost instantaneously set the face of the earth ablaze and make it entirely new'.[37]

Many other New Age writers and teachers have also developed this theme. The Indian guru Maharishi Mahesh Yogi, British biologist Dr. Rupert Sheldrake (a disciple of Jiddu Krishnamurti),[38] the New Age teacher Ken Carey,[39] and the psychiatrist Stanislaf Grof,[40] are among those who have developed this idea as part of their Neo-Gnostic philosophy. Another leading advocate in the U.K. today is Dr. Peter Russell, who is an accomplished exponent of Transcendental Meditation and a consultant on 'the development of the learning process and creativity' for such multi-national corporations as IBM, Shell, BP, Barclay's Bank, D.E.C., etc.[41] In his book, *The Awakening Earth: The Next Evolutionary Leap*, a standard New Age textbook, Dr. Russell writes:

> 'If enough people were working on inner development through such

---

[35] See Wolfgang Smith, *Cosmos and Transcendence: Breaking Through the Barrier of Scientistic Belief* (Open Court, 1984), p.9. This should be read by all scientists today.

[36] Alice Bailey, *The Reappearance of the Christ* (Lucis Press, 1922).

[37] Quoted in Peter Russell, *The Awakening Earth: The Next Evolutionary Leap* (Routledge & Kegan Paul, 1982), p.176.

[38] See Rupert Sheldrake, *A New Science of Life: Hypothesis of Formative Causation* (Blond, 1981).

[39] See Ken Carey, *The Starseed Transmissions* (Harper, 1982), and follow-up volumes.

[40] See Stanislaf Grof, *Beyond the Brain: Birth, Death, and Transcendence in Psychotherapy* (University of New York, 1985). Dr. Grof is known for his experiments in LSD therapy in Czechoslovakia in the 1950s.

[41] We will be discussing the significant influence which such people are having on the international business world in a later section.

> techniques as meditation, significant worldwide effects would be felt... The Maharishi [Mahesh Yogi] claims that if just 1% of the population were to practice [sic] the technique of TM, the course of history would be profoundly altered. The 'Age of Enlightenment' could dawn'.[42]

This 'Age of Enlightenment' is the New Age, the earthly Millennium which occultists, under their master Satan, have been working towards for almost two thousand years. Dr. Russell refers to the fulfilment of the 'Hundredth Monkey Concept' as the moment of 'Critical Mass', when a crucial number of people engaged in 'consciousness-altering' activities on the planet has been reached. In this moment, a universal change of consciousness will be effected throughout the species, bringing unprecedented effects across the globe. He puts it like this:

> 'If a person meditating does have effects such as these on the rest of society, we may well be headed towards a threshold point, or critical mass of consciousness, beyond which the momentum of rising consciousness would outweigh the inertia of the old ego-based model. If so, crossing the threshold would represent a major transition for humanity. Beyond it society might be completely transformed'.[43]

It is to this end that the Neo-Gnostic movement has been carrying out a series of what are known as 'Global Planetary Activations' designed to encourage the bringing to pass of this 'Critical Mass'. The period 1987-1992 has been a six-year preparation for the major 'awakening' in 1993 and the 'quantum leap' in human consciousness which would soon follow it. Many of the dates on which these happenings were to occur have been gleaned from the prophecies of shamans in ancient civilisations such as the Mayan people and various Indian tribes such as the Hopi. The word was put out through the New Age network and the international media for people across the globe to engage in consciousness-altering activity (e.g., meditation, visualisation, attunement to spirits, etc.) on these days. The more people who would participate in these events, the more likely it would be that the 'hundredth-monkey' point could be reached. A complete list of the dates on which this was encouraged is laid out as follows:

1. *December 31st, 1986* — This inaugurating event was sponsored by the United Nations, and was known as World Peace Meditation Day. It was the culmination of a round-the-globe run which had begun on September 16th, 1986. It was conceived and organised by a number of important Neo-Gnostics in association with the U.N., sponsored by various celebrities, and will be dealt with in full in a later section of this chapter.
2. *August 16th-17th, 1987* — This event was known as the days of 'Harmonic Convergence' and was organised on the basis of an ancient Hopi Indian prophecy.
3. *February, 1988* — codenamed Earthlink Day.

---

[42] Peter Russell, *The Awakening Earth: The Next Evolutionary Leap* (Routledge & Kegan Paul, 1982), p.177.

[43] Ibid., pp.178-179.

4. *April, 1989* — codenamed Crystal Light Link Day.
5. *November, 1989* — codenamed Time Warp Day.
6. *January 1st, 1992* — codenamed Day of the Opening of the Doorway.
7. *July 26th, 1992* — codenamed Timeshift Day.[44]

That is the Neo-Gnostic timetable in the countdown to their awaited Millennium. They are suggesting that some time around the turn of the century there will be a kind of 'Rapture' as the 'evolutionary leap' takes place. Those who seek to resist will be swept into the New Consciousness by force. In a psychic communication channelled through the New Age guru, Ken Carey, one alleged spirit-entity puts it like this:

> 'The river that is rising in this age will engulf the entire city of former human ways. Before your generation has passed away all will have entered its waters, either through their own volition or because the waters have come to them... The flood of which I speak is a current of rising vibrational frequencies'.[45]

This 'current of rising vibrational frequencies' can be seen in the many consciousness-altering activities which we have already documented. Again, speaking through Ken Carey, an ardent subscriber to the 'Hundredth Monkey Concept', this alleged spirit-being goes on to describe the approaching quantum leap in the evolution of mankind:

> 'There will be a great shift then, a single moment of quantum awakening. In this moment, the smallest interval of time measured in these dimensions...will be lengthened unto infinity. An interval of non-time will expand. Through that expansion eternity will flow. Some will experience this moment as minutes or hours, others as a lifetime... In the expanse of the non-time interval, human beings will have all the time they require to realize, experience, and remember the full consciousness of their eternal spirits and to recall the origin of their individuality in the primordial fields of being. All will have ample time to recharge their form identity and its biological projection with the awareness of who they are, why they have individualised, and why they have chosen to associate with this planet's human expression. Each one will have the choice to return to biological form or to remain in the fields of discarnate awareness. Those who choose to return to human form will do so fully aware of who they are. No longer will they be but partially incarnate; they will resume biological residence with the full memory and

---

44 This information has been gleaned from the British New Age journal *Global Link-Up*, Summer 1992, Issue 52, p.23. For further information on this concept, read the chapter entitled 'The Age of People: An Adventurous Assessment of the Present and the Impending Future', in Alick Bartholomew (ed.), *Crop Circles: Harbingers of World Change* (Gateway, 1991), pp.44-58.

45 Ken Carey, *Starseed: The Third Millennium: Living in the Post-Historic World* (Harper, 1991), pp.173-174.

> consciousness of their eternal natures, sharing the creative capacities of the Star Maker, whose reflective cells they will then know themselves to be'.[46]

Shrewd readers will notice that this is the New Age version of the 'Rapture' which many believers are awaiting. Given the propensity for self-hypnosis among these people today, it is very easy to see how millions of people across the earth could convince themselves that they have undergone such an experience. In a moment, a large proportion of the planet will have undergone a super-Satanic Initiation. And just to ensure that no one will be able to question what has happened, read the following quotation carefully:

> 'There is a new vibrational pattern descending upon your planet. Tune into it and learn an effective way of dealing with the closing years of history. You are being offered an opportunity to enter a new reality. It is already here for those with eyes to see. Soon it will be the only reality to be seen. Those who tune into the new frequencies will find life growing more wondrous every day. Those who tune into fear will find things falling apart. Two worlds of consciousness will begin to form ever more distinctly: the world of Love and Life, and the world of fear and death. There will continue to be some overlap of these worlds for several years to come, some going back and forth for certain individuals, but as the century draws to a close, the polarization will continue to intensify. The moment of birth will also be the moment of Last Judgement, the moment of final separation'.[47]

Do you see the significance of what is being said here? The scene is being set for the future so that people will not realise that the Great Tribulation is upon them and that the true Day of Judgement is fast approaching. This is because *'those who tune into the new frequencies will find life growing more wondrous every day'*. Their sense of delusion is so strong that they will believe the lie, come what may (cf. 2 Th.2:9-11). The truth is that things will really be falling apart, but only the discerning will be able to see it. In the midst of the most sinister global developments, the accomplished Neo-Gnostic will simply smile inanely and say, *'Every day, in every way, things are getting better and better'*. One could not have written a more chilling science-fiction scenario. And is this not the picture given to us by the Lord Jesus when He prophesied that on His return to earth at the time of the end, the vast majority of people on this planet will be completely unconcerned and living life as normal, as if there was nothing amiss with the world (Lk.17:26-30; 18:8b). Or that of Paul the Apostle when he prophesies that the time of the end, when *'sudden destruction comes upon them'*, will be preceded by people deluding themselves with thoughts of *'peace and safety'* (1 Th.5:3).

These ideas about the future Golden Age of raised-consciousness are not being entertained merely by a few cranks and weirdos. The words in the above quote

---

[46] Ibid., p.127.

[47] Ken Carey, *The Starseed Transmissions*, (Harper, 1982), p.31.

from a book dictated by a spirit-entity have been officially endorsed by such respected people as Sir George Trevelyan, former President of the Soil Association, founder of the Wrekin Trust in the U.K. and Younghusband lecturer for the World Congress of Faiths at the West London Synagogue in 1983. On the rear cover of the book, Sir George writes, *'If your mind is not caught down into doubt and fear, and your concern is for the birth of a new world, then for goodness sake read this book!'* Influential political leaders also embrace the Hundreth Monkey Concept. The new Deputy President of the United States, Al Gore, is an ardent advocate. In his book, 'Earth in the Balance: Ecology and the Human Spirit', Gore writes:

> 'No one can afford to assume that the world will somehow solve its problems. We must all become partners in a bold effort to change the very foundations of our civilisation. But I believe deeply that true change is possible only when it begins inside the person who is advocating it. Mahatma Gandhi said it well: "We must be the change we wish to see in the world"... Our challenge is to accelerate the needed change in thinking about our relationship to the environment in order to shift the patterns of our civilisation to a new equilibrium... The change in thinking will also follow the pattern described in Chaos Theory, with little change evident until a threshold is passed, and then, as key assumptions are modified, a flood of changes will occur all at once'.[48]

That is a pure statement of 'Hundredth Monkey Theory'. And this takes on an even greater significance when one learns that Senator Gore's boss, Bill Clinton, is every bit as much of a New Ager as his Vice-President, as has been shown in an article in *Newsweek* entitled 'The New Age President'.[49] Now that such thinking has come to dominate the minds of men in such high office and the governmental agencies of the globe (e.g., the United Nations), we must surely be fast approaching the moment when the 'hundredth monkey' in the Neo-Gnostic experiment will have succumbed to the 'rising vibrational pattern', and there will be a corresponding gigantic explosion of psychic evil across this planet. What we are faced with here is not a new approach to religion or spiritual forces. It all goes back to that ancient Law of Godless Reformation, which states that every humanistic attempt to overcome sin and evil will issue in an even worse state than that from which escape had been sought in the first instance (cf. Lk.11:24-26). The overwhelming conceit which lies at the heart of the Hundredth Monkey Concept, in all its projected forms, is that it is solely on the basis of the most intense human effort that human salvation is achieved. It is certainly no coincidence that the Hundredth Monkey Concept had its inception amongst people who have their worldview rooted in Evolution Theory, which is the icon of self-salvation. Consider this quotation from a recent book by an ardent advocate of both biological and spiritual evolution:

---

[48] Quoted in *Christian News*, Vol.30, No.37, October 12th 1992, p.9.

[49] *Newsweek*, January 25th 1993, pp.11-12.

> 'Whether or not we become all that we may be is up to us. We have been given every opportunity and facility. But we have also been given mastery of our own destiny. We are, in effect, facing an evolutionary exam — a cosmic intelligence test. We have prodigious powers at our disposal — enough to harm a planet — and before we can continue our evolutionary journey we must prove that we have a wisdom to be master of ourselves and thus use our creativity in ways that are beneficial to all'.[50]

'Mastery of our own destiny'. Here we have the fountainhead of all Gnostic teaching — the nuts and bolts of the 'Satanic Initiation' which our first parents received in the Garden of Eden. (Bear in mind that the above quote comes from a man who has responsibility for training executives in some of the world's largest industrial corporations!) In this view everything is evolving by chance to such an extent that the flowering of the future has been reduced to a mere 'cosmic intelligence test'. There is no place here for the creation and sustaining of the cosmos by a Transcendent God; and that is precisely the purpose of the 'Hundredth Monkey Concept'. It is a pure conceit of *self*-salvation. There is a great sense of irony here, as Roman Catholic Cardinal Danneels of Belgium points out in his excellent critique of the New Age Movement, 'Christ or Aquarius':

> '[The] New Age gives a very central place to the human self. It says "You have to save yourselves, and the way to do it is by using cosmic forces". Despite the company of so many constellations, of all the religions and all the gurus of the Far East, of all the remedies for happiness, and of an infinite range of psychological techniques and more or less scientific notions, the New Age leaves us completely alone. Each one of us must manage, as best we can, to be our own saviour. Thus, the New Age people are back where they started from: having searched far and wide for ways to escape the obsession with personal performance, which they loathe, they must still save themselves. The Good News is very different: we are saved freely, gratuitously, by the One who for us men and for our salvation, descended from heaven. An Other came to save us'.[51]

This is the doctrine that Satan hates. He will do anything and everything in his power to keep people from recognising that they cannot save themselves from the wrath which is to come. 'An *Other* came to save us'. Today, in this present generation, the powers of darkness, those evil spirits against which all Christians must wrestle (Eph.6:12), are doing everything within their control to take over the mind of man and lull him into believing that salvation comes from *anywhere* apart from Jehovah. The means of communication used by these evil spirits in the New Age is the subject which we will now go on to examine.

---

[50] Peter Russell, *The White Hole in Time: Our Future Evolution and the Meaning of Now* (Aquarian Press, 1992), p.223.

[51] Godfried Cardinal Danneels, *Christ or Aquarius* (Veritas, Dublin, 1992), pp.44-45.

III. HOTLINE TO HELL: Channelling Spirits of the New Age

From time immemorial, the method of communication between human beings and the spirit-world has been that of mediumship. While such communication is by no means a new phenomenon, the all-too-common, somewhat superficial, practice of making psychic contact with deceased loved-ones began to give way to a far more serious approach with the advent of the Theosophical Society near the close of the last century. At this time, Helena Blavatsky began to receive communications from alleged spirit-entities — 'Ascended Masters' who claimed to have a spiritual message for the planet (about which more later) — and this was to set the tone on mediumship for the coming century. Suddenly, contact and communication with spirit-entities was seen to be a way of penetrating lost secrets and discovering the pathway to a better future in a better world: a Golden Age ahead.

Today this form of psychic contact is known as 'Channelling' — a term which is actually derived from the UFO contactee movement. Channelling has been defined as *'a process in which information is accessed and expressed by someone who is convinced that the source is not their ordinary consciousness'*.[52] Within the past three decades, this Channelling has achieved great respectability among those in influential positions in world culture. For example, the current President of the United States of America, Bill Clinton, freely uses the term 'channelling' in his vocabulary.[53] Because the field of education is a fertile area into which Neo-Gnostics have wholeheartedly moved, schools, universities and theological seminaries have become especially prey to these influences. Dr John Rossner, the Roman Catholic lecturer in the Department of Religion at Concordia University in the U.S., has written an impassioned defence of Channelling, claiming that

> 'We can no longer afford to seal off the "open communications system" between heaven and earth by ignorance or rejection of mankind's natural and God-given psychic and spiritual faculties and/or gifts. Until this "communications system" — which has been closed off by dogmatism, doctrinalism, institutionalisation and the rivalries of religion — is opened up in a responsible and self-controlled fashion, we cannot expect the "Return to the Centre" or the revival of a religion of authentic spiritual experience'.[54]

One of the reasons for this respectablity of such phenomena must surely be the fact that a considerable quantity of data of some complexity is purportedly being channelled by highly-evolved entities, rather than the mundane information which is generally trotted out by deceased relatives in run-of-the-mill séances. Coupled with this, the assertions of influential Neo-Gnostics such as the psychologist Carl

---

[52] J. Gordon Melton, *New Age Encyclopedia* (Gale Research Inc., 1990), p.97.

[53] See the article entitled 'The New Age President' in *Newsweek*, January 25th 1993, pp.11-12.

[54] Dr. John Rossner, *Towards Recovery of the Primordial Religion, Vol.2 of the Psychospiritual Roots of Ancient Religion, Book I: 'Religion, Science and Psyche'* (University Press of America, 1983), p.117.

Jung, who claims that *'the unconscious is the only accessible source of religious experience'*,[55] have gone some considerable way towards encouraging a highly subjective 'journey within' in search of spiritual nourishment.

In the present New Age scenario, Channelling began with a vengeance with the contribution of a woman called Jane Roberts (1929-1984). In 1963, she and her husband had begun to experiment with an ouija-board and they were soon contacted by an alleged spirit-entity calling itself *Seth*. Within a short time, she found she could go into a trance during which this spirit-being would speak through her. This led to a series of best-selling books in which a great deal of occult information about every aspect of life — past, present and future — is presented in a readable style. Interestingly, it is common for these spirit-entities which channel through humans to adopt a biblical name. Whether this is the case with Jane Robert's 'Seth' is not immediately apparent. Christian believers may find it more appropriate to note that in Plutarch's 'Myth of Osiris', a character called Seth is presented as the embodiment of evil; and among the Hyksos who ruled Egypt in 1600 BC he was identified with their god Ba'al.[56]

Other well-known chanelling works are Virginia Essene's 'New Teachings for an Awakening Humanity',[57] and Amy Brown Loomis' channelled messages which were alleged to be from Jesus Christ and several of the Apostles.[58] By far the best known and most popular of all the New Age channelled works is the 1200-page book, 'A Course in Miracles'.[59] This work was channelled through psychiatrist Dr. Helen Schucman, who was Assistant Head of the Psychology Department at Presbyterian Hospital in New York and Associate Professor of Medical Psychology at Columbia University's College of Physicians and Surgeons. One of the extraordinary factors surrounding this book is that it claims to be channelled from the biblical Christ. This has led to it finding popularity among many misguided professing Christians, and it can even be found on the shelves of some Christian bookshops. The founder of the Centre for the Study of American Religion claims that the reason why the popularity of 'A Course in Miracles' has been greatest among those who have been disillusioned by organised Christianity is

> 'because it offers Westerners a scripture based on the premises of Eastern religion in a form which is compatible with the historical world-view common to Judeo-Christianity and the modern emphasis on psychology'.[60]

In fact, this is the ideal work for the aspiring Neo-Gnostic — a twentieth century 'Gnostic Gospel'. It aims to encourage in its readers the onset of 'paradigm

---

55 Quoted in *Interfaith News*, No.3, Autumn 1983, p.2.

56 John R. Hinnels, *Penguin Dictionary of Religions* (Penguin, 1984), p.291.

57 Virginia Essene, *New Teachings for an Awakening Humanity* (Spiritual Education Endeavours Publishing, 1986).

58 See Evarts G. Loomis, *Amy: The Search for the Treasure Within* (DeVorss & Co., 1986).

59 *A Course in Miracles* (Routledge & Kegan Paul, 1974).

60 J. Gordon Melton, *New Age Almanac*, (Visible Ink, 1991), p.54.

shifts' in perception (the miracles of the title) which will enable them to abandon all illusions and reawaken their 'divine consciousness'. Among the illusions which, according to this book, need to be off-loaded are the belief in the reality of space and time, sin, judgement, pain, death, disease, and so on. This book is at the sharp end of the Channelling market, and aims to cut a swathe through the teaching of the Church by presenting itself as a vital work on individual Christian growth. A superficial reading of it by an untaught believer could easily lead to it being taken on board as viable Christian teaching — especially for those who mistakenly believe the skilfully-crafted satanic lie that Divine revelation is still being given today through prophecy or 'words of knowledge'.

A major belief in Neo-Gnostic circles is that the huge growth in Channelling and reported contact with discarnates and UFOs provides conclusive evidence that we are in the process of entering the expected evolutionary psychic leap of humanity. And there is a corresponding rush to 'tune-in' to the spirit world within. One of the great works of the Channelling scene has been to encourage people to tune-in to an individual 'inner guide' through learning the art of Channelling. Today, one can attend numerous courses and workshops which will aid a person in this process. There is even an official 'School of Channelling'. Coupled with this one can attend a growing number of centres where Channelling is used as a radical part of the psycho-therapeutic process. But it does not come cheaply. At the 'Centre of Light' healing and therapy centre near Inverness in Scotland, where *'guidance is channelled from the spirit world to help unfold problems'*, it costs £20 for a one-hour psychic diagnosis of your spiritual condition, plus £55 per day just to stay for lunch. If you want to attend a course for the whole week, it will set you back another £425! Another such centre called Shambhala in Glastonbury offered individual 40-minute sessions at £25 to put people in touch with their 'spirit-guides'. This effectively restricts entry into the world of Neo-Gnosticism to professionals and the intelligentsia, which is precisely the strata which it seeks to attract. However, in opposition to this psychic rip-off, the Bible declares that the saving Gospel of Jesus Christ is absolutely free of charge and always openly available to all (Isa.52:3; 55:1-3; Jn.7:37-38; Rom.3:24; Eph.2:8).

The Channelling advocates seek support for their practice in certain biblical texts. For instance, the example is often given of the time when the Lord revealed Himself to Elijah through what one translation refers to as a *'still, small voice'* (1 Kgs.19:12, A.V.). This, say the channellers, is an example of contact with 'the God within', in which we should all indulge. They claim that true prayer means tuning in to inner voices in order to receive their divine message. But this passage has nothing to do with inner voices or inward divine revelation. As O.T. scholar C.F. Keil points out, the Hebrew here should be translated as *'a still, gentle rustling'* or *'the tone of a gentle blowing'*.[61] And if one looks at the context of this phrase, we will discover that the Lord was not communicating with Elijah through an 'inner voice'. Instead, He was demonstrating that the prophet's *'zeal*

---

[61] C.F. Keil & F. Delitzsch, *Commentary on the Old Testament* (Eerdmans reprint, 1988), p.258.

for the honour of the Lord was not in harmony with the love and grace and long-suffering of God',[62] for which reason He showed him that His divine presence was not to be found in the devastation of an earthquake, tempest or fire, but in the most delicate of whispering sounds in nature.

Again we see that, as with their ancient Gnostic counterparts, the Neo-Gnostics love to pervert the Holy Scriptures to suit their own purposes. A further example of this is shown by the fact that Channelling through contact with spirit-entities is favourably compared by its advocates to the experience of Peter, James and John when they saw Moses and Elijah *'transfigured in a cloud of ectoplasmic light'*, as one modern Gnostic scholar puts it.[63] He then goes on to justify the legitimacy of such psychic contact by claiming that it is *'akin to the experiences of apparitions of the (dead) saints to devout Christians in prayer throughout the history of the Catholic Church'*.[64] It is regrettable that within the Church there have been many claims — predominantly in the Roman Catholic camp — of apparitions of various dead saints, the Virgin Mary, and even the Lord Jesus Himself. But the sad fact is that many of these apparitions are part and parcel of the Channelling scene and thereby serve only to lend credence to the claims of the Neo-Gnostics today. This is certainly the case with the purported appearances of the Virgin Mary, who — in her discarnate 'mode' — has been claimed by many Neo-Gnostic groups to be the *'Archetype of New-Age Woman'* and one of their Ascended Masters.[65]

In the Bible, the practice today known as Channelling is referred to as 'consulting with familiar spirits', and is condemned with great severity in many places (e.g., Lev.19:31; Dt.18:10-12; 1 Sam.28:3). In Old Testament times, such practitioners were executed by order of God (Lev.20:27). King Saul of Israel was actually killed by the Lord for attempting to communicate with the dead prophet Samuel (1 Chr.10:13-14). Channelling is a sign of faithlessness towards God and His holy law. As the Messiah Himself says through the prophet Isaiah:

> 'And when they say to you, "Seek those who are mediums and wizards, who whisper and mutter," should not a people seek their God? Should they seek the dead on behalf of the living? To the law and to the testimony! If they do not speak according to this word, it is because there is no light in them' (Isa.8:19-20).

When people professing to be Christians are seen to be attempting to communicate with the dead or with discarnate spirit-entities, it provides great encouragement to unbelievers to continue in their sorceries. When we are told that *'judgement...[begins] at the house of God'* (1 Pet.4:17), the judgement which will come to those professing Christians who have not warned the world about the wickedness of wizardry can barely be conceived. The Church today must proclaim unequivocally that Channelling in all its forms is nothing but evil darkness and a tool of the satanic powers.

---

[62] Ibid.

[63] John Rossner, op. cit., Vol.2, Book 2, pp.14-15.

[64] Ibid.

[65] See, e.g., *Prayer and Meditation* (Summit University Press, 1963), p.22, illustration.

IV. THE ASCENDED MASTERS: Rulers of the Darkness of this Age

In the previous chapter, and from time to time in the present chapter, we have spoken of a hierarchy of spirit-entities known as the 'Ascended Masters' or 'Great White Brotherhood'. The widespread popularising of this phenomenon is probably the single most important contribution of the New Age Movement to the rising tide of psychic evil. These beings are alleged by Neo-Gnostics to be overseeing the spiritual and 'evolutionary' development of the human race on both an individual level and in terms of the process of global civilisation. According to the accounts, there is a distinct hierarchy of Masters in operation which — based on the the schemes upheld by H.P. Blavatsky and Alice Bailey — can be presented in the following table in order to aid understanding.

<table>
<tr><td colspan="3">The Solar Logos
Sanat Kumara
(Lord of the World)
Three Kumaras
(Buddhas of Activity)</td></tr>
<tr><td>WILL</td><td>LOVE / WISDOM</td><td>INTELLIGENCE</td></tr>
<tr><td>Manu
Vaivasvata
(1) Master
Morya
Master Jupiter</td><td>Bodhisattva Maitreya
(The Christ or World Teacher)
(2) Master Kuthumi
Master Djwal Khul
|
|
|</td><td>The Mahachohan
(Lord of Civilisation)
(3) The Venetian Master
(4) Master Serapis
(5) Master Hilarion
(6) Master Jesus
(7) Master Prince Rakocki</td></tr>
<tr><td></td><td>Four grades of Initiates
Various grades of disciples
People on the Probationary Path</td><td></td></tr>
<tr><td colspan="3">All other members of the human race at all degrees</td></tr>
</table>

The Hierarchy is pyramidic, although there are two levels of being, with the 'lower' Masters being under the guidance of still 'higher' spirit-entities known as the Enlightened Ones (the Three Buddhas). These are under yet another entity called Sanat Kumara (the 'Lord of this World') — all of which have ruling over them the 'Solar Logos', which is a crude parody of the Godhead of the Bible. The numbered Masters are also known as 'The Seven Rays'. Those Masters below the level of the Three Kumaras are the only members of the Hierarchy with whom humans can expect to communicate; and it is these who have allegedly been channelling through Helena Blavatsky, Alice Bailey and the many others who claim to have received personal visitations from the Masters.

It is not at all beyond the bounds of possibility that what is being laid out in the table above in some way reflects the *'spiritual hosts of wickedness in the heavenly places'* who are the *'rulers of the darkness of this age'*, as spoken of by the Apostle Paul in his letter to the Ephesians — a letter which, above all else, gives an overview of the place of the Church in relation to the cosmic powers (Eph.6:12).[66] One can certainly see in the above table some corroboration of the fact that *'the whole world lies under the sway of the wicked one'* (1 Jn.5:19), who is indeed *'the god of this world'* (2 Cor.4:4).

These Masters are alleged to work from a specific spiritual centre for their work in this world — an 'etheric retreat' centred on the Gobi Desert, entitled 'Shambhala'. They are also associated with a hidden location in Tibet called 'Shigatse'. A number of lesser Masters are said to inhabit the earth in physical bodies, having taken over strategically-placed bodies in order to carry out their tasks in the world. A detailed description of their sphere of operations, in one of the channelled classics in occult literature, gives further evidence of the true nature of this Hierarchy:

> 'After the great descent of the spiritual Existences [the Masters] to the earth, the work they planned to do was systematised. Offices were apportioned, and the processes of evolution in all the departments of nature were brought under the conscious wise guidance of this initial Brotherhood. This Hierarchy of Brothers of Light still exists, and the work goes steadily on. They are all in physical existence, either in dense physical bodies, such as many of the Masters employ, or in etheric bodies, such as the more exalted helpers and the Lord of the World occupy... The central home of this Hierarchy is at Shambhala, a centre in the Gobi Desert, called in the ancient books the "White Island". It exists in etheric matter, and when the race of men on earth have developed etheric vision its location will be recognised and its reality admitted... Several of the Masters in physical bodies dwell in the Himalaya mountains, in a secluded spot called Shigatse, far from the ways of men, but the greater number are scattered all over the world, dwelling in different places in the various nations, unrecognised and unknown, yet forming each in His own place a focal point for the energy of the Lord of the World'.[67]

Let us just examine some of this strange information. First there is mention of a *'great descent of the Masters to the earth'*, after which there was a systematisation of their work. Compare this with the verse in the Bible which tells us that after a mighty cosmic battle with good angels in the wake of Jesus' Ascension: *'The great dragon was cast out, that serpent of old, called the Devil and Satan, who*

[66] For an excellent discussion of the 'powers' in the Letter to the Ephesians, see Clinton E. Arnold, *Ephesians: Power and Magic — The Concept of Power in Ephesians in Light of its Historical Setting* (Cambridge University Press, 1989).

[67] Alice B. Bailey, *Initiation: Human and Solar* (Lucis Press, 1922) pp.32-33.

deceives the whole world; he was cast to the earth, and his angels were cast out with him' (Rev.12:9). Is there not a remarkable analogy between this biblical description of the fate of the fallen angels and the statement above about a *'great descent of the Masters to the earth'*? Then there is the statement that these Masters are said to be providing a *'focal point for the energy of the Lord of the World'*. The only spiritual entity to be referred to in such a way in the Bible is the devil himself, whom Paul designates *'the god of this world'* (2 Cor.4:4), and Jesus refers to as the *'ruler of this world'* (Jn.12:31; 14:30; 16:11). Furthermore, is there not a connection between the fact that these Masters are said to operate from an etheric location above the earth, while Satan and his fallen angelic accomplices are spoken of in Scripture as operating from *'the air'* (Eph.2:2) — an other-dimensional location corresponding to the atmosphere of the earth? Later in the same letter, Paul identifies the fallen angelic powers as *'spiritual hosts of wickedness in the heavenly places'* (Eph.6:12). Surely, the true identity of these entities is plain for all Bible students to see. However, according to the Neo-Gnostic worldview, the idea of the original fall of angels is neatly disposed of by claiming that it was merely part of *'the divine plan of evolution...emanating from the Mind of God'*, while the *'war in heaven'* described in Rev.12:7-9 refers to the time

> 'when the sons of God [angels]...who responded to the divine urge to experience, to serve and to sacrifice, separated themselves from the sons of God [angels] who responded to no such inspiration'.[68]

Note that some of the Ascended Masters are not discarnate but are said to operate in physical bodies in this world. Consider also that a number of Neo-Gnostic writers have drawn attention to a phenomenon known as 'Walk-Ins', *'souls who, through spiritual growth in previous incarnations, have earned the right to take over unwanted bodies'*.[69] The claim is made that if a person who undergoes a near-death experience (e.g., in a road accident, illness, or on an operating table) no longer has the will to live, he or she can be 'taken over' by discarnate entities so that after resuscitation they can be used to infiltrate earth communities. If this is true, it would signify a global build-up of true demon possession, by which Satan can manipulate earth events with 'hands-on' experience. This would also fit the description, in the Book of Revelation (e.g., Rev.9:1-12), of the demon infested conditions on earth prior to the return of the Lord Jesus Christ at the end of the Age — not to mention those in the time of Noah (Gen.6:1-6; cf. Mt.24:37).

Bear in mind here that possession by a demon does not mean that a person will grow horns or fall about the floor foaming at the mouth. This would especially be so in the cases of the 'Walk-In' phenomenon described above, where there has been a complete takeover of the individual. When demon-possession is mentioned in the Gospels, it was often only when the Lord Jesus approached demoniacs personally that they behaved in a bizarre fashion; before which they had been behaving perfectly normally and even worshipping in the synagogue (e.g., Mk.1:21-28).

---

[68] Alice B. Bailey, *The Externalization of the Hierarchy* (Lucis Press, 1957), p.118.

[69] J. Gordon Melton, *New Age Encyclopedia* (Gale Research, 1990), p.489.

However, whether or not one accepts the extraordinary claims about 'Walk-Ins' — which are by no means impossible, given a full understanding of supernatural evil — there can be no doubt that a great many extraordinary global developments are taking place which would appear to give credence to the fact that the aims of the Neo-Gnostics and their satanic Masters are being achieved on the earth today. Even near the start of this century, the work of the Ascended Masters was described in occult literature as carrying out the following functions in the world:

- Unifying Eastern and Western thought to bring about one universal church.
- Stimulating the growth of the healing arts.
- Building the world influence of occult groups such as the Freemasons, etc.
- Stimulating psychic research, the development of the intuition, and spiritualism.
- Directing the Labour Movement throughout the world.[70]

These ambitions have already been realised on a massive scale across the world a mere seventy years later. Through consciousness-altering techniques, millions of people have allegedly received visitations from these discarnates who have masqueraded as benevolent spirits, duping their hosts into believing that they are angels serving the higher needs of the Divine Plan. This kind of activity is not just confined to a few marginalised cranks. Respectable and influential figures are now avidly endorsing contact with such spirits. For example, the knighted occultist and 'Francis Younghusband Memorial' lecturer, Sir George Trevelyan, has championed an anonymously manuscript which claims that the current build-up of Unidentified Flying Objects (UFOs) is part of the work of the 'Masters' as they direct Extra-Terrestrials (ETs) which have been brought from other galaxies to patrol the 'etheric envelope' around the planet and to usher in the New Age on earth.[71] It is this phenomenon which accounts for the increasing reports of UFOs and ETs in the world's media. In reality, these occurrences are grand illusions conjured up by the demonic realm under Satan, their *'prince of the power of the air'* (Eph.2:2), not only to engender a sympathy to the concept of the existence of superbeings in the form of ET's (which undermines God's exclusive covenantal work with His people on the planet Earth), but also to engender an openness to contact with non-humanoid beings of a 'higher evolutionary order' than ourselves. To the Christian who is firmly grounded in the Scriptures, such discarnates or ET's are easily identifiable as the product of the satanic world-plan — that is, either they are actual demons (fallen angels) manifested in bodily form, or these beings are somehow projected as real into the minds of those who are open to receiving such information as true.[72] We shall have more to report about ETs and

---

[70] Alice Bailey, *Initiation: Human and Solar* (Lucis Press, 1922), pp.55-62.

[71] *A World Within a World: Transmissions from Russia on the Theory and Practice of Solar Light Radiations* (Neville Spearman/Findhorn, 1981), p.21. Sir George Trevelyan received the original manuscript anonymously and has written the foreword to this book.

[72] For an enlightening book about UFOs and ETs written from an exclusively Christian perspective, see Clifford Wilson & John Weldon, *Close Encounters: A Better Explana-*

UFOs towards the end of this present chapter, when we will be examining the growth of Neo-Gnosticism in the echelons of world government.

Occultic developments involving discarnates are being tolerated even in establishment circles. As a sure sign of the times, the 'Daily Telegraph' blandly reported that *'a psychic who says that he goes into a trance and is guided by four spirits to write a book is rceiving a grant from the Government enterprise allowance scheme'*.[73] In another example of the increasing respectability of spiritist activity, in the acknowledgements section at the front of his book extolling the twentieth century 'rediscovery' of Gnosticism, Dr. John Rossner of the Department of Religion at Concordia University in the U.S.A. makes mention of

> 'the presence of patient Unseen Forces and Beneficient Helpers who — through all of the experiences recorded in this volume — I have come to recognise as the true Architects of that new but in fact very ancient Consciousness of a "Primordial Tradition of Intuition and Insight" which is being born again into this world in our day'.[74]

Such 'Unseen Forces and Beneficient Helpers' are currently disseminating their world objectives and directing the New Gnosticism through a number of International 'Centres of Light', a phenomenon we shall be examining in the next section. Some of these 'Masters' are said to be 'perfected resurrected beings' who have worked their way through a number of highly-prestigious incarnations on earth such as Plato, Pythagoras, Francis Bacon, Francis of Assisi, Thomas More, Thomas Aquinas, etc. Neo-Gnostics claim that Jesus is also one of these beings, whose incarnation provided a vehicle for a cosmic entity called 'The Christ', which entered at his baptism and departed at the Crucifixion (an ancient Gnostic conceit) and which will return as the *Bodhisattva Maitreya* or World Teacher.

Some groups also claim that Mary, the mother of the Lord Jesus, is one of the 'Ascended Masters' who will be transmitting messages of peace on an increasingly regular basis as we draw to the close of the Piscean Age and move into the beginning of the new Aquarian Age.[75] Perhaps we can now understand the significance of the many apparitions — so beloved by Roman Catholics — of the Virgin Mary throughout the present century, in which she calls repeatedly for the setting-up of a global brotherhood to usher in an earthly reign of peace and justice. The pictorial form in which this 'Ascended Master', Mother Mary, is represented in the occult literature is virtually identical to the form of the Virgin Mary which appears in Roman Catholic visions and apparitions. The Neo-Gnostics refer to this spirit-entity as the *'Archetypal New Age Woman'*,[76] and it is difficult to

---

tion (Master Books/CLP, 1978).

73 *Daily Telegraph*, July 6th, 1987.

74 John Rossner, *Toward Recovery of the Primordial Tradition*, Vol.II, Book 3: *The Psychic Roots of Ancient Wisdom and Primitive Christian Gnosis* (University Press of America, 1983), p.xiii.

75 Elizabeth Clare Prophet, *Jesus and Kuthumi: Prayer and Meditation* (Summit University Press, 1963), p.22, illustration.

76 Ibid.

avoid the conclusion that for centuries Roman Catholics have been hoodwinked into regarding a demonic discarnate deception as a genuine vision of the mother of Jesus Christ. In other words, the Virgin Mary of the visions is an evil spirit.

One of the most renowned of the present-day apparitions is that which recurs in Medjugorje in Bosnia. This entity has been drawing countless numbers of international travellers to the village, where a select group of young men and women have ecstatic visions and report their communications to the eagerly awaiting folk in attendance. This entity has reportedly given the youngsters ten prophetic secrets to be revealed before their occurence in order to convince the world of her authenticity. In common with the other 'Ascended Masters', this apparition preaches *'Peace, peace, when there is no peace'* (cf. Jer.6:14). One occult group characterises this discarnate entity as communicating such messages as: *'I am not only your mother but your very personal friend. I ask you to take my hand, to take me to your home, to accept me as your friend'.*[77] In Medjugorje, she transmits lengthy messages which are repeatedly punctuated with the eerie, robotic phrase: *'Thankyou for responding to my call...thankyou for responding to my call...thankyou for responding to my call, etc'.*[78]

To those with whom these discarnates communicate, they claim to be acting in the higher interests of humanity by guiding scientific discovery and socio-political events. Meanwhile their advocates openly admit that their main objective is the formation of global religious cooperation and a corresponding form of international government, which will be guided by a 'World Teacher' who is predicted as coming *'towards the close of the twentieth century'.*[79] In terms of their world-view, this will constitute the commencement of the Aquarian Age — the New Age. In theosophical thought the world develops, from a spiritual standpoint, in evolutionary stages of roughly two thousand years' duration — each age corresponding to one of the astrological signs of the Zodiac, although running in reverse order. The start of each new age is heralded by a spiritual teacher and 'higher master'. Two thousand years ago, at the commencement of the Piscean age, it was 'The Christ'. Now we stand on the threshold of a New Age, the Aquarian Age (hence, the description, 'New Age Movement'), which will be characterised by an engineered 'quantum leap' in man's psychic powers — the preparatory evidence of which we can see all around us. *'This is the dawning of the Age of Aquarius'*, as the song says from the musical 'Hair'. Soon, claim the Neo-Gnostics, the World Teacher will come to assist in this process. The dates for the arrival on the world scene of this global leader vary, but all estimates are between the years 1993 and 1999. For the past one hundred and twenty years — although the majority of Christians are unaware of it — occult initiates across the globe have been trained up in preparation for two mighty events in world history, the substance of which has now been revealed in esoteric writings. These are:

---

[77] Ibid.

[78] Taken from a BBC Television *Everyman* documentary on Medjugorje, Sunday, February 8th, 1987, 2210 hrs.

[79] Alice B. Bailey, *Initiation: Human and Solar* (Lucis Press, 1922), pp.60,61.

> 'First, the coming of the World Teacher towards the close of this present century, and the other, the founding of the new sixth sub-race in the reconstruction of the present world conditions'.[80]

We are now living on the threshold of one of the greatest deceptions ever to manifest in the world, but through which the vast majority of Christians are sleep-walking. The corruption of doctrine in the Church, the vast liberal apostasy in colleges and congregations, the huge growth in occult practices, the development of the New Gnosticsm, the propagation of a New World Order — all this must be seen against the backcloth of the work attributed by occultists to these Masters in the world. Occult adepts of the higher degrees have known these secrets for decades. As the occultist Alice Bailey told her pupils:

> 'Very definitely may the assurance be given here, that prior to the coming of the [World Teacher], *adjustments will be made* so that at the head of all great organisations will be found either a Master, or an initiate who has taken the third initiation. At the head of certain of the great occult groups, of the Freemasons of the world, and of the *various great divisions of the Church*, and resident in many of the great nations will be found initiates or masters. This work of the Masters is proceeding now, and all their efforts are being bent towards bringing it to a successful consummation. Everywhere [the Masters] are *gathering in those who in any way show a tendency to respond to high vibration, seeking to force their vibration and to fit them* so that they may be of use at the time of the coming of the [World Teacher]. Great is the day of opportunity, for when that time comes, through the stupendous strength of the vibration then brought to bear upon the sons of men, it will be possible for those who now do the necessary work to take a great step forward, and to pass through the portal of initiation'.[81] [emphasis added]

Do you see the significance of this statement to the subject matter of our study? The claim is being made that there are now high-degree occult initiates hell-bent on machinating the New World Order by occupying influential positions in the Freemasons, World Government and the Church. It does not take a great deal of research to demonstrate that such a claim has indeed been realised. Alice Bailey says, regarding one particular Master, that *'certain great prelates of the Anglican and Catholic Churches are wise agents of His'*.[82] Take a moment to meditate on this. If you have been looking for an understanding as to why there should have been such great apostasy from the faith, and liberal ascendancy in the theological

---

[80] Ibid., pp.60-61. Adolf Hitler, having imbibed the occult literature, mistakenly saw himself in this role. His propagation of the Aryan ideal — based on a complete misreading of the esoteric prognostications — was a vain attempt at the *'founding of the new sixth sub-race'*.

[81] Ibid., pp.61-62.

[82] Ibid., p.57.

colleges and denominations of the world, you need look no further. For, as has also been disclosed (and remember that this was published as early as 1922):

> '[The Masters] have Their disciples and Their followers everywhere, and work through many bodies and many aspects of teaching. Throughout the world, disciples of these Masters have come into incarnation at this time with the sole intent of participating in the activities and occupations and truth dissemination in the various churches, sciences, and philosophies, and thus producing within the organisation itself an expansion, a widening, and *a disintegration where necessary*, which might otherwise be impossible. It might be wise for occult students everywhere to recognise the hierarchical vibration as it demonstrates through the medium of disciples in the most unlikely places and groups'.[83] [emphasis added]

Note well that phrase, 'disintegration where necessary'. Such a carefully controlled breakdown can be seen happening all around us in the realm of law and order, in the crisis of authority in educational institutions, in the dissolution of the sovereignty of nation-states in favour of monolithic constitutional structures (e.g., the E.E.C. or E.U. in Europe), in the corrupt capers of the financial systems of the world, in the heretical liberalisation of Christian denominations and seminaries, in the huge growth of deviant literature in Christian bookshops, and in the departure of the Gospel and Bible truth from so many church pulpits. It is also interesting to note the claim that anyone *'who in any way shows a tendency to respond to high vibration'* (i.e., who attempts to alter their consciousness through the various techniques inspired by the demonic realm) will receive every encouragement from the powers who are guiding these things in order to fulfil their purpose — all, of course, under the permissive and controlling hand of God (cf. Rev.17:17).

An interesting and significant fact is that this concept of a coming World Teacher who sets up a Golden Age on earth can be found in many world religious systems as well as in the literature of the occult. At present, numerous religious groupings are living in such an expectation. For example, the Shi'ite Muslims believe that *'God has designated a line of the family of 'Ali to act as sources of spiritual guidance to the community'*.[84] The various members of this family line are known as 'Imams'. However, in the ninth century the twelfth of the line disappeared, and this led to a hiatus in the manifestation of the Imams. However, *'the Shi'is now await the return (raj'a) of the expected Imam, who will re-establish a reign of justice and peace on earth'*.[85] The significance to world events of this expectation of the *Mahdi*, as he is called, should not be missed. For the Shi'ites believe that

> 'towards the end of the world, before the Last Day (Qiyama), a Mahdi, often identified with the returned Jesus, will establish a reign of justice

---

[83] Ibid., p.52.

[84] John R. Hinnells (ed.), *The Penguin Dictionary of Religion* (Penguin, 1984), p.161.

[85] Ibid., pp.162-164.

> on the earth. In Shi'ism the Mahdi is a vital figure, identified with the Hidden Imam who will reappear and rule by divine prescription'.[86]

The Ayatollah Khomeini was a Shi'ite Muslim and his Iranian Revolution of 1978-9 was a Shi'ite-inspired event. It is worth noting that after this Revolution, the Ayatollah Khomeini became recognised as 'Vilayat Faqih' or supreme temporal representative in Iran of the Hidden Imam or Mahdi who is still to come.[87] The power of the Shi'ites worldwide is enormous. If a World Teacher was to appear who could fulfil their expectations, his powerbase would be immense. But it is not only the many millions of Shi'ite Muslims who are expecting a World Teacher to establish a reign of peace and justice on the earth. Classical Buddhism also speaks of the expectancy of a future World Teacher to follow in the line of its founder Shakyamuni Gautama Buddha, who was alive in the sixth century B.C. Establishing the link even more profoundly, the name of their expected teacher is Bodhisattva Maitreya, which corresponds precisely with the name of the 'Ascended Master' expected to come as the World Teacher of the Neo-Gnostics (see the table earlier in this section). There is yet another interesting connection here: In Neo-Gnostic ideology, the etheric retreat where the 'Ascended Masters' are reputed to live is referred to as *Shambhala*. In the religion of Tibetan Buddhism, the same name of *Shambhala* refers to

> 'a mystic kingdom ruled by the lineage holders of the Kalachakra Tantra (Wheel of Time Tantra). It is said that King Suchandra of Shambhala received this Tantra from Buddha in the latter's eightieth year and entrusted it to his successors, the last of whom, Rigden Pema Karpo, is expected to return and establish Shambhala as a universal kingdom'.[88]

Once again, we discover in yet another religion this idea of a coming World Teacher who sets up a Golden Age on earth. Let us remember here that the Tibetan Buddhist Dalai Lama, who is so influential among the Neo-Gnostics of today, occupies a similar role to that of the Ayatollah Khomeini in terms of being the 'supreme temporal representative' of the Buddha, until the coming of the Maitreya to *'establish Shambhala as a universal kingdom'*. In anticipation of this occurrence, the Tibetan Buddhist organisation known as *Vajradhatu*, with its headquarters in Boulder, Colorado, has set up an imprint entitled the 'New Science Library Series of Shambhala', which publishes many titles propagating the New Gnosticism.

Another important factor to recognise, in relation to the global expectation of a World Teacher who will usher in a Golden Age on earth, is that the Jewish people of the world are still awaiting their Messiah (Hebrew, *Mashiyach*) to bring a reign of peace and justice on earth. This fact takes on sinister proportions when one considers that enigmatic statement of the Lord Jesus to the Jews that, although they would not accept Him as Messiah, *'if another comes in his own name, him*

---

[86] Ibid., p.198.
[87] Ibid., p.58.
[88] Ibid., p.294.

you will receive' (Jn.5:43). Here we begin to gain an insight into the true identity of this World Teacher expected by so many of the world's religions. As Augustine of Hippo (A.D. 354-430) rightly states, concerning the words of the Lord Jesus to the Jews in Jn.5:43: *'He intimated that they would receive Antichrist, who will seek the glory of his own name'*.[89]

Numerous other cults and groupings hold beliefs which are significant to this concept of the coming World Teacher. Among them, the American Indian Hopi tribe has been lending support to the spiritual timetable of the Neo-Gnostics. We have mentioned earlier the special dates which were given by Hopi prophecy as being auspicious to the approaching quantum leap in evolution which is associated with the coming of the World Teacher. Another fact pointed out by the Neo-Gnostics is that all the prophecies of the Mesoamerican Mayan culture — for whom they have great admiration — culminate in the year A.D. 2011, by which time they expect their earthly millennium to have been well-established.

What are Christians to make of all this millennial expectancy and the advent of a World Teacher? Surely, just as the idea of a future Golden Age on earth has been fabricated by Satan in his strategy of the Last Days, as a way of seducing people from the biblical fact of eternal life in the New Heavens and New Earth, so he has dredged up the idea of a coming Teacher who will set up a reign of peace and justice *on earth* — all in crass counterfeit of the Second Coming of Christ, who will establish a *heavenly* kingdom. Many Neo-Gnostics even refer to their coming World Teacher as 'The Christ' — a description which will no doubt be used to persuade untaught and undiscerning persons who profess to be Christians that this character is the actual returned Jesus Christ. Surely, it is not impossible that such a one as this expected World Teacher, who will have great occult powers and political panache, will actually come in the near future.

The people of the world today are crying out for a strong leader to take them into the twenty-first century. Naturally, such a leader would have to be highly ecumenical if he is to satisfy the requirements of all the sects and religions who are awaiting his coming. But that is not beyond the bounds of possibility, given the present syncretist outlook of the world, as we will come to appreciate in the final chapter. However, if and when such a world leader does appear, he could well be the Antichrist shown by the Bible to appear and rule on earth for a brief time as Satan's figurehead before the return of the true Jesus Christ (2 Th.2:3-11). In view of the Scriptural data, it is likely that there will be a large degree of deception about this event when it comes to pass (2 Th.2:9-11), especially when we consider that there are a great many professing Christians who are also expecting Jesus to set up a kingdom of peace and justice on the earth! We should remember the warning of the Lord that false christs can be so beguiling that they have the potential to deceive the elect, if such a thing is possible (Mt.24:24). Remember also how He added emphatically, *'See, I have told you beforehand'* (Mt.24:25).

The details that we have revealed in this section of the present chapter give some considerable credence to the idea that Satan has carefully planned out an

---

[89] Augustine of Hippo, Tractates on the Gospel According to St. John, Tractate XXIX, §8.

occult agenda which would be most compelling in its power. As an example of the skilful planning of this satanic strategy in the Gospel Age, one of these discarnates reveals in a channelled message given in the late 1970s that

> '[the] instructions [to the Masters] were to pretty much stay out of things until near the very end of the process. Then, upon receipt of a pre-arranged signal, they were to commune with the human beings on Earth at that time and assist them in awakening to their original state of unified consciousness. We received that signal nearly two thousand years ago. It has taken almost two millennia to prepare you for the message we bring. You had to be educated before communion of this nature was possible. However the time is at hand'.[90]

Ken Carey, one of the leading Neo-Gnostics of today, claims to have received information about this on the psychic plane from spirit-entities which has since been issued in book-form by the 'respectable' religious publisher, Harper (who also published John Wimber's book 'Power Evangelism' in the U.S.A. in 1986). In one communiqué referring to the work of the Masters in the affairs of the world, these beings disclose that all such developments have been taking place under the watchful eye and helping hands of their fellow discarnates. Placing the acceleration of this work firmly within the context of the hippie counter-culture of the 1960s, this statement, written in the late 1970s, maintains that

> 'We chose the years 1967 to 1969 for this first large-scale experiment, because at that time in your global civilisation there was an entire generation coming into maturity that was receptive to change on a planetary scale. The children of **this** generation will be those who will participate, on many different levels, in the great revelations of the late eighties. This will be a truly momentous time, a time when the first contractions of birth are unmistakable. A large part of the purpose of these present transmissions is to prepare the parents of this generation for something unprecedented that is to appear in their children.
>
> 'Our communications during these closing years of the seventies are reaching past the social fringe of your culture that was contacted during the sixties. This time, we are reaching deep into the heart of global civilisation. We are reaching many who are in what we call "lubricatory positions" in your society — individuals working in factories, teaching in schools, building your cities, and expanding your science. We are not in much contact yet with government officials, nor with world banks or international financiers. Our first contacts with them will occur during the more powerful transmissions of 1987 to 1989. Those who we are contacting now, nonetheless, are critical enough in the maintenance of your social systems to ensure that the world will make some incredible leaps in consciousness during the next decade...
>
> 'By the time of the eighties revelations, knowledge of our existence

---

[90] Ken Carey, *The Starseed Transmissions* (Harper, 1982), p.18.

and our work will be widespread, especially among the younger generation, the prime focus of our efforts at that time... So clear your circuitry, my friend. Great portents of change are in the air. Your physicists are speaking of these things in terms that defy explanation. Your psychologists are abandoning the sinking ships of conventional rationality. Your religions are exploding beyond the confines of their dogma in the rediscovery of Spirit... There is a new vibrational pattern on your planet. Tune into it and learn an effective way of dealing with the closing years of history'.[91]

We can see, therefore, that all these developments have not been happening of their own volition. There is a pattern to the unfolding religious influences of these present days, and it involves the global psychic influence of the rulers of the darkness of this age. As another leading occultist reveals:

> 'The Great Awakening is taking place. In the cities and towns across America, hardly a week goes by without a symposium, seminar or workshop on spiritual healing, extrasensory perception...new age living, the power within, creative imagination, the dynamics of positive thinking, mind control, awareness training, higher sense perception, the art of meditation, new dimensions of consciousness, holistic medicine, yoga... This is not by chance. According to one Advanced Soul, "Through the silent hidden work of the Masters, men and women throughout the world are beginning to intuitively understand the Truth. There is a vibration, call it the Master Vibration, that is flowing through the consciousness of mankind, turning each individual toward the Light within, and it is only a matter of time before the Dawning"'.[92]

The discernment of the true identity of this imminent *'Dawning'* is a matter of some urgency for Christians today. Never, at any stage in history, has the scene been so fully set for the manipulation of a deception of global proportions through the instrumentality of these 'Unseen Forces'. For the situation in which we find ourselves today is more bizarre and far-reaching than the most imaginative science fiction novel. Millions of people of all ages are tuning into and receiving instructions from these spirit-entities. The question is: Are these 'Masters' or spirit-guides genuine discarnate spirits with an objective life of their own — fallen angels (demons) masquerading as angels of light and servants of righteousness (2 Cor.11:14-15)? Or are they illusory characters played by the powers of darkness onto the minds of the gullible? Or are they simply the far-fetched products of a diseased imagination? The latter idea can surely be dismissed, in the light of the vast similarities of experience amongst the huge number of individuals across the globe who engage in such Channelling. Insofar as the other two possibilites are concerned, whatever conclusion one reaches, the deception is clearly of satanic

---

[91] Ibid., pp.28-31.

[92] John Randolph Price, *The Superbeings* (Quartus Books, 1981), pp.2-3.

origin because of the occultic and antichristian direction in which the initiate is subsequently led. After careful consideration of all the data available, one can only come to the conclusion that the entire charade is being masterminded by the Evil One in opposition to God, as part of a global build-up to the founding of his illusory 'kingdom' on earth. The title 'Ascended Master' has been used deliberately by the powers of darkness to challenge the uniqueness of the Lord Jesus and to usurp His unrivalled status. We have the Lord's own word for it that *'No one has ascended to heaven but He who came down from heaven, that is, the Son of Man who is in heaven'* (Jn.3:13). So, whether or not these beings are real discarnate entities (disguised as 'angels of light') or merely illusory entities conjured up by the genuine spirit-entities referred to by Paul in Eph.6:11-13, they are certainly in no way 'ascended', but have been dredged up from the bowels of hell as one of the foul 'depths of Satan'.

The 'quantum leap' being generated by the Neo-Gnostics of today, which brings men and women into contact with such beings, represents a huge escalation in the spiritual battle which has been waged by Satan against his Creator from the commencement of world history, and in which we will all be involved. It is all part of an inexorable process in which the Church on earth will be wholly engulfed. Many will doubtless fall away, and the faith of many will be tested; but if believers are intelligently informed, the element of surprise will be greatly diminished and their sense of certainty in the overruling hand of God will prevail.

V. CENTRES OF LIGHT: Satan's Satellite Dishes

In the last section, we mentioned that the satanic hierarchy of 'Ascended Masters' disseminate their teaching through special centres, focal points through which they can operate in their communications with human beings on earth. Earlier this century, Alice Bailey introduced the idea of 'Points of Light' and 'Light Groups' to channel the 'higher spiritual forces' necessary to build the New Age, and to form what is known in the jargon as a 'group soul'.[93] Today there are many such groups which are working in a highly organised way towards the bringing in of the future Golden Age on earth.

These Centres of Light, as they are now known, act as schools of psychic training to encourage the widespread practice of channelling. Instructions are channelled to Neo-Gnostic disciples, either directly, by way of an initiate, or through the ministry of a course, in order to bring them into contact with the Centres where they will be able to develop their psychic powers. In her highly influential book written earlier this century, 'Discipleship in the New Age', Alice Bailey wrote about the start of an experimental effort on the part of the 'Hierarchy' to get the momentum for the New Age going to such an extent that a new programme for the creation of 'Centres of Light' could be mobilised. To her students, she wrote:

> 'If it is successful and if the spiritual momentum set up by all of you is adequate to the effort made, and if you can carry on with persistence...it

[93] See Alice B. Bailey, *Discipleship in the New Age*, 2 Vols. (Lucis Press, 1944 & 1955).

may be possible to bring the experimental stage to an end; the Hierarchy can then recognise (as effectively established upon earth) certain *focal points of energy which can constitute magnetic centres or rallying points for the new religion*, the new medicine, the new psychology and education and the new politics'.[94] [emphasis added]

Bear in mind that these words were first published around the end of the Second World War — long before such developments were even heard of by the vast majority of people. And the development of such centres is now corroborated by many other Neo-Gnostic gurus who practice Channelling. In the mid-1980s, Ken Carey channelled the following transmission from a spirit-entity named Raphael, which places the Centres of Light squarely in the context of the coming 'quantum leap in evolution' mentioned earlier in this chapter. The message is:

> 'As you reorient toward the new way of being in the world, you will be drawn to centers where the vibrational atmosphere is more conducive to a healthy state of function. These centres will represent the focal points around which the organs of Planetary Being will form. They will be, in a sense, islands of the future in a sea of the past. Within their vibrational field, the New Age will blossom and spread organically to cover the Earth. These [centres] will be the first beachheads secured by the approaching forces, the points of entry through which the healing energies of transformation will be channelled. All of these centres will work together to prepare the human species for its collective awakening... Many such places exist at this time. Many more will arise during the remaining decades of this transitional period. By the time the next generation reaches maturity, there will be a widespread network of these islands'.[95]

The time must be fast approaching when this prediction will be fulfilled. Indeed, there is already a vast network of such centres spread around the world. A number of these are in the U.K., of which the most significant have been those situated at *Runnings Park*, in Malvern, Worcestershire; *Shambhala*, in Glastonbury, Somerset; and the *Findhorn Community* on the Moray Firth in Morayshire, Scotland. These centres are thriving communities which offer many courses to the public. The Findhorn Community was set up under the guidance of the Ascended Master entitled 'Master Rakocki'— otherwise known as the Comte de Saint Germain — the same character that Guy Warren Ballard had met at the foot of Mount Shasta. Shambhala, in Glastonbury, was apparently set up at the behest of a number of spirit-beings. Runnings Park — based in a picturesque farmhouse in extensive grounds near the Malvern Hills — was established by three couples who were leading lights in the Atlanteans, a theosophical organisation which claims to be in touch with spirit-entities from the lost continent of Atlantis. The

---

[94] Alice B. Bailey, *Discipleship in the New Age* (Lucis Press, 1944), Vol.I, p.71.

[95] Ken Carey, *The Starseed Transmissions: Living in the Post-Historic World* (Harper Collins, 1991), pp.54-55.

inspiration for Runnings Park came from one of these discarnates, known as 'Helio-Arcanophus'. David Furlong, one of the Runnings Park founders, says:

> 'What I see is places like Runnings Park acting as a focal point for translating and transmitting spiritual impulses which are coming onto the planet'.[96]

Often these centres are associated with a particular geographical location which has some esoteric importance. Glastonbury has been associated with esoteric and occult matters for many centuries. The centrality of Findhorn in the New Age scene has led to other centres being established nearby. One such place, which is actually called 'The Centre of Light', has been set up at Struy-by-Beauly near Inverness in Scotland. In the U.S., an extinct volcano in California called Mount Shasta has a long association with the magic of the native American Indians. Ever since it was reckoned to have possible links with the lost civilisation of Lemuria, esotericists and Neo-Gnostics have flocked to this mountain. Among the many centres which have sprung up there in recent years are those established by the Ancient and Mystical Order of the Rosicrucians (AMORC), the 'I AM' cult, the Ojai Foundation, the Association of Sananda and Sanat Kumara, and a community called the 'Gathering of the Ways' founded by Peter Caddy, one of the original founders of the Findhorn Foundation in Scotland. Many hundreds of individuals have moved to this site in order to tune-in to the 'energies' which they believe are emitted from the mountain.

One of the aims of these centres is to usurp the role of the Church as *'the pillar and foundation of the truth'* (1 Tim.3:15), in a counterfeit manifestation of God's people on earth. This is a fundamental part of Satan's strategy in the Last Days, so that his own methods and practices appear to be more 'churchy' than the Church itself, more 'deeply christian' than the Christianity practised by 'ordinary' believers. This principle of satanic counterfeiting is well expressed in the dedicatory epistle to 'A Discourse on the Damned Art of Witchcraft' written by William Perkins in the late sixteenth century:

> 'Touching the manner of [Satan's] practice: he has realised that the world has recognised him to be *"a liar, and the father thereof"* (Jn.8:44), and therefore if he should offer to speak in his own language, or inform an art by rules of his own devising, he might perchance incur suspicion of falsehood. Therefore, he composes his courses of action μιμητικος [Greek, *mimetikos*, counterfeit], by way of counterfeit and imitation — not according to the actions and dealings of men, *but in the manner of God's own proceeding with his Church*; holding it a sure principle in policy that actions will be much more effectual when they are carried out according to the best precedents than when they are suited to the direction of more inferior examples'.[97]

---

[96] Reported in the New Age journal *Global Link-Up*, Autumn 1987, No.32, p.10.

[97] Thomas Pickering's Dedicatory Epistle to Lord Chief Justice Sir Edward Cooke, in William Perkins 'A Discourse on the Damned Art of Witchcraft', in *Workes* (1604).

This is certainly the case with these Centres of Light, which are made to appear to those interested as if they are the true manifestation of the Church on earth rather than the counterfeit which they are. This can be seen in a book called *Christian Evolution: Moving Towards a Global Spirituality*, written by Lady Ursula Burton and Janice Dolley — one a Roman Catholic, the other an Anglican, who have been seduced into Neo-Gnosticism through their disillusionment with the institutional churches of which they were a part, and by their contact with the Findhorn Community in Scotland. In a chapter entitled 'The Role of the Church in the Next Decade', the place of these Centres of Light in the unfolding strategy of the New Age is set in its context:

> 'The early mystery schools — such as those founded by Pythagoras and Confucius — taught a select few how to bring a spiritual power into their earthly existence and thence into their daily lives. Jesus extended this concept through the example of His life and teaching. He showed that we all have the potential to open ourselves to the kingdom of heaven, to align ourselves with the will of God and act in accordance with His love. He also showed the importance of a group — 'Where two or three are gathered in my name...' Perhaps in demonstrating a sense of brotherhood He sowed the seeds for the coming of the oneness of humanity that is being realized more fully today'.[98]

The Centres of Light of today are acting very much in the mould of the ancient mystery schools, providing nerve centres which channel-in transmissions from spirit-entities in other dimensions, and from there radiating them out into the world. One can picture them as powerful satellite stations strategically placed across the globe, through which the latest messages to the world from the 'Ascended Masters' and other discarnates are 'beamed in' and then actively disseminated through further psychic communication, literature, lectures, and 'workshops' on an international basis.

VI. THE WAY OF THE SHAMAN: Restoring the Ancient Religion

One notable feature of satanic strategy is the Old Serpent's indulgence in overkill. The Evil One is not merely content to provide just a few avenues of corruption in any particular area, but instead he uses an all-embracing pincer-movement in which a dazzling array of apparently differing systems are really selling the same idea. Thus, not content merely to encourage the concept of a 'New Religion' with many 'new' techniques at its disposal, he has also created a romantic attraction for one of the most ancient of all religious phenomena — Shamanism.

Ancient Shamanism can be defined, in its most basic form, as *'the religion of North Asia, based essentially on magic and sorcery'*.[99] At the centre of this tradition is the 'shaman', who can be defined as a person who:

---

[98] Ursula Burton and Janice Dolley, *Christian Evolution: Moving Towards a Global Spirituality* (Turnstone Press, 1984), p.87.

[99] *Chambers English Dictionary* (Chambers & C.U.P., 1988), p.1351.

> 'is able, at will, to enter into a non-ordinary state of consciousness in order to make contact with the spirit world on behalf of members of his or her community'.[100]

Another source speaks of the shaman as *'One whose supernormal powers...are attributed to contact with spirits when in an ecstatic state'*.[101] This ancient religious phenomenon has greatly captivated the minds and hearts of those involved in creating the Neo-Gnostic world in which we are currently living. A number of different but complementary factors have contributed to the Neo-Gnostic attraction to Shamanism. We shall just examine these to give us a clear understanding of this facet of satanic strategy today.

First, the growth of the drug culture originating in the United States has opened up new avenues of experimentation. The intensity of interest in Shamanism can be traced directly back to the experimentation with mind-altering drugs in the 1960s. Psychedelic 'trippers' from California discovered that what they were doing had already been done for millennia by shamans in Alaska, Central and South America, and, nearer to home, the North-American Indian witch-doctors, through the use of hallucinogenic fungi, dance, rhythmic drumming and other techniques.

A second factor which has contributed to the Neo-Gnostic attraction to Shamanism is the ability of the shaman to alter his consciousness, either with drugs or by trance-inducement through the use of rhythmic sounds. The Neo-Gnostics see here a parallel with their own attempts at consciousness-raising. The psychiatrist Stanislaf Grof, who was one of the first to experiment with LSD therapy in the 1950s, had discovered that it is possible to create the same effects with a new form of psychotherapy which he calls Holotropic Therapy. This involves the use of hyperventilation (rapid breathing technique), *'enhanced by the use of evocative music or sound technology developed by various cultures specifically for the purpose of changing consciousness—for example, shamanic drumming'*.[102]

Another attraction of Shamanism for the Neo-Gnostics of today is the fact that shamans set out to make contact with the spirit world, an activity of which the New Age technique of 'Channelling' is more than reminiscent. The 'channellers' of today are the New Age equivalent of the shamans of yesterday. According to Joan Halifax, a New Age anthropologist and former director of the Ojai Foundation on the infamous Mount Shasta in California,

> 'communication with creatures and spirits...is effected in the shamanic seance; the sacred medium in trance is possessed by gods or spirits who use him or her as a means of divine transmission'.[103]

The kindling of global interest in the environment and nature during the past

---

[100] Fritjof Capra, *The Turning Point: Science, Society and the Rising Culture*, (Flamingo, 1982), p.334.

[101] John R. Hinnells (ed.), *The Penguin Dictionary of Religions* (Penguin Books, 1984), p.293.

[102] Gary Doore (ed.), *Shaman's Path: Healing, Personal Growth & Empowerment* (Shambhala, 1988), p.163.

[103] Joan Halifax, *Shaman: The Wounded Healer* (Thames & Hudson, 1982), p.13.

couple of decades — what one could call the arousal of 'Gaia Consciousness' — has also found a close kinship with Shamanism's association with the elements of nature, nature spirits, and an 'Earth-as-Mother' paradigm. Similarly, the world-wide surge of interest in alternative healing has encouraged people to turn to ancient lore and the old religions for new cures. A number of healing techniques used in the Alternative Medicine community can be traced back directly to shamanistic practices. One Polynesian shaman states that

> 'shamanic healing methods...include all faith-healings, verbal and visualisation therapies (including hypnosis), Neurolinguistic Programming affirmations, guided imagery, placebos, dreamwork, and the use of amulets and talismans'.[104]

Finally, the romanticisation of ancient heathen religions had led to the great popularity of Shamanism today. The idea has been fostered that the older a religion is, the closer it is to 'the Source of all Being' or to the spirituality of Atlantis and Lemuria, and the further away it is from the descent into the materialist consciousness of the present day. Therefore, to train in the ancient arts of Shamanism will supposedly increase one's spirituality. A little known fact is that there are a great many residual elements of ancient Shamanism in Western culture today. Some aspects of psychotherapy have been derived from the ancient way, as we will show in a later chapter on the mind-sciences. Also, most people will be totally unaware of the fact that the acting profession and a large number of modern entertainments (e.g., juggling, acrobatics, conjuring, etc.) are derived from ancient shamanistic practices.[105]

One of the most passionate advocates of Shamanism, Mircea Eliade (1907-1986), was a scholar of Comparative Religion and the editor of Collins' much-praised multi-volume Encyclopedia of Religion (1987). His book, *Shamanism: Archaic Techniques of Ecstasy* (1964) set the tone on anthropological excursions into Shamanism for decades to come. Mircea Eliade, however, has some interesting antecedents which throw considerable light on the arcane connections in the world of the New Gnosticism. Early in his life Professor Eliade had spent an influential six months on an Indian *ashram* at Rishikesh, and in the 1930s wrote a number of novels which *'were the center of a transcendental movement'*.[106] In the 1960s, he took over from the late Gnostic psychologist Carl Jung as main speaker at the ERANOS Conferences, which had originally been set up in the 1930s by a wealthy Swiss woman as *'a Summer School for the study of Theosophy, Mysticism, the esoteric sciences and Philosophies and all forms of spiritual research'*.[107] The main speaker for the first three years of these conferences

---

[104] From the chapter 'Seeing is Believing: The Four Worlds of a Shaman' by Serge King, in Gary Doore (ed.), op. cit., p.50.

[105] See Rogan Taylor, *The Death and Resurrection Show: From Shaman to Superstar* (Anthony Blond, 1985). This book is the result of the author's doctorate in psychology and religion at Lancaster University's Religious Studies Department.

[106] James Webb, *The Occult Establishment* (Open Court, 1976), p.397.

[107] Ibid., p.396.

had been none other than Alice B. Bailey of the Lucis Trust. Here we see the clear cross-currents between Neo-Gnosticism and Shamanism — the blending of which creates the Neo-Shamanism so beloved in this movement.

This Neo-Shamanism contains radical differences from the traditional tribal phenomenon. Whereas ancient Shamanism looked to a single shaman within its community, the new shamanism believes that anyone today can become a shaman, hence the growing list of workshops and seminars at which one can undergo such training. The writer on parapsychology, Brian Inglis, (better known as the television presenter of 'All Our Yesterdays' and 'What the Papers Say') believes that a change came about at the time of Pentecost (as recorded in the Book of Acts, chapter 2) which represented an opening-up of the shamanic experience for all. After asserting that Moses and the O.T. prophets were shamans, Brian Inglis claims that *'The Christian Church had grown from shamanist roots and as described by the gospel writers, Jesus is the most accomplished diviner-magician of them all'*.[108] According to Inglis, the experience at Pentecost offered the possibility of *'instantaneous transition from man to shaman'*, with Paul the Apostle as *'the most influential of the new style shamans'*.[109] And he makes the observation that *'for Paul, Christianity was shamanist, relying on inspiration rather than doctrine'*.[110] From hereon it can then be shown that simple Gospel Christianity is but a pale shadow of its former shamanistic glory, to which it is allegedly being restored by the neo-shamans (and, as we shall later see, by Neo-Pentecostalists and Charismatics). Thus, according to the Neo-Shamans, not only is Christianity a Gnostic religion, but it is a shamanistic one too. That is satanic overkill all right!

Essentially, Shamanism is witchcraft in its most untrammelled and acute form. The Bible clearly shows that witchcraft, spiritism and sorcery are in total opposition to Jehovah-Christ and His people (Dt.18:10-22). It is highly significant that these prophetic verses actually juxtapose the sorceries of the nations with the work of the true Prophet, Jesus Christ (Dt.18:14-15), who would never have sanctioned the way of the shaman. It is a solemn fact that sorcerers and rebels and all who believe the (satanic) Lie will not be admitted into the true New Age: the New Jerusalem, the New Heavens and the New Earth, the kingdom of God (Rev.21:8,27; 22:14-15; 1 Cor.6:9-10). The prophet and judge Samuel said that *'rebellion is as the sin of witchcraft'* (1 Sam.15:23). Why? Because they both deny the authority of God, the Master of the Universe, and put man on the throne in His place.

Moreover, there is a fundamental difference between genuine Divine revelation and shamanism: shamans can bring revelations from the spirits *at will, at any time, and in whatever manner they so choose*; whereas true Divine revelation happens *at the behest of God, at the times He appoints, and in the manner He chooses*. It is vital to understand this. The spirits of the shamans are *always* at their disposal, but direct Divine revelation only comes to God's people (i.e.,

---

[108] Brian Inglis, *Natural and Supernatural: A History of the Paranormal* (Prism, 1992), p.75.

[109] Ibid. p.77.

[110] Ibid. p.78.

breaks into human consciousness) when it is a necessary part of His cosmic plan. Consequently, one discovers that there have been vast periods when *'the word of Jehovah was rare in those days; there was no widespread revelation'* (1 Sam.3:1). Sometimes the Lord even withdraws any possibility of Divine revelation, so as to fulfil the purposes of His judgement (e.g., Amos 8:11-14). At the present time, now that the Messiah has come to fulfil His kingdom, there is no fresh revelation, no prophecy necessary any longer (Zec.13:1-3). However, in opposition to this, there has never been a time when shamans have been unable to practise their arts and receive their revelations. All this spells out the fundamental difference between the satanic religion and true spirituality: the giving of Divine revelation is controlled by the will of God, whereas the receiving of the satanic oracle is determined by the will of man.

Shamanism is really all about deception and the use of what Scripture calls *'lying wonders'* (2 Th.2:9). For example, when a writer says of the black magician Aleister Crowley that *'he certainly possessed shamanist powers — once, for instance, making himself invisible when attacked by muggers in Calcutta'*,[111] this allegedly shamanic ability to 'make himself invisible' is then explained by the fact that Crowley *'later admitted that he had hypnotised the muggers so that they were unable to see him'*.[112] Do you see the significance of this? Crowley's shamanic ability to 'make himself invisible' was an illusion created solely by the use of human, hypnotic mind-power, rather than any miraculous abilities. Shamanism is really about rank deception. This is hardly surprising, because Shamanism is really Satanism. Shamans are of their father the devil, and they do the desires of their father. It is through the use of just such shamanist powers that the Antichrist will be able to deceive the world into believing his lies (2 Th.2:9-12).

The neo-Shamanism of today is simply ancient Shamanism come of age and Westernised so that people can be opened up to a massive infestation of demonic activity — and all in the name of comparative religious exploration.

VII. 'INK-BLOT' INFILTRATION: Subverting Global Institutions

One highly effective tactic of warfare, used extensively by the C.I.A. during the conflicts in S.E. Asia, is that known as the 'Ink-Blot Strategy'. This involves the judicious placement of highly-trained and motivated people in a variety of different situations behind enemy lines, whose role is to gather an increasing number of allies and defectors to their cause. Each 'cell' formed in this way can be said to represent a spot of ink on a piece of blotting-paper. Once there are enough spots radiating outwards, the entire paper will be covered in ink. So it is today with the strategy of the New Gnosticism. Readers will recall the statement, in the earlier section on 'Centres of Light', in which a spirit-entity claimed that these centres being set up around the world are *'the first beachheads secured by the approaching forces [working] together to prepare the human species for its collective awakening'*.[113] That is military language, and it emphasises the fact

---

[111] *The Independent Magazine*, 27th November, 1993, p.62.
[112] Ibid.

that we are engaged in a major spiritual battle with powers which lie beyond the world of flesh and blood (cf. 2 Cor.10:3-4; Eph.6:11-13).

Today, there is a determined effort on the part of the global Neo-Gnostic community to infiltrate as many influential organisations as possible with their philosophy and practice, and to inject their ideas into as many situations as they are able. And they are highly efficient at their work. For example, when the present writer was researching for this book in the National Library of Scotland, there was not a single Neo-Gnostic book, journal or paper — no matter how obscure — which he was unable to obtain within minutes. There had been a meticulous efficiency in ensuring that their teaching was widely attainable. On the other hand, there were numerous Christian works, ancient and modern, which were found to be unavailable. Perhaps the reason for this is that as the professing Church has become increasingly earthbound, insular, parochial, fragmented and limited by sectarian aims, it has lost sight of the urgency of its original commission from Christ; whereas the advocates of the New Age constantly hold before themselves a *cosmic* image of the nature of their work, thus overcoming the fact that their sects are numerous and their ideas so disparate.

Today there is hardly an area of Western culture which has not been permeated, in some small way, by the 'Inkblot Strategy' of the Gnostic world-view. The world of the media has been especially useful in this respect, being ideally placed for such 'educational' work. An increasing number of films, television programmes and popular women's magazines (e.g., Vogue, Harper's Bazaar, etc.) are propagating the Neo-Gnostic ideals, while on the High Street, a short inspection of even the most respectable newsagents' shelves reveals a range of esoteric, occult-based journals which grows monthly.

In this concluding section, we will be taking a brief look at the key aspects of some institutions which are highly influential in terms of global manipulation through the Neo-Gnostic ink-blot strategy: First, its work in the world of commerce, business and multinational corporations; second, health, healing and the caring professions; third, its determined infiltration of global governmental agencies.

1. Neo-Gnostic Subversion in the World of Business

The Neo-Gnostic ink-blot strategy has been aimed across a broad section of establishment institutions. We have already mentioned the fact that fully-accredited degree and other graduate programmes in New Age topics are being offered in sixty-three different institutions of Higher Education in the U.S.[114] Such infiltration has also moved into the areas of national and international government, health and healing, the business community and the military. It is a most interesting fact that the business community and the military were the most responsive to the possibility of setting up New-Age-style 'transformative programs', as had been

---

[113] Ken Carey, *The Starseed Transmissions: Living in the Post-Historic World* (Harper Collins, 1991), pp.54-55.

[114] J. Gordon Melton, *New Age Encyclopedia* (Gale Research Inc., 1990), pp.517-518.

outlined in Marilyn Ferguson's book 'The Aquarian Conspiracy'.[115]

In the last couple of decades, there has been a huge growth in the introduction of Neo-Gnostic ideas, techniques and practices into the world of multinational corporations. One newspaper article showed how a personality test originally devised by the occultist and gnostic, Carl Jung, is *'sweeping through major American companies, colleges, hospitals, churches, and even the United States Army and Navy'*, as a form of assessment.[116] Many are now using various meditation, psychotherapeutic and occult techniques in their training programmes in order to create better job performance from their employees.[117] A growing number are also using astrological and psychological techniques in their assessment of job applicants.[118] One of the primary reasons for this new growth industry is the fact that so many of those who have either been a part of the counterculture of the 1960s, or who are the children of those people, have either been employed within such corporations or have started consultancies and training agencies which offer a subtle blend of practices and concepts which are conducive to the spread of their doctrine.

An organisation connected with the Findhorn Foundation (as mentioned earlier in the section on Centres of Light) is known as 'The Spirit of Business', running *'working retreats for tomorrow's business leaders'*. Courses last for one week, cost up to £750 and attract executives from a great many of the leading business corporations in the world. Among the teaching Faculty of this institution are Ian Marks, ex-Chairman of Trebor (the sweetie people) and current Chairman of the Packaging and Environmental Committee for the Food and Drink Industry, U.K.; Lynne Sedgmore, Head of Croydon Business School; and Francis Kinsman, a business consultant and journalist who has had a long association with the Findhorn Foundation. He is the founder and director of the 'Business Network' — an agency designed to promote what he calls the 'inner directed' approach to business matters — and has written a fortnightly column in the personal finance section of *The Times* newspaper for many years.

In a recently published book called *Millennium: Towards Tomorrow's Society* (New Age jargon for the Golden Age on earth), Francis Kinsman describes this new approach to the development of global business enterprise in some detail. He says that a main feature which distinguishes what he terms the 'inner directed' approach to business is that *'behind this whole vision there must always be a sense of spiritual involvement and an understanding of it as the very nature of the whole'*.[119] In what does this 'sense of spiritual involvement' in the Neo-Gnostic

[115] Ibid., p.170.

[116] *The Daily Telegraph*, March 13th, 1987, p.5.

[117] This originated in what were known in the 1960s as 'T-Groups' — training groups to facilitate 'psychological' awareness and 'sensitivity' in the participants, using the techniques of humanistic psychology. In the 1970s and 1980s, 'Human Potential Magazine' documented these developments. Other details can be obtained from the Findhorn Foundation which runs courses in a programme known as 'The New Economic Agenda'; details available from: The Park, Forres, IV36 0TZ, Morayshire, Scotland.

[118] *The Daily Telegraph*, November 3rd, 1986, p.3; December 31st, 1986.

approach to business consist? An example will demonstrate: The world's most influential computer corporation, International Business Machines (IBM) has taken a decisive step into the spiritual world-view of the New Gnosticism. In the 1960s, the company was a major sponsor of the syncretistic 'Temple of Understanding' in the U.S — an organisation designed to promote interfaith activity.[120] Recent developments show that this interest has deepened into full-blown support for New Age occult techniques and esoteric religion. In line with a growing trend among multinational companies — and in spite of complaints from some Christian workers — IBM has now developed high-powered training programmes for its workforce in which Eastern meditation, visualisation, the *I Ching* (Chinese divination), and many other such techniques are taught, *'in order to explore areas of the self not usually brought into play'*.[121] In Neo-Gnostic jargon, 'the hidden self' refers to the God-consciousness alleged to be dormant in every individual, but which can be reached through various techniques.

Originally pioneered in the U.K. by Scottish New Age centre Findhorn, these so-called 'human potential' programmes are now being utilised by many of the major business corporations in the world. The infiltration of the commercial world by the 'inner directed' approach to business management has been hugely successful. Among the top companies which Francis Kinsman lists with approval as having utilised the services of at least one of the new style consultancies are: Alcan, Allied Dunbar, Apple Computers, BCCI, BICC, Barclays Bank, BASF, Blue Circle, Boots, Bowater Scott, British Airways, British Aerospace, British Gas, BP, British Rail, BT, BUPA, Central T.V., Commercial Union, Compaq, Dept. of E., D.H.S.S., DEC, Eagle Star, Esso, FPA, Honeywell, IBM, ICL, ICI, Johnson & Johnson, Marks & Spencer, Mars U.K., Milk Marketing Board, NCR, Northern Dairies, The Post Office, Olivetti, Rank Hovis McDougall, Rank Xerox, Reed International, Shell, The Stock Exchange, Tandon, Taylor Woodrow, Texaco, Thorn EMI, TSB, Trust House Forte, Unigate, Unipart, Wang U.K., Woolwich Building Society, and the Yorkshire Water Authority.[122]

Mr. Kinsman lists eleven business consultancies in the U.K. which now offer the new 'holistic' approach to management, involving training in such areas as *'awareness raising and spiritual development as an aid to working effectiveness'* (CTC Europe). Notice that phrase 'spiritual development' again. Is it not strange to find this as an aim of a business consultancy? Since when did 'spiritual development' have an application on the world of secular business? Such spiritual development is not referring to Bible Study groups or prayer cells in company canteens. It is referring to the inculcation of Neo-Gnostic theory and practice.

---

[119] Francis Kinsman, *Millennium: Towards Tomorrow's Society* (Penguin, 1990), p.269.

[120] The origin and activities of this organisation will be dealt with more fully in Chapter 12.

[121] Information gleaned from a report on the *Focus on Faith* programme, BBC World service, 0330 hrs., September 18, 1991. Ironically, the systems of divination used by IBM have not been very successful, as recent company reports have shown world-record losses!

[122] Francis Kinsman, op. cit., pp.267-268.

Another of these consultancies (John Frank Associates) claims to be helping its clients *'towards individual and collective insights that are about the optimistic awareness of their enormously powerful inner core...the possibility of their true growth and development'.*[123]

This attainment of an 'optimistic awareness of their enormously powerful inner core' is New Age jargon for the use of a shamanistic technique designed to enable a person to realise a kind of god-like power over every situation in life. This technique is a Westernised form of ancient occult mind and word power systems today known as 'New Thought', which will be discussed in detail in a later chapter.[124] One of the training consultancies using these techniques is the Pacific Institute, whose services have been used by Scottish Nuclear Power and many other major U.K. companies. In the Pacific Institute's training manuals we discover that clients are encouraged to use such affirmations as, *'We move to and become like that which we think about'*, and through encouraging them to repeat *ad nauseam* such governing principles as, *'I easily anticipate and experience events in my imagination before they actually happen'... 'I feel warm and loving toward myself, for I am a unique and precious being, ever doing the best my awareness permits; ever growing in wisdom and love'... 'I control the present moment and with it I invent the future'... 'I guide my own destiny'.*[125] These affirmations are based on the same principles as those mentioned in the last chapter, when we examined the so-called 'I AM' Movement — a technique which we will be returning to when we examine the so-called 'Positive Confession' practice in the professing Christian Church in Chapter 11. Through the use of an overblown self-esteem coupled with visualisation and affirmation exercises, these training programmes are inculcating in their participants an utterly egocentric mindset which affirms the anthem of the godless Man, *'MY will be done'*, over and against the selfless Christian response to a sovereign God, *'Thy will be done'*. There is no place here for a Personal Transcendent God who may have other plans for us than those we have made for ourselves. In other words, true to the perennial Gnostic ambition, they put man on the throne in place of God.

This, then, is the thrust of the Neo-Gnostic business ethos which is pervading the world of the multinationals at an extraordinary pace. We are now living in an age when, to quote 'The Times' newspaper, *'IBM and General Motors send their executives on courses entitled "Metaphysics and Mysticism in business"'.*[126] Through the installation of these training programmes across the globe, the dark powers behind the New Gnosticism are manufacturing businessmen and women *en masse* who believe absolutely in themselves, who have unstoppable plans, who

---

[123] Ibid., p.268ff.

[124] This whole area of 'New Thought' systems will be discussed in considerable detail in Chapter 11 when we examine all the phenomena associated with the outer reaches of the 'mind-sciences'.

[125] Taken from material presented in the training pack *Investment in Excellence* (The Pacific Institute, 1990).

[126] *The Times*, Saturday June 18th 1988, p.10.

imagine that they are masters of their own destiny, and who envisage themselves as part of a newly-evolved breed of people with an unbridled love for the welfare of the planet and their fellow men and women. Angels of light — Satan's perfect work. The essence of Gnosis — Man become God.

2. Neo-Gnostic Subversion in Health, Healing and the Caring Professions

One of the major areas into which the New Gnosticism has moved involves health, healing and the 'caring' professions such as social work, nursing, etc. Readers will recall that one of the key components in the plan being master-minded by the occult 'Masters', and revealed by Helena Blavatsky and Alice Bailey in their writings of some decades ago, is the *'stimulation of the growth of the healing arts'*. That this has now transpired is plain for all to see. Never has there been such a focus of interest on healing of all types — especially on those which involve 'self-help' and which explore the physical and spiritual 'energies' which are alleged to lie beyond the normal field of perception. Catchphrases which were once confined to obscure foundations, such as Holistic Healing, Alternative Medicine and Complementary Medicine, have now become a standard part of the medical vocabulary. Our purpose in this chapter is not to give a detailed critique of all the alternative medical treatments and therapies; this has already been done most ably by others.[127] Rather, we are attempting to put these disciplines within the context of this present chapter by demonstrating the Neo-Gnostic influence which is being disseminated through them, coupled with the fact that this influence is rapidly becoming accepted within establishment circles in the U.K.

The word 'holistic' — so often associated with modern alternative healthcare — comes from the Greek word *holos*, meaning 'whole'. It is a very popular word with advocates of the New Gnosticism because it matches their concept of the integral oneness of everything in the universe (monism). It was first coined as a word by Jan Christian Smuts (1870-1950) as the title of his book 'Holism and Evolution' (1933), which dealt with the *'fundamental unity and continuity in nature'*.[128] Smuts was Prime Minister of South Africa (1919-1924), Prime Minister and Minister of Defence (1939-1948) and was made Chancellor of Cambridge University in 1948. He wrote a pamphlet which formed the basis of the Constitution of the League of Nations and was one of the founder-members of the United Nations, having written the preamble to the original U.N. Charter which was signed in San Francisco in 1945.[129]

The Holistic Health Movement as we know it today is based on the concept that *'we are all sentient beings who are continually creating our own realities'*.[130] That is a classic self-deifying Neo-Gnostic concept. The actual term 'Holistic Health' has been described in a manner linking it up with monistic philosophy:

---

[127] For example, from a Christian viewpoint, see P.C. Reisser, T.K. Reisser & J. Weldon, *New Age Medicine* (I.V.P., 1987). For a good secular critique, see Douglas Stalker & Clark Glymour (eds.), *Examining Holistic Medicine* (Prometheus Books, 1985).

[128] *Chambers's Encyclopaedia* (George Newnes, 1959), Vol.XII, p.619.

[129] Ibid.

[130] E. Bauman et al., *The Holistic Health Handbook* (And/Or Press, 1978), p.13.

> 'A new name for a very old concept of being. It is a reminder of the unity of all life and the essential oneness of all systems'.[131]

Illness is therefore regarded as the result of *'an imbalance of energy flow throughout the body'*.[132] Examples of the techniques used in the Holistic Health Movement are Homeopathy, Yoga, Naturopathy, acupuncture, massage (many forms: Swedish, Polarity Massage, Metamorphic, etc.), reflexology (foot manipulation), hypnotherapy, T'ai Chi, Shiatsu, visualisation, meditation, colour healing, various psychotherapies, crystal dowsing, faith healing, New Thought systems such as Silva Mind Control, and Positive Thinking, etc. Although a number of the treatments used by the Holistic Health Movement should be encouraged in these unnatural, mechanistic times — as some are not only harmless but positively beneficial (e.g., herbal medicine, some forms of massage, etc.) — an increasing number of therapeutic approaches are based on a combination of occult techniques. Some involve the utilisation of psychic powers, Shamanism and the ancient Eastern view of the body with its location and manipulation of so-called *Chakras* (energy centres) and 'meridians' (energy channels). Any therapy which claims to tune in to 'energies' is suspect.

The *exoteric* (outward) reason for the existence of the Holistic Health Movement often given by its advocates is that allopathic medicine is inhuman, mechanistic, based mainly on laboratory-manufactured drugs and does not take into account the 'whole person' when considering treatment; while most people's diet is based on refined, adulterated foodstuffs which can lead to medical problems. In many ways these are valid criticisms. We should take responsibility to look after our bodily health during our earthly pilgrimage. Let us not forget that the famous physician of the Bible and author of the third Gospel, Luke, would have used methods of diagnosis and treatment which must have been very similar to some of the natural, alternative medical practices of today.

However, despite these professed *exoteric* reasons for the existence of the Holistic Health Movement, the people who are in the forefront of these developments use the facade of this genuine and rational concern for human health as a cover for their *esoteric* (hidden) desire to propagate the occultic tenets of the New Gnosticism — that 'angel of light' syndrome again. So effective is this manipulation that many of these techniques are being practised up and down the country in health clinics, church halls and evening centres; while favourable articles appear regularly in popular women's magazines and newspapers.[133]

This occult activity in health and healing has not only operated in the predictable arena of the 'counter-culture'. In the nursing world, which has a reputation of being the most conservative of all the caring professions, the Neo-Gnostic approach to the job is now making great inroads into those seedbeds of the

---

131 Ibid., p.17.

132 W. Ohashi, *D-I-Y Shiatsu* (Unwin, 1977), p.10.

133 See, for example, an issue of *Woman*, as early as March 15th, 1986, pp.42-43. This article contained details of occult techniques such as visualisation, autohypnosis, positive thought, mind-control, etc.

profession, the colleges of nursing. In the U.S., this approach to the theory of nursing has been pioneered in the University of Colorado by Professor in Nursing, Dr. Jean Watson. In a chapter in a nursing textbook, 'Conceptual Models for Nursing Practice', she outlines her theory of nursing in a manner which makes her formative influences clear. Peppering the text with quotes from Teilhard de Chardin, Ralph Waldo Emerson and Carl Jung, she states at the outset that

> 'The process of human-to-human caring illuminates the mystery of humanity and the possibility of a higher power, order, or energy in the universe that can be activated through the nurse caring process, that can in turn potentiate healing and health and facilitate self-knowledge, self-reverence, self-control, self-care, and possibly even self-healing... Universal spirit and a central cosmic unity are identified as essential to human caring'.[134]

She then discloses that her theory of nursing reflects a *'scientific paradigm shift'*, claiming that *'the evolution of history and philosophy of science now allows some attention to metaphysical views that would perhaps have been unacceptable at an earlier point in nursing science'*.[135] The entire statement of her theory is brimming over with Neo-Gnostic code-phrases and buzz-words such as 'Universal Spirit', 'central cosmic unity', 'paradigm shift', 'the inner self' and 'spiritual evolution'; and when she says that one of her ten 'carative' factors is concerned with *'love for and trust of...our own inner power'*,[136] discerning readers will have no trouble deciphering the source and identity of this power, given all that we have so far discussed in this book. There is much in Dr. Watson's approach to nursing and caring with which we can wholeheartedly agree: not least of which is the accent on treating people as people rather than statistics or bed occupants on a system-based conveyor belt — all laudable aims in nursing practice. But these sensitive and caring aspects are just a front for an underlying metaphysical approach which brings the New Gnosticism right into the heart of the therapeutic process. This should not surprise us when we recall that saying of Irenaeus of Lyons that

> 'no false teaching desires to offer itself to our view openly, lest such exposure should lead to conviction; but, craftily putting on a plausible dress, makes itself by its outward form appear to the simpler sort to be truer than Truth itself '.

Ostensibly, this new theory of nursing is fostering a more compassionate and loving approach to the process of caring. But behind all this love and consideration, there is a hidden agenda involving what Dr. Watson calls *'existential-phenomenological-spiritual forces'* — forces which she relates to *'the inner self or essence, which allows for the development of a higher degree of consciousness*

---

[134] J. Riehl-Sisca (ed.), *Conceptual Models for Nursing Practice* (Appleton & Lange, 3rd. ed., 1989), p.220.

[135] Ibid., p.221.

[136] Ibid., p.223.

and inner strength and transcendence of the usual self'.[137] These are quite astounding phrases to discover in a standard nursing textbook. To emphasise even further the religious heart of Dr. Watson's approach, she states that *'Transpersonal caring allows humanity collectively to move towards greater harmony, spiritual evolution, and perfection'*.[138] This is an unequivocal confession of Neo-Gnosticism; and this influence on her thought is even more clearly revealed in a lecture given in March 1993, when she spoke of a *'leave-taking from the Age of Pisces, after 2000 years of the Mayan calendar'* which would lead *'into spirit-filled life, creativity and nurturing period cosmology'*.[139]

Due to the ink-blot strategy of the Neo-Gnostics, this New Age approach to medical care will not be confined to the U.S. but will spread across the world. The Colorado 'Centre for Human Caring' at which Dr. Watson is Professor of Nursing, had been scouting around for a suitable European affiliation, and they discovered that the Highland College of Nursing and Midwifery in Inverness, Scotland, was already open to such developments. This could well have been due to the fact that the director in the Highland College who set up the Colorado link was a member of the Baha'i Faith, which shares the same cosmic aspirations as Dr. Watson and her Teilhardian philosophy. However, all this will not be confined to a single college in the Scottish Highlands, but will soon be spread across the whole of the U.K., as is made plain in a report in the local newspaper:

> 'This whole field of research is being encouraged by the Government, and the Scottish Office produced a report on it recently... The Highland Health Board has given it full support... They will be setting up a network with other parts of the U.K. to share research and would like to have a very close working relationship with Colorado'.[140]

This is New Age networking on a global scale, demonstrating the efficiency of the New Gnosticism in spreading its gospel. It is not in the least surprising that Colorado should be the focus of such activity. The state is a veritable hive of Neo-Gnostic activity, partly through the offices of the folk-singer John Denver who, in 1976, started an organisation called the 'Windstar Foundation' on 1000 acres in the Rocky Mountains, whose mission is *'to call forth the spirit of transformation'*, and encourage ecological concern and a *'planetary consciousness'*. Many famous and influential personalities have participated in conferences organised by Windstar, including CNN media mogul (and partner of Jane Fonda) Ted Turner, and former Colorado governor, Richard D. Lamm.[141]

In the health world, Alternative Medicine has become increasingly accepted within the medical establishment. Many of these alternative therapies have arisen as a reaction against the almost exclusively drug-based nature of conventional

---

[137] Ibid., p.231.

[138] J. Riehl-Sisca (ed.), op. cit., p.234.

[139] Quoted in Donald M. Boyd, *New Age Nursing in the Highlands* (Free Presbyterian Religion and Morals Committee, November 1993), p.11.

[140] From a report in the *Inverness & Nairnshire Herald*, 4th September, 1992, p.1.

[141] J. Gordon Melton, *New Age Encyclopedia* (Gale Research, 1990), pp.496-497.

medicine, and they have stolen the high moral ground in this respect. However, while it is true that conventional medicine rarely takes into account the whole person, and is very often fixated on crisis intervention rather than preventative aids, the proliferation of therapies which have come in its place has led to a welter of occult techniques being invisibly seamed into the garment. As Dr. Paul Reisser states that while Western medicine grapples with its priorities,

> 'the holistic health movement continues to proclaim a lofty vision of a New Medicine for a New Age. Unfortunately...the movement's vanguard has managed to misdirect thousands of well-intentioned followers... While proclaiming the importance of individual responsibility for health, the holistic movement has provided ample opportunity for a passive "do something to me" mentality to flourish. Massage and manipulation, psychic healing and the various energy therapies all assume that something (visible or otherwise) needs to be done to the patient. Herbal concoctions, homeopathic remedies and unusual diets can easily assume the role of a magic potion.
>
> 'Above all, the holistic health movement has served as a platform for disseminating the world view of the New Consciousness and promoting occultism as an approach to health'.[142]

As an example of how contact with occult healing can lead to spiritual degeneration, the founder of the Neo-Gnostic Findhorn Community, Peter Caddy, first came into contact with the occult when his father Frederick, a crippled arthritic seeking healing, joined a spiritualist circle in which the ten-year-old Peter received a personal message from a spirit-guide which manifested itself there. In that event was the demonic root of one of the most influential Neo-Gnostic developments. In the same way today, alternative healing clinics often serve as a focal point for a great many highly undesirable practices mingled in with those which are harmless and even beneficial. However, regardless of the serious dangers of spiritualist healing and other similar forms of alternative medicine, many alternative treatments are wholesome and natural, relying on the provision of the Lord in nature. (Even a proportion of allopathic medicine is merely a laboratory version of what God has provided through the plant and vegetable world). And although the movement towards more natural and holistic medicine is to be welcomed, it is thoroughly incompatible with even basic Hippocratic principles to incorporate occult or Neo-Gnostic healing methods — which must ultimately be harmful to spiritual and physical well-being — in any approach to health and disease. To demonstrate the possibility of an occult-free transition to a more holistic approach to medicine, the 'Holistic Health Centers' founded by clergyman Dr. Granger Westburg from Chicago focus on the whole person in treatment and prevention but *'new consciousness mysticism and occultism are conspicuously absent'*.[143] It is only when Satan seeks to influence reform that spiritual corruption creeps in.

---

[142] P.C. Reisser, T.K. Reisser & J. Weldon, *New Age Medicine* (I.V.P., 1987), pp.157-158.
[143] Ibid., pp.158-159.

One area of health which the Neo-Gnostics have infiltrated is the hospice movement, where dying patients are encouraged to practise transcendental meditation, visualisation and other occult mind-power techniques, coupled with the contacting of 'spirit-guides' so as to ease their passage into life beyond the grave. This approach to the dying has been disseminated by some influential gurus of the 'near-death experience'. Foremost among these is Elisabeth Kübler-Ross, who alleges communication with the dead and has her own spirit-guide called Salem. She is the author of 'Death: The Final State of Growth', in which she claims that physical death is simply the awakening of the 'True Self' to a higher reality.[144]

In recent years, there has been a considerable degree of research by Neo-Gnostic enterprises into 'near-death experiences' suffered by people on hospital operating tables or in almost-fatal accidents. It is no coincidence that there should be this flurry of interest at this point in history: The experiences being reported by people who are on death's door completely jettison the biblical concept of 'heaven and hell', and therefore deny the need to 'flee from the wrath to come' in faith and repentance. In 1960, Karlis Osis, Director of Research at the Parapsychology Foundation in New York, sent questionnaires to thousands of doctors and nurses around the world asking them about their patients' death-bed experiences. He discovered that most people experienced a state of peace and happiness shortly before death and in many cases they received visits from spirit-beings who appeared as dead relatives.[145] Many other research programmes have been conducted which have yielded similar results. All this has led many involved with the dying to encourage the practice of techniques which will enable them to undergo an altered state of consciousness, or to have out-of-the-body experiences, and to put them in touch with spirit-beings prior to their departure from this life.

As one would expect, AIDS patients have been a particular target for this kind of therapy. One newspaper report speaks of how a former social worker with AIDS accepted the advice of a London GP *'to try meditation and Ayurvedic medicine'*.[146] Although his symptoms have been alleviated by this treatment and he has been enabled to develop *'a sense of well-being and self-confidence'*, the disease will not disappear and he will still die prematurely. But, as he says, *'I don't regard myself as a victim of Aids. If I hadn't undergone this crisis in my life, I feel that I would have missed this opportunity to know and understand myself better'*.[147] Without wishing to be at all insensitive to those dying in hospices and Aids clinics, there is surely something macabre about the way that Satan has stepped into these situations, in order to ensure that those who have a unique opportunity to come to the Lord in faith and repentance before their impending death will be sidetracked into a phoney state of temporal well-being, through an

---

[144] For a full discussion of Kübler-Ross's beliefs, see Tal Brooke, *The Other Side of Death: Does Death Seal your Destiny?* (Tyndale, 1979), pp.50-52, 92-95.

[145] Colin Wilson & John Grant, *The Directory of Possibilities* (Webb & Bower, 1981), p.139.

[146] *The Times*, 26th March 1989, p.F3.

[147] Ibid.

occult-induced 'self-knowledge' (*gnosis*) which masquerades as a development of spiritual benefit — and from thence into a state of eternal damnation.

The guru of the Neo-Gnostic treatment of Aids sufferers is Dr. Deepak Chopra, former Chief of Staff at New England Memorial Hospital near Boston, Massachusetts. He has set up a clinic in California to minister to Aids patients which has provided a model for international development. Through visits around the world (Russia has been particularly responsive), he has been able to propagate a treatment which has been devised by the 'World Medical Association for Perfect Health', an organisation set up and funded by the Maharishi Mahesh Yogi. Here in the U.K. this treatment is available at £140 a month through the 'Disease Free Society Trust', which arranges a consultation at the London Medical Centre in Harley Street, London.

There are many more examples which could be given of the ways that the Neo-Gnostic ink-blot strategy has permeated so many areas of the health, healing and caring professions. Outwardly, all these developments present themselves as a much-needed alternative to the predominantly mechanistic approach which has prevailed in recent decades. Although there is a good deal of truth in this, we see here a familiar strategy of the devil. He picks up on an extreme situation which is in need of reform, only to substitute for it yet another extreme which is at least as harmful, if not more so because it has been empowered by him.

It is true that the drug companies have ruthlessly exploited the needs of the diseased in the world, and have thereby come to dominate medical practice in a quite noxious manner, enslaving G.P.s and hospitals to their provision. But to substitute sorcery and self-centred therapies for the rapacious profiteering of allopathy is to go from the frying-pan into a fiery furnace. Similarly, it is true that nursing and the other caring professions can very easily degenerate into functional systems which fail to look at patients and clients from a 'holistic' standpoint, and wind up serving the needs of the system rather than those who should benefit from it. But to substitute Neo-Gnosticism and 'transpersonal' techniques for the depersonalising nature of functional systems in the caring professions is to lead their patients and clients from human alienation to estrangement from the divine.

Let us be in no doubt as to the true motivation behind the establishment of these practices. For they are all unfolding in the interests of an ideology — through which the Christian will become increasingly marginalised, his beliefs a source of ridicule, and in which there is no room for the transcendent, personal God of the Bible, who will one day bring this evil age to a cataclysmic conclusion in an awesome judgement of everyone who has ever received the gift of human life.

3. Neo-Gnostic Subversion and World Government

The process of national and international government is an area into which the ink-blot strategy of the Neo-Gnostics has been moving in a big way. We have already mentioned the fact that Teilhard de Chardin was one of the leading influences in the development of the New Gnosticism. In keeping with this, the French Jesuit rigorously applied his monist, evolutionary philosophy to the world political situation, leading him to advocate a vision of some kind of one-world government: *'Although the form is not yet discernible, mankind tomorrow will awaken to a "pan-organized" world'.*[148] It should come as no surprise, therefore, to learn that *'Teilhard had always viewed the United Nations as the progressive institutional embodiment of his philosophy'.*[149] However, this is not only the case from a political standpoint but from a spiritual one also; for the United Nations has long been one of the foremost world harbingers for the New Gnosticism. Seven years after the birth of the U.N., a book was published by the occultist and founder of the Lucis Trust, Alice Bailey, claiming that

> 'Evidence of the growth of the human intellect along the needed receptive lines [for the preparation of the New Age] can be seen in the "planning" of various nations and in the efforts of the United Nations to formulate a world plan... From the very start of this unfoldment, three occult factors have governed the development of all these plans".[150]

Although she did not spell out clearly the identity of these 'three occult factors', she did reveal to her students that

> 'Within the United Nations is the germ and seed of a great international and meditating, reflective group — a group of thinking and informed men and women in whose hands lies the destiny of humanity. This is largely under the control of many fourth ray disciples, if you could but realise it, and their point of meditative focus is the intuitional or buddhic plane — the plane upon which all hierarchical activity is today to be found'.[151]

To this end, the Lucis Trust (formerly Lucifer Trust), under the leadership of Foster and Alice Bailey, started a group called 'World Goodwill' — an official Non-Governmental Organisation within the United Nations. The stated aim of this group is *'to cooperate in the world of preparation for the reappearance of the Christ'.*[152] Readers should bear in mind that 'the reappearance of the Christ', as stated in Neo-Gnostic literature, is not to be confused with the biblical concept of the Second Coming of Jesus Christ, but refers to the 'World Teacher' who is expected to lead humanity into a forthcoming Golden Age on earth. But the esoteric work inside the U.N. does not stop with such recognized occult groupings. Much of the impetus for this process was initiated through the officership of two Secretary-Generals of the U.N., Dag Hammarskjöld (held office: 1953-1961) and U Thant (held office: 1961-1971) who succeeded him, and one Assistant Secretary-General, Dr. Robert Muller. In a book written to celebrate the philosophy of Teilhard de Chardin (and edited by Robert Muller), it is revealed that

---

148 Pierre Teilhard de Chardin, *The Future of Man* (Harper & Row, 1955), p.182.

149 Robert Muller (ed.), *The Desire to be Human: A Global Reconnaissance of Human Perspectives in an Age of Transformation* (Miranana, 1983), p.304.

150 Alice B. Bailey, *Discipleship in the New Age* (Lucis Press, 1955), Vol.II, p.35.

151 Ibid., p.220.

152 *One Earth,* the magazine of the Findhorn Foundation, October/November 1986, Vol. 6, Issue 6, p.24.

> 'Dag Hammarskjöld, the rational Nordic economist, had ended up as a mystic. He too held at the end of his life that spirituality was the ultimate key to our earthly fate in time and space'.[153]

In case readers may be wondering what kind of 'spirituality' Dag Hammarskjöld advocated, a leaflet about the United Nations Meditation Room written under the direction of Mr. Hammarskjöld stated that the eerie lodestone altar within it *'is dedicated to the God whom man worships under many names and in many forms'*.[154] In the final chapter, we will show how this syncretistic notion is fundamental to the development of the New Gnosticism and to the generation of its Occult Millennium.

In 1973, the U.N. Secretary-General U Thant — who was also a mystic — formed the organisation 'Planetary Citizens' with a New Age activist called Donald Keys. This is yet another Non-Governmental Organisation within the U.N. which is devoted to propagating the New Gnosticism. Since its inception, this has grown to be a global organisation which is specifically *'devoted to preparing people for the coming of the new culture'*.[155] In a revealing connection, Donald Keys has been actively involved with the New Age Findhorn Community in Scotland and writes regularly for its magazine 'One Earth'. On one such occasion, at the beginning of the 1980s, Donald Keys wrote:

> 'The New Age groups are focussing and entering a new stage — a world related stage. They are becoming mature enough to begin to shoulder some of the load of humanity's burden... The spread of New Age values as a unifying "yeast" in the human loaf may be the critical ingredient for successful emergence from the 1980s'.[156]

In this same article, Donald Keys posed the question, *'To what extent will New Age energies and values invest the human scene in the 1980s?'* And he answers: *'Without doubt it will have a major impact throughout the world on the value content of governance and the way life is lived'*.[157] That this has been the case, there can be no doubt. We now have all the talk about a New World Order, and the present President of the most influential country in the world is the most sympathetic man to the New Gnosticism that one could have in the White House. We have already shown in the previous chapter that his deputy, Albert Gore, is completely in tune with the 'Hundredth Monkey' ambitions of the New Gnosticism.

It is also surely of some significance here that Javier Perez de Cuellar — Secretary-General of the United Nations from 1982-1992 — is reputed to have been abducted by space-aliens on 30th November 1989.[158] Perez de Cuellar has

[153] Robert Muller (ed.), *The Desire to be Human: A Global Reconnaissance of Human Perspectives in an Age of Transformation* (Miranana, 1983), p.304.

[154] Quoted in R.K. Spenser, *The Cult of the All-Seeing Eye* (Christian Book Club of America, 1962), p.9.

[155] J. Gordon Melton (ed.), *New Age Encyclopedia* (Gale Research, Inc., 1990), p.357.

[156] *One Earth Image*, Magazine of the Findhorn Foundation, Vol.1, Issue 1, February/March, 1980, p.1.

[157] Ibid.

persistently refused to speak about this experience. However, in response to an enquiry about the matter from the Prince of Liechtenstein — a leading world authority on UFOs — he did not deny that it had occurred.[159] Whether or not this event really happened, its public disclosure through the international media could easily be part of a softening-up process designed by 'security agencies' to prepare people to accept the idea of a relationship between alien beings and world government leaders. Is it possible that the putting-out of films such as 'E.T.' and 'Close Encounters of the Third Kind' have also been part of the same information-feeding process, in preparation for an announcement of the 'real thing'? Admittedly, this is speculative; but there are a number of comparable intelligence reports which claim that there has been some mysterious involvement of alleged alien beings (which Christians would identify as demonic entities) with a shadow world government since around the time that the United Nations was formally set up in 1948.[160] We have also seen a number of documents propounding the conceit that the human race was originally the product of an experiment in genetic engineering by an advanced race of ETs from another world. Religious writings such as the Bible, Koran, etc., are said to contain a record of their ancient deeds, while the world religions themselves have been based on the teachings of the messengers which they sent (e.g., Buddha, Moses, Jesus, Mohammed, etc.) to prepare us for the time that the truth about all this could be revealed, and their 'Great Teacher' could finally come to earth to lead mankind into the next world-era.[161] Even the Oxford University evolutionary biologist, William Hamilton, has proposed

> 'that our planet may be a zoo controlled by extraterrestrial beings, who have "planted the seeds of evolution on Earth hoping to create interesting, intelligent creatures." Every now and then, he speculates, they see things not working very well and "so they insert a finger and just change some little thing. And maybe those are the miracles which the religious people like to emphasise"'.[162]

---

[158] *The Independent on Sunday*, 2nd January 1994, p.10.

[159] Ibid.

[160] See, e.g., 'The Secret Government: The Origin, Identity, and Purpose of MJ-12' in Milton William Cooper, *Behold a Pale Horse* (Light Technology Publishing, 1991), pp.195-235. See also 'Appendix B: UFOs and Area 51' in the same work, pp.397-443. William Cooper is a former naval intelligence operative who has linked up his 'inside information' with a formidable knowledge of the Mystery Religions, exposing all that he has seen in relation to secret world government operations and alien entities. He broadcasts regularly on the U.S. shortwave radio station, Worldwide Christian Radio.

[161] As a further twist in this strange saga, on 2nd December 1993, a quarter-page advertisement was placed on p.7 in the *International Herald Tribune*, by a French journalist who claims that ETs took him to their planet, gave him the name of Raël, asking him to spread the message that these beings will soon come back to earth, and that an embassy must be built for the occasion. Do not be surprised to find such reports increasing in the future. For further information about this gross deception, write to the International Raëlian Movement, CP 225, Geneve 8, CH-1211, Switzerland.

[162] Reported in an article entitled 'Evolutionary Faith and the Cosmic Zoo', by Carl Wie-

If this fiendishly clever idea — which has so far only been purported in academic and Neo-Gnostic circles — was to be developed into a full-blown global strategy, then we would be caught up in the most intensive spiritual battle yet, involving deception on a universal scale. It is not at all beyond the bounds of possibility that demons posing as 'highly evolved beings' from another world will be involved in the massive deception surrounding the revealing of the final manifestation of Antichrist, whose *'coming is according to the working of Satan, with all power, signs, and lying wonders'* (2 Th.2:9). Such a scenario could easily be part of the *'strong delusion'* which will be energised shortly before the time of the End among those who would rather believe the lie than love the Truth (2 Th.2:10-11).

Another major player in the Neo-Gnostic infiltration of world government is United Nations executive Dr. Robert Muller. He first came to the U.N. in 1948, and was an Assistant Secretary-General for many years. Today he is Chancellor of the United Nations University of Peace and international advocate for the setting-up of a global Council of World Religions.[163] As the editor and co-writer of a book written in honour of Pierre Teilhard de Chardin, Dr. Muller has stated:

> 'I believe that humanity on this miraculous, wondrous, life-teeming planet has a tremendous destiny to fulfil and that a major transformation is about to take place in our evolution'.[164]

This statement is wholly in keeping with the 'Critical Mass'/'Hundredth Monkey' concept which we have discussed in an earlier section of this chapter. On the syncretistic front, Dr. Muller is also the author of the book entitled 'Shaping a Global Spirituality' (Doubleday, 1982). Dr. Muller also sheds some light on the relationship of the United Nations to the New Age Movement. He rewrites the first chapter of the biblical Book of Genesis to make it refer to the creation of the United Nations. Under the title of 'The New Genesis', the first verse states:

> 'And God saw that all nations of the earth, black and white, rich and poor, from North or South, from East and West, and of all creeds were sending their emissaries to a tall glass house [the U.N. Headquarters] on the shores of the River of the Rising Sun, on the Island of Manhattan, to stand together, to think together, and to care together for the world and all its people. And God said: *"That is good"*. And it was the first day of the New Age of the Earth'.[165]

In another of Dr. Muller's books, 'Decide to Be', we see the New Age

---

land in *Creation Ex Nihilo*, Vol.15, No.4, September-November, 1993. This was a review of an article in *Time*, January 4, 1993, entitled 'Science, God and Man', in which William Hamilton's views were sympathetically reported. In that article, Hamilton was referred to as *'one of the great scientific minds of our era'*.

[163] Robert Muller was one of the keynote speakers at the 1993 Parliament of the World's Religions, where he made this proposal. This will be fully discussed in Chapter 12.

[164] Robert Muller (ed.), *The Desire to be Human: A Global Reconnaissance of Human Perspectives in an Age of Transformation* (Miranana, 1983), p.17.

[165] Ibid., p.19.

philosophy perfectly set forth. One passage which aptly demonstrates the real spiritual impetus behind the United Nations reads:

> 'Decide to open yourself to God, to the Universe, to all your brethren and sisters, to your inner self...to the potential of the human race, to the infinity of your inner self, and you will become the universe...you will become infinity, and you will be at long last your real, divine, stupendous self '.[166]

Here we have the kernel of the New Gnosticm: that the essence of God dwells unconditionally within all human creatures, and that through meditation and a variety of other techniques, we can 'tune into' this 'divine self ' and actually become God. This, of course, is not a new idea; it is at least as old as the hills (Gen.3:4-6), or even older. One has only to enter the so-called 'Meditation Room' at the U.N. Headquarters in New York to recognise the dark antichristian origins of the spiritual philosophy which has conceived and pervaded this organisation. The bare wedge-shaped room with its eerie lodestone altar, and the cryptic, Picasso-like mural on the smallest wall, symbolise the empty heart of countless esoteric religious cults down the ages. It therefore comes as no surprise to learn that the U.N. has its own official Indian meditation instructor, Sri Chinmoy, who holds two meditation sessions per week within the U.N. building, and whose speciality is to lull his audiences into trance with music! Even the normally staid Houses of Parliament in the U.K. have played host to Sri Chinmoy — at the invitation of the Speaker of the Commons — so that politicians could receive instruction in his meditation technique.[167]

In the mid 1980s there was a particular flurry of activity on the part of the United Nations Neo-Gnostic infiltrators to activate its potential global influence. This surfaced initially in the series of 'Peace Meditation' days sponsored by the U.N. and 'fronted' by a variety of celebrities who are sympathetic to New Age ideology. These two 'Peace Meditation' days were designed to frame the United Nations 'First Earth Run' which began on September 16th 1986 as a flaming torch was passed from hand-to-hand around the world, culminating on December 31st 1986 when it ignited an 'eternal flame' at the U.N. headquarters in New York. The first peace meditation was called 'The Million Minutes of Peace Appeal', while the second was entitled 'The World Instant of Cooperation'. The publicity leaflet asked the hubristic question: *'Are you ready to take the world in your hands?'*[168]

Although it was concealed from the general public, these deceptive occasions were masterminded by an international galaxy of esoteric organisations and individuals who have been working closely with the U.N., and whose spiritual beliefs, affiliations and aspirations are thoroughly in accord with the New Gnosticism.

---

[166] Robert Muller, *Decide to Be* (Link-Up, 1986), p.2. This was published by the British New Age journal 'Link-Up', which has now changed its name to 'Global Link-Up'.

[167] *The Daily Telegraph*, undated article in the 'Peterborough' column.

[168] This leaflet was obtainable from: No.4, 95, Avenue Road, St. John's Wood, London, NW8 6HY.

For these United Nations events were actually the brain-child of four leading occultists and global 'envisionists'. First, John Randolph Price, author of many Neo-Gnostic books such as 'Superbeings' and 'The Planetary Commission'. He is founder of the 'Quartus Foundation for Spiritual Research' — a Texas, U.S. based organisation dedicated to carrying out *'research and communications on the divinity of man'*,[169] and whose stated objective is

> 'to continually document the truth that man is a spiritual being possessing all the powers of the spiritual realm...that man is indeed God individualised, and that as man realises his true identity, he becomes a Master Mind with dominion over the material world'.[170]

Others involved in the conception of these United Nations Meditation Days were Barbara Marx Hubbard, whose 1983 book 'Revelation: the Book of Co-creation' called for a Hundredth-Monkey-style *'planetary pentecost which would alter the world's state of consciousness'*.[171] Then there was David Gershon, of New York, who 'envisioned' the First Earth Run as an expression of universal co-operation; and Moscow's Joseph Goldin who, in 1985, conceived a global New Year's Eve party to be held in Moscow on December 31st 1986, with satellite linkage around the world.[172] At least two of these individuals openly advocate psychic communication with spirits: Both Barbara Marx Hubbard and John Randolph Price are among the catalogue of celebrities who are quoted on the covers of Ken Carey's 'channelled' books in the 'Starseed' series published by Harper.

Such is the background to this U.N. occult jamboree, designed to introduce ordinary people of many faiths and Christian denominations to the realms of occult meditation at a global level. In fact, the organisers were living out their 'Hundredth Monkey' belief that there will be a critical point at which a *'breakthrough into a new planetary consciousness'* will take place if they can induce enough people to meditate on the planet at any one time. Among the many patrons and sponsors of these events were the Dalai Lama, James Callaghan, Yehudi Menuhin, Richard Leakey, Terry Waite, Dr. Linus Pauling, Mother Teresa, Dr. Robert Muller, composer Philip Glass, comedian Dudley Moore, actor Ben Kingsley (star of the film 'Gandhi'), Paul McCartney, paper manufacturer Bowater Scott, Brahma Kumaris World Spiritual University, The Human Unity Institute, Planetary Citizens, the Gandhi Foundation, U.N.A., Oxfam, etc.[173]

One of the major reasons that the U.N. has become the haunt of organisations and individuals seeking to bring about a one-world antichristian political and religious consciousness is that it has a ready-made global network which can be easily infiltrated and used by clandestine forces. Furthermore, it easily fulfils the preparatory plans of those secretly controlling the world government which will lead to the so-called Golden Age on earth envisaged within the New Gnosticism.

---

[169] John Randolph Price, *The Planetary Commision* (Quartus Books, 1980), foreword.
[170] Ibid., p.173.
[171] *Link-Up*, No.28, Autumn 1986, p.5.
[172] Ibid.
[173] Ibid.

The primary work of the United Nations since the time of its inception has been to soften people up to the idea of a world government which will have complete jurisdiction over the sovereignty of national governments. That is why the U.N. has suddenly come into such prominence as the 'policeman of the planet' during the late 1980s and early 1990s. This does not mean that the present U.N. and its Security Council, as it is presently constituted, will necessarily be the actual World Government itself — although it is certainly the primary harbinger.[174]

There have been a great many contributory factors in this softening-up process, of which the foremost has been the careful erosion of the concept of national sovereignty across the world. To this end, former 'Iron Curtain' countries have been systematically 'democratised' (orchestrated by the shadow world government powers) so that long-standing, covert, nationalist bitterness could once again rise to the surface, leading eventually to calls for a world government. To imagine that the dismantling of the Iron Curtain has been the result of a series of independent, spontaneous, popular people's revolutions is the height of naïvety. The present writer has seen numerous intelligence sources which show that the political structures of the Soviet Union and its satellites (e.g., East Germany, Poland, Hungary, Romania, Czekoslovakia, etc.) have been systematically dismantled by the same secret powers which originally set them in motion. Mikhail Gorbachev, former President of the U.S.S.R. and now President of the International Green Cross/Crescent, was groomed for his role in this by predecessor Yuri Andropov, and is a major protégé of the secret world government which is even now in force. One of Gorbachev's most intimate advisers is Evgeny Primakov, a member of the Club of Rome. In an article in Pravda and Izvestia in 1987, Gorbachev said:

> 'A world consultative council under the UN auspices uniting the world's intellectual elite is needed to help shape the future. Prominent scientists, political and public figures, representatives of international public organisations, cultural workers should all be involved'.[175]

Many assume that former U.S. President George Bush invented the Gnostic-Masonic term 'New World Order'. But *before* Bush assumed the Presidency, Mikhail Gorbachev, in a speech to the U.N. General Assembly in December 1988, said: *'Today, further world progress is only possible through a search for a universal human consensus as we move forward to a new world order'.*[176] In the same speech, he claimed that both the French and Russian Revolutions (1789 and 1917) *'gave a tremendous impetus to mankind's progress'* and referred to them as *'a most precious spiritual heritage'.*[177] Surely this was a coded reference to the occult Illuminist *'spiritual'* forces which lay behind both these historical events.

---

[174] The U.N. is actually a highly-inefficient and corrupt organisation. For information on this see, e.g., the article 'Does Corruption Abound?', in *Time Magazine*, August 9th, 1993, p.11, in which it is revealed that a document presented by the Heritage Foundation *'lambasted the U.N. for systematic mismanagement and corruption'*.

[175] *Toronto Star*, September 26th 1987.

[176] *Daily Telegraph*, December 8th, 1988, p.9.

[177] Ibid.

Coupled with all this Russian and European activity, we have witnessed the British monarchy coming under a welter of media smears during the past few years to soften-up the people for a removal of their office and influence throughout the once-influential British Commonwealth. The world's media moguls are also affiliated with the secret government process. The European Union (EU) is yet another brainchild of the secret government powers. As political and judicial power transfers from London to Brussels, the national sovereignty of Britain (and every other participating country) will be subsumed into the monolithic superstate called Europe. This can clearly be seen in such documents as the 'Treaty on European Union', ratified at Maastricht in 1992, in which the assertions are made that the European Union will bring about *'the creation of an area without internal frontiers'*, and that it will *'assert its identity on the international scene, in particular through the implementation of a common foreign and security policy including the eventual framing of a common defence policy, which might in time lead to a common defence'*.[178] This takes on an even more sinister aspect when we discover from this Treaty that *'every person holding the nationality of a Member State'* of the European Union is regarded as a *'citizen'* of that Union, who *'shall be subject to the duties imposed thereby'*.[179] Whatever the squirming politicians may say in their attempts at denial of a European superstate, such *'citizenship'* can mean nothing other than *governmental oversight* and jurisdiction.

Another major contributor to this world government game is the Club of Rome, which produced a confidential document, dated September 17th 1973, entitled 'A Regionalized and Adaptive Model of the Global World System', in which the countries of the world are divided into ten 'global groups'. This could provide a more manageable basis for a United Nations World Government superstructure. Watch out for major changes in the future composition of the U.N. Security Council. As far as a location of such a World Government is concerned, there is one city which would provide the perfect setting for a possible headquarters for either a World Government or a World Council of Religion (or both): that city is Jerusalem — which the Lord Jesus Christ prophesied would be *'trampled by Gentiles'* until the times of the Gentiles (the present Gospel Age) has come to an end (Lk.21:24). Its pedigree as a centre for Christianity, Islam and Judaism could well provide the ecumenical-interfaith basis for such a development. Additionally, the September 1993 accord between Israel and the Palestinians could also be an orchestrated precursor to this scenario. Only time will tell.

A vast quantity of evidence of these secret forces at work in the world can be seen today: in the systematic undermining of public confidence in law and order, in the escalation of moral degeneracy, the proliferation of inner city rioting, the introduction of AIDS into the world's population, the global sales of enslaving drugs, the incessant diet of drivel and disinformation in the world's media, the manufacture of wars (e.g., Iraq-Kuwait) to prepare people for a 'world army', the generation of upheaval and public disorder in as many areas of the world as

---

[178] *Treaty on European Union*, Title 1: 'Common Provisions', Article B.

[179] Ibid., Title II, Part Two: 'Citizenship of the Union', Article 8.

possible, the doomsday disinformation about impending environmental disasters, the multiple sightings of UFOs, the mass implementation of so-called 'family planning' strategies (e.g., abortion and contraception), the creation of uncertainty (and, ultimately, chaos) in the world's money-markets, the confederation of the world's religions into a World Council — all these, and many more, have been happening under the influence of clandestine powers who secretly control the political, informational and economic structures of world affairs. This is the *'mystery of iniquity'* in action, the aim being to fabricate the global conditions for the establishing of a world government. The abundant evidence for all this is available to anyone interested enough to do the necessary research — although many people would doubtless be too horrified to accept the results of their discoveries.

Many more examples of the occult side of world government could be given here; but there are a number of books in print which provide considerably more depth than is possible in this present work.[180] Because our main concern is to concentrate on *religious* corruption in this evil age — although this is inevitably linked-up with political corruption — we have merely sought to expose a few key aspects of the global ink-blot strategy of the New Gnosticism and its inroads into international affairs. At present, these things are in the *developmental* stage of working towards a world conglomerate which has been masterminded by Jehovah's ancient enemy. Within the next few years, the fullness of this work will become all-too-apparent to those who have eyes to see, ears to hear and the spiritual insight to understand.

The reverse side of the Great Seal of the United States of America, designed in 1782 by Freemasons. It appears on the one-dollar bank-note, brought into circulation in 1935 by order of U.S. President Franklin D. Roosevelt, a 32nd degree Freemason. Notice its Egyptian pyramid and freemasonic 'All-Seeing Eye' over the Latin inscription: *'New World Order'*.

As a further aid in the discernment of world developments we will now go on, in the following chapter, to look at a number of the identifying marks of the New Gnosticism, together with the Christian's response to them.

---

180 One of the foundational studies is John Robison, *Proofs of a Conspiracy Against all the Religions and Governments of Europe Carried on in the Secret Meetings of Freemasons, Illuminati and Reading Societies* (3rd Edition, 1798). This can be found in major libraries such as the British Library or Scottish National Library in the U.K. See also A. Ralph Epperson, *The Unseen Hand: An Introduction to the Conspiratorial View of History* (Publius Press, 3100 Sth. Philamena Place, Tucson, Arizona 85730, USA, 1985), 488pp. Also A. Ralph Epperson, *The New World Order* (Publius Press, 1990), 357pp. See also Milton William Cooper, *Behold a Pale Horse* (Light Technology Publishing, P.O. Box 1495, Sedona, Arizona 86336, USA, 1991), 500pp.

Chapter Five

THE HALLMARKS OF THE NEW GNOSTICISM

Lies, Damned Lies

'The wicked are estranged from the womb; they go astray as soon as they are born, speaking lies. Their poison is like the poison of a serpent... Break their teeth in their mouth, O God!' (Ps.58:3-6)

'The great masses of the people will more easily fall victims to a great lie than a small one' (Adolf Hitler, *Mein Kampf*, 1924)

Every religion has its hallmarks; and Satan's latest offering is no exception. Having examined the strategies of the New Gnosticism in the previous chapter, we will now survey ten of its universal hallmarks, clearly showing their deceptions and designs. Many of these hallmarks were apparent, or at least incipient, within the teachings of the Old Gnosticism; but with increased development and syncretism they found their fullness in its more recent manifestations. Some hallmarks have been specially created for the circumstances and requirements of the present time. But they all share the same motivation: to undermine the foundations of the Lord's people, to cast to one side the concept of a Transcendent Personal God, to overthrow the teachings of the Holy Bible, and to contribute towards the building of Satan's earthly kingdom.

1. THE STRAWBERRY FIELDS FACTOR: No Objective Reality

This hallmark of the Neo-Gnostic worldview is foundational to all the others — indeed, it is fundamental to Satan's entire *modus operandi*. For the acceptance of this concept immediately destroys the uniqueness of God's Word as the objective source of revelation, and the fact of Jesus Christ as the substantial fount of all Truth. Instead, it deifies individuals by holding up their personal subjective world-views as being THE truth, even when they are in contradiction with one another. This concept is a major factor in the New Age Movement and has found its expression in the vogue-phrase *'Paradigm Shift'*. A Paradigm Shift, in Neo-Gnostic jargon, refers to the process whereby one can, through a small but highly significant shift in perception or world-view, slip into another level of reality. It is rather like looking at a picture for the first time and seeing certain features, but on looking a second time one might see something completely different because a change took place in the way one viewed it. Yet both perceptions are said to be 'correct', thus negating any objective reality in the picture. A classic diagrammatic representation of such a concept is given in the drawing to the right. Is it a duck, or a rabbit? Could it be an aerial shot of the seventeenth hole at St. Andrews? Or all three?

What this concept implies is that there are as many 'realities' to a situation as there are people to perceive them: Truth is purely arbitrary and solely in the eye of the beholder. Now this can certainly be true in regard to our perceptions of many things in life, as in the example above. For there are a great many situations in which there is plainly more than one way of looking at an object. But it is a logical fallacy to deduce that this approach can be applied to every conceivable situation in the world, and even to the experience of personal existence. The reason that the drawing above can be perceived in so many ways without violating its integrity is because *there is no externally imposed control which dictates how it should be viewed.* Its identity is 'up for grabs'. But if the voice of God thunders: *'This is My beloved Son, in whom I am well pleased'*, could anyone deny that Jesus has the unmistakable identity of the Son of God? Surely reality takes on an unequivocal quality when God has imposed His objective authority upon it.

To attempt to apply the principle of 'no objective reality' to Deity, His material creation or inspired revelation (the Bible), is surely an outworking of the satanic lie in Eden ('Has God really said...?'). Perhaps such an emphasis is inevitable in a world of increasing iniquity and disobedience to God's Law. In order to bring about a complete mistrust of the concept of the Transcendent Creator God of the Scriptures, whose Word is THE Way, THE Truth and THE Life, the satanic realm has built up an assumed need for a massive paradigm shift in favour of the Eastern world-view which states that life as we know it is an illusion, that each one of us creates his own reality, that the essence of God indwells all people unconditionally, and that we can utilise this immanent 'divinity' for our own ends, both spiritual and material.

The concept of the Paradigm Shift was first formulated by science historian and philosopher Thomas Kuhn in his book 'The Structure of Scientific Revolutions'.[1] The general use of this term has since been seized upon avidly by those preaching the Neo-Gnostic 'gospel', and who have a vested interest in bringing about the Hundredth Monkey consciousness of the 'Aquarian Age' via 'quantum leaps' and 'evolutionary shifts' in psychic awareness. But the concept of 'no objective reality' has been a fundamental principle from ancient times in any situation where the Satanic Initiation is in the ascendency. In classical Hinduism, the term *Maya*, 'illusion', is used to refer to the material world, which is judged to be devoid of objective reality. As one source puts it:

> '*Maya* is originally the magical power of creating illusion or deceit, but in the *Advaita Vedanta* it refers to the illusory existence of a world of multiplicity superimposed upon the single non-dual reality (*Brahman*)

[1] Thomas Kuhn, *The Structure of Scientific Revolutions* (University of Chicago, 1970).

> by the power of ignorance (*Avidya*)...*Maya* is the power of God (*Ishvara*), which creates the illusion of a differentiated universe and conceals the divine unity behind appearances, while ignorance creates the seemingly separate self at the individual level'.[2]

The idea that each person is only 'seemingly separate' from the cosmos has grave implications for the biblical concept of personal responsibility for sin and its eternal consequences, as we shall shortly show. The uniqueness of each individual is also undermined, a fact which is illustrated in the Zen Buddhist proverb which says:

> 'Last night I dreamed I was a butterfly. Am I a man who dreamed he was a butterfly? Or am I really a butterfly who is now dreaming he is a man?'

If you meditate on that for too long, you could slip your moorings and begin to doubt your own existence: a sure recipe for self-induced psychosis. Even common sense can discern that such a statement is unmitigated nonsense. Every time we wake up, we awaken to the same world, the same circumstances, the same self; whereas, in our dreams, we enter a different world and circumstances — and very often experience ourselves as being someone else. If we accept the 'no objective reality' world-view of the East, we are entering, at best, a nursery-rhyme fantasy-land; at worst, it is the ultimate nightmare scenario, with each one of us in the starring role. Here in the West, this concept has been welcomed in the field of Transpersonal Psychology. For example, the occultist and Neo-Gnostic Carl Jung says:

> 'Our unconscious existence is the real one and our conscious world is a kind of illusion, an apparent reality constructed for a specific purpose, like a dream which seems a reality as long as we are in it'.[3]

In the 1960s, a number of psychiatrists also began to take this concept onboard in a big way as their experimental work appeared to give it confirmation. In his book 'The Politics of Experience/The Bird of Paradise' (Penguin, 1967), R.D. Laing recounted how one of his patients had suddenly undergone mental disintegration after looking at himself in a mirror and subsequently went on a ten day 'voyage' into an inner world of extraordinary hallucination. On recovering from this mind-journey, the patient felt he had undergone a profound religious experience. This persuaded Laing that reality was only relative, and he began to revere the schizophrenic and psychotic as being somehow on a higher plane with greater insight into reality than the average human being — so much so that he likened psychiatrists to *'the blind leading the half-blind'* when they counsel such people. This view was also supported by the internationally-renowned psychiatrist Stanislaf Grof, whose experiments on patients with LSD therapy in the 1950s had convinced him of the 'relativity of reality'. One is reminded here of the lyrics of the

---

[2] John R. Hinnells (Ed.), *The Penguin Dictionary of Religions* (Penguin, 1984), p.208.
[3] C.G. Jung, *Memories, Dreams and Reflections* (Routledge & Kegan Paul, 1968), p.324.

classic 1960s Beatles' song, 'Strawberry Fields', which says:

> 'Let me take you down, 'cos I'm going to Strawberry Fields;
> Nothing is real...
> Always – no sometimes – think its me;
> But you know I know when its a dream...
> It's getting hard to be someone but it all works out;
> It doesn't matter much to me'.

Lyrics rooted in a similar world of drug-induced unreality were recorded in another well-known Beatles classic, 'Lucy in the Sky with Diamonds':

> 'Picture yourself in a boat on a river,
> With tangerine trees and marmalade skies.
> Somebody calls you, you answer quite slowly,
> The girl with kaleidoscope eyes'.

It was well-known at the time that these words were inspired through the influence of the hallucinogenic drug LSD, and that the initials of the song-title were a none-too-subtle advertisement for the drug. Such 'acid-rock', as it is known, was extremely fashionable during the phase when such drug-use was being encouraged by the powers of darkness in order to cut a huge swath into the minds of the young and vulnerable children of the intelligentsia who would eventually grow into those who now hold positions of cultural responsibility and parenthood. Another development which has gone some way towards influencing this loosening of the idea of an objective reality is the huge growth of interest in Shamanism, as outlined in the previous chapter. Serge King is a Polynesian shaman who is director of the Order of Huna International in Hawaii, one of the many new schools for the training of shamans in the world today. On this subject of 'reality', he writes:

> 'The first and fundamental principle of Huna...says that "the world is what you think it is". Another, more popular way of stating the same thing is: "We create our own reality."... [Shamans] take that idea to mean that we not only attract experience by our thinking, but we actually create realities. By our assumptions, attitudes, and expectations we make things possible or impossible, real or unreal. To put it another way, by shifting mind-sets we can do ordinary and non-ordinary things in the same physical dimension that we share with everyone else... Shamans are taught as early as possible that the objective world is only one way of seeing...In shamanic thinking, the objective world is simply one more place in which to operate, and to operate effectively in any world is the shamanic goal... Shifting mind-sets or moving between worlds in full consciousness is a subtle and delicate process... With practice this becomes virtually automatic. What helps tremendously is loving yourself without reserve and trusting the God within you. But of course that is good advice whether you are a shaman or not'.[4]

---

[4] From the chapter 'Seeing is Believing: The Four Worlds of a Shaman' by Serge King, in

Do you see the implications of what is being said here? That the same shift in perception which leads to an inability to distinguish between a rabbit and a duck can be applied to the very fact of our own existence, so that we can never really be sure whether we are people or butterflies or anything. Once you have accepted this way of thinking, you then become the inventor of your own reality. Such a world-view has immense implications for the lives of those accepting it. For the whole question of where one will spend eternity becomes meaningless to a person who believes he can inhabit any reality of his own making. Thus, the purpose of this mindset in satanic strategy becomes only too obvious. (Take note of the name of the publisher of the book containing the above quotation, and things will become even clearer). And when we come to the 'official' teachings of the New Gnosticism, we find that this concept of 'no objective reality' lies at the very heart of its world-view. Findhorn guru, Peter Lemesurier, puts it like this:

> 'The only universe that you can ever perceive is *the universe that you perceive*. What you are actually perceiving...is nothing more or less than your own perceptions. The universe itself, it would seem, is random enough (scientific speculators currently prefer to explain this idea in terms of a theoretically infinite number of possible 'parallel universes') to permit your consciousness to model it in any way it wishes.
>
> 'Which has to mean, in effect, that whatever seems to you to be happening "out there" is — strange as it may seem on first consideration —ultimately a direct result of your own state of consciousness. Eerie though this realisation may at first seem, the world's problems are actually your own problems. Its divisions merely reflect your own inner conflicts; its inhumanity your own inhumanity to yourself; its famines the extent to which you are starving large parts of your own psyche; its pollution problems your proneness to smother your own inner reality with imposed beliefs and illusions; its drug addiction your refusal to face reality; its unemployment your failure to put whole areas of your awareness to work; its anti-black racialism your rejection of your own darker side; its lawlessness your disregard of the basic laws of your own being; its AIDS — along with the breakdown of the earth's protective ozone layer — your unconscious realisation that ultimately you cannot protect yourself or cut yourself off from the rest of the universe; its global warming your participation in the fever of transformation that humanity is currently undergoing; its mass-movements and mass-disasters your increasing involvement, perhaps, in the growth of some kind of new, transhuman super-entity.
>
> 'In a phrase, we do not see things as they are: we see them as *we* are. And other people...are merely particular aspects of ourselves... And so it is not so much a matter of your head being in the universe, as of the universe being in your head'.[5] [emphasis in original]

Gary Doore (Ed.), *Shaman's Path: Healing, Personal Growth and Empowerment* (Shambala Publications, 1988), pp.44-52.

Here, Peter Lemesurier reduces every phenomenon in the world to mere projections of our own consciousness. *'We do not see things as they are: we see them as we are'*. Therefore, there are as many worlds as there are people to create them. In the ideology of the Neo-Gnostic, it is not a personal God who has created the world — we each create our own worlds in every living moment out of our own consciousness. In other words, in their view, each one of us is God (cf. Gen.3:5)! It is most important that we understand the dire consequences of holding a world-view which claims that there is no objective reality. In fact, they are superbly realised in George Orwell's not-so-futuristic novel 'Nineteen Eighty-Four', in which the denial of objective reality is an integral part of the social and political philosophy of the Antichrist-like 'Big Brother' and his despotic 'Party'. At one stage in the book, the central character, Winston, stumbles on the realisation that

> 'In the end the Party would announce that two and two made five, and you would have to believe it. It was inevitable that they should make that claim sooner or later: the logic of their position demanded it. Not merely the validity of experience, but the very existence of external reality, was tacitly denied by their philosophy. The heresy of heresies was common sense. And what was terrifying was not that they would kill you for thinking otherwise, but that they might be right. For, after all, how do we know that two and two make four? Or that the force of gravity works? Or that the past is unchangeable? If both the past and the external world exist only in the mind, and if the mind itself is controllable — what then?'[6]

This way of thinking is not merely confined to the world of fiction. It is a natural consequence of the Neo-Gnostic mindset, showing clearly that the real battle-field in this world is not on any tract of national territory but in the realm of human thought-processes — a fact which becomes understandable when one realises that it is the mind which provides the interface between humanity and the demonic realm. There is a particularly chilling moment of realisation in Orwell's novel when the 'Thought Police' agent, O'Brien, during his torture and brainwashing of Winston, states:

> 'We control matter because we control the mind. Reality is inside the skull. You will learn by degrees, Winston. There is nothing that we could not do. Invisibility, levitation — anything. I could float off this floor like a soap bubble if I wish to... You must get rid of those nineteenth-century ideas about the laws of Nature. We make the laws of Nature.'[7]

'Reality is inside the skull'. This Hindu-Gnostic statement from Orwell's Thought Police is almost identical to Peter Lemesurier's claim that *'the universe*

---

[5] Lemesurier, *This New Age Business: The Story of the Ancient and Continuing Quest to Bring Down Heaven on Earth* (Findhorn, 1990), pp.230-232.

[6] George Orwell, *Nineteen Eighty-Four* (Penguin, 1984), pp.72-73.

[7] Ibid., p.228.

[is] in your head' and his other statement: *'We do not see things as they are: we see them as we are'*. Orwell's entire conception was a remarkable piece of insight concerning the future Neo-Gnostic development of human society. He saw clearly that the most powerful way to manipulate people is to claim that reality can only ever be subjective. In just the same way that Orwell's Big Brother seeks to control human minds by removing all possibility of an objective reality, so Satan seeks to regain control of the world by the same means. For without objective reality, there can be no personal God, no Divine revelation and, by dint of logic, no certain salvation. In just the same way that when there was no king in Israel everyone did that which was right in his own eyes (Jdg.17:6), so when the King of the Universe has been dethroned in the minds of men and women, reality becomes reduced to 'the imagination of man's evil heart' — which ultimately means the deification of self (cf. Gen.6:5; Dt.29:18-19; Jer.11:7-8; 23:17). If, as the 'Thought Police' agent O'Brien puts it, *'nothing exists except through human consciousness'*,[8] heaven help us all; for human consciousness, when left to its own devices and the ravages of Satan, is the psychic dustbin of the universe. And if, as Peter Lemesurier claims, other people are *'merely particular aspects of ourselves'* rather than having a *bona fide* objective existence of their own, then we have dehumanised every human being which God has brought into existence, and denied the existence of their Creator. If you want a vision of the warped future being generated by this concept, imagine a Neo-Gnostic sitting cross-legged on a human face — forever.

The world-view which holds that *'nothing exists except through human consciousness'* is actually a classic example of the well-catalogued philosophical standpoint known as 'Solipsism', which can be defined as, *'The extreme form of subjective idealism that denies that the human mind has any valid ground for believing in the existence of anything but itself'*.[9] Very few thinkers have dared to hang their hat on the solipsistic peg, although the English philosopher, Bertrand Russell, declared his ideal to be *'the establishment of physics upon a solipsistic basis'*,[10] an ideal which has now come to pass. For the so-called 'New Physics' is yet another area which has encouraged the idea that life is more or less an illusion. We will develop this more fully in the following chapter; but we are recording it here to show the full extent of such Neo-Gnostic conceptual fantasies. Because of recent scientific assertions that matter is just another form of energy, this has served to bolster the pantheistic claims of the Neo-Gnostics and their concept that material things are *only what they appear to be* within a framework of relativity. However, Dr. Ernest Lucas of the Institute for Contemporary Christianity, writing in the journal *Science and Christian Belief*, confounds such an idea when he writes: *'To say that matter is unreal because it can be converted into energy is like saying that ice is unreal because it can be converted into water'*.[11]

---

[8] Ibid., p.228.

[9] *Encyclopaedia Britannica*, 15th edition, Vol.X, p.946.

[10] *Chambers's Encyclopaedia*, 1963, Vol.XII, p.695.

[11] Quoted in an article entitled, 'New Agers Spell End for Science' in the *Times Higher*

But scientists today are not given to such rational reasoning. Instead, they have opted for the Neo-Gnostic view of reality. As one leading international physicist states in a highly regarded work: *'Physical reality does not exist independently of the observer and his experimental apparatus'.*[12] And he goes on to surmise that

> 'Perhaps *all* properties — and hence the entire Universe is brought into existence by observations made at some point in time by conscious beings'.[13]

This is entirely in accord with the Hindu-Gnostic world-view. Yet this is mainstream physics today. The presenter of a BBC science programme on the so-called 'Anthropic Principle' summed up such thinking when he made the statement: *'The centre of the Universe is in your living room'.*[14] As if this claim was not condemning enough of the solipsistic mythology of the New Physics, another physicist writes in similar vein when he claims that

> 'Physical systems cannot be said to have definite properties independent of our observations; perhaps an unheard tree falling in the forest makes no sound after all'.[15]

One can see that these statements bring into question the entire foundation of the objective material reality which has been created by the Triune God. What they are saying, in effect, is *'nothing really happens unless **I** experience it'.* Each individual, therefore, becomes the centre of his or her own universe. Man become God. Such a solipsistic nightmare has now seized the 'brilliant' minds that are at the leading edge of science today. This is in spite of the fact that the general verdict on Solipsism in current philosophical circles is that, *'presented as a solution to the problem of explaining man's knowledge of the external world, it is generally regarded as a reductio ad absurdum'.*[16] Yet this is precisely the position of all these Neo-Gnostics today, who are building a world which is about as real as that depicted in 'Strawberry Fields'.

One's blood runs cold at the thought that when the day comes that these people take full, open control of world authority (which may not be very far away), it is not beyond the bounds of possibility that they will attempt to enforce their philosophy on Christian dissidents in much the same way as the 'Thought Police' in the book '1984' — only this time not with crude electric shock treatment, but through the use of LSD therapy and other psychodynamic 'treatments' in 'rehabilitation' centres designed to alter human consciousness in the desired manner.

Education Supplement, May 8th 1992, p.6.

[12] John D. Barrow and Frank J. Tippler, *The Anthropic Cosmological Principle* (OUP, 1988), p.464.

[13] Ibid. p.470.

[14] BBC World Service science programme *Journey to the Centre of the Universe*, 0515 hrs, September 28th, 1992.

[15] J.F. Clouser and A. Shimony, quoted in John D. Barrow and Frank J. Tippler, *The Anthropic Cosmological Principle*, p.463.

[16] *Encyclopaedia Britannica*, 15th edition, Vol.X, p.946.

The notion that there is no objective reality has even permeated professing Christian organisations. The Society for the Promotion (sic) of Christian Knowledge has recently published a book entitled 'Living Illusions'. The pre-publication press release states that the book *'examines different expressions of faith...and suggests that they are all illusions'*.[17] Claiming that *'there are no hard and fast rules upon which we can pin the truth about external reality and inner life'*, the author, a lecturer at the University of Leicester,

> 'illustrates his argument with examples from studies of psychoanalysis as well as art, science, theology and mysticism, to show that our beliefs and assumptions rest only on our personal perceptions'.[18]

The solipsistic doctrine of *maya* is now standard fare in many mainstream 'Christian' circles. However, as far as the genuine Christian experience is concerned, the concept of 'no objective reality' can really be viewed as one of the 'deep things of Satan'. In the first place, there is a real ethical problem here. What happens to public (or private) morality if one can say, *'It depends how you look at it...'* every time someone commits a violation of the law. The Bible says that if someone kills in cold blood, objectively this is murder and he should lose his own life. But if there is no objective reality, then the excusatory standpoint of the murderer (e.g., 'I just lost my rag...', or 'She should never have left me...') becomes just as valid a reality as the Law of God. In other words, the moral integrity of the universe rests on the objectivity of reality.

Furthermore, the Bible shows that, far from being an illusion, our life-experience in this world is very real; and Jesus Himself revealed that the decisions we make during our sole earthly pilgrimage will affect us for all eternity (Jn.5:24). It is interesting to note that Lazarus and the Rich Man in Jesus' parable (Lk.16:19-31) did not look back on their lives as dreams, but that they retained their identity and reaped the reward for what they had done as conscious human beings. Mere dreamers cannot be held responsible for what they do in their dreams.

It is true that human beings do not have a holistic view of everything; our consciousness is tied to the present space/time dimension, and it stands to reason that our understanding and perception is limited when compared with that of God. But it is only God who has the total view, and it is only God who is *permitted* to have the total view. The desire to let go of normal consciousness and tap into 'divine consciousness' only becomes an issue for the person who wants to be like God in his understanding. But the Christian has the revealed truth that for a man to attempt to know things as God knows them was the very first deception in the cosmos (*'You will be like God, knowing...'*, Gen.3:5).

In the novel '1984', the important axiom to which Winston clung was: *'Freedom is the freedom to say that two plus two make four. If that is granted, all else follows'*. And that is also true for us in this age of Gnostic irrationality. But we

---

[17] August 1993 press release for Michael Jacobs, *Living Illusions* (SPCK, 1993).

[18] Ibid.

must also say that true Freedom is the freedom to know that a living, personal God has created this universe, and that we are all partakers in the objective world-reality which He has created, whether we believe it or not.

2. ALL ROADS LEAD TO MECCA: The Rise of Religious Relativism

This concept is a logical extension of the above Neo-Gnostic hallmark of 'no objective reality'. Based on the Hindu proverb, *'All paths lead to the top of the mountain'*, this hallmark perpetuates the delusive notion that the ultimate purpose of our earthly pilgrimage (or, in Neo-Gnostic thinking, our successive earthly incarnations) is an ecstatic mystical union with the 'Supreme Being'. The underlying idea is that the pathways which lead to the realisation of this union are many and varied, and that we must choose the path which most suits our own personal requirements. If all roads lead to Mecca, then who are we to say which one is the right road? Naturally, if you believe that the universe exists only as a projection of what is in your own head, then you will deny that there is just one objective way back to God, and will instead assert that there are as many ways to 'realising divinity' as there are people to experience it. The ancient Hindu scripture, the Bhagavad Gita, puts it like this: *'Every man's faith is according to his nature'*.[19] Here in the modern West, this view is epitomized in the following assertion by a leading U.K. advocate of the New Gnosticism:

> 'We are on the brink of the Age of Aquarius when everyone will learn to become his or her own person, directing life and knowledge in an individual way... No one can direct your path but yourself, guided by your inner self, and the gods and goddesses if you desire to know them... The Age of Aquarius is the age of the individual selecting his or her own path from the many offered'.[20]

The expression 'inner self' is Neo-Gnostic jargon for 'the god within', and the 'gods and goddesses' who direct the initiate's pathway are the 'spirit guides' and discarnates that we have mentioned previously. In this world-view, all religions and spiritual pursuits are equally valid, while salvation is universally applicable. In order to progress spiritually, one simply chooses whatever happens to **feel** right, shopping around from a vast assortment of techniques. Such an approach cuts across the teaching of Scripture (Isa.5:21; Prov.12:15; 16:25; cf. Jdg.17:6).

This world-view of religious relativity is not confined to the outer reaches of the Neo-Gnostic empire. Even the former Anglican Archbishop of Canterbury, Dr. Robert Runcie, has said that *'all religions possess a provisional, interim character as ways and signs to help us in our pilgrimage to Ultimate Truth and Perfection'*.[21] And Pope John Paul II of Rome said, regarding the many religions of the world, that:

---

[19] Bhagavad Gita, XVII, iii.

[20] Marion Green, *Magic for the Aquarian Age* (Aquarian Press, 1983), pp.8, 106.

[21] Dr. Robert Runcie, Archbishop of Canterbury, from a transcript of his 'Sir Francis Younghusband Lecture' to the World Congress of Faiths, published as *'Christianity and World Religions'* (World Congress of Faiths, n.d.), p.10.

> 'though the routes taken may be different, there is but a single goal to which is directed the deepest aspiration of the human spirit as expressed in its quest for God'.[22]

One might ask: to which summits of which mountaintops do Scientology, Satanism or Snake-Handling lead us? We will be taking up this entire question of true religion in relation to syncretism in the final chapter of the book.

3. PURPLE HAZE: The Inducement of Mental Minimalism

In the thinking of the New Gnosticism, because 'spirit' is ethereal and non-corporeal — beyond words and logic — and because the Fall was a fall into matter, therefore the use of the human mind provides an obstacle which must be tamed, suppressed and ultimately overcome if one is to be able to make contact with one's 'inner self' (New-Age-speak for our alleged Godhood) and become truly spiritual. Wherever the New Gnosticism is operating, this assertion of the inferiority and hindrance of the mind to proper spiritual development will be very much to the forefront. The reason? To allow Satan easy entrance to our faculties.

Within the professing Church, this is a primary reason why the foundational techniques of the Christian sect known as the Charismatic Movement involve trance-inducing practices such as prolonged, repetitious chorus singing, a suggestion-induced swoon known as being 'slain in the spirit', and ecstatic babbling mistaken for the spiritual gift of languages revealed in the Bible. In fact, the present writer has heard it said, by a number of members of this sect, that the mind or intellectual reasoning presents a real stumbling-block to the Christian experience. Given the attraction to trance-inducing, mystical religion amongst this sect, it is not surprising to discover that leaders in this movement create an unnatural division between 'spirit' and 'intellect', advising those who attend their meetings and conferences to *'leave their minds at the door with their shoes'*, in much the same way as one would find in a *darshan* meeting led by Bhagwan Shree Rajneesh. A great many Christians are being hoodwinked today by this satanic call to abandon intellectual discernment.

For example, former Quaker and rock guitarist John Wimber, founder of the highly influential, neo-Pentecostal, Vineyard ministries in California, openly advocates a 'paradigm shift' away from thinking with Western logic into the exclusively experiential way of oriental thinking — a concept thoroughly in line with the mystical ideology of the New Gnosticism.[23] He also claims that *'first century Semites did not argue from a premise to a conclusion; they were not controlled by*

---

[22] Pope John Paul II, *'Redemptor Hominis'*, n.11.

[23] John Wimber, *Power Evangelism* (Hodder & Stoughton, 1985), p.89. But read all of his Chapter 5 in this first edition to appreciate where Wimber is leading his readers. His 'Paradigm Shift' is directly parallel with that advocated by all mystics, gnostics and New Age syncretists. To back up his argument, he even includes a 'subjective reality' picture like the rabbit or duck illustration shown earlier. In the more recent edition of his book (1992), the material has been expanded somewhat but it still retains the original thrust (see pp.129-149).

rationalism'.[24] This is a highly erroneous and mischievous statement. Not only is it historically inaccurate but it also attempts to denigrate logic, as if this is something to be shunned. It also epitomises the considerable confusion in the Charismatic Movement in terms of its failure to identify the difference between (unhealthy) *rationalism*, whereby the miraculous is denied and the supernatural work of the Spirit is blasphemed, and (wholesome) *rationality*, whereby the Christian exercises necessary discernment and chooses that which is compatible with the law of God. Because of this misunderstanding, it is often said in Charismatic circles that the use of the mind is destructive to true spirituality, and there is a general belittlement of the intellect over against what is deemed to be 'the Spirit'. But there could be no more demonic suggestion than this. The suspension of the rational has been the stuff of mysticism and cultdom since the beginning of human history. Far from suspending the activity of the mind, the indwelling Holy Spirit actually transforms and sharpens it so that it works powerfully and in the full service of the Lord Jesus Christ (Lk.21:12-15; 1 Cor.2:15-16; Mt.22:37; Rom.12:2; Eph.4:23; 2 Tim.1:7).

In stating that *'first century Semites did not argue from a premise to a conclusion'*, John Wimber is also showing his profound ignorance of both history and the Bible. The ultimate first century Semite was surely the Lord Jesus Christ; yet He continually used the most devastating logic to demolish His opponents. One simple example: *'He who is of God hears God's words; therefore you do not hear, because you are not of God'* (Jn.8:47). If A, then B. If not A, therefore not B. Pure logic: arguing from a premise to a conclusion. Many other examples could be given; but two more will suffice. Again, He said: *'If you were of the world, the world would love its own. Yet because you are not of the world, but I chose you out of the world, therefore the world hates you'* (Jn.15:19). If A, then B. If not A, therefore not B. Pure logic. Again, He said:

> 'What man is there among you who has one sheep, and if it falls into a pit on the Sabbath, will not lay hold of it and lift it out? Of how much more value then is a man than a sheep? Therefore it is lawful to do good on the Sabbath' (Mt.12:11-12).

That is pure logic: arguing from a premise to an irrefutable conclusion. And it was used by a first century Semite as a matter of course. Arguing in this manner, from the lesser to the greater, was a common first-century Semitic form of logic. Another first century Semite, Paul the Apostle, used exactly the same technique: *'He who did not spare His own Son, but delivered Him up for us all, how shall He not with Him also freely give us all things?'* (Rom.8:32). Paul regularly used the most devastating logic. When he was taking the Corinthians to task because there were some among them who — although continuing as believers — said that there is no resurrection of the dead, he used a straightforward logical argument: *'If the dead do not rise, then Christ is not risen. And if Christ is not risen, your faith is futile; you are still in your sins!'* (1 Cor.15:16-17). He used logic to show

---

[24] John Wimber, Ibid., p.74.

them the irrationality of their position, just as Jesus used logic to show the Pharisees and Sadducees the irrationality of their position. And we need to use logic today to show their modern successors the futility of their position. Without logic, we will never be able to *'[cast] down arguments and every high thing that exalts itself against the knowledge of God, bringing every thought into captivity to the obedience of Christ'* (2 Cor.10:5). The Christian mind is actually a hyper-logical mind. So, we find that the first century Semite who had been born blind and who had spent his life as a beggar on the streets of Jerusalem, after he had been healed and brought into a saving relationship with Christ (the *Logos*), found that he was able to use the most withering logic against the Pharisees. His triumphant logical syllogism at the climax of his interview with the Pharisees (Jn.9:30-33), who had accused Jesus of being a sinner (Jn.9:24) and of not being from God (Jn.9:29), goes like this:

> *Major Premise*: 'Only those who are worshippers of God, who do His will and who are not (impenitent) sinners are heard by Him.'
>
> *Minor Premise*: 'This man was heard by God, because He opened the eyes of one who was born blind — something previously unheard of.'
>
> *Conclusion*: 'This Man is from God. If He were not from God He could do nothing. He must definitely not be an (impenitent) sinner'.

What is most interesting about this exchange is that this beggar was actually using the same kind of reasoning as the Pharisees in order to defeat them. First century Semites engaged in logical combat. We can see from this that it is twentieth century Charismatics who cannot argue from a premise to a conclusion — not only because of their muddled reasoning but because their fundamental premises are profoundly mistaken. They confuse 'rationality' with 'rationalism', and reject both. It is significant to note that when Jesus was refuting the Sadducees — the supreme rationalists of the day — and their dumb attempts to prove that there was no resurrection, He does not accuse them of being rationalists but instead demolishes them with one logical argument after another and then upbraids them for *'not knowing the Scriptures'* (Mt.22:29) — an accusation which should be levelled at all those who would dare claim that *'first century Semites did not argue from a premise to a conclusion'*. It is not at all 'rationalistic' to argue from a premise to a conclusion: it is the only way to establish the truth — whether you are a first century Semite or a twentieth century Anglo-Saxon!

So let us wholeheartedly reject humanistic *rationalism*, with its bland denial of the supernatural; but let us at the same time exercise the God-given faculty of *rationality*, by which healthy discernment is established, sound logic is embraced and every false way shunned. Never before has a 'sound mind' been so necessary in the life of the Church. To substitute mysticism for rationalism is the spiritual equivalent of moving from a one-dimensional world into a black hole.

Perhaps, in these matters, the children of the world are often wiser than the childen of light. When the Lord uses the secular press to make observations that expose the absurdity of sects in today's professing Church, we should sit up and take notice. In a brilliant extended editorial on the Charismatic Movement in the *Sunday Telegraph* entitled 'That New Black Magic', Sir Peregrine Worsthorne wrote:

> "Charismatic religion is very much part of the New Age. That is to say, it is part of the flood of mindlessness that appears to be spreading throughout Western countries. From various brands of oriental meditation to witchcraft to little green men in UFOs, there is evidence that more and more people are seeking refuge from the difficulties of life in mysticism, mysteries and superstition".[25]

It is in these ways that the Charismatic Movement is very much a part of the worldwide Neo-Gnostic renaissance. The Eastern mystic seeks an ultimate experience of spiritual enlightenment, which is called in Sanskrit, *Nirvana*. It is highly significant that this word is translated as *'a blowing out of the mind'*, which involves the dissolving of the individual ego and a blending of oneself into the 'cosmic soup'. In a world-view which regards reality as being merely subjective, the individuated consciousness is seen as obstructive to spiritual progress. The Neo-Gnostic of today — whether Charismatic or New Age — has simply followed in this 'mind-blowing' tradition. We have already mentioned above the many techniques which are utilised in order to effect this state: meditation, psychic exploration, consciousness-altering, drugs, psychotherapies, asceticism, gurus, and a variety of trance-inducing practices such as repetitive singing and ecstatic babbling.

In refutation of this Hindu-Gnostic tenet of faith, the Scriptures reveal that in order to come to God, we must first *believe* that He **is** (Heb.11:6) — a perception which does not involve the snuffing-out of the mind but, rather, a heightened exercise of it. The right use of the mind is an integral and essential part of Christian experience. The worship of God involves using the mind in equal proportion to all other cooperating agencies of the human constitution (Mt.22:37; Lk.10:27). Accordingly, when a person becomes a Christian under the power of God, his mind is also a vital part of the transformation process (cf. Rom.12:2), rather than something to be left behind or — as some mystics describe it — *'put in a cloud of unknowing'*. It is certainly true that over-intellectualism and scholasticism will hold the Spirit at bay; but the solution to that can never be found in going to the other extremes of mystic mindlessness or ecstatic indulgence.

4. AN UNDISCERNING EYE: The Stifling of Judgementalism

A recurring feature of Satan's occultic plan is the pressing into his service of a number of Bible verses which are taken out of context and thus given a distorted meaning. A classic example of this occurs with the use of that saying of the Lord Jesus Christ: *'Judge not, that you be not judged'* (Mt.7:1). Satan, in the garb of an angel of light, would have us interpret this verse as meaning that we must never make any judgement which paints something or someone in a negative

---

[25] *Sunday Telegraph*, 14th. April 1991.

light. Such an interpretation, however, has no foundation whatsoever in the Bible. Firstly, Jesus was referring primarily in this verse to our indulgence in hypocritical, condemnatory judgement of another person concerning faults which we have not confronted in our own lives, or things about which we are ill-equipped to make such judgements. This is clearly borne-out by the context in which it is set (cf. Mt.7:1-6), coupled with the supplementary statement of Jesus that we should not *'judge according to appearance, but judge with righteous judgement'* (Jn.7:24).

Obviously then, we are supposed to make judgements — even negative judgements — but from the solid foundation of righteousness rather than from mere superficiality. In other words, our yardstick for judgement should be the God-breathed Scriptures rather than our own petty human traditions and values. Furthermore, we should never ignore the fact that there is a vital artery running throughout the length of the Bible, which overrides the respectful rapport which should normally exist between all peoples, and which instead emphasises the importance of discerning the difference between true and false teaching.

It is true that we cannot make infallible judgements about individual hearts — only the Lord can do that (Jer.17:10) — but we are repeatedly urged to use the gift of discernment in relation to sorting out positive spiritual influences from negative ones (Mt.24:4; Mk.13:21-23; Rom.16:17; 1 Cor.2:12-16; Eph.5:6; Jas.5:19,20; 2 Pet.3:17; 1 Jn.4:1). In fact, the Greek word in the New Testament which is translated as 'discernment' is *diakrisis*, a compound of *dia*, between, and *krisis*, judgement. Discernment means to make a distinguishing judgement. As disciples of Christ, we are faith-bound to exercise such judgemental discernment in all our relationships, always bearing in mind the clarifying statement in Jn.7:24: objective, righteous, Scriptural judgement, rather than egocentric, superficial, legalistic condemnation. The same holds true for our need to censure doctrine which threatens the stability and soundness of the Church on earth. As the Anglican Bishop J.C. Ryle expressed this more than one hundred years ago:

> 'There is a spiritual instinct in most true believers which generally enables them to distinguish between true and false teaching... Let us beware of despising this spiritual instinct. Whatever a sneering world may please to say, it is one of the peculiar marks of the indwelling of the Holy Ghost'.[26]

It is supremely ironic that the Neo-Gnostics, who claim that the Spirit of God indwells all human beings unconditionally and who would also advocate non-judgementalism towards other 'faiths', not only fail to exercise any discernment whatsoever, but also employ a blasphemous and utterly condemnatory judgementalism against all those who seek to be faithful to the Lord God and Christ of the Scriptures. For they are most scathing when referring to true Christians.

There is, of course, a hidden agenda here: For it is Satan's sincerest wish that

---

[26] J.C. Ryle, *Expository Thoughts on the Gospels: John, Vol.II* (James Clarke, 1985), pp.198, 199.

we should never make a negative judgement about those who set out to destroy the Church and its foundations, or who spread deadly heresy and false doctrine. Correspondingly, the real reason that human non-judgementalism in any form is becoming so fashionable in this age is that it makes the concept of a judging, avenging God seem ridiculous, anachronistic and implausible — a clever ploy on Satan's part to fool the world as his own inevitable doom approaches. In spite of Jesus' repeated warnings of such judgement, people would rather gloss over this awesome cosmic reality — the Lamb who *'treads the winepress of the fierceness and wrath of Almighty God'* (Rev.19:15) — emphasising in its stead the infinitely more comfortable concept of the ineffability of a loving, all-embracing Universalist God. Until there is a realisation that the avenging wrath of a judging God is an *integral part* of the unsearchable love of God, there will be little true repentance on this bedevilled planet.

5. THE MARCIONITE MALADY: Rejection of the Old Testament

Another hallmark which is consistent with all manifestations of Gnosticism, whether Old or New, is the rejection of the Old Testament Scriptures and their relegation to the level of mythology or fable. One of the first people to make his mark in this way in the history of the Church was a man by the name of Marcion (died *c.*160), who concocted a personalised blend of Gnosticism and formed his own canon of Scripture consisting of an abridged Gospel of Luke and ten of the Pauline letters. He believed that the God of the Old Testament was unjustifiably violent and vastly inferior to the Father of the Lord Jesus in the New Testament. That gentle Church father, Polycarp (*c.*70 – *c.*155/160), referred to Marcion as the 'first-born of Satan', and his teaching wielded great influence in the Church until the fifth century when it was absorbed into Manichaeism. However, his anti-Old Testament legacy has lingered long, and regularly features as a hallmark of all those who seek to undermine the person and work of Jehovah-Christ.

The reasons for this rejection of the Old Testament are easy to discern. First, there is a continuity between the Old and New Testaments which, if they are rent asunder, makes both portions of Scripture meaningless. As Augustine of Hippo put it, *'The New in the Old is latent; the Old in the New is patent'*. Let us not forget the fact that Jesus regarded the entire Old Testament as the inspired Word of God which could never be broken (e.g., Jn.10:35; Lk.24:27,44). He frequently quoted it authoritatively, and both He and the Apostles clearly viewed His life and death as a fulfilment of Old Testament prophecy (*'It is written...'*).

In the Neo-Gnostic view, the Old Testament is reduced to the 'fabulous' — a series of allegorical fables designed to show certain spiritual realities. This can take many contrasting forms. In the early 1970s, a book came out by John Marco Allegro, professor of Semitic Languages at Manchester University and translator of the Dead Sea Scrolls, entitled 'The Sacred Mushroom and the Cross'. In this work, it was claimed that the Bible — the Old Testament in particular — was an elaborately woven fabric of allegorical tales put together by an hallucinogenic, mushroom-eating fertility cult. In this work it was claimed, among many other things, that Esau (who was a ruddy, hairy man) symbolised the red-topped and hairy psychedelic fungus *Amanita Muscaria.* One had to marvel at the ways in which familiar Bible stories could somehow be forced to support this theory — all of which had eluded students of the Bible for almost two thousand years. Naturally, the author became rich on the proceeds and retired to a tax haven in the Isle of Man!

There is no end to the methods used by the Neo-Gnostics to twist and subvert the Old Testament Scriptures in support of their cause. The present writer once attended a series of seminars unfolding this 'fabulous' understanding of the Bible, in which it was claimed that the Children of Israel's flight from Egypt into the wilderness symbolises the escape of the 'Inner Self ' from enslavement to the ego-mind, that Joseph's multi-coloured coat represented his etheric 'aura', that Goliath symbolises the outsized human-ego which has to be 'killed' through the resolve of the childlike 'Inner Self ' (David), and so on, *ad nauseam.*

It is certainly true that there are many symbolic elements in the Old Testament — 'types', as they are known. But we would interpret the symbolism in a very different way from the Gnostics. Far from reducing the O.T. to a series of mere myths, these symbols strengthen and highlight its infallible connection with the New Testament. For all these types find their 'antitypes' or fulfilment in the N.T., and were prefiguring later events so that they would be more easily understood and accepted when they came to pass. For example, the judgement of the Flood prefigured the Final Judgement to come, the O.T. sacrifices prefigured the sacrifice of Christ, the deliverance of the Children of Israel from Pharaoh typified the deliverance of believers from Satan, the slaying of Goliath by David prefigured the destruction of the Antichrist (and his mentor, Satan) by the Lord Jesus Christ, and so on. However, the crucial difference between the Christian believer's understanding of these symbolic elements and that of their Gnostic counterparts is that these events were not only symbolic of future events but that they were also *real historical events in themselves.* The great strength of this symbolism lay in the fact that God had actually foreordained that historical events should provide a matrix in which the Old Testament people could apprehend the future, and, conversely, that through these events in the past we in the Church can today have an even fuller understanding of the more recent episodes which they prefigured.

The crucial importance of the Old Testament to the Christian faith cannot be stressed enough. Yet many believers have scant regard for it today, believing it to have been superseded by the New. Such a mistake has grave consequences for the future of Christianity. As one writer warns:

> 'The fact that Gnosticism, like certain later movements, ties rejection of the Hebrew Old Testament to fresh superstitions and an interest in the occult, helps us to see the cardinal importance of the Old Testament for Christian orthodoxy. The major doctrines of Christianity are indeed drawn from the New Testament, and superficially it might appear as though the Old Testament is of interest chiefly as background. As a matter of fact, however, it is the Old Testament that guarantees the

> rootedness of Christ, his person, and his work in real history. Whenever the Old Testament is ignored or reduced to mere Jewish religious thought, Christians fall prey to various mythologies and occultism'.[27]

The sinister potential of such an allegorical approach to the Bible for the satanic strategy becomes all-too-clear when one recalls that saying approved by the Neo-Gnostic scientist, Lyall Watson, *'When a myth is shared by large numbers of people, it becomes a reality'*.[28] Therefore, believers must fight tooth and claw for the *unique historicity* of the Old Testament; for without it — as Satan knows only too well — the integrity of the New Testament is brought into question, and thereby the very foundations of the Christian Gospel. The two Testaments must stand or fall together.

6. 'DELIVERANCE' FROM EVIL: The Depersonalising of the Devil

One of the most far-reaching aspects of the world-view of the New Gnosticism is its flat denial of the objective fact that evil has taken root in the cosmos, due to the original intervention of wicked angelic hosts. There is never the remotest hint in all the material being channelled from spirit-entities about an ongoing spiritual battle of primitive origins. It is always assumed that all channelled messages come from benign beings, and that any evil aspects in the Universe are a mere projection of the minds of people who are not very highly evolved. To make any suggestion of conflict in these circles will elicit accusations that one is projecting one's own 'screwed-up state' onto the world and that one should immediately seek psycho-spiritual help to get sorted out.

Readers will recall how the New Age business training consultant Peter Russell claimed that the biblical references to Jesus Christ depict the 'Inner Christ' in all people, and that Satan or Antichrist represents the individual 'ego-mind' which must be eliminated. It is easy to discern the reason behind such an allegorisation of the Book of Revelation. Once Satan has been effectively depersonalised and made to symbolise the human ego, not only is the structure of the Bible completely transformed, but its entire eschatology is radically altered, as we can see from Peter Russell's subsequent interpretation of the New Jerusalem as symbolising

> 'a world freed from the dictates of our ego-mind, a world in which a liberated mind is the norm rather than the exception... There will, at last, be peace on earth — the inner peace we have been seeking all along".[29]

Contrary to this teaching, Jesus tells us not to imagine that He came to bring peace on earth, saying, *'I did not come to bring peace but a sword'* (Mt.10:34). He taught that the Gospel will naturally divide groups and families, and that this

---

[27] Harold O.J. Brown, *Heresies: The Image of Christ in the Mirror of Heresy and Orthodoxy from the Apostles to the Present* (Baker, 1984), p.51.

[28] Lyall Watson, *Lifetide* (Hodder & Stoughton, 1979), p.158.

[29] Peter Russell, *The White Hole in Time: Our Future Evolution and the Meaning of Now* (Aquarian Press, 1992), p.178.

will not be resolved until the end of the Age when *'the angels will come forth, separate the wicked from the just, and cast them into the furnace of fire'* (Mt.13:49-50). This separation, which heralds the beginning of the New Jerusalem, has nothing whatsoever to do with 'Inner Selves' being liberated from 'ego-minds'. It is a real event which happens to real, morally responsible individuals, and which will cause considerable *'wailing and gnashing of teeth'* (Mt.13:50).

Because, in the world-view of the Neo-Gnostic, the being called Satan is merely a symbol of the human ego, conflict only occurs as a result of the ego-mind standing in the way of psychic liberation. Eradicate the ego and the world will be transformed. This, in turn, determinines the Neo-Gnostic comprehension of evil and the presence of malfunction in the cosmos. In the light of these claims, certain questions must be raised: Who or what were the demons which Jesus cast out of so many people during His earthly pilgrimage? Were they just projections of malicious 'thought forms', as the Neo-Gnostics suggest? Or was Jesus merely paying lip-service to the religious ideas of the time by speaking in demonological terms, as the theological modernists believe?

The Bible clearly shows that the Lord Jesus Christ accepted the concept of a vast pantheon of demons which operate under the leadership and authority of an evil personal being called Satan (Mt.12:22-28). He also taught that *'the devil and his angels'* were morally responsible personal beings who were destined to spend eternity in hell when the Final Judgement comes at the end of this present age (Mt.25:41; cf. Rev.20:10). Furthermore, Jesus clearly spoke of Satan as having been a real person who was *'ruler of this world'* at the time of His Incarnation, and who He had come to overthrow (Jn.12:31). He also depicted Satan as a personal being who invented the lie at the outset of human history and who brought death into the world (Jn.8:44). The Apostle John concurs with this when he says that the devil was a being who was morally responsible, having *'sinned from the beginning'*, and that the Son of God had become incarnate precisely to *'destroy the works of the devil'* (1 Jn.3:8). All the writers of the New Testament mention the actuality of demons or evil angels as personal beings (e.g., 1 Cor.10:20-21; 1 Tim.4:1; Jas.2:19; Rev.6:14).

The many people who were portrayed as afflicted with demons in the Scriptures are not shown to be the victims of their own intransigent egos, but are depicted as being oppressed and possessed by actual entities with a personality who were addressed as such by the Lord Jesus and those He empowered to cast them out (e.g., Lk.8:2 & 30). The Apostle Paul speaks in very clear terms about the fact that believers are involved in a cosmic spiritual battle against all *'the wiles of the devil'* under whose jurisdiction operates a vast horde of spirit-entities, who are *'the rulers of the darkness of this world'* (Eph.6:11-12).

It is clear that Satan has written the agenda of the Neo-Gnostics concerning the devil and his wicked henchmen. To teach that evil spirits are merely projections of the evil minds of 'unevolved' people and that Satan represents the human ego which must be overcome through tuning into 'the Christ within', is one of the most consummate ploys he has yet vomited into the minds of men. In the next section we will look at one of the key derivative ideas to emerge from this depersonalisation of the devil, and from the denial of demonic reality.

7. THE GOOD WITHIN: Denial of Original Sin (and Guilt)

Following closely on the heels of the Neo-Gnostic's mythological representation of the devil comes his denial of the original sin of our first parents. In depicting the Fall as a gradual descent into gross matter and ego-consciousness, the doctrine of the imputation of Adam's sin to all humanity (as taught by the inspired Apostle, Rom.5:12; 1 Cor.15:21-22; cf. Gen.3:1-6; Isa.43:27) is bundled neatly into obscurity.

The New Gnosticism upholds the notion that humanity is basically good, and that if we could only be reformed with meditation, better parenting, vegetarianism, realignment of body energies, relating to 'spirit-guides', surrendering to peace and justice movements, psychotherapy, green thinking, etc., we would be able to get together across the globe and create a beautiful planet teeming with lovely people. It is not difficult to discern the reason why this delusion has come about. Satan has no greater wish than to conceal from his offspring the fact that there has been a Fall into lawlessness, and thereby to deny the great claim of the true Gospel that our subsequent inherent sinfulness has rendered us helpless, lost, without salvation, and in need of a gracious Saviour (Jn.15:5). The Neo-Gnostics' mythologising of Satan and twisted symbolisation of the early Genesis material has so strongly coloured their understanding of the Fall into which humanity has been plunged, that there is no place whatsoever for the idea of the innate sinfulness of mankind. For the modern Gnostic, therefore, the presence of evil in the world is solely a product of human perception rather than having an objective reality. As an example of state-of-the-art Neo-Gnostic thinking on these matters, Findhorn guru Peter Lemesurier rejects the idea of a personalised Satan by claiming it is old-fashioned dualism, and then says:

> 'There seems to be no alternative but to accept the fact that the world was always perfect, humanity was always perfect, and *no imperfection ever entered the picture at all.* What, then, did enter the picture? What entered the picture was *human consciousness* — not merely the generalised awareness of the right brain, but also the focussed, analytical consciousness of the left. It was this latter form of consciousness that then started to divide up the world into categories which formed the basis of all thought and language... The imagined imperfection of the world was always a mere illusion from the beginning. What had happened was that humanity had lost sight of reality as it was. And the only way to improve the situation was — and is — to put human consciousness back in touch with that reality, not least by re-establishing contact with our direct perceptions, uncontaminated by the entirely theoretical categories and judgements of our rampant left-brain consciousness'.[30] [emphasis in original]

[30] Peter Lemesurier, *This New Age Business: The Story of the Ancient and Continuing*

The recommended way here to bring improvement to human existence is 'to re-establish contact with reality', that is, one's 'Inner Self '. Evil and malfunction in the world are simply cured by a shift in perception — a leap in consciousness. Surely, Peter Lemesurier is speaking for every Neo-Gnostic alive today when he goes on to make the remarkable claim that

> 'The Illusion is that the world is imperfect and divided against itself, that the Garden of Eden has been lost to us and needs to be restored. The reality is that all is absolutely perfect as it is, and that the Garden of Eden has never ceased to be'.[31]

These extraordinary words could have been written by Satan himself, as they eradicate every vestige of his evil work from the start of human history. Not only that; an inevitable outworking of this denial of original sin is the teaching that all people who have ever lived will be saved. Although it is true that all people are God's *creatures* and owe their very lives and sustenance to Him, our creaturehood is **not** the guarantee of our adoption into the family of God (Jn.1:12; Rom.8:8-17; 9:8; 2 Cor.6:18; Gal.4:5-6). The erroneous teaching that *all* are in God's family — and thereby in His favour — ignores not only countless references to the special election and predestination of those chosen by God in His mercy to be a part of His family and kingdom (e.g., Mt.11:25; 20:16; 25:34; Lk.8:10; 10:20; 18:7; Jn.6:37-39,44-45; 10:2-4,25-29; 17:2,6,9; Rom.8:28-30; Eph.1:4-5,9-11; etc.), but also the many statements by the Lord Jesus Himself which proclaim the uncomfortable truth that not all are going to be saved (e.g., Mt.13:24-30,38-42; 22:11-14; Lk.20:45-47; Jn.3:36; 5:28-29; etc.).

8. THE GOD WITHIN: Universal Divine Consciousness

Another favourite teaching in the satanic gospel of the New Consciousness is that because man was created in the image of God, there is something of the essence of God in each one of us — known in Neo-Gnostic jargon as *'The Divine Consciousness'* or *'The Doctrine of the Inner Light'* or *'The Higher Self'*. As we have already shown in the previous chapter, the claim is made that we can readily tap into this inner divinity through consciousness-altering techniques and thereby attain personal Godhood. This teaching of 'the God within' is not only the most fundamental of all the tenets of the New Gnosticism , but it has been the mainstay of shamanism and Eastern mysticism for millennia. It is our strong conviction that during the coming years, this teaching will become one of the prime ways that the corrosion of the Christian Gospel will be hastened. For this reason, it is most important for believers to be able to refute entirely the idea that all people have God indwelling them. For if this is true, then it removes the exclusive nature of Chrisian salvation over against the claims of all the world religions.

Once again we find that this concept has come about through the diabolic characteristic of plucking texts from the Bible, then applying them out of context in

---

Quest to Bring Down Heaven on Earth (Findhorn Press, 1990), pp.213-214.

[31] Ibid., p.232.

order to support a personal philosophy and to claim biblical endorsement for teachings which are entirely at variance with the mind of God. Three Old Testament passages are used by Neo-Gnostics to support their claim that all people have a spark of indwelling divinity. Let us examine these texts.

A prime Old Testament passage used to support the Gnostic idea of God indwelling every creature occurs in Psalm 46:10, from which an erroneous rendering is constructed so that it reads: *'Be still, and know God'*. The idea is that all people have to do is to 'be still' — which is usually interpreted in Neo-Gnostic circles as the act of transcendental-style meditation or other activity to numb the mind — and then they will attain 'God-consciousness', i.e., 'know' that they are God. Again, this is a perversion of the Scripture, removing it from its true context. The text does not advise readers to *'be still, and know the God within'*. Instead, as the context makes clear, the Lord is commanding His enemies (and those of His people) to cease from their battling and recognise His divine authority and power in the earth. The Hebrew word translated as 'still', *raphah*, means 'cease' or 'desist'. So when God says, *'Be still, and know that I am God'*, He is really saying here: *'Cease from all your foolish turmoils and recognise that **I am** God, and that you cannot resist Me or confound My people'*.

The second Old Testament text used by Gnostics to prove the doctrine of 'the God within' occurs in the Book of Job (34:14-15), in which some translations of a saying of Elihu can give the impression that God's Spirit indwells every person. Turning to the original Hebrew, a literal translation reads:

> 'If He sets his heart on man, if He gathers to Himself his spirit and his breath, all flesh shall perish together, and man shall turn again to dust'.

It is the spirit and breath *of man* — his God-given life-force — which is being referred to here as being withdrawn, not the indwelling Holy Spirit of God (note the capitalisations of the pronouns referring to divinity). As John Gill points out in his comment on this verse, the *'spirit'* which is 'gatherered in' to God in Job 34:14 is

> 'not His own Spirit and breath, drawing in and retaining that within Himself, and witholding the influence of it from His creatures; but the spirit and breath of man, which are from God, and which, as He gives, He can gather when He pleases'.[32]

In fact, in support of this, Elihu makes a statement earlier in his discourse in Job, saying, *'The Spirit of God has made me, and the breath of the Almighty gives me life'* (Job 33:4). This does not at all imply that Elihu believes God has imparted a spark of divinity into his being. It simply refers to the creative and upholding power of the Spirit in his life. King Solomon also refers to the same phenomenon when he says that at death *'the spirit (or breath) will return to God who gave it'* (Eccl.12:7). Again, although human life is certainly created and upheld by God's Spirit, it is the spirit (lifeforce) *of man* that is being referred to by

---

[32] John Gill, *An Exposition of the Old Testament* (Mathews & Leigh, 1810), Vol. III, p.466.

Solomon, not the Holy Spirit of God or any form of indwelling divine essence.

This same idea holds true in Psalm 104:29-30, another text alleged to support the Gnostic doctrine of 'the God within'. Here, in a wonderful outburst extolling God's creation and His sovereignty over it, the psalmist says to the Lord, *'You take away their breath, they die and return to their dust. You send forth Your Spirit, they are created; and You renew the face of the earth'*. However, there is no suggestion here of the pantheistic notion of indwelling divinity in God's human creation. All that these verses show is that all life is dependent on God for its sustenance, and that it is the Spirit of God which is involved in creation and renewal.

However, having shown that these texts in the Book of Job and the Psalms refer to the lifeforce which God upholds by His Spirit rather than the indwelling Spirit of God, it would be most beneficial for us to turn our attention to the original creation of the first man Adam. For, in doing so, we will learn much about the true nature of the spiritual relationship between God and man, as well as about Satan's strategy in respect to this doctrine of 'the God within'. In the Book of Genesis, there is one verse on this matter which says:

> 'And the LORD God formed man of the dust of the ground, and breathed into his nostrils the breath [spirit] of life; and man became a living being' (Gen.2:7).

When the Neo-Gnostics come to this text, they read it as if it proves that the 'spirit of man' is of the same essence as the Spirit of God. For example, the Franciscan monk Brother Ramon, states:

> 'God breathed his life-giving *ruach* [Hebrew for spirit or breath] into Adam's nostrils and he became a living soul... In the Bible the breath of man is a manifestation of the breath of the Eternal Being'.[33]

Here he simply assumes that the human spirit (the 'breath of man') can be directly identified with the Spirit of God and that this is every person's natural heritage. This is tantamount to the deification of man. The claim is made by all Neo-Gnostics that through the degeneration of human consciousness, human beings have lost contact with that original 'god within' imparted to man in the creation. Having been obscured by the development of a 'false self', they assert that all that is necessary to 'rediscover' it, or 'rekindle' it, is to use certain meditation techniques which will radically alter our consciousness and bring us once more into contact with our ancient heritage. How do these claims square up to the biblical data?

It is certainly the case that Adam must have had the indwelling Holy Spirit as part of his original creation when God breathed the breath of life into him; but this is not at all to be identified with the Gnostic's 'god within' or the mystical notion of a universal indwelling 'spark of divinity'. The teaching that Adam had the indwelling Holy Spirit is surely a fundamental canon of the Christian faith,

---

[33] Brother Ramon, *A Hidden Fire: Exploring the Deeper Reaches of Prayer* (Marshall Pickering, 1985), pp.71-72.

resting primarily on the relationship between Adam and Christ. The Apostle Paul says that Adam, to whom he refers as *'the first man Adam'* (1 Cor.15:45), was *'a type of Him who was to come'* (Rom.5:14), that is, the Lord Jesus, whom he refers to as *'the last Adam'*. In Rom.5:12-14 and 1 Cor.15:20-49, Paul shows the clear analogy between the two Adams: The first Adam brought sin and death into the world through his seduction by Satan; the Last Adam overturns this through His obedience and successful resistance of Satan. If the last Adam had the Spirit, then by analogy the First Adam must have done also. As George Smeaton puts it in an analysis of Gen.2:7 in his excellent work on the Holy Spirit:

> 'The doctrine that man was originally, though mutably, replenished with the Spirit, may be termed the deep fundamental thought of the Scripture-doctrine of man. If the first and second Adam are so related that the first man was the analogue or figure of the second, as all admit on the authority of the Scripture (Rom.5:12-14), it is clear that, unless the first man possessed the Spirit, the last man, the Healer or Restorer of the forfeited inheritance, would not have been the medium of giving the Spirit, who was withdrawn on account of sin, and who could be restored only on account of the everlasting righteousness which Christ brought in (Rom.8:10)... No one, in fact, can read the action of Christ on the first evening after His resurrection, and consider the symbolic breathing on the disciples [Jn.20:21-22], and the words which fell from Him in conveying a new gift of the Spirit, without an impress that *these two acts were counterparts* — the one [in Gen.2:7] the original gift, the other [in Jn.20:22] the restoration of what was lost'.[34]

Does all this mean that people have God unconditionally indwelling them, as the Gnostics would claim? Not at all. For the Holy Spirit was withdrawn from Adam as a result of his fall into sin. The one who had been made in the pure image of God could no longer be described as such. Now it could be said of him: *'The heart is deceitful above all things, and desperately wicked'* (Jer.17:9) and *'the imagination of man's heart is evil from his youth'* (Gen.8:21). From the following generation onwards, men could only cry out: *'Behold, I was shapen in iniquity; and in sin did my mother conceive me'* (Ps.51:5, A.V.). The Lutheran Formula of Concord (1580) makes a sweeping affirmation on this post-Fall human condition, which brilliantly sums up its totality:

> 'Original sin in human nature is not only a total lack of good in spiritual, divine things, but at the same time it replaces the lost image of God in man with a deep, wicked, abominable, bottomless, inscrutable, and inexpressible corruption of his entire nature with all its powers,

---

[34] George Smeaton, *The Doctrine of the Holy Spirit* (Banner of Truth, 1974), pp.15-17. George Smeaton was Professor of New Testament Exegesis at Free Church of Scotland College in Edinburgh from 1857-1889. His two books on the Atonement (Banner of Truth) and that on the Holy Spirit cannot be recommended enough. They shed a good deal of highly original light on the Scriptures, yet never straying beyond them.

> especially of the highest and foremost powers of the soul in mind, heart and will.
>
> 'As a result, since the Fall man inherits an inborn wicked stamp, an interior uncleanness of the heart and evil desires and inclinations. By nature every one of us inherits from Adam a heart, sensation, and mindset which, in its highest powers and the light of reason, is by nature diametrically opposed to God and his highest commands and is actually enmity against God, especially in divine and spiritual matters'.[35]

In the Scots Confession of 1560 there is a similar emphasis concerning the result of the Fall on the image of God in man:

> 'Because of this transgression, commonly called Original sin, the Image of God was utterly defaced in man, and he and his posterity of nature become enemies to God, slaves to Satan, and servants unto sin'.[36]

Far from continuing to possess the gift of the indwelling Holy Spirit — which Gnostics and Mystics interpret as a spark of original God-given divinity or a 'Hidden Self' which can be tapped through meditational techniques — the Belgic Confession (1561) boldly states:

> 'Since man became wicked and perverse, corrupt in all his ways, he has lost all his excellent gifts which he had once received from God. He has nothing left but some small traces, which are sufficient to make man inexcusable. For whatever light is in us has changed into darkness, as Scripture teaches us: the light shines in the darkness, and the darkness has not overcome it (Jn.1:8); where the apostle John calls mankind darkness'.[37]

Consistent with this verdict, in the Heidelberg Catechism, the question is asked: *'But are we so corrupt that we are totally unable to do any good and inclined to all evil?'* To which the answer is given: *'Yes, unless we are regenerated by the Spirit of God'.*[38] The condition of man as bereft of the Holy Spirit and no longer in the pure image of God has spread to every man and woman after Adam and Eve. This is why the Lord could say, shortly before the judgement of the Flood, *'My Spirit shall not strive with man forever, for he is indeed flesh'* (Gen.6:3). Man had so descended from grace as a result of the Fall that he was indeed just 'flesh', bereft of the indwelling Spirit of God. This is corroborated by Jude when he describes sinful man as *'not having the Spirit'* (Jude 19). The Lord Jesus clearly differentiated between two classes: *'That which is born of the flesh is flesh; and that which is born of the Spirit is spirit'* (Jn.3:6); the one is merely 'in Adam', the other 'in Christ'. From the First Adam, the human race has inherited a physical body; from the Last Adam, believers inherit a spiritual body also (1 Cor.15:45). And Paul also made a clear distinction between those who do not

---

35 Formula of Concord, Solid Declaration, Article I, §11.
36 Scots Confession, Article III.
37 Belgic Confession, Article 14.
38 Heidelberg Catechism, Lord's Day 3, Question 8.

have the indwelling Spirit and those who do:

> 'So then, those who are in the flesh cannot please God. But you are not in the flesh but in the Spirit, if indeed the Spirit of God dwells in you. Now if anyone does not have the Spirit of Christ, he is not His'.
>
> (Rom.8:8-9)

Those who do not have the Spirit of Christ are those who are merely the physical descendants of Adam — once born — whereas those who do have the Spirit of Christ are those who have been 'born again' through the regenerating power of God (Jn.3:3). The original sin of the First Adam caused the withdrawal of the Spirit from man; the (sinless) Last Adam restores the Spirit in those who come to Him in faith and repentance. It is only those who repent and believe that have this original gift restored to them (Col.3:10; Eph.4:24). All this means that the Neo-Gnostic claim of a universal 'God within' is a sheer fantasy which goes against both the plain evidence of the Holy Scriptures and the witness of the Church. Perhaps we can now recognise the importance of upholding this original indwelling of the First Adam by the Holy Spirit and the subsequent loss of the Spirit at the Fall. For the only way one can have the indwelling Holy Spirit today is through His restoration in those who believe in the Second Adam, the Lord Jesus Christ.

Strangely, the doctrine of Adam's original possession of the Holy Spirit has received little recognition since the writings of a great many of the Church Fathers who vigorously upheld it. It may be that the neglect of this doctrine is because of a fear that it panders to a Pantheistic view of creation and appears to support the Gnostic world-view of universal indwelling divinity.[39] But this fear is unfounded when the relationship between Adam and Christ is properly understood, and the full effects of the Fall have been grasped. Indeed, the proclamation of this doctrine actually works against the view of the Gnostic, as it clearly places every one of them outside the realm of those who have the Spirit of God!

One of the New Testament texts advanced by the Gnostics in support of their doctrine of 'the God within' is that saying of the Apostle Peter *'...you may be partakers of the divine nature'* (2 Pet.1:4). However, yet again this passage works against the Neo-Gnostic view because it is not addressed to all people everywhere but to *'those who have obtained like precious faith with us by the righteousness of our God and Savior Jesus Christ'* (2 Pet.1:1). Even on their own admission, Gnostics uphold the idea of knowledge (*gnosis*) rather than faith for salvation. So

---

[39] For example, the Jewish philosopher, Philo, who lived at the time of Christ's earthly ministry, argued against the idea that it was God's Spirit which was breathed into man, on the basis that such an interpretation deifies sinful man (*Allegorical Interpretation*, 1:13). But there are two oversights here. In the first place, Adam was not sinful when he was created, and did not become so until he was seduced by Satan. Secondly, Philo makes the typical pagan error of imagining that to have the indwelling Holy Spirit means that a person becomes deified, becomes a god. It is precisely this error which has been propagated in the Gnostic approach to those texts which speak of the relationship between the Spirit and mankind.

this letter could hardly apply to those who propagate the New Gnosticism, who do not rely in faith on the imputed righteousness of Christ for their salvation, but on their own systems and techniques. True Christians, by having the imputed righteousness of Christ and the indwelling Holy Spirit of God, become — through their fellowship with Christ — partakers in the divine nature. *But this does not at all mean that they are partakers in the divine essence.* Being a 'partaker in the divine nature', as one Christian writer has put it so well,

> 'does not mean that man shall give up one nature and assume another, but that he shall become the recipient, through grace, of what the Bible has termed "the glory" of God. What Christianity proclaims is an eternal participation in the Life of God — but not an identity'.[40]

That is the fundamental difference between the orthodox, biblical, Christian concept of the relationship between God and man, and the 'divinisation-of-man' conjecture of all the Satan-inspired religions and cults of the world. To be a participant in the life of God and a recipient of the glory of God — as Adam was and as all believers are — is very different from the notion that one can achieve divinity through contacting 'the God within'.

There is one further New Testament text which is used in support of the Gnostic claim that all human beings unconditionally have a spark of God indwelling them which is waiting to be kindled into flame by consciousness-altering techniques. This is the statement by the Lord Jesus to the Pharisees that *'the kingdom of God is within you',* (Lk.17:21). The rendering of the Greek *entos humon* as *'within you'* in this translation is technically imprecise — and especially so within this particular context. A far more reliable translation is *'in your midst'* or *'among you'*, in support of which J.P. Lange states the following three grounds:

> '**1)** That in this way the antithesis between the external coming [of the kingdom] and the being already actually present is kept more sharply defined; **2)** That the kingdom of God had not been truly set up in the hearts of these Pharisees; **3)** That in Jn.1:26; 12:35; Luke 7:16; 11:20 the same thought which is expressed in our translation is expressed in another way; while, on the other hand, for the apparently profound but really not very intelligible statement, that the kingdom of God is found *in* the man, no other proofs are to be found in our Lord's words'.[41]

An important factor in these verses is that Jesus is not speaking of the *inwardness* of the kingdom, but of its *presence.* The kingdom of God does not come into a person — for that is occult mysticism. Rather, a person becomes an inhabitant of God's kingdom at conversion, as can be shown from many other places in Scripture (cf. Col.1:13; Mt.25:34; Jn.3:5; Acts 14:22).

The successful refutation of the Gnostic teaching of the universal 'God within' is an absolute necessity for believers today. Many foundational aspects of Christianity are made void if this concept is held to be true. A few examples follow:

---

[40] Wolfgang Smith, *Teilhardism and the New Religion* (TAN Publishing, 1988), p.128.

[41] *Lange's Commentary on the Scriptures*, Vol.VIII, Part.2 (Zondervan, 1975), p.266.

- If it can be proved that all people at every stage in history have had an indwelling spark of divinity, then the entire biblical concept of the Fall and subsequent loss of the indwelling Holy Spirit is denied.
- The loss of the Holy Spirit in the wake of the Fall meant that man would die — spiritually as well as physically. The restoration of the indwelling Spirit in believers is their guarantee of eternal life (Eph.1:13-14; 2 Cor.5:5). If all people still have a spark of Divinity which can be activated through various techniques, then this removes the need to receive eternal life from Jesus Christ, who is described as a *'life-giving spirit'* (1 Cor.15:45).
- If all one needs to do for salvation is to 'tap into' the 'God/Christ within' through certain foolproof techniques, then the necessity for the historical event of Jesus' atonement for sin is swept to one side.
- The need for the Son of God to become incarnate is rendered entirely meaningless in the face of a universal 'Inner Christ' who is available 'on tap' to all people at every stage of history, without the need for repentance. For if the first Adam had not lost the indwelling Holy Spirit as a result of sin, then there was no need for the last Adam (Christ) to be manifested in the flesh and to restore the Holy Spirit to those who would follow Him.

If the teaching of the universal 'God within' is true, the list of Christian doctrines which would fall could go on forever. In fact, it is precisely for this reason that it has come to play such a prominent role in the satanic strategy of the Gospel Age. For at the heart of this teaching we find that original satanic lie that human beings can become God (Gen.3:4-6). When Satan told our first parents that they would be like God and never die if they obeyed him rather than their Creator, no sooner had they done so than God's judgement brought decay into the world and the indwelling Holy Spirit was taken from them — which was the complete opposite of what the devil had originally promised! Truly, he was a liar *par excellence*; and he continues to be just as much of a liar today by hoodwinking his subjects into believing that they still have the original 'spark of divinity' — which is how Gnostics will always view the indwelling Holy Spirit — which was given to Adam. And when they 'tune-in' to this 'God within', the 'Higher Self ', in order to awaken it, the Old Serpent ensures that they will have all the experiences necessary to perpetuate the Lie.

9. GONE TODAY, HERE TOMORROW: The Great Reincarnation Hoax

Having shown how that original lie that man can become God is perpetuated by the teaching of the 'universal God within', we will now discover the primary manner in which Satan perpetuates that other original lie that man would never die if he disobeyed his Creator and followed him. Although this lie is perpetuated, to a large extent, through alleged mediumistic contact with the spirits of the dead and through out-of-the-body experiences, by far the most successful teaching has been that of reincarnation, the acceptance of which is now worldwide.

The concept of reincarnation is fundamental to Neo-Gnostic belief. Having been a basic teaching of the Eastern religions from time immemorial, an integral part of many Gnostic and Cabbalistic sects, and part of the teaching of Plato and Pythagoras, reincarnation (or metempsychosis, as it is sometimes called) has developed in the West as a result of the confluence of certain circumstances which have worked in its favour, as well as by the overt propaganda of various individuals. During earlier centuries, the colonisation of Oriental countries by Western powers meant that numerous administrators and officials were exposed to such beliefs and brought them back to the West. Earlier this century, the visits of such gurus as Swami Vivekananda to the Parliament of the World's Religions in 1893 in Chicago, coupled with the wide dissemination of the theosophical teachings of Helena Blavatsky, Rudolf Steiner and Alice Bailey, enabled belief in reincarnation to flourish widely. In theosophical thought — which is the quintessence of modern Western reincarnational belief — each individual comprises a higher self whose natural abode is in a higher dimension than that in which the material cosmos exists. In order to grow into full perfection, each higher self must come down to the material cosmos in a series of lifetimes through which he or she learns and develops spiritually. Conscious cooperation with this process will speed things up to a perfect conclusion. The Ascended Masters mentioned in previous chapters are allegedly those who have come to the end of their incarnational cycle and no longer have need for a material body (although they are apparently able to use one as a vehicle to fulfil their purposes).

The notion of a single 'higher self', which comes in a different bodily manifestation on a repeated basis just does not make sense. For it works out as a kind of docetism as people only *appear* to be individual people but are really phantasms of a mysterious 'higher self ' which is the real thing, but which no one ever sees. But what exactly is this mysterious 'Higher Self '? It is bizarre to suggest that behind every human being there is really an ethereal being which is the 'real person' but which never reveals itself and which just hops from one incarnation to the next like an actor in a one-man show wearing one costume after another? Is each individuated personality just a heap of clothing — a prop — which can be discarded forever by a performer in a cosmic play after he has milked the part for all he can get? There is also an ethical problem in that one can do an evil act without ever having a conscious realisation of its value or effect in this life; and when the time comes in a future incarnation for one to pay the consequences for that act of an earlier lifetime, there is still no conscious realisation of the evil carried out in earlier incarnation. In short, reincarnation creates an ethical nightmare.

Today a number of Primal Therapy groups not only encourage participants to delve back into natal and intra-uterine experiences, but to go beyond into former lives which allegedly have an effect upon our personalities today. In one group attended by this writer, a man was told that he suffered from paranoid tendencies because, in a former incarnation, he was allegedly thrown down a well by his mother as a child in medieval times.[42] A noticeable feature of those who believe

---

[42] This form of suggestion on the part of the therapist to the patient in secular groups is very similar to the suggestions given in the so-called 'word of knowledge' which occurs

in reincarnation is that whenever they speak about their past lives, they never see themselves as, say, a cockroach or a beggar. They have always been some high and mighty personage or great sage. The same holds true whenever one visits a psychic who claims to be able to tell one about one's past lives. Prior to his conversion, the present writer was told by various mediums that he has been an American Indian medicine man, a leading bishop in the early Church, and a famous Indian poet! Somehow, one is never told that one has been a thoroughly evil character or an insignificant insect. Flattery is a great aid to the development of Gnostic spirituality!

The Church first became concerned about this ancient doctrine when the reincarnationist teachings of Origen of Alexandria (185-254), who had been influenced by Gnosticism, began to find many sectarian adherents among believers. His teachings on these matters were officially condemned at the Second Council of Constantinople in A.D. 553. The doctrine of reincarnation was further condemned at the Councils of Lyons (1274) and Florence (1439). The entire concept of reincarnation presents a full-frontal challenge to the Christian doctrines of bodily resurrection and Divine judgement. For the Bible plainly teaches that at the end of the present age, each individual who has ever been alive will be reunited with his or her body.[43] The model for this is Jesus Christ himself, who died, was buried and on the third day rose again from the dead, reunited with exactly the same body which was buried in the tomb. But if it is true that a 'higher self' reincarnates through many lives, there would be some considerable confusion as to which body it would be reunited with! The teaching of the Bible is clear: a person *'passes away and does not come again'* (Ps.78:39). Every human being, without exception, is *'appointed...to die once, but after this the judgement'* (Heb.9:27).

Intimately connected with reincarnation is the concept of Karma, the teaching that bad and good deeds are compensated for in successive lives. However, this doctrine contradicts the substitutionary atonement of the Lord Jesus Christ on the Cross. For it is only through this that one can be wholly absolved of one's sin (Heb.10:1-4), rather than the Karmic teaching that one must work out one's bad Karma through good works in a successive incarnations.

In the parable of the Rich Man and Lazarus (Lk.16:19ff.), we are given a rare biblical glimpse into the world beyond the grave. Although this is indeed a

---

in many Charismatic 'Inner Healing' groups today.

[43] For those who may wonder how a soul can be reuinited with a body which has long since decayed or which was hopelessly deformed, or which has been obliterated in fire, explosion or other trauma, Augustine of Hippo writes: 'Nor does the earthly material out of which men's mortal bodies are created ever perish; but though it may crumble into dust or ashes, or be dissolved into vapours and exhalations, though it may be transformed into the substance of other bodies, or dispersed into the elements, though it should become food for beasts or men, and be changed into their flesh, it returns in a moment of time to that human soul which animated it at the first, and which caused it to become man, and to live and grow', *Enchiridion*, Chapter 88, in *The Writings of the Nicene and Post-Nicene Fathers* (Eerdmans, 1956), Vol.III, p.265. For further information on this subject, read the whole section from Chapter 84-91.

parable, there are certain fundamental principles which come across clearly in this teaching of Jesus. First, there is a retention of identity with the life which was being lived prior to the death. Lazarus did not revert to some 'higher self' after death, but continued to be Lazarus. The Rich Man did not have to suffer the working-out of Karma in future lives to pay for his sins as the Rich Man; instead he was held responsible for his sins immediately after he had died. In other words, it was appointed for him — like every other human being — *'to die once, but after this the judgement'*. In all of Jesus' teaching, He never once gave the remotest intimation that He upheld the doctrine of reincarnation, which is simply another manifestation of the unconditional eternal life (*You will not surely die'*, Gen.3:4) which Satan promised to our first parents in Eden at the beginning of human history.

10. THE OMEGA POINT: Satan's Endtime Fantasy

Our final hallmark of the New Gnosticism involves a spiritualised form of evolution theory which asserts that all things are moving inexorably towards absolute perfection. This utopian theory has been most fully developed by the French Jesuit Pierre Teilhard de Chardin, and has been incalculably influential on the theories of the New Gnosticism. De Chardin believed that the movement of evolution is towards greater complexity and ever higher consciousness, culminating in what he called 'Point Omega'. He puts it like this:

> 'Mankind, at the end of its totalization, its folding-in upon itself, may reach a critical level of maturity where, leaving Earth and stars to lapse slowly back into the dwindling mass of primordial energy, it will detach itself from this planet and join the one true, irreversible essence of things, the Omega point...An escape from the planet, not in space or outwardly, but spiritually and inwardly, such as the hypercentration of cosmic matter upon itself allows'.[44]

Although Teilhard's language was always rather obtuse, the implication here is clear. For those who require a succinct summary of Teilhard's theory of life, culminating in the Omega point, John Ferguson, the former Dean of the Open University in the U.K. and ardent advocate of 'metaphysics', writes:

> 'Man has the power of understanding and transforming the evolutionary process. The movement of history is towards greater cohesion, culturally and psychically. There is a threefold convergent evolution, chemical, organic, psychosocial, in what Teilhard calls the hydrosphere, the biosphere and the noosphere. Mankind is converging into a kind of super-organism'.[45]

This Neo-Gnostic teaching that the whole of humanity — good and evil, regenerate and unregenerate — is 'converging into a kind of super-organism' is

---

[44] Pierre Teilhard de Chardin, *The Future of Man* (Harper & Row, 1964), pp.123-124.

[45] John Ferguson, *An Illustrated Encyclopaedia of Mysticism and the Mystery Religions* (Thames & Hudson, 1976), p.192.

Universalism on a grand scale, for which the Neo-Gnostic claims biblical support in two verses. The first is from Paul: *'that in the dispensation of the fullness of the times He might gather together in one all things in Christ, both which are in heaven and which are on earth—in Him'* (Eph.1:10). The second is from the words of Jesus: *'And I, if I am lifted up from the earth, will draw all to Myself'* (Jn.12:32, author's translation). But these verses have been plucked out of context to support a teaching which cannot be upheld from the Bible. Furthermore, the choice of these verses is highly selective as, in each case, they occur in the context of other statements which completely contradict the teachings of Neo-Gnostics. In his letter to the Ephesians, Paul writes that salvation is an entirely unearned gift from God (Eph.2:4-10), whereas the Gnostic believes that he has to achieve salvation by his own efforts. He also states that Christians are involved in spiritual warfare with evil spirits who rule from the heavenlies over the darkness of this age (Eph.6:12), a view which would be regarded as anathema within Neo-Gnostic circles. Similarly, when the Lord Jesus uttered the words above, they were immediately preceeded by a statement that the world was under the rulership of an evil personal being who he was about to overthrow (Jn.12:31), which the Apostle John informs us elsewhere was the undergirding purpose of His incarnation (1 Jn.3:8).

While the Church warns people to *'flee from the wrath to come'*, the demonic realm whispers in the ears of the world that 'peace and justice can be created on the earth'. But what the recipients of this message do not realise is that it is just *'when they say, "Peace and safety!" then sudden destruction comes upon them'* (1 Th.5:3). Their belief in Satan's lies will mean that, for them, the return of the Lord will overtake them as a thief in the night (1 Th.5:2,4; 2 Pet.3:10).

The place of this teaching in satanic strategy is not hard to discern. For the Old Serpent knows full well from the Word of God the fate which lies in store both for him and his followers. The concept of a future convergence of the creation into a kind of 'super-organism' denies many vital Bible truths such as Satan's 'little season', the bodily Resurrection and personal return of Christ, global judgement, and so on. It represents a spiritualised, planetary version of Emil Coué's positive-thought epigram: *'Every day and in every way, I am getting better and better!'* — a concept which is contradicted by the fact that the Bible shows that the world situation has first to get a whole lot worse, to the point of planetary destruction! Just as he does with other teachings which are fatal to his ambitions, he has invented his own counterfeit version of the time of the end, in which there is no place for the debacle which will overtake him. The utopian conceit of the New Age is an earthbound, satanic concept which does not even begin to qualify as a pale reflection of the reconstituted universe to come.

CONCLUSION

Here we conclude our three-chapter survey covering the founding of the New Gnosticism and its hallmarks. In these chapters, we have traced the development of the spiritual subterfuge of Satan throughout this Gospel Age, and observed the fact that the work of the devil has now come out into the open after centuries in comparative secrecy. Today, in the twentieth century since the coming of the Lord Jesus Christ, we can see the fruits of these centuries of accumulative subversive warfare. As the Church continues to be battered with a welter of Gnostic teachings, one can begin to understand that prophetic saying of the Holy Spirit that the time would come when those in the visible Church would *'heap to themselves teachers, having itching ears; and they shall turn away their ears from the truth, and shall be turned unto fables'* (2 Tim.4:3-4, A.V.). The word *'heap'* here is most appropriate. Never has the flood of false teachers and false prophets within the Church been so torrential. But let us understand well here. The sole purpose of Satan bringing teaching into this world which contradicts that of the Word is in order to destroy the **Church**, rather than the world. This is a profound truth. For he does not need to deceive the children of the world — they are already his. He owns them lock, stock and barrel! But those who have escaped from his authority into the waiting arms of Christ cause him no end of anguish.

The Christian depicts himself as one who is reaching up towards a God whom he can only know through the ministry of the one Mediator, the Lord Jesus Christ; whereas the Gnostic depicts himself as having already manifested his own divinity. Moreover, if Gnosticism was the true Christian doctrine as delivered to the Church by Jesus Christ and the Apostles, then it would never have gone underground with its doctrine for more than a thousand years, while perpetuating itself through secret teachings. That occult path is not the way of the true Christian, who is exhorted to proclaim the Gospel openly. The holders of Christian truth would never go 'underground' with the Gospel in order to keep it hidden for a thousand years or more. It is a mark of the true Christian that he faces persecution with a brave face and speaks the truth boldly without fear of what mere men can do to him. As Jesus said to His disciples: *'Whatever I tell you in the dark, speak in the light; and what you hear in the ear, preach on the housetops'* (Mt.10:27). Let us remember those words of the Lord Jesus, describing His own life, saying, *'I spoke openly to the world. I always taught in synagogues and in the temple, where the Jews always meet, and in secret I have said nothing'* (Jn.18:20). These words alone prove that there can be no 'secret wisdom tradition' or 'esoteric gnosis' in the perpetuation of Christian doctrine.

The Neo-Gnostics of today consist, in the main, of many millions of deceived, idealistic, spiritual vagrants, who want to escape the boundaries of their ordinary consciousness and build their science fiction playgrounds; always searching but never coming to a knowledge of the truth (cf. 2 Tim.3:7). But behind all this, these deluded wanderers are being shepherded, wittingly or unwittingly, by those who are steeped in occult wickedness, but whose minds have been blinded by Satan into believing the lie that they are sublime spiritual beings serving the 'higher purposes' of humanity. Gnosticism, the New Consciousness, the New Age Movement — call it what you will — is nothing more than the deification of man. The devil's perfect work.

The New Gnosticism is Satan's religion rendered respectable to Western atheistic society, and has grown into a deception of international proportions which surely has the potential to fulfill the conditions, foretold in many places in Scripture, of the time when man finally establishes the global basis for Satan's long-awaited earthly kingdom. But our story has only just begun. Having now exposed the biblical background, historical foundations, global strategies and universal hallmarks of the New Gnosticism, in the remaining chapters we will be examining the many avenues and disciplines through which this 'Golden Age' is being effected in science, psychology, women's liberation, mysticism, the professing Church and world religion. All these are caught up in the all-embracing work of the beast whose power and authority are wholly derived from Satan (Rev.13:2), the doomed strategist of an evil age.

Chapter Six

KNOWLEDGE FALSELY SO-CALLED

Science and the Satanic Dream

'O, Timothy, guard the deposit, having turned away from the profane empty babblings and opposing theories of the falsely named knowledge, which some having asserted have missed the mark concerning the faith' (1 Tim.6:20-21).

Having shown the development and growth of the New Gnosticism, together with its vast inroads into the world-system today, we have prepared the ground for an exploration of its work in three key areas of modern culture: Science, Psychology and Feminism. These subjects will form the concerns of the remaining three chapters in this second part of this book, entitled 'the Gods of the Nations'. First, we turn to consider the ancient and modern developments of the discipline of science.

It is commonly held in most Christian circles that the human discipline known as Science, with its manifold researches, is an integral component of the general grace of God towards mankind. In this view — especially popular among theistic evolutionists and creation 'day-age' theorists — the Lord is believed to be gradually pushing back the barriers of existence and enabling the eventual quality of human life on earth to be greatly improved through the collective work of the scientific 'community'. But such a naïve understanding of this branch of human wisdom overlooks a number of highly important factors; not least of which are the total depravity of mankind, the continuing dominion of Satan over his corrupt and doomed world-system, together with the disastrous effects which these have on even the best laid plans of mice and men.

In this chapter, we aim to show that in certain significant branches of modern-day scientific research, the prevailing impetus is not one of altruism but is, rather, the tightening of Satan's grip on the collective unregenerate human mind, alongside a determination to annihilate the already beleaguered biblical concept of the Transcendent Jehovah God of the Bible and the primacy of His unique Deity.

When the Hindu mystic, Swami Vivekananda appeared as the 'star' of the First Parliament of the World's Religions in Chicago in 1893, he claimed that his great ambition was for the realisation of a global, syncretistic dream which would involve the creation of *'a society compounded of Western Science and Socialism and Indian Spirituality'.*[1] We have already discovered, to a large extent, the role

[1] John Ferguson, *Encyclopaedia of Mysticism and the Mystery Religions* (Thames &

played by the latter two elements as components in the New Gnosticism — we revisit Indian mysticism in Chapter 9 — and in the final chapter we will come to understand the role they have played in the development of a crusading, ecumenical, interfaith superchurch. In the present chapter, we will establish where developments in Western Science fit into the spiritual battle for Truth at this crucial time in church history.[2]

Many Christians have a very naïve view of the true aims of the men and women who compile the corpus of knowledge which we call *science,* believing that it is wholly composed of very clever people who are essentially altruistic, hard working and dedicated to the establishment of God's truth on earth. This is an unfortunate illusion. On a mundane level, many scientists are actually involved in the ruthless quest for personal kudos. A great number are vitally interested in undermining the revelation of God in the Holy Scriptures. A few of influence are even hell-bent on taking over the role of God Himself. This may seem to be a very derogatory view of the scientific 'community'; but if we fail to have a true comprehension of what God requires of His created humanity, as revealed in the Bible, then we will have a poor grasp of what is true science and of what is 'science (knowledge) falsely so-called'.

In our Scripture quotation at the beginning of this chapter, the apostle Paul is warning Timothy to turn away from the profane, empty babblings and opposing theories of that which is falsely given the name of *'knowledge'* or, in the Greek text, *gnosis.* Now Paul is not here belittling *every* kind of knowledge, but specifically *those forms of knowledge which do not deserve to be so-called* because it is based on empty, unsanctified theories which oppose the cause of God and truth.[3] The Latin equivalent of the Greek word, *gnosis*, is *scientia*, from which our word 'science' is derived. In harmony with Paul's dictum, we do not seek to condemn *all* science; but only that which does not deserve to be so-called. Science (knowledge) which is falsely so-called can be identified as that which is not in harmony with the righteousness of God's Law, as revealed by the Lord Jesus Christ: Genuine love for the true God and for our neighbours (Lk.10:26-27; 1 Cor.10:31).

Now most, if not all, branches of modern science would claim that they are carrying out their researches for the good of humanity — i.e., out of a love for their neighbour — and this claim could seduce many Christians into believing that all scientists are therefore fulfilling the Law of God. But, even if this was so (and we will dispute it), unless the researches initiated by human wisdom are motivated primarily out of a love for God — with the desire to work in His service and to bring about His sole glorification — then their fruits, by default, will be of

Hudson, 1976), p.207.

[2] Let us not forget that *all* history is church history (after all, it's **His** story!); for all things are for the sake of the Lord's people (2 Cor.4:15) and all things work together for the good of those who are the called according to God's purpose (Rom.8:28).

[3] For example, this is why Isaiah speaks of idol-worshippers as people who *'have no knowledge'* (Isa.45:20). Any ideas that idol-worshippers hold about their idols do not even deserve the title of 'knowledge'. To give it such a title would make it 'knowledge falsely so-called'.

particular service to the cause of Satan. Man cannot serve two masters. This bears out a *leitmotif* which constantly haunts the pages of this book: the 'Law of Godless Reformation'. This law states that all exclusively humanistically-inspired attempts to reform the world (and those who populate it) will lead to even deeper demonic bondage than that from which it was imagined to have been delivered (cf. Lk.11:24-26; Mt.12:43-45).

So often, professing Christians seem to forget that the devil, from the very beginning, has not only been a liar and a murderer, but has also been hell-bent on setting up his kingdom on earth as a demonstration of his imagined superiority to Jehovah, his God and Creator, and in gross, earthly imitation of the spiritual Kingdom of God which the Lord is building. This has been his aim from the commencement of human history. Remember that the 'initiation' which our first parents received from the devil in Eden involved that threefold lie: First, that they could be like God; second, that they could acquire a level of wisdom over and above that with which they had been endowed by their Creator; and third, that they could achieve unconditional eternal life (Gen.3:4-6). Part and parcel of this 'Satanic Initiation' — into which all the offspring of Adam have also been inducted (Rom.5:12) — was the receiving of the fruit of the Tree of the Knowledge of Good and Evil, which, as we showed in the first chapter, involved an intrusion into and a usurping of that knowledge which belongs exclusively to God.

Because that attempted kingdom-building by Satan has never abated throughout the whole of history, it should come as no surprise to discover that many of the areas into which Western Science is now probing with unsanctified gusto can be perfectly harmonised with the parallel Neo-Gnostic developments in Socio-Political Utopianism and Eastern Mysticism. These developments — as we come to the close of the twentieth century — are vitally shaping the cultural, political and religious aspirations of the majority of the world's population. Of course, we accept that there are a number of Christian scientists whose goals are very different to those which we are presenting in this study; but we are here concerned with that which represents the leading edge of secular scientific intent at the close of the twentieth century, especially in the realm of Theoretical Physics: Man attempting to determine his own fate, and that of the universe — the fruit of the usurped Knowledge of Good and Evil.

One of the principal components in the self-determination process which was initiated by the Fall has been the proliferation of religious developments designed to enhance the humanistic aspirations of the world. Accordingly, the massive increase in scientific 'discoveries' throughout the past one hundred and fifty years has led to a comprehensive reassessment of the truths of the Bible — the spread of which had been so influential on the cultural life of Europe and the Americas. A radical part of this reassessment has centred on the interpretation of the nature and attributes of God.

Most scientists — indeed, most non-scientists also — would regard the Bible as a largely irrelevant document, and the biblical God as a hopelessly outmoded concept. For example, Walter Schwartz, the religious affairs correspondent of the liberal U.K. newspaper *The Guardian*, spoke for them all when he publicly expressed the privately-felt question of many: *'Can God be brought up to date?'*. In this highly impious article, he claimed that science has conclusively shown that God can no longer be regarded as omnipotent because *'for millions of years the earth didn't have enough oxygen for him to create life, and for millions of years after that he could apparently do no better than create monkeys'*.[4] Following on from that, he pleaded for the creation of a new religion and a new church which brings together all the strains of the New Gnosticism — including the modern discoveries of the New Physics:

> 'A modern God will need a modern church. Its bishops will include nuclear physicists to teach us about the new frontiers that have made atoms unimportant, demoted the status of matter itself and questioned the distinction between observer and observed. Other bishops will be psychologists. Revealed scriptures will include Bach oratorios. Theology will be an empirical science, constructing its theories on the raw material of religious experience, including, but not restricted to, the shattering events of the Old and New Testaments. It will need, of course, to be a universal global-village church, as attentive to East as to West, but most attentive to the fate of the whole world. An emphatically ecological church'.[5]

We see here Swami Vivekananda's all-embracing syncretistic dream fully realised. Then, as if to emphasise the ephemeral nature of all human knowledge, he goes on to say that this Church of the New Age, which would be wholly rooted in the New Science, *'will have no dogma. Only theories, valid until they are disproved. If creation is evolution, religion must be reformulated continuously'*.[6] 'Only theories, valid until they are disproved'. Surely that is the quintessence of the modern scientific paradigm. For this reason alone, it is a great mystery that so many Christians should devote their energies to attempting to harmonise Scripture with the scientific theories of men, which, on the admission of those who devise them, have a validity only until they are disproved. Note also in this quotation, the fact that it is acknowledged that evolution theory renders a permanent and final revelation of God (as represented in the Scriptures) to be impossible, due to the fluctuating nature of all things which evolve — religion included. Scripture, however, is unequivocal: Heaven and earth (which includes the pathetic theories of men) will pass away, but God's Word will *never* pass away.

Throughout the remainder of this chapter our purpose will be to show that in much of the development of scientific research and methodology, the prime

4 *The Guardian*, 17th March 1986. This quotation, alone, shows how important it is to maintain the miraculous, Creationist account of the origins of the universe. Those Christians who advocate a billion-year-old earth, involving massive geological ages instead of literal days, are advocating the same 'impotent God' theory which causes so much ridicule from these secular commentators.

5 Ibid.

6 Ibid.

motivations have been the killing-off of the transcendent God of the Bible and the promotion of Satan's monist and pantheist philosophy.

I. THE OCCULT DEVELOPMENT OF MODERN SCIENCE

As we have already stated, we are not at all opposed to scientific exploration and research which is rooted in a genuine love for our neighbours and for the one true God. But a major departure from such aspirations has been accelerated at certain points in history, and especially as a result of what historians call the 'Age of Enlightenment', which began in the seventeenth century and climaxed in the eighteenth. We discussed some of the implications for Christianity of this period of history in Chapter 3. Just to remind ourselves of the importance of this in the context of the present chapter, we shall revisit a quotation from a historian who showed that the occult order of the Rosicrucians in the seventeenth century was of great influence in terms of the ensuing 'Enlightenment' and its scientific developments. He wrote that

> 'The denial of the dogmatically rigid restrictions and regimentation of the church, the passionate belief in natural science as the way to all-round progress, the possession of an open world view and the yearning for religious unity and mutuality, the...striving for the harmony of religion and science and above all the call for a general reformation of "the whole wide world" — all of these are integral parts of the secret fraternity of the Rosicrucians. Thus Rosicrucianism, as a transition between the Renaissance and the scientific societies of the seventeenth century, forms a point of crystallisation. In its mode of thinking, one can discern an early form of the Aufklärung [awakening] which in many respects was seminal to the further development of European science and culture'.[7]

The battle between the Word of God and the world of Satan in the arena of human science took on a major esoteric twist with the inauguration of the Royal Society. This respectable national scientific organisation has an interesting pedigree, with its primitive roots in the occult arts rather than in the natural sciences. One researcher refers to this early period of the establishment of scientific endeavour with the observation that

> 'Certain of the individuals most active in [Freemasonry] formed themselves into an English version of the "Invisible College" of the Rosicrucians — a conclave of scientists, philosophers and "esotericists" in the vanguard of progressive ideas. During the English Civil War and Cromwell's Protectorate, the "Invisible College" — now including such luminaries as Robert Boyle and John Locke — remained invisible. In 1660, however, with the restoration of the monarchy, the "Invisible

---

7 Christopher McIntosh, *The Rosecross and the Age of Reason: 18th century Rosicrucianism in Central Europe and its Relationship to the Enlightenment* (E.J. Brill, 1992), pp.34-35.

> College" became, under Stuart patronage, the Royal Society. For the next twenty-eight years, Rosicrucianism, Freemasonry and the Royal Society were not just to overlap, but virtually to be indistinguishable from one another'.[8]

These occult influences are well understood by a wide variety of researchers. According to Christopher McIntosh, a leading scholar of seventeenth century occultism, the stream of Rosicrucian philosophy

> 'constituted one of the influences behind the formation of the Royal Society...Robert Boyle, one of the most active early members of the Society, refers in a letter to an "Invisible College" which he sometimes attended and which may have been some sort of precursor to the Royal Society. And John Wilkins, another leading Royal Society man, knew of the Rosicrucian legend and refers to it in his *Mathematicall Magick* (1648). It seems likely that the Royal Society, founded in 1660, was an attempt to realize in practical terms the Rosicrucian ideals of a brotherhood of learning and enlightenment which would help to usher in the kind of Utopia visualized by Bacon, Andre, Comenius and others'.[9]

Here we have a summary of the major thrust behind the development of modern science: the ushering-in of the humanist Utopia, which is nothing less than the kingdom of Satan which has struggled to come into existence since the time of the Fall. It is this same dominion which Satan's lackeys today seek to exercise in the field of scientific endeavour. Fallen human beings, at the instigation of Satan, have continually attempted to reassert that dominion over nature and the powers of the universe which was given to Adam *before* the Fall; and the scientific drive which began in the seventeenth century was a major expression of that. As the eminent historian, Oxford Reader Frances Yates, puts it:

> 'Bacon's view of the future of science was not that of progress in a straight line. His "great instauration" [renewal] of science was directed towards a return to the state of Adam before the Fall, a state of pure and sinless contact with nature and knowledge of her powers. This was the view of scientific progress, a progress back towards Adam, held by Cornelius Agrippa, the author of the influential textbook on occult philosophy. And Bacon's science is still, in part, occult science'.[10]

It is this 'occult science' of Francis Bacon (1561-1626) which, via the Enlightenment inspired by Rosicrucianism, has provided the impetus for modern science. As the authoritative 1987 'Encyclopedia of Religion' has stated,

> 'The Hermetic axiom, "As above, so below", typical of Rosicrucian teaching, had a profound effect on early modern scientific thought, and

---

[8] Michael Baigent & Richard Leigh, *The Temple and the Lodge* (Jonathan Cape, 1989), p.145.

[9] Christopher McIntosh, *The Rosicrucians* (Thorsons, 1987), p.64.

[10] Frances Yates, *The Rosicrucian Enlightenment* (Routledge & Kegan Paul, 1975), p.119.

> Rosicrucianism — like other occult paths — has been credited with having helped to prepare the way for the rise of modern science".[11]

In an earlier chapter we discussed a document called 'The General Reformation of the Whole Wide World' — the Rosicrucian manifesto which first saw the light of day in 1612 — which was highly influential on seventeenth century esotericism and on later political developments in Europe, including the French Revolution and other movements of 'people-power' in Europe and the U.S.A. Another primary area of the influence of this manifesto was the advocation of a far-reaching reformation in science, of which the Royal Society was the historical and spiritual beneficiary, as well as being the instigator of a stream of scientific development. As one scholar puts it:

> 'Rosicrucian vision was therefore both traditional and radical, both theological and scientific... It looked forward to an age when religion and science would work hand in hand'.[12]

Religion and science working hand-in-hand. There was, therefore, a *hidden agenda* behind the work of the occultists and esotericists of the seventeenth century and the more humanistic perpetrators of the Enlightenment who came in their wake. That hidden agenda concerned the overthrow of biblical doctrine and the religious ideas of the Church which claimed to represent the same. In the pursuit of this aim, science was seen to be the most influential area in which this hidden agenda could operate; and by the mid-nineteenth century, enough ground had been gained for the inception of the most radical, antichristian, scientific concept yet: The Theory of Evolution.

It is no exaggeration to say that the heart of antichristian reformation in the development of Western science really began in earnest with the advent of evolution theory or 'Darwinism', as it should perhaps more accurately be known. This theory has had a monumental impact on contemporary politics, philosophy, religious systems and the whole panorama of science itself. In many ways, it has provided the ideal backdrop to the satanically-planned demise of the Christian faith and of biblical authority. Charles Darwin himself, according to biographers Adrian Desmond and James Moore, *'had written in his covert notebooks that the human mind, morality and even belief in God were artefacts of the brain'*.[13] Once such a view of Deity is held — that God is simply a product or figment of the human psyche — a great many facets at the heart of human existence become similarly relegated to the realms of mere relativism. That the developments in science in the wake of Darwin have paralleled the global demise of Christianity, can be seen in this jubilant statement from the thesis of a researcher in the Religious Studies department of Lancaster University:

---

[11] Mircea Eliade (ed.), *Encyclopedia of Religion* (Macmillan, 1987), Vol.12, p.477.

[12] Christopher McIntosh, *The Rosecross and the Age of Reason: 18th century Rosicrucianism in Central Europe and its Relationship to the Enlightenment* (E.J. Brill, 1992), p.26.

[13] Adrian Desmond & James Moore, *Darwin* (Michael Joseph, 1991), p.xviii.

> 'For the past two hundred years, the established religion of Christianity has been on the wane and its churches fast emptying of believers. The old God was losing ground before the demonstrable, repeatable and explainable wonders of modern science. The optimistic scientists of a hundred years ago were positivists. *They were positive that it was just a matter of time before science superseded religion as the highest expression of man's quest for knowledge.* First had come magic and superstition, then religion and faith, now science and certainty. How fortunate we were then'.[14] [emphasis added]

The quaint, Victorian philosophy of evolution — standing in stark opposition to the biblical doctrine of the primitive perfection of our first parents and their subsequent fall into sin — can be shown to be not only wholly unscientific but also reliant on ancient ideas of a distinctly satanic origin.[15] The true basis for its widespread acceptance lies not in any inherent veracity but in the popular desire to be free from responsibility to a personal God and Creator who judges as well as loves, who requires inward righteousness as well as outward worship.

It must be said here that true religion upholds the simultaneity of both the transcendence (objective omnipotence) and immanence (omnipresence) of the Godhead, while false religion generally seeks to deny the concept of a Transcendent, Creator God and upholds the sole concept of a pantheistic, universal spirit ('God is in everything and everything is God'). This is the difference between mysticism and true spirituality. The satanic approach to deity is always based on this pantheism which exalts the element of divine immanence — thus paving the way for the deification of the creature — and nullifies the element of divine transcendence, thereby removing all possibility of a God who judges, or destroys, or saves, or loves, or hates, or just plain ***is***.

The development of evolution theory has been a major component in the realisation of every unregenerate person's dream: namely, the dream of 'deicide' — the killing-off of this God who is 'wholly other' than His creation, which he created *ex nihilo,* out of nothing. For almost one hundred and fifty years, this has been the concerted aim of many in the scientific community. Five years after the publication of 'The Origin of Species' by Charles Darwin, a secret group of nine leading British scientists was formed which was to have a powerful influence on the future course of Western Science. This 'X' Club — as it was known — containing T.H. Huxley and other avowed evolutionists, is credited with having as its business

> 'the politics of the learned societies, projects of new museums and journals, the periodical *warfare with religion* and the classics, [and] the place of science in contemporary education'.[16] [emphasis added]

---

[14] Rogan Taylor, *The Death and Resurrection Show: From Shaman to Superstar* (Anthony Blond, 1985), p.12.

[15] For a far-reaching development of this theme, see Henry Morris, *The Long War Against God* (Baker Book House, 1989).

[16] W. Irvine, *Apes, Angels and Victorians* (Weidenfeld & Nicholson, 1956), p.183.

For thirty years this group of antichristians and opposers of biblical authority wielded enormous influence in the world of religion, education and science. There can be no doubt that their campaign has been a resounding success, for today we find leading churchmen, such as the Anglican Archbishop of York, Dr. John Habgood, bemoaning the fact that

> 'there are still some Christians who try to protect themselves against what they regard as scientific threats to their faith by reiterating that evolution is only a theory. This is a delusion. Though scientists are certainly not infallible, and though sciences change and develop, it cannot be stated too clearly that evolution is not a theory which might be upset by contrary evidence tomorrow or the day after; *it is the only conceivable basis for modern biology*'.[17] [emphasis added]

The view of the Archbishop of York is that of a scientist and philosopher rather than a Christian pastor. He is one of many professing Christians who have 'killed' God and the Bible with their worldly wisdom — gnosis: science. More than four hundred years ago, John Calvin said of such people:

> 'I know quite well that there is no sport more grateful to you Academics than the rooting out of all faith from the hearts of the godly by casting a shade of doubt over all that they hold dear'.[18]

Dr. Habgood is only one among a majority in the scientific community who bear witness to the pernicious effect of evolutionary theory on both the world of science and our institutions of learning. But it is by no means the case that all intellectual heavyweights support evolution theory. For example, Dr. Wolfgang Smith, the Professor of Mathematics at Oregon State University, shows in his superb book debunking the theories of the French Jesuit pseudo-scientist Teilhard de Chardin, that there are many in the scientific field who do not share the Archbishop of York's opinionated belief that evolution theory is 'the only conceivable basis for modern biology'. On the contrary, as Dr. Smith discloses:

> 'The fact is that in recent times there has been increasing dissent on the issue within academic and professional ranks, and that a growing number of respectable scientists are defecting from the evolutionist camp. It is interesting, moreover, that for the most part these "experts" have abandoned Darwinism, not on the basis of religious faith or biblical persuasions, but on strictly scientific grounds, and in some instances regretfully, as one could say'.[19]

---

17 John Habgood, *A Working Faith: Essays and Addresses on Science, Medicine and Ethics* (Darton, Longman & Todd, 1980), p.4.

18 John Calvin (trans. Henry Cole), 'A Treatise on the Secret Providence of God', in *Calvin's Calvinism* (Reformed Free Publishing Association, n.d.), p.259.

19 Wolfgang Smith, *Teilhardism and the New Religion* (TAN Books, 1988), p.1. Dr. Smith's demolishion of Teilhard de Chardin's evolutionary hypothesis is a joy to read — as is the manner in which he brings out the clear connection between Teilhard and the New Gnosticism. For a solid exposition on biblical creation and a worthy debunk-

In his book, Dr. Smith demonstrates that the main problem with Darwinism has been its complete failure to differentiate between *macro*evolution and *micro*-evolution. In the words of Dr. Smith, the latter involves *'relatively minor changes in the structure and function of plant and animal forms...which is precisely what Darwin has very convincingly detailed in "The Origin of Species"'*.[20] Macroevolution, on the other hand, involves *'a change in the underlying form, the very prototype of the organism. Such a transformation would constitute a leap from one of the major taxonomic groups to another'*.[21] As Dr. Smith points out, microevolutionary transformations can indeed be observed, whereas macroevolution — like the so-called 'Hundredth Monkey Theory' we examined in Chapter 4 — is a wholly fictitious projection, an untenable myth developed out of observable data. It would serve us well here to recall the Neo-Gnostic scientist Dr. Lyall Watson's assertion: *'When a myth is shared by large numbers of people, it becomes a reality'*.[22] For this turning of a myth into 'reality' has not only occurred in the claims of the Neo-Gnostics — who are awaiting man's next 'quantum leap' in evolution into a 'psychic superman' — but it is also what has happened in the field of evolution theory. As Dr. Smith states:

> 'The salient fact is this: *if by evolution we mean macroevolution...then it can be said with the utmost rigor that the doctrine is totally bereft of scientific sanction*. Now, to be sure, given the multitude of extravagant claims about evolution promulgated by evolutionists with an air of scientific infallibility, this may sound strange. And yet the fact remains that there exists to this day not a shred of *bona fide* scientific evidence in support of the thesis that macro-evolutionary transformations have ever occurred'.[23]

The significance of the bogus theory of macroevolution to the progress of Satan's earthly ambitions and his strategy during the Last Days cannot be overemphasised. As one writer puts it: *'Every attack on the Christian Faith made today has, as its basis, the doctrine of evolution'*.[24] What so many Christians have failed to realise is that the secret impulse behind the theorising of the evolutionists has been to kill off God. Sometimes this impulse will not only be alluded to but will even be explicitly stated. For example, on the biology shelves of our universities one can pick up an academic textbook at random in which one finds the following explicit assertion of the hubristic claim which lies in the hearts of more scientists than is generally realised:

> 'How can I be so sure that God is dead? How do I know that it is not just a superficial passing of the name of God?— just the death of a

ing of Evolution Theory, see also Vol.6 in Carl F. Henry, *God, Revelation and Authority* (Word, 1976-1983).

20 Ibid., p.5.

21 Ibid.

22 Quoted in Lyall Watson, *Lifetide* (Hodder & Stoughton, 1979), p.158

23 Wolfgang Smith, *Teilhardism and the New Religion*, op. cit., pp.5-6.

24 Wallace Johnson, *Evolution?* (TAN Books, 1992), p.114.

> superstitious understanding foisted upon us by tribal traditions? No, it is the death of the Christian God, One who is now, in our age, absolutely, totally and irrevocably dead! By what right have I to say how he was killed, to describe the method in such detail? I'll tell you how I can do all these things: *because I was there! Because I killed God!* There seems to be no place for Him in our organisation today. He had to go. Man will not play junior partner in a firm he thinks he can run better himself. That is why I killed God'.[25]

These words, written as the conclusion to this biology textbook by a Roman Catholic Dominican priest who is also a scientist, chillingly highlight the extreme hubris which lies behind all satanic inspiration, of which evolution theory is a prime example. The quintessence of evolution does not reside in the fact that it is a scientific theory dreamed up by antichristian scientists of the nineteenth century. It actually has its roots in a dominant idea of the ancient satanic religion: the same idea which forms the ground of the doctrine of reincarnation. This mystical doctrine — the spiritual counterpart of biological evolution — claims that individual souls evolve through a series of incarnations on Earth, on the pathway to 'perfection'; and if there is a single doctrine of modern science which has given major impetus to the modern rise of Neo-Gnosticism it is the Theory of Evolution. It provided the basis for the theosophical speculations of Helena Blavatsky enshrined in her landmark work *The Secret Doctrine*. Indeed, the Theory itself is a wholly Gnostic idea. This concept needs to be grasped. As Dr. Wolfgang Smith puts it so well:

> 'As a scientific theory, Darwinism would have been jettisoned long ago. The point, however, is that the doctrine of evolution has swept the world, not on the strength of its scientific merits, but precisely in its capacity as a Gnostic myth. It affirms, in effect, that living beings create themselves, which is in essence a *metaphysical* claim... Thus, in the final analysis, evolutionism is in truth a metaphysical doctrine decked out in scientific garb. In other words, it is a scientistic myth. And the myth is Gnostic, because it implicitly denies the transcendent origin of being; for indeed, only after the living creature has been speculatively reduced to an aggregate of particles does Darwinist transformism become conceivable. Darwinism, therefore, continues the ancient Gnostic practice of depreciating "God, the Father Almighty, Creator of Heaven and earth". It perpetuates, if you will, the venerable Gnostic tradition of "Jehovah bashing"'.[26]

In the occult echelons of Freemasonry (which also has its roots in the ancient

---

[25] John N. Deely and Raymond J. Nogar (eds.), *The Problem of Evolution: A Study of the Philosophical Repercussions of Evolutionary Science* (Appleton-Century-Crofts, 1973), p.402, n.19. This book was found by the present author on a 'Biology' shelf in the University of York Library.

[26] Wolfgang Smith, *Teilhardism and the New Religion* (TAN Books, 1988), pp.242-243.

Mystery Religions), there is also a great emphasis on Evolution Theory. In W.L. Wilmhurst's book 'The Meaning of Masonry', it is stated:

> 'This — the evolution of man into superman — was always the purpose of ancient mysteries... Man, who has sprung from the earth and developed through the lower kingdoms of nature, to his present rational state, has yet to complete his evolution by becoming a god-like being and unifying his conscience with the Omniscient'.[27]

The theory of evolution is, therefore, the scientific equivalent of 'the Emperor's new clothes' — a belief which becomes 'the only conceivable basis for modern biology' if a person has a vested interest in the death of the transcendent God of Christianity and the promotion of the *gnosis*. It is, essentially, an occult ideology which blasphemes our Creator and logically leads to the deification of the creature.

II. THE STOLEN MANTLE OF CREATOR SPIRITUS

Two of the primary functions of Western Science in the twentieth century — ignoring, for the moment, any philanthropic intentions or the ubiquitous quest for personal kudos — have been, firstly, to find ways of nullifying the effects of the Fall (which, of course, the unregenerate man does not recognise as such) and, secondly, to devise methods of undermining the transcendent existence and sovereignty of God and our true relationship with Him.

In the fields of Genetics and Embryology these aims are being most efficiently realised. Here decisions are taken about matters which should lie under the sole jurisdiction of God. Leaving aside the rampant, faithless, 'family planning' indulged in by so many Christians, such disciplines as eugenics, genetic engineering, 'test-tube' babies, womb implantation, together with other fertility treatments and embryological experimentation must surely be an abomination to our Sovereign Creator.[28] There is even discussion today of using eggs from aborted foetuses in test-tube fertilisation programs — leading to the grotesque prospect of creating children whose true mothers have never been born.[29] The rapid rise of *in-vitro* fertilisation during the past decade has resulted in a growing bank of left-over embryos being kept on ice. It is estimated that there are at least ten thousand frozen embryos suspended in liquid-nitrogen baths in the U.S. which are

> 'stuck in a kind of icy limbo as their would-be parents sort out the options. Do they let the embryos thaw out and die? Do they give them away? Do they have the right to sell embryos to the highest bidder? And who gets custody – or the cash – in a divorce?... "This is the dawn of the eugenics era," declared Jeremy Rifkin, founder of the Foundation

---

[27] W.L. Wilmhurst, *The Meaning of Masonry* (Bell Publishing, 1980), pp.47, 94.

[28] We are not referring here to research which is being humanely executed and which is genuinely seeking to ameliorate the human condition — especially congenital disorders such as *Spina Bifida*, etc.

[29] B.B.C. Radio Four news report, 0015 hrs, 3rd January 1994.

> on Economic Trends, a biotechnology-watchdog group in Washington, [who painted] a dark picture of "standardized human beings produced in whatever quantity you want, in an assembly-line procedure".[30]

When it was announced in the U.S. in 1987 that new forms of animal life currently being created in the laboratory through gene-splitting could be patented, it marked a significant development in this usurpation of the divine role.[31] One Patent Office official has actually acknowledged that this decision could easily lead to the patenting of new human traits — the direct result of a 1980 Supreme Court decision ruling that patent laws include *'anything under the sun that is made by man'*.[32] Through genetic engineering, viruses have now been designed in order to combat agricultural pests. It is one thing to modify one substance into another, but to interfere with the genetic coding of creatures, while creating new creatures by substance, is properly the place of God, which Man is here, in his conceits, usurping to himself. The payoff for such sin could one day be beyond our imagination. Prof. John Lawton of Imperial College, London, claimed that the new genetic engineering technology

> 'is a little like a nuclear power station. It is usually very safe, but if it does go wrong, it goes horribly wrong'.[33]

However, the key threshold in this area was crossed in October 1993, when it was reported to the American Fertility Society in Montreal that an experiment had occurred in which two scientists at George Washington University had successfully cloned human embryos — producing forty-eight clones from just seventeen microscopic embryos.[34] The first recorded animal cloning took place as early as 1952 when frogs were cloned from tadpoles; but agricultural researchers had used such a cloning technique for more than a decade before the George Washington University experiment. However, this was the first time that it had been used for *human* cloning. Although the practice of cloning is outlawed in Germany, Japan and the United Kingdom, it is only a matter of time before the work in the U.S. is reproduced across the world. What will happen then is anybody's guess. As one reporter has put it: *'Technology tends to develop a momentum of its own'*.[35]

The reason for this huge upsurge of work in these taboo areas (in which humanists just love to trample) is not too difficult to understand. As the forces of evil have gathered increasingly in momentum and intensity, so all the multifarious (and often seemingly disparate) factions of antichristian origin will make their own idiosyncratic contribution to the process of world apostasy and accumulated evil. Is it not a fact that *'Wherever the carcass is, there the eagles will be gathered together'?* (Mt.24:28).

---

30 *Time Magazine*, November 8th 1993, pp.66-67.
31 *Daily Telegraph*, 18th April, 1987, p.3.
32 Ibid.
33 *Daily Telegraph*, 22nd August, 1990, p.5.
34 *Time Magazine*, November 8th 1993, pp.63ff.
35 Ibid.

Although the Lord has certainly given us the means whereby we can *ameliorate* some of the ways that the Fall has adversely affected the world and our bodies, there is a definite boundary over which many physicians and scientists have boldly stepped, in their desperate attempts to *reverse* the effects of the Fall. Thus, we find that the thrust behind so much scientific research is either a denial that such a Fall has ever taken place, or else an attempt to recreate the conditions which existed before the Fall occurred. For, if it can be shown that there is no original sin, then there has never been any necessity for the historical intervention of a divine Saviour, and therefore everything can be seen within the context of perpetual improvement.

III. PROBING THE SECRETS OF GOD

Meanwhile, over in the Theoretical Physics department, under the auspices of the 'New Physics', scientists are working flat out to prove that there is no need for the universe to have been created by a transcendent personal God. Although Darwin, Huxley, and the 'X' Club had done a fine job in undermining the Genesis account of the Creation in the popular mind, there still remained the problem that even if the theory of evolution could be proved, God could still be given the credit for having set the ball rolling in the first place. In other words God just might have banged the Big Bang! Scientists have therefore been struggling to rectify this problem. Thus, by way of example, in 1983 — when it was reported that a tiny particle of matter had been discovered which scientists called the 'W Vector Boson' — the physicists declared that it provided *'the key to a new theory for unifying the basis forces of nature'*.[36] This is 'new-physics-speak' for the fulfilment of Man's dream of discovering the secret of life itself — an accomplishment to which he has always aspired.

But is it really a healthy pursuit to probe into the energies and microscopic particles of nature in order to discover the secret of life? Many would say — even many Christians — that it is perfectly natural and wholesome for Man to search for the key to the riddle of life through scientific pursuit. But is it? We wish to challenge this idea, for three primary reasons: Firstly, everything to which the unregenerate man applies himself is destined, ultimately, to issue in chaos and disorder. Secondly, every technological or scientific discovery which is made by unregenerate man will eventually be used in the service of his immediate master, the devil. Thirdly, we should also consider the fact that the Bible, as the Word of God, is the only source for discovering the 'secrets' of life; and even then, only insofar as the Creator has revealed them to us (Dt.29:29). The Christian rests on this revealed knowledge alone, not needing to accrue hidden knowledge solely in order to satisfy his curiosity (Ps.131), for he knows that the desire for such knowledge was a fundamental part of the 'Satanic Initiation' which brought about the Fall of our first parents.

It is true that it was an original 'creation mandate' of God for Man to have dominion over all nature (Gen.1:26-29). But that mandate was given before he fell

---

[36] *The Times*, 25th April, 1983.

into sin, before he brought himself under the powerful sway of Satan, before he lost the image of God (apart from a few small traces) in which he had originally been created. It is, perhaps, significant that this dominion mandate was not identically reiterated by God in His post-Flood covenant with Noah (Gen.9:1-2). Whether or not it is significant, even though fallen human beings have continued to exercise that dominion in the wake of the Fall, they now do so in the service of their master, Satan (cf. 1 Jn.5:19). We are not saying that the original dominion mandate has been abrogated, any more than we would say that the original marriage mandate has been annulled. But just as fallen man corrupts the God-given institution of marriage, so he exercises this continuing dominion over nature in a fallen and corrupt manner. This is a fact which is sadly misunderstood by many present-day Christians who mistakenly believe that the Lord, through something called 'common grace', is gradually building up 'civilisation' on the earth through the manifold endeavours of Man — including those in the field of science.

It is interesting to note that the modern scientific belief that the key to all life can be found through the probing of material nature and particles of matter bears a remarkable similarity to the pantheistic conviction of the Gnostics during the first few centuries A.D., that 'imprisoned' in all matter is a spark of divinity which has fallen from heaven and into which a man can probe to further his spirituality. Just as the Gnostics strove to free the spirit from its fallen state in matter through various mystical practices, so the scientists of today are frantically trying to 'liberate' this 'entrapped' energy on another level; which explains why the mystical occultists of East and West are so keen to encourage them in this work.[37]

The New Alchemy

The 'spark of divinity' alleged by Gnostics and Neo-Gnostics to permeate all things — the so-called *élan vital* — has been sought after by countless mystics and occultists throughout history. Now it is the turn of the psychologists and scientists to do the same. To the Taoists and Japanese Buddhists it is known as *Ch'i* or *Ki*. To the Indians it is *Prana*. To the transcendental magician it is the 'Grand Elixir' or the 'Philosopher's Stone'. To Mesmerists it is the 'Magnetic Fluid'. To the occultist Colin Wilson it is 'Faculty X'. To the psychologists following in the footsteps of the Freudian protégé Wilhelm Reich it is 'Orgone Energy'. To the New Physicist it is known as the 'Superforce'.

Let us not forget that threefold lie communicated to our first parents by Satan in Eden: that Man can be God, that he can have superhuman wisdom, and that death does not exist. The entire thrust of fallen man's every quest ultimately involves the confirmation of these three elements. Through science Man will seek to promote every avenue of possibility for both playing at God and discovering immortality. This is the modern realisation of alchemy.

One renowned British physicist, Professor Paul Davies, relishing the prospect

[37] As we have said in an earlier chapter, for the Gnostic (as for the Buddhist, Hindu, etc.), the idea of a historic Fall does not involve a fall into sin, but the metamorphosis of Man from being a spiritual entity to a material one. In other words, to be made of gross matter is to be fallen.

of science 'cracking the code of life' has written the following statement which clearly demonstrates not only the satanic nature of modern scientific research, but also its links with the occult and alchemical traditions:

> 'Letting imagination have free rein, it is possible to envisage mankind one day gaining control over the superforce. To achieve this would enable us to manipulate the greatest power in the universe... With the superforce unleashed, we could change the structure of space and time, tie our own knots in nothingness and build matter to order. Controlling the superforce would enable us to construct and transmute particles at will, thus generating exotic forms of matter. We might even be able to manipulate the dimensionality of space itself, creating bizarre artificial worlds with unimaginable properties. Truly we should be lords of the universe'.[38]

This is pure witchcraft. Such words could have come from the pen of any occultist, ancient or modern. Yet they come from the current Professor of Theoretical Physics at the University of Sydney, Australia (formerly Professor at Newcastle University, U.K.). In fact, it is the ancient occultic art of *alchemy* that is represented here in modern garb — the use of forbidden knowledge in order to play at being God through altering the structure of matter and consciousness. The two fundamental ideas of alchemy are the unity of all matter, and the existence of a potent transmuting agent. These ideas have their roots firmly planted in the magical practices of Babylonia, Egypt, India and China, coupled with influences from the later Greek Pythagorean and Platonic Schools.[39] In order to demonstrate the similarity between the ambition of Professor Davies and the ancient occult stream of alchemy, Christopher McIntosh, an acknowledged expert on Rosicrucianism and hermetic philosophy, writes:

> 'God, according to the alchemist, has deliberately placed at man's disposal the spiritual and material means by which perfection can be achieved... The alchemist realises that in order to overcome subservience to matter man must understand how matter works and master its processes'.[40]

This 'mastering of the processes of matter' in order to overcome 'subservience' to it is one of the major thrusts in the New Science of today; yet its true origins can be traced back through seventeenth century occultism to the fount of all human 'wisdom': the Satanic Initiation in Eden. In recognition of the fact that sorcery and modern science have become intertwined, the internationally-renowned witch and High Priestess of the Covenant of the Goddess, Starhawk, has written that *'the theoretical model that Witches use to explain the workings of magic is a clear one and coincides in many ways with the "new" physics'.*[41] This is surely

---

[38] Paul Davies, *Superforce* (George Allen & Unwin, 1986), p.1.

[39] *Chambers's Encyclopaedia*, Vol.I, (George Newnes, 1959), p.229.

[40] Christopher McIntosh, *The Rosicrucians: The History, Mythology and Rituals of an Occult Order* (Crucible, 1987), pp.77-78.

an apocalyptic statement.

Not surprisingly in these apostate times, even professing Christian leaders are voicing their approval of the new hubris in science. The Archbishop of York, the scientist Dr. John Habgood, in his contribution to a fourteen-page special scientific report entitled 'In the Beginning there was the Program' — a secular look at the origins of life — concluded with the extraordinary statement:

> 'There is the world of material things, on the whole operating by fixed laws. Science depends on this fixity. And this is *'the earth'*. Then there is the future and the realm of possibility. That is *'heaven'*. We need the past. We learn by it and are guided by it. But sometimes we are trapped by it. But we are creatures of freewill. We have the choice. We can be freed from the past. That is what Christians mean by salvation. Whatever has been written in The Program of the past, it is possible for each one of us to rewrite it for the future'.[42]

One could write a book on the discrepancy between this statement and the truth of the Holy Scriptures. The fact that two of the Archbishop's co-authors in this special report were the New Age biologist and Krishnamurti protégé, Dr. Rupert 'Morphic Fields' Sheldrake, and the 'new physics' Professor, Paul 'Superforce' Davies, sheds much light on the direction of science in the twentieth century and its interaction with religious principles and 'church' leaders. Alert readers will recall that the hidden agenda of occultists of a few centuries ago involved the harmonising of religion and science. As one historian has put it:

> 'Rosicrucian vision was therefore both traditional and radical, both theological and scientific... It looked forward to an age when religion and science would work hand in hand'.[43]

This agenda has now been firmly realised.

No Place for the God who is 'Other' than His Creation

A torrent of data is being produced by these scientists which similarly incorporates many facets of occult-mysticism, establishing a clear link between heathen mysticism and the researches of the New Physics, while at the same time striking at the heart of the Holy Bible. While a recent £½M bequest by the late Arthur Koestler to Edinburgh University founded a Chair in Parapsychology (scientistic witchcraft), books such as 'The Tao of Physics' and 'The Turning Point' by U.S. physicist Dr. Fritjof Capra (Berkeley University); 'Wholeness and the Implicate Order' by Krishnamurti protégé Prof. David Böhm (London University); 'The New Science of Life' by another Krishnamurti protégé Dr. Rupert Sheldrake; 'God and the New Physics' and 'Superforce: the Search for a Grand Unified

---

[41] Starhawk, *The Spiral Dance: A Rebirth of the Ancient Religion of the Great Goddess* (Harper & Row, 1979), p.112.

[42] *Sunday Mirror*, 8th November, 1987.

[43] Christopher McIntosh, *The Rosecross and the Age of Reason: 18th century Rosicrucianism in Central Europe and its Relationship to the Enlightenment* (E.J. Brill, 1992), p.26.

Theory of Nature' by Prof. Paul Davies (formerly of Newcastle University, now of the University of Sydney, Australia); and many more, have all made a major contribution towards the presentation of the Transcendent sovereign Lord and Father of the Scriptures as an irrelevant anachronism. To gain a sense of what it is that Western Science is now working towards, note these words which were written some years ago by one of the top physicists in the U.K:

> 'There is a growing feeling that science, especially what is known as the New Physics, can provide answers where religion remains vague and faltering... I believe the New Physics sweeps away much of the traditional imagery of God 'out there', embedded in absolute time. Outmoded concepts have been replaced by an astonishing collection of new ideas, abstract and sometimes bizarre, *which could dictate the shape of religion in the coming generations.* The richness and subtlety of the New Physics is proving compulsive to those searching for a modern explanation of existence'.[44] [Emphasis added]

It is not surprising that the New Physics and Eastern mysticism should have so much in common. They are both wilfully attempting to probe the hidden energies by which God sustains the universe — their projected *élan vital* — for their own selfish ends. The new physicists are working to trace and catalogue its manifest qualities in *outer space,* while the mystics and transpersonal psychologists are seeking to become unified with it through personal experimentation in *inner space* (e.g., meditation, trance, hallucinogenic drugs, psychotherapy, etc.). As the gnostic psychologist, C.G. Jung put it, writing in 1951:

> 'Sooner or later, nuclear physics and the psychology of the unconscious will draw closer together, as both of them, independently of one another and from opposite directions, push forward into transcendental territory... If research could only advance far enough, therefore, we should arrive at an ultimate agreement between physical and psychological concepts'.[45]

What has happened is that both these groups have stumbled upon the fact that they are chasing the same pot of gold at the end of the metaphysical rainbow: the new physicists working from the 'outside' inwards, the mystics and transpersonal psychologists working from the 'inside' outwards. Both approaches reduce God from the personal, omnipotent, transcendent Creator God of the Bible to a 'Universal Spirit' — a 'Superforce' which they hope will provide the key to unlocking their own ability to gain absolute mastery of themselves, their destiny, and that of the universe. Thus, they become gods, festooned in immortality — the embodied satanic dream.

This arrogant desire to gain intimacy with the mind of God is tellingly illustrated in the populist work of such men as Prof. Stephen Hawking of Cambridge

---

[44] Paul Davies writing in the *Sunday Telegraph Magazine*, 1983, month unmarked.

[45] C.G. Jung, *Aion: Researches into the Phenomenology of Self* (Routledge & Kegan Paul, 1981), p.261.

University. Along with the majority of leading scientists today, Prof. Hawking is seeking to 'probe the divine' but without the benefit of the only true source of divine revelation, the Bible. The concluding paragraph of his best-selling book bringing New Physics to the masses reads:

> 'However, if we do discover a complete theory, it should in time be understandable in a broad principle by everyone, not just a few scientists. Then we shall all, philosophers, scientists, and just ordinary people, be able to take part in the discussion of why it is that we and the universe exist. If we find the answer to that, it would be the ultimate triumph of human reason — for then we would know the mind of God'.[46]

Cobbling together a complete theory of the origin of the universe may represent the *'ultimate triumph of human reason'*, but it will not bring human beings a jot nearer to knowing the true mind of God. For the 'mind of God' (whatever that may be) does not provide a focus for speculative probing by unsanctified theoreticians. God has revealed Himself through His written Word, the Bible, and His incarnate Word, Jesus Christ; He has also revealed Himself in nature (Rom.1:19-20); but these scientists are not open to the simple truths of these founts of revelation. They are too busy seeking a 'triumph for human reason', which is nothing other than the acquisition of wisdom beyond that with which human creatures have been endowed by their Creator (cf. Gen.3:6).

However, in spite of their rejection of the transcendent God of the Bible, Scientists in general, and physicists in particular have, in the last few years, been compelled to come to the conclusion that there might, after all, be a purpose in the unfolding of the universe. This has led to a radical application of evolutionary ideas concerning the development of life, and a seduction of many Church leaders into believing that science and religion now have some kind of meeting-point. Cardinal Basil Hume, for example, naïvely reckons that

> 'science and religion are not in conflict. The new physics and the explosion of astronomic knowledge in fact lead humanity into an inward and outward exploration of reality whose conclusions can only as yet be glimpsed but which appear to be most stimulating'.[47]

However, what Cardinal Hume and so many other professing Christians have failed to realise is that when the theoreticians of the New Physics speak about 'God', they are not referring to the transcendent Jehovah of the Bible or His creative work in the cosmos — an objective Creator who is other than His creation: When they speak of getting in touch with the so-called 'mind of God', they are not interested in discovering what the Lord God has given to the world in His revelation, the Bible. Just like the mystics and shamans, they are referring to a god which is more or less a pantheistic concept. In fact, they will accept anything as God so long as it does *not* resemble the biblical God, the Creator of heaven and

---

46 Stephen W. Hawking, *A Brief History of Time* (Bantam, 1988), p.175.

47 Cardinal Basil Hume, *Towards a Civilisation of Love: Being Church in Today's World* (Hodder & Stoughton, 1988), p.169.

earth. In a newspaper article focusing on Professor Stephen Hawking's ideas and asking the question *'How did the universe begin?'*, we are told that space and time *'can be finite in extent, and yet have no boundary; the universe could have a finite age, and yet have no actual starting point'*.[48] This idea has far-reaching implications. As the writer states:

> 'Hawking's "no boundary" proposal has a far more profound implication. If there was no beginning, then there is no need for something to cause the universe to exist. In short, the "no boundary" idea appears to rule out the need for a Creator... In 1947, American scientists showed that sub-atomic particles are indeed being created and destroyed all around us... A number of researchers now believe that the entire universe may have similarly just "popped" into existence, without the aid of a Creator... It seems that, once again, the physicists have found a way to make God redundant'.[49]

Similarly, when Professor Paul Davies asks the question, *'Should we conclude that the universe is a product of design?'*, he answers by saying that

> 'the new physics and the new cosmology hold out a tantalizing promise: that we might be able to explain how all the physical structures in the universe have come to exist, automatically, as a result of natural processes. We should then no longer have need for a Creator in the traditional sense'.[50]

So what kind of a God do the New Physicists envisage? In his book, 'God and the New Physics', Professor Davies questions whether the 'discoveries' being made in the realm of the New Physics deny the existence of God. *'Indeed not'*, he writes. But he then goes on say that

> 'It makes redundant the idea of God-the-creator, but it does not rule out a universal mind existing as part of that unique physical universe: a natural, as opposed to supernatural God'.[51]

This is the thinking of one of the most popular scientists in the world — a man who brazenly states: *'In my opinion science offers a surer path to God than religion'*.[52] The New Physics is proffering its own religion to the world today. It is a religion which speaks about an 'Ultimate Observer' to describe something akin to what we may call 'God', and refers to an 'Anthropic Principle' in relation to the necessity for the existence of created beings. One physicist speculates that

> 'there is some Ultimate Observer who is in the end responsible for coordinating the separate observations of the lesser observers and is thus responsible for bringing the entire universe into existence'.[53]

---

[48] *Sunday Telegraph*, March 22nd, 1992, Review Section, p.viii.

[49] Ibid.

[50] Paul Davies, *Superforce*, op. cit., p.243.

[51] Paul Davies, *God and the New Physics* (Pelican, 1984), p.223.

[52] Ibid., p.ix.

And he goes on to make the extraordinary statement that

> 'perhaps *all* properties — and hence the entire Universe is brought into existence by observations made at some point in time by conscious beings'.[54]

In a recent BBC World Service radio programme entitled *Journey to the Centre of the Universe*, Professor John Barrow again claimed that *'we are all participants in bringing about something of the universe in the distant past'*.[55] It is impossible to reconcile such statements with the Bible, which opens its revelation with the fact that *'In the beginning God created the heavens and the earth'* (Gen.1:1). In spite of what Basil Hume, John Habgood and other professing Christian leaders may believe, science and Christianity **are** in conflict — and at the most fundamental of levels.

Other influential scientists are also advocating an alternative to the Jehovah of the Bible. The physicist and lecturer at Berkeley University, California, Fritjof Capra — who has written a highly-esteemed book on the connections between the New Physics and Eastern Mysticism[56] — avidly approves the fact that *'feminist spirituality will have a profound influence not only on religion and philosophy but also on our social and political life'*.[57] He is referring here to the goddess worship and witchcraft which is now so prevalent in the Feminist movement. He goes on to say:

> 'The image of a female deity seems to embody this kind of spirituality more accurately than that of a male god. Indeed worship of the Goddess predates that of male deities in many cultures, including our own, and may also have been closely connected with the ancient Taoist tradition'.[58]

Dr. Capra also advocates the way of the shaman (ancient witchcraft) in national health programmes, claiming that

> 'Shamanism can teach us a lot about the social dimensions of illness... The great variety of psychological techniques that shamans use to integrate the patient's physical problems into a broader context offer many parallels to recently developed psychosomatic therapies'.[59]

If we bear in mind that this is one of today's leading scientists in the field of Theoretical Physics, whose writings have been applauded by many 'respectable'

---

53 John D. Barrow and Frank J. Tippler, *The Anthropic Cosmological Principle* (OUP, 1988), p.470.

54 Ibid.

55 BBC World Service science programme *Journey to the Centre of the Universe*, 0515 hrs. September 28th, 1992.

56 Fritjof Capra, *The Tao of Physics* (Flamingo, 1988).

57 Fritjof Capra, *The Turning Point: Science, Society and the Rising Culture* (Flamingo, 1982), p.463.

58 Ibid., p.462.

59 Ibid., p.338. Dr. Capra devotes a whole section here to shamanism.

journals (such as *Nature*), we can appreciate where all this research is really heading. Accordingly, it should not surprise us to learn that the leading New Age journal in the U.K. has said, *'It marks a particular point in history that scientists have started to make these discoveries and are beginning to speak the same language as mystics'.*[60] The prevailing world-view in the New Physics fraternity involves a blend of syncretism and mysticism which discerning Bible students would immediately recognise as more closely aligned with witchcraft and sorcery.

IV. THE 'SCIENTISTIC' RELIGION OF THE NEW WORLD ORDER

The sad fact is that when true religion has been stifled, the people will always be quick to invent a false one (Rom.1:20-23). We now live in a world which scoffs at the devil, angels, demons and miracles of the Bible, yet which earnestly embraces the concepts of ET's, supernatural mysteries, telepathic communication and many other forms of parapsychology (sorcery in a white coat). The need to ruminate on the nature of Black Holes, Quasars and the 'unification of nature' (a monistic idea in scientific garb), has now taken precedence over meditating on the deep things of God. The New Gnosticism — which essentially involves the denial of the biblical Jehovah and the true worship of Him in Christ — has created a scientistic religion which even the Atheist can wholeheartedly embrace. This religion of the New Age — which will provide the spiritual base of the much vaunted 'New World Order' — can be espoused by a Gorbachev or a Dalai Lama, an Adolf Hitler or a fat Gautama, a U.S. President or a 'Holy Father', a scientist or a Swami Rama. It is the religion of the world: the harmonising of socialism, Western science and Eastern mysticism.

Nowhere has the truly ecumenical nature of this new religion been better realised than in the former U.S.S.R., the home of official Atheism. It is a little known fact that in the Soviet Union and now in its successor, the Russian 'Commonwealth', there is more official scientific research into the realm of the supernatural than in any other country in the world. The popular, military, hegemonic image of the former Soviet Union had, in the past, tended to blind the eyes of the world to this phenomenon. More recently, the so-called *perestroika* had a similar bedazzling effect. Yet a large portion of its scientific work — and that of its successor, Russia — has been given over to the study of such subjects as UFOs, extraterrestrials, hypnotism, telekinesis (the ability to move objects with thought-control), Kirlian Photography (a photographic technique which exposes 'bio-energy' emanations from living matter), extra-sensory perception and other aspects of parapsychology (scientific sorcery).

The germane connection between hypnosis and parapsychology is clearly demonstrated in this statement by Prof. Paval Bul of the Leningrad Hypnotarium at the Pavlov Medical Institute:

> 'We are also concerned with the secret powers of the human mind and the mystery of the human psyche. The human brain is the most fantastic of all tools on this Earth. We try to control it, and the

[60] *Global Link-Up*, Editorial, Issue 49, October/November 1991.

parapsychologists try to harness it in a different way... The question is, what sort of matter is involved? Is it what parapsychologists call bio-energy?' [61]

Once again, that *élan vital* forms a pivotal part of this research. There have been many more sinister connections concerning the parapsychological research which was carried out in the Soviet Union. For example, when Leonid Brezhnev gave a speech in the Kremlin on June 13th 1973 *'urging the U.S.A. to agree to a ban on research and development of new kinds of weapons 'more terrifying' than existing nuclear weapons'*,[62] the New York Times reported:

> 'There is no evidence that Brezhnev was referring to something in the field of parapsychology. But it is a possibility that has occurred to some observers, because of the vacillating treatment of parapsychologists, the evident involvement of the KGB with the subject, and what some regard as a traditional Russian interest in mysticism'.[63]

However, Larissa Vilenskaya, editor of 'PSI Research: East West Journal of Parapsychology', confirms that *'official Soviet scientists are interested in using psychic powers primarily to develop* ***extended means for mental influence at a distance'*** [64] [emphasis in original]. This is simply the dressing-up of shamanism in scientific clothing. Interest in this subject is endemic in Russian society. Writing in the journal 'Scientific American', Professor Sergei Kapitsa, president of the Soviet Physical Society, has expressed concern at the huge growth of interest in Russia in ESP, UFOs, clairvoyance, mystic cults and mesmeric healing.[65]

Parallel to the development of scientific sorcery in the Russian empire is the race to make communication with beings from other worlds. The Soviet astronomer, Prof. Mirzoyan, of the Byakuran Observatory in Armenia, has said:

> 'I am certain that we are on the threshold of a major breakthrough in interplanetary communication... It is no more a matter of wondering if there *could* be somebody out there, but *how* to establish the first interplanetary dialogue... We are working round the clock to sift data'.[66]

Recently, a new scholarly journal called 'Social Sciences and Modernity' published by the Academy of Sciences in Russia had an announcement on its back page headed 'Voice from Space', which stated that it would publish *'dialogues with the Cosmic Mind'*.[67] Bear in mind that all this frantic research to develop the 'secret powers of the mind' and to make contact with extra-terrestrials was

---

61 Henry Gris and William Dick, *The New Soviet Psychic Discoveries* (Souvenir Press, 1979), p.233.

62 Ibid., p.291.

63 Ibid.

64 Russell Targ and Keith Harary, *The Mind Race: Understanding and Using Psychic Abilities* (New English Library, 1983), p.239.

65 *Daily Telegraph*, 28th September 1991.

66 Henry Gris and William Dick, op. cit., p.125.

67 Ibid.

initially developed in a country which was supposedly dedicated to Atheism; but it has by no means abated even in the wake of the political changes which have taken place. Here we have clear proof of the fact that unsanctified scientific research, which does not seek to glorify God and which is not done out of a love for Him and for our neighbour, is always in the service of the devil.

It therefore becomes far easier to understand why — even in the 'bad old days' — the Soviet Union was so fêted by such a great variety of liberals and occultists, and why, according to the Times Literary Supplement, the occult writer Colin Wilson is *'among the most discussed English authors in Moscow University circles'*.[68] It also explains why, at a so-called 'Peace Forum' in 1987 in Moscow to which 800 international 'celebrities' had been invited, the Tibetan Buddhist Chief Lama of Ladakh could make the extraordinary statement: *'The Soviet Union is a country of spiritual freedom promoting humane attitudes to the world'*.[69] In fact, what was the U.S.S.R., and is now the Russian Federation, has had a long history of the co-mingling of religion and science. Those Rosicrucian ideals of the seventeenth century have certainly made their mark on the European land mass.

Let us not be deceived: Western Science, Socialism and Eastern Mysticism make up the soup-of-the-day in the progressive cultural, political and social circles of the world. The empty platitudes of the political and religious fraternities will continue to feed the cherished illusions of the people, who clutch onto straws and put their trust in flesh.

V. THE GREAT CHRISTIAN SELL-OUT

We have taken a brief look at some aspects of scientific development today, in order to show the extent of the fulfillment of Swami Vivekananda's dream that science would one day be linked with political-utopianism and Eastern mysticism. Let us be quite clear that in the fields of the New Physics and Parapsychology, it is not mere objective scientific interest or humanitarian altruism that motivates the research. For there are two major scientific discoveries which, in the warped mind of fallen man, hold the key to destroying the biblical concept of the Transcendent Creator God, thereby preparing the way for the 'establishment' of Satan's kingdom on earth. The first 'discovery' would be the 'proof' of extra-terrestrial life; the second would be the 'discovery' of that elusive *élan vital* — the secret energy code of life. It is for this reason, above all others, that Western Science — whether in the Massachusetts Institute of Technology or the Moscow Academy — is concentrating on these areas so avidly. This is the hidden agenda in the world of science: to make the biblical Jehovah a redundant force in the world of man.

---

[68] From the dust jacket of Colin Wilson, *The Occult* (Hodder & Stoughton, 1971). Is it not extraordinary that a professing Christian publishing house should be the publisher of one of the world's most influential and propagandist occult works?

[69] *The Daily Telegraph*, 16th February, 1987. This article refers to what one could call the 'Symposium of Useful Idiots' held in Moscow by Mikhail Gorbachev on 13th-15th February 1987.

But this is no recent phenomenon. The rot set in long before the inception of the Royal Society in the seventeenth century. For the true thrust of human endeavour will always have its roots in the primordial, prototypic desires of fallen nature. It is most significant that science and technology had their first beginnings amongst the ungodly seed of Cain. Derek Kidner's comment on the birth of technology and its subsequent corruption as shown in Gen.4:19-24 is most appropriate to our study:

> 'The immediate conversion of metal-working to weapon-making is... ominous. Cain's family is a microcosm: its pattern of technical prowess and moral failure is that of humanity'.[70]

Great technical prowess and continual moral failure: that sums up the history of our 'glorious civilisation' and its scientific endeavours. Yet most unbelievers imagine that the world is somehow going to stagger through this present evil age, moving ever closer to world peace and technological utopia, the pinnacle of the evolution of man. Many Christian believers, preferring to believe what men tell them rather than what God has revealed, fall into the same erroneous belief (cf. Ps.20:7). How strange it is that so many Christians today — far from turning away from the falsely-called knowledge which opposes the cause of God and truth — are avidly embracing the theories of the pseudo-sciences. The harmonising of Scripture with some of these theories — especially those connected with cosmogony and cosmology — has emerged as one of the great modern arts of neo-evangelical 'scholarship'. Every new discovery revealed by the scientific establishment which *appears* to contradict biblical revelation will be squeezed into an accommodating system in order to 'protect' the integrity of Scripture. In this way, many of the supernatural elements of Scripture have been explained away. But the overriding factor is always the same: that Scripture must never be seen to be contradicting 'known' facts. In the language of the scientist, the term *'a known fact'* refers to anything which *appears* to have been proven by secular science. However, as we have already noted, the work of modern science, on its own admission, is *'only theories, valid until they are disproved'*. At the close of the twentieth century, Evangelical Christians have gone soft on gainsayers. They have become altogether secular.[71]

Yet, far from attempting to harmonise every whim of human wisdom with the revelations of Scripture, we are exhorted — using our spiritual weaponry — to pull down strongholds, to demolish reasonings, and every lofty thing which raises itself up against the knowledge of God (2 Cor.10:4-5). However, we have allowed the modern latitudinarians — the 'gentlemen of a wide swallow' — to dictate the agenda in the relationship between the church and the world with its pseudo-science, perverse politics, childish wargames, corrupt media, depraved pleasures and putrid pastimes. In our misplaced anxiety to avoid alienating the unbelieving

[70] Derek Kidner, *Genesis: An Introduction and Commentary* (Tyndale, 1967), p.78.

[71] The word secular is derived from the Latin *saeculum* meaning 'an age'. That which is secular is, therefore, that which belongs to this present age or aeon, the true calibre of which is exposed in Gal.1:4; Eph.6:12; etc.

masses with unnecessary stumbling-blocks to the Gospel, we have forgotten the fact that Christ has no fellowship with Belial, and that believers should never be unequally yoked together with those outside the household of faith (2 Cor.6:14).

The unsaved scientist comes to his craft with an entirely different mindset from the one who has been redeemed by Christ, and whose life and actions are therefore determined by God's word and enacted to His glory. Discerning believers should not be indulging in fanciful thinking about the benign progress of Western science. Just as the mystic who delves within in order to tap into a supposed 'divine spark' is hopelessly deluded in his quest, so the scientist who seeks to 'create new life forms' or to 'know the mind of God' through probing particles and outer space is chasing a futile dream that can never be realised. The only god either will find is the one who has inspired their quest in the first place: the one who has been a liar, a murderer and their father from the very beginning — *'the god of this [evil] age'* (2 Cor.4:4; with Gal 1:4 and Jn.8:44).

Chapter Seven

SORCEROUS APPRENTICES

(1) The 'Mind-Sciences' in the World

'Do not be conformed to this world, but be transformed by the renewing of your mind, that you may prove what is that good and acceptable and perfect will of God' (Rom.12:2).

'Even if our gospel is veiled, it is veiled to those who are perishing, whose minds the god of this age has blinded...' (2 Cor.4:3-4).

In the third chapter, we identified six seeds of corruption that were implanted by Satan in world culture during the late nineteenth century in order to undermine the true Gospel and bring the swell of lawlessness to its tidal-wave proportions. These were Evolution Theory, Theological Liberalism, Comparative Religion, Socio-Political Utopianism, the Mind-Sciences, and Theosophy. These six seeds became the harbingers of many anti-Christian offshoots. In the present chapter — the first of a two-part treatment of the subject — we turn our attention to what we call the 'mind-sciences'. Under this heading we place all those developments which would concern themselves with the therapeutic and non-therapeutic causation of change in human consciousness and with the deep manipulation of the minds of men and women.

In the present chapter, we will expose the occult origins of the mind-sciences in psychology and test the claims of psychotherapy against the teachings of Scripture. In the second part of our examination of the mind-sciences, in the eleventh chapter, we will survey many disturbing developments within the professing Christian Church in which the use of trance, hypnosis, visualisation techniques, and other systems for the exploitation of 'mind-power' or the raising of consciousness have become popular.

As we have journeyed through the subject-matter of this book, you will no doubt have come to appreciate how deeply the collective mind and imagination of this fallen world have become the playground of the demonic realm, although travelling under the many euphemisms of the New Gnosticism. These areas provide the ideal interface between the dimension of the spirit-world and that of humanity: They are the spheres in which they can best utilise their permitted powers. We have also noted that the world of professing Christianity is to be no exception to this state of affairs.

In citing the mind-sciences as a seed of corruption, we are not restricting ourselves to the *clinical* study of the mind and human behaviour. Rather, we are referring to the entire development of techniques and systems designed to alter human consciousness. Whether in the realms of the New Physics, the networking of the New Age Movement, or in the outer reaches of Holistic Medicine, there is a concerted effort to bring about profound changes in matter and consciousness through a variety of sorcerous methodologies — all of which have their ultimate roots in ancient religious developments which have been opposed to the cause of God and truth for millennia.

Because of the spiralling deterioration in faithfulness to the Bible and adherence to orthodox Christian doctrine during the last couple of decades, fertile ground has also been provided in many denominations and fellowships for the practice of various forms of the mind-sciences, such as trance and hypnosis (with its associated suggestion and auto-suggestion), psychism, psychotherapies (which travel under the trade names of 'Inner Healing', 'Rebirthing' and the 'Healing of the Memories'), meditation techniques and *mantras*, visualisation (imaging), the inducement of hysteria, unbiblical exorcistic rites, and many others. We will deal in detail with these sundry phenomena in the churches — the result of varying degrees of manipulation in the realm of the mind and imagination — in the eleventh chapter. In the present chapter, we will examine the overall background to the mind-sciences by tracing the development of psychotherapy as a 'respectable' and widely-used technique.

Because the practice of a variety of psychotherapeutic techniques is now so widespread throughout the churches, a number of radical questions need to be raised. Are Christians really aware of the true historical roots of psychotherapy? What are the aims of its advocates? What purpose does it serve in the outworking of world history today? Is there any support for psychotherapy in the Bible? Should the Christian seek the services of a secular or even of a Christian psychotherapist in the event of behavioural or perceptual problems developing in his mental or emotional life?

For many Christians, the answer to this last question is simple. When one is physically ill one goes to a body doctor (physician); therefore, when one becomes 'mentally ill' one must go to a 'mind doctor' (psychiatrist or psychotherapist). But there is a grand delusion inherent in such a concept, which we intend to expose. Psychotherapy, as one of the key modern mind-sciences, is a major growth industry in the world. There are something in the region of 200 different therapeutic approaches and over 10,000 specific techniques available in the marketplace today.[1] This is an extraordinary phenomenon. Many of these techniques contradict one another at radical levels. Naturally, in the world-view of the New Gnosticism this is not a problem, as truth is relativistic and one simply chooses the particular pathway which seems most appropriate to one's own personal 'lifestyle'.

Our concern here is not to delve into all the various schools of psychological

---

1 Martin & Deirdre Bobgan, *The Psychological Way: The Spiritual Way* (Bethany House, 1979), p.23.

thought in order to criticise them from a Christian perspective. Our aim is, rather, to show clearly the spiritual and philosophical roots of the mind-sciences and their exponents, both ancient and modern — especially in relation to their influence on the development of the New Gnosticism and the ease with which they have been able to infiltrate the structures of the professing Church and its practices through a variety of channels. The most notable of these are the liberal-humanist clergy and the Charismatic Movement, whose abreactive therapies such as 'Clinical Theology', 'Inner Healing', and 'Healing of the Memories' have almost become household phrases among Christians today.[2]

There are a number of reasons why we have chosen psychotherapy as our introduction to the mind-sciences. First, because it is especially illustrative of the many deceptions currently being wrought by the demonic realm in the imaginal life of humanity, while clearly evidencing the role they are fulfilling in this world of gathering lawlessness and apostasy. A second reason why we are dealing with psychotherapy as an introduction to the mind-sciences, is because it very often forms a starting point for the demonic realm to foster an interest in the deeper realms of the human psyche — thus providing a springboard for gradual immersion in the more esoteric aspects of the New Gnosticism.

The entire field of psychology has not developed in a vacuum during the past century. From the dawn of 'civilisation', people have sought to find a system which will rationalise and explain the inner workings of the human mind, with a view to the alteration of consciousness. The resulting world-views have generally been according to the prevailing level of social and scientific development, in an attempt to meet the cultural needs of the society in which they have been spawned. Consequently, in late twentieth-century Western society — in which the notion of Truth as an absolute is anathema — there are as many systems of thought to interpret human behaviour as there are people to invent them. However, whatever schools of thought have been in the ascendancy throughout this century, there has been an increasingly visible movement, within its closing decades, to unify the techniques of Western psychology with the fundamentals of Eastern mysticism.

This has occurred primarily within the Humanistic and Transpersonal schools of psychology, and has been especially fruitful in terms of their psychotherapeutic application. We are not merely speaking here of a few fringe organisations and obscure quacks peddling an eccentric form of therapy. What we now have is a truly global development within the very establishment itself. The probing of 'inner space' through various techniques — once the sole province of occultists and mystics — has now, through such things as meditation and psychotherapy, become as respectable as the exploration of outer space.

The 'psychedelic' 1960s provided a watershed in this development, which moved from being the province of the beard and caftan to that of the white-coated professional. Over twenty years ago, an international meeting attended by

---

[2] The word *'abreactive'* is being used here to refer to those psychotherapies which advocate *'the resolution of a neurosis by reviving forgotten or repressed ideas of the event first causing it'* (Chambers English Dictionary, 1988).

psychiatrists, psychologists, theologians, physicians, mathematicians, physicists and engineers, called '*The Interdisciplinary Conference on the Voluntary Control of Internal States of Consciousness*', stated in its official invitation:

> 'We have reached the point in history at which the exploration of 'internal states' has become not only legitimate, but also a high-priority business of science. In addition, many people are conducting their own explorations in consciousness with unknown chemicals in psychoactively-unknown doses in an attempt to enhance life or escape from it. This can be a dangerous route to 'freedom'. The Conference Committee feels that at this moment it is especially important for stabilising forces to be brought to bear that link what is useful from the past with the present and the future, uniting in some degree the existential wisdom and psychology of the East and the different psychological insight of the West'.[3]

However, not only is Western psychology being synthesized with Eastern mysticism, but its psychotherapeutic approaches are rooted in occultism at a far more basic level than is generally understood — even by the so-called mental health professionals. Although many people may be entirely unaware of the developments related to the Conference on *'internal states of consciousness'* mentioned above, a brief historical survey of the key influences on modern psychotherapy reveals some surprising links with the occult and esoteric of both near and distant past, giving a clear indication of the origin and aims of the mind-sciences. So, before we expose the unfortunate delusion which lies behind the notion that one must go to a 'mind doctor' with 'mind problems', let us examine the origins of the 'mind doctor' in both his white coat and his animal skin. We will then be in a better position to respond to this pressing pastoral issue.

I. THE FATHERS OF THE MIND-SCIENCES

We will examine the fathers of the mind-sciences by looking first at those who have been the more recent founders, under the heading 'Mystics, Gnostics and Esotericists'. In the second section we will discover the ancient fathers: Shamans, Witches and Wizards.

1. The Modern Founders: Mystics, Gnostics and Esotericists

In this section we will survey, in chronological order, the life and work of four key modern influences on psychotherapy as we know it today: Franz Mesmer, Gustav Fechner, plus Sigmund Freud's favourite pupils Wilhelm Reich and Carl Jung.

i. The Legacy of Mesmerism

One of the most controversial but highly important influences on the development of the mind-sciences in relation to today's growing New Consciousness is

[3] Quoted in William Johnston, *Silent Music: The Science of Meditation* (Collins, 1974), p.23. Incidentally, this book, by a modern Jesuit mystic, was obtained in the Bookshop at York Minster — a major Anglican cathedral in England.

the Austrian physician Franz Anton Mesmer (1734-1815). At his graduation in 1765, Mesmer had presented his Paracelsus-inspired thesis which dealt with the influence of the planets on the human body, maintaining that such influence was exerted through their effects on a 'subtle fluid' which was present in the human form. The ethereal 'energy' which he thought he had identified was the equivalent of the 'bioenergy' or 'inner light' with which occultists, mystics, new physicists, gnostics and parapsychologists throughout the ages have been preoccupied.

Ten years later, having been further influenced by the occult work of a Jesuit priest, Maximillian Hehl,[4] one of Maria Theresa's court astrologers who had used magnets to cure people, Mesmer went on to develop his famous theory of 'Animal Magnetism' which resulted in the equally famous faith-healing sessions in Paris. One description of these sessions, in a major book on the occult, reads as follows:

> 'His patients sat round a large oak tub which was filled with water, iron filings and powdered glass, and from which iron rods protruded. The patients applied these rods to the afflicted parts of their bodies while Mesmer marched about majestically in a pale lilac robe, passing his hands over the patients' bodies or touching them with a long iron wand. The results varied. Some patients felt nothing at all, some felt as if insects were crawling over them, others were seized with hysterical laughter, convulsions or fits of hiccups. Some went into raving delirium, which was called 'The Crisis' and was considered extremely healthful'.[5]

Sometimes the participants would hold hands to form a circle, and it was not uncommon for waves of communal singing to take place.[6] Another description of Franz Mesmer's therapy sessions is even more graphic:

> 'Some are calm, tranquil and experience no effect. Others cough, spit, feel slight pains, local or general heat, and have sweatings. Others, again, are agitated and tormented with convulsions. These convulsions are remarkable in regard to the number affected with them, to their duration and force. They are preceded and followed by a state of languor or reverie... Patients experienced more or less violent perspiration, palpitations, hysterics, catalepsy, and sometimes a condition resembling epilepsy. When the crisis was at its height, the patient was carried by attendants into one of the adjoining "Salles de Crises"; he was there laid on a couch, and usually he subsided gradually into a deep sleep from which he awoke refreshed and benefitted'.[7]

Some perceptive brethren will, at this point, be making some interesting connections with certain phenomena which have so bewitched numerous churches

---

4 *Chambers's Encyclopaedia*, Vol.IX, p.306.

5 Richard Cavendish, *The Magical Arts* (Routledge & Kegan Paul, 1984), p.180.

6 James Webb, *The Occult Underground* (Open Court, 1974), p.25.

7 The historian Bailly being quoted by R.B. Ince in the book *Three Famous Occultists* (Gilbert Whitehead, 1939), pp.87-88.

today. Communal singing to warm things up, the laying on of hands, powerful physical sensations, agitation, hysterical laughter, raving delirium, convulsions, all followed by a deep sleep or state of reverie. These events, however, whether within the professing Church or in Anton Mesmer's therapy clinic, are sheer manifestations of hysteria induced through the heady power of hypnotic suggestion — the mind-sciences in action. The true significance of these sessions was not lost on those with insight who were Mesmer's contemporaries. In 1784, the King of France appointed a Commission to examine Mesmer's claims. The resultant 'Report of the Faculty of Medicine of the Academy of Sciences' and 'Report of the Royal Society of Medicine' stated:

> 'that man can act upon man at any time, and almost at will by striking his imagination; that the simplest gestures and signs can have the most powerful effects; and that the action of man upon the imagination may be reduced to an art, and conducted with method, upon subjects who have faith'.[8]

In fact, Mesmer's discovery that his patients could be controlled by his will is generally acknowledged as being a great foundation-stone of hypnotism, as well as exerting a profound influence on succeeding generations of occultists of many traditions, ranging from the Cabbalist magician Eliphas Levi, to the U.S. Spiritualist Movement of the nineteenth century, which had discovered that in the mesmeric trance a person could readily make contact with discarnate entities or 'spirit-guides'. Moreover, because these deep links between hypnotism and the occult were more easily accepted and understood within a culture which was steeped in such traditions, it is therefore no surprise to learn that a Mesmeric hospital was actually set up in 1845 in Calcutta, India — the very home of the Eastern mystical tradition — a harbinger of the Western mind-sciences.[9]

Mesmer's own 'Memorandum' on the force which he termed 'Animal Magnetism', made the following propositions:

1. A responsive influence exists between the heavenly bodies, the earth, and all animated bodies.

2. A fluid universally diffused, so continuous as to admit no vacuum, incomparably subtle, and naturally susceptible of receiving, spreading and communicating all motor disturbances, is the means of this influence.

3. This reciprocal action is subject to mechanical laws with which we are not yet familiar.[10]

Such a theory was, of course, nothing new; it is actually a pseudo-scientific rendering of ancient mystical pantheism. This 'Magnetic Fluid' of Mesmer is the equivalent of the Taoist's and Japanese Buddhist's *Ki* or *Chi*, the Hindu's *Prana*, the transcendental magician's Grand Elixir, and a whole host of other titles given to it in the ancient religions of the world. More than anything else, this view has

---

[8] Ibid., pp.107-108.

[9] James Webb, *The Occult Underground*, op. cit., p.25.

[10] Ibid., p.24.

led to the prevailing 'green' approach which views the earth as being a personification of the goddess, the 'Great Mother', Gaia. As C.G. Jung puts it:

> 'According to [the alchemist] Basilius Valentinus, the earth (as *prima materia*) is not a dead body, but is inhabited by a spirit that is its life and soul. All created things, minerals included, draw their strength from this earth-spirit. This spirit is life...and it gives nourishment to all the living things it shelters in its womb'.[11]

This alchemic earth-view is also remarkably similar to a major area of research in the realm of the 'New Physics' — what scientists are calling 'The Superforce'.[12] However, although a special commission (including Benjamin Franklin) at the French Académie des Sciences had, in 1784, rejected Mesmer's magnetic theory, it had nevertheless conceded the phenomenon itself, albeit imputing it to the effects of the imagination.[13] Thereafter, almost a century later, the mantle of hypnotic research fell onto the shoulders of Jean-Martin Charcot (1825-1893), a physician working at the Paris hospital for nervous diseases, the Salpêtrière. His role was to try and disentangle the discipline of hypnosis from the occultism with which it had become associated in Mesmeric circles, thus rendering it as a purely materialist science. However, as much as the scientific establishment would have liked to distance itself from the realms of mesmerism, there can be no doubt, as one researcher of the occult has noted, that

> 'the phenomena that are now defined as 'hypnotic' emerged from the faith-healing activities of Mesmer at the turn of the eighteenth and nineteenth centuries'.[14]

Charcot himself was to become an important influence on another founding father of the mind-sciences, Sigmund Freud (1856-1939). Although Freud came from a background in which hypnotic phenomena were regarded as more occult than scientific,

> 'he became absorbed in them, and, though Charcot himself looked on them purely as branches of neuropathology, for Freud they meant the first beginnings of the investigation of the mind'.[15]

Here we see that a direct lineage from Mesmer to Freud is established. We shall shortly learn in what ways this was to manifest itself when we examine the occult activities of Freud's protégés at his Viennese School. The long-lasting significance of Mesmer's influence can be seen in this statement from a prominent psychiatrist writing in the prestigious Journal of the Royal Society of Medicine:

> 'What is important is the impact and influence [Mesmer] had on the

---

[11] C.G. Jung, *Psychology and Alchemy* (Routledge & Kegan Paul, 1957), p.329.

[12] This has already been dealt with in the previous chapter.

[13] *Chambers's Encyclopaedia*, Vol.IX, p.306.

[14] James Webb, *The Occult Establishment* (Open Court, 1976), p.352.

[15] James Strachey & Angela Richards (eds.), *The Pelican Freud Library*, Vol.IV, *The Interpretation of Dreams* (Penguin, 1976), p.16.

subsequent development of psychiatry. It would indeed be no exaggeration to say that he was one of the world's first psychotherapists'.[16]

The truth embodied in this observation by the medical profession of today will be plain to see by the time we have completed our study of the mind-sciences.

ii. The Fechner Connection

It is widely recognised that one of the principal founders of modern psychology was a man called Gustav Theodor Fechner (1801-1887), the German philosopher, physicist, and son of a Christian pastor. He spent the majority of his life in Leipzig, becoming professor of physics at the university there in 1834. Within a few years of his appointment, he suffered a strange illness akin to a 'nervous breakdown' which had been partly induced by his personal participation on research into after-images.[17] The occultist and writer, Colin Wilson, claims that Fechner's own lengthy account of this illness *'makes it sound oddly like the troubles that afflicted Gopi Krishna after he had accidentally awakened the Kundalini serpent'*.[18] This is a reference to the acute distress suffered by an Indian man which was revealed in his renowned book on the effects of Tantric Kundalini Yoga. Such a 'crisis experience' is very common in the development of the 'New Consciousness' of the occultist/magician/esotericist — often being a precursor to a deeper initiation into these things — and Gustav Fechner was no exception to this norm.

Thereafter, in the words of one authority, Fechner *'spent the rest of his long life in expounding science and pantheism to a wide and grateful public'*.[19] This mystical pantheism was enshrined in his writings, in which he laid claim to an actual consciousness which permeates all creation — that 'superforce' again — exemplified in his books *'Nanna'* (The Soul Life of Plants, 1848), and *'Zend-Avesta'* (Star-Life, 1851). The notion that plants have a 'soul-life' was by no means new in modern occult-mystical circles. Fechner's compatriot, Johann Göethe (1749-1832) — who was to have a profound influence on the teachings of the occultist and founder of the Camphill Schools, Rudolf Steiner — had made similar claims after serious illness had resulted in an interest in alchemy, astrology and the works of mystics such as Giordano Bruno (1548-1600) and Emanuel Swedenborg (1688-1772).[20] The history of such conceits does not stop there: The original expositors of this essentially pantheistic theory are none other than the Neoplatonists. The connections here are highly significant. William Inge (1860-1954), Dean of St. Paul's, London, from 1911-1934, and a leading Anglican scholar who had a major role in re-arousing ecclesiastical interest in mysticism, had also *'recommended Fechner and admitted that Christian mysticism owed a debt to the Greek Mysteries'*.[21] Here we can see that this is yet another

[16] *Journal of the Royal Society of Medicine*, Vol.85, no.7, July 1992, p.383.

[17] *Chambers's Encyclopaedia*, Vol.V, p.606.

[18] Colin Wilson, *Mysteries* (Granada, 1979), p.595.

[19] *Chambers's Encyclopaedia*, Vol.V, p.606.

[20] *Chambers's Encyclopaedia*, Vol.VI, p.406.

[21] James Webb, *The Flight from Reason*, Vol.I of *'The Age of the Irrational'* (Macdonald,

example of how all these streams are but different tributaries of the same polluted river.

Gustav Fechner was also known to have attended the experiments conducted by the astronomer Johann Zöllner, a fellow professor at Leipzig, in which spiritualist séances were conducted in order to prove the existence of a 'fourth dimension'.[22] However, the most interesting occult link with this founding father of psychology — and certainly the most significant — is the claim that Gustav Fechner was visited in Leipzig by one of the so-called 'Ascended Masters',[23] the discarnate entities first recorded in historic Tibetan Buddhism, who are alleged to be masterminding history, and are the alleged spiritual force behind all the developments of the New Gnosticism in the past hundred years.[24] Known as 'Master Kuthumi', this unearthly being apparently attended Leipzig University in human form in 1875 before retiring to a lamasery in Shigatse, Tibet, from where he sent his esoteric teachings by mail throughout the world, and which are now actually on file in the British Museum.[25]

These various background experiences of Gustav Fechner become doubly significant when one learns from the editors of Sigmund Freud's 'Complete Works' that *'the psycho-physicist Fechner had a great influence on Freud's theories'*.[26] We should bear in mind that Freud was the acclaimed father of modern psychotherapy. The Viennese school which he founded was not only the training ground of some of the modern fathers of psychology and psychotherapy, but it was also a harbinger of the subsequent major schools which have shaped the world-view of the New Gnosticism and received avid acceptance within the professing Christian Church. In fact, there was more than a whiff of esotericism about Freud's School — especially highlighted by his use of a secret insignia which was only issued to those in the 'inner circle'. As James Webb discloses: *'[The Committee]...formed a secret society of seven and wore gold rings in which they mounted Greek intaglios given them personally by Freud'*.[27] Two of the main protégés of Freud were his favourite students, Wilhelm Reich (1897-1957) and Carl Gustav Jung (1875-1961). These two men and their twin philosophies were to become the main progenitors of the New Gnosticism and the consciousness-altering psychotherapies with which the world is becoming so infatuated, and by which many churches are being bewitched.

1971), p.179.

[22] James Webb, *The Occult Establishment*, op. cit., pp.42 & 364.

[23] Kuthumi, *Studies of the Human Aura* (Summit University Press, 1971), from the jacket cover note.

[24] As discussed in Chapter 4.

[25] Kuthumi, op. cit., jacket cover note.

[26] James Strachey and Angela Richards (eds.), *The Pelican Freud Library*, Vol.I., *'Introductory Lectures on Psychoanalysis'* (Penguin, 1974), p.119. For further information on this, see Chapter 5 of Freud's 'Autobiographical Study' in Vol.XIV of *The Pelican Freud Library*.

[27] James Webb, *The Occult Establishment*, op. cit., p.382.

iii. The Mysticism of Wilhelm Reich

Although the name of Wilhelm Reich is little known outside the circle of faithful *cognoscenti* who have carried his torch throughout the past forty years or so, his philosophy and innovations in the field of psychology have had a profound influence on the new generation of humanistic and transpersonal psychotherapists, while at the same time contributing to the growing East/West syncretism and inspiring the 'sexual revolution' of recent decades.

Reich was responsible — in Western psychology — for establishing the concept of a 'bioenergy' which he believed permeates all matter, including the human organism. In the psychologically healthy person, whom Reich termed the 'Genital Man', this energy flows freely. However, in those who have experienced emotional trauma and/or sexual repression in early life, blockages of this bioenergy become pathologically ingrained within the organism — what Reich called 'character armour' — resulting in an adult who is riddled with neuroses and other psychological problems. In his book, *'The Murder of Christ'*, he claimed that the Fall expounded in the third chapter of Genesis was an allegorical tale depicting the beginnings of sexual repression in human society, while Christ — who he claimed was the ultimate 'Genital Man' — came to give humanity an example of perfect sexual and energetic health. The reason that the Lord Jesus Christ was killed by the people, according to Reich, was because the sexually-maladjusted world could not take His dynamically-healthy sexual energy.[28] The mass outworking of this individual 'character armouring' was termed as 'The Emotional Plague' — a condition which he claimed was responsible for such negative global developments as war, fascism, etc. His primary thesis consisted in the assertion that

> 'it is solely the re-establishment of the natural love-life of children, adolescents, and adults which can rid the world of character neuroses and, with the character neuroses, the emotional plague in all its forms'.[29]

The cure for these global problems was to be found in his crudely named 'Vegeto-Therapy', later to be called 'Orgone Therapy', in which the patient was led into emotional release and abreaction through suggestion, physical manipulation and exercises, known today as 'Bioenergetics'. He also used gadgets known as 'orgone accumulators' — small booths constructed of specialist materials in which the patients would sit in order to bring about an 'adjustment' in their psychic energies.

Reich believed passionately that the experiencing of a full and healthy orgasm was the key to emotional health (and he was not above having sexual encounters with his own patients if he thought the situation called for it). This experience of full orgasm, he claimed, was dependent on being free from blockages in the character structure caused by faulty development in early life. Significantly, as the

---

[28] See Wilhelm Reich, *The Murder of Christ* (Farrar, Straus and Giroux, 1953).

[29] Wilhelm Reich, *Character Analysis* (Farrar, Straus & Giroux), p.539.

champion of radical changes in education and child-rearing techniques, these ideas led to Reich becoming the main influence on the philosophy of the well-known libertarian school, Summerhill, and long-term psychotherapist to its founder and headmaster, A.S. Neill, who first popularised the humanist term 'Self-Regulated Child' — i.e., a child who is free to develop without the authoritarian interference of his parents.[30]

In his book, *Charakteranalyse* (1933, 1945, 1948), Reich gave a full exposition of his theories together with details of the therapeutic measures he practised. In its third and final version (1948), we can see the full influence that his ideas were to exert in the bringing together of Western psychology and Eastern mystical philosophy and anatomy — although it is doubtful if the man himself was aware of these links. Indeed, Reich's whole concept of 'bioenergy' was astonishingly parallel to many other seemingly disparate manifestations of similar phenomena in both East and West. We have already mentioned these phenomena both in this chapter and in previous chapters: the life-force, Mesmer's 'Magnetic Fluid', the New Physicist's 'Superforce', the spiritualist's *Élan Vital*, the Taoist's and Japanese Buddhist's *Ch'i* or *Ki*, the Hindu's *Prana*, the alchemist's Grand Elixir, the occultist's *Philosopher's Stone*, Colin Wilson's 'Faculty X', and so on.

There can be no doubt that there is far more to the human anatomy than meets the eye; and without a doubt there are a great many phenomena connected with living matter of which we are entirely unaware. But to attempt to penetrate, manipulate or harness any invisible 'energies' — human or otherwise — in order to *'increase our potential'* or to *'realise the fullness of our being'* is the province of the sorcerer, and must have no place in the life of the biblical Christian, who recognises the limitations imposed on him living in a fallen world, and patiently waits for the return of the Lord to discover what he is really made of (1 Jn.3:2; cf. Dt.29:29; Ps.131).

In his later years, Reich sought to harness this energy in increasingly outlandish experiments, some of which involved the use of radioactive substances.[31] These attempts to probe manifestations of energy have been carried out by occultists through the ages in order to gain power over God's creation; recently they have become the province of Western psychology and science. The anti-Christian world-system always seeks to control and subdue the creation for its own ends, vainly hoping to achieve (or rather, recover) the original God-given dominion

[30] See the paper by A.S. Neill entitled *'The Self-Regulated Child'* in David Boadella (ed.), *In the Wake of Reich* (Coventure, 1976), p.103. In this essay, Neill confesses in the opening sentence: *'I never heard the term self-regulation until my friend Wilhelm Reich used it, and if he did not invent it, he, more than any other man, has understood and used the method'* (p.103).

[31] Trevor Constable, *The Cosmic Pulse of Life* (Neville Spearman, 1976), pp.326-327. Two chapters in this book are especially enlightening regarding Reich's deepening esotericism: Chapter 18, *'From Orgasm to UFOs'*; and Chapter 19, *'Cosmic Breakthrough'*. For a full exposition of Reich's life by a sympathetic researcher, which particularly highlights the occultic aspects of Reich's work, see Colin Wilson, *The Quest for Wilhelm Reich* (Granada, 1982).

mandate in Eden (Gen.1:28) — only this time, without God's involvement.

A major hypothesis in Reich's therapeutic model, which also brings together East and West, is his division of the body into seven principal 'energetic' segments running laterally from the head to the base of the spine.[32] Reich claimed that each of these segments needed 'opening up' sequentially through psychotherapeutic techniques, the end-result of which would be a 'streaming' through the entire body of what he termed 'orgone energy' — i.e., ecstasy. This theory of the seven bioenergetic segments of the body is virtually identical to the essential elements of Tantric Yoga.

The Tantric branch of the Yogic disciplines identifies seven *Chakras* or energy centres which correspond precisely to Reich's segments. In the practice of Tantra, the unblocking of these *Chakras* leads to the ultimate experience of *Kundalini* energy-activation, known in Tantric literature as 'Serpent energy' — the ecstatic experience of pure Cosmic Consciousness, *ãnanda*. Reich had no apparent knowledge of Eastern anatomy yet, independently, he proffered an almost identical analysis of psychic life to that of the Eastern Tantrist. This shows the universality of occult phenomena.[33] Furthermore, Reich's emphasis on the importance of the full utilisation of sexual energy and the genital relationship to produce ecstatic 'orgonotic streamings' was virtually identical to the philosophy of Tantrism, which does not limit sexual intercourse to procreation and marital bonding. Indian scholar, Ajit Mookerjee, explains how this works:

> 'Through the ages, the sex act has been generally associated with procreation or gross physical satisfaction. Tantrikas [adepts in Tantric Yoga], however, realized the immense potentiality of sex energy, and, through tantra-ãsanas [sexo-yogic postures], transformed the energy of sex and freed it to a plane of cosmic awareness. Sex is seen as divine in itself, and a source of a vital energy capable of acting with tremendous force on the physio-psychic state, which in turn reacts on the higher cosmic plane'.[34]

The generation of sexual energy through this method is an intrinsic element of the ritualism of all occult and esoteric groups, theories and organisations — from Taoism and Tantric Buddhism to Theosophy and Transcendental Magic. For instance, an early twentieth century German occult society specialising in such sex-magic, known as the Order of the Templars of the Orient, boasted Rudolf Steiner among its membership; while the head of the British branch of the same organisation was that master of the black arts, Aleister Crowley, who gave himself the

---

[32] Wilhelm Reich, *Character Analysis*, op. cit., pp.368-390.

[33] One can only surmise what influence came to bear in order for Reich to make these connections. Remember, in an earlier chapter we identified that one of the claims for the 'Ascended Masters' is that they have been manipulating events on this planet so as to unify Eastern and Western thought and to stimulate the growth of the 'healing arts' — amongst which is numbered modern psychotherapy.

[34] Ajit Mookerjee, *Kundalini: The Arousal of the Inner Energy* (Thames & Hudson, 1978), p.59.

infamous nickname 'The Great Beast – 666'.[35]

This exploration of sex and sexuality forms a vital cog in the psychotherapeutic development of the New Gnosticism, and the Tantric legacy of sex-magic is flooding the West in a variety of guises. For example, the interfaith organisation 'The Temple of Understanding' — a Non-Governmental Organisation in the United Nations and main organiser of the 1993 Parliament of the World's Religions in Chicago[36] — had, as one of its original U.S. sponsors, Dr. John H. Zitko, founder of the 'World University' and author of a book entitled *'New Age Tantric Yoga'*.[37] This is just another example among thousands which could be given, of the ever-repeating connecting points in the growth of global iniquity through the burgeoning influence of the New Gnosticism.

All this should not surprise us. The mesmeric power of corrupt sexuality lies directly under the sway of the demonic realm. The proper and only place for the sexual union is the marriage bed — and even then, in conditions of chastity and

---

[35] Richard Cavendish, op. cit., pp.40-41. Rudolf Steiner was the founder and guru of the Camphill Steiner Schools; for details of his involvement in the Order of the Templars of the Orient, see James Webb, *The Occult Establishment*, op. cit., p.489.

[36] See the final chapter for full details of this 'Temple of Understanding' and the Parliament of the World's Religions.

[37] Dr. Zitko's written works are extensive. Details can be obtained from The World University Development Program, P.O. Box 68, Huntington Park, California, U.S.A. His book *'New Age Tantric Yoga'* includes explicit details of sex-rituals amongst couples which will allegedly result in the siring of babies who will be naturally attuned to the New Gnosticism. This is more or less using sexual ritualism as a way of forming a pact with the devil, whether or not the performer is aware of it. In another book by Dr. Zitko, entitled *'The Lemurian Theo-Christian Conference'*, he claims that *'advanced intelligences on other planets of our solar system are again becoming active in human affairs after a lapse of some ten thousand years'*. This is a common claim among Neo-Gnostics. The increasing number of UFO sightings, however, has nothing to do with genuine extra-terrestrial civilisations, but is part of an ongoing strategy of the *'powers of darkness'* (Eph.6:12), under the direction of their *'prince of the power of the air'* (Eph.2:2), who are engaged in convincing the minds of the gullible that 'something out there is trying to contact us'. To those whose minds are attuned to such contact, demonic beings will actually manifest themselves as benign 'extra-terrestrials' (ETs) who wish to offer help to humanity — an offer that will, if it presents itself more openly, be avidly received as the influence of the New Gnosticism develops in world culture. If it can be 'proven' that ETs do exist, and that they are on a 'higher plane' than the inhabitants of planet Earth, this will go a long way towards vindicating the claims of the Neo-Gnostics, as well as establishing the suppositions of the New Physics and the evolutionary theories of secular humanism. If this was to be supplemented by an alleged scientific 'discovery' of the secret of the 'life-force', the way would be paved for some truly cataclysmic changes on this planet. We should not be at all surprised if these developments occur in the near future as part of the advancing strategy of the powers of darkness to discredit the Gospel, debunk the Bible, and eradicate the concept of a transcendent Creator God. The world will then be ready to believe the Lie which Satan has always sought to perpetuate, and the global conditions will be in place for the revealing of the ultimate Man of Sin (2 Th.2:3-12).

lovingness. The uses of sex as a 'personal growth' technique for the achievement of ecstasy or as a method of producing spiritual enlightenment are pure manifestations of a 'Satanic Initiation', whether or not the users are aware of it.

Late on in life, when he began to experiment with machines utilising energy rays (including a 'Cloudbuster' to affect the weather), Reich became increasingly convinced that his work was being monitored by extra-terrestrial beings. Without a doubt, he had become aware of those demonic forces which had inspired his entire life's work — from his beginnings as a radical Marxist psychiatrist offering therapy on the cheap to the workers, to his final desperate explorations into the realms of cosmic energies. He died of a heart-attack in 1957 in a U.S. state penitentiary, having been imprisoned for refusing to submit to a Federal Order not to ship his 'orgone accumulators' across state borders.[38]

Today, the legacy of Wilhelm Reich lives on in many ways: The contemporary exploration of sexuality and sexual 'freedom' (the so-called 'sexual revolution' has been directly attributed to Reich); many of the psychotherapies such as Feldenkrais technique, Structural Integration, Rolfing, Primal Therapy, Rebirthing, Bioenergetics, etc., are direct offshoots of the therapeutic pathway trodden by this strange, obsessive protégé of the Viennese School of Sigmund Freud. His theories provided considerable reinforcement to the development of the New Gnosticism — of which he is a declared hero.

iv. The Gnosticism of Carl Jung: The Archetypal Alchemist

As congregational counselling from the pulpit through powerful biblical preaching has disappeared from the vast majority of professing Christian churches, so there has been a parallel rise in the pastoral practice of its secular substitute, psychotherapy. By far the most popular technique to emerge is that developed by the Swiss psychiatrist and philosopher, Carl Jung. In this section, the true spiritual fountainhead of his life's work is laid bare, leaving no Christian in any doubt about the darkness enshrouding the legacy he has left behind.

Of all the forms of psychotherapy to be adopted by the churches for their pastoral application, none has enjoyed greater success than the teachings of Carl Gustav Jung (1875-1961), golden pupil of Sigmund Freud. Moreover, of all the Freudian protégés, Jung has been the most avidly received throughout the entire international psychotherapeutic community during the last twenty years.

The fact that the same welcoming accolade for Jung can also be seen in the response of many churches is a matter of no small moment. Although most Christians have been unable to accept the teachings of Freud because of his obvious anti-Christianity, or could dismiss Wilhelm Reich because of his bizarre eccentricities and sexual proclivities, Jung has been avidly promoted by professing Christians of all sects — especially within the Charismatic Movement, where his

---

[38] In view of the harsh way that Reich was treated for a relatively minor offence by the U.S. government at the end of his life, and taking into account his interests before he was arrested and the manner in which he was dispatched from this world, one cannot help wondering if he had stumbled on some closely-guarded secrets regarding 'alien' activity in which world government agencies were clandestinely involved.

teachings have provided the power behind so-called 'Inner Healing', with its visualised images of Jesus and the Virgin Mary.[39] This branch of the mind-sciences will be dealt with in detail in Chapter 11.

One of the principal reasons for this deceiving of so many professing Christians is Jung's synthesis of an apparent 'spirituality' with his psychological investigations. This is a mould which holds great appeal for the multi-faith, ecumenical pluralists in the late twentieth century church — especially the Roman Church with its rich history of mysticism and idolatry, and the other mainline denominations which have removed the Bible as their rule of faith and practice. However, Jung's spiritual investigations had nothing to do with the spirituality of the Bible, but were primitive elements of the ancient satanic religion dressed up in 'psychobabble' to increase their widespread intellectual appeal. He was, in fact, the supreme twentieth century occultist, gnostic and transcendental sorcerer, who went deeply into a 'Satanic Initiation', mapping his psychic experiences to allure others to follow, and, as such, was the modern founder of what is known as 'Transpersonal Psychology' — the exploration of archetypal, mystical states of consciousness (ecstasy, visions, ego dissolution, etc.) through various techniques such as trance, hallucinogenic drugs, meditation and visualisation.

Jung's original teacher, Sigmund Freud, had also been far more interested in the occult than is generally known. Although he liked to present himself primarily as a scientist, he could happily make the statement that

> 'Behind all so-called occult phenomena lies something new and important: the fact of thought transference, i.e., the transferring of psychical processes through space to other people'.[40]

However, in his dealings with Jung, Freud found his pupil's deepening interest in the occult, mysticism and esoteric religion to be more than even he could bear. A tension developed between them on this issue, and a climax came during an extraordinary episode in Vienna in 1909, described by Jung's biographer thus:

> 'Busily engaged in arguing about occult experiences...Jung suddenly felt *'as if my diaphragm were made of iron and were becoming red hot — a glowing vault'*. Immediately afterwards came a loud report from a bookcase which made them jump up in alarm fearing it was going to topple over on them'.[41]

Jung then predicted that there would be a second explosion from the bookcase, which then duly occurred. These events marked the turning point in their

---

[39] A lengthy list of names could be cited of those professing Christian leaders advocating Jungian-style psychotherapy dressed up in Christian clothing. Some of these are Agnes Sanford, John and Paula Sandford, Morton Kelsey, John Wimber, David Seamonds, Jamie Buckingham, the Arbuthnotts, Richard Foster, Paul Yonggi Cho, Denis and Rita Bennett, the Linn brothers, Francis MacNutt, etc.

[40] Edoardo Weiss, 'Sigmund Freud as Consultant', p.69; quoted in Paul Roazen, *Freud and his Followers* (Penguin, 1979), p.250.

[41] Vincent Brome, *Jung: Man and Myth* (Paladin, 1980), p.113.

relationship: Freud had a rational explanation for them, whereas Jung's was supernatural; and these idiosyncratic interpretations clearly indicated the paths down which each man would go.

A few years after this event, Jung was to undergo a mental breakdown, characterised by a variety of exceptional experiences which are the hallmark of those who take an intense interest in the psychic realm. It was during this period that he was first visited by his spirit-guide, a discarnate entity called 'Philemon', who conjured up — to use Jung's own description — *'an Egypto-Hellenic atmosphere with Gnostic colorations'*.[42] Jung advocated contact with such entities which he regarded as 'archetypes' — psychic emanations which were throwbacks to former civilisations, held in what he called the *'collective unconscious'*. To this practice — now identified by modern occultists (the Neo-Gnostics) as 'visualisation' — Jung designated the title *'active imagination'*. Through interacting with the discarnate entities invoked by this visualisation process, it is maintained that one can mature psychologically and become his or her 'true self'. For these 'archetypes' would counsel their hosts and act as inner guides or psychotherapists. In Chapter 11, we will be exposing this technique as being the manipulation of the human race by demonic forces on a vast scale.

The Philemon archetype recognised by Jung actually took on the embodiment of a separate personality with whom Jung would converse. Around this same time, his life began to be plagued by visions and hauntings which created a continuous nightmare for his family. Spirit-beings tormented his children in the night, along with other weird supernatural effects. On one occasion, the front-door bell of his house began to ring for an interminable length of time, independent of any human agent. As his biographer discloses:

> 'The whole family looked uneasily at one another and Jung knew that "something had to happen". It was, he wrote, as if *"a crowd were present"*, and the whole house *"crammed full of spirits. They were packed deep right up to the door and the air was so thick it was scarcely possible to breathe"*'.[43]

Apparently, these discarnate entities then cried out in chorus with the words, *'We have come back from Jerusalem where we found not what we sought!'*.[44] Amazingly, these demonic occurrences are merely interpreted by Jung and his followers as being part of a *'creative nervous breakdown'* or an *'encounter with the archaic materials of the collective unconscious'*. The discerning Christian cannot but regard such episodes as being indicative of a severe case of demon infestation.

In 1952, towards the end of his life, Jung's book 'Answer to Job' appeared — the mature reflection of an old man nearing the end of his life's work. But far from showing any understanding of the deep things of God, as revealed in the Scriptures, this work shows Jung's true spiritual condition. For it was the

---

[42] Ibid., p.164. It is a point of some interest that demons will often take on biblical names when they declare themselves to those exploring their realm.

[43] Vincent Brome, op. cit., p.167.

[44] Ibid.

ultimate expression of hubris, in which he gave vent to his outrage at a God who can allow evil to exist in the world.

It is a singular fact that the unregenerate person has no conception whatsoever of how and why evil has come about, and will always be perplexed by it, raging at God that such a situation should exist. Such a one — always implicitly, often explicitly — will make the claim that God must be the actual originator of evil, rather than accepting His sovereignty as the great Orderer and Controller of it. However, the Christian who is rooted in Scripture has no problem accepting this mighty fact, coming to understand, though the revelation of the Spirit, why evil exists and why God permits it to do so (cf. Isa.45:7; Prov.16:4; Rom.9:22,23, etc.).[45] In contrast to this, after sixty years of 'spiritual' searching and concentrated mystical experience, Jung could only say that God had become for him *'a contradiction in terms...an ailment that man has to cure'*.[46] In the light of all this, is it not extraordinary that so many professing Christians allow themselves to be influenced by this man?

Jung spent his entire life trying to marry Eastern mysticism and Western philosophy. One form that this took was in his use of the *Mandala* — a complex geometrical image which is the visual counterpart of the *Mantra* — as a tool for self-discovery and meditation.[47] The *Mandala* is known as a 'power diagram', having its origins in Tantric Buddhism, which is designed to alter consciousness and awaken the Kundalini energy in an individual, thereby leading to 'enlightenment' or the realisation of personal divinity. In other words, it is another vehicle for the 'Satanic Initiation'. In some oriental traditions, the *Mandala* — like its verbalised counterpart, the *Mantra* — is believed to contain *'centres of power or energy related to a specific god or demon'*.[48] Carl Jung was also one of the most avid proponents of the *'I Ching'* — an ancient Chinese form of divination, now very popular in the New Age Movement — in which one casts a number of sticks or coins to determine the future by the pattern in which they fall.[49] Is this practice one which should encourage Christians to have confidence in Jung's teachings? The method embodied in the *I Ching* — the casting of sticks (or arrows) — is shown in Scripture to be a Babylonian occult divination practice (Ezk.21:21). The art of divination, that is, attempting to forecast the future through occult means, is expressly forbidden in both the Old Testament and the New (Lev.19:26; Dt.18:10-14; Acts 16:16-18).

Another important connection in respect of Jung's involvement with things

[45] For further help in coming to terms with this profound subject, see the article 'Tested by Fire' in the journal *Diakrisis*, Summer 1992, Issue 4, available from the author.

[46] C.G. Jung, 'Letters', Vol.II, 5th January 1952. Quoted in Vincent Brome, op. cit., p.255.

[47] The Eastern mystical practice of the *Mantra* — a spell or collection of words chanted repetitively so as to alter consciousness — will be examined in detail in Chapter 9.

[48] Raymond Van Over, *Total Meditation: Mind Control Techniques for a Small Planet in Space* (Collier Macmillan, 1978), p.135.

[49] See Jung's commendatory preface to the authoritative edition of the *I Ching* edited by Richard Wilhelm (Routledge & Kegan Paul, 1970).

Eastern and esoteric occurred in his participation in what were known as the Eranos Conferences.[50] These were annual meetings initiated in 1930 by the wealthy socialite Olga Froebe-Kapteyn, in a specially erected auditorium in the grounds of her home by Lake Maggiore, Ascona, in Switzerland, at which *'scholars, mythologists and psychologists of Jungian sympathies have expounded their views of the spiritual problems faced by modern man'*.[51] In 1930, Olga Froebe sent out personal invitations for *'a Summer School for the study of Theosophy, Mysticism, the Esoteric Sciences and Philosophies and all forms of Spiritual Research'*.[52] From 1931-1933, the main lecturer at these conferences (and personal guest of Olga Froebe) was Alice B. Bailey, founder of the Lucis Trust (formerly the Lucifer Trust), an influential neo-gnostic occult group now working within the United Nations and the author of an extensive library of books foundational to the growth of the New Gnosticism.[53] Then Jung himself took over as the leading light of Eranos after Alice Bailey retired to New York in 1933. After his death in 1962, the office passed to Mircea Eliade, whose works 'Yoga, Immortality and Freedom' (1950) and 'Shamanism: Archaic Techniques of Ecstasy' (1964) are also basic textbooks of the New Gnosticism.[54] The revealing sequence of key speakers at Eranos — First, Alice Bailey, then Carl Jung, then Mircea Eliade — has prompted a researcher of the occult to claim that

> 'The theories of Carl Jung have passed into the hands of the modern representatives of the 19th century Occult Revival. Jung's psychology inspires the inheritors of those traditions which once inspired him. The Eranos Conferences are a compendium of all the elements of the Occult Revival, and an extension of all the elements of Jung's work'.[55]

Considering the occult involvement of Jung, and the willingness of occult organisations to embrace him and his teachings, it does seem strange that he should be accepted by so many professing Christians — and especially ironic that his teachings should be utilised by those in the professing Christian sect known as the Charismatic Movement, who claim to have great discernment of occult and demonic activity!

Another little-known fact — much played down by those professing Christians

---

[50] *Eranos* is a Greek word denoting a meal to which all participants contribute. In this context it signifies the syncretic and eclectic nature of these gatherings.

[51] James Webb, *The Occult Establishment* (Open Court, 1976), p.395.

[52] Ibid. p.396.

[53] The occultist Alice Bailey was the subject of some discussion in Chapter 3. Her books were all allegedly written under dictation from a discarnate entity known as 'Djwal Khul', or Master D.K. Her key publications are *Initiation: Human and Solar* and *Discipleship in the New Age*. A full list is available from the Lucis Trust, 866, United Nations Plaza, New York. 10017-1888, or from Watkins Books, 19, Cecil Court, London, WC2N 4EZ. A number of her titles are also available from the Anglican St. James Church, Piccadilly, London.

[54] For further details of Mircea Eliade, see p.162 in Chapter 4.

[55] James Webb, *The Occult Establishment*, p.397.

who have been seduced by Jung's teachings — is that the satanic stream of Gnosticism played as important a role in his life's work as did Eastern mysticism and Western esotericism. In the same way that his use of the *Mandala* was derived from Tantric Yoga, he drew his theory of psychological types directly from Gnostic philosophy. In view of the evidence throughout the entire history of the Church of the anti-Christian nature of these streams of thought, it is astounding that so many of those professing to be followers of Christ have found a place for Jung's theories in their formative influences, claiming him unashamedly as their guide in mapping out an understanding of human psychology. *Gnosis* (the Greek word for 'knowledge') refers to that secret knowledge which mystics seek in order to achieve personal 'divinity'. In one of his many works, Jung freely admits: *'My investigation seeks, with the help of Christian Gnostic and Alchemical symbols, to throw light on the change of psychic situation within the Christian aeon'.*[56] In a less esoteric vein in his own 'Reminiscences', Jung wrote:

> 'I had stumbled upon the historical counterpart of my psychology of the unconscious. The possibility of a comparison with alchemy, and the uninterrupted intellectual chain back to Gnosticism, gave substance to my psychology'.[57]

Whether his purportedly Christian followers care to admit it or not, C.G. Jung was really one of the main protagonists of the New Gnosticism today. As one Jungian theosophist has openly stated in a lecture:

> 'Jung's insights need to be considered as one of the latest and greatest manifestations of the stream of alternate spirituality which descends from the Gnostics'.[58]

On Jung's eightieth birthday, the C.G. Jung Institute of Zurich presented him with a highly unusual present: an original papyrus manuscript of some of the Gnostic writings found at Nag Hammadi in Egypt in 1945, including the 'Gospel of Truth', the 'Gospel to the Egyptians' (known as the 'Sacred Book of the Great Invisible Spirit') and the two counterfeit 'Gospels' according to Thomas and Philip. These had been obtained through blackmarket channels and represented the writings of the Gnostic School founded by Valentinus in the second century. This collection of works is now officially known as the 'Jung Codex'. Church Father, Irenaeus of Lyons, towards the close of that same century, wrote a chapter in his great work 'Against Heresies' entitled *'How the Valentinians Pervert the Scripture to Support their own Impious Opinions'.*[59] We can just as easily apply

---

[56] C.G. Jung, *Collected Works*, Vol.XI, Pt.2, Foreword, p.ix. Quoted in Vincent Brome, op. cit., p.253.

[57] C.G. Jung, *Memories, Dreams and Reflections*, p.196. Quoted in Vincent Brome, op. cit., pp.232-233.

[58] Stephan A. Hoeller, *The Gnostic Jung and the Seven Sermons to the Dead* (Quest Books, 1982), p.32.

[59] Irenaeus, *A Refutation of Knowledge Falsely So-Called* or *Against Heresies*, Bk.I, Chap.viii.

this statement to include Jung, the Jungians, and the modern 'Christian' psychotherapists who follow him!

Lest the significance of this birthday gift to Jung — and the influence of Gnosticism on his work — be underestimated by some readers, the 'Gospel According to Philip' includes within its pages the claim that the person who achieves 'gnosis' is *'no longer a Christian, but a Christ'*.[60] This is a classic statement of the Satanic Initiation — the true thrust behind Jungian psychology, emphasised by the fact that the man himself has actually been referred to as the *'semi-mystical Messiah'*.[61] This self-divinisation of Jung is brought out especially clearly in the following account of an occasion in Africa:

> 'Deliberately walking away from his companions, Jung further isolated himself and savoured what he described as the extraordinary feeling of recreating the world — for himself. *"In an invisible act of creation"*, he put the *"stamp of perfection on the world by giving it objective existence"*. His old Pueblo friend who helped the sun to journey across the sky came into his mind. Now Jung went beyond that experience to become *"the second creator of the world"*'.[62]

As we have so often mentioned within these pages, this is the ultimate goal of all mysticism and occultism: the achievement of personal 'divinity' through transcendental experience. To the Gnostic, knowledge of self is identical to knowledge of God. As Jung's biographer relates, *'God-Jung...believed in his own divinity'*.[63] Yet, on a personal level, even after this surfeit of 'divinity' and a lifetime of mystical searching, Jung was far from being a godly man. The greater part of his life had been spent having an extra-marital relationship with at least one of his patients,[64] which his wife was forced to endure painfully without question, and of which he never repented. To the end of his days, he would regularly fly into rages over trivialities, while any spare time he had was frittered away in the reading of detective stories and thrillers — a strange occupation, indeed, for a 'semi-mystical Messiah'!

In view of the information given in these pages concerning the life and work of Carl Gustav Jung, is it not extraordinary that he should so often be a source of uncritical reference for many professing Christians today? For example, in 'Living the Faith: A Call to the Church' — a collection of papers recently published by the influential Open Synod Group of the Church of England (which includes MPs, Theology Professors and Bishops) — the name *'C.G. Jung'* constitutes the laudative opening words of the first chapter, while his book 'Memories, Dreams and Reflections' is among the brief list of *'selected further reading'*.[65]

---

[60] R. McL. Wilson, (ed)., *The Gospel of Philip*, 67:26-27 (Mowbrays, 1962), p.43.

[61] Vincent Brome, op. cit., jacket cover.

[62] Ibid., p.203.

[63] Ibid., p.204.

[64] Notably Toni Woolf, who herself went on to become a well-known Jungian psychologist and author.

[65] Kathleen Jones (ed.), *Living the Faith: A Call to the Church* (OUP, 1980), pp.9, 51.

The Anglican Church has a large Jungian following, with Dr. Martin Israel — a leading counsellor in that denomination — being an avid proselyte of the Jungian worldview. Similarly, the Anglican St. James Church, Piccadilly — the leading Neo-Gnostic Church in the U.K. — is permanent host to the work of the 'Pastoral Guild of Psychology', which was founded by Jung. As Satan leaves his fingerprints in his favourite haunts, it is worth noting that this Guild has as its symbol a holy grail-style communion cup from which a serpent is drinking! The list of 'Christian' adherents of Jungian philosophy is extremely large today, as the cult of Jungianism forms a central pivot of the psycho-gospel throughout the entire church — especially the Charismatic Movement's 'Inner Healing' techniques[66] — and including, often unwittingly, many in the Evangelical wing.[67]

It does seem extraordinary that the man himself has been regarded by numerous high-ranking clergymen as a great spiritual thinker and philosopher. But how and why has this happened? The answer becomes clear when one realises that all psychological research, therapy and introspection, when carried out by the unregenerate person, can only ever be in the service of Satan — whose special realm of control in man is the mind. As Satan's cardinal lie to man involved the ideas that Man can become God, attain superhuman wisdom and have unconditional eternal life (Gen.3:4-6), it is hardly surprising that he uses these mind-control techniques to foster such illusions. Jung's teachings involve the foundational Gnostic idea that one can become God (the fulfilment of Satan's Edenic promise to his children: *'You will be like God'*), coupled with the Satanic evolutionary doctrine of reincarnation (perpetuating Satan's Edenic promise to his children: *'You will cnot surely die'*). Jung himself was one of the two principal fathers of the New Gnosticism as manifested in the New Age Movement.[68] Jung was even knowledgeable of the coming Aquarian Age, as evidenced by the fact that he referred to *'the Christian aeon of the Fishes [Pisces], now running to its end'*.[69]

Satan has been most thorough in his work of deception. Neo-Pentecostal and Charismatic Christians who publicly attack the occult are actually promoting it in teaching visualisation and inner healing. They have dressed up Jungianism with

---

66 As proof of this, a reliable Christian reference work states: 'One sector of the Charismatic movement, a sector that could be called "The Jungian School" — Agnes Sanford popularised the approach — takes dreams very seriously and finds in the intricate psychological writings of Carl Jung a theoretical basis (Kelsey, 1964, 1968). 'Inner Healing' was an understandable development that emerged out of that school' (S.M. Burgess & G.B. McGee, *Dictionary of Pentecostal and Charismatic Movements* (Zondervan, 1988), p.808.).

67 A notable example of this phenomenon is Richard Foster, whose bestselling book *A Celebration of Discipline*, published by Hodder and Stoughton, has been acclaimed by many evangelical organisations, and contains a commendatory foreword by David Watson, late Anglican vicar of St. Michael le Belfrey in York.

68 Jesuit priest Pierre Teilhard de Chardin was the other father of the New Gnosticism in the twentieth century, while Alice Bailey was the 'mother'.

69 C.G. Jung, *Aion: Researches into the Phenomenology of Self* (Routledge & Kegan Paul, 1981), p.62.

a few grossly-misapplied biblical texts, while many 'evangelical' bookshops — presumably for the sake of filthy lucre — are eagerly promoting these destructive teachings. Such undiscerning behaviour represents yet another brick in the wall of the growing 'kingdom' of the prince of darkness. Paul could not have been more prophetic when he predicted that there would come a time when professing Christians would heap up for themselves false teachers through whom they would be turned aside to myths (2 Tim.4:3-4). The teachings of Carl Jung represent the ultimate in mythology. As the discerning Professor of Mathematics at Oregon State University, Dr. Wolfgang Smith has said:

> 'In the final analysis, what Jung has to offer is a religion for atheists and a mysticism for those who love only themselves... It is an Ersatz, or as Reiff puts it, "a religion of a sort — for spiritual dilettantes, who collect symbols and meanings as others collect paintings"... Jung has ransacked the religions and secret doctrines of the world to provide himself with an impressive pantheon of god-terms... What makes the Jungian cult of self-worship especially seductive — and perhaps more dangerous to religion than any other ideological system presently in vogue — is its pan-religious and scientific garb, which disarms almost everyone... Here at last is an anti-creed that could indeed "deceive the elect"!... In churches all over the land it would appear that Jung has already gained admittance into the sanctuary'.[70]

Unless Christians wake up to these facts, the true work of Pastors and Teachers will continue to be eclipsed by the counterfeit work of pseudo-therapists, occultists and countless other charlatans.

* * * * * * *

Having now examined the modern founders of the mind-sciences, it is surely no exaggeration to say that a great many of the psychotherapeutic models on offer today — especially the Humanistic and Transpersonal branches, and including the 'Christianised' abreactive therapies ('Healing of the Memories' and 'Clinical Theology') mentioned near the beginning of this study — have their roots in the life-work and theories of one or more of the above four men. But these explorations into the hinterland of human experience are not without an even more antique pedigree. Let us therefore now turn our attention to those who are their spiritual forebears — the ancient ones.

2. The Ancient Founders of the Mind-Sciences: Shamans, Witches and Wizards

Having now examined some of the instigators and begetters of the mind-sciences in the last couple of centuries, we have established how their ideas were

---

[70] Wolfgang Smith, *Cosmos and Transcendence: Breaking Through the Barrier of Scientistic Belief* (Open Court, 1984), pp.130-133. This is a most intelligent and stimulating book. The chapter on Jung, 'The Deification of the Unconscious', is the most devastating (and unanswerable) annihilation of Jung's views ever published.

embedded in various aspects of magic, sorcery and esotericism rather than in any kind of true science. However, as readers will by now have noticed, the occult roots of these matters always extend considerably further back into history than the formulation of the cult concepts of the more recent centuries. Any excursion through the antecedents of the mind-sciences would, therefore, be incomplete without looking at those cultures and religious traditions in which magic, sorcery and esoteric knowledge (without the 'benefits' of academia or a spurious white coat!) have held sway since ancient times.

In previous chapters, we have had cause to mention a religious tradition known as 'Shamanism' — a form stretching back through millennia. At the centre of this tradition is the 'shaman', who can be defined as a person who *'is able, at will, to enter into a non-ordinary state of consciousness in order to make contact with the spirit world on behalf of members of his or her community'.*[71]

For this purpose, the shaman uses hallucinogenic plants, self-hypnosis, ecstasy and other techniques to alter his consciousness and connect with the spirit-world. This tradition goes back many thousands of years and constitutes the very heart of the ancient satanic religion, under the sway of which the whole world has lain — either openly or in deception — since the earliest era of history. Shamanism is generally regarded anthropologically as a Northern Asiatic religious phenomenon, but regardless of superficial differences, the same transcultural, transpersonal pattern reveals itself — from Tibet, Mongolia and Siberia to Africa, Alaska, North and South America. As one reference works states:

> 'The main aspects of the Asiatic Shaman's procedure...are found to be of well-nigh universal occurrence in connexion with healing, discovering the will of the spirits or gods, or prophesying'.[72]

The shaman is a wizard who uses magic and sorcery for a variety of functions in the community, such as healing, confronting demonic forces, divination (foretelling of events) and religious ritual. Anthropologist Joan Halifax (whose husband Stanislaw Grof was a prime instigator of LSD therapy in the 1950s) writes:

> 'For the shaman, all that exists in the revealed world has a living force within it. This life energy force, like the Polynesian *mana* or the Sioux *wakanda* is conceived of as a divine force which permeates all. The knowledge that life is power is the realization of the shaman. Communion with the purveyors of power is the work of the shaman. Mastery of that power: this is the attainment of the shaman'.[73]

Perhaps we can now understand the context in which Anton Mesmer discovered his so-called 'Magnetic Fluid', or the New Physicist posits his 'Superforce', together with all the other references — whether ancient or modern — which we

---

[71] Fritjof Capra, *The Turning Point: Science, Society and the Rising Culture* (Flamingo/Collins, 1982), p.334.

[72] James Hastings (ed.), *Encyclopaedia of Religion and Ethics* (T.& T. Clark, 1920), Vol.XI, p.446.

[73] Joan Halifax, *Shaman: The Wounded Healer* (Thames & Hudson, 1982), p.9.

have repeatedly made to this concept of *'a divine force which permeates all'*. Moreover, the identity of the above *'purveyors of power'* is not difficult to discern, in the light of our understanding of 'spirit-guides' and our knowledge of the discarnate entities known in theosophical and New Age circles as the 'Ascended Masters' or the 'Great White Brotherhood'. It was one such 'purveyor of power' which manifested itself as the spirit-guide *Philemon* to Jung, although Jungians would naïvely regard such an entity as a *'helpful structure in the personality deriving from the collective unconscious'*.

To put it bluntly, these demonic entities are purveying the same knowledge to the shaman — knowledge *'desirable to make one wise'* — as that given to our first parents as a result of their eating from the *'tree of knowledge'* at the dawn of human history (Gen.3:6). A knowledge based on the twin illusions of divinity and immortality. This is, without a doubt, the primary *leitmotiv* in our explorations of the spiritual battle between the serpent and the Cross which has extended from Eden to the present day. The knowledge purveyed by these demons to shamans and other explorers of *'non-ordinary states of consciousness'* is actually forbidden knowledge (Gen.2:17). The Hebrew word translated as *'wizard'* or *'familiar spirit'* (A.V.) in the Bible (e.g., Lev.19:31; 20:6; Dt.18:11) is *yiddeoni*, which means, literally, *knowing one*, implying *'esoteric knowledge not available to the ordinary person'*.[74] The English word 'wizard' also comes from an Old English root 'wis' meaning *to know* (from which our word 'wise' is also derived). This is the knowledge received from the demonic realm which fosters the twin illusions of divinity and immortality. The shaman, therefore, is a focal point for the transmission of a 'Satanic Initiation' — both for himself and for those who come to him for counsel. And within his own culture, he is regarded as an agent of change, the solver of problems — in fact, an early form of psychotherapist to whom one went to confess one's sins.[75]

The link with Western psychotherapy here is not merely a fanciful idea on the part of the present writer. It is, in fact, a highly significant prototype for the concept of the 'mind doctor' which is so popular in Western society today. Indeed, there is more than a superficial similarity between the function of the shaman of the ancient satanic religion and that of the psychotherapist of today. As Berkeley University physicist and Neo-Gnostic advocate, Dr. Fritjof Capra, points out:

> 'Shamans used therapeutic techniques such as group sharing, psychodrama, dream analysis, suggestion, hypnosis, guided imagery, and psychedelic therapy for centuries before they were rediscovered by modern psychologists'.[76]

'Rediscovered by modern psychologists'. Truly, there is nothing new under the sun! Modern humanistic and transpersonal psychotherapies are, in fact, a subtle

---

74 R.L. Harris, G.L. Archer Jr., & B.K. Waltke, *The Theological Wordbook of the Old Testament* (Moody Press, 1980), Vol.I, p.367.

75 James Hastings (ed.), *Encyclopaedia of Religion and Ethics*, Vol.XI, T. & T. Clark, p.444.

76 Fritjof Capra, op. cit., p.337.

rehash of many of the techniques of ancient pagan religion. The purveyors of the modern mind-sciences have actually resurrected the atavistic practices of the shaman and blended them with the modern techniques of the Viennese School and its offshoots — all hiding behind a smokescreen of acceptable scientific jargon. It was precisely such syncretism which was manifested in the key speakers at the ERANOS conferences in Switzerland, when a leading proponent of *shamanism*, Mircea Eliade, took over from the *psychotherapist* C.G. Jung who, in turn, had taken over from the Neo-Gnostic *theosophist* Alice B. Bailey. Shamanism, psychotherapy and theosophy are but different manifestations of the same root phenomenon, equal partners in the satanic outworking of the mind-sciences, the result of a global deception in which an increasing number of people are coming under the direct influence of the powers of darkness — deceiving spirits who masquerade as angels of light.

In the following two sections, we will examine the fallen world conditions and human state of mind which provide the fertile seed-bed for all the deceptions of the mind-sciences.

II. THE TRAP OF ENTRANCEMENT

1. The god of this Age

Since the creation of our first parents, the powers of darkness, as permitted by the Lord, have continually been working towards the complete control of the world, in order to make it the kingdom of Satan rather than being under the dominion of God. That Satan considered himself to be in such control is demonstrated by his offer to the Lord Jesus Christ in the wilderness of all the kingdoms of the world (Lk.4:5-7). This bid for control operated on two levels: firstly, through the political aspect of the nations, kingdoms, powers and principalities of the world, and, secondly, through the religious developments of the nations. On two notable occasions, God has taken major supernatural action in the cosmos in order to prevent this demonic control and iniquity from coming to its fullness: first, with the Flood (Gen.6:5-7, 11-13), and then at Babel (Gen.11:1-9).

However, when the Lord Jesus Christ won His victory on the cross at Golgotha, Satan was cast out of his role as *'prince/ruler of the world'* (Jn.12:31; Col.2:15). Since that time, the devil has been stalking the environs of the earth with the wrath of a roaring lion, seeking whom he may devour (Rev.12:12; 1 Pet.5:18), in the role of the usurper prince without any real kingdom, awaiting the sentence of judgement to be finally enacted upon him (Rev.20:10). Nevertheless, although Satan has been well and truly vanquished, he and his fellow demons still have some permitted powers of operation in the world during this span of time between the Ascension of Christ and His Second Coming, the Gospel Age — a period of history that Scripture calls *'the last days'* (Acts 2:17; Heb.1:2; 2 Pet.3:3). But the devil is under restraint from working publicly among the nations (as he did prior to the Cross) in open enmity against God and His people (Rev.20:1-3) — which is why the Gospel has been able to flourish so well. He has, therefore, been forced to operate in a more clandestine fashion.

This occult activity of Satan throughout the Gospel Age has again worked on both political and spiritual levels. Politically, it has been working unceasingly behind the scenes in order to bring about a confederated form of world government and economic system which will be in open enmity to the one true God and His Christ. Spiritually, it has operated through the collective mind and imagination of unregenerate humanity — especially through the development of occult techniques and practices which alter consciousness and lead to a kind of initiation involving the twin-illusions of divinity and immortality (cf. Gen.3:5-6: *'You will not surely die...You will be like God.'*). In previous chapters, we have looked in some detail at these practices: the repetition of *mantras* and other forms of auto-hypnosis, mysticism and meditation techniques, the inducement of mass trance-states through powerful suggestion procedures, consciousness-altering drugs, sorcery, etc. These practices form a major component in the more esoteric aspects of any of the world religions and cults.

In order to understand the magnitude of the conflict we are here exposing, we must realise that from the Fall to the present day, Satan and his fellow angels (demons) have cast a 'veil' over humanity through which people's minds are blinded to the reality of spiritual truth and seduced into the ways of lawlessness. Such spiritual blindness is the natural condition of the human mind in its unregenerate state (Jn.14:17a; 1 Cor.2:14). Such a man cannot even 'see' the kingdom of God (Jn.3:3), for his mind is *'darkened'* (Eph.4:18). It is in such a context as this that Paul makes the assertion that *'even if our gospel is veiled, it is veiled to those who are perishing, whose minds the god of this age has blinded'* (2 Cor.4:3-4).

Who is the *'god of this world'* that blinds the minds of those (unbelievers) who are perishing? It is none other than Satan — that wicked one whom Paul calls *'the prince of the power of the air, the spirit who now works in the sons of disobedience'* (Eph.2:2); while the entire demonic realm is referred to collectively as *'the rulers of the darkness of this age'* (Eph.6:12). Redemption through Christ means that this veil is lifted and the mind is released from the clutches of the powers of darkness (Col.1:13). This is why Paul spoke of himself as being sent to the Gentiles by Christ in order *'to open their eyes and to turn them from darkness to light, and from the power of Satan to God'* (Acts 26:17-18). Echoing this fact, Paul told the believers at Ephesus: *'You were once darkness, but now you are light in the Lord'* (Eph.5:8). The prophet Isaiah predicted this gift of salvation when he said, *'Then the eyes of the blind shall be opened, and the ears of the deaf shall be unstopped'* (Isa.35:5). A Christian is one who both sees and hears the Truth.

What is clear here is that spiritual regeneration involves an emerging from the compulsive, hypnotic power of the serpent into the loving, protective shadow of the Cross. The fact that unbelief is equivalent to being in a hypnotic state is alluded to in a number of places in Scripture. Sometimes, the Lord confirms a person in this blind haze of unbelief for judicial purposes. For example, when addressing the disobedient Israelites, Isaiah says:

> 'Pause and wonder! Blind yourselves and be blind! They are drunk, but not with wine; they stagger, but not with intoxicating drink. For

> the LORD has poured out on you the spirit of deep sleep, and has closed your eyes' (Isa.29:9-10).

And again, speaking of idolaters:

> 'They do not know nor understand; for He has shut (Hebrew, *tuach*, smeared over) their eyes, so that they cannot see, and their hearts, so that they cannot understand' (Isa.44:18).

Such judicial blindness from the Lord prevented many of the Jews from believing in Christ when He walked among them in Israel. On one occasion, Jesus warned the Pharisees that He had come into this world for judgement, *'that those who do not see may see, and that those who see may be made blind'* (Jn.9:39). He was saying here that those who humbly confess their spiritual blindness will be given spiritual eyesight, whereas those who proudly imagine themselves to have this eyesight by nature will only be made more blind. John confirmed this fact when he quoted from Isaiah:

> 'He [i.e., the Lord] has blinded their eyes and hardened their heart, lest they should see with their eyes and understand with their heart, lest they should turn, so that I should heal them' (Jn.12:39-40; cf. Mt.13:14-17; Mk.4:10-12).

It is in this same context of judicial blindness and hardening that the Gentiles — having turned from the worshipping of God the Creator to that of the creature — are spoken of as having been *'given over* [by God] *to a reprobate mind'* (Rom.1:28, A.V.). Similarly, when unbelievers give their full allegiance to the Antichrist, the Lord *'will send them **strong delusion**, that they should believe the lie'* (2 Th.2:11). To be under the power of Satan and deceived by false doctrine is tantamount to being *mesmerised* — which is why Paul asks the deceived Galatians, *'Who has **bewitched** you that you should not obey the truth?'* (Gal.3:1).

The tragedy of this world is that Satan and the demonic realm wield a kind of **mass hypnosis** over all those who are not saved by the power of Christ. This chasm between saved and unsaved is amply highlighted by the apostle John when, writing as one of the elect to his brothers and sisters in Christ, he says: *'We know that we are of God, and the whole world **lies under the sway** of the wicked one* [i.e., Satan]*'* (1 Jn.5:19). The regenerated person who has found salvation in Christ has been rescued from being under this sway of the wicked one, set free by the Truth (Jn.8:32), delivered from the power of darkness (Col.1:13), renewed in the spirit of his mind (Rom.12:2; Eph.4:23), given *'the mind of Christ'* (1 Cor.2:16), the mind *'which was also in Christ Jesus'* (Phil.2:5) — a mind which cannot be mesmerised by the forces of darkness or their earthly agents (cf. Mt.4:1-11), a mind which is so *'sound'* (2 Tim.1:7) that it cannot be *'tossed to and fro and carried about with every wind of doctrine, by the trickery of men'* (Eph.4:14). To such a person, the arm of the Lord has been revealed (Is.53:1). Revealed means unveiled, from the Latin *revelare*, to draw back the veil — the veil with which Satan blinds the minds and hearts of his subjects, even as he himself has been blinded to the knowledge of his own sin (cf. Isa.44:20).

2. The Battle for the Mind

All of this may seem to be something of a digression in a study on psychology and the mind-sciences; but we are, in fact, dealing with the very crux of the issue, which is this: That the collective mind and imagination of unregenerate humanity is under the power and control of the wickedness of Satan and the demonic realm. This has profound implications for any study of the human mind; because, in its unregenerate state, it is a mind held pathologically in abject delusion and darkness, a mind that is indeed *mad*, in that it is alienated from the 'Father of spirits'. In other words, we are dealing with a mind which can easily be psychically-controlled and programmed by the powers of darkness. Such is the mind that psychology attempts to map, and psychotherapy to treat.

We live in an age in which there have been many enhancements in the ease with which the mass mind of humanity is able to be programmed. The use of media such as television, newspapers, magazines, films and advertising have darkened the mind to spiritual truths, while at the same time encouraging the reception, in almost every home, of all manner of satanic specialities such as violence, pornography, occultism, ridicule of biblical Christianity, promiscuity, denigration of marriage and the family, syncretism, evolution theory, etc. Indeed, the very act of watching television and films has a progressively *mesmeric* effect which encourages the development of a *passive mind* — a psychic dustbin programmed to receive, without discernment, all that the enemies of truth can throw into it. Surely the television of today should cease to have pride of place in the living-room of the godly Christian home which seeks to fulfil its responsibilities towards children.

It is clear from Scripture that the whole of human history is built around a battle involving the *'rulers of the darkness of this age'*, a vast pantheon of wicked spirit-entities of varying rank and abilities, under the rulership of a once-mighty but now fallen angelic being (Eph.2:2; 6:10-18). These evil entities have invaded the imaginal life of humanity at every level — much of which we just take for granted — tempting, perverting, twisting and deceiving, posing as angels of light in order to bring to fruition the aims of this evil aeon. This is not to say that people can blame demons for their sinful behaviour in the same way that they like to blame their early-life traumas or their parents for their 'neurotic' behaviour; but that as the world chooses, through its own sinful desire, to plunge ever deeper into debauchery and godlessness, so it is given over by God to a reprobate mind and the resultant increased enslavement to demonic powers.

There can be little doubt that the mind-sciences are developing into globally acceptable phenomena. This is why psychotherapy, hypnotherapy, hallucinogens, Eastern Meditation and psychic research have become such vogue pursuits, even within the scientific 'community'. For this same reason, shamanism, spiritism, rebirthing, transpersonal psychology and theosophy — with their spirit-guides, Ascended Masters, visions and other demonic manifestations — are also becoming so widespread, even in establishment circles. Through these things, coupled with the use of the media, the world is gradually being flooded with habits, ideologies, practices and techniques which will render it into the ideal pre-hypnotic state of extreme suggestibility for the implementation of the final phase of the satanic world-kingdom. The stark reality is that as the world falls ever deeper into hubris and sin, it will be increasingly hardened and given over to being controlled with even greater might by these forces of evil — although it will all take place under the disguise of angels of light.

3. The Pre-Hypnotic Condition of the World

Truly, the unregenerate mind is *'deceitful above all things and incurably sick'* (a literal translation of the Hebrew in Jer.17:9). It will scream and wail ecstatically at the sight and sound of media-manufactured personalities. It will sit riveted for hours on end by a soap opera or similar base entertainment. It is a mind as easily addicted to nicotine, television and alcohol as it is to heroin, 'crack' and cocaine. It will slavishly follow the fashions and fads of the day. It will gleefully gawp at the icons of royalty. It will mindlessly follow a football team to the four corners of the earth, singing its praises and stabbing those who differ. It will incinerate whole nations of peoples if instructed to do so by men in white coats with clipboards and 'Joe 90' spectacles.[77] It will bow down before the grim Mullahs of Islamic cultdom and chant collectively at the pre-set signal. It will believe the collective lies of generations of political skullduggery. It will condemn pornography with its mouth, yet its mind and eyes will spend the rest of their time engrossed in visual and printed media which exclusively peddle such degrading material.

This tragic, powerfully pre-hypnotic condition of humanity and its ability to be manipulated has even been officially recognised within the field of psychotherapy — although not as a tragedy but as a field ripe for further exploitation. One senior psychotherapist has tellingly stated, in a training session on hypnosis with other therapists:

> 'One of the most fascinating things you will discover once you are fully

---

[77] We are not referring particularly here to the situation in Nazi Germany during World War II. Because most people would say, *'we would never do that'*, it would be more revealing to cite the 'Milgram Experiment'. In the 1970s, an experiment was carried out at City University, New York, by Professor of Psychology Stanley Milgram. In a research programme designed to discover whether apparently decent people can commit atrocities, he set up an artificial situation in a laboratory where volunteers from 'respectable' backgrounds were given to believe (wrongly) that they were administering electric shocks to other experimental subjects in a neighbouring room. Amazingly, the majority of these people were prepared to give fatal shocks to the subject (who could often be heard screaming for mercy) in the cause of science, when requested to do so by a seemingly respectable academic scientist. In the U.S.A. 62% went all the way; while figures in Rome, South Africa, and Australia were much higher. In Germany, the figure was a staggering 85%! Details of this controversial but highly revealing experiment were published in *Obedience to Authority: An Experimental View* (1974), and in an article entitled 'Behavioural Study of Obedience', in the *Journal of Abnormal and Social Psychology*, Vol.67, 1963, pp.371-378.

> competent in using the ritualistic notions of traditional hypnosis, is that you'll never have to do it again. A training program in hypnosis is not for your clients. It's for **you**, because *you will discover that somnambulistic trance is the rule rather than the exception* in people's everyday 'waking activity''.[78] [emphasis in original]

Here, it is being frankly admitted by a professional trainer of psychotherapists that 'trance' is the normal state of the unregenerate human mind. In other words, such a mind is a walking bundle of susceptibility to hypnotic suggestion. There has been a glut of psychological research which backs up this phenomenon. In one such study, a psychologist discovered that he was unable to find a single thing within the bounds of professional ethics that normal, awake subjects would not do under the power of suggestion.[79] And it is this all-pervasive condition which has enabled the mind-sciences in their many forms to proliferate to such an extent — even in the ecclesiastical scene, as we shall see in Chapter 11. In an extraordinary admission concerning the real nature of psychotherapy, the above trainer of therapists goes on to give the following truly apocalyptic advice to his students:

> 'You will discover that most of the techniques in different types of psychotherapy are nothing more than hypnotic phenomena'.[80]

Here is a senior psychologist revealing the truth of his craft, exposing the manipulation that lies at the back of the mind-sciences — deception and suggestion working in harmony with one another. *'Nothing more than hypnotic phenomena'*. It is the suggestible, trance-like, hopelessly-dependent state of the fallen human mind which provides the receptive ground on which the hypnotic techniques of psychotherapy can do their work. And these are techniques which many Christians have been duped into believing are in line with Scripture, when we can now see that they conform much more closely to the subterfuges of shamanism and ancient sorcery.

What we are really dealing with here are mind-games on a vast scale. For the collective unregenerate imagination is a vast, open canvas on which the 'powers of the air', in conjunction with the corruption of the world, can paint whatever suggestion the observer, through his own inherent sinfulness, is open to receive — whether it is a vision in keeping with his religious tradition, the illusion of an acquired 'divinity', the belief that one's leg has been lengthened by a faith-healing session, the urge to murder or steal, a recurrent sexual obsession, the re-experiencing of an early life trauma, or (as any advertising magnate will aver) the desire to buy a particular brand of baked beans! Whatever a person's proclivity,

[78] Richard Bandler and John Grinder, *Frogs into Princes: Neuro-Linguistic Programming* (Real People Press, 1979), p.100. It should be noted that 'Neuro-Linguistic Programming', a subtle kind of hypnotherapy, has enjoyed a major cult following in the British social work and psychology scene — having been vogue in the so-called 'caring' professions in the U.S. for many years beforehand.

[79] M.T. Orne, 'On the Social Psychology of the Psychological Experiment', in *American Psychologist*, No.17, 1962, pp.776-783.

[80] Richard Bandler and John Grinder, op. cit., p.100.

so it will be exploited to the full, providing the bed-rock for besetting sins, as well as a multitude of excuses for them. It is for this reason that the apostle Paul advises the Ephesian believers not to *'give place to the devil'* by allowing sinful anger to persist and thereby become enstructured within the personality (Eph.4:26-27).[81] He knew well that the demonic realm feeds on the ready-made foibles of the sinful human mind.

It is not without significance for our study at this point that even the scientists are beginning to recognise these things as they become involved in parapsychology and transpersonal research — although their conclusions differ radically from those of the biblical Christian. For example, Dr. Elmer Green of the Menninger Foundation is a leading neuro-psychiatrist in the U.S.A., who has also worked for fifteen years as a physicist on rocket and guided missile research. He was one of the pioneers in terms of bridging the gulf between Western science and Eastern mysticism, following his research in 1970 into the psycho-physiological states of Yoga, using the Indian guru Swami Rama as his laboratory subject. In one paper treating of the exploration of transpersonal states, he writes:

> 'According to various warnings, the persistent explorer in these... realms...*brings himself to the attention of indigenous beings who, under normal circumstances pay little attention to humans...* If he is not relatively free from personality dross, it is said, they can obsess him with various compulsions for their own amusement and in extreme cases can even disrupt the normally automatic functioning of the nervous system, by controlling the brain through the *Chakras* [energy centres in Tantric anatomy].[82]

In spite of the misleading elements in this statement (e.g., that these 'beings' pay little attention to humans) it is an acknowledgement, from a leading Western psychiatrist, that malign discarnate entities can have access to the human psyche. As we have already noted in an earlier chapter, it is necessary for good communication between the demonic realm and humanity that the inner life or imaginal capacity (consciousness) of a person should be 'expanded' to its maximum, thus creating an openness to manipulation. This fact accounted for the huge growth in recent decades of the use of 'mind-expanding' drugs, and all the other techniques which are being used to expand consciousness and create the illusion of realised divinity. As one psychologist rightly claimed more than fifteen years ago:

> 'In my experience and thinking, the single major event forcing this development [of transpersonal psychology] has been the widespread use and abuse of psychedelic or mind-manifesting substances such as

---

[81] The Greek word translated as 'place' here is *topos*. Another eminently suitable translation would be 'foothold' or 'opportunity'. What Paul is saying is that if you don't resolve your sinful anger, you give the devil an immediate foothold or place of opportunity in your life.

[82] Dr. Elmer Green, *On the Meaning of Transpersonal*, Journal of Transpersonal Psychology, Vol.XIII, No.1, 1971.

marijuana, LSD and mescaline [an hallucinogenic Mexican cactus]... The psychedelic drugs gave incontrovertible proof that altered states of consciousness had reality and that paths toward transcendent experience existed... We were hunting for ways to stay high forever and bring home the New Jerusalem, the Whole Earth'.[83]

The 'psychedelic sixties' were, as we have shown, paving the way for the gathering wave of global demonic manipulation. At the same time, Eastern mysticism made a major assault on the West by cashing in on this new transcendentalism. Within a matter of years, Western science also began to tell us to *'leave our minds at the door with our shoes'* when we entered its territory. Such practices have contributed to the creation of a New Consciousness which is finely tuned to the promptings of the demonic realm. It is because of these developments that there is the great need for a rational, discerning mind and the Christian concept of **objective reality** which have become such objects of disparagement in the ethos of this New Gnosticism.

In the light of the pedigree of Western psychotherapy which we have traced out in this study, we believe that Christians should be eschewing all involvement in its techniques. Apart from the pressing fact that there is no record of any kind of psychotherapy for the Christian in the Bible, we must apply ourselves to discovering what should be the response of the Christian to human problems which are generally identified as 'emotional' or 'mental health' issues. Let us now therefore examine some important concerns affecting the mind of man.

4. It's All in the Mind

In the same way that pathology in medicine (unwittingly) involves the study of the effects of the Fall on the physical constituents of the human body, so psychology is essentially (and also unwittingly) concerned with the study of the effects of the Fall on the imagination and behaviour of the human mind. All the research that has ever been gathered in this field is simply a cataloguing of the characteristics and propensities of a corrupted and fallen nature. The vast pantheon of psychotherapies which have been developed in the wake of such study and research merely signifies the desperate *humanistic* attempts which have been made to try to rectify the tragedy of the human condition: alienation from God.

In order to understand how this has come about, one must first understand that all secular psychology is concerned with researching and gathering data on the behaviour of what the apostle Paul called the *'old man'*. This is the fallen sinful nature, in its unregenerated state, which is *'enmity against God'* (Rom.5:12; 8:7). Thus, the human being suffers and brings about suffering. His condition of alienation from God prevents him from partaking in the benefits of His saving grace. When the Fall of our first parents took place, the Lord Himself decreed that human existence would be filled with hardship (Gen.3:16-19). Thus, the

---

[83] John Heider, *'Catharsis in Human Potential Encounter'*, Journal of Humanistic Psychology, No.14, 1974. Quoted in John Rowan, *Ordinary Ecstasy: Humanistic Psychology in Action* (Routledge & Kegan Paul, 1976), p.103.

scene was set for problems of every kind: mental, emotional, physical, personal, environmental — with spiritual and physical death as the centre-piece of the tragic scenario.

Essentially, the province of psychotherapy is the reformation of 'mind' problems and the toll they take on the emotional well-being of the individual. There is, however, a world of difference between this kind of Godless, humanistic reformation and the true spontaneous regeneration initiated by the Holy Spirit in those who have been called according to His purpose. In the same way that mysticism involves the utilisation of certain practices in order to induce in a person the experience of a pseudo-regeneration, so psychotherapy has devised a variety of techniques to effect a simulated sanctification. In contrast to this, true religion is *'born, not of blood, nor of the will of the flesh, nor of the will of man, but of God'* (Jn.1:13).

Both mystical practices and psychotherapeutic techniques are designed to bring about a counterfeit experience of the profound spiritual changes which take place in the Christian who is quickened by the Holy Spirit. Although it is true that psychotherapy can indeed bring about changes in the personality and behaviour of an individual — and we will later see in what it is that those changes consist — true regeneration transforms those parts of the person which psychotherapy can never reach. Furthermore, the work which God does in those He saves is not in the least dependent on any prior therapy or treatment. In fact, the process of Spirit-inspired regeneration can take place in the heart of the most seemingly hell-bent psychopath. Whatever your condition — whether riddled with neuroses, nervous tics, phobias, obsessions or any other personal problem — if the Lord wants you, He will have you!

Because of this provision, the unregenerated nature — what the New Testament calls the *'old man'* — of the one so converted will be spontaneously and irreversibly transformed into the *'new man'* (Col.3:9-10). He or she will become *'a new creation'* in Christ (2 Cor.5:17). In such a manner as this, the Lord has indeed provided the most remarkable cure for the sick personality of the fallen human being. This is the kernel of the Gospel message. Those who have faith to call upon His Name will be spiritually transformed and brought back into communion with their Creator (2 Cor.5:18-21; 2 Pet.1:4), while their alienated, fallen natures will be crucified with their Saviour (Rom.6:6).

Such a transformation makes psychotherapy, by comparison, seem like a shoddy game in which the participants merely manage to make each other *feel* better — 'feelings' always being the central concern in this field. Confession without absolution is the name of the game. With psychotherapy, one papers over the cracks and polishes the paintwork of a person, but he just becomes like the house which is *'empty, swept and put in order...and the last state of that man is worse that the first'* (Mt.12:43-45). In other words, the perennial effect of a psychotherapeutic 'cleansing' on the unregenerate person will be to leave him in a state of openness to a subtle but even more powerful form of bondage than that in which he had been, prior to the therapy. Only the regenerating power of the Holy

Spirit has the ability to set in motion a complete reversal of the Fall in its ontological effects on the personality of the human being.

However, this does not mean that the believer's problems, fears, diseases and other afflictions immediately disappear. Far from it! The Bible does not speak of one mighty experience which erases, in an instant, all the problems connected with having a corruptible body and living in a fallen world. But it does mean that when a man or woman is made a new creature in Christ, there is the beginning of a wholly new way of dealing with any problems which present themselves in the life of the believer — involving the twin processes of *Sanctification* and *Mortification*, about which we shall have more to say shortly. Although on one level it is true that the Christian has been 'definitively sanctified' — that is, cleansed and set apart from the world — through his or her regeneration (cf. Eph.2:5-6), there is a subsequent lifelong process of transformation in the personality and being of the believer, during which he or she must walk every (often painful) step of the way under the leadership and guidance of the Holy Spirit (cf. Rom.8:12-17; Gal.5:16-18; Phil.2:12-13).

Although it is true that from a spiritual standpoint the Christian has already *'crucified the flesh with its passions and desires'* (Gal.5:24), he still continues to exist, from an anthropological standpoint, *in the flesh* — demonstrated by the fact that Paul exhorts the Galatian believers not to use their Christian liberty *'as an opportunity for the flesh'* (Gal.5:13; cf. 1 Pet.2:16). Because of this ongoing condition — arising from the 'not-yetness' of the kingdom, which has so far come only *in grace* but not yet *in glory* — the Christian can find himself in some considerable turmoil if he does not exercise biblical self-control (Pro.25:28; Gal.5:23; 1 Cor.9:27; Rom.6:11-14; Jas.4:7).

From a spiritual standpoint, therefore, the chief concern of the Christian is not how to find ways of being free from the traumas of life but to discover how to respond to them with spiritual wisdom and acceptance — walking by faith rather than by sight (Rom.8:18; 2 Cor.4:17; 5:7). In the time of the apostolic Church the majority of children would have had a traumatic early-life experience, unshielded from the gritty hardships of life and death; yet the main focus of the apostles was on the fostering of *spiritual* growth, regardless of the psychological problems of life and in spite of any past traumas. Indeed, there is no biblical record of a believer seeking or receiving any kind of psychological therapy for his hang-ups. The 'denial of self' prescribed by Christ stands in complete opposition to the obsession with Self which characterises all psychotherapy.

When Paul asked the Lord to remove a nagging problem (that famous *'thorn in the flesh'*), he wasn't sent by Him to see the nearest shaman or healer. Instead, he received the reply: *'My grace is sufficient for you, for My strength is made perfect in weakness'* (2 Cor.12:9). That should give the Lord's people pause for thought whenever the urge to go rushing off to therapists with the least problem presents itself. The only truly healthy mind is that which possesses *'the mind of Christ'* (1 Cor.2:16). Such a mind can say with assurance: *'I can do all things through Christ who strengthens me'* (Phil.4:13). The focus for the believer must be on the

Lord Jesus Christ as his 'role model', rather than on himself or his therapist (Heb.12:1-3).

The uncomfortable truth is that no matter how super-straightened-out we may imagine we have become through the techniques of the mind-sciences — even if we manage to transform ourselves into the model New Age Renaissance Human Being — in the eyes of the Sovereign Lord of the universe we are spiritually unclean until we have come to the foot of the cross and begged for that mercy and forgiveness which can only be found in the saving blood of the Lord Jesus Christ (Jn.3:3-6).

5. The Great Christian Therapy Hoax

In spite of these biblical truths, there are many in the professing church who advocate the use of various psychotherapies — especially the abreactive types — in preference to the Christian way of sanctification and mortification. Indeed, drinking from the fountains of Egypt has become a major pastime in many areas of life in Evangelical circles. That this should be the case with psychotherapy is extraordinary, in view of the fact that the psychotherapeutic approach to behavioural and perceptual problems is rooted in the conceptual framework of ancient shamanism and more recent occult phenomenology. In some circles, the saving power of psychotherapy has been given a higher status than that of the preaching of the true Gospel, which would be considered to be outmoded. Indeed, the 'Psycho-Gospel' has become as powerful an ecclesiastical pursuit as its stablemate, the 'Social Gospel', with Jesus being presented as 'the Great Psychotherapist' as well as 'the First Socialist'! One 'Christian' psychotherapist puts it like this:

> 'We, as therapists, like Christ, are human channels. We try to develop the gifts of knowledge, understanding, intuition and caring that we have been given, to the best of our ability. The Holy Spirit cannot work through us as therapists unless we use our brains, continually enlarging and deepening our insight into human nature and our knowledge as to how personality develops as well as our understanding of the kind of things that can go wrong. We must not assume that God will do the whole job himself. At times he needs a human channel, but we must realise we are a channel or a catalyst to help a person to grow and become healed of past emotional hurts'.[84]

It is this kind of statement which is deceiving so many Christians today. For the unwary, it all sounds so caring and plausible. But the Lord Jesus Christ is not merely, like the therapist, a 'human channel'; He is the eternal Son of God (Jn.8:58), by whom all things were created (Col.1:16-17). Furthermore, the Holy Spirit is dependent on nothing in man for His operations within people, otherwise there would be no human salvation! It is true that the Lord often uses human instruments to bring His works to fruition, but there is not even a hint in Scripture

---

[84] Barbara Gage, *Channels: Journal of the North of England Christian Healing Trust*, September 1985, p.8.

that psychotherapy or its practitioners are among them.

In this same article, examples are given of people in the Gospel writings with alleged 'emotional problems' whom Jesus helped therapeutically: people such as the Prodigal Son, his brother and father, the rich young ruler, the woman with the alabaster box, Zacchaeus, the woman at the well of Samaria, etc.[85] Such an interpretation of these parables and narratives bears no relation to the true intent of those who were divinely inspired to write them down for us. The idea that the Gospel stories provide us with a model for Christian psychotherapy would be laughable, were it not so destructive of the real sense of the Scriptures. This psychotherapist, in conjunction with many others today, claims to be following Christ by making people 'whole' through

> 'forming a relationship with the sufferer which is so deep it reaches the level of early emotional hurts, so reliable and loving that they can safely be recalled, sometimes relived and then healed by love'.[86]

The kind of abreactive therapy being expounded here is a well-used secular technique in which the patient, through hypnosis or powerful suggestion by a therapist, is taken back to early life experiences — even to birth and the intra-uterine state — in order to 'undo' the harmful hold they allegedly exert over our behaviour. The *'deep'* relationship with the sufferer referred to by this therapist is what Freudians call the 'Transference', a significant stage of the therapeutic process in which the person undergoing therapy transfers onto the therapist the affections and authority which would normally characterise his relationship with his parents. This places the counselee/client in a very vulnerable position, through which he becomes easily manipulated and open to all manner of suggestions from the therapist — including the idea that he needs to relive past hurts in order to be 'cured'. This mind-manipulation, involving the power of suggestion, was clearly exposed in a recent cover-article in 'Time' magazine, which claimed that *'repressed-memory therapy is harming patients, devastating families and intensifying a backlash against mental health practitioners'*.[87]

The theory behind all abreactive therapy is that traumatic experiences in one's formative years (e.g., parental ill-feelings towards the foetus in the womb, an obstetric rather than a natural birth, cruelty towards the child, anything which does not fully meet the child's needs) build up defensive postures like bricks in a wall, until he or she is hedged in and cut off from real living. Neuroses are cracks in that wall; more serious disorders (known as schizophrenia or psychosis) occur when the wall starts to topple down. Abreactive psychotherapy involves the systematic dismantling of these walls in people through various techniques.[88]

---

[85] Ibid., p.7.

[86] Ibid., p.8.

[87] *Time Magazine*, November 29th, 1993.

[88] The film, *'The Wall'*, by the Pink Floyd rock group, was a thematic representation of this theory, as the group's leader, Roger Waters, had become infatuated with psychotherapy. They performed a special show of the music from the film in Berlin after the Berlin Wall came down. Esotericists and Neo-Gnostic psychotherapists today believe

This therapy travels under a variety of names such as Primal Therapy, Regression Therapy, Psychodynamic Therapy, Rebirthing, Bioenergetics, Structural Integration, etc. Within Christian circles the same conceptual framework has simply been rehashed, mingled with elements of Christianity, and peddled under the umbrella headings of 'Inner Healing' (prime mover, Agnes Sanford), 'Healing of the Memories' (devised by Methodist minister David Seamonds), and 'Clinical Theology' (invented by Dr. Frank Lake).[89]

However, it must be understood that psychotherapy takes insufficient account of the dynamic profundity of the transformation which is effected in the life of the one who is delivered out of the power of darkness into the kingdom of Christ. Formerly illiterate and ignorant people become children of wisdom with an insatiable appetite for Christian literature and the ability to read it. Previously violent thugs are stilled like the storm on the sea of Galilee and the man with the legion of demons. The chronically shy are changed into communicative creatures, filled with zeal. Hardened addicts of all kinds are released from bondage into a love-filled liberty of life. Such is the transforming power of God, which is just as capable of vaporising mental and emotional turmoil in a person — provided it is His will to do so and the biblical guidelines for treatment are being followed.

As far as the non-Christian is concerned, the *beginning* of a cure for mental and emotional difficulties is to come to Christ in repentance for one's sin. All other forms of cleansing will leave the last state of that person worse than the first — even if psychotherapy gives him the *illusion* of health. Thereafter, he must submit to the Word of God and seek help from his new-found brethren and the newly indwelling Holy Spirit. However, conversion does **not** mean an instantaneous remission of all behavioural disorders. But the new convert will now have a *biblical* framework in which to view his distresses, and a godly strategy with which to begin to cope with them.

Although the unbeliever will generally seek his own immediate well-being in these circumstances, the Christian must seek primarily to know God's will in every instance of his life. Thus, for the Christian who is suffering from psychological difficulties, disturbances of the mind or behavioural problems, the beginning of a 'cure' consists in the acknowledgement that his life is now governed by the fact that he is *a new creation in Christ* rather than an autonomous individual.

Because he recognises this undergirding fact, the psychologically-suffering Christian — provided the source of his problems is not organic disease — will seek help, if necessary, *from other Christians*, rather than from unbelievers. And these Christians from whom he will seek help will not have to be trained in the arts of secular psychotherapy; neither will they be purveyors of a synthesis of this

---

that their work is bringing about a gradual breaking-down of the psychological barriers within people, through which they hope to generate the breaking down of physical, national, geographic and religious barriers between people — all leading to the one-world, globalist, interfaith outlook which they so desire.

[89] The teachings of these Christian healers, along with other ecclesiastical diversions, will come under intense scrutiny in Chapter 11.

and some fuzzy biblical thinking. It is our heartfelt, Bible-based conviction that Western psychotherapy is unfit to diagnose the true problems of the unbeliever, let alone the Spirit-indwelt believer. Indeed, it has been ably demonstrated that psychiatric diagnosis is a wholly unreliable process, stigmatising people for life with worthless labels.[90] For these reasons, when the believer subjects himself to a so-called 'Christian' psychotherapist, who has simply rehashed the theories of his secular counterparts, he has sold his birthright for a veritable mess of potage.

We will look further into the process of biblical counselling later in our study. First, we are laying bare the true causes of behavioural problems in life. Unless we have a full understanding of the universal underlying reasons for human disorders, we will contine to dream up solutions based on false or inadequate premises.

III. THE BASIC FAULT

This now brings us to a vital issue, and a most revealing one. In the early 1970s, a little book which has been highly influential in psychotherapeutic circles first appeared. Entitled 'The Basic Fault', by psychiatrist Michael Balint, this work related his conviction that behind all neurosis, psychosis or schizophrenic disorder, there is a root cause which can be traced back to either foetal experience in the womb, the trauma of birth itself, or life-threatening experiences during the first few days of life.[91] There is a burgeoning number of Christian psychotherapists who also subscribe to this theory — additionally maintaining that these experiences prevent the development of a satisfactory relationship with God. Treatment with psychotherapy, therefore, is alleged to lead not only to emotional wholeness but also to the resultant ability to enjoy a closer relationship with God. But does this theory — assuming for a moment it is true — really reach into the *basic* fault in humanity? This we will now examine.

1. Original Sin

Although there are certainly some elements of truth in this highly deterministic concept of human development — in that people can indeed be profoundly affected by environmental influences — it actually represents a very superficial understanding of human development, and does not go nearly far enough in its assessment of the true condition of man. The conditioning element of any early environmental influences is not the real root factor in the emotional or psychic hurts of mankind.[92] Our early-life parental relationships may well cause distortion of other interpersonal relationships in later life, but that early-life deprivation **is itself a consequence of another far more profound factor**. For it is our primordial separation from God through the Fall of our first parents which actually predetermines a distorted relationship in the first instance.

---

[90] For evidence of this, see Martin & Deidre Bobgan, *The Psychological Way: The Spiritual Way* (Harvest House, 1979), pp.53-63.

[91] Michael Balint, *The Basic Fault: Therapeutic Aspects of Regression* (Routledge & Kegan Paul, 1973, 1990).

[92] As can be seen by the fact that even Pavlov's dogs lost their conditioning when a laboratory accident befell them!

Of course, this concept of 'original sin' does not figure at all in the work of the psychotherapists, whether secular or 'Christian'. Dr. Frank Lake — a professing Christian psychiatrist who was profoundly influenced by Wilhelm Reich — suggests, in his book 'Clinical Theology', that we become mad (or sinful) through being the innocent victims of our parents' sin in their neglect of us at an early age.[93] But this is completely at loggerheads with the teaching of the Bible, where it is shown that all human beings have sinned *'in Adam'* (Rom.5:12ff.; 1 Cor.15:22) and are steeped in sin *right from the moment of conception* (Ps.51:5), rather than our sin being the result of a traumatic intra-uterine experience or birth-process. Unregenerate human beings *'are estranged from the womb'* (Ps.58:3), are *'by nature'* deserving only of God's wrath (Eph.2:3), and, as Jesus Himself showed, are destined for eternal damnation in hell (Jn.3:36; Lk.13:3,5).

It is that original sinful nature, alienated from God and in enmity towards Him, which then craves self-gratification in such a way that it can never be properly satisfied by any human comfort. In other words, man — in his natural, unregenerate state, without hope and without God in the world (Eph.2:12b; 1 Th.4:5b) — is **mad** in the truest sense, regardless of how 'civilised' he may appear to be or how 'straightened out' he may become through psychotherapy. As the prophet Jeremiah puts it: *'The heart is deceitful above all things, and **incurably sick**'* (a literal translation of the Hebrew in Jer.17:9). One can relive and resolve every single childhood trauma under the powerful suggestion of adult psychotherapy and yet still be among the most hell-bound of sinners.

In his play *'Huis Clos'*, Jean-Paul Sartre had his principal 'damned' character say that *'Hell is other people'*; but that is an insane inversion of the truth. Hell is *alienation* from other people (Mt.22:13) and from God (Mt.27:46; cf. 2 Th.1:9). In its ultimate manifestation, Hell is madness fixed for eternity, in which there will be a wailing and gnashing of teeth that will make the worst bear-garden appear like a genteel tea party. In the same way that the Church is the suburbs of Heaven, so the world of the unregenerate is the outskirts of Hell. Although it serves as God's device for making life in this world tolerable for His people, the historical process known as 'civilisation' is humankind's wallpaper over the cracks that lead to Hell.

When our first parents sinned in Eden by denying the authority of God their Father, they were disowned from what would have been their family inheritance: eternal life in fellowship with God (Gen.2:17; 3:22-24). From that point on human beings would be rootless vagabonds in the world, without any real home or family — outside of a relationship with God, a law unto themselves. It is as if the Lord had said to Adam and Eve (and thereby to all their descendants, Rom.5:12-14):

> 'Well then, since you have chosen to do without my good offices as your Father, and you have turned to the devil; therefore I henceforth disown you, and you can have Satan as your father instead'.

---

[93] Frank Lake, *Clinical Theology* (Darton, Longman and Todd, 1986), p.12.

Because of this alienation and *orphanism*, man makes desperate attempts to compensate through establishing his own futile powerbase in the world in his own name (Gen.4:17; cf. Ps.49:11-12; Zech.5:11), under the fatherhood of Satan. Having no hope and without God in the world (Eph.2:12b), mankind became the children of the devil (Mt.13:38; 1 Jn.3:10; cf. Mt.12:34; Jn.8:44). The only way out of this misery is to be adopted back into the family of God through faith in Jesus Christ. According to the Bible, one is either *'in Adam'* or *'in Christ'* (cf. 1 Cor.15:22), insofar as our spiritual family heritage is concerned. The former means being under the fatherhood and influence of the devil; the latter means being under the Fatherhood of God and thereby a brother or sister of the Lord Jesus Christ. When a person is converted by the power of the Gospel, he receives the Spirit of adoption who enables him to cry out *'Abba, Father'* and who witnesses to his spirit that he is now one of the children of God (Rom.8:12-17). In short, he is adopted back into the family of God and receives the Holy Spirit as a guarantee or downpayment ('earnest', A.V.) on his future inheritance of eternal life and glorification (2 Cor.1:21-22; 5:1-5; Eph.1:13). This explains the 'recognition' felt by the new Christian that he or she has 'found' (or, rather, has been found by) the One whom he had unknowingly sought all along. Conversely, those who never come to Christ in repentance choose to remain as orphans, without hope and without God in the world.

However, because of this intrinsic alienation from God the Father and the spiritual vacuum it creates, every single human being — in spite of a wilful predisposition towards selfishness and pride — inwardly craves some measure of restoration and reconciliation, although not that provided by God Himself. This condition of unfulfilment manifests itself in one distorted form or another throughout our entire lives. It is especially noticeable in relation to the universal need man has for religious practice. And it is this primordial *spiritual* need for reconciliation which gives rise to an insatiable and essentially unrealizable *psychological* desire to be unconditionally loved by an earthly substitute. And not only loved, but constrained too. Is it not true that each one of us cries out for boundaries and external control — authority, law? And is this not because we are born in a state of lawlessness apart from God? Our earthly parents are, in a sense, *in loco parentis* for God, our true but lost Parent (cf. Gen.18:19; Ex.20:12; 21:15-17; Ps.78:5; Pro.22:6; 23:13-14; Eph.6:4).[94]

Consequently, in order to compensate for his alienated state, man spends his infancy, childhood and adolescence making impossible demands on his earthly parents, and later in adulthood on his spouse, who is unable to provide for his true needs, because they are essentially spiritual rather than psychological. It is, therefore, hardly surprising that we grow into adulthood with all manner of unmet

[94] It is not without significance that trendy, libertarian methods of education and child-rearing have become vogue in recent years. It is in the interests of the satanic realm to emphasise the importance of an environment in which the 'self-regulated' (and self-oriented) child can develop *without restraint*. This is all part of an education for the New Age.

needs.[95] It is pointless to blame our parents for these neuroses, probing the recesses of our minds for their cause. The true reason for their existence and the sole panacea lie so much deeper than even our earliest possible memory. The **real** basic fault does not lie in our early-life traumas but in our being *'in Adam'*. The sad reality is that even after a lifetime of therapy in which every painful memory imaginable has been brought to the surface, a person will still be spiritually unregenerate and destined for eternal death, unless his heart is turned to Christ in repentance and faith — for he will still be partaking in the original sin of Adam, and thus outside of the family of God.

Therefore, in opposition to the claims of psychotherapy that others cause our madness and therapists provide the cure, we proclaim that the cause of madness is ourselves (and the dilemma of who we are), while the cure of madness is Christ (and the fullness of who He is).

2. Structural Sin

Let us now take this matter of the inadequacy of the psychotherapeutic model of human development even further still: We have seen that a psychological framework which views early-life traumas as the root of all 'mind' problems is woefully inadequate — in that it has no concept of original sin and its effect of alienation. Similarly, it can also be said that any psychotherapeutic approach which claims to deal with such problems on the basis of that inadequate framework will also be hopelessly deficient.

The disorders which are classified as 'mental illness' in Western culture are fundamentally the result of man's fallen state. As we have seen, on a universal level, **original sin** predisposes human beings to such difficulties (Gen.3:16-19). However, quite apart from the ontological problems that man has through having sinned *'in Adam'*, the behavioural and perceptual problems which Western psychology calls 'mental illness' very often form a strategy that is directly rooted in **personal sin**. What the world does not know (and many Christians fail to realise) is that sin is not so much an outward behavioural problem but an inward *structural* dilemma. Sin is described by Paul the Apostle as if it was an actual entity — an impelling force which is embedded within the very structure of a person and which powers all his outward actions (Rom.6:6). The Lord Jesus also said:

> 'Hear Me, everyone, and understand: There is nothing that enters a man from outside which can defile him; but the things which come out of him, those are the things that defile him. If anyone has ears to hear, let him hear!' (Mk.7:14-15).

Jesus identified those defiling 'things which come out of a man' as being such disturbed behaviours as

> 'evil thoughts, murders, adulteries, fornications, thefts, false witness, blasphemies, covetousness, wickedness, deceit, licentiousness, an evil

[95] The fact that the majority of 'pop' songs bewail such unmet relationship needs is yet another poignant testimony to this dilemma.

eye, pride, foolishness' (Mt.15:19 with Mk.7:21-23).

The modern psychotherapists would attempt to blame these things on our early-life traumas — on contingencies outside of ourselves — but Jesus says: *'All these evil things come from within and defile a man'* (Mk.7:23). There is never a hint in Jesus' teaching that our behaviour is ultimately the result of the sin of others affecting our lives. Jesus was here identifying the fact of human depravity, the structural sin which is an outworking of our original sinful nature. The behaviours known as 'mental illness' are actually extreme outworkings of this inbuilt sinful structure — one which can continue to harass the Christian, even though it no longer has dominion over him (Rom.7:17-18,23 with 6:14).

It is certainly true that many disorders of this nature (phobias, anxiety, depression, morbid thoughts and feelings, palpitations, pains, obsessions, hallucinations, delusions, etc.) can be precipitated by organic disease (e.g., hormone and chemical imbalance, coronary disease, genetic disorder, Parkinson's Disease, etc.); and such possibilities should be vigorously investigated by the proper medical experts when such behavioural problems present themselves. It is likewise true that such difficulties can be brought on by dietary deficiencies, inadequate exercise, allergies, chemical food additives and poor sleeping patterns. In which case, the treatment can be relatively simple and quickly effected.

However, in the event of these contingent factors being discounted or of organic illness being invalidated, there is no requirement whatsoever for us to invoke the clinical, medical model in order to diagnose, understand or cope with presenting emotional or behavioural problems. In fact, we believe that the medical model or clinical approach to these afflictions in such circumstances is a serious error — the inevitable product of a culture which will not face up to its spiritual failures, responsibilities and deficiencies. Accordingly, we view these problems as essentially spiritual rather than clinical — rooted ultimately in the structural sin of man rather than in his early-life experiences, which are preceded by it.

For example, if a person develops a handwashing ritual which must be carried out every fifteen minutes without fail in order to avert a feeling of doom, the psychotherapist calls it an 'Obsessional Neurosis'. But such a behavioural problem is actually a manifestation of superstition which has been allowed to take root deep in the personality structure. It is the grown-up equivalent of the childhood fetish of avoiding cracks in the pavement! Such a person is relying on his own powers to save him from doom, rather than having faith in the Lord God (cf. Isa.31:1). *That is sin.* Similarly, if a person develops a massively inappropriate fear, Western psychotherapy calls it a 'phobia' and proceeds to look for a deterministic cause. But such a behavioural disorder is really caused by faithlessness and an inability to comprehend the holding arms of God. *That is sin.* In the unbeliever, this is because he has no faith in the first place; but in the believer, it involves a highly-radical lack of faith in the promises and assurances which have been given to him so lavishly in the Word of God (e.g., Rom.8:15; 2 Tim.1:7). Then, if someone is found to be eating vast quantities of food in secret 'binges' followed by self-induced vomiting, often in order to control the weight, psychiatry calls this a disease and gives it the label 'Bulimia' (literally, the appetite of an ox, from the Greek, *bous*, an 'ox', and *limos*, 'hunger'). But this is an exhibition of extreme greed, gluttony and self-indulgence, all in the interests of personal vanity. *That is sin* (cf. Prov.23:20-21). Such orgiastic eating and wanton indulgence belongs to the old 'earthly' nature and is characterised by the Apostle Paul as a form of idolatry which should be decisively 'put to death' by the uniquely Christian art of 'mortification' (Col.3:5). Again, if a person makes claims that he is God or Christ, Western psychotherapy claims this as symptomatic of 'Schizophrenia' or a 'Psychotic Delusion'. But such bizarre behaviour is really an extreme exhibition of the cardinal sin into which our first parents were tempted in Eden — belief in their own 'divinity' (Gen.3:5-6). *That is sin* — the ultimate sin!

A great many more examples could be given; but these clearly show that many of the behavioural and perceptual problems that Western psychotherapy calls 'mental illness' are actually aspects of structural sin finding its outworking in extreme and often bizarre forms. This is indwelling sin manifesting itself 'with-a-vengeance'. All humans *by nature* are superstitious, unfaithful, idolatrous, greedy and deluded about their status in the world. However, such *structural* sins normally continue their operations in a person behind the scenes, fuelling all their actions, but without necessarily drawing themselves to the world's attention with such ferocity. But when such sinfulness breaks out in these disturbing manifestations, the world — which is under the sway of the wicked one (1 Jn.5:19) — devises a theory to ensure that it is regarded as an 'illness' deriving from an outside source rather than from the indwelling sin which is a radical component of the fallen human nature.

We recognise that just as the Christian will — in spite of his regeneration and spiritual transformation — continue to be subject to physical disease and decay, he will also continue to be under mental and emotional stress and prone to suffer from various 'psychological problems'. For the believer, the forms of bondage which Western psychotherapy calls 'Obsessional Neurosis', or 'Phobia', or 'Delusions of Grandeur' are caused by the 'flesh' rearing its ugly head, fuelled on occasion by the devil and his associates.

3. Mortification: The Ultimate Christian Therapy

What has just been said above does not mean that we can negate personal responsibility for our own sin, as if it was caused by something outside of us over which we have no control. Western psychotherapy removes that personal responsibility, places the blame on the environment or other people's treatment of us at an early age, then packs us off to professionals devoid of true spiritual wisdom. That may be the way that the children of the devil handle their difficulties; but it is not the way of the biblical Christian. The promise to all believers is that sin shall *not* have dominion over them (Rom.6:14). The Christian is not in bondage to anything (Gal.5:1) and he is a 'hyper-conqueror' through Christ who loves him (Rom.8:37). The failure of believers to appreciate the full significance of these promises is, more often than not, responsible for the majority of their pastoral difficulties.

However, the turmoil of the true conversion experience can bring out (or, rather, *should* bring out) the very worst in a person; and this is a lifelong process. Becoming a Christian means being redeemed from every lawless deed and purified as Jesus' own special people (Tit.2:14). Although it is true that we are already cleansed — in the sense that our sins are counted as having been laid on Christ on the Cross — the fact is that *'everyone who has this hope in Him purifies himself, just as He is pure'* (1 Jn.3:3). In the aftermath of a genuine conversion experience, all the dark recesses of our personalities — those awkward, previously-hidden, shame-inducing aspects of our natures — should repeatedly disclose themselves for mortification, a vital part of this lifelong process for the serious disciple of Christ. The 'therapeutic' model for the Christian is, therefore, *mortification*. This is the true Christian pathway to a healthy mind and behaviour; and it involves the decisive slaying and cutting out of sinful problems at their root rather than merely tackling their symptoms. Mortification is the removal of all that which creates a stumbling-block to our spiritual progress and which hinders our relationship with Christ (Rom.8:13; Col.3:5). Mortification — a vital part of our sanctification process — is possibly the most neglected Christian doctrine of recent times. What does it involve? First, the most profound desire to be rid of your sin, no matter how small it may appear (after all, Christ died even for the smallest of our sins). Second, a heartfelt cry to the Lord to help you overcome sin by the power of His Spirit. Third, the implementation of decisive moves to cut it out of your life, to 'put it to death' forever. Fourth, if necessary, the bringing in of your brothers and sisters in Christ to assist you with wise and godly counsel (Gal.6:2). That process is the greatest therapy in the world — a therapy the world knows nothing about. Mind therapy. Heart therapy. Soul therapy.

What most Christians fail to realise is that all secular psychotherapy is an attempted counterfeit of this Spirit-led process through humanly-devised techniques: It attempts to create a 'new man' by merely remoulding the 'old man'; whereas the biblical transformation demands nothing less than the *'putting off'* of the old man and the *'mortifying'* of the flesh — an act which comes through faith and which can only be initiated by God through His Spirit (Rom.6:6; Col.3:5-10; Eph.4:22-24).

Having said all this, the greatest love, care and sensitivity must be shown to those who are suffering from such a devastating outbreak of their indwelling sin. They may have fallen apart to such an extent that they are unable to cope with living without constant help and attention — and this should be provided by fellow-believers. Sometimes, such problems can be precipitated by the enormous weight of an emotional shock (e.g., bereavement), serious accident or recent debilitating disease, all of which can bring normally undetected problems to the surface. One should also consider the feasibility of direct demonic activity — perhaps due to occult involvement, sexual perversion or other extreme sinful behaviour, past or present — in the life of the one so-afflicted. However, in view of the hysteria being generated in some circles of the Church on this subject, it ought to be added that this should be explored in a sensitive and unsensational manner. But whatever the cause of behavioural or emotional problems, sufferers must never be stigmatised or thought to be more sinful than others who do not exhibit such disorders. We are all equally prone to sin; it is just that some — due perhaps to inadvertent neglect, traumatisation, divine chastisement, or just a plain lack of detection of a deep sin — are smitten in an especially devastating manner. This could happen to any one of us at any time. Such occurrences offer an occasion for real counselling and provide a (personal) growth-inducing opportunity for the exclusively Christian art of mortification.

All that we are saying here is not new. Over three hundred years ago, one of Oliver Cromwell's chaplains, John Owen, wrote an extensive treatise on the indwelling nature of sin and the need for its mortification. He, too, believed that sin is the root cause of madness: that it

> 'will darken the mind, extinguish convictions, dethrone reason, interrupt the power and influence of any considerations that may be brought to hamper it, and break through all into a flame'.[96]

The use of psychotherapy to deal with these explosive outbursts of indwelling sin is based on the same false premise which moved some men in the early Church (e.g., Origen) to castrate themselves in order to overthrow unlawful sexual desire. Such desire comes out of the sick heart of man — his essentially sinful structure — and can never be eradicated by any superficial action. As Jesus said: *'All these evil things come from within and defile a man'* (Mk.7:23). He knew only too well the true nature of man's sinful structure (Jn.2:24-25). Secular psychotherapy has come into being because of a complete ignorance of sin and its structural nature. Christian psychotherapy has been developed in those circles which have a deplorably deficient doctrine of sin.

IV. SEVEN CAVEATS AGAINST PSYCHOTHERAPY

We began this study by asking the fundamental question: *'To whom is the mentally or emotionally suffering Christian to turn with his afflictions?'* We then acknowledged that for many the answer is simple: if one goes to a body doctor (physician) with a somatic disorder, then one goes to a mind doctor with a 'psychological' disorder. But this is based on the false notion that there is such a thing as mental 'illness' in the same way that there is physical illness.[97] We then

---

[96] W.H. Goold (ed.), *The Works of John Owen* (Banner of Truth, 1967), Vol.VI, p.28. See also p.206. This volume is essential reading for the diligent Christian, although the language is, admittedly, difficult.

[97] Long before the present writer was saved, when he was employed as a social worker in a Child Guidance Clinic, co-running therapy groups and working with families with 'problem' children, he came to the conclusion — through reading books by Dr. Thomas Szasz and other 'anti-psychiatrists' — that mental illness is a Western culture-generated myth and that the clinical model of psychotherapy was a hoax. It was all the more surprising, after conversion, to find that Christians were devouring these secular theories wholesale. This was at least as astounding as the discovery that other professing Christians did not believe in a literal, bodily Resurrection of Jesus Christ!

surveyed the background of all psychotherapy and saw the key influences to consist of a number of pathetically-deluded hypnotists, occultists, mystics and sophists sheltering in the shanty towns of the ancient shamans. This we followed by examining the effects of the Fall on the mind of man, together with an exposition of the range of 'mind-games' which are the joint province of the demonic realm and the sinful nature of man.

Thereafter, we showed that the *basic* fault in the psychological character of mankind is not rooted in early-life traumas which must be relived one-by-one in order to find true mental health. Rather, man's basic fault lies in a twofold problem of sin — original sin and the structural sin which is a natural outgrowth of it. Such a perspective is unique to the Christian world-view, gleaned from the Bible and ratified in his own life. Many believers have grown so used to drinking from the fountains of Egypt in other areas of their lives that when it comes to 'mental health' problems their first instinct is to do likewise and bow to the worldly wisdom, 'professional' prowess and spiritual blindness of the white-coated ones. Accordingly, we maintain unequivocally that psychotherapy should have no place in the life of the Spirit-indwelt believer.

There will be further practical discussion and criticism of 'Christian' psychotherapy in the second half of 'Sorcerous Apprentices', when we come to examine the application of the mind-sciences in the Christian scene. In these closing pages of this chapter we catalogue seven primary reasons why believers should not consider psychotherapy as a valid cure for behavioural and emotional disorders.

1. Psychotherapy is Wholly Absent from Scripture

If, as the Christian psychotherapists claim, the sanctification of the believer involves the probing and abreaction of early memories, why is there no mention of these techniques in Scripture? Why have millions of Christian men and women down the centuries had to live their lives without the benefit of these things? Was the Holy Spirit dependent on the advent of Freud and his protégés for more effective forms of sanctification? Why did it take almost two thousand years for this apparently vital aid to sanctification to be 'discovered' and foisted onto a naïve and largely ignorant ecclesiastical scene? From the biblical data, it is clear that this technique was never used by the Lord Jesus Christ throughout His entire ministry. Neither is there a reference to it or record of its use in the other New Testament writings or works of the early Church. Surely if abreactive psychotherapy is so vital to Christian growth, there would be a mention of it somewhere in the N.T. record; but there is not even the remotest hint. The reason for this is that Jesus and His disciples were not so much concerned with sorting out the emotional hang-ups of individuals as with the need for spiritual rebirth and subsequent ongoing growth in sanctification. In the Christian life, emotional growth takes place *naturally* in the wake of spiritual growth (e.g., 2 Cor.5:17; Rom.12:2).

2. Psychotherapy Ignores the Sovereignty of God

In psychotherapy, the sovereignty of God is ignored in terms of the providential sending of affliction and chastisement to His people, including His prerogative to remove it, according to His will. It is taken for granted by all psychotherapists that everyone has an immediate right to what they regard as full mental health. Yet the mental state of the Christian is wholly in the Lord's hands, rather than in those of any psychotherapist. For not only does He have the power to visit a person with sudden physical illness according to His will (e.g., Num.12:9-10; Dt.24:9), but it is also in His jurisdiction to plunge any of His creatures into extreme mental anguish at any given moment, if — in His inscrutable wisdom — He so wills it (e.g., 1 Sam.16:14-15; Dan.4:16-17).

The children of Israel were warned that if they broke the covenant, *'The LORD will strike you with madness and blindness and confusion of heart'* (Dt.28:28). Conversely, He also has the power to deliver one from such afflictions, as He so orders (1 Sam.16:16, 23; Dan.4:34-37). For all we know, the *'thorn in the flesh'* — given by the Lord and administered by His unwitting servant, Satan — which plagued the apostle Paul may well have been something which we would regard as an unpleasant psychological affliction. But, whatever it was, the Lord saw fit that he should continue to be plagued by it, precisely because it would prosper his sanctification rather than hinder it (2 Cor.12:1-10).

This does not mean that the afflicted Christian should refuse to seek medical or pastoral help on the basis that *'it is God's sovereign will that I should be ill'*. Such fatalism is far removed from the thrust of biblical truth. For the Lord has also ordained that there should be expert medical assistance available whenever it is necessary. We must never assume that illness always comes as a divine chastisement. But when it does, we should recognise it as such and discover what it is that the Lord wants us to learn from the experience.

It would never occur to the 'Christian' therapists that the Lord may actually desire that a person be mentally or physically unwell in order to provide an aid to his ultimate Christian growth; yet, we must admit this if we are to maintain a testimony of the sovereignty of God over all His creatures together with an understanding of the wisdom of divine chastisement, through which all genuine children of God are being trained (Heb.12:5-11). However, whatever afflictions and hardships He decrees for one of His people, we may be sure that He will also provide a corresponding strength to bear it (1 Cor.10:13), and a great reward for enduring it (Rom.8:18; 2 Cor.4:17).

3. Psychotherapy Denies the Power and Sufficiency of the Word

A third caveat against the Christian indulging in psychotherapy is that it undermines the authority of Scripture. All the teaching and information necessary for the personal growth of the believer is contained in the Word of God, the Bible. One of the great characteristics of Scripture is its ability to make the man of God complete and thoroughly equipped for every good work (2 Tim.3:17). We ignore this claim at our peril. Why settle for wholly inferior man-made alternatives when the very best has already been provided by God? It is the greatest manual of psychology and counselling that a person could have. When Paul writes to the Hebrews that the Bible is:

> 'living and powerful, and sharper than any two-edged sword, piercing even to the division of soul and spirit, and of joints and marrow, and is a discerner of the thoughts and intents of the heart' (Heb.4:12),

we must apply that to the power of our pastoral ministry and not confine it to an evangelistic exhortation. A major problem today is that the God-breathed Scriptures have become so wrapped up in leather-bound, version-competitive presentation kits, that the all-surpassing, dynamic spiritual power of the Word of God has been reduced to just another marketable commodity. Many professing Christians today think that the Bible has been surpassed in its insights by the secular scientific and psychological discoveries of today. A more profound error could not be made. Both Evolution and Psychoanalytic Theories have been spewed out by Satan in these closing days of history as ways of undermining the truthful principle of *Sola Scriptura.*

This does not mean that nothing that can be learned from secular counselling procedures. For instance, in a Rogerian Counselling textbook, one will read that the counsellor must *'listen to the music behind the words'* of the one needing counsel; for the presenting problem is rarely the essential difficulty. Insights such as these are very valuable. But beware... Firstly, the music which the Christian counsellor listens for is very different from that which his secular counterpart seeks to hear. Secondly, it is a fact that any useful insight in secular counselling already has its biblical parallel. The Rogerian gem of wisdom above — that a person's presentation may differ radically from what is in his heart — can also be found in many places in Scripture (e.g., Ps.28:3; 55:21; Pro.5:3; 26:24). Thirdly, if you immerse yourself in a Rogerian Therapy training programme instead of the Bible, you will have to take onboard a wholly unbiblical world-view. So why settle for teaching which — even if it does contain valid human insights — is not only inadequate, but is also likely to lead the undiscerning into serious error?

If you steep yourself in the Scriptures as your counselling textbook and use its insights in all your relationships, you will be a wise counsellor indeed — far, far wiser than any secular psychotherapist, and far more incisive than any therapist who has dressed up secular psychotherapy's theories in some outwardly appealing Christian clothes.

4. Psychotherapy Dissolves Human Responsibility

A fourth caveat against the Christian seeking psychotherapy for his inner difficulties is that it denies the individual's personal responsibility for his actions before God. The vast majority of psychotherapies involve a deterministic ideology which attempts to absolve the counsellee/patient from accepting accountability for his difficulties. How much more convenient it is to blame our parents or our environment for the effects of original sin and the outworkings of the structural sin which stems from it. One of the greatest aids to recovery from 'mental illness' is the initial acceptance that we ourselves — under the indwelling power and leading of the Holy Spirit of God — are to take responsibility for our lives now that we are Christ's (Phil.2:12-13). Nothing could be more harmful to the spiritual life or neglectful to mental health than to chase after the innumerable hidden memories of traumas under the guidance and suggestion of a psychotherapist. People go to therapists hoping that they will be able to pin-point something outside of themselves to which they can attach blame for their condition. But Jesus warns us to eschew such an approach to human sin, asserting that

> 'there is nothing that enters a man from outside which can defile him; but the things which come out of him [those things which...come from the heart] those are the things that defile a man' (Mk.7:15 with Mt.15:11).

The real origin of our 'mental illness' (if it does not have an organic cause) is our own sin — not the sin of our parents in maltreating us, as the abreactive psychotherapists claim, but our own sinful responses to it. Until we are prepared to take responsibility for that, we will continue to suffer unnecessarily and seek unnecessary help to be free of it.

5. Psychotherapy is Self-Centred Rather than Christ-Centred

The ultimate aim of almost all psychotherapeutic techniques is to build up *self*-esteem in the client/patient. But this approach is the direct antithesis of the way of counsel advocated by the Bible. The true disciple of Christ must esteem himself less than others, abase himself, deny himself and take up his cross daily. He knows the great spiritual secret (foolishness to the world) that abasement and humiliation always lead to exaltation, whereas the one who seeks to exalt himself will be abased (Mt.23:12; 16:25; Lk.14:11; 17:33; 18:14; Jn.12:25; cf. Phil.2:3-11).

A common phrase used in psychotherapeutic circles is 'Personal Growth'. We freely acknowledge that inner growth is necessary for a person to come to maturity. However, the psychotherapist's idea of personal growth is very different from that of the Christian. The unbelieving therapist enables a person to grow through focussing on self, encouraging self-esteem to flourish — thus the Self becomes both the aim and object of all attempts at reformation. The 'Christian' psychotherapist also mimics his secular counterpart in fostering a similar approach to personal growth. *'Self-esteem'* is one of the most popular phrases in the 'Christian' psychotherapy literature. The way of Christian growth, however, is through a sanctification process which involves focusing exclusively on Jesus (Heb.12:1-3) and imitating Him, rather than becoming obsessed with ourselves.

Did Moses, Gideon, Job, David and Isaiah have low self-esteem when they confessed themselves to be as nothing before the Lord (Ex.3:11; 4:10; Jdg.6:12-15; Job 40:4; Ps.51:2-5; Isa.6:5)? No. They simply had a realistic estimation of themselves — the heart of true humility. The Bible does not call us to false modesty or nihilistic self-disparagement; but we are expected to cultivate a realistic attitude to the evil heart of human nature and the realisation that every good thing the Christian has is a gift from God. It is for this reason that the Apostle Paul can say: *'For I know that in me (that is, in my flesh) nothing good dwells'* (Rom.7:18). Heaven preserve us from the pedlars of self-esteem, whose estimation of themselves prevents them from grasping their innate unworthiness. To such people, a handful of pithy questions shout out from Scripture:

> 'Who makes you differ from another? And what do you have that you did not receive? Now if you did indeed receive it, why do you glory as if you had not received it?' (1 Cor.4:7).

The Christian must make Christ the centre of his life, not himself; for he can say with great assurance, *'I have been crucified with Christ; it is no longer I who live, but Christ lives in me'* (Gal.2:20). He hears those words of his Master saying: *'Because I live, you will live also'* (Jn.14:19).

Not only must the Christian refrain from making himself the focus of his life, but he must also avoid putting any therapist on a pedestal. We have already referred to a powerful therapeutic influence called 'The Transference', by which the counsellee becomes obsessed with the therapist as an authority figure. However, in a genuine pastoral relationship, the Christian's allegiance should be transferred to his Saviour, rather than to a psychotherapist. In any pastoral relationship — if there is to be true spiritual growth — the focus must always be Christ, His doctrine and His word. A true Christian counsellor or pastor will always point his counsellees in that direction. He is our ultimate 'role model' (2 Cor.3:18). When Paul told other believers to imitate him, he was careful to add the words: *'just as I also imitate Christ'* (1 Cor.11:1). Psychotherapy betrays its true roots by focusing on the self rather than on Christ. It makes man into a little god.

6. Psychotherapy Negates the Work of the Body of Christ

The advocating of psychotherapy for the behavioural and emotional problems of the Christian *professionalises* a process which should really be the province of the Body of Christ. *'Confess your trespasses to one another, and pray for one another, that you may be healed'* (Jas.5:16); *'Bear one another's burdens, and so fulfil the law of Christ'* (Gal.6:2). No therapist's couch here! Christians are to minister to one another — and are specially equipped to do so (Gal.6:1). Although all in the assemblies can counsel to some extent, some brethren will be especially gifted by the Lord to be very skilled in this (Rom.15:1). It is the place of Christian pastor-elders to oversee the counselling needs of the local church, ensuring that those with special gifts have the opportunity to develop them. It is essential that all such problems as those under discussion in this study, when they break out in people in our fellowships, should be dealt with within the Body of Christ, as collective problems, insofar as that is possible. When one member hurts, the whole body should feel it.

Many different contributions can be made by members of the congregation to the counselling process. For example, a brother or sister in an acute state of depression or suffering from what is popularly described as 'Schizophrenia' may need to live-in with a family in the congregation: this will provide an opportunity for one who has the gift of hospitality, as well as for developing sensitivity in the skills necessary to counsel in such a situation.

Often, a great problem is that as soon as someone in the family develops a so-called 'mental health' problem, many people — because of their understandable alarm and ignorance of these matters — act with great haste in washing their hands of it all by immediately handing the person over to the state medical authorities for reform. It is our view that such a pathway for the Christian is an abdication of responsibility among the brethren. This is not to say that allopathic medication should never be used. Certainly, in the event of problems in an acute phase, such contingencies may well be necessary, under the guidance of a physician. Moreover, the greatest tact is necessary when dealing with the various health authorities who may become (or desire to become) involved. But where it is possible, without violating the law of the land or jeopardising health and safety, Christians must take control of a member of their fellowship who is hurting.

We recognise that it takes great courage for a fellowship to embark on assisting one another in this process of mortification and mutual counselling. Many bodies of believers are so hooked-into a style of ministry which negates the priesthood of all believers and gives one man too much power in the assembly, that great changes of heart would be necessary in order for the life of the Church to be enhanced. The prevailing infantilism in the churches caused by such unbiblical church order is not only holding many believers back from growing into the fully-fledged Christians which they should be, but it is often responsible for causing emotional problems in those who suffer at the hands of authoritarian leaders.

We need to find new and creative ways of dealing with these problems, so that a total Christian solution — and an alternative to the unsanctified therapy provided by the state — can be offered to those in need of spiritual counsel, while giving other believers openings to develop their own skills as servant- counsellors.

7. Psychotherapy Neglects the Work of the Holy Spirit

Perhaps the most important reason why the believer should avoid psychotherapeutic techniques as a way to 'mental health' is that it completely neglects the work of the Holy Spirit in the life of the believer. The fact is that in psychotherapy the therapist becomes a substitute for the **true** Christian Counsellor — the Holy Spirit. Jesus said that He would ensure that His people would not be left as orphans in His absence, but that He would send them *'another Parakletos'* who would abide in them (Jn.14:16-18). This Greek word *parakletos* can be variously translated as Comforter, Counsellor, Helper, Advocate, Intercessor. It is a compound of two Greek words, *para*: alongside, and *kaleo*: to call. The Holy Spirit is, literally, One who is called right alongside the believer in all his trials and tribulations — as if He was the child of God's best friend. So, the first counsellor to whom the Christian turns in the event of emotional or psychological difficulties is **the** Counsellor — the Holy Spirit of God — to assist him in the discovery and mortification of the sin which may lie at the root of his problem. And the first prayerful consideration when undergoing any of these difficulties is for the afflicted one — in conjunction with a Christian counsellor, if necessary — to ask that the Holy Spirit will reveal to him why these things are happening to him, and what lessons does the Lord desire him to learn (cf. Heb.12:11).

For the spiritually unregenerated person, psychotherapy represents an attempt to climb into the sheep-fold by another door. For the Christian believer, it represents a denial of the prescriptions of the word of God and a rejection of the ministrations of the Holy Spirit. If you are truly led by the Spirit, you have no need to be under a psychotherapist!

CONCLUSION

For many believers, much that we have said in this chapter will be very new, and the practical enactment of its findings will not be easy to carry through — given the pressures from 'mental health' professionals and the practices of many fellow-believers. But it will not be the first time that the Lord's faithful ones have had to hold out against the world. The many gulfs which separate the Church of God from the world of man are being eroded in our time. The gulf between psychotherapy and biblical counselling is no exception. As the Bobgans have well said:

> 'The psychological way originates with man, utilizes man-made techniques and ends with man. The spiritual way originates with God, employs gifts and fruits of the Spirit, and leads a man to a greater awareness of God and himself as created by God... The psychological way is a combination of techniques and theories, but the spiritual way is a synthesis of love and truth... The psychological way involves changing standards and flexible morals. The spiritual way follows the unchanging standard and authority of the Word of God... The psychological way has self at the centre, while the spiritual way is centred in Christ... The psychological way attempts to change a man's thinking and behaviour through the mind, will and emotions. The spiritual way changes a person's thinking, emotions, and behaviour through his spirit'.[98]

Many Christians would say that psychotherapy 'works', therefore it must be a good thing. One can certainly undergo a process under the influence of powerful suggestion and the manipulation of a therapist, in which one relives a traumatic early-life experience, and obtains catharsis and release from a specific 'neurosis' or other problem. But that only melts one particular *symptom* of the undergirding structural sin. It does not come anywhere near mortifying the sin itself — which lives on, ever ready to ensnare one in some other aspect of one's life.

An important point to remember here is that just because something appears to 'work' does not mean that it is beneficial. One of the biblical caveats concerning a false prophet is that although his sign or wonder may come to pass, it will lead people into idolatry (Dt.13:1-3). Similarly, psychotherapy — even when it appears to work — leads its victims into a welter of other ungodly (often occultic) interests, produces a false sense of well-being and generates a denial of the leading and power of the Holy Spirit. The presenting problem actually provided a unique opportunity for major surgery on its root cause. In carcinogenic language,

[98] Martin & Deidre Bobgan, *The Psychological Way: The Spiritual Way* (Bethany House, 1979), pp.176-177.

psychotherapy operates on a secondary growth, leaving the root cancer free to run riot in numerous unseen ways. Christian mortification, on the other hand, views mad behaviour as indicative of deep structural sin which will require some *spiritual* resources if it is to be neutralised.

It is tragic that so many Christians are attracted to the ways of the world and lack the discernment to distinguish between the spiritual way and the psychological way. Through the influence of the mind-sciences — of which psychotherapy is but one component — the world is rapidly being conditioned, at the mystical level, to accept the most phenomenal hoax worked by Satan since his effecting of the Fall in Eden. The tragedy is that large numbers of professing Christians are working right alongside him in the field of the mind-sciences — a development which we shall be examining in great detail in the penultimate chapter. If we are looking for the reasons behind this, it is certainly no coincidence that the growth of the 'Christian' psychotherapy movement has been temporally parallel to the downgrading of the Word of God and the decline in adherence to *'the faith which was once for all delivered to the saints'* of the apostolic Church.

Almost two thousand years ago, the Lord Jesus Christ warned His disciples that false christs and false prophets would attempt to deceive even the elect of God (Mt.24:24). How sad it is that this warning has gone largely unheeded in so many churches today.

Chapter Eight

DAUGHTERS OF BABYLON

Rebellion, Witchcraft and Women's Liberation

'Rebellion is as the sin of witchcraft' (1 Sam.15:23)

In this final chapter in the second part of the book entitled 'The Gods of the Nations', we turn to one of the most widely reputed humanistic movements of modern times: Women's Liberation. Having looked at the Neo-Gnostic influences in science and psychology — both highly influential in the development of modern culture — we now focus on another movement which has shaped late twentieth-century thinking to a similar degree. Equal opportunities, abortion on demand, housewife emancipation, woman-power. Amidst the jingoistic sloganeering, it is often difficult to discern the real background to this growing global development. However, true to the iceberg tradition, there is another, deeper, darker side to Feminism of which most people are entirely unaware. In view of the fact that an increasing number of professing evangelicals believe that there is such a thing as 'Christian Feminism', this chapter sets out to reveal the true roots of all Feminist ideology and to show that the growth of this movement forms a vital component in satanic strategy at this point in history.

I. THE RISE OF FEMINIST PHILOSOPHY

During the last twenty-five years the Western world has witnessed the phenomenal rise of the Women's Liberation Movement. There is, of course, nothing very new about this: the public campaign for women's 'rights' reaches back to the last century when the Suffragettes sought to obtain the vote for women and draw attention to the wider need for the emancipation of women from the constraints of what they deemed to be a male-dominated society. Yet, in the last two decades there has been a re-emergence of this campaign on a considerably wider scale, resulting in an international movement which has begun to gain a good deal of political clout and credibility.

This movement has no central organising body; neither does it have a corporate manifesto — yet it has captured the aspirations of many women from all walks of life who feel that they live in a world which is badly governed by men. The chief result of this state of affairs, they claim, has been repeated wars, violence, oppression, exploitation (especially of women), pollution, increasing immorality and materialism. Feminists are convinced that it is precisely because the world has been run and dominated *by men* that these problems exist at all, and that a change from our current patrifocal society to a matrifocal one, which many feminists believe was the prevailing pattern in ancient cultures, would result in a more humane, compassionate and peaceful world.

Now, it is true that we do live in what tends to be a male-dominated culture — one might even say a male chauvinist culture.[1] And this male domination has often tended to work itself out in ways contrary to those which the Lord intended when He originally assigned to us our genders and our roles. It might even be fair to say that, in some ways, those who have formulated a philosophy of Women's Liberation have had genuine reasons for doing so. They have rightly observed that there is something fundamentally flawed with this world and with a great many of the male/female relationships within it — women often being treated as though they were lower than the animals, sometimes beaten and subjected to gross sexual exploitation and manipulation. It is a deplorable fact of this world that many men believe that women are inherently incapable of anything other than housekeeping and childcare, and feel threatened by any attempt on a woman's part to do otherwise. There is, indeed, a widespread subjugation of women which cannot be justified from Scripture, whether we care to admit it or not.

Consequently, the world has sought to find solutions to this 'battle of the sexes' — solutions which are essentially humanistic. However, as we have often asserted, any form of political or personal reformation in a Godless society, although often having an appearance of humanitarian benefit, actually leads in the long term to increased evil (cf. Lk.11:24-26; Mt.12:43-45) — what we have called the Law of Godless Reformation. That this was the case with the development of Feminism can easily be shown.

1. Politics and 'Spirituality'

The late twentieth century renaissance of the Women's Liberation Movement — in common with so many other 'liberation' movements — had its beginnings in the 'alternative society' counter-culture of the 1960s. At that time, many traditional concepts were being questioned by the emerging, rebellious, hippie generation. Although hippie culture, in the opinion of many Feminists, was itself highly 'oppressive' towards women,[2] the rebellion against traditional societal and religious values which was being fomented, coupled with the sexual revolution spearheaded by Wilhelm Reich and other psychologists, meant that the place of women in society became one more social issue to go into the melting pot, resulting in the development of a worked-out humanistic philosophy of Feminism.

This philosophy developed along two primary lines: one *political*, and the other

---

1 The word 'chauvinist' is derived from the name of Nicolas Chauvin, an extreme French patriot and ardent follower of Napoleon. A chauvinist can be defined as someone who has an extravagant attachment to any group, place, cause, etc.

2 Actually, hippie culture of the 1960s, in spite of its 'love 'n peace' sloganeering, held a concealed contempt for women. Female partners were described as 'chicks', were expected to do menial work and were often abandoned with children in the 'free love' climate. The men, immature and oversensitive, tended to reflect the contemporary rock-star 'macho' image, using their 'chicks' as an ego boost and mother substitute.

psycho-spiritual. The former had its roots in the Marxist-utopian, intellectual, academic circles of the universities — eventually working its way onto the wider international political and social scene. The other wing of the feminist movement has emerged from the psycho-spiritual questionings of the hippie counter-culture, which had led to a great upsurge of interest in hallucinogenic drugs, Transpersonal Psychology and numerous mystical, pagan religious forms — all of which also contributed towards the founding of the New Gnosticism.

The political grouping of Feminism is the one with which most people are familiar. These political feminists have sought to bring about change in women's circumstances through political and educational channels, and it is this grouping which has made its voice heard in universities and in local and national government bodies. The growing number of university 'Women's Studies' departments, the Equal Opportunities Commission and the many local authority 'Women's Committees' which have been set up around the U.K., all owe their existence to the lobbyists and pressure groups from the various Feminist organisations.

Political feminists come in a variety of hues, ranging from the predominantly heterosexual, Guardian-reading, libertarian/socialist, to the hard-line lesbian-separatist. Until comparatively recently, the lesbian wing of Feminism was viewed as extremist, even by other feminists; but the tide has now turned, and it is obvious that an anti-heterosexual philosophy has become increasingly influential, both within the Women's Liberation Movement and outside it. On the surface, the two wings of Feminism developed their lesbianism from rather different perspectives. The political feminists got into Lesbianism to make a political statement about their non-dependence on men, while the psycho-spiritual feminists became Lesbians as a religious expression of pure woman-power.

2. The New Sodom

One of the radical effects of this anti-heterosexuality was to cause many women to become confused about their sexual orientation. One woman pathetically expressed this confusion in a letter to the upmarket Feminist magazine 'Spare Rib':

> 'Recently I have been giving a lot of thought to the question of whether Feminism and heterosexuality are compatible... I am currently living in this world as a heterosexual (living with a man but with virtually no sexual relationship due to my confusion about the above issues). I am now seriously questioning how much longer I can do so and am going to a lot of women only/lesbian socials to see if I want to be a lesbian'.[3]

Such confusion is becoming increasingly common as greater numbers of women allow themselves to be taken to the outer reaches of a philosophy which views men and maleness as intrinsically bad, and accuses heterosexual women of 'consorting with the enemy' because they associate with men. One popular women's health book, available in all High Street bookstores, openly declares that *'the endless assumptions by heterosexuals that they are the 'normal' people has constantly to be challenged'.*[4]

---

[3] *Spare Rib*, No.155, June 1985.

From the mid-1980s onwards, this anti-heterosexual influence has made a special effort to worm its way into many areas of our national life. The world of politics is of course a prime target. The Greater London Regional Labour Party, for instance, issued guidelines asking that in future all literature distributed to the public by prospective Labour candidates should not feature a photograph of the candidate's heterosexual family situation for fear that it would be prejudicial to homosexual candidates, who would be unable to do so.[5] As another example, the Islington-based Centre for Homosexuals set up by the Greater London Council received rates relief from Islington Council to the tune of 25% after running up a deficit of £44,000.[6] Six months later, the same council refused an application for rating relief from the charity for the mentally handicapped, 'Mencap'.[7]

This move to undermine heterosexuality and promote homosexuality (the result of a merger of interests between the 'gay' and Feminist pressure groups), has even been forcing its way into the classrooms of our schools. Recently, the woman head teacher of a school in the London Borough of Hackney refused to allow a class to attend the Shakespeare play 'Romeo and Juliet' because it was *'a blatantly heterosexual love story'*.[8] She openly stated that *'until books, films and the theatre reflected all forms of sexuality, she would not be involving her pupils in heterosexual culture'*.[9] The significance of the fact that the head teacher is a lesbian who lives in a relationship with another woman was not lost on the media.[10] Even more disturbing is the fact that the parents and the governors of the school have given their full backing to this head teacher. This shows the extent to which sexually deviant ideas have become the norm among ordinary people, and how successful Sodomite propaganda has become.

This form of 'social engineering' in schools has its roots in the radical watershed of the mid-1980s, when a so-called 'Lesbian and Gay Unit' was set up by the London Borough of Haringey with a £250,000 budget and full-time staff of six. This council sub-committee wrote to all head teachers proposing courses on homosexuality and lesbianism for all pupils from nursery schools to further education. Another report claimed that

> 'Teachers in inner London have been urged in a booklet sent out by the education authority [ILEA] to make use of material from pressure groups promoting lesbianism, homosexuality and anti-sexism'.[11]

Whether or not people realise it, there has been an all-out endeavour on the part of feminists to infiltrate every area of civic life and propagate their warped view of the world. It is only the presence of certain conservative influences and the sway

---

4 Angela Phillips & Jill Rakusen, *Our Bodies Ourselves* (Penguin Books, 1978), p.98.

5 *Daily Telegraph*, June 5th, 1986.

6 *Daily Telegraph*, August 8th, 1986.

7 Ibid.

8 *The Times*, January 27th, 1994, p.6.

9 *The Times*, January 21st, 1994, p.6.

10 *The Times*, January 28th, 1994. See also *The Sun*, January 22nd, 1994, p.1.

11 *Daily Telegraph*, August 7th, 1986.

of tradition which have so far prevented this situation from running out of control. But one wonders how much longer it will be before the acceptance of sexual deviancy as the norm, as has happened in Kingsmead Primary School in Hackney, will become a much more widespread phenomenon. This is something about which all responsible Christian parents should be extremely concerned.

However, all this has not been happening in a vacuum. It is just one more component in a process of disintegration in many areas of national and religious life, behind which lies an occult plan of global proportions. Let us go into this a little.

3. The Secret Aim of Feminism

The promotion of homosexuality may seem a long way from the simple issue of Feminism. However, as we have already stated, all humanistically inspired attempts to disguise the effects of our depravity will lead to a worse state than the original. Unless they are inspired by the indwelling Holy Spirit, even the most well-intentioned gestures become corrupted with one or more of a number of satanic hallmarks such as sexual immorality, violence, greed, self-exaltation, sorcery and a hatred of Jehovah and the Son of God, Jesus Christ. Moreover, the Lord Himself will often recompense the commission of one kind of grave sin by permitting the person committing it to be 'given over' in judgement to another, even worse, sin (cf. 2 Th.2:11-12). Accordingly, the gross sin of homosexuality is one of the principal results of the previous sin of idolatry — a rejection of the one true God (cf. Rom.1:26).

In this respect, the philosophy and practice of Feminism was destined to be among the most doomed of all the modern reforming movements for the simple reason that its anti-male, anti-patriarchal stance was bound to become anti-Christ, because God is represented in Scripture as 'He' or 'Father', and God incarnate, Jesus Christ, was a male. In common with many other developments in this era, the Women's Liberation Movement and its Feminist ideology is essentially (to the unregenerate woman) an externally-appealing humanistic philosophy (to the unregenerate woman) which enshrouds a pernicious occult function. The *real* Feminism — as opposed to the champagne-socialist, Guardian-reading, armchair variety — makes no bones about its true aims and its dedicated opposition to Christianity and the Holy Scriptures, a fact about which most Christians are entirely ignorant. As a leading example of this antichristian heart of Feminism, the renowned U.S. Feminist 'theologian', Naomi Goldenberg, claims that

> 'Every woman working to improve her own position in society or that of women in general is bringing about the end of God. All feminists are making the world less and less like the one described in the Bible, and are thus helping to lessen the influence of Christ and YAHWEH on society'.[12]

Once these occultic aims of Feminism are exposed, it is revealed as a stark declaration of war on God and His eternal world-plan. In fact, Goldenberg unashamedly states that *'The Feminist movement in Western culture is engaged in the slow*

[12] Naomi R. Goldenberg, *Changing of the Gods* (Beacon Books, Boston, 1979), p.10.

execution of Christ and YAHWEH'.[13] This may well prove to be an awkward truth to swallow for the many 'soft' feminists who merely wish to see an end to discrimination against women at work and in the home. It will be especially awkward for those who profess to be 'Christian' feminists. They will have to decide whether or not they are going to be aligned with those who have declared war on the Lord God of all creation — with those who assert that

> 'God is going to change... We women are going to bring an end to God. As we take positions in government, in medicine, in law, in business, in the arts and, finally, in religion, we will be the end of Him. We will change the world so much that He won't fit in anymore'.[14]

In short, Feminism is nothing less than a manifestation of the ancient Gnostic art of Jehovah-bashing. This planned eradication of the God of Judeo-Christianity has inevitably demanded the invention of new religious forms to take the place of those which revere Him. This has been more than adequately provided by the *psycho-spiritual* wing of Feminism, which has tended to work along procedures outwardly differing from its *political* counterpart. The main thrust of the hippie counter-culture in the 1960s involved a rejection of the materialism of the earlier generation, coupled with the search for spiritual forms which would reflect a mystical approach to living (e.g., the New Age Movement, Hinduism, etc.). In much the same way, the psycho-spiritual feminists coupled their rejection of our culture — which they perceived as thriving on the subjugation and denigration of women — with the search for religious practices which would reflect their emerging mystical concept of an elevated womanhood. It was not long before one emerged.

II. THE 'NEW' WOMEN'S RELIGION

For many years, the political and psycho-spiritual wings of Feminism regarded each other with mutual suspicion. The former saw the latter as woolly-minded religionism; the latter saw the former as too materialistic and politicised. However, towards the end of the 1970s a significant cross-fertilisation took place which completely altered the composition of the Feminist movement.

The initial meeting point between these two wings was their shared attitude towards human sexuality. The political feminists' advocation of homosexuality and exaltation of the status of womanhood blended well with the psycho-spiritual feminists' need to find a suitable religious form which satisfactorily fitted the requirements of the principles of Women's Liberation. In other words, they were seeking a religious system which would exalt women's spirituality over and above the traditional religions, which they perceived as serving primarily the exclusive interests of men, and responsible for all the ills of the world.

Inevitably, as it sought a suitable reflection of exalted womanhood, Feminism found its spiritual counterpart in the ancient religion of the Goddess, manifesting a significant return to the religious conditions of biblical times — a rebirth of the

---

[13] Ibid., p.4.

[14] Ibid. p.3.

fertility and goddess cults whose opposition to Jehovah (through the attempted subversion of His chosen people, Israel) is faithfully catalogued in the Old Testament and whose confrontation with the early Church is well-illustrated in the Acts of the Apostles and in the Epistles.[15] The amalgamation of the previously incompatible political and psycho-spiritual wings of the Women's Liberation Movement was now sealed, enabling High Priestess Z. Budapest to say as early as 1980:

> 'No longer are Goddess worshippers mocked as silly in the Feminist Movement, no longer are we seen as threatening clouds on political horizons, but *as the very essence of Women's Politics'*. [16]

This revival of the religion of the goddess is the new witchcraft. Miriam Simos (alias Starhawk), is a licensed minister of the Covenant of the Goddess — a legally-recognised church in the U.S.A., and main sponsor of the 1993 Parliament of the World's Religions in Chicago. She puts it like this:

> 'Goddess religion is unimaginably old, but contemporary Witchcraft could just as accurately be called the New Religion. The Craft [witchcraft] today is undergoing more than a revival, it is experiencing a renaissance, a recreation. Women are spurring this renewal, and actively reawakening the Goddess, the image of the legitimacy and beneficence of female power'.[17]

Thus, the *Feminist Witchcraft Movement* was born, and the ancient religion of the goddess was revived. Through this development a brand new women's worldview came into being which would change the face of the women's movement and bring forth a new generation of women's literature in support of the cause. In a prime example, 'The Women's History of the World', by Rosalind Miles, sets out to prove that God was originally a woman and that deity only became male as a male-dominated agriculture took over from women's horticulture.[18] She writes: *'In the beginning, as humankind emerged from the darkness of prehistory, God was a woman'*.[19] Later, she says,

> 'there arose the belief that woman was divine, not human, gifted with the most sacred and significant power in the world; and so was born the worship of the Great Mother'.[20]

But none of this proves that God is a woman. All it demonstrates is that the image which was worshipped as a god (or goddess) was female and that sinful men and women had deified woman. God never was a woman; people just

---

[15] See, for example, Ex.20:3-5; Jdg.2:13; 3:7; 1 Sam.12:10; 1 Kgs.11:5; 18:19-40; Acts 17:16; 19:21-41; 1 Cor.10:7; Gal.5:20; 1 Pet.4:3, etc.

[16] Z. Budapest, *The Holy Book of Women's Mysteries*, Part II (Susan B. Anthony Coven No.1, USA), p.219.

[17] Starhawk, *The Spiral Dance: The Rebirth of the Ancient Goddess* (Harper & Row, New York, 1979), p.8.

[18] Rosalind Miles, *The Women's History of the World* (Paladin, 1989), p.64.

[19] Ibid., p.36.

[20] Ibid., p.39.

imagined he was. Perhaps we can now understand why God has put such checks on women, both in His judgement in the wake of the Fall (Gen.3:18) and through His Apostles in the early Church (1 Tim.2:9-15). Just as Eve took the lead in Eden and usurped her husband's position, so women have sought to do so ever since, culminating in today's feminist movement.

1. Hex, Hex, Hex

It may perhaps be difficult for many people to appreciate the connection between the movement for 'women's rights' and that of witchcraft, but this must be understood from an occult standpoint if it is to be adequately grasped. As Feminist witch Starhawk writes:

> 'The Feminist movement is a magico-spiritual movement as well as a political movement. It is spiritual because it is addressed to the liberation of the human spirit, to healing our fragmentation, to becoming whole. It is magical because it *changes consciousness,* it *expands our awareness* and gives us *a new vision.* It is also magic by another definition: the art of *causing change in accordance with the will'.*[21] [emphasis added]

The four italicised phrases in this statement show clearly the occultic background to Feminism. They represent the nuts and bolts of the New Gnosticism which is now at the heart of the rising culture, shaping the minds and hearts of a growing multitude of men and women who have enthusiastically embraced a Satanic Initiation. Thus we can see why this same witch, Starhawk, should be such a popular guest lecturer at the Anglican St. James' Church, Piccadilly, in London. And it is in this process of 'changing consciousness', coupled with the use of 'the will' to bring about this change, that we find the great connecting points between women's politics and magic or witchcraft. As that doyenne of Feminist theology, Naomi Goldenberg, proudly states: *'To witches, magic is the ability to bring about change in the world'.*[22] To the feminist, it matters not a jot whether that change is political or religious. Goldenberg continues: *'In witchcraft, a woman's will is sacred. Once she has learned to visualise her wishes, a witch uses her will to bring them to reality'.*[23] This visualisation to which she is referring is one of the most popular practices in the New Gnosticism, and has even taken hold of many in the churches today who appear to be oblivious to its sorcerous origins.[24]

As early as 1976, several hundred women attending a conference on 'Women's Spirituality' in Boston were advised by Zusanna Budapest, High Priestess of the Susan B. Anthony Coven, that

> 'witches were functioning as prophets... They were beginning a large-scale religious movement whose goal is to strengthen the mind and will of every woman in Western civilisation'.[25]

---

21 Starhawk, op. cit., p.196.
22 N. Goldenberg, op.cit., p.100.
23 Ibid., p.102.
24 Further details of these developments are given in Chapter 11.

At that same conference the goddess-worshipping participants, who represented the Feminist Witchcraft Movement in embryo, were also told to place mirrors on their altars *'to continually remind them that they were the goddess and that they had divine beauty, power and dignity'*.[26] This is self-exaltation in the highest, and provides yet another echo of that original promise to our first parents, *'You will be like God'* (Gen.3:5). Such is the chilling revelation concerning the true background to all Feminism. Their literature is filled with advice on the conducting of various magical rituals, the invocation of spirits and the incantation of spells. One such book, by the witch Starhawk, is published in the 'Women's Studies' imprint from the 'respectable' religious publisher Harper and Row, who also publish Christian literature. Entitled 'The Spiral Dance: The Rebirth of the Ancient Goddess', this book is described by the publishers as *'highly informative, poetic, and extremely readable'*. This, in spite of the fact that it includes within its pages itemised details of how to 'hex' an enemy using a small doll.[27]

The casting of spells and hexing are an important part of witchcraft. Our modern word 'witch' is derived from the old English word for witch, *wicce*, a derivative of the Swedish word *vika*, meaning 'to bend'.[28] This etymology finds its way into a number of modern words. For example, the Rowan tree is known as the 'Witchen' because of its extreme pliability. We also have the words 'weak' (i.e., compliant), 'wicked' (literally, bent!), and 'wicker', referring to the craft of bending and weaving twigs for baskets and chairs. This, in turn, is connected with the word 'web' which comes from the German word 'weben', to weave.

It is for this reason that one will repeatedly find the use of a spider's web as a prominent symbol in Feminist Witch activities. For example, the web was the main symbol of the 'Women for Life on Earth' organisation, a 'green' group promoting ecology and 'woman-power' founded by Feminist Witches.[29] This is the same group which founded the 'peace-camp' at Greenham Common Airbase in Berkshire in the early 1980s. The symbol of the web could be seen on all the

[25] N. Goldenberg, op. cit., p.96.

[26] Ibid., p.94.

[27] Starhawk, op. cit., p.126. A HEX is the witch's word for putting an evil spell on another person. It comes from the Greek word for the number SIX. This number is of great importance in magic as witnessed by the use of six-sided forms in all magical invocation and ritual. It is also suggested that the number six is associated with Satan's work among men (cf. Rev.13:18) because of its incompleteness and *'the falling short of the repose and bliss of the divine sabbatism'* which is shown in the number seven which is identified with God (see Patrick Fairbairn, 'The Imperial Bible Dictionary', Vol.V, Blackie & Son, 1888, p.37, for a fine article on biblical numerology).
The number six is also associated with Venus, the goddess of female sexuality (see references in *Transcendental Magic* by Eliphas Levi, Rider Press, 1979). The sign of Venus is actually used as the worldwide symbol of Feminism.

[28] C.T. Onions (Ed.), *The Oxford Dictionary of English Etymology* (Oxford University Press, 1966).

[29] One will repeatedly discover the use of this term 'Gaia' in these circles. Gaia was the goddess or personification of Earth in Greek mythology. In eco-speak it represents the concept of Mother Earth — the earth as an actual living organism in the cosmos.

peace-camp's badges and posters. Although it is not generally known (even by many in the national Campaign for Nuclear Disarmament), this 'peace-camp' functioned effectively as a witch's coven throughout its duration. On the camp itself, many occult ceremonies were held, during which airforce personnel on the base would be 'hexed', pentagrams would be drawn on the runways and were used in secret night-time rituals, while wool was woven web-like around the entire perimeter fence as symbolic of the spells which were being woven by the women and directed at the United States Airforce operation. U.S.A.F. sources will bear out this testimony. They knew they were up against both libertarian politics **and** witchcraft.[30]

This spellmaking and hexing provides an important insight to the background of Feminism. As the Feminist theologian Naomi Goldenberg claims:

> 'Witches are very concerned with weaving in a metaphoric sense — with weaving spells and learning how to bend the world to their will'.[31]

As an example of the manner in which witchcraft is a complete inversion of biblical integrity, consider this advice offered by Goldenberg to feminist hexers:

> 'Hexing is dangerous because a witch becomes involved with destructive thoughts that can rebound in her own life. If someone else has wronged a witch, however, she is perfectly safe in avenging herself to whatever degree she suffered harm'.[32]

Such 'avenging' is in complete opposition to the Christian position:

> 'Beloved, do not avenge yourselves, but rather give place to wrath; for it is written, "Vengeance is Mine, I will repay," says the Lord. Therefore "If your enemy is hungry, feed him; If he is thirsty, give him a drink; for in so doing you will heap coals of fire on his head." Do not be overcome by evil, but overcome evil with good' (Rom.12:19-21; cf. Mt.5:38-48).

One can imagine what chaos there would be in the world to which the feminists aspire, where men are the enemy on whom to seek revenge, together with the additional hexing and counterhexing between the witches themselves! Yet, perhaps this sorcerous 'star-wars' is not as far-fetched as it may appear. With an increasing number of people intruding into the psychic realm, such spiritualistic activity is likely to increase accordingly. Scripture bears witness to the growth of demonic activity in the latter days, leading up to a truly awesome climax (1 Tim.4:1ff.; 2 Tim.3:13; 2 Th.2:3ff.; Rev.9; 20:7-10; etc.).

---

[30] The present writer speaks from first-hand knowledge as he was a prominent 'peace-activist' in the early 1980s. At one time, he spent a week living on the 'peacecamp' at Greenham Common and personally knew a number of the core instigators and perpetrators.

[31] N. Goldenberg, op.cit., p.96.

[32] Ibid., p.102.

2. The Goddess Archetype

What is one to make of a movement which is given over to the worship of womanhood, whether it is in the form of a goddess or as a generic concept? The sharpest dividing line exists between the serpent-inspired pagan and the Spirit-indwelt child of God. The latter knows that man was originally made in the image of God; the former continually makes gods and goddesses in his or her own image. A goddess is a humanly manufactured image — an idol — which, in itself, is utterly meaningless, futile, a work of errors (1 Cor.8:4; cf. Jer.10:5,11,15). The demonic reality which lies at the back of such idols and imaginings is made clear by the apostle Paul (1 Cor.10:20).

We have already shown in an earlier chapter, that the heathen cults and religions which claim their roots in the primitive past are in fact extensions of the practices which arose out of the divinely-appointed scattering which took place at Babel on the plains of Shinar (Gen.11:1-9). Witchcraft is no exception. Indeed, the Feminist Witchcraft Movement itself acknowledges its atavistic nature:

> 'Witchcraft is a religion, perhaps the oldest religion extant in the West. Its origins go back before Christianity, Judaism, Islam — before Buddhism and Hinduism, as well, and it is very different from all the so-called great religions'.[33]

Alongside the admitted ancientness of witchcraft, the timeless quality of the evil supernatural power inherent in all idol worship is chillingly illustrated by one of the earliest U.K. advocates of the Feminist Witchcraft Movement:

> 'I believe that the ancient Women-cultures are NOT just of the past, but that they coexist with us now... And if we tune into the real wisdom and power in our own Being we can *reach out towards them and make contact* — renew our ancient contact — and finally come to understand who they were then, who we are now, and who we will become again'.[34] [emphasis added]

This 'tuning-in' to lost psychic powers which allegedly existed in ancient civilisations is a hallmark of all occultism and Neo-Gnosticism. Based on the erroneous notion that our earliest ancestors had 'got it right spiritually', the proponents of this visualisation practice allege that if we make contact with them through techniques of meditation and visualisation, they will become our 'inner guides' and will impart secret knowledge to us. This doctrine of deception has become a major hallmark of the New Gnosticism, opening people up to demonic interference on a vast scale. For the discarnate entities with which 'contact' is made are either deceptive figures conjured up by the powers of darkness or they are actually the multitude of fallen angels of old, whom the Bible designates as demons. Such demonic contacts have a profound effect on a person's being. As a counterfeit of the Christian's 'renewing of the mind' — the new creation which takes

[33] Starhawk, op. cit., p.2.

[34] Monica Sjöö & Barbara Mor, *The Ancient Religion of the Great Cosmic Mother of All* (Rainbow Press, Trondheim, Norway, 1981), p.6.

place at conversion — so the servant of the devil, wizard or witch, undergoes a deep transformation of mind during his initiation, by which he becomes enslaved to the devil. As one Feminist puts it:

> 'Traditionally, apprentice witches were required to study for 'a year and a day' before they could be initiated.....Magical training cannot take place overnight. It is, as we have said, *a process of neurological repatterning*, which requires time'.[35] [emphasis added]

The way that this 'neurological repatterning' occurs is usually through some kind of course or training programme. There are a great many such programmes available today for the aspiring goddess-seeker. One workshop for women is known as 'The Goddess Training', weekend workshops in a Victorian Gothic Castle on the Bristol Channel, led by a witch who has called herself Christina Artemis.[36] In her advertising leaflet, she writes:

> 'Goddesses create their own lives. I appeal to each woman to welcome her own goddess into her life...This weekend [workshop] is the beginning of an exciting process of realizing who you really are, experiencing the joy of being yourself, reclaiming your personal power, realizing how birth and childhood affect us all, dissolving the limitations of our mind to open up to the life force itself and to let it permeate all our thoughts and deeds...The time is now...the more we heal ourselves the more we heal Mother Earth...Let us make this a golden age for the woman in us...Awaken the Goddess within you'.[37]

All the usual Neo-Gnostic ingredients are here: you create your own life in your own strength; you discover your true self; you dissolve your mind and discover the 'life-force'; you experience pantheistic identification with the earth; you create a golden age; you discover the god/goddess within. Notice also the reference to the effects of birth and childhood. One of the primary ways that Satan is infiltrating human minds is through encouraging the use of therapies which take people back to early life or even to the womb itself. In this situation, a person becomes highly vulnerable to the powerful suggestions of the leaders of these 'workshops'.[38] Most of the participants are inadequate people who are searching for some meaning in their lives. Satan's strategy in attracting them to these meetings is a cross between that of the vampire and the piranha. And he finds a willing prey.

The chief reason that Feminists propound the romantic notion of rediscovering ancient matriarchal civilisations of the past is in order to provide women with an 'Amazonian' image, a suitable 'role-model' with which they can identify. However, Susanne Heine, Professor of Practical Theology and Psychology of Religion

---

[35] Starhawk, op. cit., p.160. Bear in mind that this is the Feminist Witch who is a popular guest lecturer at the Anglican St. James' Church, Piccadilly.

[36] Witches and Neo-Gnostics often change their names to suit their new identity. Artemis is the goddess Diana whose cult-centre was in Ephesus (cf. Acts19:21-41).

[37] From the advertising leaflet put out by the organisers.

[38] See Chapters 7 and 11 for further details of this phenomenon.

in the Faculty of Theology at the University of Zurich, exposes the fact that *'on closer historical examination the evidence whether there ever was a matriarchy proves negative'*.[39] Professor Heine, herself a passionate although moderate feminist, goes on to add that *'the thesis that the patriarchy was introduced through popular movements into what were formerly matriarchal cultures also proves untenable on closer examination'*.[40] Professor Heine's research into and exposure of the fallacy of the feminist mythology machine provides us with a powerful example of the importance of distinguishing between scientific truth and *scientistic myth*. When the light of her research is shone onto that shibboleth of the feminist movement, the concept of an ancient matriarchy, she brings forth the ironic fact that

> 'These characteristics of a whole matriarchal world as we have come to know it from feminist literature, and which represent the result of female science and the feminist method, do not stem from a woman but from a nineteenth-century philosopher who died in 1918: Georg Simmel. What is offered us today as the result of feminist scholarship was invented by men a century earlier'.[41]

However, in spite of the fact that such respected feminist scholars have proven that the notion of a superior lost matriarchal civilisation is historically insupportable, this does not deter many from persisting with the promotion of such imagery. The simple reason for this is that in the matter of lost matriarchies,

> 'most witches are more concerned with that concept as a psychological and poetic force than as an historical veracity'.[42]

This is very much in line with that saying of Dr. Lyall Watson concerning the 'Hundredth Monkey Concept', that *'When a myth is shared by large numbers of people, it becomes a reality'*.[43] In other words, one can make up the history of one's religion in order to suit ones personal requirements — in this instance, to prop up the imagined primordial superiority and divinity of women. When the question is asked, 'Why are goddesses so attractive to feminists?', we can only answer with Professor Heine that it is because they are *'so powerful, erotic, aggressive and destructive'*.[44]

To this end, feminists will seek to make psychic contact with goddesses which they believe are genuine manifestations of divine power. In other words, like their

---

[39] Susanne Heine, *Christianity and the Goddesses: Systematic Criticism of a Feminist Theology* (SCM Press, 1988), p.97. It is also interesting to read Professor Heine's other work dealing with feminist matters, *Women and Early Christianity: Are the Feminist Scholars Right?* (SCM Press, 1987).

[40] Ibid., p.99.

[41] Ibid., p.151.

[42] N. Goldenberg, op. cit., p.89.

[43] Quoted in Lyall Watson, *Lifetide* (Hodder & Stoughton, 1979), p.158.

[44] From a lecture by Professor Susanne Heine at Edinburgh University Theological Society, March 9th, 1993.

Neo-Gnostic male counterparts who seek to tune in to 'the god within', feminist witches are attempting to energise 'the goddess within'. To take 'the inward pathway' in the hope of rediscovering a supposed lost inner divinity, is one of the greatest spiritual deceptions ever dreamed up by Satan. One of the methods devised by the Feminist Movement is based upon the strange idea that when a father dies, the offspring tend to become introspective, therefore if one removes all male gods from the world then women will be able to move inward to their lost spiritual heritage: the female divinity within. Naomi Goldenberg puts it like this:

> 'Since introspection does follow the death of fathers, then the death of father gods could mean the onset of religious forms which emphasise awareness of oneself and tend to understand gods and goddesses as inner psychic forces'.[45]

These 'inner psychic forces', although often representing themselves as helpful spirit-guides, are in reality *demonic* forces plying their victims with notions of their own divinity and the awakening of intrinsic lost powers.[46] This dangerous practice often masquerades as a psychological technique:

> 'Modern witches are using religion and ritual as psychological tools to build individual strengths. They practice [sic] a religion that places divinity or supernatural power within the person. In a very practical sense they have turned religion into psychology'.[47]

It is no coincidence that many of those in the forefront of the Feminist Witchcraft Movement are psychotherapists, primarily with a Jungian background. We can certainly notice that there is an interconnecting narcissism between occultism and psychotherapy and, lest readers think that we have left the political Feminist far behind, we are told that

> 'A major difference between witches and psychotherapists is that witches see the mental health of women as having important political consequences. Although every modern coven does not call itself a Feminist coven, all covens support Feminist ideology to some degree'.[48]

Again we have a clear lead concerning the link between political and psycho-spiritual Feminism. In reality, they are one and the same thing because they seek to destroy God through subterfuge and the undermining of His eternal Laws. When Miriam Simos states that *'the essence of Witchcraft and of political Feminism is acrostic vision'*,[49] she is referring to the current worldwide process of asserting that there is no true norm for anything: no God-given gender, no true religion, no objective reality, no Absolute Truth.[50]

---

[45] N. Goldenberg, op. cit., p.41.

[46] See Chapter 11 for details of the use of 'inner guides' to expand consciousness and receive spiritual advice.

[47] N. Goldenberg, op. cit., p.89.

[48] Ibid., p.91.

[49] Starhawk, op. cit., p.187.

3. The Goddess in the Church

A number of Christian women today have embraced Feminism of a sort; and evangelicals appear to be falling over themselves to root out incipient 'sexism' and to uphold the fundamental tenets of feminist ideology. Even the respected writer, John Stott, has made the extraordinary remark, *'We must engage in a double listening, both to the voice of feminists and to the voice of God'.*[51] However, what all these well-meaning folk fail to realise is that Feminism and Christianity are diametrically-opposed world-views. Of course, we must be sensitive to others in terms of our evangelism; but this does not mean that the Christian who is rooted in the fullness of Scripture can have anything to learn from the secular ideology of Feminism. It is certainly true (and very sad) that the special gifts of women have often been ignored, and even suppressed, within many churches, due to the paranoia of certain men who have given themselves an unbiblical level of authority. But the antidote to this dilemma lies in obedience to the overall position of the Bible on the work of women in the Church, rather than in being deferential to the philosophy of women's liberation (feminist-utopianism), behind which lies the increasingly popular religious expression of goddess-worship and witchcraft. How can Christian believers engage in listening to the voice of feminist ideology which is deliberately setting out to turn women away from God by telling them that

> 'Jesus Christ cannot symbolise the liberation of woman. In order to develop a theology of women's liberation, Feminists have to leave Christ and the Bible behind them'.[52]

This is also the opinion of the Roman Catholic Feminist leader, Mary Daly, who teaches at the Jesuit school, Boston College, in the U.S. Many professing Christian theologians and ministers are now lending support to the religion of the Goddess under the thin disguise of the 'Eternal Feminine' and on the erroneous basis that God Himself is both masculine and feminine — a hermaphrodite spirit. At a recent public lecture in Houston called *'Recalling the Elemental Powers of Women'*, Dr. Daly said:

> 'I don't like to see women ordained in any Christian church because I think it perpetuates an illusion. I understand very well the argument, especially from Protestant women, but to me the great danger is assimilation, tokenism and illusion... What I would like to see them do is simply to leave the Catholic Church — and all of Christianity'.[53]

Dr. Daly, whom many would regard as merely a political or philosophical Feminist, described her journey through life in the following statement, which

---

[50] An 'acrostic' is a poem or puzzle in which the first or last letters of each wordline spells another word or sentence. It is being used in the present context to denote a situation in which there is no way of discerning what is true reality.

[51] Kathy Keay (Ed.), *Men, Women and God* (Marshall Pickering, 1987), p.vii.

[52] N. Goldenberg, op. cit., p.22.

[53] Reported in *Christian News*, 8th January, 1990, p.23.

reveals a great deal about the true nature of her feminist 'spirituality':

> 'I see the process as a voyage. The craft that I'm in is like my own craft or strength. It's also witchcraft. It's also my craft as a writer, as a philosopher. So 'craft' has multi-meanings. And the sea I'm talking about contains a deep, deep background knowledge'.[54]

Dr. Daly is one of many leaders and teachers in the professing church who have moved into the new Feminist religion. For example, a Lutheran minister's wife now uses the term 'Goddess' to refer to God while teaching her Bible study classes.[55] A great many Roman Catholics have joined Mary Daly in her mystical quest away from the biblical understanding of God. A number of Roman Catholic nuns are now engaging in private Goddess worship. Sr. Judy Vaughan, executive director of the National Association of Religious Women in Chicago, has publicly stated that she *'believes in the Goddess'* and that such practices are a growing phenomenon among religious and Feminist Catholic women. Sr. Vaughan also said: *'Some of the traditions keep Mary subservient, the handmaiden. There are movements to re-define Mariology and focus on her as a goddess figure'*.[56]

The big push is also on in theological seminaries, to destroy their Christian foundations. Margaret McManus of the Center for Women and Religion at the Graduate Theological Union in Berkeley, California has said: *'The issue is no longer equality... The issue is transformation of our religious institutions'*.[57] One Christian Reformed Church minister, Marty Rienstra of Douglas, Michigan, is currently working on a book paraphrasing the Psalms by converting all pronouns from masculine to feminine. Rienstra has stated that

> 'It is unfair for critics to cry 'idolatry' just because God is referred to as Goddess. In fact, the idolatry has already happened with the masculinization of God as King... Jesus said God is Spirit. To make God just male is to make God a masculine idol'.[58]

In a later section we will show the profound misunderstanding at the heart of this statement. Rienstra's assertion is that the Church needs to *'reclaim the female face of God'*. The claim is made that because Protestants do not have a Virgin Mary to worship, nor women's religious orders, the feminine aspect of God is defaced and the Almighty Himself becomes imbalanced. Therefore, *'Among the Protestants, the movement is the strongest to reclaim the female face of God'*.[59] In this manner, both Catholic and Protestant groupings on a large scale have been sucked into Feminist dogma and goddess-worshipping religion.

Feminists believe that men have created God in their own image in order to establish male domination on the earth. They see the worshipping of God as

---

[54] Ibid.

[55] *Christian News*, 17th September 1990, p.19.

[56] Ibid.

[57] From the article 'Feminism and the Churches', *Newsweek*, February 13th 1989.

[58] *Christian News*, 17th September 1990, p.19.

[59] Ibid.

consisting in men worshipping a male image of themselves, while women are forced to worship the male principle in the form of God the Father, resulting in a world which regards them as second-class citizens with all the attendant conditions of low pay, low status, poor opportunities.

Looking at the wider planetary affairs, feminists conclude that such problems as war, pollution, violence, etc., are only in existence because men, in the main, have cornered the leadership roles. They therefore deduce that if women could change the gods which people worship from male to female, then women will be exalted instead of men and the world will become a better place. They firmly believe *'that by selling women a male God, Judaism and Christianity have denied women the experience of seeing themselves as divine beings'.*[60] This bears out the universal truth of our statement in an earlier chapter that the political, social and religious freedom which is sought by unregenerate human beings — regardless of any high-sounding ethical aims — will always be used ultimately *'to develop the divine reality within themselves'*, that is, to make little gods out of themselves. In any case, Christianity does not *'sell women a male God'*, as the feminist theologians try to claim. Neither is there any truth at all in Mary Daly's feminist rallying-cry in 1974 that *'Since God is male, the male is God'.*[61] As Roland Frye points out, in his excellent booklet on the subject of inclusive language for Deity,

> 'Daly's slogan is full of errors, both of interpretation and deduction. Ancient Greek and Roman gods such as Zeus showed that they were 'male' in every sense, as the myths of their incessant sexual exploits demonstrate, but God the Father is not sexually male either in the Bible or in Christian doctrine... 'Since God is male' begins with an assumption that the mainstream of biblical religion has consistently denied... The Fathers of the Church spoke to the same effect... The pervasive biblical references to God as Father do not teach that 'God is male'.
>
> 'Neither do they teach that 'the male is God'. The claim of divine status for any human individual, group, or ideology is the originating sin from which all other sins derive... To act as though 'the male is God' is not a logical outcome of biblical religion, but a rejection of it.
>
> 'Daly's slogan that 'since God is male, the male is God' has exerted great influence. It also evidences the disparity between understandings of God in much feminist theology and in historic Christianity'.[62]

This is the main problem which believers face in the feminist literature — the constant misrepresentation of biblical, historic Christianity. The misrepresentation of one's opponent is the first refuge of those who are insecure in their argument. Those who **know** they have truth on their side do not need to indulge in such philosophical sleight of hand. The ultimate aim of Feminism is, in fact, to

---

[60] N. Goldenberg, op. cit., p.90.

[61] Mary Daly, 'The Qualitative Leap Beyond Patriarchal Religion', *Quest*, Vol.I, 1974, p.21.

[62] Roland M. Frye, *Language for God and Feminist Language: Problems and Principles* (The Handsel Press, n.d.), pp.3-4.

destroy the apparently 'male' image that the world has of the biblical Jehovah. Thus, toward that end, they will not accept a world which has men in leadership roles. But it is not merely this male image of God which they want to destroy, but God Himself, along with the entire teachings of the Bible and the Christian faith. They are really using the philosophy of Feminism to establish the elementary principles of Satan on a worldwide scale in the form of exalted womanhood. One may begin to wonder where men will fit into the New World Order envisaged by feminists. In answer to this, one of their number decrees that *'men...can serve as helpful sons of women and, perhaps, as lovers, but they should not be considered as equal to women in divinity'.*[63]

The stark truth is that Feminism is not, and has never been, about the attainment of equality for women but the seizing of superiority over men — all in fulfilment of Satan's desire to invert God's prescribed order.

4. Initiation into the Goddess

Perhaps some readers may still be having a little difficulty in grasping the connection between the simple worldly concerns of the political feminists (women's supposed rights, etc.) and the seemingly extreme assertions of the Feminist Witchcraft Movement. But there is a systematic deepening from one level to the next in the Feminist genre. As with all occultic ideologies, the progression from a superficial understanding to full maturity — from noviciate to initiate — is always gradual: by degrees (to use a Masonic term). The path which runs from the first glimmer of concern for the treatment of women in society to full membership of a Feminist Witch Coven (of which there are now many) is paved with a number of ever-deepening 'initiations'.

The commonest form of influence in the early stages of initiation is known as a 'consciousness-raising group', wherein various strategies (pro-lesbian, anti-male propaganda, etc.) and techniques (visualisation, encounter group methods, etc.) are used to inculcate a 'women's consciousness' and open up the participants to using the full rein of their female power. It might be more accurate to describe the noviciate women's groups as 'consciousness-*changing* groups', as their occult function is to prepare women for the higher grade groups where they will develop a personal, inner relationship with the primitive matriarchal civilisations which they project out of their new perception of the world and its development. The high-grade group or coven is described by the feminist-witch Starhawk as

> 'a Witch's support group, consciousness-raising group, psychic study center, clergy-training programme, College of Mysteries, surrogate clan, and religious congregation all rolled into one'.[64]

Once this stage has been reached, a whole subculture opens out for the woman entering into it: the subculture of the Lesbian. Here we should try to fathom some of the external, human factors which make a woman turn to another woman for a physical relationship. We do not go into this in order that it might be condoned,

---

[63] N. Goldenberg, op. cit., quoting Zusannah Budapest on p.103.

[64] Starhawk, op. cit., p.35.

or to engender sympathy for it; but in order that we may have a real understanding of the experiences of these people, so that we can appreciate the need to present them the Gospel out of that understanding, rather than displaying a mere knee-jerk reaction of hatred (of which many Christians are profoundly guilty).

In this atheistic world of ours a great many men behave in an appalling manner towards women. Our culture — regardless of any high-sounding noises to the contrary — actively encourages a pornographic mindset with its exploitation of, and violence towards, women. Movies and television programmes often portray a picture of hostility towards women which is inexcusable, treating them as capricious sex-objects. In many places it is impossible for a woman to walk in the streets for fear of being raped or sexually assaulted or insulted. Such are the fruits of our fallen world, which Satan then exploits for his own purposes. Because of this, it becomes easy for many women to fall straight into the unthreatening arms of another woman — to take refuge in a seemingly safe place in an otherwise hostile world. Thus, one slips into a lesbian lifestyle and with it an important initiation takes place, which we will now examine.

5. Lesbianism is Witchcraft

The word 'lesbian' is derived from the Greek island of Lesbos which, in the sixth century B.C., was host to a group of women dedicated to the worship of the female principle and the service of Aphrodite and Artemis.[65] These two goddesses are of some biblical significance: Aphrodite was the goddess of sex-magic, the Greek version of the Roman goddess Venus, the Babylonian Ishtar, the chief goddess of Tyre, Asherah, and the Canaanite Astarte/Ashtoreth. In the Old Testament, she was referred to as the *'queen of heaven'* (Jer.44:17,18,25) and was the idolatrous object of apostate Hebrews, and the downfall of Solomon (1 Kgs.11:5).

The other Lesbian goddess, Artemis, was the Greek version of Diana, the Roman goddess whose main centre of worship was at Ephesus in the Roman state of Asia, and whose worship was characterised by sensuous orgies and ceremonial prostitution.[66] Feminist writer and researcher, Barbara Walker, has observed that

> 'Diana's cult was so widespread in the pagan world that early Christians viewed her as their major rival, which is why she later became 'Queen of Witches''.[67]

Feminists believe that they are invoking a primordial female principle when they worship these goddesses, giving themselves something with which they can genuinely identify as the unique province of eternal womanhood. However, the various goddesses of love in Syria and Asia Minor originated in the earlier Babylonian Ishtar through Astarte/Ashtoreth; and one must come to the wholly ironic conclusion that the Feminist Movement has concocted a mythology, to suit their

---

[65] It is from the name of Aphrodite that we get our word 'aphrodisiac'.

[66] Read Acts 19:23-41 for an account of the obsessive nature of the Diana goddess worshippers.

[67] Barbara G. Walker, *The Woman's Encyclopedia of Myths and Secrets* (Harper & Row, 1983), p.535.

purposes for today, out of goddess cults which were actually *established by men* to suit their own sexually immoral needs and desires! Ashtoreth and Diana (who are essentially the same sex-goddess of Asia), far from being wonderful examples of woman-power and Amazonianism from a primitive era, are actually classic examples of female images which man has set up out of the evil imaginations of his own heart and then worshipped. Rather than providing a heroine model for would-be feminists, these idols and ideas personify man's foul, fornicatory lusts, made in his fallen image and after his own likeness. To put it bluntly, Feminists are today worshipping the pornographic imagery of ancient times: The goddess idols, the groves, the sacred shrines and temples of the ancients were actually the primitive versions of the blow-up dolls, sex-shops, peep-shows and whore-houses of today, which, ironically, modern feminists claim so vehemently to oppose!

Homosexuality was rife in these primitive cults, as it is in all situations which are devoid of true religion. The lesbianism of today is a modern outworking of the demonically-inspired goddess cults of biblical times which opposed Jehovah-Christ. This is the reason it can serve as the interface between the Women's Rights Movement and the Feminist Witchcraft Movement. The initial desire to improve one's lot as a woman — because it is essentially a futile, God-less search for personal 'liberation' — becomes the object of exploitation by satanic forces which provide a very credible alternative philosophy and lifestyle, amounting to a Faustian kiss of sorcery, sodomy, and self-exaltation: the true nuts and bolts of Feminism, inevitable under the Law of Godless Reformation.

Lesbianism is a direct defiance of and challenge to the Creator God of this universe, the development of which is well-documented by the Holy Spirit in the first chapter of the epistle to the Romans (1:18-32). The Women's Liberation Movement in its outworking is ultimately a Lesbian Movement; even its heterosexual adherents support the principles of homosexuality, or 'Gay Liberation' as they call it. So we can see from Scripture that there is nothing new about the religious practices of Feminism, which are merely a resurrection of the man-made, Israel-opposing, pagan cults recorded in the Old Testament, rather than those of any lost matriarchal civilisation. However, the Holy Spirit also has much to tell us concerning the issues raised by the political feminists: gender roles, marriage, men/women relationships, etc. And these we shall now explore, insofar as they pertain to this present study.

III. MAN AND WOMAN IN CREATION

We are confronted, in the opening pages of the Bible, with the endowment of gender-gifts in the creation of man and woman. This is the climax of God's creative activity. Although the fact that the creation of the man took place before the woman does hold some significance, this is not an indication of male superiority and female inferiority. In spite of the assertions of many people down the ages, there is no justification for relegating woman to a second-class status in God's eyes simply because she came into being after man. All true Christians recognise this, as did the Puritan pastor and teacher William Perkins in the late sixteenth century, when he wrote the well-known words which have been plagiarised by many later commentators (including Matthew Henry):

> 'The duty of the husband [is] to honour his wife...in three ways: First, in making account of her as his companion or yoke-fellow. For this cause, the woman, when she was created, was not taken out of the man's head, because she was not made to rule over him; nor out of his feet, because God did not make her subject to him as a servant; but out of his side, to the end that man should take her as his mate'.[68]

God created both the man **and** the woman in His image, a fact that is strongly emphasised in the text (Gen.1:27; 5:2). Coupled with this, it should be stressed that God Himself is neither male nor female; but neither is He androgynous, as some Christians seem to believe. In fact, because He is spirit (Jn.4:24) He transcends any kind of gender definition (cf. 1 Sam.15:29). This is why all the talk about changing the biblical pronouns which refer to Deity in Scripture is utterly futile — a fact which we will be going into more fully later in this chapter.

Feminists — especially those within the churches — have always been very vocal on the 'women's ordination' issue; and the exegetical gymnastics of the feminist-sympathising evangelicals concerning the controversial Pauline texts have been truly breathtaking. Paul could not have been clearer in the things he said about church leadership, the exercise of authority and the role of women in the assemblies — what he calls *'the house of God'* (1 Tim.2:9-15; with 3:15). Yet, because so many people in the churches today use modern cultural (predominantly feminist-inspired) norms as the yardstick against which the biblical data should be measured, everything possible is done to bend, twist and squeeze his words into something more acceptable to the kind of people who construct their life-norms out of 'Cosmopolitan' magazine and 'The Guardian' newspaper.[69]

The stark truth is that the Word of God excludes women from the eldership in local churches, and also from shaping the authoritative teaching of the Church, on the basis of Eve being created after Adam and also being deceived by Satan into falling from grace (1 Tim.2:11-15). Admittedly, these concepts are rather alien to the modern world; but this does not render them null and void. The idea of a soul-saving blood-sacrifice is also an alien concept in late twentieth century Western culture; but that does not prevent the atonement of Christ from being the central pivot upon which the whole of human history turns, from creation to eternity. The Apostle's authoritative teaching about women in the churches does not designate women as being more obnoxious or less gifted than men. Paul is simply revealing and ratifying the consequences through the ages of God's original judgement on the actions of the first woman in history. Neither does his teaching

---

[68] William Perkins, 'A Short Survey of the Right Manner of Erecting and Ordering a Family, According to the Scriptures', in *Workes*, Vol.III (Cantrell Legge, 1613), p.691.

[69] For a straightforward but sensitive treatment of the role of women in the churches, see Derek Prime, *Women in the Church: A Pastoral Approach* (Crossway, 1992). The great virtue of this book is that it studiously avoids the tortuous, back-bending scholarship which characterises so many modern evangelical treatments of this subject.

imply that Christian men are more honourable than their female counterparts. Let us not forget that Christian men, as well as women, were once *'darkness'* (Eph.5:8) and *'dead in trespasses and sins'* (Eph.2:1), because of the sin of the man, Adam, which brought death into the world (Rom.5:12).

In spite of all the attempts to force equality on the world today, there are fundamental God-ordained differences between men and women which are vital to the working out of His plan on earth. The Hebrew word for woman or wife, *ishah*, is derived from a root which means 'soft' or 'delicate'.[70] Although this word is similar to the Hebrew word for man, *ish*, there is actually an intentional contrast in meaning, as this *ish* appears to be derived from a root which means 'to be strong'.[71] So there is a deliberate and complementary contrast in our gender-gifts from God, ensuring that men and women recognise a completion and fulfilment in their relationship with one another. This is the true mystery of marriage, and also provides a stunning symbol of the relationship between Christ and His Church (Eph.5:22-33). Adam recognised this unity of the male with the female when he said of Eve: *'This is now bone of my bones and flesh of my flesh'* (Gen.2:23). So man and woman, although having individual sexual characteristics and roles, are intended by God to engage in a lifelong bond in conformity with His spiritual purposes: *'Therefore a man shall leave his father and mother and be joined to his wife, and they shall become one flesh'* (Gen.2:24).

Here we can perhaps understand the significance of the devil's undermining of marriage between man and woman. If such a union has been — and still is — of supreme spiritual importance for the outworking of God's plan,[72] then by attempting to destroy all manifestations of this union, it may be possible to undermine the plan itself. Marital discord and breakdown is a part of this element in the spiritual battle, but the most far-reaching tactic in the satanic destruction of marital integrity between man and woman is the widespread growth of homosexuality. It may be unfashionable but it is certainly no exaggeration to say that homosexuality is a sin — a profound sin. It is a sin, not simply because it is 'disgusting', or 'perverted', or 'unhealthy' (these words are really secular judgements), but above all because it is *disobedient to God's will.* When we deny that heterosexuality is normal, we deny our Creator, and we must then have recourse to euphemistic words such as 'gay' in our efforts to cover up the intrinsic sinfulness of homosexuality and to deny the spiritual significance of the heterosexual union in marriage. This process of becoming 'one flesh' (Gen.2:24) is referred to in the New Testament a number of times, and Jesus Himself reiterates the creation and union of man and woman, adding the rejoinder: *'therefore, what God has joined together, let not man separate'* (Mt.19:6). The apostle Paul, in his first epistle to the Corinthians,

---

70 *The New Brown, Driver, Briggs and Gesenius Hebrew-English Lexicon of the Old Testament*, 1906 edition (Hendrickson, 1979), p.61.

71 Ibid., p.35.

72 The Saviour of the world — the Seed (offspring) of the woman (Gen.3:15) — came to incarnation through a long line of generations. His people also come into being in the world as a result of marriage between the male and female.

also stressed the sanctity of this union when he warned its recipients not to have sexual contact with prostitutes: *'For "the two," He says, "shall become one flesh"'* (1 Cor.6:16), thus defiling their bodies which are *'not for sexual immorality, but for the Lord'* (1 Cor.6:13).

The sanctity of marriage has become increasingly eroded in recent years and we can expect this erosion to continue as the iniquity of the satanic world-system comes to its fullness. A common phrase in relation to male-female relationships is the 'battle of the sexes'. That such a state of affairs should have arisen is hardly surprising. The entire problem began at the time of the Fall of our first parents recounted in Genesis 3. Neither Adam nor Eve would take responsibility for their disobedience to God, and when Adam behaved with such cowardice, blaming Eve for his own waywardness (Gen.3:12), the scene was set for a strife-torn relationship between men and women which has persisted to this day, resulting in the 'lovers' tiffs', jealousy, marital stress, separation and divorce which are now so prevalent in our culture.

Naturally, the more people attempt to ameliorate these difficulties through their own strength (cf. 1 Sam.2:9b), the more they will become entrenched in their problems — that Law of Godless Reformation once again. But the key to this immense problem cannot be found in Feminism or in any other attempted humanistic or utopian solution. The real key to the problem lies throughout the Bible: it is *submission.* This is not a popular form of demeanour in this day and age — especially for feminists. For they believe that women are already too submissive to men. However, the submission advocated in the Bible operates in a very different way from the submission which Feminism finds so offensive. When Paul said: *'Wives, submit to your own husbands, as to the Lord. For the husband is head of the wife, as also Christ is head of the church'* (Eph.5:22-23), he was not giving men *carte blanche* to subjugate their wives in a master/slave capacity. It is the wives who should, *of their own volition,* submit to their husbands to the glory of God. The husbands are not told to *force* their wives submit to them. In fact, the husbands are told: *'Love your wives, just as Christ also loved the church and gave Himself for her'* (Eph.5:25). In other words, theirs is to be a life of self-sacrifice.

God's structure for human relationships works through two principal means: First, the *submission* of the one under authority; second, the *self-sacrifice* of the one in authority. The kind of male-female domination and submission so prevalent in our culture is actually a complete antithesis of the relationship advocated by the apostle here, because it is generally enforced in an entirely unreasonable manner — and that by unregenerate men. Similarly, the remedies offered by the Women's Liberation Movement are equally unbiblical because they merely offer at best, reactionary political reform; at worst, they initiate a descent into witchcraft.

God gives men leadership in the family as well as in the Church. As the Apostle writes: *'I want you to know that the head of every man is Christ, the head of woman is man, and the head of Christ is God'* (1 Cor.11:3). This is the divinely-appointed hierarchy in the Church for the remainder of this age. This headship of the man can be learned from a number of Scriptures, which show that it goes back to the original creation. Paul argues for the fact that women should not have rule or give authoritative teaching in the Church when he says: *'Adam was formed first, then Eve'* (1 Tim.2:13). Again, he says: *'For man is not from woman, but woman from man. Nor was man created for the woman, but woman for the man'* (1 Cor.11:8-9). This echoes that primal Scripture: *'The LORD God said, "It is not good that man should be alone; I will make him a helper comparable to him"'* (Gen.2:18). Finally, he also asserts that the man *'is the image and glory of God; but woman is the glory of man'* (1 Cor.11:7). Now it is true that this is not at all in line with current worldly opinion; but the true purpose of Christian doctrine has never been to please the world (cf. Lk.16:15). Rather, it is to build up the Church and provide norms for people who dwell in a new spiritual kingdom. We are to be conformed to the Word — not to the world. As the Apostle says:

> 'Now we have received, not the spirit of the world, but the Spirit who is from God, that we might know the things that have been freely given to us by God. These things we also speak, not in words which man's wisdom teaches but which the Holy Spirit teaches, comparing spiritual things with spiritual. But the natural man does not receive the things of the Spirit of God, for they are foolishness to him; nor can he know them, because they are spiritually discerned' (1 Cor.2:12-14).

You must have the indwelling Holy Spirit to appreciate, discern, and obey the Word of God — especially in the area of relationships. That is why unbelievers and impostors in the Church will never really understand what Paul is talking about, and will always feel obliged to make his words say other than what they really mean. Like the false religionists of Christ's day, they fall into error because they neither know the Scriptures nor the power of God (cf. Mt.22:29).

In the original creation, the headship of the man would have involved a beautiful and harmonious relationship. But after the Fall, that relationship became hugely distorted. So it has been throughout history, during which relationships between men and women have been shot through with striving. But when husbands and wives come to Christ, that original relationship between man and woman is restored. Christian wifely submission and husbandly self-sacrifice bring the most wonderful things to a marriage. In many ways, the Lord's requirement of the man's love toward his wife is the more demanding of the two roles, for to love his wife *'as Christ also loved the church'* (Eph.5:25) represents the ultimate in self-sacrifice, as Christ became the Suffering Servant and laid down His life for His people, the Church. How many men can honestly claim to love their wives in this way? There can be no more beautiful harmony in relationship than when a husband is in submission to Christ, a wife is in submission to her husband, and the children are obedient to their parents. And all in submission to God and His Word. God blesses those who obey His Word and live according to the structures He prescribes. This applies in any sphere of life.

There are a number of key factors with respect to this 'submission' in the relation of the wife to the husband: First, it is voluntary. Biblical submission does not involve oppression, repression, coercion or cruelty. Biblical submission has nothing to do with the woman being a mouse or a doormat. A woman can be a very strong and outgoing personality, and yet still be submissive according to God's command. Submission does not at all mean that a woman becomes an insignificant blob without any real identity of her own. In fact, motherhood and homemaking are the most highly esteemed roles for a woman in Scripture — in spite of the fact that they are regarded as inferior in many quarters today. Scripture even envisages the possibility of working wives — although always operating within the domestic sphere (see Prov.31:10-31).

A second key factor in relation to a wife's submission to her husband is that it is always envisaged as being under the patronage of God: *'Wives, submit to your own husbands, as is fitting in the Lord'* (Col 3:18). What is implied here is that the submission of the wife is part of her obedience to Christ, and this lifts it out of the realms of the mundane and invests it with great spirituality. In sum, biblical submission simply means that, on a voluntary basis, out of love and reverence for the Lord and His Word, the wife accepts the authority of her husband in matters belonging to the family sphere. This does not mean that she is prevented from vitally contributing to family decisions. It is simply a question of deference to the headship appointed by God. Now the usual response to all this talk of submission from those who find it hard to swallow is that 'it says somewhere in the Bible that there is neither male nor female in Christ Jesus'. Aren't we therefore all equal in the eyes of God? Let us just have a look at this text:

> 'After faith has come, we are no longer under a tutor. For you are all sons of God through faith in Christ Jesus. For as many of you as were baptized into Christ have put on Christ. There is neither Jew nor Greek, there is neither slave nor free, there is neither male nor female; for you are all one in Christ Jesus. And if you are Christ's, then you are Abraham's seed, and heirs according to the promise' (Gal.3:25-29).

The context here has nothing whatsoever to do with marriage, but is about the standing of people before God in relation to salvation. Insofar as all believers are children of God, all distinctions between people pale into insignificance. The gift of salvation is not at all determined by our cultural, ethnic or gender characteristics. The only thing that matters is whether or not you are Christ's; for, if you are Christ's, then you are God's children and recipients of the inheritance — eternal life. However, despite this equality in terms of salvation, insofar as we are part of human structures in God's creation, there is a divine order: a sacred hierarchy. The husband and wife are one in Christ Jesus; and they are one flesh in their relationship. But that relationship involves a structure, an order determined by God for its harmonious outworking. And who are we to argue with that?

So the woman's position in relation to the man, as designated by God, does not indicate outright inferiority but a difference in office and administration. We must not superimpose the secular concept of male domination/female subjugation onto the biblical doctrine of submission within the family — for then we merely play into the hands of the feminists. The difference between the role of the man and that of the woman is one of *office* rather than consisting in superiority and inferiority. Yet, paradoxically, her submission to the man is totally liberating rather than enslaving when the man himself is in submission to God, because this is the relationship that God intended for His spiritual purposes. The beauty and enigma within this relationship require long meditation if they are to be understood.

This divinely-instituted headship of the man over the woman was never a sorrowful or distraught event in the original creation, but became distorted only after the Fall. So, when the Lord God said to Eve, after her lapse from His Law, *'your desire shall be for your husband, and he shall rule over you'* (Gen.3:16), He was not spitefully laying down a tyrannical rule, but was, in judgement, frankly predicting how the male-female relationship would have to be worked out in the world as a result of human disobedience. Far from being able to exercise the equivalent of God's knowledge and handling of good and evil — as Satan had suggested (cf. Gen.3:5) — the woman would now herself be the victim of evil over which she would be unable to exercise control. Such is the power of God. This saying of God was prophetic of the universally-recognised heartache felt by women in relation to men, and which can be worked out only in the complete acceptance of that relationship's demands (cf. 1 Tim.2:15). All attempts to avoid the opportunity to carry the cross of this curse can only lead to a further distancing of oneself from the Lord. The Feminist movement has, in many ways, correctly recognised the effects of this curse, but because they are blinded to its true spiritual origins and significance, they choose to bypass this heartache by taking refuge in political reform, lesbianism and fanciful occult religious practices, rather than restoring a relationship with their Creator through His prescribed pathway to Life and freedom (Mt.11:28-30; Jn.8:31-32).

These extraordinary truths are outside the understanding of the worldly women of today; but when a man and a woman dedicate their lives and their marriage to the Lord God, their eyes are opened to the necessity of this cross and it becomes a positive joy to carry. In other words, without this marital structure which the Lord has provided there would be much chaos and heartache. As the biblical model of marital and family life becomes further eroded by our humanistic culture, so the chaos and heartache associated with it will increase. God has ordained structure in human affairs for very special purposes. Francis Shaeffer puts it like this:

> 'In a fallen world (in every kind of society — big and small — and in every relationship) structure is needed for order. God himself imposes it on the basic human relationship... It is not simply because man is stronger that he is to have dominion. But rather he is to have dominion because God gives this as structure in the midst of a fallen world'.[73]

Yet, because we live in a fallen world, there has even been an abuse of the very structure which was ordained for us to alleviate the effects of the Fall and bring us to repentance. The maltreatment and enforced subjugation of women by men is surely a gross corruption of the divinely-ordained principle of headship and

---

[73] Francis Shaeffer, *Genesis in Space and Time* (Inter Varsity Press, 1972), p.94.

submission. But Feminism can never bring about any real change in this world-wide problem because feminists have chosen to ignore a vital truth: *that Christianity itself, through the mediatorial office of Jesus Christ, is the only true force of liberation, for women as well as for men.* Let us now turn to this lovely theme.

IV. JESUS, THE TRUE LIBERATOR

Although the brutalising effects of the Fall on male-female relationships in general have continued unabated (in spite of the veneer of 'civilisation') throughout the millennia, the advent of the Lord Jesus Christ brought — for the first time in the history of humanity — a complete transformation in this area. As one writer puts it:

> 'Jesus never called a woman His own and yet He had a warm appreciation of women. He was the first in all the world to recognise her as a moral personality and He placed her on an equality with man before God... Thus it was Jesus who first brought woman to honour, and Frenssen is right when he says, 'Women of all the world, be grateful to Him!'' [74]

The apostle Paul stresses the lack of any inferiority between Christian men and women in their standing in the kingdom of God, when he says: *'There is neither male nor female: for you are all one on Christ Jesus'* (Gal.3:28). Thus, the Women's Liberation Movement and Feminism are tragic anachronisms, because Jesus Christ has already done all the 'liberating' necessary for all those who will receive Him. It is only *'in Christ Jesus'* that men and women can become 'one'. In this light, it is completely unnecessary for women to become embroiled in tortured debate about whether or not the Bible is offensive to them because of the constant references to God as 'Father' and 'He', or because the Redeemer of the world incarnated in a male body. Obviously we can have no truly complete conception of God, but we can certainly say that He is neither exclusively male nor exclusively female, since both men and women were originally made in His image. It is just as mistaken, also, to speak of God as being androgynous — i.e., *both* masculine and feminine — as some evangelicals do today, in line with their Jungian analysis of human psychology. The Lord transcends gender altogether, in spite of the fact that the Bible speaks of God with male pronouns.

But why do these male pronouns occur in the Bible? Is there not a good reason for this? The Scriptures could never refer to God as 'It', for that would remove the personal nature of the Almighty. Men and women are not made in the image of an 'It'. The use of specifically masculine pronouns most likely does occur for very special reasons. Professor Roger Nicole puts this issue into perspective when he shows that God had to be represented as a male in the Bible because

> 'To do otherwise would have undoubtedly severely curtailed the understanding of his majesty; and the licentious developments in religions

---

74 Otto Borchert, *The Original Jesus* [*Der Goldgrund des Lebensbildes Jesu*] (Lutterworth Press, 1933), p.288.

where female deities are found would manifest the appropriateness of avoiding this representation in O.T. times'.[75]

It is no coincidence that the very people who are clamouring for the removal of male pronouns which refer to Deity in the Bible are those who are avidly worshipping the goddess today. There is nothing new under the sun. God's wisdom in representing Himself as male can therefore be seen to be very astute. Furthermore, to take away the male pronouns in reference to Deity would be to do irreparable damage to the doctrine of the Trinity — Father, Son and Holy Spirit — upon which a true understanding of the Godhead of Scripture depends. Above all, we speak specifically of the 'Father' and the 'Son' because Jesus did (Jn.6:40; 10:36; 14:13). Even more to the point, we can wholeheartedly pray to God as Father because Jesus did (e.g., Jn.17:1). Only the most rebellious persons would dare to set themselves against the pattern laid down by the founder of the Christian faith. In truth, the entire Gospel message is offensive to the entire unregenerate human race, and no mere tampering with a few pronouns will remove that offence. The attempted detection of so-called 'sexism' in biblical literature is an utterly vain and superfluous activity.

Feminism asserts that Christianity and the Bible portray women in a poor light, creating the precedent for their alleged ill-treatment today. Yet any biblical study will show that precisely the opposite is true. Although women in O.T. times held a second-class position legally, on an everyday basis their actual status was one of dignity, and disrespect toward them was severely punished (Lev.20:9; Dt.27:16). Mothers were in fact recognised as being equal with fathers in many places in the O.T. (e.g., Ex.20:12; Prov.1:8; 6:20; 10:1).

Women were involved in the arts (Ex.15:20; Jdg.21:19-21; 2 Chr.35:25), were skilled weavers (Ex.35:25-26), rebuilt the Wall of Jerusalem (Neh.3:12), were involved in business ventures (Pro.31:16; Acts 5:1), and in the manufacture and sale of linen garments and tents (Pro.31:24; Acts 16:14; 18:2-3). Women were also judges (Deborah, Jdg.4:4-5), prophetesses (Miriam, Ex.15:20; Num.12:2; Deborah, Jdg.4:4-5; Huldah, 2 Kgs.22:14; Noadiah, Neh.6:14; Anna, Lk.2:36; Philip's daughters, Acts 21:9), and queens (Athalia, 2 Kgs.11; and Esther).

The advent of Jesus Christ brought about a complete transformation in the legal and spiritual status of women, who were regarded by the contemporary Hellenistic culture as the lowest of the low. Because *'His mercy flowed like a broad stream, seeking the low levels of life'*,[76] His coming was to be especially significant for the sinner (Mt.9:13; Lk.15:7; 19:10; 1 Tim.1:15), the unsophisticated (Lk.10:21; 1 Cor.1:26-29),[77] the suffering and the downtrodden (Mt.5:10-12; Jn.15:19-20)

---

[75] Walter A. Elwell (Ed.), *Evangelical Dictionary of Theology*, (Baker Book House, 1985), p.1177.

[76] O. Borchert, op.cit., pp.288-289.

[77] The Greek word used for 'wise' in these verses is *sophos*, from which we obtain our word 'sophisticated' — a class of persons defined in Chambers Dictionary as *'adulterated, falsified, worldly-wise, devoid or deprived of natural simplicity'*. In other words, people who are *'wise in their own eyes'* (Prov.3:7; Isa.5:21) and therefore unable to have

Naturally enough, in this order of things, women were among Jesus' main beneficiaries, and one can hardly begin to imagine the consternation which must have been generated by His 'preservation of women's rights' during the discourse on marriage and divorce (Mt.5:27-32; 19:3-9), or when He healed on the Sabbath a woman to whom He referred as a *'daughter of Abraham'* (Lk.13:16).

Moreover, it was to a woman — and a Samaritan, too! — that Jesus first openly admitted that He was the Messiah (Jn.4:25-26). He had many close and caring relationships with women (Lk.8:2-3; 10:38-42; 24:10; Jn.11:5; 12:2-7; etc.) and women were in the majority in the circle of disciples at the Cross. It was also women who were the first witnesses of the Resurrection. This was a revolutionary thing for the time, as under Roman law a woman was unable to serve as a witness, which probably contributed to the sceptical response of those who were the first to receive the good news of the risen Christ (Lk.24:11).

If there is this vast wealth of evidence in the Scriptures concerning the worth of women, why should there be such a hue and cry from the feminists about the subjugation of women at the hands of Christianity? Unfortunately, throughout the past nineteen-hundred years, a host of unbiblical persecutory acts carried out by people professing to be Christians has led to a souring of the essential Gospel message of Christianity for many people in the world. This is especially relevant when considering the development of the Feminist movement, which has made such political and emotional capital out of the mass slaughter, by professing Christians, of many women through the centuries who were believed to be witches. Understandably, they conclude that such atrocities must reflect the teachings of Christ, and are the natural, misogynous outcome of a male-dominated Christian society.

However, these appalling and barbaric actions — by both Protestants and Roman Catholics alike — were the result of a flawed application of the Mosaic Law which advocated capital punishment for practising witches (Ex.22:18). In redemptive historical terms, this practice was a necessary deterrent at the time in view of the magic and occultism practised within the cults and religions of the nations surrounding the people of Israel, and the fact that the religion of Israel had to be preserved until the coming of the Messiah (Gal.3:22-24). Although it is true that the Lord's judgement on these gross practices will never change (cf. Rev.22:15), the manner in which they were dealt with under the Mosaic Covenant is totally transformed in the New Covenant in Jesus Christ. Since His coming, it has been fully revealed that it is through Christ's blood — *'shed for many'* (Mk.14:24) — that Satan and all his works are overcome (Rev.12:11). The weapons of our warfare against the works of the devil are spiritual, not carnal (2 Cor.10:4). We sing a new song. We have a Gospel to preach. We have the fulfilment of the types. The Church is not the nation Israel.

The invocation of the Mosaic Law as a justification for the execution of witches during the past two millennia (by whatever method) is more an expression of the

---

fellowship with God until they have been humbled. All those sponsoring humanistic liberation movements must fall into this category.

hatred and depravity of the perpetrators rather than a manifestation of post-crucifixion Christianity. To apply John 15:6 to the execution of witches, as did certain deluded professing Christians in earlier eras, represents not only a heinous twisting of Scripture but also a serious misunderstanding of the movement of redemptive history and the manner in which the Christian deals with demonic principalities and powers. This truth must be proclaimed to the Feminist movement; for it would be no exaggeration to say that the Feminist philosophy has been constructed on the mountainous ashes of the witches who they are determined to commemorate and eulogise.

Let it be fully proclaimed that biblical Christianity has always acknowledged the dignity and worth of womanhood, as laid down in the Scriptures. True followers of Christ should be ready to condemn any harsh treatment or subjugation of women. In 1728, the devotional writer William Law wrote, concerning women: *'The corruption of the world indulges them in great vanity, and mankind seem to consider them in no other view than as so many painted idols that are to allure and gratify their passions'.*[78] Law was way ahead of his time in this view of the manner in which our culture perverts women. Consider the crass treatment of women in the media and advertising today. Almost all film and television series turn their leading women into sex objects. Law rightly recognised that women were perverted *'by an erroneous education'* which mistakenly led people to the view that they are *'naturally of little and vain minds'.*[79] He deplored this abuse of womanhood, declaring: *'There is a finer sense, a clearer mind, a readier apprehension, and gentler dispositions in that sex than in the other'.*[80] Such a statement cuts right across the grain of secular culture. While it is true that the corruption of the world indulges women in great vanity, and the general mass of mankind seems to view them as so many painted idols to satisfy their deluded passions, the Scriptures give the true picture of womanhood, both fallen and redeemed — a picture to which all believers should subscribe and conform. Until they do, there will be no real understanding of the true ministry of women in churches today.

When Scripture places demarcation lines between the roles of the sexes, it is not in order to accentuate division or promote subjugation but, rather, to fulfil God's unique and holy purposes. These purposes (some revealed, some concealed) can never be fulfilled in a context which is devoid of love, or which ignores the essential unity of the Body of Christ in Christ Jesus Himself.

EPILOGUE: THE SIX SATANIC INFLUENCES IN FEMINISM

Having now revealed the true spiritual background to Feminism, together with some of the biblical data on gender roles and female achievement, let us conclude by drawing together some of the prevailing influences in this movement.

---

[78] William Law, *A Serious Call to a Devout and Holy Life* (Macmillan & Co., 1898), pp.218-219.

[79] Ibid., p.218.

[80] Ibid.

1. Anger

One of the first things that one notices in a Feminist bookstore is that the literature is filled with expressions of the most extreme anger and griping. It erupts from the page like a flood of molten lava: burning fiercely, but destined to turn to a wilderness of stone. Words such as 'roaring', 'fury', 'fight' and 'raging' are often applied to the internal condition of these women in their writings. One popular book, available from many High Street bookstores, is called *'Woman and Nature — the Roaring Inside her'*. This is a 250-page 'stream-of-consciousness' invective against the ills of the world, with the Feminist error of blaming its 'menfulness' rather than its Godlessness for its history of ever-deepening ills.[81]

In another example, underneath a drawing of a 'Great Mother Sphinx',[82] one popular early Feminist poster makes the statement: *'Women are the real Left. We are rising with a fury older than any force in history. This time we will be free or no one will survive'*.[83] Another pamphlet is entitled *'Raging Womyn'*.[84] Even from its earliest days, the salute of Feminism has been an upraised clenched fist held high above the head — an extreme symbol of anger which it shares with Marxist-socialist causes throughout the world. And the badge that feminists wear (see right) is a picture of that fist ringed by a symbol of Venus.

Many of these women have deep, unresolved hurts, a root of bitterness laid down from bad experiences and abuses which they have suffered at the hands of harsh fathers, cruel boyfriends and insensitive husbands. It is unfortunate that this suppressed pain has emerged as a vast, collective, unforgiving anger known as the Women's Liberation Movement. Such anger can only be dissolved through repentance before Jesus Christ, regeneration through the Holy Spirit, followed by wise Christian counsel.

2. Violence

One of the oldest chestnuts of the Feminist Movement is the concept of 'abortion on demand'. This goes back to the very foundations of the Women's Liberation Movement. What more serious form of violence could there be than the wilful murder of a foetus through abortion? The growing acceptance of abortion as a contraceptive technique, coupled with its enabling legislation marks a more than coincidental return to the licentious conditions prevalent in early Roman times. Abortion and infanticide have always been endemic in pagan cultures.[85] It

---

[81] Susan Griffin, *Woman and Nature: the Roaring Inside Her* (Women's Press, 1984).

[82] The Sphinx is a monster in Greek mythology which has the head of a woman and the body of a lioness. This creature proposed a riddle to travellers, strangling those unable to solve it! Our word 'sphincter' has the same derivation.

[83] This wall poster first appeared in 1969.

[84] Jean Freer (alias Carol Lee), *Raging Womyn* [sic] (The Wymyn's [sic] Land Fund, Islington, 1984). Feminists often spell the words 'women' and 'woman' in ways which prevent the word 'men' or 'man' from having any part of it, e.g., 'wimmin' or 'womyn'.

was a problem in biblical times for the Children of Israel, as they fell under the influence of the surrounding nations who worshipped Molech — a deity to whom children were sacrificed (Lev.18:21), and who, with Ashtoreth, was responsible for the fall of King Solomon (1 Kgs.11:7).

The methods of abortion which can be used today are legion. One widely-used Feminist health book even gives a detailed account of how one can carry out a 'psychic' abortion using certain meditation and visualisation techniques, which are advocated as being the humane and spiritually responsible way of disposing of unwanted children.[86] This combination of selfish sexuality and sorcery is the inevitable outcome of the godless reforms and demoniacal demands of the Feminist Movement.

3. Sexual Immorality

One of the leading features of all occultic developments is the use of an appealing external philosophy to attract people who are unable to see beyond it, through which adherents can then all the more easily be ensnared with the real doctrine which lies behind it. One of the main appeals of the Feminist Movement lies in its stance against pornography — especially that which degrades or exploits women. This is a laudable position; yet, ironically, Feminism itself is a hotbed of sexual immorality with its advocation of sodomy and its bevy of goddesses, which are really deific objects of worship from ancient sexually-amoral cultures. Women within the Feminist Movement are unable to see this 'doublethink' in their philosophy, having been sold the lie that they are 'goddesses' themselves.

The twilight world of Prostitution is another area of immorality which the feminists have eagerly promoted. In October 1986 an extraordinary event, known as the 'Second World Congress of Whores', was held in Conference Room 63 of the European Parliament building in Brussels. According to one newspaper report, this conference was *'overloaded with a heavy European feminist lobby'*, and it noted that *'although a sexy little high-heeled shoe is the logo for the Congress, the radical feminist prostitutes wear baggy trousers and flat shoes'*.[87] Having been sponsored by numerous international women's groups, the Belgian and Dutch governments, and the Australian Prostitutes Collective, this 'Congress' was set up *'to promote the image of prostitution as a legitimate industry'*, and one of its recommendations was to introduce the term 'sexual services industry' instead of the commonly-used word 'prostitution'.[88] When we learn that this 'World Congress of Whores' was *'booked in by the European Green Party and the Women's Organisation for Equality'*,[89] one may well wonder how such fornication can possibly be promoted by those who claim to be taking a firm stand against the 'rape'

---

[85] See Francis Shaeffer et al., *Whatever Happened to the Human Race? — Study Guide* (Marshall, Morgan & Scott, 1980), p.36.

[86] Jeannine Parvati, *Hygieia: A Woman's Herbal* (Wildwood House, London, 1979), pp.201-205. *Hygieia* was the name of the Greek goddess of health.

[87] *Daily Telegraph*, October 3rd, 1986.

[88] Ibid.

[89] Ibid.

of the earth and the exploitation of women! Such is the doublethink of the Neo-Gnostics today.

So proud and arrogant are these feminists, they are prepared to flaunt their perversity in the face of the Lord of all creation (cf. 2 Pet.2:10). At the Boston Conference on 'Women's Spirituality' mentioned earlier in this chapter, the lecture audience in the church-building specially hired for the occasion ran amok after listening to speeches on the theme of 'Womanpower: Energy Resourcement'. In a scene reminiscent of the riot at Ephesus (Acts 19:21-41), they chanted *'The Goddess is Alive — Magic is Afoot'* and, in the words of one eyewitness, they *'evoked the Goddess with dancing, stamping, clapping and yelling. They stood on pews and danced barebreasted on the pulpit and amid the hymnbooks'*.[90]

Such an intense, rampant hatred of the Lord is a classic outworking of the combination of demonic influence and unashamed human evil.

4. Self-Reformation

Alongside all the so-called 'consciousness-raising' groups mentioned earlier, the Feminist movement is a veritable antheap of various tendentious therapies and training techniques. These can involve anything from learning Martial Arts (protection against all those oppressive men) and counselling rape victims, to acquiring skills in a job which requires a boiler-suit, e.g., bricklaying, plumbing, joinery, etc. One of the most popular and widely available of these feminist attempts at self-reformation is known as 'Assertiveness Training', during which a woman, through role play, etc., learns techniques to develop her will and to avoid being submissive or passive in her dealings with others — especially men. One would expect such a therapy within the Feminist movement, as the assertion and building-up of the will forms a necessary part of the noviciate training in classic witchcraft — a fact borne out by Naomi Goldenberg when she states that:

> 'A woman with a strong will is admired and considered an asset in the coven's work. The negative image society has of the headstrong, wilful, determined woman is completely reversed in witchcraft. Witches find most of the world's 'bitchy', 'pushy' females endearing'.[91]

Obviously, women — in both secular and Christian communities — do need to find ways of dealing with the shabby and unbiblical way that they are treated by men in many areas. However, the assimilation of a handful of secular techniques to bring about personal and relationship change can only lead, as previously stated, to that *'state [which] is worse than the first'* (Mt.12:45).

5. Self-Exaltation

The supreme exaltation of self is a manifest characteristic of the Feminist movement, in which a woman seeks to raise her consciousness and assert her own 'personhood'. There is a kind of pride known in English as *hubris*. This word was used by the apostle Paul in its Greek noun-form *hubristes* (Rom.1:30), to

---

[90] N. Goldenberg, op.cit., p.92.

[91] Ibid., p.104.

describe one of the resultant characteristics of accepting the Lie — the substitution of the creature for the Creator — and is translated variously as 'despiteful', 'insolent', 'violent'. In the list in Romans, it comes immediately after a word for 'God-haters' and immediately before words for 'arrogant' and 'boastful', which J.B. Phillips neatly amalgamates in his translation into *'insolent pride and boastfulness'*. Hubris was the cardinal sin of Satan — the pride which makes a person act with violent, wanton insolence against both God and man. It leads him to forget his creaturehood and to exalt himself against God. This condition of *hubris* is endemic in the fallen creature and provides one of the primary footholds for the outworking of satanic forces. Considering the detail given in this chapter, can there be any doubt about its application to the Feminist movement?

6. Sorcery

This particular satanic foothold in the Feminist movement, which by now needs no introduction, is both the essence and final expression of a movement which is attempting to liberate womanhood from the effects of the Fall without repentance and humility, and to steer it into the cultivation of witchcraft as the women's religion coupled with an imagined sense of its reclaimed 'divinity'.

The presentation of this lie as a viable way of life can only be perpetuated through deception — i.e., magic, witchcraft — because it is essentially the same Lie as that proposed by Satan to the human creation at the dawn of history, the manifestation of which has been repeatedly realised throughout human history (and exposed throughout the course of this book). This compound lie involved the promise of unconditional eternal life, the kindling of the desire for forbidden wisdom and the illusion of personal divinity. This is the true meaning of mystical *Babylon* in the Scriptures. These very characteristics were derided by the Lord in the prophecy of Isaiah when He mocked the Babylonians more that two and a half thousand years ago for trusting in sorcery, while exalting themselves above their true worth. The words of these verses are just as applicable to the daughters of Babylon of today:

> 'Come down and sit in the dust, O virgin daughter of Babylon; sit on the ground without a throne, O daughter of the Chaldeans! For you shall no more be called tender and delicate... For you have trusted in your wickedness; you have said, 'No one sees me'; your wisdom and your knowledge have warped you, and you have said in your heart, 'I am, and there is no one else besides me'... Stand now with your enchantments and the multitude of your sorceries, in which you have laboured from your youth... Behold, they shall be as stubble, the fire shall burn them' (Isa.47:1,10,12,14).

The modern Daughters of Babylon — the Feminist movement — are acting as earthly agents, wittingly or unwittingly, for the same demonic forces which battled with the Lord of Creation in biblical times. Satan has always turned the ways of the Lord upside down. As the father of lies, he specialises in inversions. The Lord's Prayer is recited backwards; the creature is worshipped rather than the

Creator; men and women seek sexual relations with their own gender in ways which are too shameful to describe. Feminism is an ideal which does not, in reality, seek 'equality' for women but, rather, as implied in the word itself, it seeks the 'headship' of women over men — a complete reversal of God's preferred order.

All *-isms* are humanisms — human thought-systems, which are inevitably futile (Ps.94:11). Although it is indeed true that women need liberating from human enslavement to fallen, impenitent men and the world-system they have perpetuated together, true liberation can only come through the saving power of Jesus Christ. There can be no liberation of any kind until we put our trust in the Sovereign Lord of all creation, begging for His help and strength in the face of our former rebellion and pride.

With this, we come to the close of the section of our book on religious corruption in the world-system. Next we turn to examine the inroads that such corruption has made into the professing Church. But before doing so, having exposed the rebellious mindset of modern woman, let us consider a prayer spoken three thousand years ago by a godly woman whose name in Hebrew means 'Grace'. With these words, Hannah dedicated her life to the one, true God with such humble simplicity and compelling power that it makes a fitting exhortation to the feminists of today to do likewise:

> 'My heart rejoices in the LORD; my strength is exalted in the LORD. I smile at my enemies, because I rejoice in Your salvation. There is none holy like the LORD, for there is none besides You, nor is there any rock like our God. Talk no more so very proudly; let no arrogance come from your mouth, for the LORD is the God of knowledge; and by Him actions are weighed... For by strength no man shall prevail. The adversaries of the Lord shall be broken in pieces; from heaven He will thunder against them. The LORD will judge the ends of the earth' (1 Sam.2:1-3, 9-10).

PART THREE

THE DEFILEMENT OF THE TEMPLE

Religious Corruption in the Churches Today

'So He brought me to the door of the court; and when I looked, there was a hole in the wall. Then He said to me, "Son of man, dig into the wall"; and when I dug into the wall, there was a door. And He said to me, "Go in, and see the wicked abominations which they are doing there"' (Ezekiel 8:7-9)

Chapter Nine

THE SECRET LADDER

The Corruption of Christianity with Eastern Mysticism

'Can you search out the deep things of God? Can you find out the limits of the Almighty? They are higher than heaven — what can you do? Deeper than Sheol — what can you know?' (Job 11:7-8).

'The secret things belong to the LORD our God, but those things which are revealed belong to us and to our children for ever' (Dt.29:29).

In an earlier chapter, we recognized that Satan's pincer movement in his war against the Church in these last days involves the deceptions of Syncretism and Mysticism. Syncretism involves the blurring of the distinctive boundaries between Christianity and the various religions, philosophies and ideologies of the world — a phenomenon which we will be discussing in the final chapter of this book. Mysticism embraces the contrived suspension of rational human faculties, together with the conceit that Divine power can be tapped through learnable systems and techniques. In this present chapter, we will examine the growth of mysticism in the Church from the first century to the present day, and discover how this leads naturally into a most destructive form of syncretism.

Mystical practices are among the oldest religious activities in the world. Yet, in spite of this ancientness, people have often found the word extremely difficult to define. Indeed, W.R. Inge (Dean of St. Paul's, 1860-1954), writing at the beginning of this century, cited twenty-six different definitions![1] The word 'mystic' is derived from the Greek word *mustes*, 'the initiated', from *mueo*, 'to initiate into the mysteries'. It was first associated with the mystery religions and Gnostic cults which abounded in the first few centuries A.D., with their esoteric rites and ceremonies. Many of these cults were a loose admixture of Greek philosophy, Christian teaching and oriental religion, and the apochryphal writings of this era reflect such syncretism.

The dictionary definition of 'mysticism' is *'the habit or tendency of religious thought and feeling of those who seek direct communion with God or the divine'*,[2] while a mystic is defined as *'one who seeks or attains direct intercourse with God in elevated religious feeling or ecstasy'*.[3] In line with these definitions

[1] William Johnston, *The Inner Eye of Love: Mysticism and Religion* (Collins/Fount, 1981), p.15.

[2] *Chambers English Dictionary* (Chambers/C.U.P., 1988), p.950.

[3] Ibid.

of mysticism, such spiritual endeavour has been a radical part of every world religion from time immemorial. It was first the foundation of ancient Shamanism, and from there it passed to the Yogic traditions of the East. However, it is also true that a similar mystical dimension has flourished within the professing church from early in the history of Christianity, while mystical and contemplative orders of monks and nuns of varying degrees are an accepted part of the Christian scene today. Yet, has this always been the case in the life of the Church? What is the true source of this mystical thread which has become so much a part of the mainline denominations in the Christian Church? Does it lie in the life and teachings of Jesus? Are there any teachings concerning mystical and ascetical theology within the doctrines of the Bible? These questions will lead us onto many surprising pathways as we discover the revealing parallels between the mysticism of the East and that which professes to be Christian.

In this chapter, before showing the errors of all forms of mysticism, exposing its true sources and giving a comparison of 'Christian' mysticism with the Christianity of the Bible, we will first examine the historical and present-day development of mysticism in the professing Church.

I. THE DEVELOPMENT OF MYSTICISM IN THE CHURCH

Although the concepts of a universal indwelling divinity and the corresponding use of techniques to 'tap' into it have been highly influential throughout the entire history of heathen and pagan spiritual practice — particularly in the Orient — they were in distinct contradiction to the teachings of the Apostolic Church, which had sought to establish its new and revolutionary spring of true spirituality in a world polluted with a vast quantity of mystical-occultic developments. One could even say that the fact that God was uniquely manifested in the flesh in the person of the Lord Jesus Christ, completely overthrows the pagan notion that *any* human being can become God. The unique deity of Christ refutes the possibility of the deification of man.

Even monotheistic Judaism had degenerated into occultism through the Essenic cults in Israel, which had borrowed in large measure from Persian Zoroastrianism and other oriental mixtures. During the early Church period, this Jewish mysticism was to develop into the teachings of the Kabbalah — a complex esoteric and magical system which applies occult symbolism to the Old Testament, in much the same way as the Freemasons. As mentioned in previous chapters, this Kabbalah subsequently became the foundation stone of occult organisations such as the Rosicrucians and various magical practitioners such as Eliphas Lévi (1810-1875) and Aleister Crowley (1875-1947).

It was not long before there was an intrusion of these occult-mystical teachings into the infant Christian Church. As an introductory example, in the so-called *'Gospel According to Thomas'* — a second century Gnostic work which claims to be a collection by the Apostle Thomas of one hundred and fourteen sayings of Jesus Christ — there is the unmistakable influence of oriental spirituality. When the writer of this pseudo-gospel states: *'The Kingdom is within you and without you'*,[4] it bears a remarkable similarity to that central statement in the Hindu Indian *Upanishads* (800-400 B.C.): *'What is within us is also without. What is without us is also within'*.[5] It is interesting to note, in this connection, the inclusion of a song called 'Within You, Without You', on the Beatles album 'Sgt. Pepper's Lonely Hearts Club Band' (1967), which was written by George Harrison after his experiences in India with the guru Maharishi Mahesh Yogi. Elsewhere in this 'Gospel of Thomas', the alleged Jesus makes the equally mystical assertion:

> 'When you make the two one, and make the inside like the outside, and the outside like the inside, and the upper side like the under side, and (in such a way) that you make the man [with] the woman a single one, in order that the man is not the man and the woman is not the woman...then you will go into [the] Kingdom'.[6]

This absurd statement bears no resemblance to any saying of the biblical Christ. It is, in fact, pure Tantric Yoga. In the Tantric worldview,

> 'The consummated human being is man and woman fused into a single unit. When the idea of basic unity, that the two are inseperable, emerges, the state of ananda, of infinite joy or perpetual bliss, is reached'.[7]

As a well-known Tantric rhyme states: *'So 'ham: I am He, or Sa 'ham: I am she, for There is no difference between Me and Thee'*.[8] In occult-gnostic circles, there has always been an attempt to demonstrate that Christianity is derivative of pagan and Eastern mystical religious influences. For this reason, the 'orientalisation' of Christianity was a recurring feature during the first few centuries in the life of the Church, as part of Satan's strategy to undermine the unique truth of the Christian Gospel. Correspondingly, the Neo-Gnostics of today regularly make the claim that Jesus was really an Eastern-style guru, who spent His youth, prior to His public ministry, in India training in the ways of the mystic East.[9] What could be the purpose of this tendency — which first began so soon after the victorious Ascension of Christ — but to disguise the basic tenets of Oriental mysticism behind a facade of Christian teaching?

One very good reason for this is that the Lord Jesus, who so clearly stated that the only way to God is through Him (Jn.14:6), had actually destroyed the spiritual 'monopoly' which Satan had enjoyed prior to His Incarnation. No longer were the

---

4 Robert M. Grant & David N. Freedman (trans. & eds.), *The Secret Sayings of Jesus: According to the Gospel of Thomas* (Fontana, 1960), p.115.

5 Swami Prabavanda & Frederick Manchester (trans. & eds.), *The Upanishads* (Mentor, 1957), p.51.

6 Robert M. Grant & David N. Freedman, op. cit., p.136.

7 Ajit Mookerjee, *Kundalini: The Arousal of the Inner Energy* (Thames & Hudson, 1982), pp.62-63.

8 Ibid., pp.61-62.

9 See, for example, Elizabeth Clare Prophet, *The Lost Years of Jesus* (Summit University Press, 1984).

nations to be almost exclusively in the grip of spiritual abominations and absurdities. The Lord Jesus had asserted the essential depravity of the human heart (Mk.7:21-23; Jn.2:23-25), the unrivalled promise of salvation and eternal life through a personal Divine Saviour (Jn.3:16-18), the unique fact of His Resurrection (1 Cor.15:17), coupled with a liberating truth which could be known by all who seek it (Jn.8:32). All this, in conjunction with the Apostolic teaching that one comes into a right relationship with God by faith in Jesus Christ rather than by one's own religious actions (Rom.5:21; Eph.2:8; Gal.2:16; Phil.3:9), and that a person dies just once, after which he comes to divine judgement (Heb.9:27; cf. Ps.78:39). Such doctrines are in complete opposition to religions which teach that all people have a spark of divinity which can be kindled through their own efforts, that life is an illusion, and that one's existence consists of a series of progressively-perfecting reincarnations, between which there are no judgements, divine or otherwise.

It is easy to see why the devil has had to find powerful ways of waging war against the truth of Christ which had overturned the satanic lie of many millennia standing. Not content with having dredged up the heresies of Gnosticism, Docetism, Montanism, Arianism, Sabellianism, Patripassianism, Pelagianism, Manichaeism, Apollinarianism, Nestorianism, and Eutychianism, and being determined to *'make war'* with those *'who keep the commandments of God and have the testimony of Jesus Christ'* (Rev.12:17), the devil brought into being a more subtle development which would have a profound impact on the historical course of professing Christendom. We have already documented the various mystery religions, cults and gnostic sects having a seductive quasi-Christian philosophy which flourished in those first few hundred years after the end of Jesus' earthly ministry. We also showed how they were forced to go 'underground' into secret societies and subversive movements in order to do their work among the nations. However, alongside of this secrecy in the world-system, another equally important aspect of the 'mystery of lawlessness' was the creation of a new 'gospel' *within the Church itself* — a gospel which would also embrace the wolfish tenets of the various mystical systems of the world. Throughout the rest of this section, we shall develop this claim by examining the historical and present influences of mysticism in the life of the Church.

1. The Primary Mystical Influences on the Church

We have already mentioned an apochryphal writing of the second century; many other similar Gnostic works would appear in the ensuing three centuries. But once Gnosticism had disappeared from view, a stream of written works would appear which would bring Eastern mysticism right into the mainstream of the Church. Where Gnosticism had been unable to accomplish its ambitions, this New Mysticism would prove to be highly successful, being artfully couched in Christian terminology so as to deceive the gullible. The most primitive example of this process involved the implanting of Neoplatonism into Christianity. This, coupled with other influences such as the sect known as Hesychasm, wielded a powerful and lasting formative influence on the work of mysticism in the Church, especially on those known as the 'medieval mystics'. Later, the work of the Jesuits (Society of Jesus) would also make its contribution to the modern mystical practices. Let us now develop these themes.

i. The Dionysian Deception: Neoplatonist Infiltration

In the late fifth or early sixth century A.D., a mysterious Syrian monk wrote a number of theological treatises to which he fraudulently affixed the name of 'Dionysius the Areopagite', who is mentioned briefly in the Book of Acts as a convert of the Apostle Paul (Acts 17:34). These works represented an attempt to reconcile Christianity with the Neoplatonic thought which had pervaded Graeco-Roman culture. Neoplatonism was a Greek ascetic metaphysical system operating from about the end of the second century until the middle of the sixth. Its chief architect was a man named Plotinus (*c.*205-270), who *'advocated asceticism and the contemplative life, though he seemed to live in some style himself'.*[10] The actual system of Neoplatonism originally arose as a hostile response to the claims of Christ, absorbing the earlier Platonic mystery school to become the syncretic religion of the age. One leading pupil of Plotinus, Porphyry, wrote a massive tome of fifteen volumes entitled 'Against the Christians'. In the words of one researcher, the Neoplatonists

> 'tried to concentrate all the forces of Greek thought and religion and of oriental religion in a defence of Graeco-Roman civilisation against the rising tide of Christianity and became increasingly antichristian'.[11]

In this way, almost as a 'Parthian shot' at the purity of Christianity from a corrupt but dying civilisation, the Neoplatonists attempted to revive the mystery cults and the ancient religions under one all-embracing, monistic, pantheistic theology, whose spiritual aim was

> 'to transform all men into one man; all souls into one soul — the World-soul; all minds into one mind — the World-mind; all gods into one god; and all things, whether spiritual or material, into the One'.[12]

In spite of the fact that this Neoplatonism *'provided the philosophical basis for the pagan opposition to Christianity in the fourth and fifth centuries'*,[13] its syncretic co-mingling with a profession of Christian faith was carried out by Satan with great stealth, and provided the religious foundations for all 'Christian' mysticism. Even William Inge, Dean of St. Paul's, London from 1911-1934, and a leading Anglican scholar who had a major role in re-arousing ecclesiastical interest in mysticism, *'admitted that Christian mysticism owed a debt to the Greek Mysteries'*.[14] The dissemination of all these carriers of syncretistic mysticism was

---

[10] Magnus Magnusson (ed.), *Chambers Biographical Dictionary* (Chambers, 1990), p.1172.

[11] *Chambers's Encyclopaedia* (Newnes, 1962), Vol.IX, p.756.

[12] Ibid.

[13] Walter J. Elwell, *Evangelical Dictionary of Theology* (Marshall Pickering, 1984), p.257.

[14] James Webb, *The Flight from Reason*, Vol.I of 'The Age of the Irrational' (Macdonald,

carried out through the offices of such men as Gregory of Nyssa (335-394) and his brother Basil of Caesarea (330-379).[15] Gregory, in particular, specialised in the wildly allegorical approach to the Scriptures in the tradition of the universalist Origen (185-254); and by the time that pseudo-Dionysius appeared on the scene, the way had been paved for the compounding of a quasi-Christian mystical theology which would be mistaken by many for Christianity itself.

This Neoplatonist Syrian monk who took the name of the Pauline convert, Dionysius, for his own — presumably to guarantee his writings acceptance within Christian circles — was an advocate of what is known as the *via negativa* (the negative way), whereby through asceticism and certain meditation practices one gradually eliminates from the mind all that is not God in order to penetrate the mystery of His *'dark no-thingness'*. The leading features of pseudo-Dionysius' written works are *'the exaltation of the via negativa above revealed theology'*, coupled with *'the doctrine of the perfection by ecstasy'*.[16]

All this is certainly not biblical Christianity. It is not the *'faith which was once for all delivered to the saints'* of the early Church, for which all believers must strive to maintain (Jude 3). The entire concept of the *via negativa* is almost a carbon copy of the Buddhist doctrine of *'neti, neti'* — 'not this, not this' (lit. 'No, No') — by which one practices the same process of elimination of 'that which can be thought', leading to an ecstatic absorption into the cosmos through the pursuit of 'emptiness' and non-attachment to the material world. An identical *via negativa* concept lies at the heart of many other Eastern traditions, including Taoism, which states that *'the Tao that can be told of is not the Absolute Tao'*.[17] All this comes in contrast to that great saying of Jesus that the Christian will *'know the truth, and the truth shall make you free'* (Jn.8:32). Christianity has a Gospel which does not hide behind dark mystical teachings.

The most influential work written by this pseudo-Dionysius is known as the *Mystica Theologia*. Fraudulently addressed to Paul's disciple of five hundred years earlier, Timothy, this brief treatise was translated into English for the first time in the fourteenth century by the anonymous author of another mystical work, entitled 'The Cloud of Unknowing'. However, as this translator acknowledges in his introduction, in order to render the *Mystica Theologia* more acceptable to the Christian reader, he doctored the text with appropriate changes to bring it more into line with Christian doctrine.[18] This is syncretism in the making — a classic early example of the fusion of Christianity with Eastern mysticism. In spite of this 'doctoring', there is not a hint of the true Gospel within its ten pages; and

---

1971), p.179.

[15] John Ferguson, *Encyclopaedia of Mysticism and Mystery Religions* (Thames & Hudson, 1976), pp.70-71.

[16] *Chambers's Encyclopaedia*, op. cit., Vol.IV, p.534.

[17] Alan Watts, *Tao: The Watercourse Way* (Penguin, 1979), p.39.

[18] Clifton Wolters (trans.), *The Cloud of Unknowing and Other Works* (Penguin, 1961), pp.202, 207. See also William Johnston, *The Inner Eye of Love: Mysticism and Religion* (Collins/Fount, 1981), p.19.

there is barely a thought or sentiment which cannot be found in one of the mystery cults or oriental religions of the world. As an example, in the closing pages, we read:

> 'For the perfect and unique cause of all is of necessity beyond compare with the highest of all imaginable heights, whether by affirmation or denial. And this surpassing non-understandibility is un-understandably above every affirmation and denial'.[19]

This gibberish is hardly representative of biblical, Apostolic Christianity. In fact, it is pure Eastern mystical philosophy. This is confirmed when we discover that one scholar of mystical writings has said that within the *Mystica Theologia*,

> 'the controlling idea is the possibility of the soul's union with God, with the consequent deification of man. This is achieved by the soul's putting aside all knowing obtained through reason and the use of the senses and by its entry into a "cloud of unknowing"'.[20]

Such a description could have applied equally to a work on Yogic meditation, which also involves the suppression of the mind, coupled with the attainment of personal divinity. However, for nearly fourteen hundred years, this piece of writing — bereft of the merest hint of the true Gospel of Jesus Christ and brimming over with Eastern mystical thought — was believed (especially among those circles for whom it was spiritually expedient) to be a genuine communication to the biblical Timothy from the Pauline convert, Dionysius! It was actually accepted as sound doctrine at the Council of Constantinople (A.D. 533) and the Lateran Council (A.D. 649), while this pseudo-Dionysius himself came to be regarded in the West as *'the first of non-canonical Christian writers'*.[21] As we shall shortly be learning, his writings exerted enormous influence upon the flow of medieval mystical practice within the church; and it was not until the nineteenth century that the authorship and dedication of *Mystica Theologia* were uncovered as a forgery. However, even this discovery did not diminish its acclaim and following among Christian mystical circles, for the simple reason that it supported the rudiments of their mystical gospel, eclipsing the message of the true Gospel which was to be preached throughout the world.

This osmosis of Oriental mysticism into the Church through Neoplatonic infusion continued steadily from pseudo-Dionysius onwards; and we will be returning to examine this in our refutation of Christian mysticism towards the end of the present chapter. However, as we continue to trace the landmarks in the orientalising of Christianity, we arrive in the fourteenth century to consider one particular group in the Eastern Orthodox Church which became the first real focal point of theological controversy in the development of Christian mysticism. To this we now turn.

---

[19] Ibid., p.218.
[20] Ibid., p.202.
[21] *Chambers's Encyclopaedia*, op. cit., Vol.IV, p.534.

ii. Christianised Yoga in the Making: Hesychasm and Beyond

A natural outcrop of the pseudo-Dionysian teachings is the mystical tradition known as 'Hesychasm', from the Greek word *Hesuchia*, meaning 'quiet'. This doctrine is generally traced back to an eleventh century Studite mystic named Simeon the New Theologian (940-1022) who posited a 'Doctrine of the Divine or Inner Light'. By the time of the fourteenth century, a Byzantine contemplative order had been established on Mount Athos which came to bear the official title of 'Hesychasts'. They claimed that their meditation technique brought illumination through experiencing what they called the 'Uncreated Light of Tabor' — which they alleged to be the mystical light manifested in the Transfiguration of Jesus on Mount Tabor, as recounted in the synoptic Gospels (e.g., Mk.9:2-13). The 'Hesychasts' believed that the experience of this 'divine light' would gradually transform the seeker until he became divine himself. A major link between the mysticism of both East and West is the Doctrine of the Inner Light, and Indian mysticism is full of references to this mystical teaching. One modern Eastern sect which has been very active in Western countries is known as the 'Divine Light Mission', founded in the 1970s by the boy-guru Maharaj Ji. In Buddhism, the goal of the adept is the realization of the *'pure cosmic Light within the heart'*.[22] Comparative religion scholar Mircea Eliade also claims that

> 'for Indian thought the Light mystically-perceived denotes transcendence of this world...and the attainment of another existential place — that of pure being, of the divine, of supreme knowledge and absolute freedom... One who reaches the Light and recognisies himself in it reaches a mode of transcendent being beyond the reach of the imagination'.[23]

Earlier, we spoke of the Hesychast's experience of the 'Uncreated Light of Tabor', which is drawn from the same source as that of the Eastern mystic. St. Gregory of Palamas, the Greek Orthodox Archbishop of Thessalonica (1347-1359) and Hesychast apologist, also claimed that experiencing the 'Light which dwells within' is a prerequisite of true mystical experience. The same experience gripped the founder of the sect of the Quakers, George Fox, who devised his universalist doctrine of the 'Inner Light of the Living Christ' in all people, from the beginning of time.[24] Fox taught that truth *'is to be found primarily not in Scripture or creed but in God's voice speaking to the soul'*.[25] Such a reliance on experiential revelation is one of the major hallmarks of all mysticism, and everywhere that it is found there will be the manifestation of extreme error and the most profound demonic interference.[26] In the Hindu Upanishads, we also find this doctrine of the Inner Light expounded in a meditation instruction which reads:

---

[22] John Ferguson, op. cit., p.106.

[23] Ibid.

[24] Ibid., p.88.

[25] Walter J. Elwell (ed.), op. cit., p.425.

[26] We see it today especially in the Charismatic Movement, which imitates many aspects of the mysticism which has plagued the Church down the centuries.

'Now that light which shines above this heaven, higher than all, higher than everything, in the highest world, beyond which there are no other worlds, that is the same light which is within man'.[27]

This is just another way of saying that there is a 'spark of divinity' in every person. The Benedictine nun, Hildegard of Bingen (1098-1179), claimed that she, too, from infancy had *'seen this light, in my spirit...more brilliantly than the sun'*.[28] Her incessant visions caused her to name God 'Lux Vivens', and she acquired the reputation of a prophetess for her ability to foresee the future, although her oracles and revelations were *'highly coloured and often no less highly mysterious'*.[29] Alongside this doctrine of the 'Inner Light', accessible by meditation, the underlying doctrine of Hesychasm claimed that

'the unregenerate human condition resembles the sleep of death, where no remembrance of God is possible. This state is called "prelest". In prelest, the fallen human being mistakes the "mirage" world in which he lives for the real world, and thus can never have a real relationship with himself or God. The "sleeping" self needs to be awakened through the process of contemplation and spiritual awakening".[30]

This 'awakening' of the sleeping self and the alleged illusory nature of the material world are yet further examples of Eastern mystical doctrines, known respectively in Sanskrit as *moksha* and *maha-maya*. Readers will recall our discussion in an earlier chapter that the fundamental tenet of ancient Gnosticism is the notion of a 'sleeping self' — a spark of divinity in every person — which needs awakening. Such Gnostic teaching was originally derived from Oriental mysticism. That mysticism which calls itself Christian is also derived from the same source. The whole purpose behind Yogic practice is the discovery or awakening of the 'hidden self', which, it is claimed, is actually the 'God within'. This 'real' but 'sleeping' or dormant 'self' travels under a wide variety of names, depending upon the religious tradition followed. For example, the Zen Buddhist Hui-Neng (A.D. 638-713), claimed that

'within our mind there is a Buddha, and that Buddha within is the real Buddha. If Buddha is not to be sought within our minds, where shall we find the real Buddha? Do not doubt that a Buddha is within your mind, apart from which nothing can exist'.[31]

In the same way, the Hindu Upanishads are littered with such imagery:

'As people who do not know the country walk again and again over a gold treasure that has been hidden somewhere in the earth and do not discover it, thus do all these creatures day after day go into the

---

[27] F. Max Müller (ed.), *The Sacred Books of the East: Vol.XV* (OUP, 1900), 'The Upanishads', Vol.1, Part.1, p.47.

[28] John Ferguson, op. cit., p.105.

[29] Donald Attwater (ed.), *Penguin Dictionary of Saints* (Penguin, 1982), p.168.

[30] Walter J. Elwell, op. cit., p.509.

[31] John Ferguson, op. cit., p.35.

> Brahma-world...and yet do not discover it, because they are carried away by untruth, they do not come to themselves, i.e., they do not discover the true Self in Brahman, dwelling in the heart'.[32]

It is clear that the Hesychasts, in spite of their purported profession of Christianity, were simply another syncretistic mystical sect propagating the blasphemous notion that the purpose for the human being is to tap into the 'God within' through asceticism, mind-control, meditation systems and yogic practice. It should come as no surprise to learn that the various techniques used by Hesychasts were borrowed entirely from Eastern Yoga. For example, they would sit in a yogic posture, head forward, chin on chest, gazing at the region around the navel, to examine the 'inner heart', waiting for the experience of 'the Light'.[33] While adopting this posture, the Hesychast would continuously repeat what would later become known as the 'Jesus Prayer': *'Lord Jesus Christ, Son of God, have mercy on me, a sinner'* — with alternate phrases on the in-breath and the out-breath. This 'Jesus Prayer' had evolved through the teachings of such men as Diadochus of Photice in the middle of the fifth century and John Climacus in the early seventh century, who recommended the continual repetition of the name of Jesus in prayer and meditation — a practice which eventually evolved into the extended version of the Hesychasts.[34]

The Hesychastic assertion that it is possible to experience the eternal and uncreated Divine Light of God was eventually challenged in 1337 by a Calabrian monastic theologian called Barlaam, who regarded Hesychasm as mere superstitious practice. However, after considerable debate, the views of St. Gregory of Palamas, Archbishop of Thessalonica and chief advocate of Hesychasm, were accepted by the Councils of Constantinople (1341, 1347 & 1351). This was effected on the basis of a submission by Gregory that the Hesychast's experience of God was *'of His energies rather than His essence'*.[35] In other words, mystics in the Church could legitimately continue practising Yogic meditation under the tactically adjusted claim that their ecstatic experiences were not the result of a direct union with the essence of God Himself, but merely with cosmic energy which emanated from His Being!

These absurd ecclesiastical decisions set the scene for Christian mysticism to pervert the Gospel for centuries to come. Whatever cover-up tactics were employed, the techniques for meditation propagated by the vast majority of Christian mystics during the first millennium and a half after the coming of Christ, were ultimately plundered from the ancient yogic traditions of the East, and were suitably clothed to give them the appearance of Christianity. The Jesus Prayer itself is nothing more than what the Hindus call a *mantra* — a repetitive chant, prayer or

---

[32] F. Max Müller (ed.), *The Sacred Books of the East: Vol.XV* (OUP, 1900), 'The Upanishads', Vol.1, Pt.1, p.129.

[33] This is the origin of the derogatory saying, *'navel gazer'*!

[34] John Ferguson, op. cit., p.92.

[35] John R. Hinnells (ed.), *The Penguin Dictionary of Religion* (Penguin, 1984), p.147. See also Walter J. Elwell, op. cit., p.509.

spell designed to alter the consciousness of its user — only now dressed in Christian garb. Former Benedictine priest, Dom Henri le Saux, who was one of the earliest pioneers of Hindu-Christian dialogue — eventually transforming himself into the Indian Guru Abhishiktananda — demonstrates this inescapable relationship between Eastern and Christian mysticism:

> 'Hesychasm...and the "Jesus Prayer" which goes with it, embody methods of spiritual discipline and contemplation which are perfectly familiar in India. The Jesus Prayer had its counterpart in *nama-japa,* the continual repetition of the name of the Lord'.[36]

The use of such a technique to blank out the mind in the mistaken attempt to attain Divinity (or blend into His 'energies'), must be an abomination to the Sovereign Lord of all creation, regardless of whether or not it utilises the Holy and Precious Name of Jesus (cf. Ex.20:7; Lev.19:12; Mt.6:7). In the Orient the right use of the *Mantra* has always been an esoteric doctrine, available only to initiates, and regarded as carrying a supernatural power of great intensity. As one esoteric handbook puts it:

> 'The Mantra is not merely a *technique of awakening*; it is actually and in itself a state of being, indicative of the *presence of divinity*.....The Mantra bestows no magic power from the outside; rather it *releases latent forces* within each person which are normally suppressed by the ego. Proper use of the Mantra enables the adept to control and direct these forces, primarily towards *dissolving the ego* and opening himself to the universe within and around him. This control is crucial and is the reason for much of the secrecy around Tantric yoga'.[37] [emphasis added]

'Technique of awakening', 'presence of divinity', 'releases latent forces', 'dissolving the ego'. Such mystico-magical practice has been a radical part of the satanically-inspired religions for millennia; while twentieth century occult-mystical sects such as Maharishi Yogi Hesh's Transcendental Meditation (TM) and Swami Prabhupada's Hare Krishna Movement still teach this ancient practice of the repetition of the name of a deity or other *mantra* in order to bring about an internal 'paradigm shift' in a person, leading to personal transformation in the psychic realm. However, lest anyone imagine that there is a vast difference between the Vedic mantras of the Upanishads and those which use the word 'Jesus', modern occultists and New Consciousness advocates recognise only too well that *'traditional mantras brought down through the ages in Hinduism...are similar to the Holy Name mantras of Christianity'*.[38]

The plain fact is — as any Neo-Gnostic will affirm — that the practice of

---

[36] Abhishiktananda, *Hindu-Christian Meeting Point* (ISPCK, 1969), p.23.

[37] Ajit Mookerjee, *Kundalini: The Arousal of the Inner Energy* (Thames and Hudson, 1982), pp.29, 30.

[38] Raymond Van Over, *Total Meditation: Mind Control Techniques for a Small Planet in Space* (Collier Macmillan, 1978), p.147.

'chanting or using a mantra is indeed a universal method for invoking God's presence'.[39] However, the god that is invoked by these techniques cannot be the God of the Holy Bible, as such invocations are in complete opposition to a divine commandment. When Jehovah declared: *'You shall not take the name of the LORD your God in vain'* (Ex.20:7), it was a direct repudiation of the satanic use of 'name-magic', the invocation of a god through the ritual repetition of its name, as practised by heathen cults for millennia. As Geerhardus Vos puts it, in his discussion of this Third Commandment:

> 'It is not sufficient to think of swearing and blasphemy in the present-day common sense of these terms. The [use of the] word is one of the chief powers of pagan superstition, and the most potent form of word-magic is name-magic. It was believed that through the pronouncing of the name of some supernatural entity this can be compelled to do the bidding of the magic-user... It is, as all magic is, the opposite to true religion'.[40]

Similar Yogic values to those of the Hesychasts prevailed among the medieval mystics of continental Europe and England. In Paris, there were the Victorines at the Abbey of Sainte-Victor. In Germany, men such as Johann Tauler (*c.*1300-1361) and his mentor Dominican priest Meister Eckhart (*c.*1260-1328) were highly influential in the subsequent development of a Christian-clothed mystical system. They both adhered to the view that a union with God is possible because of a divine *'grund'* or spark within each human soul. The teachings of Eckhart in particular bordered closely on pantheism and the Neoplatonism which had been digested through the writings and teachings of pseudo-Dionysius and the Dominican philosopher and theologian Thomas Aquinas (*c.*1225-1274). It is worth noting that in his magnum opus *Summa Theologica*, Aquinas quotes pseudo-Dionysius one thousand seven hundred and sixty times,[41] clearly demonstrating the powerful influence that the initiation of this Syrian monk had on the infiltration of syncretic mysticism into mainline Christianity.

---

[39] Ibid. It is for this same reason that the Charismatic Movement uses the repetition of simple choruses to 'invoke' what they believe to be the Holy Spirit — thus betraying this Movement's true origins. Charismatic leaders have been known to recommend to people attending their meetings that they should *'leave their minds outside'*. The same recommendation was also given by guru Bhagwan Shree Rajneesh (died 1990) to those devotees attending his meditation sessions.

[40] Geerhardus Vos, *Biblical Theology* (Banner of Truth, 1975), pp.137, 138. This name-magic technique is still practised today in the mainline denominations. One popular Roman Catholic book claims to reveal *'a tremendous secret almost unknown today — the amazing power of the Holy Name of Jesus'*. In this book, it is said that *'by repeating reverently and often [even hundreds of times a day] the Holy Name of Jesus we can glorify God,...pay our spiritual debts, assist the souls in Purgatory, obtain graces, receive protection from the Devil, obtain the grace of a happy death, be preserved from disasters and even regain our physical health!'* (Fr. Paul O' Sullivan, *The Wonders of the Holy Name*, TAN Books, 1993).

[41] John Ferguson, op. cit., p.196.

One of the earliest English mystics who came from this lineage was the anonymous author of the famed fourteenth-century work 'The Cloud of Unknowing', a classic synthesis of all its predecessors, with the usual generous sprinkling of superficial Christianity to render it the appearance of orthodoxy. Thus, in this work, we find the wholly unbiblical assertion — based on a highly faulty exegesis of Lk.10:38-42 — that, of the Lord's people, some are chosen to salvation (so-called 'actives', like Martha), others to perfection (so-called 'contemplatives', like Mary).[42] In spite of some charming prose and occasional shrewd spiritual advice, this book has many other links with Eastern mysticism. For instance, it gives the instruction to budding contemplatives to put a *'cloud of forgetting between us and the whole created world'*.[43] This is followed by the suggestion of a *mantra* in the form of a short word, preferably of one syllable, a word like 'God' or 'Love'. *'Choose which you like, or perhaps some other'*, he says, *'so long as it is one syllable'*.[44] The reason? *'With this word you will suppress all thought under the cloud of forgetting'*.[45]

Such ascetic mind-control has no place in the spirituality of the Bible. The Lord Jesus did not pray that His people should be taken out of the world. Although we are not *of* the world (Jn.17:14-15), nor to be conformed to it (Rom.12:2), we are certainly expected to be *in* it — involved with it — although without being corrupted by it. We have already shown in an earlier chapter that one of the hallmarks of Gnosticism is the depreciation of the mind or intellect. Soon, we will come to understand that the same hallmarks apply to its flip-side, Mysticism. The Christian is nowhere advised to 'suppress all thought', but is instead called upon to use his transformed mind in the service of the Lord (cf. Mt.22:37). The idea that thought-processes *per se* are a stumbling-block to the development of spirituality is not a biblical one. Once again, in spite of the Christian window-dressing, the leading influences within the pseudo-Dionysius-inspired 'Cloud of Unknowing' can be shown to be firmly rooted in Eastern traditions such as Buddhism, whose avowed goal is that state called 'Nirvana', which means in Sanskrit a 'blowing-out-of-the-mind'.[46]

This use of a monosyllabic *mantra* to annihilate the mind and invoke divinity is also nothing new. For thousands of years the favourite and most universally effective Hindu *mantra* has been the syllable AUM. This mystic *mantra* carries many esoteric magical meanings, far too numerous to mention. For example, apart from its reputed *'sound frequency-vibration'* — which has been alleged from ancient times to have a paradigm-shift-style, supernatural effect on the human psyche[47] — it is worth mentioning the far lesser known fact that the individual letters in this *mantra 'also stand for the [Upanishadic] mantra Tat Twam Asi [Thou Art That],*

---

[42] Clifton Wolters, op. cit., pp.81-90.

[43] Ibid. p.66.

[44] Ibid.

[45] Ibid., p.69.

[46] This is the origin of the drug-user's phrase 'blowing your mind'.

[47] Ajit Mookerjee, op. cit., p.22.

the realisation of man's divinity within himself'.[48] Today, many thousands of years later, the mantric key to a Neo-Gnostic 'relaxation-meditation' mind-control programme devised by the Harvard University TM researcher, Dr. Herbert Benson, involves *'the use of any single syllable sound'*.[49] This is precisely the same system as that advocated within 'The Cloud of Unknowing'. Truly, there is nothing new under the sun!

But the orientalising of Christianity did not stop here. For around this same medieval period, a development took place within the Roman Church which was to be of lasting influence on the status of mystical practice within Christianity and its absorption of the so-called 'wisdom of the East'. Let us now turn to these.

iii. Stairway to Nothingness: The Secret Wisdom of John of the Cross

Many occult-mystical sects had flourished during the sixteenth and seventeenth centuries in Europe. Groups such as Les Illuminés (1623) and Les Guerinets (1634) in France had probably developed out of the earlier Spanish Los Alumbrados (the Illumined Ones, 1520), who advocated an ecstatic mystical union with Divinity. One famous sixteenth century mystic of the Roman Catholic Counter-Reformation was the Spanish Carmelite monk, St. John of the Cross (1542-1591). Having studied under the Thomas Aquinas theology of the Dominicans at Salamanca — which had well absorbed the Dionysian *via negativa* — St. John of the Cross was rooted in the Neoplatonic thought of his predecessors.[50] The Spanish mystics, believing that the pseudo-Dionysius's *Mystica Theologia* was a genuine work of the Pauline convert, were greatly influenced by it. As the editor of the works of John of the Cross states:

> 'The pseudo-Dionysius was another writer who was considered a great authority by the Spanish mystics. The importance attributed to his works arose partly from the fact that he was supposed to have been one of the first disciples of the Apostles; many chapters from mystical works of those days all over Europe are no more than glosses of the pseudo-Areopagite'.[51]

However, the work of John of the Cross is less straightforward to analyse than many of the other mystics as it does contain flashes of profound wisdom and insight. Yet, at the same time, this man's work came to consist of an incongruous mixture of Christo-centricity and an accentuated Eastern mysticism which was derivative of the Neoplatonism of pseudo-Dionysius.

One can see a good example of the latter in his elaborate drawing of Mount Carmel, the Mount of Perfection which symbolises the ascent to mystical union

---

[48] B.K.S. Iyengar, *The Concise Light on Yoga* (George Allen and Unwin, 1980), p.43.

[49] Raymond Van Over, op. cit., p.170. It is interesting to note that Transcendental Meditation teachers recommend *The Cloud of Unknowing* to their initiates. See, for example, Peter Russell, *The TM Technique* (Routledge & Kegan Paul, 1976), p.44.

[50] John Ferguson, op. cit., p.93.

[51] E. Allison Peers (trans. & ed.), *St. John of the Cross: Ascent of Mount Carmel* (Burns & Oates, 1935), pp.xli-xlii.

with God on the mountain. The entire conception of the spiritual life as an arduous ascent up a mountain which culminates in union with divinity at its summit is a singularly Eastern mystical idea. For example, *'There are many paths up the mountain'* is an ancient Hindu saying which refers to the many religious routes which allegedly lead to union with the divine. On the pathway of the mystic in John of the Cross's drawing is written six times the word *Nada* (Spanish for 'nothing').[52] Higher up the mountain he adds, *'and even on the mountain Nothing'*.[53] This concept of *nada*, 'nothingness', as the goal of spirituality is fundamental to his written works. We can see clearly the connections with Eastern religion when John of the Cross makes such statements as, *'In order to arrive at being everything, desire to be nothing. In order to arrive at knowing everything, desire to know nothing'*.[54] In the light of this statement, it is hardly surprising to learn that *'some distinguished Christian writers have labelled St John of the Cross [as] Buddhist'*.[55] Indeed, this entire concept of 'nothingness' as the centrepiece and goal of religious enterprise lies at the very heart of Zen Buddhism, where it is known by the word *'Mu'* (Japanese for No-Thing). In an old Zenrin poem which speaks of mystical illumination, the above statement by John of the Cross is echoed with the words: *'You cannot get it by taking thought; you cannot seek it by not taking thought'*.[56] Another Zen teacher puts it like this: *'Only when you have no-thing in your mind and no-mind in things are you vacant and spiritual, empty and marvellous'*.[57]

Repeatedly in mysticism of both East and West, we find this 'emptying of the mind' so that one can experience the 'no-thingness' of God. Johann Scheffler (1624-1677), a Lutheran who converted to Roman Catholicism because of the rejection by the Reformers of the *Mystica Theologia* of pseudo-Dionysius,[58] wrote a lengthy series of verses under the pseudonym Angelus Silesius, in which he brings out this concept of the suppression of self in order to experience personal divinity. Three brief examples will suffice: 1) *'God is sheer nothingness. Whatever else He be, He gave it that it might be found in me'*.[59] 2) *'Let go of the Me as of a worthless thing — unless you abdicate, you will not be King'*.[60] 3) *'I was inside God before I became Me and shall be God again when from my Me set free'*.[61] Although it is true that Jesus spoke of the need to deny ourselves if we wish to follow Him (Mt.16:24), any similarity between these words of our Lord and the

---

52 Ibid, p.xiii.
53 Ibid.
54 Ibid., p.59.
55 William Johnston, *The Inner Eye of Love: Mysticism and Religion* (Collins/Fount, 1981), p.115.
56 Alan Watts, *The Way of Zen* (Penguin, 1962), p.156.
57 Ibid., p.151.
58 John Ferguson, op. cit., p.14.
59 Frederick Franck (trans. & ed.), *The Book of Angelus Silesius* (Vintage-Random, 1976), p.140.
60 Ibid.
61 Ibid., p.130.

suppression of thought, self-annihilation and ego-death sought after in Eastern mystical religions is purely superficial. It has been a fatal error of mystics down the centuries to imagine that the teachings of Jesus and the apostles were merely a first-century A.D. Semitic expression of the 'eternal ancient truths' of the Orient. The vast gulf between the two will be more fully discussed later in this chapter; for now it is enough to observe the depth of the deception, which has been perpetuated by the vast number of pseudo-Christian manuscripts which appear to support these concepts — the *Mystica Theologia* being a prime example.

The pursuit of the mystic goal of 'perfection' during this earthly life is a quest for salvation through one's own actions, and one which can be perfomed by anyone of whatever religion. Sooner or later, the mystic goal becomes a quest for a union with the 'god within' and its attendant ecstasies and supernatural phenomena. One of the underlying teachings within the writings of John of the Cross — who practised self-flagellation — is *'the mystical theology which theologians call secret wisdom'*.[62] In his 'Dark Night of the Soul', he maps out *'ten degrees of the mystic ladder'* by which souls, through this secret wisdom, may come to a union with divinity.[63] This esoteric concept of the ever-ascending stages of a 'secret ladder' which leads to an ecstatic union with God is a common one throughout the works of Christian mysticism — one definitive example being Walter Hilton's 'Ladder of Perfection' (*c*.1390). But such a concept is also firmly rooted in the Yogic meditational traditions of the East. For example, an Indian prayer says:

> 'I salute Adisvara (the Primeval Lord Siva) who taught first the science of Hatha Yoga — a science that stands out as a ladder for those who wish to scale the heights of Raja Yoga'.[64]

Yoga involves a rigorous discipline of asceticism, postural exercise and meditation in order to suppress the mind and prepare it for an experience of the divine. In this, there is little difference between the mystic of the East and the one who professes to be Christian. They each display very similar characteristics, whether or not the Christian version makes a show of the name of Christ and peppers its writings with references to the Bible. The modern Christian mystic, Father William Johnston, following in the tradition of all his predecessors in the history of his church, recommends

> 'control of the mind, control of the breathing, control of the body. These three approaches converge at the desired goal of heightened awareness and even, under certain circumstances, at enlightenment'.[65]

Similarly, the Eastern mystic says:

> 'One who has conquered his mind, senses, passions, thought and

---

[62] Benedict Zimmerman (trans. & ed.), *St. John of the Cross: The Dark Night of the Soul* (James Clarke, 1973), p.157.

[63] Ibid., pp.166-176.

[64] B.K.S. Iyengar, op. cit., p.vii.

[65] William Johnston, *The Inner Eye of Love: Mysticism and Religion* (Collins/Fount, 1981), p.189.

> reason is a king among men. He is fit for Raja Yoga, the royal union with the Universal Spirit. He has Inner Light'.[66]

Regardless of the apparent Christo-centrism of the Christian mystics, there is little fundamental difference in their techniques and goals. In common with those mystics who had gone before him, John of the Cross had been deceived into believing that the *Mystica Theologia* of pseudo-Dionysius was a work of Apostolic teaching which all Christians should follow. Because the Roman Catholic Church gave at least as much authority to the ex-canonical teachings of the Church as to canonical Scripture, the *Mystica* came to be regarded as the most important of non-canonical writings within the Church. Satan's key Last Days strategy of counterfeiting Christian writings had paid great dividends in his attempted destruction of the Church from within — a strategy which involved both Gnosticism and Mysticism. In one brief mystical publication, he ensured that the greater part of professing Christians would believe that the way to God would not be through repentance, discipleship and simple faith in Jesus Christ, but through the same religious techiques and practices with which he had been deceiving the heathen nations from the very beginning.

iv. Spiritual Marriage in Teresa of Avila

Another major feature of Christian mysticism is the concept of a 'spiritual marriage' with God in ecstatic visions and experiences. This is brought out most clearly in the writings of Teresa of Avila (1515-1582), a close colleague of John of the Cross who became a Carmelite nun in 1533.[67] In an attempt to explain her sensations of the marriage union of the soul with God, Teresa uses an interesting metaphor which strongly highlights the syncretic nature of the Christian mystical experience. She describes it as identical to

> 'what we have when rain falls from the sky into a river or fount; all is water, for the rain that fell from heaven cannot be divided or separated from the water of that river. Or it is like what we have when a little stream enters the sea, there is no means of separating the two'.[68]

This metaphorical description is almost identical with that used in the Upanishads to express the Hindu monistic conception of the relationship between all created things and the divine:

> 'These rivers, my son...go from sea to sea (i.e., the clouds lift up the water from the sea to the sky, and send it back as rain to the sea). They become indeed the sea. And as those rivers, when they are in the sea, do not know, I am this or that river. In the same manner, my son, all these creatures, when they have come back from the True, know not

---

[66] Ibid., p.7.

[67] These two mystics shared a strange, celibate, ecstatic relationship. There is a well-known story of an occasion on which a nun in the convent they shared allegedly found the two of them levitating above the ground in an ecstatic trance!

[68] Kieran Kavanaugh & Otilio Rodriguez (trans. & eds.), *Teresa of Avila: The Interior Castle* (SPCK, 1979), p.179.

that they have come back from the True'.[69]

The Christian mystic's experience of a spiritual 'marriage' with God is nothing more than the ecstatic monistic absorption into the cosmos sought by the yogic devotee of the East. Dressed up in different terminology, it has a Christo-centric appearance, but this is purely superficial. Furthermore, the whole concept of marriage to a deity is among the oldest throughout the entire history of false religion. Mystics the world over, from time immemorial, have experienced the rapturous sensation of a sexual embrace on a spiritual level with the deity of their choice. The 'god', who or whatever that may be, is usually the bridegroom and the soul of the nun/monk/initiate/yogin is the bride:

> 'The concept of the spiritual marriage is used all over the world to express the relationship between a spirit and the inspired human. Thus, in Ethiopia the *zar*-initiate is called a bride...In Voodoo in Haiti men and women contract spiritual marriages with one of the *loa* [spirits]...Among the Saora of Orissa dedication of the inspired priest is celebrated by marriage with a female spirit...Among the Chukchee of the Arctic the male shaman often has a spirit wife'.[70]

In many parts of Africa, the medium who undergoes a trance and possession by a spirit is called *'wife-of-god'*, and *'he, or generally she, undergoes a course of training which aims at binding spirit and human being together in a sacred marriage'*.[71] Similarly, in an Indian Sikh hymn of Guru Nanak (1469-1538), the devotee chants: *'I would repeat the holy Name of the Lord; thus let the soul step-by-step mount the stairs to the Bridegroom and become one with Him'*.[72] Notice how this line contains the three universal elements of mysticism: *mantra*, secret ladder and mystical marriage. In Indian religious thought, the dualistic cosmogenic conception (origin) of the universe is expressed by the equal twin forces of *prakti* (nature, female) and *purusa* (spirit, male). In China, these twin-forces are known as *yin* and *yang*. There are also numerous early cosmogonies the world over which claim that the cosmos is formed from sexual intercourse between the male power of the heavens and the female power of the earth.[73] In Taoism, for example, the sexological writings identify thirty 'heaven-and-earth positions' of intercourse, while the union of sky and earth was an important part of Greek religious thought in the concept of 'Sacred Marriage'.[74] So we can see that there are a great many parallels between these manifestations of pagan cosmology and the experiences of Christian mysticism.

Another characteristic which often comes across through the various writings of the Christian mystics on this subject of spiritual rapture is their intense sexual

---

[69] F. Max Müller (ed.), *The Sacred Books of the East: Vol.XV* (OUP, 1900), 'The Upanishads', Vol.1, Part 1, p.102.

[70] John Ferguson, op. cit., p.84.

[71] Geoffrey Parrinder, *Mysticism in the World's Religions* (Sheldon Press, 1976), p.79.

[72] Ibid., p.105.

[73] John Ferguson, op. cit., p.168.

[74] Ibid., p.174.

imagery. Take this somewhat pornographic offering from Teresa of Avila:

> 'Though I often have visions of angels, I do not see them... In [one angel's] hands I saw a great golden spear, and at the iron tip there appeared to be a point of fire. This he plunged into my heart several times so that it penetrated my entrails. When he pulled it out, I felt that he took them with it, and left me utterly consumed by the great love of God. The pain was so severe that it made me utter several moans. The sweetness caused by this intense pain is so extreme that one cannot possibly wish it to cease, nor is one's soul then content with anything but God'.[75]

It is hardly surprising that people living in unnatural monastic seclusion — having imbibed the mystical theology of the pseudo-Dionysius, practising asceticism with all manner of strange meditations, without ever knowing the sexual fulfilment of a marital relationship — should begin to undergo bizarre hallucinations with such overtly sexual overtones! With this vision in mind, one can understand why this ecstatic sexual union with divinity should often be described as a 'rapture' — a word which is derived from the same Latin word as 'rape'. It is interesting to note here that when Teresa was in middle years and well-experienced in meditation, the supernatural phenomena which attended her were pronounced as *'diabolical'* by her spiritual directors. The only people who assured her otherwise (and thereby encouraged her further) were two Jesuit priests who had set up residence nearby in Avila.[76]

Although we will be examining the entire mystical concept of 'union with God' later in this chapter, the dual question must be asked here: What is the biblical foundation for the intense experiences of these mystics, and what is their true source? The main proof texts offered by Christian mystics for the concept of a 'Spiritual Marriage' — in which the individual soul is *'oned with God'*,[77] as the Cloud of Unknowing calls it —are the passages in the Book of Revelation which speak of the 'Marriage Supper of the Lamb' (Rev.19:7-9), the passage in Eph.5:22-33 dealing with the marital relationship of the Christian, coupled with the entire contents of the Song of Solomon. What we have here is yet another classic case of 'first choose your philosophy, then find the Scriptures which appear to support it'. The references to the 'Marriage Supper' in the Book of Revelation are concerned solely with the relationship between Jesus Christ and the Spirit-united universal Church of all true believers. The Marriage Feast refers to that glorious moment at the end of this Gospel age when Jesus will personally return for His Church, the Body of Christ (1 Cor.12:27), to *'gather together His elect from the four winds, from one end of heaven to the other'* (Mt.24:31). It has nothing whatsoever to do with the individual ecstasies of certain characters during this earthly life. The Marriage Feast refers to a historical event in Church history, *not*

---

[75] Geoffrey Parinder, op. cit., p.169.

[76] *Chambers's Encyclopaedia*, op. cit., Vol.XIII, p.543.

[77] Clifton Wolters, op. cit., p.46.

to an individual personal experience. Similarly, when Paul says, *'Husbands, love your wives, just as Christ also loved the church and gave himself for it'* (Eph.5:25), he was making an allusion to the bridal status of the entire Church — chosen by God to be His people from before the creation of the world — rather than the rapturous experience of a few individuals professing to be part of that Church, who happen to have practised the right *mantras* and meditations.

The exegetical interpretation of the relationship between the bride and bridegroom in the Song of Solomon as being allegorical to an ecstatic mystical union between the soul and God is wholly spurious. Such an interpretation originated with Origen (*c*.185-253), renowned for his allegorical destruction of biblical truths, and who himself gave rise to a mystical teaching among some Palestinian monks of the mid-sixth century called 'Origeniast'.[78] Surely it is not wise to trust the allegorising of a man who was prepared to take Mt.19:12 literally by castrating himself, who believed that pre-existent souls who had behaved badly were incarnated on earth for their purification, and who asserted that Satan and his fellow demons would ultimately be restored by the grace of God! However much there is a legitimate application of the Song of Solomon to the loving relationship between Christ and His Church (cf. Eph.5:22-33), it stands alongside that of a positive endorsement in the Word of God of the beauty and legitimacy of human sexuality, and of the marital love which was originally intended to illustrate the oneness within the Godhead (cf. Gen.1:27; 2:24; 1 Cor.6:16-20). This last point is especially ironic in view of the fact that the mystics generally eschewed normal marital and sexual relations as being unfitting for one who desires to attain a higher level of spirituality!

Having shown how steeped are the Eastern traditions in this imagery of the ecstatic, quasi-sexual, monist absorption of the human soul into the 'Ultimate Being', one cannot avoid noticing its similarity to the corresponding experience of the Christian mystic. We can now see clearly the pattern of parallels between the practices of the 'Christian' mystics and the mystics of the world's religions. In fact, what is starting to emerge here is an understanding of how the ecumenical meeting point for a universal religious confederacy can indeed be found in the mutual 'mystical dimension' in all the different religious traditions of the world — a point which we shall take up both in the conclusion to this present chapter and in the final chapter, 'Strangers, but not Pilgrims'.

v. The Jesuit Connection

Another syncretic point of contact between the mysticism of the 'Church' and that of the Eastern religions comes through the monastic order of the Society of Jesus (Jesuits), which was founded in 1534 by Ignatius of Loyola (1495-1556). He is best remembered for his 'Spiritual Exercises' which comprise a four-week series of meditation techniques utilising visualisation, verbal repetition and rhythmic breathing — all of which are used in Eastern mysticism. All occultists recognise the connections between the exercises of Ignatius and their own

---

[78] *Chambers's Encyclopaedia*, op. cit., Vol.X, p.243.

practices. In a chapter entitled 'The Emergence of a New Consciousness', Lady Ursula Burton — a former Roman Catholic who has converted to Findhorn-style Neo-Gnosticism — highlights the relationship between Ignatius' exercises and Eastern Mysticism when she says:

> 'The Church tends not to recognise that the teaching of Christ was often of a psychological nature and concerned with bringing out the full potential that lies within each individual. Within the Catholic Church, a method used to *find the 'hidden self' and help it come alive* is by following the Spiritual Exercises of St. Ignatius Loyola. St. Ignatius, a Spaniard born in 1495, recognized the significance of the unconscious and, indeed, *used some of the methods that twentieth century psychotherapists have rediscovered*'.[79] [emphasis added]

She is referring here to the Eastern meditational practice of 'visualisation', which we shall be examining in detail in our penultimate chapter. Notice also her reference to 'the hidden self' — a classic hallmark of mystical religionism. Yet another occult researcher and practitioner, demonstrating (amongst other things) how Himmler's Nazi S.S. was modelled on Ignatius' Society of Jesus, affirms that

> 'These 'spiritual exercises' are a carefully graded visualisation programme encompassing certain archetypal scenes designed to bring the individual practitioner closer to the Inner Christ. *'The Kingdom of God'*, Jesus told his disciples, *'is within you'*. And the Jesuits are among the very few orthodox churchmen actually trying to make contact with it. The context of Jesuit visualisations differs radically from that of the exercises used in many of the occult schools, but there is an uncanny similarity in the techniques'.[80]

Prior to the setting up of the Jesuit order, Loyola had often been denounced to the Inquistion for his unauthorised brand of Christianity; but somehow he was always eventually declared orthodox. After seven years of study in Paris and the founding of his order, the Jesuits were officially authorised by the Roman Catholic Church in 1540. This powerful organisation then became ostensibly *'the stormtroops of the Counter-Reformation'*,[81] zealous to stamp out those Protestants who had broken away from the corrupt and unbiblical bonds of the Vatican. They also officially adopted the pseudo-Dionysian-influenced Thomas Aquinas as their theologian, while at the same time placing the accent on human action in the process of salvation rather than on grace.[82]

---

[79] Ursula Burton & Janice Dolley, *Christian Evolution: Moving Towards a Global Spirituality* (Turnstone Press, 1984), p.112.

[80] James Webb, *The Occult Establishment*, (Open Court, 1975), p.320.

[81] *Chambers's Encyclopaedia*, op. cit, Vol.VIII, pp.80-81.

[82] Walter J. Elwell (ed.), op. cit., p.1030. This is another form of the early Church heresy known as Pelagianism, which was first proferred by a British monk, Pelagius, in the fifth century. He taught that human beings have freewill, that sin is not inheritied, and that grace is merely an aid to (rather than the sole source of) salvation.

However, the methods of the Jesuits were far more subtle than those of the Inquisition, relying instead on mission work, the founding of schools and colleges, coupled with skilful diplomatic liaison with political and governmental agencies. Not surprisingly, their international activities brought them into many disputes with other orders and individuals, but, strangely enough, never with the Vatican. Moreover, their subtlety led to an extreme flexibility in accommodating Roman Catholic doctrine to the prevailing needs and prejudices of the time. It is of great significance to our subject in this present chapter that Jesuit missionaries in the Orient were prepared to *'soften the transition from oriental modes of thought to Christianity'.*[83] This tendency has persisted to this present day, when it is common to discover Jesuit theologians in India saying: *'The fact that members of the higher religions, such as Hindus and Buddhists, do not convert may be a sign that they are not meant to convert'.*[84]

It is interesting to note the references to the Jesuits in the writings of the French mathematician and Christian apologist, Blaise Pascal (1623-1662), who was convinced that they were *'truly the forces of evil'.*[85] He saw clearly that in their Counter-Reformation activities the Jesuits *'oblige people either to accept error or swear that they have done so',*[86] and he laid on them the charge that they *'have tried to combine God and world, and have only earned the contempt of the world'.*[87] It is also worth noting that the occult-mystical sect of the 'Illuminati' — who, like the Jesuits, are reputed by many researchers to have been instrumental in manipulating world politics and economics during the last two hundred years — was founded in Ingolstadt on the first of May 1776 by Jesuit-trained Professor of Canon Law, Adam Weishaupt.

Today, the 'Spiritual Exercises of St. Ignatius' form the focal point of many mystical retreats being organised within the professing Church, while the Jesuits themselves run some four thousand schools worldwide and eighteen American universities.

2. The New Mysticism Within the Church

Having looked at some of the key influences in the historical development of mysticism in the Christian Church, we now turn our attention to the manifestations of mysticism in the Church today. It is a sad fact that the Roman Catholic Church has always provided a fertile ground for heresy. In spite of its ministry of exorcism, its numerous Inquisitions, its censors and its aspirations to social and ethical morality (known in the jargon as 'peace and justice'), it has persistently been unable to cleanse its own doorstep of false doctrine and downright evil. Although there have been many distinguished apologists and upholders of the flag of truth in the Roman Church, alongside that stream of orthodoxy there has flourished unhindered a great number of people who have perverted the word of God.

---

[83] *Chambers's Encyclopaedia*, op. cit, Vol.VIII, p.81.

[84] From an article by Denis Murphy in the Jesuit magazine *America*, August 25, 1979.

[85] Blaise Pascal, *Pensées* (Penguin, 1966), p.17.

[86] Ibid., p.355.

[87] Ibid., p.353.

Many of these have been fêted and canonised within its churches, convents and monasteries. Coupled with this, the great prevalence in the Roman Church through the ages of so-called 'contemplatives' and mystics has provided the perfect seedbed for a major development in Satan's strategic purposes.

So far in this chapter, we have traced the manner in which a Christian form of mysticism has been concocted from a syncretic brew of Neoplatonism, Eastern mysticism and Yogic practice. However, it is fair to say that, in general, the Christian mystics of earlier ages did not consciously seek to build a bridge with the oriental religions of the world. Their activities were founded, in the main, on ignorance and the fact that they had been deceived by the spurious contents of the pseudonymous *Mystica Theologia*. The situation today is somewhat different, because the modern mystics in the Church are deliberately setting out to forge a common bond with those of the East. In just the same way that there has been the creation of a New Gnosticism in the West, which was built on many of the ancient Gnostic teachings (coupled with other influences), so there has been the development of a parallel movement towards a New Mysticism which has been founded on the teachings of earlier mystics, coupled with strains from Hinduism, Buddhism and other eclectic sources.

This Neo-Mysticism is such a growth industry in the Church today that it is difficult to be selective in providing examples. A vast number of writers and teachers in the Roman Catholic Church have been especially instrumental in the founding of it; but here we give a few important examples in three areas of Roman Catholic input.

i. Hindu-Catholicism

One of the most successful weddings between Eastern and Christian mysticism has taken place in the meeting between Hinduism and the Roman Catholic Church. Two men have been particularly instrumental in this respect. The first is Dom Henri le Saux (d.1974). He is a Roman Catholic monk who went to live in India and changed his name to Abhishiktananda. He has written a great deal on the grafting together of Hindu and Christian spiritual practices, especially the uniting of Indian mantras with certain biblical invocations in the manner of the Hesychasts. He advocates the repetitive invocation of the Name of God as a way of achieving 'enlightenment', claiming that the Bible invites us to chant 'Abba, Father' as *'a sacred mantra which opens the doors of eternity'*,[88] while he claims that the parallel use of the *mantra* 'AUM' *'introduces man into the mystery of the Holy Spirit'*.[89]

In similar vein, the Benedictine monk Fr. Bede Griffiths runs an ashram called 'Shantivanam' ('Forest of Peace') near Hyderabad in India, and has written extensively on the integration of Eastern and Christian mysticism. Books such as *Essays Towards a Hindu-Christian Dialogue* (Collins, 1966), *The Marriage of East and West* (Collins, 1982), and *Cosmic Revelation: The Hindu Way to God* (Collins, 1983) have been instrumental in this process. On his ashram, Fr. Griffiths

[88] Abhishiktananda, *Prayer* (SPCK, 1967).

[89] Ibid.

has amalgamated Christianity and Hinduism by holding interfaith Eucharists offering bread and wine and the four elements of water, earth, air and fire. *'The idea'*, he says, *'is that it represents the cosmic sacrifice. Christ assumes the whole creation and offers it to God'*.[90] What is extraordinary is that this kind of mystical twaddle has been officially approved by both the bishops and the Holy See.[91] Fr. Griffiths has also incorporated the development of yoga into the life of his community, to which people from all over the world travel — including those of great influence in the religious world. Here is how he describes this experiment:

> 'One of our monks is an expert in yoga and is now very interested in Kundalini yoga. He has developed an interesting method of Christian yogic meditation with asana [posture], pranayama [rhythmic breathing] and the name of Jesus. We use the mantra "Jesu" on the inbreath and "Abba" on the outbreath. We're beginning to get into this idea of *transformation of energy*'.[92]

It is worth noting here that Kundalini, as a branch of Tantric Yoga, is one of the most powerful and dangerous of all forms of Yoga, involving practices designed to release what is known as 'serpent energy', which allegedly lies dormant in the cerebro-spinal system. This can lead to a variety of psychic experiences akin to those achieved through the use of drugs such as LSD. Many of these practices have been held as secret doctrines by Tantrists for millennia, but are now being released into the West on a huge scale through a variety of gurus. Indeed, there are many mystical and so-called 'charismatic' practices which travel under the banner of Christianity that have far more in common with the activation of Kundalini energy than with manifestations of the Holy Spirit.

Father Griffiths claims that what he calls the 'One Reality' has revealed itself through two essential but different traditions: the Semitic (i.e., Judaism, Christianity and Islam) and the Oriental (i.e., Hindu, Buddhist, Taoist, etc.), both of which are equally valid.[93] In common with all modern mystics of East and West, he claims that all religions are based on the same fundamental principles and rooted in the same essential deity. Precisely the same approach has been adopted at another Hindu-Catholic ashram, also called 'Shantivanam', which exists in the U.S.A. This is run by former Roman Catholic parish priest, Fr. Edward Hays, who set up his syncretistic 'house of prayer' after returning from an extended visit to the East in search of inspiration for *'freshness in spirituality'*.[94] In the words of

---

[90] From an interview with Fr. Griffiths in the *Laughing Man Journal*, Vol.5, No.3, 1984, p.36. This journal was published by a U.S. Neo-Gnostic organisation headed up by a self-styled guru called Da Free John who believes he is 'God Incarnate'. At the time of this interview, Fr. Bede Griffiths was an official visitor to Da Free John's cult retreat in California. See Chapter 11, pp.477-478 for further information about Da Free John.

[91] Ibid.

[92] Ibid., p.37.

[93] Ibid.

[94] Randy England, *The Unicorn in the Sanctuary: The Impact of the New Age on the*

Roman Catholic New Age watcher Randy England, Fr. Hays *'blends Christianity with the other religions and puts Jesus in the same class as "Buddha and the other holy saviours... "*.[95] Recommending the use of *mantras* and breathing exercises, coupled with the celebration of the ancient Celtic festivals, Fr. Hays' ashram has the full backing of Archbishop Strecker of Kansas City.[96]

ii. Zen-Catholicism

The marrying of Eastern mysticism with the trappings of Christianity moved into overdrive with the teachings of a U.S. Cistercian (Trappist) monk called Thomas Merton (1915-1968). He had first entered the monastic life at an early age after being seized with guilt as a result of making a young woman pregnant. After many years of what he called 'elected silence' (the Trappists are a silent order), he became the international champion of a dialogue between the many contemplative traditions of the East and the mystical orders in the sphere of the Church. His written works include *Zen, Tao et Nirvana* (Paris, 1970), *The Zen Revival* (Buddhist Society of London, 1971), and *Thomas Merton on Zen* (Sheldon Press, 1976).

Thomas Merton believed passionately that there is an 'original unity' to all religions which can be experienced through mystical states. In a posthumously-published book entitled *Contemplation in a World of Action*, Thomas Merton called strongly for a renewal of the monastic life, mysticism and contemplative practices. Little did he know that within twenty years of his death, the world would be overrun with gurus of every shape and colour, and that his own books would become so popular across the globe. One Roman Catholic researcher, deploring the growth of New Age practices in his denomination, reports that

> 'Some Buddhists revere Merton as a reincarnated Buddha, while one spirit medium reports that Merton has escaped the cycle of reincarnation and is now the Ascended Master "Davog", whose task is to prepare for the Second Coming of Jesus'.[97]

Another champion of the marriage between Zen Buddhism and Christianity is the Benedictine monk Dom Aelred Graham, whose book 'Zen Catholicism' is a classic of the genre. Back in 1963, Graham claimed that

> 'Catholic spirituality — at least as expounded in its most satisfying form by Aquinas — moves at the same profound level as the metaphysical tradition behind Zen Buddhism'.[98]

Similarly, D.T. Suzuki, the Zen Buddhist missionary to the West, wrote a book called 'Mysticism: Christian and Buddhist', in which he *'demonstrates the superficial differences between the Zen...and Christian schools and stresses the deep*

Catholic Church (TAN Books, 1991), pp.72-73.

[95] Ibid., p.73. Randy England is here quoting Edward Hays' book *Secular Sanctity* (Forest of Peace Books, 1984), p.16.

[96] Ibid.

[97] Ibid., p.76.

[98] Aelred Graham, *Zen Catholicism* (Harcourt, Brace & World Inc., 1963), p.39.

affinities between them'.[99] Of course such a statement becomes possible only when one makes a comparison between Zen and Christianity at the level of mysticism and the religious experiences of the respective mystics. The 'Christian' model used by Suzuki in his comparison with Zen is none other than the Dominican monk Meister Eckhart (1260-1328), who would better be described as a Neoplatonic pantheist rather than a Christian. Readers will recall from an earlier chapter that Eckhart was identified as one of the four streams of thought which contributed to the making of Rosicrucianism in the seventeenth century.[100]

iii. Eclectic-Catholicism

In the previous sections we have looked at examples of modern Christian mystics who have a special interest in uniting one particular discipline of Eastern mysticism with Christianity. In the present section, we will examine the teachings of three men whose mysticism has been gathered from a variety of different sources. Such eclecticism brings them closer to the Neo-Gnostic position and shows the clear links between the two streams.

Our first example of the eclectic type of modern mystic is the Franciscan friar and Guardian of Glasshampton Monastery in Worcestershire in the U.K., Brother Ramon. He has written a widely-read book published by the 'Christian publisher' Marshall Pickering entitled 'A Hidden Fire: Exploring the Deeper Reaches of Prayer'. This work is really an updating of the techniques of Christian, Buddhist, Zen and Taoist mysticism through the ages, mingled with the newer secular psychological techniques of relaxation and autohypnosis — all sprinkled liberally with a deceptive dash of Bible Christianity. Here is a passage on the preparation necessary for successful prayer to God:

> 'Now as a prerequisite to your chosen posture, practise an exercise in relaxation. It is best to wear either singlet and shorts or a track suit — nothing tight-fitting and no footgear. Everything free, everything easy, no strain. Now lie down upon the ground on your back, and very simply enumerate the parts and areas of your body, from your feet...to your face and head. As you enumerate, stretch and gently relax each part...letting go...letting go...until you have drained the tension away and are at rest. Resting naturally and resting in God. I have found, after becoming familiar with this form of meditation, that it is an appropriate way to meditate upon one's death'.[101]

Unless one was familiar with this exercise, one would be entirely unaware that it is the yoga posture (*asana*) known as *'Savasana* or *Mrtasana*, which is used as the rudimentary preparation for all meditation. *'Sava* means 'corpse' and *Mrtis* means 'death' (cf. our word 'mortal') in Sanskrit, leading to this position being

---

[99] Taken from an advert for D.T. Suzuki's book, *Mysticism: Christian and Buddhist* (George Allen & Unwin).

[100] See p.81 in Chapter 3, 'The Founding of the New Gnosticism', part 1.

[101] Brother Ramon, *A Hidden Fire: Exploring the Deeper Reaches of Prayer* (Marshall Pickering, 1985), p.68.

known in English as the 'position of the corpse'. The authoritative Indian *Hatha Yoga Pradipka* tells us:

> 'Lying upon one's back on the ground at full length like a corpse is called *'Savasana*. This removes the fatigue caused by other asanas [postures] and induces calmness of mind'.[102]

Nowhere in his book does Bro. Ramon tell his readers that he has derived these techniques from the art of Yoga. Everything is presented as normal Christian practice. But one does not have to indulge in such exercises in order to 'open a channel to God'. That is the ancient way of Satan-inspired religion. Under no circumstances can one imagine any of the great prayers of the Bible being preceded by this kind of self-indulgence (e.g., 1 Sam.2:1-10; Neh.2:4; Acts 4:23-31). This exercise is a precursor to Eastern meditation and Yoga (union with 'the god within' through our own efforts), and is entirely inappropriate as a prerequisite to biblical prayer (communion with God the Father through Jesus Christ). The biblical concept of prayer involves rational communication between one objective person and another, rather than 'mellowing out' or attempting to 'blend into the infinite' through total body relaxation and blanking out the mind.

In common with all other mystics, Brother Ramon claims that the 'spirit of man' is of the same essence as the Spirit of God:

> 'God breathed his life-giving ruach [Hebrew for spirit or breath] into Adam's nostrils and he became a living soul...In the Bible the breath of man is a manifestation of the breath of the Eternal Being'.[103]

We have already made extensive reference to this error in earlier chapters, showing the fallacy which lies at its heart.[104] He then goes on to advise his readers to *'experiment with breathing'*, using rhythmic breathing techniques with the 'Jesus Prayer', which is all reminiscent of the exercises of the Hesychasts. All these techniques are an aid to hypnosis or self-hypnosis and are used by many psychotherapists today. The effects which they induce (often the result of hyperventilation) are mistaken by mystics for genuine spiritual experience. Vast numbers of people today are under the illusion that the experience of well-being produced by these ancient yogic practices is the work of the Spirit of God, when it is purely of psycho-physical origin. It is hardly surprising to learn that Brother Ramon finds that during his autohypnotic programming of rhythmic breathing and mantric repetition he begins to speak in an ecstatic babbling which he mistakes for the biblical gift of tongues.[105]

---

[102] *Hatha Yoga Pradipka*, Chap.I, v.32. Quoted in B.K.S. Iyengar, op. cit., p.183. This practice is also described in many other books on meditation and mind-control. See, e.g., Raymond Van Over, *Total Meditation: Mind Control Techniques for a Small Planet in Space* (Collier Macmillan, 1978), pp.175-176.

[103] Brother Ramon, op. cit., pp.71-72.

[104] See the section in Chapter 5 on 'The god within'.

[105] Ibid. p.75. Many people in the Christian sect known as the Charismatic Movement are also labouring under the same illusion.

Other prayer techniques and enhancements recommended by Brother Ramon are *'certain forms of charismatic and aerobic dance'*, in which one dances before the Lord in a *'personally choreographed or completely spontaneous manner'*.[106] This he couples with 'prayer walks' and 'prayer jogging' which are based on the trendy U.S. practice of Zen walks and Zen jogging. There are many touching passages in Brother Ramon's book, and he is obviously a man of great sensitivity. Unfortunately, like so many other spiritual seekers today, he has missed the entire thread of the Bible and its redemptive-eschatological teachings, having been seduced by the syncretistic practices of the New Mysticism and New Gnosticism. In one passage which sheds considerable light on the true source and nature of Brother Ramon's teachniques, he states:

> 'Because of the work of men such as Carl G. Jung, we have become aware of levels of being that go much further than conscious awareness. They may be thought of as interpenetrating layers of being which include the conscious subliminal consciousness...and the collective unconscious... Pioneers in the field of psychology such as Freud, Jung and Adler have done a service to Christian and secular man in calling attention to dimensions of being in which biblical modes of thought may operate freely. Certainly, their findings may help us in an understanding of the deeper reaches of prayer'.[107]

From this one must deduce that the prayers of all the saints prior to the advent of Freud's Viennese School were somehow deficient in their profundity. Regrettably, Brother Ramon's book is not about prayer to the Transcendent God of the Bible; it is about a psychological awareness, altered consciousness and a tuning-in to 'the god within'. Brother Ramon is typical of a growing number of Neo-Mystics who are setting the agenda in the professing Church for the next decade. His book is not really a Christian book at all; it is a handbook to the New Mysticism and New Gnosticism posing as Christian spirituality, skilfully marketed by a professing Christian publishing firm, and all true Christians should be aware of this deception.

Another influential character worthy of a mention here is the professing evangelical, Richard Foster. Although not strictly a Roman Catholic as such, he has certainly drunk at the same tainted fountain, bringing techniques foreign to the pages of the Bible right into the heartlands of Protestantism. In his book 'A Celebration of Discipline', which was recommended by Anglican vicar David Watson, he has laid out for the Christian believer the perfect Eastern mystical meditation sequence, dressed up in biblical clothing. In spite of his superficial differentiation between Eastern and Christian meditation, there is considerable use of the techniques and jargon of Eastern traditions, psychotherapy and occultism.[108] Again, we are confronted with the usual preliminary 'meditation' exercises as a

[106] Ibid., p.81.
[107] Ibid., p.132.
[108] This occultic aspect in Richard Foster's writings will be developed in Chapter 11.

preparation for prayer. Richard Foster calls this period *'centering-down'*.[109] To those 'in the know' this is an original Zen Buddhist term for the pre-meditation period when one 'finds one's centre', collecting oneself by stilling the mind in preparation for deeper meditation. Any advocate of Eastern meditation or Neo-Gnostic of today would instantly recognise such a term as a part of his own vocabulary. We are then given two meditations with which to 'center-down'.

The first of these exercises is called *'palms down – palms up'*, a well-known psychotherapeutic relaxation exercise which releases anxieties through downward facing palms, followed by upturning the palms to *'allow the Lord to commune with your spirit, to love you'*.[110] The second exercise in the 'centering-down' sequence involves the renowned rhythmic breathing cycles. In Richard Foster's version, it goes like this:

> 'Having seated yourself comfortably, slowly become conscious of your breathing. This will help you to get in touch with your body and indicate to you the level of tension within. Inhale deeply, slowly tilting your head back as far as it will go. Then exhale, allowing your head slowly to come forward until your chin nearly rests on your chest. Do this for several moments, praying inwardly something like this: "Lord, I exhale my spiritual apathy, I inhale your light and life". Then , as before, become silent outwardly and inwardly. Be attentive to the inward living Christ. If your attention wanders to the letter that must be dictated, or the windows that need to be cleaned, "exhale" the matter into the arms of the Master and draw in His divine breath of peace. Then listen once again'.[111]

We have written this out in full so that you will realise the true source (and deception) of Richard Foster's meditations. This is not Christian prayer. In which of the great prayers of the Bible do we find this sort of practice advocated? It is a standard pre-meditation exercise used in Eastern mystical practice before 'tuning in to the god within'. As a matching parallel of Richard Foster's exercise, compare this example from the Tibetan Buddhist Mahayana tradition which simply uses the image of the Buddha in place of Richard Foster's 'Lord' and 'Master':

> 'Having seated ourselves on a properly prepared cushion in the manner described, we should first attend to our motivation: the state of mind in which we are entering the meditation. If we discover that our mind is full of wild, uncontrolled thoughts, we should try to eliminate them... mental disturbance can be overcome by paying attention to our breath in the following manner. Breathe normally through your nostrils, without haste or noise, and mentally count "one" upon completion of the first cycle of incoming and outgoing breaths... We can also visualise all our non-virtues, delusions and disturbances in the form of thick, black

---

[109] Richard Foster, *Celebration of Discipline* (Hodder & Stoughton, 1980), pp.24-25.
[110] Ibid.
[111] Ibid., p.25.

smoke that flows out of our mind with the outbreath and disappears in the far distance. When we breathe in we can visualise the blessings of all the buddhas entering our nostrils in the form of pure, yellow light which then dissolves into our entire body and fills us with inspiration'.[112]

Just compare these two accounts: We see the need for correct seating arrangements; the subduing of the mind; the attention to one's breathing rhythms, and so on. Richard Foster 'inhales' the 'light and life' of his 'Lord'; the Tibetan Buddhist breathes in the 'blessings of all the Buddhas' in the form of 'pure, yellow light'. This is the New Mysticism in action in its Eastern and Western clothing. Breathing out bad things and breathing in good things is a basic psycho-magical, auto-hypnosis technique used by many professional psychologists and occultists. This exercise has nothing whatsoever to do with bringing oneself into the presence of God but rather with the alteration of consciousness. What it does is induce what are known as 'Alpha-waves' in the activity of the brain.

Normally, during the focused consciousness of wakeful existence, the brain-wave pattern registered on an electro-encephalograph is described as 'Beta', which is between thirteen and twenty-six cycles per second. However, another brain-state has been identified in which there is a more diffuse awareness, registering between eight and thirteen cycles per second. It is this state which the yogi and the mystic seek to attain through meditation. This Alpha-wave brain-state is, in fact, a pre-hypnotic state in which the person is extremely open to suggestion — human and otherwise. One meditation/mind control manual describes this state as *'floating, pleasant blankness, or shifting consciousness, peaceful meditation'*.[113] It is the Alpha-wave feeling of well-being induced by these rhythmic breathing and mantric exercises which the person experiences, and which he confuses with an experience of the 'presence of the Lord', which, if such was the case, would truly be awesome! Such a state can just as easily be induced with a biofeedback machine as it can with these exercises.

The real irony is that if one's relationship with God was truly God-centred rather than being so *self*-conscious, one would not have to resort to these humanistic techniques in order to approach the throne of grace. The reason that the Eastern mystic needs to use these relaxation exercises is because he is attempting to blank out his mind and tune in to 'the god within' — the natural result of his pantheistic worldview. This has nothing whatsoever to do with the biblical practice of prayer, which is primarily discursive — a two-way conversation between a creature and his or her Creator. It is not bodily *relaxedness* which determines the quality of the believer's prayer-life but, rather, a sense of total dependence on God and an awareness of His cosmic transcendent power. The substitution of the seductive inducement of Alpha-waves for the saving power of the true Alpha (and Omega) is an entirely self-centred and Spirit-less exercise.

---

[112] Geshe Kelsang Gyatso, *Meaningful to Behold* (Wisdom Publications, 1980), pp.226-227.

[113] Raymond Van Over, op. cit., p.107.

Richard Foster has also included, in his chapters on 'Christian' meditation, extensive instructions in the ancient occult art of 'visualisation' — the use of guided imagery to effect material and spiritual changes in oneself and in one's environment. This is one of the principal techniques used to prepare a novice for the deeper realms of Eastern meditation. The deceptive nature of this practice, its true origins and its widespread advocation in the Church today will form the subject matter of the penultimate chapter of this book.

Among the 'eclectic' Catholics, one of the most ardent propagandists of the New Mysticism has been Father William Johnston (b.1925). Originally from Northern Ireland, he joined the Jesuit order and went to Japan in 1951, where he received a doctorate in Mystical Theology from the Jesuit Sophia University. He has been the director of the Institute of Oriental Religions in Tokyo since 1980. As the author of numerous books, including one entitled 'Christian Zen', Fr. Johnston claims to have discovered that

> 'Mysticism is the exquisitely beautiful queen before whom the other branches of theology bow down with awe and reverence like lowly handmaids. I also saw clearly that this queen is the Lady Wisdom for whom all religions search and in whose presence all religions meet'.[114]

It is interesting that he should refer to Mysticism as 'Lady Wisdom'. The Greek for wisdom is *sophia* — the name of Fr. Johnston's University. *Sophia* was also the name that the Gnostics gave to the Holy Spirit in their cosmology. In a passage which shows the clear parallels between Mysticism and *gnosis*, Fr. Johnston reveals his willingness to advocate the use of drugs, biofeedback machines, and 'anything-which-works' in order to gain the desired effect of mystical trance and ecstasy:

> 'Inner space is going to be quite as enthralling as outer space. LSD, Mescalin and suchlike drugs (whatever may be said about their abuse) do reveal a new environment, a new world, another dimension of reality; and the psychophysiology of awareness promises to be one of the most exciting adventures of our exciting age. In short we find ourselves at *the threshold of a new science*. This is the *science of consciousness, of mind-expansion, of enhanced awareness*'.[115]

This is the tragic 'gospel' that these modern mystics and gnostics have to offer. In common with the spiritually lost folk of all ages, they spend their time *'in nothing else but either to tell or to hear some new thing'* (Acts 17:21). It is little wonder that all the world's religions think that Christianity is just another religion like theirs. Indeed, Fr. Johnston gives them even further assurance of this with the announcement:

> 'One need be no great prophet to predict that Western theology of the next century will address itself primarily to dialogue with the great

---

[114] William Johnston, *The Inner Eye of Love: Mysticism and Religion* (Collins, 1978), p.10.
[115] William Johnston, *Silent Music: The Science of Meditation* (Collins, 1974), p.22.

religions of the East...when we or those who come after us will forge a common way of speaking and even some kind of common theology'.[116]

Fr. Johnston will not need to wait any longer. Just fourteen years after writing those words, these developments have already occurred, as we shall be cataloguing extensively in the final chapter of this book. When Fr. Johnston recognises that *'at the end of the twentieth century we again find ourselves at a great crossroads in the history of mankind'*, he goes on to say that this *'demands a new theology, a re-statement of the Gospel message, and answer to the peculiar problems that confront us'*.[117] He then identifies two cultural influences which will enable this to happen:

'First...the switch to "interiority". That is to say, the whole emphasis is, and will be, on the inner world, the world of the mind, the human consciousness. Secondly, the new culture will certainly be a world culture profoundly influenced by all the great religions: Hinduism, Islam, Buddhism, Judaism as well as Christianity'.[118]

This is the agenda within the New Mysticism for the remainder of this present decade: the alteration of human consciousness and the building of a global religious confederation. In these ambitions they become united with the Neo-Gnostics in the fulfilment of a plan which is designed by Satan as part of his own strategy to destroy the Church and the unique claims of Christ. As Fr. Johnston rightly acknowledges: *'One of the great challenges to a new Christian theology will be mysticism, particularly oriental mysticism'*.[119] How are true Christians going to meet such a challenge today? Are they sufficiently equipped apologetically to do so? These developments had been foreseen many years beforehand. Way back in 1851, the philosopher and mystic Arthur Schopenhauer, made an extraordinarily apocalyptic statement:

'At present we may perceive shining through in the writings of the learned, the nature pantheism of India, which is destined sooner or later to become the faith of the people. *Ex oriente lux* [from the East comes light]'.[120]

We can now appreciate the extent to which this has become a reality. The development of mysticism within the Church over the centuries has played a major role in satanic strategy as it brought about a gradual corruption of the Christian Gospel throughout Christendom. Knowing these things, Schopenhauer was able to predict with confidence that

'in India, [Christianity] will now and never strike root: the primitive wisdom of the human race will never be pushed aside by the events of

---

[116] William Johnston, *The Inner Eye of Love: Mysticism and Religion*, op. cit., pp.9-10, 16.

[117] Ibid., p.57.

[118] Ibid.

[119] Ibid.

[120] Arthur Schopenhauer, *Parerga*, 3rd edition, Vol.II, p.59. Quoted in F. Max Muller (trans. & ed.), op. cit., Vol.I, *Sacred Books of the East*, pp.lxi-lxii.

Galilee. On the contrary, Indian wisdom will flow back upon Europe, and produce a thorough change in our knowing and thinking'.[121]

This mystical philosopher was here predicting, more than one hundred years before the event, the phenomenon which has fulfilled every ambition of Gnosticism and Mysticism, ancient and modern. Within the remainder of the final decade of the twentieth century, those who uphold biblical Christianity and are waiting for the return of the Lord Jesus Christ will be hard-pressed to respond to the apparently overwhelming claims of the New Mysticism. Throughout the rest of this chapter, in order to equip the saints to respond to this phenomenon, we shall first construct an apologetic comparison between mysticism and biblical Christianity, followed by an exposé of the occult origins of all mysticism.

II. THE THREE ERRORS OF ALL FORMS OF MYSTICISM

In common with all other philosophies, ideologies and religions of the world, the teachings of Eastern mysticism and Yoga do contain a number of characteristics which can give them the superficial appearance of having similarities with certain biblical truths. Consequently, one finds in many Eastern religious traditions such qualities as an attention to purification, avoidance of gross personal sin, the upholding of moral values, eschewing of materialism, development of humility, cultivation of non-violence, even devotion to a transcendent 'god' in those traditions where a preliminary form of theism is encouraged. However, in any comparison of a religion or philosophy with Christianity one should not make the classic error of looking merely for superficial similarities. This is the stuff of ecumenical appeasement, in which it is considered negative to highlight the differences between things.

It is not the similarities between two things which confirm their compatibility or reveal their true relationship: for if this was the case, one would find that even a hydrogen bomb and a raindrop shared common ground through the fact that they both fall from the skies! Yet, the one is a source of replenishment while the other is incomparably destructive. Seemingly innocuous similarities, taken on their own, can mask something far more serious. It is only through the added knowledge of the differences between two things that one can come into the full truth of their relationship. Such an understanding is especially pertinent in the Christian pilgrimage, during which we are to demolish antichristian ideological strongholds, *'casting down arguments and every high thing that exalts itself against the knowledge of God, bringing every thought into captivity to the obedience of Christ'* (2 Cor.10:4-5).

We have already shown that the three leading tenets of all forms of mysticism are:

1. A universal indwelling divinity (known as the 'Inner Light' or 'True Self') which is masked by a false, conditioned self.
2. The use of techniques to suppress or annihilate that false self, resulting in:

[121] Ibid., p.lxiv.

3. A complete (and usually ecstatic) union of the indwelling personal divinity with the 'Universal Spirit'.

We shall now examine these three teachings, highlighting the all-important differences between them and the biblical data.

1. The Doctrine of the Inner Light

We have mentioned previously that there are a large number of meeting-points between the principles of Neo-Gnosticism and those of the New Mysticism. One such principle is the teaching of a 'universal God within'. The starting point of all mysticism — whether of the East or West — is that a spark of God indwells every human being unconditionally. As the Professor of Comparative Religion at London University, Geoffrey Parinder, puts it:

> 'God breathes into man the breath of life, which is the Holy Spirit, and must be by definition immortal. It would appear that the living soul in man is God himself, and there could hardly be a closer union'.[122]

This statement perfectly sums up the central doctrine of both Mysticism and Gnosticism (as well as the teaching of modern apostate academics); but it is seriously in error in a number of ways. The first error is in assuming that *'the breath [spirit] of life'* which our first parents received from their Creator can be identified as the Spirit of God — as if each individual human soul is, as Professor Parrinder puts it, *'God himself'*. This is pantheism and is far removed from the biblical data, which simply shows that Adam had life 'breathed' into him by his Creator and thus became 'a living soul' (Gen.2:7). It is true, as we have shown in Chapter 5, that as part of his creation, Adam will have received the gift of the indwelling Holy Spirit; but this simply means that before the Fall he reflected God's image, having been created in knowledge, righteousness and true holiness. Because of this, it can be said that Adam was certainly a partaker of the divine nature (cf. 2 Pet.1:4), *but he was not at all a partaker in the divine essence.*

The second error in the above statement of Professor Parrinder is in thinking that because our first parents were originally endowed with the indwelling Holy Spirit at the dawn of history, therefore all human beings subsequently born have that same gift. When we examined the hallmarks of the New Gnosticism in an earlier chapter, we showed that although our first parents were indeed originally endowed with the indwelling Holy Spirit, they lost that privilege because of their disobedience. Since that time, every human being born in this world does *not* have that indwelling Spirit of God but is merely *'flesh'* (Gen.6:3). It is only those who repent and believe that have this original gift restored to them (cf. Col.3:10; Eph.4:24). However, even the mystics' conception of the indwelling Holy Spirit is faulty; for they imagine that the soul itself is the very essence of God. As we have said previously, to have the indwelling Holy Spirit is to be a *'partaker of the divine **nature**'* rather than a sharer in the Divine essence.

As we have already examined the main Bible texts used by the Neo-Gnostics to

---

[122] Geoffrey Parrinder, *Mysticism in the World's Religions* (Sheldon Press, 1976), p.113.

uphold their erroneous concept of 'the god within', our purpose in this present section is to examine some of those texts offered by the Neo-Mystics as support for their doctrine of the universal Inner Light. One of their main 'proofs' occurs in the Apostle Paul's sermon in the Areopagus when addressing the Athenians, as recorded in the Book of Acts:

> 'And He has made from one blood every nation of men to dwell on all the face of the earth, and has determined their preappointed times and the boundaries of their habitation, so that they should seek the Lord, in the hope that they might grope for Him and find Him, though He is not far from each one of us; for in Him we live and move and have our being, as also some of your own poets have said, "For we are also His offspring"' (Acts 17:26-28).

One Roman Catholic commentator quotes this text with approval in support of his mystical doctrine, claiming that it supports *'a fundamental belief which is to be found in the New Testament...that God dwells in every man as the author and sustainer of his being'.*[123] However, as we shall see, such an interpretation upholds the very doctrine which Paul was trying to overturn. Although God does indeed sustain all creatures, this does not provide a precondition for the indwelling of God. The above verses have to be seen against the national and cultural background in which they were set, coupled with their biblical context, before they can be properly understood. Let us follow through Paul's thought in this highly skilful sermon (Acts 17:16-34).

The Apostle, knowing full well that *'Greeks seek after wisdom'* (1 Cor.1:22), was addressing the adherents of various Greek philosophical systems and was carefully building his words so that he took the crowd with him before presenting them with his real message. First he acknowledged the sect known as the Epicureans by going along with their avowed concept (compatible with Christianity) of the self-sufficiency of the divine nature (*'Nor is He worshipped with men's hands, as though He needed anything [from us]'*, v.25a). Then he carefully follows that with some words which challenged their philosophy of the remoteness of divinity (*'He gives to all life, breath and all things'*, v.25b). He then makes out to resonate with the pantheism of the Stoics in vv.27-28; but notice how careful he is to say that we have our being *'in Him'* rather than God having His being *'in us'*, which would have been far closer to the Stoic view. Paul is here shedding some much-needed Judeo-Christian light on the half-truth of heathen pantheism by stressing the omnipresence of God (*'He is not far from each one of us'*, v.27), which is not 'God identified with nature' or the indwelling divinity of the mystics. Indeed, as the 'immanence' of God is only half the truth, Paul then goes on to emphasise the nature of His *transcendence* by shrewdly quoting one of the leading heathen philosophers of the time: *'For we are also His offspring'* (v.28).

The stark truth behind this sermon in Acts is that it could never be used as a

---

[123] Article by Bede Frost entitled 'Mysticism', in *Chambers's Encyclopaedia*, op. cit., Vol.IX, p.648.

justification for advocating a mystical union with the alleged 'god within' all people. The fact that God is the author and sustainer of our being does not mean that He can somehow be 'plugged into' through an ecstatic experience. On the contrary, Paul was trying to preach the true Gospel to the Stoic philosophers whose pantheism had already led them to think in terms of such inner divinity. For this reason alone, he would have been at pains to ensure that he would not say anything which might give the impression that the new Christianity supported the same theory. Having originally come from Tarsus — a Stoic stronghold — he would have known that their philosophy and worldview was incompatible with the Christianity that he was preaching. In fact, so removed was the cosmology of Stoicism from that of Christianity that just a few decades later it served as a leading influence on that twin of mysticism, and avowed enemy of Christianity, Gnosticism.

Another proof text for the Christian mystic's 'universal Inner Light' is found in the enigmatic beauty of the first chapter of John's Gospel. The particular verse which has given the 'indwelling divinity' schools (especially the Quakers) their greatest impetus is the one which describes the Lord Jesus Christ as *'the true Light, which lighteth every man that cometh into the world'* (Jn.1:9, A.V.). The translation deliberately given here is that of the Authorised Version, for it is this which makes it seem as if everyone is born with the Inner Light or Divine Essence within him. But this translation makes the phrase *'cometh into the world'* refer to *'every man'*, thereby giving the verse a universalist flavour which cannot be sanctioned either from this Gospel or from Scripture as a whole. However, every other version since the KJV has rendered the phrase *'comes into the world'* as being linked to *'the true Light'*. This agrees with the parallel statement of Jesus in Jn.3:19 that *'the light has come into the world'*. Jesus Christ, the true Light, does not enlighten everyone being born into the world and is not received by all, as the author of this Gospel is often at pains to bring out (e.g., Jn.1:11-13; 5:21; 6:44,53,64-65; 10:14,26-28; 13:18; 17:9). On this basis, a suitable paraphrase would be: *'The True Light, which enlightens everyone who receives Him, was in the act of coming into the world'*. It has nothing whatsoever to do with a universal inner divinity — a concept which would have been abhorrent to John, who had recorded the words of our Lord that some of the Pharisees belonged to the devil rather than being among the sheep of God (Jn.8:44-47). So this verse cannot mean, as the mystics would claim, that every man who comes into the world receives a measure of Christ's divinity in the form of his or her own soul.

We cannot stress the point enough, that the Holy Spirit of God does not indwell all people unconditionally. The Holy Spirit indwells only those who are numbered among Christ's people (1 Cor.12:27; Eph.1:22-23; 4:15-16; Col.2:19), creating in each individual who receives Him what Paul calls the *'new man'* (Eph.4:17-24; Col.3:8-10); 2 Cor.4:16; 5:17; Rom.6:4-6; 7:6; 12:2). Jesus Christ indwells those who *'live by faith in the Son of God'* , and lives in the hearts of those whom He has loved and for whom He gave Himself on the cross (Gal.2:20). As Paul solemnly declares, *'Now if anyone does not have the Spirit of Christ, he is not His'*

(Rom.8:9; cf. Jude 19). This clearly implies that not only is this indwelling of the Holy Spirit confined to the Lord's chosen ones, but that there are also people who do *not* have this Spirit. This is confirmed when the Bible reveals that it is only those who are adopted into God's new family who receive the indwelling Spirit from Him (Gal.4:6; cf. Rom.8:14-15).

Surely this is proof enough that the Holy Spirit is not already the essence of the souls of all people in all ages from the time of their birth. Such a notion is blasphemous at any stage of history. Just as the Holy Spirit brought to completion God's original creation (Gen.1:2), so He brings to completion God's new creation in men and women — the elect Church (2 Cor.5:17; Gal.6:15). These are the true facts concerning the 'God within'. The doctrine of the unconditional Divine Inner Light within every person coming into the world is therefore in complete contradiction to biblical Christianity and is an abominable doctrine. As G.K. Chesterton rightly says:

> 'If I were to say that Christianity came into the world specially to destroy the doctrine of the Inner Light, that would be an exaggeration. But it would be very much nearer to the truth... Of all conceivable forms of enlightenment the worst is what these people call the Inner Light. Of all horrible religions the most horrible is the worship of the god within. Any one who knows any body knows how it would work; anyone who knows anyone from the Higher Thought Centre knows how it does work. That Jones shall worship the god within him turns out ultimately to mean that Jones shall worship Jones... Christianity came into the world firstly in order to assert with violence that a man had not only to look inwards, but to look outwards, to behold with astonishment and enthusiasm a divine company and a divine captain. The only fun of being a Christian was that a man was not left alone with the Inner Light, but definitely recognised an outer light, fair as the sun, clear as the moon, terrible as an army with banners'.[124]

The Christian assertion of the Outer Light over against the worldly experience of the Inner Light will be one of the great battlegrounds of the faith, as the Gospel comes under increasingly violent attack in the closing days of world history.

2. Religion by Numbers: Techniques for Spiritual Advancement

Having examined the first principle of mysticism — that all people have a spark of divinity indwelling them — we now come to the second principle. Because one error leads to another in the spiritual life, the mystic's belief that he has indwelling divinity leads him to seeks ways of tapping into it. One of the first elements which is noticeable in the writings of the mystics and their advocates in all ages is the use of techniques and systems in order to effect some kind of religious 'experience'. There is a constant search for new and better *methods* with which to achieve the desired spiritual goal. But Jesus said: *'No one can come to Me unless the Father who sent Me draws him... No one can come to Me unless it has been*

[124] Gilbert K. Chesterton, *Orthodoxy* (John Lane, The Bodley Head, 1908), pp.135-137.

granted to him by My Father' (Jn.6:44,65). We do not have eyes to see the Light of life until God has opened them. We are completely dependent on the Lord for everything: *'It is the Spirit who gives life; the flesh profits nothing'* (Jn.6:63).

The foremost system used in mystical religious experience is that of meditation, whether in the religions of the East or in the Christian mystical tradition. However, the meditation techniques of East and West are very different from the meditation which is prescribed by God in the Bible. For the mystic, the ultimate goal which he seeks through techniques and systems of meditation is an ego-dissolving 'union with the Divine' — an experience which we shall be discussing in some detail in the next section. The ever-present goal of the true Christian, rather than attempting to become *'oned with God'* in this mystical manner, is to glorify God (1 Cor.6:19-20), obey His commandments (Jn.10:27; Acts 5:29; Phil.2:12-13), and follow the guidance of the Holy Spirit (Jn.16:13; 1 Cor.2:10-13). The use of techniques to achieve spiritual goals must surely have no place in the Christian's earthly pilgrimage.

Is it really conceivable that Jesus, Peter, Paul and John ever encouraged new converts to practise rhythmic breathing, systems of mind concentration or repetitive chants to block the mind from interfering with their spiritual achievements? True Christian meditation is based on a study of the Bible which is both devotional and discursive, and, secondly, is centred on the contemplation of the wonders of God's creation and His relationship with His people. The greatest examples of such meditation occur in the Psalms, where David and others meditate not only on the glory of the Lord (Ps.63:5-6; 104:34) and the wonder of His works (Ps.143:5) but also the Scriptures themselves. *'How I love Your law!'*, says David, *'It is my meditation all the day'* (Ps.119:97; cf. Jos.1:8). In a further example of biblical meditation, we are told that *'Isaac went out to meditate in the field in the evening'* (Gen.24:63). There is no evidence whatsoever that Isaac was here practising a Yogic type of meditation. The Hebrew word which is translated here as 'meditate' is said to be

> 'used of silent meditation on God's works (Ps.77:12) and God's word (Ps.119:15,23,27,48,78,97,148). In the second instance it is used of rehearsing aloud God's works (1 Chr.16:9; Ps.105:2; 143:5)'.[125]

To sum up: The true pathway of meditation for the Christian involves constant prayer (1 Th.5:17; Eph.6:18) and study of the deep truths of the Bible — especially the redemptive work of God throughout the history of His creation. It is our place to glorify God rather than to seek the attainment of 'God-Realisation' through meditative techniques. Christian meditation is the rational contemplation of objective truths; whereas mystic meditation is the irrational arousal of subjective feelings. It is not by following the systems of human devising that we find spiritual salvation; but through faith, and a subsequent obedience to the commandments of Christ (Jn.14:15; 15:10).

---

[125] R. Laird Harris, G.L. Archer & B.K. Waltke, *Theological Wordbook of the Old Testament* (Moody Press, 1980), Vol.II, pp.875-876.

3. Attainment of 'God-Consciousness': The Essential Lie

Having examined the first two tenets of all forms of mysticism — that all people have a spark of divinity indwelling them, and that they must first perform some spiritual exercises in order to 'awaken' this inner divinity — we now come to the third of the leading tenets: That the spiritual work which the mystic must perform is to achieve ecstatic union with God. Again, this is based on a fundamental error. Not only is it erroneous for the mystic to imagine that the use of meditation techniques will bring him true spiritual advancement, but he is also profoundly mistaken in the object of that advancement, which is union with God, an absorption into the Divine, so that one actually becomes God — often known in mystic circles as 'God-realisation'.

As we have already shown, there is not a single verse in the Bible which states that each human being is Divine by nature, or has a 'Divine spark' which can be tapped into through certain techniques. The only place where it is said that man can be *'as God'* is the occasion when Satan spoke to Eve about what would happen when she followed him (Gen.3:5). Neither is there a solitary reference advising us to seek an ecstatic union with God in order to experience divinity. It is most important that we distinguish here between the identification of the Christian believer with God which is portrayed in Scripture and the ecstatic union with the Divine which is the aim of the mystics of both East and West. When the mystic speaks of 'union with God', he is referring to an experience which he seeks to undergo through ever-deeper meditation practice, which he hopes will eventually put him in touch with the divine spark which he believes lives at the heart of his being. In the reckoning of the mystic, this is an experience which is open to anyone of any religious belief-system. As William Johnston claims:

> 'In the mystical life one passes from one layer to the next in an inner or downward journey to the core of the personality where dwells the great mystery called God — God who cannot be known directly, cannot be seen (for no man has ever seen God) and who dwells in thick darkness. This is the never-ending journey which is recognizable in the mysticism of all the great religions. It is a journey towards union because the consciousness gradually expands and integrates data from the so-called unconscious while the whole personality is absorbed into the great mystery of God'.[126]

We see here that union with the Divine is viewed by the mystic as *'an inner or downward journey'* which can be made by anyone in the world at any point in history, regardless of their religious affiliation, and always in the same direction: *'to the core of the personality where dwells the great mystery called God'*. The search for union with God thus becomes the search for union with the 'Self' which lies at the core of the individual personality. And it is at this point that we can see the similarity between the Christian mystics and those of the East; for in

---

[126] William Johnston, *The Inner Eye of Love: Mysticism and Religion* (Collins/Fount, 1981), p.127.

the Mandukya Upanishad of Hinduism it is clearly shown that the Divine is identified with the individuated Self. In his book on mysticism, the philosopher W.T. Stace frankly admits that *'the Christian [mystical] experience is basically the same as that which is described in the Mandukya Upanishad'*.[127] And when union with this Self/god is achieved, the result is enlightenment for the Hindu, and 'deification' for the followers of the pseudo-Dionysius. For the mystic, therefore, union with God is essentially an ecstatic religious experience — a uniting of the Self and the Divine Essence — which is brought into being through consciousness-altering techniques and exercises. In the East, those exercises are called Yoga; among Christian mystics, as we have seen, meditation exercises similar to those of the yogi are used.

Over against the mystical view of achieving union with God, the biblical view is entirely different. It is true that the Apostle Peter used the phrase *'partakers of the divine nature'* (2 Pet.1:4); but this was addressed to believers in the Lord Jesus Christ rather than to the whole human race, and besides, as Thomas Watson (d.1689) points out, this partaking in the divine nature *'is not by identity or union with the divine essence, but by a transformation into the divine likeness'*.[128] Likewise, A.A. Hodge (1823-1886) states that *'this union does not involve any mysterious confusion of the person of Christ with the persons of his people'*.[129] Similarly, Augustus Strong (1836-1921) asserts that the nature of the union of the believer with Christ is not *'a union of essence, which destroys the distinct personality and subsistence of either Christ or the human spirit — as held by many of the mystics'*.[130] As Robert Dabney (1820-1898) has rightly pointed out, the Christian believer, after he or she has been indwelt by the Holy Spirit, is

> 'still a separate person, a responsible free agent, and a man, not a God. The idea of a personal or substantial union would imply the deification of man, which is profane and unmeaning'.[131]

In a compelling section on 'Union with Christ' in his Systematic Theology lectures, A.H. Strong shows that the union of the believer with Christ is

> '*An organic union*,— in which we become members of Christ and partakers of his humanity...*A vital union*,— in which Christ's life becomes the dominating principle within us...*A spiritual union*,— that is, a union whose source and author is the Holy Spirit...*An indissoluble union*,— that is, a union which, consistently with Christ's promise and grace, can never be dissolved (Mt.28:20; Jn.10:28; Rom.8:5,39; 1 Th.4:14,17)...*An inscrutable union*,— mystical, however, only in the sense of surpassing in its intimacy and value any other union of souls which we know (Eph.5:32; Col.1:27).[132]

---

[127] W.T. Stace, *Mysticism and Philosophy* (Collins, 1960), p.100.
[128] Thomas Watson, *A Body of Divinity* (Banner of Truth, 1968), p.46.
[129] Archibald A. Hodge, *Outlines of Theology* (Thomas Nelson, 1879), p.483.
[130] Augustus H. Strong, *Systematic Theology* (Pickering Inglis, 1981, f.p.1907), p.799.
[131] Robert L. Dabney, *Systematic Theology* (Banner of Truth, 1985, fp.1871), p.615.

The true nature of the union of the believer with God is brought out in numerous Scriptures which show that Christ, through His Holy Spirit, indwells all true believers in order to bring about a radical transformation so that they can be *'renewed in knowledge according to the image of Him who created [us]'* (Col.3:10). This is a renewal in influence *not* in essence, as John reveals it to be an *'anointing from the Holy One'* (1 Jn.2:20), an act which comes from a transcendent God restoring us to the spiritual state in which we were at the beginning of history, only this time without the potential for a Fall (Ps.37:23-24; 1 Pet.1:5). Such transformational work in believers is being undertaken so that they shall be once more in His likeness, having divine qualities, being *'partakers of His holiness'* (Heb.12:10), and renewed in the spirit of their minds, in righteousness and true holiness (Eph.4:23-24).

Having said all this, it is important to stress that a genuinely mystical change does take place at the most radical level within the person when he or she becomes united with Christ. It is an unfortunate fact that the erroneous writings and experiences of the mystics and charismatic sects throughout the history of the Church have tended to engender a knee-jerk reaction among many believers, leading to what can be a very superficial view of the indwelling Holy Spirit, so that this becomes little more than a benign influence in the life of the Christian. George Smeaton highlights this reactionary problem when he writes:

> 'Divines sometimes hesitate to accept the idea of inhabitation [by the Spirit] in the full sense of the term, lest they should seem to fall into excess or to adopt the language of the enthusiasts. We are as fully [aware] as they can be to the duty of speaking with sobriety and caution, when we recall the language of the mystics of medieval times and the extravagances of the heady high-minded sects of the time of Cromwell, which produced a recoil from the Scripture doctrine of the Spirit, from which many have not recovered to this day. But we ought equally to be on our guard against the opposite extreme of erring by defect, lest we obscure or misrepresent the supernatural work of the Holy Spirit'.[133]

So we must not let a reaction against the mystics — whether Montanist, medieval or modern charismatic — intimidate us into quenching the Spirit or lessening the intensity and immediacy of the relationship which the believer has with Christ. For, as A.H. Strong puts it:

> 'It is this [union with Christ] and this only which constitutes him a Christian, and which makes possible a Christian church. We may, indeed, be thus united to Christ without being fully conscious of the real nature of our relation to him...Christ and the believer have the same life. They are not separate persons linked together by some temporary bond of friendship,—they are united by a tie as close and indissoluble

[132] A.H. Strong, op. cit., pp.800-801.

[133] George Smeaton, *The Doctrine of the Holy Spirit* (Banner of Truth, 1974), pp.231-232.

> as if the same blood ran in their veins. Yet the Christian may never have suspected how intimate a union he has with his Saviour; and the first understanding of this truth may be the gateway through which he passes into a holier and happier stage of the Christian life'.[134]

However, although this is so very true, and worthy of our meditation, the entire idea of an *essential* union with Divinity and the *accomplishment of perfection* during this earthly life are completely erroneous mystical concepts for which there is not a shred of evidence in the Bible. So, when it is said that *'Christians of the "twice-born" type (especially evangelical Protestants) have often been strongly anti-mystical'*,[135] we can perhaps now understand the reasons for this. The 'twice-born' type of Christian has no need to experience a monistic absorption into the 'immanent energies' of Deity. He is far too sensitive to the fact that union with God is an **ongoing vital reality** in the life of the believer, rather than a moment or series of moments to be achieved through meditation techniques. The 'twice-born' Christian is too keenly aware of the *awe*-ful transcendence of God the Creator and his own place of servanthood, to seek an essential union with divinity. He is too conscious of his own sin and imperfection to aspire to such a lofty station. He is also too well-versed in the truths of Scripture to imagine that the indwelling Holy Spirit, which he has received by faith as a gift from God, is some universal divine spark which can be kindled into flame by his own efforts so that he can experience 'God-consciousness'. Above all, the 'twice-born' Christian is painfully aware of the fact that the original Fall of Man, which gave rise to the need for a Saviour in the first place, was rooted in a positive response to the demonic promise, *'You will be like God'* (Gen.3:5). And it is in response to that same perpetual promise that the so-called mystics through the ages have been propagating that original Fall and the same initiation into satanic practice which was a radical part of it.

Finally, the mystical idea that human beings have to go in search of God through the labyrinths of the mind, in order to climb some 'mountain of perfection' and achieve 'God-consciousness', is a complete inversion of the pathway of true religion. We do not need to first ascend into heaven and bring Christ down to us from above (see Rom.10:6); for God *has already come down to us and dwelt among us*, full of grace and truth (Jn.1:14). He calls upon us simply to *'repent, and believe in the Gospel'* which He proclaims (Mk.1:15). It is these facts that we are challenged to respond to and grasp wholeheartedly. If we confess with our mouths the truth about the Lord Jesus and believe in our hearts that God has raised Him from the dead, we will be saved (Rom.10:9). This is no mere superficial assent — it involves the dynamic, life-changing acceptance of the way that God has graciously provided, because He knows only too well the sheer depravity of human nature and that no one is capable of any spiritual achievement without Him (Jn.15:5).

---

[134] Augustus H. Strong, op. cit., p.802.

[135] H.P. Owen, 'Christian Mysticism', in *Religious Studies*, 1971, pp.40f. Quoted in Geoffrey Parrinder, *Mysticism in the World's religions* (Sheldon Press, 1976), p.154.

III. THE ORIGINS OF CHRISTIAN MYSTICISM

Having looked at some of the key errors of mysticism in its broadest sense, we will now turn to examine the origins of mysticism in the Church. We will follow two tracks in our analysis: first, we will trace the movement of Eastern philosophy into the mainstream of professing Christianity; then we will examine the growth of Christian monasticism in the mystical scene.

1. How the East Came West

At the beginning of this chapter, we looked at the manner in which Christianity became corrupted by mysticism through Neoplatonism, which all happened as a result of one man putting a false name to a document so that it would appear to have been written in the Apostolic era by a Pauline convert. Is it not extraordinary that people who claim to be serious about religion and the pursuit of divine knowledge should be so happy to ground themselves in such a spurious treatise? Could any genuine Christian development have come about through such dishonest means? Surely this just proves that those who are willing to accept these documents as valid religious material are merely seeking a crutch to support their own preconceived ideas, rather than believe the objective truths which reflect divine revelation. It would seem that with mysticism we are in the same world as that of the Gnostic, who writes pseudo-gospels, hoping to pass them off as inspired works of Holy Scripture. In fact, Gnosticism and Mysticism (whether Christian or otherwise) are merely two different words to describe the same essential influence — both being derived from 'the ancient religion'. This is fully understood by all Eastern mystics and occultists. For example, when discussing the progress of mystical-occultism through the historic march of Christianity, theosophist Annie Besant identified two chief components: Gnosticism and Christian mysticism. She writes:

> 'Two streams may nevertheless be tracked through Christendom, streams which had as their source the vanished mysteries. One was the stream of mystic learning, flowing from the Wisdom, *the Gnosis*, imparted in the Mysteries; the other was the stream of *mystic contemplation*, equally part of the Gnosis, leading to the ecstasy, to spiritual vision'.[136] [emphasis added]

However, although the Neoplatonic stream of mysticism was to continue to be the official standard-bearer of mystical-occult *gnosis* in Christianity through the centuries to the present time, the actual tradition of Gnosticism — the Mystery Religions — went underground. So, while the *gnosis* was shrouded in a secret wave of esoteric societies for centuries (before being revealed within the last hundred years through the modern theosophists), *the initiation into Satan's religious experience was brought right into the midst of the Church by the mystics* — a very cunning move on the part of Satan.

Exactly where does the Christian mystical tradition find its roots in the

---

[136] Annie Besant, *Esoteric Christianity* (Theosophical Publishing House, 1901), p.80.

religious experience of the East? It all began with Pythagoras (581-497 B.C.) who founded an occult mystery school in Crotona, Southern Italy, around 530 B.C., of the same type as the mystical cult-societies associated with the name of Orpheus.[137] Here, he trained initiates until the community was disbanded in the fifth century B.C. Although little survives of his written output, Pythagoras is believed to have visited India, where he underwent an 'initiation' and developed many of his spiritual ideas, including the theories of the transmigration of souls, the kinship of all living things and various ritual rules of abstinence.[138] One researcher states that *'what Pythagoras taught was that the truth of the human was an occult self'*.[139] We have already discussed, earlier in the chapter, the idea of a hidden (divine) self which is awaiting to be 'discovered'.[140] This is a fundamental concept of Eastern philosophy, and it is widely recognised that Pytharoras's doctrine of reincarnation was directly *'borrowed from Hinduism'*.[141] Likewise, with great similarity to the Gnostics, Pythagoras encouraged *'study aimed at purifying the soul and releasing it from "entombment" in successive bodies'*;[142] and the way of life in his 'school' was one *'in which union or likeness with God is to be sought through knowledge'*.[143] Knowledge, of course, in this context, means the *gnosis*.

A century or so later, the philosopher Plato (427-347 B.C.), heavily influenced by the mystical mathematician, was the natural successor to the Pythagorean Mysteries. From there such esoteric knowledge passed to the Neoplatonists alongside other syncretic thought-systems. The esoteric nature of this transfer of mystery *gnosis* is brought out by the occultist Rudolf Steiner with the following disclosure:

> 'Plato's later disciples, the Neoplatonists, credit him with a secret doctrine which he imparted only to those who were worthy, and then under the "seal of secrecy". His teaching was looked upon as secret in the same sense as the wisdom of the Mysteries'.[144]

The links between Neoplatonism and Eastern mysticism could not be clearer. Indeed, as the *Encyclopaedia Britannica* reveals:

> 'The most striking similarity of Greek and Indian thought is the resemblance between the system of mystical gnosis (esoteric knowledge) described in the *Enneads* of the Neoplatonic philosopher Plotinus (3rd century AD) and that of the *Yoga-sutras* attributed to Patanjali, an Indian religious teacher sometimes dated in the second century A.D. The Patanjali text is the older, and influence must be suspected...'.[145]

---

[137] *Chambers's Encyclopaedia* (George Newnes, 1963), Vol.XI, p.392.

[138] Magnus Magnusson (ed.), *Chambers Biographical Dictionary* (W. & R. Chambers, 1990), p.1202.

[139] Mircea Eliade (ed.), *Encyclopedia of Religion* (Collier Macmillan, 1987), Vol.XII, p.114.

[140] See pp.345-346.

[141] John Ferguson, op. cit., p.152.

[142] *The Macmillan Encyclopedia* (Macmillan, 1988), p.1005.

[143] *Chambers's Encyclopaedia* (George Newnes, 1963), Vol.XI, p.392.

[144] Rudolf Steiner, *Christianity as Mystical Fact* (Rudolf Steiner Press, 1972), p.47.

It was through such Neoplatonists as Plotinus (A.D. 205-270, Iamblichus (died *c.* A.D. 330) and Proclus (A.D. 410-485), that the Hindu-Buddhist Pythagorean occult-mystical legacy would have worked itself into the writings of pseudo-Dionysius in the late fifth or early sixth centuries. It is these teachings which gave rise to the *Mystica Theologia*, **not** the doctrines of the Bible. However, it was not until the ninth century that these pseudo-Dionysian works were translated into Latin for the first time by John Scotus Erigena (*c.*810-877), a philosopher and theologian whose major work, 'De Divisione Naturae' (*c.*865),

> 'tried to fuse Christian and Neoplatonic doctrines...but his work was later condemned for its pantheistic tendencies and eventually placed on the Index [of Prohibited Books] by Gregory XIII in 1685'.[146]

Erigena's translations into Latin made pseudo-Dionysius's works accessible to the vast array of medieval mystics who were to follow. Thomas Aquinas, the Victorines of the Abbey of St. Victor, Meister Eckhart, Johann Tauler, the author of *The Cloud of Unknowing*, John of the Cross, Teresa of Avila — all these drank in some way from the fountain of Neoplatonism, either directly or indirectly. We make no judgement about the spiritual status or eternal destiny of these men and women. It is their teachings with which we take issue. Nevertheless, a full grasp of the importance of the transmission of such writings as those of the unidentified pseudo-Dionysius is vital if the *occult significance* of the mystical succession is to be understood. The modern mystics and Neo-Gnostics are themselves only too well aware of the shrouded 'initiatory' role that lies behind the ancient mystical concept which advocates an absorption into God-consciousness. This is especially brought out in the lectures of Rudolf Steiner when he states:

> 'The Christian-mystical initiation was given to the West in the form in which it flowed from the Initiator, the "Unknown One from the Highlands", to St. Victor, Meister Eckhart, Tauler, etc.'.[147]

It is intriguing to ponder on the identity of this mysterious 'Initiator', this 'Unknown One from the Highlands', whose initiation flowed to the later Christian mystics. Could it have been this pseudo-Dionysius, whose work was to lay the foundations for an occult initiation disguised behind the trappings of Christian-sounding words and phrases? Readers may remember our disclosure in Chapter Three that the mystical pantheistic teachings of Eckhart and Tauler formed one of four significant streams which had flowed through the Europe of the sixteenth century to create the Gnostic manifestation of Rosicrucianism, the fount of twentieth century Neo-Gnosticism. Eckhart and Tauler had received their mystical teaching via the Erigena translations of the *Mystica Theologia* by pseudo-Dionysius. It is now beginning to emerge that a Mystery-Occult tradition

---

[145] *Encyclopaedia Britannica*, Vol.XX, fifteenth ed., p.524.

[146] Magnus Magnusson (ed.), *Chambers Biographical Dictionary* (Chambers, 1990), p.484. According to tradition, after he became Abbott of Malmesbury, Erigena was stabbed to death by his scholars with their pens 'for trying to make them think'!

[147] Robert A. McDermott (ed.), *The Essential Steiner* (Harper & Row, 1984), p.20.

stretching back to ancient Hinduism via pseudo-Dionysius, Neoplatonism and Pythagoras — coupled with other intermediate occult inputs — has, through the canonised mystics, become an official part of the teachings of the Roman Catholic Church. Occultists are only too well aware of this phenomenon. The theosophist Annie Besant brings home the full implications of this, when she writes:

> 'You must not limit your thought on religion to the few hundred years since the Reformation, to the minority of Christians that you find in the so-called Protestant communities. You must take a larger view than that: go back over the whole of Christian antiquity and further back still over the ancient religions of the East, and then you will find that identity of knowledge which is the mark of reality, which is the keynote of Mysticism.
>
> 'And so you find the existence of a Path and a method declared by which the supreme knowledge may be gained. The Roman Catholic has always kept a knowledge of that Path and he calls the end of it by a startling name. Generally the word Union is used, but take up some great book of Roman Catholic theology and you will find the startling word which I have in mind; they call it 'Deification', the deification of man, man become God, for nothing less is meant by 'Deification'. And the Hindu and the Buddhist call it 'Liberation', the setting free of the human spirit from the bonds which have tied him down, from the matter which has blinded him. The meaning is the same, the method the same, the thing the same.[148]

For these reasons, all occultists and Neo-Gnostics regard the Vatican as the standard-bearer of the ancient *gnosis* through its contemplative mysticism. Because they mistakenly confuse Roman Catholic religion with Christianity, they conclude that there is no difference between the experience of the Eastern mystic and that of his Christian counterpart. As the well-known occultist and author, Paul Brunton, writes in his book *The Secret Path*:

> 'What the advanced Indian Yogi experiences as *Nirvana* is substantially the same condition as what the advanced Christian mystic experiences as God. If either, in recording or describing this sublime state, tacks onto it theological or local doctrines peculiar to his race or land, we must ascribe these accretions to their true source: the personal prejudices or mental bias of the seer, and not to the illumination itself'.[149]

We can now see how religious syncretism has been a natural child of mysticism. For a similarity between Eastern mysticism and Christianity can only be claimed *at the level of mystical experience*, which is the common denominator in all the world religions.[150] Christian mysticism is not only *derived* from oriental

---

[148] Annie Besant, *Mysticism* (Theosophical Publishing House, 1914), p.15.

[149] Paul Brunton, *The Secret Path* (Rider, 1934), pp.134-135.

[150] Not including Christianity, which is *not* a religion, as we will learn in Chapter 12.

religious practices and experiences, but it has also been the *carrier* of the *gnosis* within the Church for many centuries — the fruits of which will be shown in the final chapter when we examine the growth of religious syncretism and universalism.

2. Christian Monasticism: The Alternative Church Movement

In this second section of our examination of the true source of Christian mysticism, it will help our overview of the origins of Christian mysticism if we look at the way that monastic practice has developed within the Christian Church. For it is through the offices of the monastery and convent that mystical practice has been able to obtain an influential, international foothold in the midst of the professing Church. Indeed, more than this, the founding of Christian monasticism has practically provided an alternative to the manner in which the true Church should be established on earth.

From the time of the coming of Jesus Christ, monasticism was totally unheard of in the Christian Church until the so-called 'desert fathers', e.g., Antony the Hermit and Pachomius, set up their hermitages in the desert areas and waste places of Northern Egypt around A.D. 300. From that time until the sixth century, others followed suit in Palestine and Syria — of which the pseudo-Dionysius who wrote the *Mystica Theologia* will have been a prime example. It should be said that the process of adopting the permanent lifestyle of a hermit in order to further one's spiritual development has no foundation in Scripture. Although some may point to certain characters in the Bible who appear to have led a monastic type of lifestyle, closer examination of the circumstances and nature of their calling removes any support for the practice of monasticism. In just the same way that at special times in history, the Lord has suspended His natural laws of the universe to enact a sign-miracle to herald something of vital importance, so He has also ordained selected people to live on the hinterland of worldly life, in order to deliver special messages on spiritual matters of pressing importance in redemptive-historical terms. Elijah in the Old Testament and his New Testament counterpart, John the Baptist, are two cases that spring easily to mind — both of whom were deliberately linked by Jesus in Mt.17:10-13.

The fact that an ascetic, hermit-like existence has been the ordained lot of some of God's people prior to the beginning of the Gospel Age does not mean that such a life is advocated for others. On the contrary, a definitive statement of the Triune Godhead at the very start of human history states: *'It is not good that man should be alone'* (Gen.2:18). The Christian is one who should readily seek active fellowship with other believers (Heb.10:25a; cf. Jude 19). However, this does not mean that there will never be times when one should retire into seclusion for a while for replenishment and recreation. After the Apostle Paul underwent a most profound conversion experience and change of life, he went to sojourn in what he refers to as 'Arabia' for three years before launching out with the Gospel into the nations of the world (Gal.1:17-18). Why did he spend this time in Arabia? As Professor Richard Longenecker writes:

'Many have supposed that it was for the purpose of missionary outreach. But it could just as well be argued that it was principally for solitude to rethink his life and learning from the perspective of Christ's revelatory encounter, away from Jewish jurisdiction and pressures'.[151]

Such temporary retreat from the world may well be beneficial for those who have an important and responsible office to take up in the Church. Indeed, John Calvin writes about Augustine showing that a monasticism existed in the early church which *'supplied the clergy for the church'* — thus forming a vital part of a man's preparation to the work of the ministry, rather than cultivating it as a way of life separated from the life of the true Church.[152] But it is plain that this practice degenerated into a wholly indulgent eremetism, reclusion and wilderness-living, wherein the monastic life became an end in itself. As Calvin rightly observed, in relation to the monks of his own day,

'Our monks are not content with that piety to which Christ enjoins his followers to attend with unremitting zeal. Instead, they dream up some new sort of piety to meditate upon in order to become more perfect than all other people'.[153]

So what could have motivated the 'desert fathers' to become lifelong hermits in the Egyptian wilderness? Egypt, of course, had been no stranger to mystical orders in the first few centuries A.D. Many of these were monastic. The syncretic 'Hermetica' and the Gnostics, for example, were well-established there with their sorcery and initiation ceremonies. The words 'monk' and 'monastic' are derived from the Greek word *monachos*, meaning 'solitary' or 'single one' — a word which is frequently used in the Gnostic Gospel of Thomas to describe a Gnostic. The infiltration of the Church with Gnostic doctrine — itself a derivative of the religions of the Orient — has been traced back to Simon Magus, the sorcerer who crossed swords with the Apostle Peter in Acts 8:9-24. This meeting can be considered to be a landmark of some significance in the process of Church history: Peter the Apostle — ordained by God, on whose confession of Christ the Church was founded (Mt.16:15-19) — being confronted by Simon Magus, the originator of 'Christian' Gnosticism, a child of Satan who was blasphemously called by people *'the great power of God'* (Acts 8:10).[154]

---

[151] Richard N. Longenecker, *Word biblical Commentary: Galatians* (Word Books, 1990), Vol.41, p.34.

[152] F.L. Battles (trans.), *Calvin: Institutes of the Christian Religion*, [IV.xiii.8] (Westminster Press, 1960), Vol.II, pp.1261-1262.

[153] Ibid., p.1265 [IV.xiii.10].

[154] There are great similarities between the life and workings of Simon Magus and the legend of Faust. Dr. Georg Faust was evidently a real character who came from Knittlingden, studied in Cracow and died in 1540. He had a reputation for eccentric scholarship, miraculous powers, was a homosexual, and was described by Lutheran reformer Philip Melanchthon (1497-1560) as *'a sewer filled with devils'* (J. Ferguson, op. cit., p.59). The *Hastings Bible Dictionary* lists the resemblances between Faust's life and that of Simon Magus as being: 1) The relationship with a woman partner called Helena; 2) The

Although it is only foreshadowed in the Bible, Simon Magus is reputed to have become one of the prime spiritual counterfeiters of the age. Irenaeus (*c.* A.D. 130-200), in his great anti-gnostic work 'Against Heresies', tellingly reveals the background and elementary tactic of this Simon and of all heretics when he discloses that

> 'All who in any way adulterate the truth, and damage the preaching of the Church...are disciples and successors of Simon the sorcerer of Samaria. Although in order to seduce others they profess not their master's name, yet they teach his opinion. Holding forth the Name of Christ Jesus as an allurement, while in various ways they bring in Simon's impiety, they destroy many, by the good Name foully corrupting their views, and by the sweetness and glory of that Name holding out to them the bitter and malignant venom of the Serpent, the beginner of apostasy'.[155]

With this in mind, it must surely be relevant to learn that the monastery run by Pachomius (*c.* A.D. 290-346), one of the first of the so-called 'desert fathers', was within sight of the cliff where the second century Gnostic pseudo-gospels were found at Nag Hammadi in 1945. Moreover the scholar Frederick Wisse has suggested that this very monastery *'may have included the Nag Hammadi texts within their devotional library'.*[156] This could well provide yet another important background feature — alongside the parallel influence of Neoplatonism — to the Christian mystic's notion of finding the Light/God within. The Gnostic Gospel of Philip, for example, claims that the person who achieves 'gnosis' is *'no longer a Christian, but a Christ'.*[157] Similarly, according to Hippolytus of Rome (*c.* AD 170 – *c.* 236), Simon Magus claimed *'that each human being is a dwelling place, and that in him dwells an infinite power...the root of the universe'.*[158]

It is beginning to come clear that the monasticism which travelled under the label of Christianity in the desert places of Egypt was not a natural outgrowth of the true Gospel. Neither did it develop in a vacuum. It was merely imitating the prevailing occult-mysticism of the surrounding area. The Gnostics and Neo-Gnostics reject gross matter as being the product of the Fall and turn inwards to change their own consciousness. In the same way, the monastic and reclusive 'Christian' mystics are also indulging in a similar gnostic activity by withdrawing from the material world in favour of isolation and navel-contemplation. One of the Nag Hammadi Gnostic texts, *Zostrianos*, provides a formula for the monk/initiate to achieve union with the divine:

---

name Faustus (Simon, in the Gnostic Clementine Homilies, changes himself into someone called Faustus); 3) The idea of the homunculous; 4) The fact that in Simon Magus himself there is more than a hint of Mephistopheles.

155 John Keble (trans.), *The Five Books of St. Irenaeus Against Heresies,* I.xxvii.4 (A.D. Innes, 1893), pp.79-80.

156 Elaine Pagels, *The Gnostic Gospels* (Weidenfeld & Nicholson, 1979), p.120.

157 R. McL. Wilson (ed.), *The Gospel of Philip*, 67:26-27 (Mowbrays, 1962), p.43.

158 Quoted in Elaine Pagels, op. cit., pp.134-135.

> 'First, he had to remove from himself physical desires, probably by ascetic practices. Second, he had to reduce "chaos in mind", stilling his mind with meditation. Then, [the author of *Zostrianos*] says, "After I set myself straight, I saw the perfect child" — a vision of the divine presence'.[159]

This Gnostic prescription is a carbon copy of Eastern mystical techniques for spiritual 'advancement', and a summation of those practised within the cloisters of the Christian monastic movement. Another contributory factor for our consideration is that for some time prior to the establishment of the 'Christian' monastic life in the Egyptian desert in the third century, Buddhist missionaries had been proselytising a short distance away in the city of Alexandria.[160] So the twin influences of Buddhism and syncretic Gnosticism flourished in this heretically-fertile area, providing the perfect bedrock for the monachism of those 'desert fathers' who have subsequently been canonised by the Vatican.

Another major influential grouping in Northern Egypt, the mystical-occult sect known as the *Therapeutae*, flourished near Alexandria during the first three centuries A.D., having also absorbed a good number of their spiritual twins from Palestine, the Essenes, who had faded out towards the end of the first century.[161] It is highly likely that these Essene-reinforced *Therapeutae* — having also made an important contribution to the regional Gnosticism — had a great influence on early monastic Christianity. Many of the Essenes, after their demise, had simply blended into the new Christian scene, presumably taking their influences with them and contributing to the burgeoning gnostic syncretism in the early Church. It is not at all inconceivable that such mystical groupings as the Essenes and *Therapeutae* were the intended recipients of Paul's warnings about mysticism in his letter to the church at Colossae (Col.2:8-10,15-23).

There can be little doubt that the 'desert fathers', the founders of monastic, mystical Christianity, rather than being influenced by the true Gospel and the need to proclaim it openly in the world, were swayed not only by Gnosticism but also by the Essene-*Therapeutae* way of life, coupled with an infusion of Eastern mysticism with its withdrawal from the world, rigid asceticism and search for spiritual perfection. This is not to say that all the mystics and monastics in the Christian Church have been followers of Satan. On the contrary, many were clearly devout men and women who lived exemplary lives which were committed to the care of others. Antony the Hermit (*c*.251 – 356), who could be described as *the* original 'desert father', had a profound effect on Athanasius (*c*.296 – 373) who wrote a biography of the man, and both men championed the faith against the Arian heresy of the time.[162] But the syncretic influences which these hermits had imbibed paved a crooked pathway for others to follow and led them into a way of

---

[159] Ibid., p.135.

[160] Ibid., p.xxi.

[161] *Chambers's Enclopaedia*, op. cit., Vol.V, p.395.

[162] Indeed, it is said that when he was 104 years old, Antony journeyed to Alexandria specifically to dispute with the Arians there.

life which is not compatible with the will of Christ, who specifically prayed to the Father that He should not take His disciples out of this world (Jn.17:15). The deluded escapism of the monastic life could not be more clearly encapsulated than in this anecdote concerning Arsenius, one of the 'desert fathers':

> 'When Abba Arsenius was in the palace, he prayed to God and said, "O Lord, direct me how to live", and a voice came to him, saying, "Arsenius, flee from men and thou shall live". And when Arsenius was living the ascetic life in the monastery, he prayed to God the same prayer, and again he heard a voice saying to him, "Arsenius, flee, keep silence and lead a life of silent contemplation, for these are the fundamental causes which prevent a man from committing sin"'.[163]

According to the Bible, these are not at all the fundamental causes which prevent a person from committing sin. Yet this anecdote has been hailed as the essential paradigm for all monasticism! Simply hiding away from the world as a hermit — even if you hive off up the tallest pole imaginable — does not solve the root problem of sin, which does not disappear merely through a reduction of the external opportunities available. The only remedy for sin lies in Jesus Christ, who *'has appeared to put away sin by the sacrifice of Himself'* (Heb.9:26). Believers are no longer under the dominion of sin (Rom.6:14) and, *'having become slaves of God, you have your fruit to holiness, and the end, everlasting life'* (Rom.6:22). The Christian will certainly have problems with 'the flesh', but nevertheless we are to live in the world, relying on the Lord and His grace for our sanctification, rather than the *'fuge, tace, quiesce'* ('flight, silence and contemplation') of the mystics and monastics. How often has it been true that the monastic lifestyle has inculcated *'unbridled self-mortification for its own sake, competitive fasting, an "orgy of the supernatural"'*.[164] The comments of a nineteenth century Anglican Bishop of Bristol ably sum up the folly of the monastic life in relation to true Christian spirituality. Building his case to highlight *'the follies and extravagances which were the natural fruits of the eremetical and monastic modes of life'* and *'the mischievous consequences of setting up any one mode of life as pre-eminently pure and holy'*, he shows that

> 'These speculative notions, [which were] originally derived from the Platonic School, no sooner gained a footing in the Church than they were reduced to practice. Men began to affect a life of solitude and contemplation, and to deem all intercourse with the world a positive hindrance to the attainment of that spiritual elevation at which the Christian ought to aim. Overlooking the clear intimations supplied by the constitution of their nature, that man is designed for society — overlooking the express declarations of Scripture and the example of

---

[163] E. Wallis Budge (trans.), 'The Paradise of the Fathers' (London, 1907), Vol.II, §3. Quoted in Thomas Merton, *Contemplation in a World of Action* (George Allen & Unwin, 1980), p.273.

[164] Donald Attwater, op. cit., p.47.

our Blessed Lord, whose ministry was one continued course of active benevolence — they took Elias and the Baptist for their models, without reflecting for a moment either upon the peculiar circumstances in which those holy men were placed, or the peculiar objects which they were appointed to accomplish. Thus...they succeeded in persuading themselves and others that they were treading the path which leads to Christian perfection, and pursuing the course most pleasing in the sight of God — that they were the especial objects of His regard, were holding habitual intercourse with Him, and enjoying a foretaste of that ineffable bliss which would be their portion, when removed from this world of sin and misery to His immediate presence'.[165]

Like all other mystical sects in the history of Christianity, the early Christian monastics simply continued an occultic succession which goes back to the antiquities of the East and beyond — right back to Eden, in fact. Clothing the pious spiritual deadwood of the past in the trappings of Christianity, and even using the name of Christ Himself to support their cause, it was a skilful way of perpetuating the war against the genuine Gospel of truth. Such a phenomenon is at the heart of the spiritual battle in the Church today. When the occultist and Gnostic psychologist, C.G. Jung, in the twentieth century, predicted that *'the West will produce its own Yoga, and it will be on the basis laid down by Christianity'*,[166] he was already well behind the times. The subtle synthesis of Christianity and yoga had already been fused many centuries earlier during the first few millennia A.D., through the compound influence of the Essenes, the Therapeutae, the Gnostics, the Neoplatonists, the 'desert fathers', pseudo-Dionysius, the Victorines, the Hesychasts, the medieval mystics, and all the rest who teach a system of sanctification derived from the Eastern religions.

Moreover, monasticism brings into the Christian arena a religious system which is in direct opposition to the biblical way that the Gospel should permeate the world — namely, through active, localised cells of Christians who live and work in the community and who meet together for worship and instruction. That is what *ecclesia* is all about. It is through local churches that Christianity is meant to flourish. Monasteries bring in an alternative which has its roots in the religions of the East rather than in the pages of the Bible.

IV. COMPARISON OF CHRISTIANITY AND MYSTICISM

As we draw to the close of our analysis of mysticism, we shall conduct a brief comparison of mysticism with biblical Christianity. First, we will discover whether or not Jesus and His Apostles indulged in a mystical form of Christianity or practised Eastern yoga. Second, we will find out if the Bible in general teaches mysticism. Third, we will expose the dark, primitive root of all mysticism.

---

[165] John, Bishop of Bristol, *The Ecclesiastical History of the Second and Third Centuries* (Griffith, Farran, Okeden & Welsh, 1825), p.211.

[166] Quoted in Ursula King, *Towards a New Mysticism: Teilhard de Chardin and World Religions* (Collins, 1980), p.222.

1. The Benchmark Question: Were Jesus and the Apostles Mystics?

The decisive question in discovering the truth about mysticism is this: Did the Lord Jesus or His Apostles lead a contemplative lifestyle and advocate mystical techniques and practices? The answer must surely be in the negative. The ascetic withdrawal from the world had been a way of life among the heathen nations for millennia prior to the coming of Christ; but there is not a single verse of Scripture which could lead one to view Jesus as advocating a life of contemplative mysticism. He was ever in the public eye, rubbing shoulders with crowds of ordinary people, aware of His need to work incessantly in the world (Jn.9:4-5), which even kept Him from His food (Mk.3:20) and exhausted Him to sleep (Mk.4:38).

Our Lord did, however, often retire from the glare of public life for a brief time to replenish Himself and commune with the Father (Mt.14:23; Mk.1:35; 6:46; Lk.6:12). This should be an example to each one of us. One may well need to withdraw from the 'hubbub of Vanity Fair' to spend time in devotion, prayer and Bible study, seeking the continual infilling of the Spirit. However, we should always bear in mind that our work, like that of the Lord Jesus Himself, is centred on proclaiming salvation to a needy world into which we have been sent (Jn.17:14-19; Mt.28:18ff.).

The accent on relentless spiritual work in the outside world rather than occult teachers peddling secret doctrines is equally present in the lives of the Apostles. There is not even the faintest hint of the world of the mystics and contemplatives in their lives. For example, when Paul was waiting in Athens to be joined by Silas and Timothy, he did not spend his time hiving off to a desert place or holing himself up in a secret society (Acts 17:15-34). Instead, because *'his spirit was provoked within him when he saw that the city was given over to idols'* (Acts 17:16), he spent the entire time preaching the Gospel in the market-place. In other words, he contended for the true faith with other human beings, rather than practising the syncretic mysticism which abounded in the Near East at that time, or trying to forge an inclusivist ecumenical-interfaith dialogue with the spiritual leaders of the Grecian capital! Indeed, throughout the entire output of Paul's breathless testimony to the churches as recorded in Acts or in the Epistles, he never once refers to the necessity to practise asceticism or permanent withdrawal from the world in the Christian walk. 'The Way', as Christianity had come to be nicknamed by its followers (Acts 9:2; 19:23; 24:22), had no place for such superficially religious egotism.

It is also often claimed by occultists, Gnostics and Neo-Gnostics that Jesus was a kind of Guru (teacher) like those of India who have been flooding the West throughout the past century. There are a great many reasons why this cannot be so. A primary hallmark of all Gurus is that they have always been initiated by another Guru into the 'secret path', whom they clearly acknowledge to be their master whenever they are involved in teaching. Jesus specifically repudiated the revering of any teacher other than God Himself (Mt.23:8-10). Eastern mysticism also stipulates that certain practices must be undertaken in order to attain spiritual perfection. But this too is foreign to the life and teachings of Jesus. For example,

B.K.S. Iyengar, in his classic work on Yoga, claims that: *'In course of time, the practitioner of Yoga has to adopt a vegetarian diet, in order to attain one-pointed attention and spiritual evolution'.*[167] That Jesus was no vegetarian is a well-attested fact (Mk.6:32-44; Mt.26:17-19), but far more important is Jesus' declaration that a person is defiled by what comes **out** of his mouth rather than what goes into it (Mt.15:11).

In noticeable contrast to the spiritually-elitist Gurus of the East and Mystery Initiators, who hole out in their 'ashrams' and temples, Jesus deliberately sought out the company of sinners and the common people (Mt.9:10-11). He also said, concerning the true spiritual pathway: *'Narrow is the gate and difficult is the way which leads to life'* (Mt.7:14), whereas the mystics of the East say: *'The Great Way is gateless, approached in a thousand ways. Once past this checkpoint you stride through the universe'.*[168] Or, they assure us that *'the Way is broad, reaching left as well as right'.*[169] Or, again, they sweetly say, *'The path to bliss is straight and wide'.*[170] In complete contrast with these recipes for spiritual attainment from the Satan-inspired mystic Gurus, the Lord of the universe said, *'Enter by the narrow gate; for wide is the gate and broad is the way that leads to destruction'* (Mt.7:13; cf. Num.20:17). It cannot be stressed enough: although it is indeed possible to find apparent similarities between certain teachings of Jesus and those of other cults and religions, it is in the differences that the truth shines through.

On the question of whether or not Jesus was an occult teacher who gave out secret doctrines, we have His own testimony on the matter. When questioned by the High Priest about His disciples and His doctrine, He simply said: *'I spoke openly to the world. I always taught in synagogues and in the temple, where the Jews always meet, and in secret I have said nothing'* (Jn.18:20). Even more pointedly, He specifically stated to the twelve apostles when He sent them out on a mission to potentially hostile towns:

> 'Therefore do not fear them. For there is nothing covered that will not be revealed, and hidden that will not be known. Whatever I tell you in the dark, speak in the light; and what you hear in the ear, preach on the housetops' (Mt.10:26-27).

In a marvellous Trinitarian statement, the Son had made a similar pre-incarnation pronouncement through Isaiah when He said:

> 'Come near to Me, hear this: I have not spoken in secret from the beginning; from the time that it was, I was there. And now the LORD God and His Spirit have sent Me' (Isa.48:16).

In the same vein, again emphasising the wonderful openness of the work and

---

[167] B.K.S. Iyengar, *The Concise Light on Yoga* (George Allen & Unwin, 1980), p.25.

[168] Katsuki Sekida (trans. & ed.), *Mumonkan and Hekiganroku: Two Zen Classics* (Weatherhill, 1977), p.26.

[169] D.C. Lau (trans.), *Lao Tzu: Tao Te Ching* (Penguin, 1963), p.93.

[170] Jhan Robbins & David Fisher, *Tranquillity Without Pills: All About Transcendental Meditation* (Souvenir Press, 1973), p.29.

Gospel of Jesus Christ, the Apostle Paul told King Agrippa:

> 'For the king, before whom I speak freely, knows these things; for I am convinced that none of these things escaped his attention, since *this thing was not done in a corner*' (Acts 26:26). [emphasis added]

There are no secret doctrines in Christianity. The true Church does not act in a corner but in the full light of day. It is certainly true that the revelation of Jesus Christ was *'the mystery which was kept secret since the world began'*; but it has now *'been made manifest, and by the prophetic Scriptures has been made known to all nations'* (Rom.16:25-26; cf. Mt.13:35). Of course, there are many things which the Lord has not yet revealed to us. But He reveals them when the time is right and not before — His time, not ours (Dt.29:29). As Jesus said to His disciples, *'I still have many things to say to you, but you cannot bear them now'* (Jn.16:12). God's timing, not ours.

The teachings of Jesus and His Gospel were never secret doctrines. When the Lord wants us to know something, He tells us loud and clear: *'Write the vision and make it plain on tablets, that he may run who reads it'* (Hab.2:2; cf. Isa.45:19). For the mystics and esotericists to claim that the spiritual pathway must be hidden in secret teachings is a clear contradiction of Scripture. For if the Gospel is veiled, *'it is veiled to those who are perishing'* (2 Cor.4:3). But the glaring truth is that *'when one turns to the Lord, the veil is taken away'* (2 Cor.3:16). This is why Jesus said that the spiritual understanding of the *'mysteries of the kingdom of heaven'* is restricted to those who have become truly spiritual (Mt.13:11; cf.1 Cor.2:6-16). Pearls should never be cast before swine to be merely trampled underfoot (Mt.7:6). Although the mystics and Neo-Gnostics will point to these verses to support their assertion that Jesus was an occult Master who revealed selected exoteric teachings to the common people in the form of parables, while reserving the real esoteric doctrine for the initiated inner circle (Mt.13:9-17; Mk.4:11-12), they fail to grasp the important fact that for the believer the revelation of true doctrine is imparted by the Spirit rather than through the initiation rites of human origin. Only those who have their ears and eyes opened by the Lord will truly understand and respond to the Gospel. The truth is stated openly but will only be understood by those who have ears to hear. This is not occultism — it is the mystery of election and the sovereign grace of God, which defies the wisdom of the theosophists.

2. Does The Bible Teach Mysticism?

As in all heresies, there is a partial truth in the theology and practice of the Christian mystics. Without an appearance of truth and a superficial similarity to the real thing, no heresy could ever begin to establish itself. For example, the mystic claims that we have to suppress the 'self' in a 'Cloud of Forgetting' in order to reach the goal of union with God. We have already shown that true union with God is an ongoing reality in the Christian life rather than a single, higher, sought-after experience enjoyed in the hot flush of ecstasy after prolonged meditation and other consciousness-altering techniques. However, in regard to the idea of suppressing the 'self' in a so-called 'Cloud of Forgetting', there is a biblical sense in which this is true, but it has been stretched well beyond its bounds in the cloisters of Christian monachism. This has occurred through an over-literal interpretation of a handful of Scriptures coupled with the ascetic influences of Oriental, Hellenist and Gnostic philosophies — all having a superficial resemblance to the true holiness of Christianity but, in reality, being radically different. In this respect, the core teaching of Jesus which has been seized upon by the ascetics and mystics is: *'If anyone desires to come after Me, let him deny himself, and take up his cross and follow Me'* (Mt.16:24). The mystics interpret this command to deny self as referring to asceticism, navel-gazing, self-torture and suppression of individuality in order to achieve their ultimate goal of ecstatic union with Christ in this earthly life. Not only is this a complete misunderstanding of the requirements of discipleship, it is, ironically, a harbinger of extreme egocentricity.

The denial of self to which Jesus is referring is the cutting off of the 'old man' — the mortification of those works of the flesh which manifest in sinful conduct. As Paul exhorts the Ephesian church: *'put off concerning the former manner of life the old man, which is corrupt according to the deceitful lusts'* (Eph.4:22). As he writes elsewhere: *'Even though our outward man is perishing, yet the inward man is being renewed day by day'* (2 Cor.4:16; cf. Rom.12:2). As William Hendriksen puts it:

> 'To deny oneself means to renounce the old self, the self as it is apart from regenerating grace. A person who denies himself gives up all reliance on whatever he is by nature, and depends for salvation on God alone. He no longer seeks to promote his own predominantly selfish interests but has become wrapped up in the cause of promoting the glory of God in his own and in every life, and also in every sphere of endeavour'.[171]

The denial of the self is not an abandonment of the ego, or an annihilation of the personality, or a fusing of the soul with the 'Universal Spirit' of God. It does not involve suppression of one's individuality but a complete renewal of it. Jesus both acknowledged and encouraged individuality, as He demonstrated by His differing approaches to human circumstances of apparent similarity. For instance, some whom He healed were told to tell no one (Mt.8:4), while others were not; a rich man is told to sell all that he has (Mt.19:21), while others are allowed to retain some or all of their possessions (Lk.19:8; Mt.27:57). It is worth noting here that Jesus did not lay down a 'rule of poverty' as a condition of true discipleship, as shown by the fact that some of His disciples who possessed property were not required to give it up (e.g., Mt.26:1-13; Lk.19:1-10). The fact that a rich man is described by Jesus as being unable to get into heaven (Mt.19:24) has not so much to do with his actual wealth but with his relationship to it. Jesus shows that things need abandoning only when they interfere with our spiritual progress (cf. Mt.5:29-30).

---

[171] William Hendriksen, *The Gospel of Matthew* (Banner of Truth, 1973), p.656.

Christian self-denial is a surrendering to God of the will, not the abandonment of one's individuality. Denying ourselves does not mean that we must be merged into the essence of God; but that we must follow in Jesus' footsteps, in imitation of Him (1 Cor.11:1). His own life provides a model of self-denial in order to do the will of God. As He said Himself, *'My food is to do the will of Him who sent Me, and to finish His work'* (Jn.4:34), *'For I have come down from heaven, not to do My own will, but the will of Him who sent Me'* (Jn.6:38). And in Gethsemene, to the Father who sent Him, He said, *'Nevertheless, not as I will, but as You will'* (Mt.26:39). If there is such a thing as true Christian mysticism, it is this: the alignment of the human will with the will of God, to be *'crucified with Christ'* (Gal.2:20), the perishing of the old self and its renewal through the inward regenerating work of the Holy Spirit whereby the believer can say: *'I live'* — 'I still am an individual person with all my individual character traits and personality' — *'yet no longer I, but Christ lives in me'* — 'in spite of my individuality, I and Christ are in union' (cf. Jn.14:23) — *'and the life which I now live in the flesh I live by the faith of the Son of God, who loved me, and gave himself for me'* — 'and this union that I have with Him is rooted in His sacrificial death' (Gal.2:20). This is the great mystical fact of the Christian life. The indissoluble union of the believer with Christ. It is not an experience of ecstasy or personal perfection, attained through a system of meditation or an ascetic lifestyle; but it is the natural fruit of the Spirit in the life of all those who come to Christ through repentance and faith.

3. Back to the Garden: The Primitive Roots of Mysticism

As we have already stated, one of the core teachings of occult mysticism is that there is an esoteric body of truth hidden behind the exoteric doctrine of the Bible — a 'secret ladder of wisdom' by which any would-be mystics of East or West can ascend to an ecstatic union with God. The mystics of the East claim that the Bible which Christians have today is merely a collection of spiritual superficialities to provide secure anchors for the great mass of common people, while those chosen for 'higher' knowledge and spiritual development find their succour in the deeper mysteries and secrets which have been handed down through the ages in initiatory groups. In this respect, the Christian mystics — although retaining a professed adherence to the Bible — have aligned themselves with the Eastern mystics and occultists through their addition of new teachings which are a radical departure from the teachings of Scripture. The *Mystica Theologia* of pseudo-Dionysius is a classic example of this, taking its impetus from Neoplatonist doctrine rather than that of the Bible.

The question must here be asked: What is the true origin of this idea of a secret doctrine or esoteric knowledge through which one can supposedly achieve wisdom and union with Deity? What is at the root of the widespread development of the doctrine of the universal 'Inner Light' or 'God within'? Professor Ferguson, Dean of the Open University and an ardent advocate of mysticism, lists five generalised points which one can identify in any manifestation of mysticism. When we read these, we will see clearly the true origins of all mystical endeavour. He writes:

> 'First, mystics believe that there is an Ultimate Being, a dimension of existence beyond that experienced through the senses...[which] is often, though not invariably, conceived in personal terms and called God...Second, mystics claim that the Ultimate can in some sense be known or apprehended...Third, the soul perceives the Ultimate through inward sense...Fourthly, it would be widely held by mystics that there is an element in the soul akin to the Ultimate, a divine spark...a holy spirit within. In this way to find God is to find one's true self ...Fifth, mysticism has as its zenith the experience of union with the Ultimate...The mystic seeks to pass out of all that is merely phenomenal, out of all lower forms of reality, to become Being itself'.[172]

We can see from this description of mysticism, first, that God is reduced to a pantheistic *'dimension of existence'* beyond the normal senses, although this is sometimes called 'God' for convenience; second, that there is an element of this divinity, a divine spark, a *'holy spirit within'* all people; third, that it is possible to tap into this 'inwardly' so that one is absorbed into it, and can even become that 'Ultimate Being' oneself; fourth, the relegation of this life to a *'lower form of reality'*, something *'merely phenomenal'*. Finally, notice also the idolatrous and even blasphemous assertion that *'to find God is to find one's true self'*.[173] Although Professor Ferguson will certainly not have intended it to be received in this way, we have here a summation of all the characteristics of false religion which were initiated into humanity through the Fall which was engendered by Satan — that we can be like God and that we can attain a wisdom beyond that with which we have been endowed by creation (Gen.3:4-6).

The mystic seeks to attain an ecstatic oneness with the cosmos and a mystical union with the Supreme Being, Universal Spirit, or whatever he or she may believe that to be. In mystical belief, the different names that man has invented for the gods and goddesses of his many religions are merely varying cultural expressions of the same essential 'Ground of Being' with which the mystic seeks to achieve an identification. Among mystics, there exists the belief that there is a common body of knowledge running through all the religions and cults of the world — a 'secret wisdom tradition' which contains instructions on how to achieve the ultimate *gnosis*. We have touched on these matters so many times throughout this book; indeed, they form the very foundation of our thesis. For the teaching that all people have a spark of God unconditionally indwelling them is among the greatest of Satan's many strategies in these last days, being an original part of the 'Satanic Initiation' into which our first parents entered at the beginning of human history when the serpent said, *'your eyes will be opened, and you*

---

[172] John Ferguson, *An Illustrated Encyclopaedia of Mysticism and Mystery Religions* (Thames & Hudson, 1976), p.127.

[173] What a supreme irony it is that religious people everywhere seek to equate themselves with God, yet, when the only One who can truly claim to be God comes to earth as 'Saviour of the world', they muster all the forces available to them in order to kill Him (see e.g., Jn.8:58-59; 10:30-33)!

will be like God' (Gen.3:5). This was the knowledge which was *'desirable to make one wise'* (Gen.3:6) — the clear implication being that there was some hidden knowledge which would give access to superhuman, godlike wisdom. The teachings of the mystics and occultists throughout the ages echo precisely this principle. They, like our first parents at the dawn of human history, are too impatient to wait for the Lord to lead them into the ripeness of wisdom, *as He would give it* — preferring instead the quickening of occult *gnosis*. However, in the midst of this supreme folly, human beings from our first parents onwards have deliberately chosen to ignore the stark fact that

> 'the inward, hidden content of God's mind can become the possession of man only through a voluntary disclosure on God's part. God must come to us before we can go to him'.[174]

Instead, in a fundamental misunderstanding of the holy life, these men and women in the world of mysticism, seeking the enhancement of mind and spirit through methods not revealed to us in the Word of God, would utilise such techniques to aid their spiritual development and growth in wisdom. The author of the *Cloud of Unknowing* actually calls his techniques *'spiritual dodges'*.[175] The true believer does not need to use these humanistic 'dodges' to make headway in his or her spiritual growth. Prayer (us speaking to God), the devotional study of Scripture (God speaking to us) and a willingness to be led by the Holy Spirit, are the only methods prescribed by the Bible as aids to Christian progress.

Within the verses of Scripture which depict the Fall of humanity we have the root of all occultism, mysticism, sorcery, ungodliness and sin — which is lawlessness. The mysticism of this ages-old satanic 'wisdom' has been passed down through the ancient religious doctrines of the East, through all the other cults offering 'mystery *gnosis*' — the Pythagoreans, the Platonists, the Neoplatonists, the Essenes, the Gnostics, and so on — to become what we know today as Christian Mysticism, the brazen act of *'oneing the soul with God'* through the suppression of thought and the exercise of mind-control. If we understand the true nature of this process, we have the key to the whole history of mysticism throughout the ages: the achievement of personal 'divinity' through the acceptance of Luciferic knowledge — the cardinal sin of the universe, the Lie.

CONCLUSION

Readers will by now have grasped the fact that Gnosticism and Mysticism are merely two different words to describe the same influence. They both offer a Satanic Initiation into that original *gnosis* proffered by Satan to our first parents. Now we can understand those words of the theosophist, Annie Besant:

> 'Two streams may nevertheless be tracked through Christendom, streams which had as their source the vanished mysteries. One was the

---

[174] Geerhardus Vos, *biblical Theology: Old and New Testaments* (Banner of Truth, 1975), p.3.

[175] see Clifton Wolters, op. cit., pp.97-100.

> stream of mystic learning, flowing from the Wisdom, *the Gnosis*, imparted in the Mysteries; the other was the stream of *mystic contemplation*, equally part of the Gnosis, leading to the ecstasy, to spiritual vision'.[176] [emphasis added]

In just the same way that the New Gnosticism provides a link to ancient Eastern mysticism and beyond, so Christian mysticism provides a link between the ancient *gnosis* and the Church. Gnosticism, Eastern mysticism and Christian mysticism all share the same characteristics which can be traced back to the spiritual corruption inherent in the original Fall of Man.

As we approach the close of the twentieth century, there is no necessity for the doctrines of demons to infiltrate the Christian Church from without, for the devil saw to it that such practices would already be within and reckoned respectable many years beforehand. Through this subterfuge, with superlative satanic subtlety, that old serpent has fostered the delusion that there is an ancient link between the faith initiated by Christ and all the religions which Satan has inspired on this planet: that all religions, including Christianity, are fundamentally the same.

For those who may believe that these excursions into an examination of Christian mysticism have no relevance today, the seriousness of the matter can be seen in the fact that it is precisely in this area that traditional Roman Catholicism shares so much in common with the religions of the world — especially those of the Orient. And when one considers the frantic moves that are taking place today on the interfaith front, we can perhaps begin to appreciate the significance of the material we have uncovered in terms of religious developments throughout the remainder of this age. As the Jesuit monk, mystic and teacher William Johnston puts it: *'The most profound encounter of world religions takes place at the level of mysticism'*.[177]

Because there has been a huge rise in the popularity of Eastern mystical techniques and systems in the past decade, their many adherents have become aware of the multitude of similarities with the Christian version of mystical practice. The obvious projection which they make from this is that Jesus is just another occult-mystical guru, and the resultant Christianity — which they see enshrined in the practices of Christian mysticism — is just another expression of the 'primitive wisdom' behind all the religions of the world. And when the practices of the Christian mystics are compared to those of the Orient, there is indeed little difference between them. It is for this reason that mysticism, and especially the mystical dimension of prayer and meditation, has come to play such an important role in the development of interfaith dialogue. This dialogue has mainly been forged between the Roman Church and various Eastern mystical traditions. But when the true teachings of the Bible as a whole are compared with those of the religions of the world, an unbridgeable gulf opens up before us.

---

[176] Annie Besant, *Esoteric Christianity* (Theosophical Publishing House, 1901), p.80.

[177] William Johnston, *The Inner Eye of Love: Mysticism and Religion* (Collins/Fount, 1981), p.31.

Apart from the profound biblical and theological ignorance which pervades the world of the Christian mystics, the major reason that they have been so seduced by the mysticism of the Orient is their acute lack of spiritual discernment — most especially in the area of original sin and its subsequent outworkings. One of the leading promoters of mysticism at the present time exemplifies this ignorance in the following statement:

> 'I was educated in a philosophy which taught...that the norm of morality is human nature and that by obeying the fundamental dictates of human nature one's activity is right. Original sin, of course, is there. But it is a wound which weakens, without corrupting human nature. I believe that all the great religions hold ultimately that man's basic nature is good since at the core of his being is Brahman or Atman or the Buddha nature or the Holy Spirit'.[178]

Such a syncretist belief in the inherent goodness of Man, and that obedience to 'the fundamental dictates of human nature' makes one's activity right, is the equivalent of handing an open cheque-book to the devil. Theological ignorance, lack of discernment and a hopelessly inadequate understanding of human depravity, are the foremost factors that have led the visible Church into the dire state in which it finds itself today. In the remaining three chapters, we will show the degree to which this ecclesiastical corruption has been effected, and the enormous extent to which mysticism and the *gnosis* have penetrated those organisations claiming to represent the unique cause of Christ.

---

[178] Ibid., p.158.

Chapter Ten

THE GOSPEL OF DARKNESS

Church Seduction in the New Age

'Thus says the LORD: "Stand in the ways and see, and ask for the old paths, where the good way is, and walk in it; then you will find rest for your souls. But they said, 'We will not walk in it.'" (Jeremiah 6:16)

'For the pastors have become stupid, and have not sought the LORD: therefore they shall not prosper and all their flocks shall be scattered' (Jeremiah10:21)

In the last chapter, we looked at the manner in which Mysticism, old and new, has come to exercise such a hold over large sections of the Church. This has especially been the case with the 'mainline' denominations. We now turn to examine the extent to which the New Gnosticism has come to wield a similarly powerful influence in such professing Church circles. In order to illustrate this, we will concentrate on the infiltration of 'New Age' thinking into the Church of England during the past couple of decades, through the pervasive influences of three representative ministries.

An event which gives us important insights into this development occurred in November 1989 when Dr. Robert Runcie, the then Archbishop of Canterbury, addressed the *Senior Evangelical Anglican Clergy Congress* at the Swanwick Conference Centre in Derbyshire. Among the subjects he covered was the relationship between the Church and the New Age Movement. Dr. Runcie himself had been personally criticised by evangelical ministers for allowing an interfaith festival with New Age overtones to be held at Canterbury Cathedral earlier that year. He was now taking the opportunity to clear the air and defuse the objections of his critics on this issue. In the faithful manner of diplomacy, Dr. Runcie made certain noises about the Movement *'not according with the Christian way'*. However, although such statements may serve to placate the less discerning among his flock, Dr. Runcie's overriding message was one of appeasement and highly skilful subtlety, as he endeavoured to defuse any challenge to his authority while attempting to hold all the diverse elements of Anglicanism in unity.

However, Dr. Runcie, as an *episkopos* — **the** *arch-episkopos* — of the established Church in England, not only failed to give the lead on this issue, but he deliberately ignored the extent to which his own denomination, in common with all the other mainline denominations, is actually a harbinger of the New Gnosticism within the Church. There are two principal elements in Dr. Runcie's speech which demonstrate this: First, he said that to speak about the New Age Movement too precisely would give it *'a coherence which it does not possess'*. And he went on to say: *'Indeed, it would be difficult to condemn it since there is scarcely an identifiable "it" to condemn'*. Second, he concluded with the recommendation that *'a spirit of engagement [with the New Age Movement] rather than of condemnation will serve us best'*.

Now, the first statement is categorically untrue. The New Age Movement as a major spearhead of Neo-Gnosticism is, in its widest sense, a somewhat amorphous body; but — as we have already shown in earlier chapters — a large part of it is highly organised and deliberately moving towards a number of very specific goals. The second statement cuts right across the thrust of the true Church, which has never dealt with false doctrine in a mere *'spirit of engagement'*. Such 'engagement' is the way that the 'establishment' Churches have generally attempted to deal with these problems (e.g., the *homousios* party in the Arian controversy at the Council of Nicea in A.D.325), but it is not the biblical way.

Michael S. Northcott, lecturer in Christian Ethics and Practical Theology at New College in Edinburgh, takes a similar line to that of Dr. Runcie when he writes in his monograph, 'The New Age and Pastoral Theology': *'The Church, far from rejecting the New Age in paranoia, should rather embrace its agenda'*.[1] Here he is using one of the oldest ploys in the book: throw out one extreme (which, in any case, is a caricature) and then replace it with another. He is engendering a false 'either-or' situation; you have two choices: you can either reject the New Gnosticism out of paranoia, or you can embrace its agenda. What nonsense! Although it is true that we must be prepared to engage with unbelievers in a firm but compassionate dialogue which is overtly evangelistic, this does not mean that there will be no condemnation of antichristian teachings. One would have to be completely ignorant of the New Age agenda in order to imagine that one could embrace it without violating the Word of God.

The Christian is called to judge between true and false doctrine, and to make such judgements plain. He is to turn away from that which is falsely-called 'knowledge'. But the leaders of denominations such as the Church of England are politicians and diplomats rather than pastors and defenders of the faith. They have gone a-whoring with the religions and cults of the world because they do not know the Scriptures or the power of God. They have failed to preserve the body of teachings enshrined in Christianity which Apostolic decree exhorts us to uphold unswervingly (2 Th.2:15; 1 Tim.6:3,20; 2 Tim.1:13; 2:2; Tit.1:9; Jude 3).

We have already shown in earlier chapters that the New Age Movement is not the amorphous collection of fringe activities that Dr. Runcie would have us believe. It is working with great alacrity through many international bodies and organisations at both governmental and non-governmental levels. Moreover, we

---

[1] Michael S. Northcott, *The New Age and Pastoral Theology: Towards the Resurgence of the Sacred*, Contact Pastoral Monograph No.2, (Contact, 1992), p.31.

can easily prove that as respectable a body as the Church of England is one of the principal collaborators in the dark work of the burgeoning antichristian brotherhood which lies behind the 'mystery of iniquity'. In fact, there are a multitude of Neo-Gnostic practices openly advocated, and thereby officially sanctioned, within the Anglican Church itself.

The fact is that Dr. Runcie, during his time of office, not only played the part of a politician in the classic establishment Church tradition, but he was also a false teacher who allowed Neo-Gnostic ideas to proliferate to a great extent during his time of office. Therefore, rather than being politely entertained at an 'evangelical' conference, he should be exposed as a deceiving figurehead in the professing Church of Christ. Such exposure may seem unnecessary in view of the fact that he has now retired from his Archbishop's post; but, in view of the fact that there has been no appreciable change of direction since his retirement, the contents of this chapter should provide a warning of equal intensity to his successor, Dr. George Carey.

Let us now direct our attention to some of the extensive activities of the New Gnosticism within the Church of England.

THE NEW AGE: ANGLICAN STYLE

We could very easily here show that the so-called New Age Movement now operates in a wide variety of ways throughout the entire international professing Church and has done so on an increasing basis during the past twenty years or so. But our purpose is limited here by our aim to refute Dr. Runcie's hopelessly deficient handling of this issue — especially his professed ignorance of such activities within his own denomination. We have already revealed that the central ethos of this New Age Neo-Gnosticism is the claim that humanity is now poised on the brink of a worldwide 'paradigm shift' or 'quantum leap' of psychic energy which will take the world into a new spiritual and evolutionary dimension, facilitated by explorations of the inner psychic realm through meditation, psychotherapy, and other techniques. This same philosophy is also rapidly finding a foothold within the establishment Church.

The Rt. Rev. Stephen Verney was, until recently, the Anglican Bishop of Repton, with the major responsibility in the Church of England for training clergy *'to take part in the renewal of the Church in the last part of the twentieth century'.*[2] As early as the 1970s, Bishop Verney had written a book entitled 'Into the New Age', in which he perfectly mirrored the Neo-Gnostic 'Hundredth Monkey' philosophy so prevalent in the secular world. He puts it like this:

> 'The human race is approaching *an evolutionary leap forward in the realm of the spirit* and at the same time is being swept towards catastrophe... The new age will have a new style of politics, of education, of medicine, of architecture and city planning, of art, work, leisure, technology, family life, *and religion.* It is already being explored by men and women in all fields, and it is already coming to birth

[2] Stephen Verney, *Into the New Age* (Collins, 1976), p.1.

through their combined endeavours'.[3] [emphasis added]

He then cites — with emphatic approval — four examples of the *'emerging picture of humanity which could guide us into this new age'.* The first entails a conference which asked the question: *'What is Man?'* and which is answered by him in terms with which monists and psychotherapists would be able to identify. The second example he gives of the *'emerging picture of humanity which can guide us into the new age'* is the tale of a young girl who, in a time of crisis, perceived *'that the trees and the grass and the rain were in me, and that nature and me and everyone, including God, were all one'.* This is a textbook example of the unbiblical pantheism which is so characteristic of Neo-Gnosticism. Bishop Verney's third example concerns a Catholic priest who — having written a book about the hidden Christ at the heart of Hinduism — also led a multi-faith conference group (consisting of Hindus, Buddhists, Sikhs, Jews, Christians and Moslems) into recognising *'that each of our six religious traditions contained within itself insights which could develop and grow in the direction he was indicating'* (i.e., a 'holistic' view of life instead of a theocentric one). The fourth example cited by Bishop Verney as an *'emerging picture of humanity which can guide us into the new age'* involves a psychotherapist who, he claims

> 'is so much a man of the new age that he has founded — or rather allowed to come into being and to form itself — the New Era centre, an international group of people who, while continuing to work in the old structure, are exploring the possibilities of living in the *new consciousness*'.[4] [emphasis added]

The New Era Centre has been in the forefront of pioneering New Age activities within a Christian setting. These four examples of the *'emerging consciousness'* of humanity, which have so captured the Bishop's imagination, are the nuts and bolts of the very New Age Movement which Dr. Runcie claimed as being *'incoherent'* and *'scarcely identifiable'.* Yet, these ideas have been masterminded within the ranks of Dr. Runcie's own denomination by both himself and his episcopal peers, and have been so for a number of years — as witnessed by the date of publication of Bishop Verney's book.

It is important to note that through the late 1970s and during the whole of the 1980s, Bishop Verney was vested with the major responsibility in the Church of England for training clergy *'to take part in the renewal of the Church in the last part of the twentieth century'.* That has involved no small influence within the denomination, and has meant that the New Age circus within the Church of England was able to grow with great rapidity. As we shall see, this has not involved a handful of esoteric extremists. All the men who form the subject of this chapter are highly respected and prominent teachers in the Church of England. This is exactly the way in which, according to its own teachers, the Neo-Gnostic's

---

3 Ibid., p.13.

4 Ibid. This, and the above three examples given by Bishop Verney of the *emerging consciousness* which can usher in the New Age appear between pp.35-51 of his book.

conspiratorial dream is destined to unfold. Readers may recall the statement given in an earlier chapter by the occultist Alice B. Bailey of the Lucis Trust that

> 'Very definitely may the assurance be given here, that prior to the coming of the [World Teacher], adjustments will be made so that at the head of all great organisations will be found either a Master, or an initiate who has taken the third initiation. At the head of certain of the great occult groups, of the Freemasons of the world, *and of the various great divisions of the Church*, and resident in many of the great nations will be found initiates or masters'.[5]

The architects of the New Gnosticism are claiming that there are people who have, in some way, been initiated into the occult who are now occupying influential positions in the Church. Indeed, regarding one particular 'Ascended Master', Alice Bailey claims that *'certain great prelates of the Anglican and Catholic Churches are wise agents of His'*.[6] How aware these Church leaders would be of their spiritual sponsorship is a matter for conjecture. The stark significance of these statements will become only too apparent at the conclusion of our study, when we will understand the power which lies behind the activities of Archbishop Runcie, Bishop Verney and the many other Anglican dignitaries whom we will have cause to mention.

There are a great many ways in which the New Gnosticism has manifested itself within the Church over which Dr. Runcie presided. Rather than deal with the plethora of illustrations available, we will confine our study to one example in each of three categories. First, we will look at the way in which forms of Christianised Yoga have taken hold so firmly in the Church of England. Second, we will examine the work of a leading Anglican teacher who has been heavily influenced by Theosophical Mysticism. Third, we will examine a certain Anglican-Episcopalian parish church in London which provides a model of the ultimate New Age church.

1. Christianised Yoga

We have already referred to the increasing use of meditation techniques in the secular world during the past thirty years. This popularity has been paralleled in the Church. It is now very 'chic' in a number of Church circles to hold retreats with multiple 'workshops', where one learns various techniques in meditation and healing which purport to be Christian in origin. An example of this can be seen in a handbook written in 1977 and distributed in Anglican churches entitled *Towards Contemplation: A Practical Introduction for Prayer Groups*, by the Rev. Peter Dodson, the former Anglican vicar of St. Helens in York and a former director of the Northern Office of the Association for Promoting Retreats — an organisation which worked in collaboration with the Roman Catholic Retreat Group and the Methodist Retreat Group. The pamphlet has since been updated, considerably expanded and republished in a one hundred page book by the Society for the

---

5 Ibid., pp.61-62.

6 Ibid., p.57.

Promotion (sic) of Christian Knowledge in 1987 — a book commended by Joyce Huggett *'to anyone who is hungry for God'*.[7]

It is always interesting to discover the source of a teacher's knowledge — especially if he claims to be a Christian teacher. Even more revealing is the account of a person's conversion experience. In his book, 'Contemplating the Word', Peter Dodson gives some intriguing facts about *'what I can only describe as some kind of conversion'*.[8] Apparently, while walking in the hills as a young man serving in the Army, he became aware of a 'presence', as if someone or something was with him. On one occasion, this 'presence' began to take control of his hands and used them to make mysterious gestures over his body. When he sought to understand what was happening to him, he says that the answer came in two stages: *'First, I came to know in my bones that I was being loved better, and secondly, that the regular gestures formed a sign of the cross'*.[9]

He took all this as some kind of religious experience which was designed *'for his healing and restoration'*, and which involved *'the healing power of the cross of Christ'* — a concept which was reinforced by the fact that this 'presence' would stretch out his body as if it was being crucified amidst great pain.[10] The upshot of all this was that he went to see his regimental chaplain who lent him a book which introduced him to the whole realm of Christian mysticism and 'contemplative' meditation. One can only conclude from this account that Peter Dodson was converted to mysticism and contemplation — with its universalism, physical postures and psychological techniques — rather than to the Gospel of biblical Christianity, which speaks of an atoning sacrifice for sin (Mt.20:28; Rom.3:25; Col.1:13-14; Rev.5:9; 7:14), the need for repentance (Mk.1:14-15), the division of society by the Gospel (Lk.12:51), the judgement to come (Jn.5:27-30; Rev.20:4; Heb.9:27), and a kingdom for believers in, and disciples of, the Lord Jesus Christ (Mt.25:31-34).

Amazingly, Peter Dodson brazenly states that one does not need even to believe in God in order to practise his form of religion, citing Anglican liberal Don Cuppitt as an example of such 'Christian atheists' — i.e., those who are attracted to the human being called Jesus Christ but have no time for all this 'God-talk', as he calls it.[11] The Bible, on the other hand, clearly states that *'without faith it is impossible to please Him, for he who comes to God must believe that He is, and that He is a rewarder of those who diligently seek Him'* (Heb.11:6). Peter Dodson then issues the warning that *'the Christian atheist needs to take extra care how he*

---

7 Peter Dodson, *Contemplating the Word: A Practical Handbook* (S.P.C.K., 1987), rear cover.

8 Ibid., p.8.

9 Ibid., p.9.

10 Ibid.

11 Ibid., pp.56, 103-104. He also says that he meets this 'Christian atheism' — the ultimate contradiction in terms — among *'recent post-ordination students'*. A liberal education in an Anglican theological seminary is clearly enough to induce this condition. It is, therefore, hardly surprising that the ministry of the Anglican church has become so apostate in recent years!

or she uses the dangerous tool of contemplation'.[12] Dangerous tool? What kind of Christianity is that? An examination of his writings will provide us with the answer.

In his ten-page booklet, 'Towards Contemplation', Peter Dodson sets out to provide a model for a prayer-group session consisting of a dozen or so people, using a series of techniques and calling itself a *'contemplative prayer exercise'.*[13] It is divided into three parts purporting to deal with the mind, the heart and the will. After bidding its readers to go through a typical yogic pre-meditation relaxation routine: *'Attend to the spine, head, neck, mouth, eyes, forehead, feet, hands, breathing',*[14] the first part of this prayer exercise consists in a classic Christianised auto-hypnotic technique to tranquillise the mind through the repetition of words of Scripture alternating on the inbreath and the outbreath. Peter Dodson explains his technique in this way:

> 'In my experience, the Word of God itself has a power to help us to come to a wonderful point of stillness, using words like those from St. Matthew 11:28 and Ps.46:10: *'Come to ME, all whose work is hard, whose load is heavy; and I will give you rest...' 'Be still and know that I AM God...' 'Come to ME... Be still...and rest...Come...rest... Come...rest'.* We spend just a couple of minutes, allowing those two 'words' to become part of the rhythm of our breathing and of our life; *'Come...*[as we breathe in]*...rest...* [as we breathe out]. *Come...rest... Come...rest'.*[15]

We have here a complete misunderstanding of what the Bible means when it speaks of the Word of God as being *'living and powerful, and sharper than any two-edged sword, piercing even to the division of soul and spirit'* (Heb.4:12). The power of the Word of God does not lie in its ability to bring about tranquillity or ecstasy when repeated hypnotically; that is a Luciferic deception: worse, it is magic — the same magic as that which lies behind the Eastern *mantra* which we examined in the previous chapter. The true power of the Word of God lies in its ability to quicken the dead souls of those chosen by God for new life. *'Faith comes by hearing, and hearing by the word of God'* (Rom.10:17). The way in which Scripture works in a person is by rational, propositional communication, via the mind of the recipient. The quickening of dead souls does not occur as the result of some other sort of magic as distinct from Gnostic magic. It is by rational, objective means. Peter Dodson's 'prayer exercise' then continues with a meditation on Isa.43:1,4: *'You are MINE...You are precious in MY eyes, and honoured, and I love you'.* He then tells his readers:

> 'The spirit and life of those words has the power to give us a renewed awareness of our own immense worth and value, to overcome any

---

[12] Ibid., p.56.

[13] Peter Dodson, *Towards Contemplation* (Sisters of the Love of God Press, 1977), p.8.

[14] Ibid., p.5.

[15] Ibid., p.4.

> negative attitude we may have about ourselves, to heal any inferiority complex. If we dare to take God at his word, we are bound to discover that, deep down, we are precious and highly honoured people — people lovable enough even to die for'.[16]

The group is then recommended to let the words *'You are precious... I love you'* become *'part of the rhythm of our breathing and our life: You are precious [as we breathe in]...and I love you [as we breathe out]... You are precious...and I love you, etc'*.[17]

It is important to realise that those attending Peter Dodson's workshops are not necessarily Christians. Many are probably the sort of people described by him as 'Christian atheists'. Furthermore, these verses of Scripture in Isa.43 never were addressed to every person in the world unconditionally. They were addressed by God specifically to His chosen people Israel, and, by extension (as shown incontrovertibly in Isa.43:7) to the whole of the Lord's elect, including those called into the Church under the New Covenant. Moreover, God does not choose His elect people on the basis of their *'immense worth and value'* (cf. Dt.7:6-7) but simply *'according to His good pleasure which He purposed in Himself'* (Eph.1:5,9). It is not God's intention to soothe any negative image one may have of oneself. He wants us to see ourselves as we really are (as **He** sees us); then, perhaps, He may grant us the gift of repentance .

Peter Dodson is using this exercise as a form of therapy in order to hypnotise (brainwash) people into holding a false image of themselves as being so meritoriously lovable that Jesus died for them. Satan must be very grateful to him for the immense service he is contributing to his cause. The truth of the biblical Word is actually the complete reverse of what Peter Dodson is teaching his helpless retreatants. In countless places in Scripture we learn of people voluntarily recognising their unworthiness before the Lord, rather than mindlessly brain-washing themselves into a carnally-satisfying but spiritually false self-worth.

Was Moses mistaken when, after being empowered by God to deliver the children of Israel from the Egyptians, he expressed only self-doubt and self-depreciation (Ex.3:11; 4:10)? Was that *'mighty man of valour'* Gideon deceived when, after being commissioned by the Angel of the Lord to do battle with the Midianites, he could only mutter about his family being *'poor in Manasseh'* and himself being *'least in my father's house'* (Jdg.6:12-15)? Was Job deluded when, after being confronted by the majesty and power of the Living God, he cried out: *'Behold, I am vile; what shall I answer You?'* (Job.40:4)? Was King David deranged when, after being cursed and insulted by the Benjamite Shimei, he said: *'Let him curse; for so the LORD has ordered him'* (2 Sam.16:11). Was the great prophet Isaiah misguided when, at the sight of the glory of the Lord, he could only say: *'Woe is me, for I am undone! Because I am a man of unclean lips'* (Isa.6:4-5)? Was Paul the Apostle misled when, after being *'caught up to the third heaven'*, receiving visions and revelations and hearing *'inexpressible*

[16] Ibid., p.5.

[17] Ibid.

words', he could only say that he would rather boast of his infirmities and take pleasure in his weaknesses (2 Cor.12:1-10)?

Did all these godly men of the Bible have an inferiority complex — a negative image of themselves which needed straightening out in one of Peter Dodson's therapy sessions? For that is what his 'prayer exercises' are: an eclectic smorgasbord of relaxation therapy, auto-hypnosis and emotional catharsis, hiding behind the respectable cover of Scripture. Herein rests the satanic lie behind all such therapy. For you can be freed from every neurosis under the sun and imagine that God has healed you, yet you will remain the most depraved, hell-bound sinner in the world. The awful truth is that Satan uses the above breed of 'prayer-exercise' to contradict this inescapable fact and to try to prevent people from coming to the only Physician given by God who can truly heal us and in the only manner prescribed by Him for it: true repentance and faith in the atoning sacrifice of the Lord Jesus Christ. It is only by His stripes (His sacrificial death, Isa.53:5-6) that we can be healed (receive forgiveness of our sin, 1 Pet.2:24-25).

This fashion in Anglican retreats and prayer groups of snuffing out the mind with word-repetition and breathing techniques has its roots wholly in Eastern meditation. We have already shown in the previous chapter how the osmosis of oriental mysticism into the Church came initially through the Neo-Platonism of the fifth century Syrian monk, pseudo-Dionysius, who passed himself off as living in the Apostolic era and wrote a treatise which claimed to be addressed to Paul's helper, Timothy. Then, passing through the Hesychasts and medieval mystics, this essentially Eastern doctrine became established as the mystical wing of the Roman Catholic Church and other denominations which developed a mystical tradition.

Today, these exercises and practices do not need to infiltrate the Christian Church from without, for the devil saw to it that such practices would already be within it and reckoned respectable many years beforehand. Through this subterfuge, with superb subtlety, that old serpent has fostered the delusion that there is an ancient link between the faith initiated by Christ and all the religions which Lucifer has inspired on this planet: that all religions, including Christianity, are fundamentally the same. Peter Dodson is fully aware of this link, although he does not see anything sinister in it. But he does feel the need to advise the leaders of Christian meditation retreats to keep quiet about the relationship between Eastern meditation and that advocated by Christians today. He says:

> 'It is, however, unwise for the leader to refer too much to, say, Buddhist or Hindu meditative disciplines, or to use the foreign words and phrases associated with them. I have learned to 'button my lip' about matters relating to Eastern religions other than Christian, mainly because some Christians are doubtful about Eastern styles of meditation but also because there is really no need to refer to them. *The valuable things they have to offer have, in recent years, been well and truly incorporated into Western Christian thinking and practice*'.[18] [emphasis added]

[18] Peter Dodson, *Contemplating the Word*, p.40.

It is for this reason that Peter Dodson, and the many other meditation gurus in his church circles, can get away with such rank deception. For such exercises now have a respectable pedigree in many of the churches today. When Bishop Stephen Verney, in his book 'Into the New Age', advises that if we want to become aware of the presence of God, *'we need some kind of aid or focal point'*,[19] what profundity does he recommend to us for this mighty task? None other than the universal Christianised 'mantra' which has been the focal point of satanic influence in the Church for centuries. He writes:

> 'An example of such a focal point is the 'Jesus Prayer' which is taught in the Orthodox Church, and which consists in saying again and again one simple phrase *'Jesus, have mercy'*. As this phrase is repeated the mind grows still around it. Many people combine it with breathing slowly in and out', etc., etc.[20]

All this is just as the occultist and Gnostic psychologist, C.G. Jung, predicted some fifty years ago: *'the West will produce its own Yoga, and it will be on the basis laid down by Christianity'*.[21] Thus, a mystical activity which has its roots in Hindu and Tantric occultism and its fulfilment today in the rituals of the New Gnosticism, is now practised in an increasing number of church halls and Retreat Centres across the country.

2. Gnostic Mysticism

Our next excursion into the infiltration of the Anglican Church by New Age concepts and practices involves a somewhat different approach. Our subject example here is Dr. Martin Israel, priest-in-charge of Holy Trinity with All Saints Church, London. Dr. Israel is — as the blurb on his book jackets claims — one of the most sought-after healers and counsellors in the country, as well as a renowned leader of retreats. He has managed to dress up just about every possible mark of the New Gnosticism in Christian clothing. To enter one of Dr. Israel's books or attend one of his lectures is indeed a unique experience. It is a world of parapsychology, spiritualism, theosophy, necromancy, universalism, Jungianism, mysticism and syncretism. He has actually blended all these elements with traditional Church doctrine to create his own hybrid religion which — in spite of his protestations — is entirely compatible with the New Gnosis. In order to find one's way around, it is helpful to know the jargon so that these influences can be properly identified.

First, Dr. Israel believes that the sacred history of God's spiritual revelation to humanity has been progressively given in history through what he calls the *'Chinese, Indian and Hebrew dispensations'*, culminating in the Advent of Christ.[22]

---

19 Stephen Verney, op. cit., p.92.

20 Ibid.

21 Quoted in Ursula King, *Towards a New Mysticism: Teilhard de Chardin and World Religions* (Collins, 1980), p.222.

22 Martin Israel, *Coming in Glory: Christ's Presence in the World Today* (Darton, Longman & Todd, 1986), p.11.

Now, it is a major Theosophical teaching, adopted by the New Gnosticism, that the teachers and gurus, ancient and modern, of the religions of these countries have a similar and complementary contribution to make to human spirituality: Taoism, Confucianism, Hinduism, Buddhism, Judaism, Christianity and Islam — all are relevant to the spiritual evolution of mankind. As an illustration of this, the original interfaith 'Temple of Understanding' building which was planned to be erected on the bank of the Potomac River in Washington had six wings, each to be accorded to one of the so-called world faiths: Hinduism, Judaism, Buddhism, Confucianism, Christianity and Islam[23] — all representatives of what Dr. Israel calls the *'Chinese, Indian and Hebrew dispensations'*. Dr. Israel goes on to add credence to his syncretic notion by claiming that, *'we need only think of the amazing spiritual literature of China and India to see how intensely the ardent human soul was infused with the power of God'*.[24] This appears to support the syncretic notion that all religions are of God.

We should remember here that the Lord Jesus Christ clearly pronounced that all those with messianic pretensions who came before Him were *'thieves and robbers'* (Jn.10:8). He also told the Samaritan woman that her fellow-Samaritans worshipped what they did not know and stated that salvation is of the Jews (Jn.4:22).[25] The Apostle Peter declared that apart from the Lord Jesus Christ *'there is no other name under heaven given among men, whereby we must be saved'* (Acts 4:12). Moreover, his fellow-Apostle Paul clearly stated that, at the final judgement, the vengeance of God will be poured out on two categories of people: first, the heathen of all time — described in Scripture as *'those that do not know God'*; second, all those who refuse to believe the gospel in the post-Christ era — described as *'those who do not obey the gospel of our Lord Jesus Christ'* (2 Th.1:8).

Let us not forget that the religious gurus of what Dr. Israel calls the 'Chinese and Indian dispensations' have generally presented themselves as being God-incarnate — a downright blasphemy. Swami Vivekananda, as an example of the religious impulse behind the 'Indian dispensation', *'rejected the Christian idea of sin, and taught that by living a virtuous life you can realise God in yourself'*.[26] As we have already stated elsewhere, the apparent wisdom and devotional aspects of Chinese and Indian spirituality are a mask of devotion and good works, behind which lurk the elementary principles of sorcery and the quest for personal divinity. Indeed, Dr. Israel confirms his adherence to the satanic doctrine of personal divinisation by stating that the purpose of man is *'to realise God in our being'*.[27] This is a typical Gnostic misconception, based on the erroneous notion that a

[23] The original artist's impression of this 'Temple' can be seen on the rear cover of Robert Keith Spenser, *The Cult of the All-Seeing Eye* (The Christian Book Club of America, 1964).

[24] Martin Israel, *Coming in Glory*, op. cit., pp.28-29.

[25] The Samaritans were a syncretic people who had been formed out of the residue of Israelites left in the land after the Assyrian invasion in 721 B.C.

[26] Don Cuppitt, *The Sea of Faith: Christianity in Change* (BBC, 1984), p.175.

[27] Martin Israel, op. cit., p.96.

'spark of divinity' exists within all people — a conceit which we have already shown to be manifestly untrue.[28] The true purpose of man is to *glorify* God *with* our being, not to 'realise God *in* our being'.

One interesting feature of many Christian syncretists and occultists is an alleged disavowal of syncretism and occultism. Consequently, we find in Dr. Israel's works the pretended criticism of *'esoteric cults and gnostic philosophies'*, together with a professed rejection of

> 'a rootless, spineless syncretism that sees all forms as virtually the same and can therefore borrow indiscriminately from them to fashion a hybrid religion'.[29]

However, this stance is inexplicably contradicted throughout his entire output. In one notable example he speaks of his admiration for *'a Benedictine monk who has an ashram in India and has played a notable part in bringing the deeper spirituality of Hinduism into harmony with the Catholic faith'*.[30] He is referring here to one such as Father Bede Griffiths, examined in the previous chapter, who — since the death of Thomas Merton — has probably done more towards creating a syncretic religion than any other man alive today, having established a Hindu-Christian ashram, inaugurated a Hindu-Catholic Eucharist, advocated the mantric repetition of the Jesus Prayer together with the practice of Kundalini Yoga and propagated the notion of a common source of all faiths.

On an eschatological level, Dr. Israel reckons that the Second Coming of Christ *'is as much contingent on our ability to receive him as on the inscrutable will of God'*.[31] This is a contradiction of the Scriptural teaching on this subject. There is a predetermined time for Christ's return and, far from being contingent on the ability of humanity to receive Him, it is ineradicably linked with such things as the times of the Gentiles being fulfilled (Lk.21:24), man's iniquity having reached ripeness for judgement (2 Th.2:1-12; Rev.17 & 18; 20:7-10), and the full number of the elect having been brought in (Rev.6:9-11). The reason that Dr. Israel makes Christ's return dependent on the ability of humanity to receive Him is because it upholds his own unbiblical position of universal salvation. His incredible account of the Parousia is a classic case of 'enfleshing' the teachings of Holy Writ with personal ideas, as these extracts show:

> 'When the cosmic event is at its height, the forces of darkness set on universal destruction evenly balanced by the forces of light intent on a victory for their cause, there will come a moment of dark poignant silence. The minds of all rational creatures will be focused on a point of absolute awareness which will contain nothing. Out of the dark silence there will come a luminous glow that will be intensified rapidly until it becomes a light so radiant that its rays will transfigure all the world.

---

[28] See the section 'The God Within' in Chapter 5.
[29] Ibid., pp.54, 39.
[30] Ibid., p.57.
[31] Ibid., p.viii.

> The Lord will come to claim his own, who are all created things, but now they will be utterly transfigured...
> 'And then all will meet on the summit of the mountain of transfiguration, each bringing their own kind with them in their own heaven. As they reach the top, men of all races and religions will establish their common unity as they have penetrated their own tradition to its heart and attained its summit. They will find that they now speak with one language and know one Christ who is the destination of all the great religions, to whose coming again they had all looked forward according to their own tradition... When this happens, the second great advent leading to the final appearing of the Lord, time will have been lifted up into eternity.
> 'The advent could be very soon, but in fact time is only a symbol of our present incompleteness. When we are ready he will appear as a supreme cosmic event. He will also change the hearts of all from stone to flesh, the flesh of the spiritual body. None will be excluded'.[32]

Needless to say, this science-fiction scenario, far from being a biblical account of Christ's return, is the product of Dr. Israel's imagination, with a smattering of biblical phraseology thrown in for good measure. Yet, this teacher is not on the fringes of the Anglican scene. He is highly esteemed. On the cover of the book from which the above extracts are taken there is a passionate commendation by fellow-Anglican Richard Holloway, Bishop of Edinburgh. But this book could well have been written by Satan himself, for it eliminates a most important aspect of the Second Coming: namely, the Day of Judgement. The reason for this is that Dr. Israel, in his superior reckoning, feels that

> 'the state of heaven has to include everyone, because the absence of even one creature diminishes it, and it is therefore not completely heavenly'.[33]

In spite of the superficial appeal of this sentimental, human viewpoint, it is completely at loggerheads with Jesus' many sobering accounts of *eternal* damnation (e.g., Mk.9:43-49; Mt.13:41-42,49-50; 25:41,46; Jn.3:36; cf. Dan.12:2; Mt.3:12), not to mention the verse in the apocalyptic vision of John which unequivocally states that, at the time of Christ's return, *'anyone not found written in the Book of Life was cast into the lake of fire'* (Rev.20:15). However, Dr. Israel manages to get round this problem by claiming, in another book, that Jesus mellowed after His crucifixion experience, thereby altering His eschatological decrees. He puts it like this:

> 'The man Jesus who uttered the words of terrible judgement when he was alive in the flesh has himself grown to a greater perfection through the experience of suffering and death: Gethsemane and Calvary have opened even his compassion to the full tragedy of the human situation.

---

[32] Ibid., pp.115-116.
[33] Ibid., p.102.

> No one is ultimately beyond healing, so much are we all parts of one body'.[34]

One is forced to ask: from where did Dr. Israel receive this extra-biblical information? Is such doctrinal innovation subject to the disapproval of the overseers of his Church? On the contrary, for the commendatory foreword in this very book is written by none other than Dr. Robert Runcie himself, as it was published as the Archbishop of Canterbury's 1987 Lenten Book! In his foreword, Dr. Runcie writes:

> 'In [this book] Martin Israel shares his wealth of understanding and wisdom. There is penetrating and sensible psychology. There is profound knowledge of the Bible, sensitively applied. There is a powerful style of exposition, the more authoritative for its simplicity'.[35]

In this same book, Dr. Israel significantly refers to the Sovereign Lord as the *'supreme No-Thing'*,[36] a classic term in Zen Buddhism (known as *Mu*, which is Japanese for 'nothing') and in Neo-Platonist writings, as we have already covered in the previous chapter. Other Neo-Gnostic influences visible in Dr. Israel's eclectic writings are evidenced by such vogue phrases as *'the collective unconscious'* (Jungian terminology), *'one-pointed awareness'* (Buddhist terminology), and numerous references to *'a psychic osmosis between the living and the dead'* (spiritualist terminology). If one needs further evidence of New Age influence, in a crowning statement in another of his books (and in flat contradiction to the Scriptural teaching in Heb.9:27 and Ps.78:39), he confesses belief in the evolutionary doctrine of reincarnation when he claims, *'It seems likely that many souls do assume an earthly body on a number of occasions in their spiritual journey'*.[37] Again, we ask, from where does Dr. Israel receive his extra-biblical information? What are the true sources of his unique exposition of the Scriptures? We need not look far for our answer. Neither should we be too surprised. When a book-cover biographical note tells us that Dr. Israel

> 'became increasingly involved in *psychological and spiritual investigation*, that culminated in his ordination to the Anglican priesthood in 1975' [38] [emphasis added],

we may well wonder what form these investigations took. Perhaps it would help if we were also told that Dr. Israel became a leading light in the Churches Fellowship for Spiritual and Psychical Studies — an ecumenical body (with a large Anglican following) exploring the province of psychic phenomena, exorcism, mysticism, necromancy, meditation and spiritual healing.[39] Dr. Israel's

---

[34] Martin Israel, *Gethsemane* (Collins, 1987), p.102.

[35] Ibid., p.9.

[36] Ibid., pp.17, 110.

[37] Martin Israel, *Summons to Life* (Mowbrays, 1974), p.145. Dr. Israel also asserts this fact on his tape 'Communion of Saints' (see below).

[38] Martin Israel, Gethsemane, op. cit., p.1.

[39] Michael Perry, Archdeacon of Durham, is also a leading light in the spiritualist fellow-

work in this field has brought him into contact with many allegedly discarnate beings, which he believes to be the souls of dead people. As he himself puts it:

> 'When the dead come to me — as they do frequently — they come as a shaft of light. They announce themselves to me in pure intelligence and I know them, and I listen to what they say, and what they say is always important. And this is the way in which the risen ones work'.[40]

In other words Dr. Israel is into the Neo-Gnostic practice of 'Channelling'. He claims that the 'communion of saints' is all about psychic communication between the living and the dead as well as with others on the planet — through *'telepathy and other extra-sensory means'*.[41] He believes that the highest Christian service is to pray for deceased war-criminals and others who have committed atrocities (e.g., Hitler) because *'if they are not healed, we will not be healed'*.[42] He claims that such dead people, rather than being in hell — which state he refers to as *'childish make-believe'* — are actually

> 'wandering around in the lower psychic realms, and their fear and evil emanations cause untold damage, not only in their realm but in our realm as well'.[43]

He believes that atrocious crimes committed by people on this earth are instigated through the person *'being infested by the evil thoughts and powers of those on the lower astral'*.[44] Underpinning his whole philosophy is that pervasive universalism. After confessing his belief in individual guardian angels, his counsel to the bereaved is this:

> 'Remember, ultimately the only way in which you move beyond the horror of bereavement is by being involved in the horror of the world. And then your loved ones will help you on the other side to resurrect the world'.[45]

The communion of saints is thus reduced to this: the gradual psychic healing of all creatures — both living and dead — through meditation and psychic communication between mediums and spiritists on the earth, and all those on 'the other side' (i.e., the discarnate dead). Hell, of course, is non-existent. All this is what has been taught by theosophists, spiritists and esotericists down the ages. Such activity, into which Dr. Israel has been completely immersed, is necromancy and is expressly forbidden in Scripture (Dt.18:11-12). As the prophet of old has said:

---

ship to which Dr. Israel belongs. Michael Perry has also written a book called 'Psychic Studies' which is published by the Aquarian Press — a leading New Age publishing house.

[40] From a tape recording of a sermon by Dr. Israel on sale at his church, entitled 'The Communion of Saints'. No date.

[41] Ibid.

[42] Ibid.

[43] Ibid.

[44] Ibid.

[45] Ibid.

> 'And when they say to you, "Seek those who are mediums and wizards, who whisper and mutter," should not a people seek their God? Should they seek the dead on behalf of the living? To the law and to the testimony! If they do not speak according to this word, it is because they have no light in them' (Isa.8:19-20).

In the light of the fact that Dr. Israel receives his primary spiritual communication and doctrinal information from discarnate entities — alleged spirits of the dead — rather than from the infallible Scriptures, which he merely uses in highly cavalier fashion to back up his theosophic ideology, perhaps we can understand the true nature of the source from which his teachings are emanating.

The man whose views we have been examining is not just an ordinary Anglican vicar; he is *'one of the most sought-after healers and counsellors in the country'*, as we are told on the covers of his books. In view of the seriousness of his antibiblical views and practices, does it not seem extraordinary that Dr. Israel is so revered — not only within his own denomination but even in the wider evangelical world? One leading Reformed evangelical journal, which prides itself in upholding biblical Christianity, reviewed his eschatological book *'Coming in Glory'* and warmly commended it for its *'spirituality'*.[46] This verdict on a book which teaches universalism and syncretism is somewhat strange for such a publication: when the blind lead the blind, they will all surely fall in the ditch. It would seem from this that there is great confusion in Christian circles — and even in the evangelical party — concerning the difference between *mysticism* and *spirituality.*

At this point, one may wonder why Dr. Martin Israel should be a minister in the Anglican Church — a denomination with which, at least historically, his views are wholly inconsistent? Perhaps it would help if we knew that, as early as 1963, the name 'Dr. Martin Israel' appeared on the list of British sponsors of the syncretic, interfaith organisation, the 'Temple of Understanding', which is a Non-Governmental Organisation of occult origins operating within the United Nations, and which did a great deal towards the setting-up of the Second Parliament of the World's Religions in 1993.[47] We know that many sponsors on that original 'Temple of Understanding' list were eager to turn the Christian denominations towards religious globalism. We have received personal testimony that a number have deliberately gone into the Church for this express purpose.

Here we are forced to ask a revealing question: could there be any connection here with the claim of the Neo-Gnostics that discarnate entities (which we have already identified as a product of the demonic realm) are ensuring that occult initiates will be in positions of authority and influence in the mainstream denominations in preparation for their coming World Teacher and the associated quantum leap in consciousness? To many, such a suggestion will appear somewhat far-fetched. But we would suggest that they have not properly considered the true

---

[46] Dr. J. Gordon McConville writing in *Evangel*, Winter 1986, published by the evangelical Church of Scotland centre at Rutherford House in Edinburgh.

[47] Taken from an official 1963 compilation of the List of Sponsors of the Temple of Understanding, held in the present writer's possession.

nature of the spiritual warfare in which the Church will continue to be embroiled until the end of the present evil age (Gen.3:15; Mt.10:34-36; Eph.6:10-18; 2 Th.2:3-12; Rev.12:17; etc.).

We are presently on the threshold of the greatest battle the Church has yet faced; and it will take more than a few millennial fantasies to dissolve that monumental fact.

3. The Model New Age Church

The next category of infiltration by the New Age of the Church of England involves the same variety of Neo-Gnosticism as propagated by the highly-organised Centres of Light mentioned in an earlier chapter. For our primary example in this third category of Church of England infiltration by the New Age, we need only nip a stone's throw down the road from Lambeth Palace to the rather lovely, tourist-attracting, Christopher Wren-designed, St. James' Church, Piccadilly. Here we find a classic manifestation of the church in the New Age.

First on offer here is the 'Whole Bookshop', containing a wide selection of New Age books on divination (e.g., numerology, tarot, runestones, I Ching, astrology, etc.), magic, sorcery, theosophy, feminism, yoga, Zen, psychotherapies, the after-life (spiritualist-style), Essenism, holistic health and healing, auto-hypnosis, and so on. The Rector of St. James', Donald Reeves, has allowed his church building to be used by many (mainly non-Christian) individuals, groups and organisations who are busily propagating the global universalism of the New Age. There is a Health and Healing Centre utilising every kind of 'holistic' and occult healing technique available; there are frequent 'workshops' and lectures in all the practices of the New Age, ranging from shamanism, Zen Meditation and Christianised Yoga, to interfaithism, witchcraft, transpersonal psychology, visualisation and prosperity consciousness. As an example of what this Anglican church has to offer, on the very evening that these words are being written, a lecture was given by the co-Principal of the 'School of Channelling', entitled 'Handling Psychic Energy Safely'.[48] Is this an example of what Dr. Runcie called *'a spirit of engagement'* with the New Age? Does the inclusion of this occult lecture in an Anglican church mark what Dr. George Carey — in reference to the 1993 'Parliament of the World's Religions' — described as *'the growth of mutual respect and understanding between different faith communities'*?[49] Does the 'School of Channelling' qualify as a 'faith community'? In view of the fact that the 'Covenant of the Goddess', a witchcraft-based organisation, was amongst the official sponsors of that Parliament, perhaps the expression 'faith community' needs to be redefined!

These workshops and lectures at St. James' Church are organised under the umbrella heading 'Alternatives' — a 'human potential' style programme which was founded in 1982 as 'Turning Points'. Among the stated aims of these sessions are to:

- Create networks of like-minded people.

---

[48] Held at St. James' Church, Monday January 10th 1994.

[49] *The English Churchman*, No.7357, August 20th-27th, 1993, p.1.

- Transform consciousness by providing group experiences.
- Build bridges between radical Christians, Humanists and the New Age.
- Inspire those who are disillusioned by formal religious institutions.
- Offer a gateway to new opportunities of thinking, living, being, exploring.
- Become an institution where 'leading edge' thinkers can commune with their audience and together discover knowledge.[50]

St. James' Church is actually a realistic model of what the coming new church will be. It is *the* church of the New Age. Now we can understand the meaning of the term 'leading edge' — it is the thin end of the wedge of the attempted destruction of the true Gospel of Christ. But how has all this come about? What has led to this Anglican Church being seduced by the New Gnosticism? Surely it cannot have escaped Dr. Runcie's notice that the Rector of St. James' Church was an ardent promoter of the New Age Movement. As early as 1982, Donald Reeves had written in the pioneering New Age journal, *The New Times*, extolling the benefits of the modern religious cults and sects (and what he significantly calls *'the ancient religion'*) over and above his caricature of mainstream Christianity:

> 'The cults and sects and the discovery of the ancient religion offer the possibility of a genuine "religion" experience often under the guidance of a charismatic leader who knows the truth. How far removed from your local vicar struggling to keep together a congregation, and to raise money for old buildings'.[51]

Because he is well-known for his pro-New Age stance even in New Age circles, Donald Reeves was a guest speaker at a conference in October 1985 organised by the Findhorn Foundation — the occult 'Centre of Light' in Morayshire, Scotland.[52] On his return he delivered a sermon in his church concerning his impressions of the community in Findhorn, in which he claimed that

> 'It is largely as a result of our decaying life-denying institutions where the Spirit has been firmly quashed, that places like Findhorn exist. Had we been doing our job I believe that the Church would have been part of the mainstream of the New Age. Therefore it is always in penitence that we approach communities like Findhorn'.[53]

With his analysis of the establishment Church as decaying into a life-denying, Spirit-quashing institution we would most heartily agree! But he has created a false 'either/or' situation — a common problem in these illogical times. For what

---

50 *Turning Points* Programme, January-May, 1986, back page. This programme is quoted to demonstrate the antiquity of the organisation at St. James' Church — yet further testimony that Dr. Runcie cannot plead ignorance to both the level of organisation of the New Age Movement and his own denomination's propagation of it.

51 *The New Times*, No.6, November 1982 – January 1983, p.5.

52 See the section entitled 'Centres of Light' in Chapter 4.

53 Donald Reeves, Sermon given at St. James' Church, Piccadilly, on Sunday 20th. October 1985. Transcripts are available from the Rector.

is the advantage in exchanging such a spiritually-dead institution for one which is steeped in occultism and the deification of man? In his sermon, Donald Reeves also declared how impressed he was by the fact that the directors at Findhorn *'laid themselves open to the guidance [of meditation] and to what they call the God within'*, adding that this experience, known in New Age circles as *'attunement'*, is practised by all members of the community.[54] However, Donald Reeves failed to tell his congregation that at Findhorn they are 'tuning in' to discarnate entities with names such as 'Master Rakocki' and 'Limitless Love and Truth', who direct the lives of the meditators in accordance with demonic strategy. He also failed to disclose in his sermon the fact that the then official spiritual guru of Findhorn, David Spangler (a former student of Alice B. Bailey), openly advocates what he calls *'a Luciferic Initiation'*. To elucidate, here are a few telling extracts from Mr. Spangler's teachings concerning the spirit-entity, Lucifer:

> 'Lucifer, like Christ, stands at the door of man's consciousness and knocks. If a man says, *'Go away because I do not like what you represent; I am afraid of you'*, Lucifer will play tricks on that fellow. If a man says, *'Come in, and I will give to you the treat of my love and understanding and I will uplift you in the light and presence of the Christ, my outflow'*, then Lucifer becomes something else again. He becomes the being who carries that great treat, the ultimate treat, the light of wisdom...Lucifer, then, is neither good nor bad in his true essence. He is completely neutral. He is an agent of God's love acting through evolution.
>
> 'Lucifer works within each of us to bring us to wholeness, and as we move into a new age, which is the age of man's wholeness, each of us in some way is brought to that point which I term the Luciferic Initiation, the particular doorway through which the individual must pass if he is to come fully into the presence of his light and his wholeness...It is one that many people now, and in the days ahead, will be facing, for it is an initiation into the New Age'.[55]

So, an initiation into the New Age is a 'Luciferic Initiation'. This *'ultimate treat'*, as David Spangler calls it, is actually nothing less than a reassertion of the same 'Satanic Initiation' with which Lucifer seduced our first parents in the Garden of Eden: the illusion of personal divinity and the promise of wisdom beyond that with which we have been endowed by God in creation (Gen.3:4-6). This is a great challenge to all those who do not think there is anything in the New Age about which Christians should be concerned. Naturally, there is no reference to Lucifer in Donald Reeves sermon, although he must certainly be well aware of these teachings; for not only are David Spangler's books available in the St. James' Church 'Whole Bookshop', but they are also recommended at the conclusion of Rev. Reeves' published sermon transcript. In another of David Spangler's

---

[54] Ibid.

[55] David Spangler, *Reflections on the Christ* (Findhorn Publications, 1978), pp.41-45.

books he — or rather, his spirit-guide — states that *'throughout the last century there has been the release of information and concepts held confidential for centuries within select occult groups'*.[56]

This information is, says David Spangler, being disseminated through such groups as the Theosophical Society, the Lucis Trust, the Anthroposophical Society (Rudolph Steiner Schools/Camphill Trust Villages), New Thought Movements (Christian Science, Visualisation, Positive Thinking, Prosperity Consciousness, etc.), the writings of Teilhard de Chardin, coupled with this late twentieth century blending of the cultures and beliefs of East and West. All this occult data — held confidential for centuries, as David Spangler rightly claims — is now being disseminated through such centres as St. James' Church, Piccadilly. Satan must obtain a great deal of satisfaction at the thought that his evil doctrine is actually being propagated within the walls of a professing Christian church. One can therefore comprehend the context of the following statement in which this vicar, who has received the 'Luciferic Initiation', makes the claim that:

> 'There is a great need for a massive spiritual and intellectual effort to create some sort of framework in which the new sensibilities can flourish — actually the framework will not be new but it will reclaim some *ancient wisdom* which we have almost lost'.[57] [emphasis added]

This *'ancient wisdom'*, so frequently referred to by Neo-Gnostics, is none other than the 'wisdom' originally dispersed through our race by Satan in Eden (Gen.3:4-6) — a 'wisdom' which so corrupted humanity that it led to the tragedy of the Flood, a 'wisdom' which was subsequently redeveloped at Babel in post-diluvian Sumero-Mesapotamia, and from there scattered throughout the globe in the form of shamanistic pagan religion and idolatry. The secrets and mysteries of this wisdom are now being spread — not only in the midst of our culture, but in the heart of the professing Church — by the advocates of the New Age.

The statement of Donald Reeves concerning the need for *'some sort of framework in which the new sensibilities can flourish'* was made eight years before the writing of this present work. There has now been ample time for such consolidation to take place — and indeed it has, throughout the duration of Dr. Runcie's office and into that of Dr. Carey. One only needs to visit the St. James' Church to corroborate this sober fact. Therefore, Dr. Runcie's claim that there is nothing structured about the New Age Movement is an utter sham — for his own denomination is making a major contribution towards the building of that structure.

There appears to be a pattern of development in these New Age circles. It may begin with a professed desire for a deeper spirituality than the established Church institutions are offering (which can seem very reasonable), coupled with a subsequent seduction into some form of gnosticism by way of alternative. This is a classic satanic strategy: the false 'either-or' situation. Both Spirit-less churches and gnostic cults are bad places to be (although in the former one has less chance

---

[56] David Spangler, *Revelation: The Birth of a New Age* (Findhorn, 1971), p.124.

[57] Donald Reeves, op. cit.

of being eaten alive!). However, within a short time, the person who receives such an initiation begins to open up to the whole range of techniques and practices on offer in the Neo-Gnostic imbroglio — divination, UFOs, meditation, rebirthing, Channelling, magic, prosperity consciousness — it makes little difference, for in their view every pathway leads to the top of the mountain eventually. This is the broad way: the Luciferic principle of multiple diversity in opposition to the narrow way: the one Way in Christ.

We could delve considerably further into the activities in the Church of England — both at St. James' Church and elsewhere — but this chapter would then become the book! What is being propagated at this Church of England attraction is nothing less than that old heresy of Gnosticism, decked out in modern garb; the ancient religion of Babylon hiding behind clerical collars and cassocks. One of the most popular guest speakers at the St. James' 'Alternatives' evening programme is the leading American witch known as 'Starhawk' (alias Miriam Simos), High Priestess of the Covenant of the Goddess, who has written books on goddess worship and on how to cast spells.[58] She is openly billed in the St. James' Church literature as an exponent of *'earth and goddess mysteries'*. A confessed witch invited to peddle her wares in a professing Christian church! This is what the Church of England has come to — in which every member of that denomination wittingly or unwittingly conspires. How such activities could flourish so readily under the episcopal oversight of both Dr. Runcie and Dr. Carey is a question which both men will have to answer on the Day of Judgement.

EPILOGUE

This brings us to the conclusion of our study on the way in which New Age ideology has been steadily infiltrating the establishment Church of England, and indeed every other mainline denomination. In view of all that we have set forth in this chapter, Dr. Robert Runcie was being highly disingenuous in his assertion that the New Age Movement is so insubstantial that it cannot be condemned. Look back at our earlier quotation from the Lucis Trust literature about the infiltration of the major religions and denominations by New Age initiates. Think carefully about their stated aims. Recall all that we have discussed in the course of our study. Observe the manner in which these things are being fulfilled — as are the Scriptures on this subject (Mt.24:23-27; Mk.13:5-6; 1 Tim.4:1; 2 Tim.4:3-4; 1 Jn.2:18; Rev.17:5). Observe the increasing number of Anglican cathedrals and churches which hold interfaith pagan celebrations at strategic times in the Church calendar. The truth is that the Church of England can no longer be called a *Christian* denomination: it is actually a leading edge of the New Gnosticism in religious culture today.

One cannot be impartial in this situation. In the spiritual battle, we are not dealing with flesh and blood but with principalities and powers in the heavenlies. How do we imagine that Satan and his cohorts spend their time in this run-up to their eventual, inevitable destruction? To be sure, on an individual-microcosmic

[58] Starhawk, *The Rebirth of the Ancient Goddess* (Harper & Row, 1986).

level they put much energy into tempting people into sin and apostasy; but at the global-macrocosmic level they are involved in a full-scale build-up to war with the Most High and His saints. The placement of people like Dr. Runcie and his friends — overseers who do not pastor but who, by neglecting this duty, destroy — into positions of influence in the various denominations of the world, whether these men realise it or not, is a vital part of that warfare and must be exposed. In the light of all that we have said, consider these questions in the Old Prayer Book which are asked of the ordinand at the consecration of a Bishop or Archbishop:

> 'Brother, are you persuaded that the holy Scriptures contain sufficiently all doctrine required of necessity for eternal salvation through faith in Jesus Christ? And are you determined out of the same holy Scriptures to instruct the people committed to your charge; and to teach or maintain nothing as required of necessity to eternal salvation, but that which you shall be persuaded may be included and proved by the same?
> 'Will you then faithfully exercise yourself in the same holy Scriptures, and call upon God by prayer, for the true understanding of the same; so as you may be able by them to teach and exhort with wholesome Doctrine, and to withstand and convince the gainsayers?
> 'Are you ready, with all faithful diligence, to banish and drive away all erroneous and strange doctrine contrary to God's Word; and both privately and openly to call upon and encourage others to do the same?'

To all these questions the prospective Bishop or Archbishop must answer emphatically in the affirmative. In the light of the knowledge contained in this study, can you read these questions without weeping? Can Dr. Runcie read them without throwing himself to his knees in repentance? For he has made a major contribution to the upbuilding of the false church. The Belgic Confession (1561) cites three signs of the True Church:

> '1) It practises the pure preaching of the Gospel. 2) It maintains the pure administration of the sacraments as Christ instituted them. 3) It exercises Church discipline for correcting and punishing sins. It short, it governs itself according to the pure Word of God, rejecting all things contrary to it and regarding Jesus Christ as the only Head'.[59]

The established Church in England is a denomination in which these signs have been virtually liquidated. What could be the solution to this crisis in the Church? The only course of action for the knowing and concerned Christian is to expose the deception involved and then to replace it with faithful and effective biblical teaching. Leaving aside personal responsibility for individual apostasy, one of the principal reasons that so many within the Church are seduced by every wind of doctrine is that they lack a genuine understanding of fundamental Christian teaching — a state of affairs which has accrued over many decades. The pastors have not tended to the flocks; indeed, in many cases — as in that of Dr. Runcie — they have spiritually abandoned them altogether and fed them poison.

---

[59] Belgic Confession, Article XXIX.

We know that there are many within the Church of England who will find the contents of this chapter as harrowing as we do. We have great sympathy with their position. But the manifold activities of that denomination provide us with a model for the deterioration which has been happening in the majority of Christian organisations throughout the past century: first, theological liberalism in the colleges, then, after a period in which this influence can inseminate the churches, there follows a rapid declension of Gospel truth and an eclipse of biblical preaching and teaching.

In the next chapter, we will examine the manner in which a number of Neo-Gnostic teachings posing as Christianity have been able to flourish in those churches where a solid grounding in the Scriptures has given way to the supremacy of subjective religious experience. By the conclusion of that chapter, we will have begun to understand why these developments should have been taking place at this particular point in history.

Chapter Eleven

SORCEROUS APPRENTICES

(2) The 'Mind-Sciences' in the Church Today

'Blessed are those who do His commandments, that they may have the right to the tree of life, and may enter through the gates into the city. But outside are dogs and sorcerers...and whoever loves and practises a lie' (Rev.22:14-15).

In a previous chapter, we identified six seeds of corruption that were implanted by Satan in world culture during the late nineteenth century in order to undermine the true Gospel and bring the swell of lawlessness to its tidal-wave proportions. These were Evolution Theory, Theological Liberalism, Comparative Religion, Socio-Political Utopianism, Theosophy and the Mind-Sciences. These six seeds became the harbingers of many anti-Christian offshoots. The last of these six seeds forms the subject of this present chapter — the second part of our examination of the mind-sciences. In Chapter 7, we examined the occult origins of the 'mind-sciences' and the ease with which a person can fall under the powerful suggestions and manipulations of another through the auspices of secular psychotherapy. Not only was this seen through the life and work of four founding fathers of the psychology of the New Gnosticism — Franz Mesmer, Gustav Fechner, Wilhelm Reich and Carl Jung — but also through the ancient religious stream of Shamanism and its present-day revival.[1] We came to see how the entire Godless world lies under the sway of Satan, relating this specifically to the manipulation of the imaginal life of the unregenerate mind and the development of various techniques and systems designed to 'tap into' the spiritual realm. We affirmed that biblical counselling rather than secular psychotherapy should be the resource of the Christian in the event of emotional and behavioural crises.

In the present chapter, we will survey the pervasive influence of the mind-sciences on many disturbing elements within the present-day professing Christian Church which are masquerading as genuine phenomena of Christian spirituality — especially those churches which describe themselves as 'Charismatic' or 'Pentecostal'. We will show that these developments have far more in common with the ancient sorcery of the pagan cults than with historic, orthodox, biblical

---

[1] The term 'Shamanism' originally referred to the religion of N.E. Asia which utilises magic and sorcery through a priestly leader known as the Shaman; but its essential principles can be found in religious groupings all over the world. For a fuller discussion of Shamanism, see pp.160-164, and pp.266-269.

Christianity. We are speaking of such influences as 'Visualisation' (otherwise known as 'Imaging' or 'Imagineering'), spirit invocation, verbal incantations, faith-healing, techniques of trance-inducement, and exorcistic ritualism. These have not only provided the perfect interdenominational, ecumenical focal point among professing Christian churches, but they have also unwittingly introduced many Christians to the realms of interfaith syncretism and the corresponding generation of mystical experiences. One can wholly understand the existence of these developments in non-Christian circles, for they have Satan as their master (1 Jn.5:19b), and they feel the need to resort to superstition and ritual in order to gain some illusion of control over their lives. But when these concerns begin to be practised within the professing Church, it calls for an alarm to be sounded and an apologetic to be raised. These we will seek to do in the present chapter.

INTRODUCTION: The A-B-C of Ancient Magic

At the close of the twentieth century — as a result of the crusading marriage of Neo-Pentecostalism, Roman Catholic Charismatic 'renewal', and syncretistic liberalism — various shamanistic, occult practices are being advocated by an increasing number of churches around the world. One of the primary claims of this chapter is that the Charismatic Movement has unwittingly provided a convenient foundation-shaking foothold for Satan through which he can seduce gullible believers into hankering after the mystical, inveigling them into utilising 'Christianised' occultic and psychic practices within the Church itself.

During the last fifteen years or so, a welter of books has emerged from allegedly Christian sources which are actually promoting these occult and mystical practices — although without the authors or publishers discerning them as such. A perusal around almost any Christian bookshop today will reveal shelves full of literature with flashy covers containing detailed advice on 'How to Lead a Totally Successful Life', 'How to Claim your Healing', 'How to Walk in the Miraculous', 'How to Discover the Power Within', 'How to Speak in an Angelic Language', 'How to Cast Demons out of your Budgie/Cat/Wife/Car/Self/Home/Pulpit/Neighbourhood, etc.', and so much more. It has virtually reached the stage now where any Christian bookshop which does not stock such literature would be considered to be dull, lifeless and 'lacking in the Spirit'.

Although an increasing number of believers are under the illusion that the contents of these works are perfectly acceptable Christian writings, we will show that they constitute one of the most cunning deceptions which Satan has masterminded in the history of the Church. Scandalous as it may seem, for almost a century Christians have been learning to practise magic in the name of Christ. This is all the more ironic for the fact that the principal perpetrator of this subterfuge is the sect known as the Charismatic Movement — a body which claims for itself great powers of spiritual discernment. Unfortunately, many of these believers have been so busy locking the front door against imaginary demons, that they have left the backdoor wide open to the real thing.

The practices that we will be examining fall into the general category of magic, and we will tackle them by first concentrating on their secular occurrence, followed by a detailed exposé of their manifestation in the churches and in the literature which is so often on display in many Christian bookshops today. Before we examine the basic elements of all magic and sorcery, let us just be informed as to what is meant by these terms.

Magic can be defined as *'a system of beliefs and practices by which it is believed that man may control the natural and supernatural forces that affect his life'*.[2] The crucial component in this definition is that it is **man** who does this controlling of natural and supernatural forces out of *sheer creature-strength* — the starting-point for every manifestation of magic and sorcery in the unfolding of human civilisation. However, before proceeding, it is worth pointing out a common misconception. For there are many people who try to make a differentiation between *white* magic (which presents itself as being of noble pedigree, intending to heal, and spiritually beneficent) and *black* magic (which is associated in the popular mind with the insertion of pins in dolls, ritual human and animal sacrifice, satanism, etc.). This is actually a false distinction, because *both* can be shown to be serving the secret purposes of the devil. Even if it were not a false distinction, the plain fact is that the purportedly milder body of witchcraft which calls itself 'white' is *'the worser of the two'* — as William Perkins (1558-1602) states in his superb monograph on witchcraft.[3] The reason for this is that whereas most people would run a mile from outright black magic, 'white' magicians present satanic teaching in the garb of an angel of light, thus successfully carrying away many more souls into Satan's clutches and thereby into outer darkness.

The development of magic in the religious life of the human race is an outworking of that original 'initiation' which our first parents received at the dawn of history, when Satan seduced them into believing that they could be little gods (*'You will be like God, knowing good and evil...'*), that they could have unconditional eternal life (*'You will certainly never die...'*), and that they could gain access to wisdom which was over and above that with which they had been endowed by their Creator (Gen.3:4-6). We have already discussed these fundamental principles of satanic strategy on many occasions in earlier chapters. Readers will recall how we have shown that a number of far-reaching developments in the religious beliefs and practices of humanity were to arise out of this 'Satanic Initiation' in Eden, its pre-diluvian and post-diluvian development, and the scattering around the world of its many facets after the debacle at Babel. Among these have been: A doctrine of the 'god within' — an alleged 'spark of divinity' in all people which can be 'tapped' through prescribed techniques; a substitution of the creature for the Creator as the object of worship and the focus of religious power; and teachings which support the notion of unconditional eternal life, e.g., reincarnation, spiritualism, out-of-the-body, 'after-death bliss' experiences, etc. These three factors are a recurring feature throughout all pagan religions.

---

2 *Macmillan Encyclopedia* (Macmillan, 1986), p.759.

3 William Perkins, 'A Discourse on the Damned Art of Witchcraft' in *Workes*, Vol.II (Cambridge, 1613).

However, alongside of these factors, two other major outworkings can be clearly seen. For when people believe that they have an indwelling 'spark of divinity', and that this is a power which can be 'tapped into' through various techniques, certain magical practices will naturally arise in the religious life. These are:

1. **'Mind-Power' techniques**, operating through the concentrated use of the imagination and visualised images.
2. **'Word-Power' techniques**, working through personal fiats, affirmations, and spoken commands addressed directly to the powers of darkness and the conditions they allegedly cause; coupled with various religious rituals which are used to effect them.

An examination of every aspect of these two practices will form the subject matter of this present chapter, alongside a comparison of these with the teachings of the Word of God. We shall, therefore, first take a detailed look at the use of the imagination as a visualising tool in occult-based mind-power techniques; followed by an examination of the use of verbal affirmations and ritualistic commands as a method of manipulating matter and human consciousness.

I. IN YOUR MIND'S EYE: The Occult Art of Visualisation

The term *'mind-power'* is being used here to refer to the use of the imagination in creating objects or beings in the mind, which are then exploited for a variety of purposes. The person practising this 'imaging' technique can then create a personal relationship with these imaged objects (or beings), or they can be manipulated into material benefits which will manifest in his or her life. Fundamental to our study is the fact that the development of the imagination through 'visualisation' exercises is one of the most ancient and widely used occult techniques for expanding the mind and opening up the psyche into new (and forbidden) areas of consciousness. It is found in all ancient religious traditions, especially in shamanistic cults and Tibetan Buddhism. It plays a highly important role in occult training and forms the background to Transcendental Magic and the ancient art of *Wicca* (witchcraft). More recently, it has become a recognised technique in the fields of humanistic and transpersonal psychology, as well as being a fundamental consciousness-raising practice in the New Age Movement.

In earlier chapters, we have already charted the way in which breathing techniques and hypnotic relaxation exercises are being used as an introduction to occult meditation in many churches today. In this section of the present chapter, we will concentrate specifically on the use of visualisation as a means of opening a person up to occult influences, together with its infiltration into the professing Church.

The practice of visualisation can be used in a variety of ways, but they all fall into three main types. **Firstly**, they can be used to provide a doorway into what psychologists call a 'non-ordinary state of consciousness'. **Secondly**, they can be used as a means towards something called 'Inner Healing' or 'Healing of the Memories'. **Thirdly**, they can provide an instrument for the manipulation and recreation of matter and consciousness. We shall now examine each of these categories in turn.

1. Visualisation: The Doorway to Altered Consciousness

This category of visualisation probes deep layers of the psyche and involves entering what psychologists call *'non-ordinary states of consciousness'*. We will first look at this practice in the secular world, followed by its corresponding practices in the Christian scene today.

i. Secular Practice of Consciousness-Altering Visualisation

Two ancient examples of this form of visualisation are the visualising of highly detailed pictorial representations of deities in Tibetan Buddhist meditation, or a visualised *mandala* (complex patterned circle) in Tantric Yoga to assist the 'awakening' of Kundalini serpent power. In this type of deep visualisation it is quite common to encounter spirit-entities which are known in the jargon as 'inner guides' or 'sub-selves', depending on whether you follow the esoteric tradition or the psychotherapeutic model.[4] A classic manifestation of this phenomenon, as we discussed in Chapter 7, is the spirit-entity called Philemon, which Carl Jung encountered in his own 'journey within'. The serious student of visualisation is positively encouraged to seek out these 'inner guides' in order to assist him in the journey to the centre of his mind, as they communicate with the consciousness of the explorer, giving him guidance and light on the next step in the process.

Such consultation with spirit-entities, via the 'journey within', had always — until comparatively recently — been the province of the Eastern mystic, psychic medium, Shaman or other sorcerer. But now the Western psychologists have devised their own versions of these practices to make them more palatable to the uninitiated Westerner. New Age scientist, Dr. Fritjof Capra, rightly states that

> 'Shamans used therapeutic techniques such as group sharing, psychodrama, dream analysis, *suggestion, hypnosis, guided imagery*, and psychedelic therapy for centuries before they were rediscovered by modern psychologists'.[5] [emphasis added]

The psychologists of today have simply rediscovered the techniques of the ancient shamans. One of the earliest champions of this type of visualisation in Western psychology was Roberto Assagioli, a pupil of Carl Jung who, in 1910, devised a system known as *psychosynthesis*, which used guided visualisations as an aid to the discovery of so-called 'sub-selves' which could be integrated and synthesised within the personality — an experience which is *'often associated with some kind of experience of ecstasy or insight'*.[6] In a revealing statement on the

---

[4] The *esoteric* tradition of visualisation is universal in practice but Eastern in origin, having its roots in Shamanism and Tibetan meditation. The *psychotherapeutic* model of visualisation is a Westernised adaptation of the esoteric tradition.

[5] Fritjof Capra, *The Turning Point: Science, Society and the Rising Culture* (Flamingo/Collins, 1982), p.337.

[6] John Rowan, *Ordinary Ecstasy: Humanistic Psychology in Action* (Routledge & Kegan Paul, 1976), p.68.

true roots of this psychotherapeutic system, a former chairman of the U.K. Association of Humanistic Psychology makes the claim that the psychosynthesis model of visualisation *'can be seen as related to the Mandala, and also to the Tarot'*,[7] although he does not elaborate on how this works out in practice. Readers should note the significance here of the fact that a leader in the field of so-called 'humanistic' psychology has no problem accepting the validity of the religious symbols of the *Mandala* and *Tarot.*

The *bona fide* occult initiate is invariably encouraged to practise visualisations which will bring him into contact with an 'inner guide' and, ultimately, the spark of 'divinity' allegedly residing within each person — known in transpersonal jargon as the 'Higher Self'. To this end, he will meditate on one of many deities, a fixed image such as a *mandala*, or on fluid, unfolding, 'archetypal scenes', such as a journey down a dark tunnel or a trip into outer space — anything which takes the visualiser out of his rational mind and into the unpredictable world of the imagination. One present-day psychologist advocating visualisation in order to discover one's 'inner guides' describes them in this way:

> 'Not only do inner guides exist, but many exist. They are persons from the past, present or future who belong to spheres of consciousness outside the conscious sphere. They can be of either sex and can be young or old. They are extremely knowledgeable, especially about ourselves'.[8]

In one visualisation exercise, the reader is told to switch on an imaginary television set:

> 'Once it is on, wait for the male figure to form on the screen. When it does so, you will be able to converse with him. This is not unusual, it is merely a method of reaching your other selves. You can ask him questions or ask for advice. Now indicate to him that you will be finishing your conversation and thank him and say that you would like to call on him again'.[9]

It takes little discernment to realise that this exercise is a blatant piece of auto-suggestion. Significantly, the author has written two other books entitled

---

Paul, 1976), p.68.

[7] Ibid. The word *Mandala* means 'circle' in Sanskrit and is used in Hindu and Buddhist ritual, art and meditation. In a number of religious traditions, the *Mandala* is *'believed to contain centers of power or energy related to a specific god or demon'* (Raymond Van Over, *Total Meditation: Mind Control Techniques for a Small Planet in Space*, Collier Macmillan, 1978, p.135). The *Tarot* is a card-based system of divination or fortune-telling — an activity which is inspired by demons (cf. Acts 16:16) and expressly forbidden in Scripture (Dt.18:10-12).

[8] Ronald Shone, *Creative Visualisation: How to Use Imagery and Imagination for Self-Improvement* (Thorsons, 1984), p.35. This book, along with Shakti Gawain, *Creative Visualisation: Use the Power of your Imagination to Create what you want in your Life* (Whatever Publishing, 1978), are the two secular classics on this subject.

[9] Ibid., p.36.

'Autohypnosis' and *'Advanced Autohypnosis'*. It may require a little more discernment to realise that such an exercise is a sure way of bringing oneself into contact with the demonic realm. This concern is heightened when he says

> 'After some time you will be able to recognise your inner guides very easily, you will know which sphere of consciousness they belong to and what type of advice or information they will be able to supply you with. They may even bring in other persons to help you!'.[10]

This great hoax of the 'inner guides' is just one more component of the extensive range of techniques currently being used by the powers of darkness to bring humanity more extensively under their sway. In this manner, the initiate is brought within easy access of the demonic realm, ready to receive instructions from demons masquerading as angels of light. Yet, similar kinds of visualisation exercises are being practised in meditation sessions across the world by many who are keen on 'raising their level of consciousness' — including professing Christians such as bishops, theologians, ministers and others blinded by the seductive power of Jungian psychology. Children — especially those who are prone to day-dreaming — are particularly vulnerable to this experience, as their imagination is more highly developed than that of the adult. The present growth in the use of computer games exploits this faculty to a sinister extent. Moreover, the entities observed by children, which are sometimes referred to as 'imaginary friends', can perhaps be seen in a different perspective in the light of this knowledge.

It should come as no surprise to discover that the increasingly sought-after experience of contacting and receiving advice from 'inner guides' should find its way into a suggested checklist for school activities, recommended in an education newsletter by the 'respectable' U.S. Association for Humanistic Psychology. This document recommends that students should

> 'do Yoga each morning before class; interpret their astrological charts; send messages via ESP; mind project; heal their own illnesses; *speak with their 'Higher Selves' and receive information necessary for joyful living*; lift energies from the power Chakra to the heart Chakra; practice skills necessary for color healing; hold an image of themselves as being perfect; *receive advice from personal guides*; merge minds with others in the class to experience the collective consciousness of the group'.[11]

Some people may think this sounds a long way from their neighbourhood school! But in the U.S., the New Gnosticism is considerably more developed in educational circles than in the U.K., especially through such influences as 'Confluent Education'. Moreover, this was the U.S. thirteen years ago; and what the U.S. did thirteen years ago happens today in the U.K. Recently, an eleven-year old boy who attends the prestigious Edinburgh Academy, reported to the present

---

[10] Ibid., p.38.

[11] *Education Network Newsletter* of the Association for Humanistic Psychology, published in the U.S. in May-June, 1979.

writer that his class had been obliged to sit cross-legged on their desks by the Mathematics teacher and practise meditation for the duration of the lesson.

ii. 'Christianised' Consciousness-Altering Visualisation

The visualisation involving 'inner guides', and the taking of an inner journey through mental imagery, is not merely confined to the spiritual practices of the heathen nations and the 'personal growth' techniques of psychology. It also has a rich history of infiltration into the Church. The earliest influence in this field was the Jesuit priest, Ignatius Loyola (1495-1556), whose renowned 'Spiritual Exercises' use visualisations involving Christ and biblical stories to achieve their mystical goal. All occultists recognise the connections between the exercises of Ignatius and their own lore. In a chapter entitled *'The Emergence of a New Consciousness'*, Lady Ursula Burton — a former Roman Catholic who has converted to Findhorn-style New Ageism — highlights the relationship between Ignatius's exercises and the mind-sciences when she says:

> 'The Church tends not to recognise that the teaching of Christ was often of a psychological nature and concerned with bringing out the full potential that lies within each individual. Within the Catholic Church, a method used to *find the 'hidden self' and help it come alive* is by following the Spiritual Exercises of St. Ignatius Loyola. St. Ignatius, a Spaniard born in 1495, recognized the significance of the unconscious and, indeed, *used some of the methods that twentieth century psychotherapists have rediscovered*'.[12] [emphasis added]

Concerning the occult connections of the Jesuits, the former Reader of History at Oxford, Frances Yates, writes that

> '...of all the branches of the Roman Catholic Church it was the Jesuits who were most like the Rosicrucians. The Renaissance esoteric influences behind the formation of the Jesuit Order have not yet been fully studied. The Order made great use of the Hermetic tradition in appealing to Protestants and to the many other creeds which it encountered in its missionary work. The Hermetic and occult philosophy of the Jesuits received a tremendous formulation in the work of Athanasius Kircher, whose vast work on Hermetic pseudo-Egyptology was published in 1652'.[13]

It is noteworthy to discover that the Roman Catholic priest turned occultist, Eliphas Levi, intended to include a section on *'the magical side of the exercises of St. Ignatius'*, in his classic work 'Transcendental Magic'.[14] In a further pointer to the esoteric nature of the formation of the Jesuits, another researcher writes:

---

[12] Ursula Burton & Janice Dolley, *Christian Evolution: Moving Towards a Global Spirituality* (Turnstone Press, 1984), p.112.

[13] Frances A. Yates, *The Rosicrucian Enlightenment* (Routledge & Kegan Paul, 1972), p.230.

[14] Eliphas Levi, *Transcendental Magic* (Rider, 1968, first published 1896), p.xxx.

> 'Ignatius Loyola was a Basque... Some German occultists had claimed that the Basque people was the last remnant of the Atlantean race... Himmler [head of the Nazi S.S., Ed.] believed that [Loyola's Spiritual Exercises] had been handed down from the Masters of Atlantis, and that now he was the man chosen by the 'higher powers' to use them in the reactivation of Vril for the dominance of the Teutonic race over all others'[15]

Yet another occult researcher and practitioner, demonstrating (amongst other things) how Himmler's Nazi S.S. was modelled on Ignatius's Society of Jesus, affirms that

> 'These 'spiritual exercises' are a carefully graded visualisation programme encompassing certain archetypal scenes designed to bring the individual practitioner closer to the Inner Christ. *'The Kingdom of God'*, Jesus told his disciples, *'is within you'*. And the Jesuits are among the very few orthodox churchmen actually trying to make contact with it. The context of Jesuit visualisations differs radically from that of the exercises used in many of the occult schools, but there is an uncanny similarity in the techniques'.[16]

As this observer rightly points out: *'The real heart of magical training is systematic visualisation'*.[17] This connection between visualisation and magic is crucial to the integrity of our study. As another leading magician states:

> 'The developing practitioner of advanced magical arts must have grounding and experience in the following disciplines: meditation, concentration, *visualisation*, and ritual pattern-making'.[18] [emphasis added]

However, as another occult writer points out, *'This notion of the magical power of the imagination is not confined to the Western tradition; it can be found all over the world'*.[19] So we find Alice Bailey of the Lucis (formerly Lucifer) Trust receiving this 'message' from one of the so-called 'Ascended Masters', Djwal Khul: *'The clue to all this esoteric work demanded by Shambhala is to be found in the development of the Art of Visualisation'*.[20] This is a fact which needs to be

---

15 Nigel Pennick, *Hitler's Secret Sciences: His Quest for the Hidden Knowledge of the Ancients* (Neville Spearman, 1981), pp.104-5.

16 James Webb, *The Occult Establishment*, Vol.2 of *The Age of the Irrational* (Open Court, 1975), p.320.

17 Ibid.

18 R.J. Stewart, *Advanced Magical Arts: Visualisation, Meditation and Ritual in the Western Magical Tradition* (Element Books, 1988), p.8.

19 Colin Wilson, *Mysteries: Investigation into the Occult, Paranormal and Supernatural* (Hodder & Stoughton, 1978), pp.246-247.

20 Sir John Sinclair, *The Alice Bailey Inheritance* (Turnstone Press, 1984), p.154. Shambhala is the name of the etheric headquarters of the 'Ascended Masters'. We have already given details of Alice Bailey and the Lucis Trust in Chapter 4.

grasped. Most of the people being seduced into the practice of visualisation — especially those within the Church — have not the faintest conception of the occultic aim which lies at its root. In spite of the attractions and harmless benefits put forward by its advocates, visualisation is a primary gateway for demonic infiltration into human consciousness — a deception currently being worked on a truly grand scale. That this deception is so complete in relation to the Church can be seen in the large number of Christian writings advocating visualisation practices. Of course, these books do not necessarily speak of *'non-ordinary or altered states of consciousness'* (although some do), but rather of *'contemplation'* and *'deeper faith experiences'*. It all seems very devotional and proper, unless one knows the jargon and the hallmarks.

One such book, by the Quaker, Richard Foster, is widely read within Evangelical circles and has a commendatory foreword by the late Charismatic vicar, David Watson. Entitled *'Celebration of Discipline: The Path to Spiritual Growth'*, it is published by the 'Christian' publisher, Hodder and Stoughton. Richard Foster, having freely confessed to being influenced by faith-healer Agnes Sanford, the psychology of the self-styled Gnostic Carl Jung and the Spiritual Exercises of Ignatius Loyola, writes that *'the inner world of meditation is most easily entered through the door of the imagination'.*[21] Because the Christian is encouraged to meditate on the Scriptures, Richard Foster concludes that one should indulge in visualisation exercises so that they can *actually* enter the stories within its pages — *'not as a passive observer but as an active participant'.*[22] He then claims that

> 'Since Jesus lives in the Eternal Now and is not bound by time, this event in the past is a living present-tense experience for Him. Hence, you can *actually* encounter the living Christ in the event, be addressed by His voice and be touched by His healing power. It can be more than an exercise of the imagination; it can be a genuine confrontation. Jesus Christ will actually come to you'.[23]

This process of meeting a visualised 'Christ' in the imagination is a recurring theme in the writings of the Christian visualisers; and we must be very discerning in order to break through to a proper understanding of what is involved in this work. Such an encounter will often result in the practitioner receiving advice and information from this visualised entity. Morton Kelsey, an Episcopalian priest and theologian who has greatly influenced Richard Foster, writes that *'religious experience is found by turning inward and using one's imagination as a tool with which to contact the reality of the spiritual world'.*[24] This practice, he claims,

> 'can be learned by most people with little determination, [and] opens up various levels and depths of reality in the inner realm that can be

---

[21] Richard Foster, *Celebration of Discipline* (Hodder and Stoughton, 1980), p.22.

[22] Ibid., p.26.

[23] Ibid.

[24] Morton Kelsey, *The Other Side of Silence: A Guide to Christian Meditation* (SPCK, 1977), p.136.

met and explored as one deals with the images that rise'.[25]

Therefore, through stepping into *'the events recorded in the New Testament or into the stories told by Jesus'*, one can have a personal meeting with a visualised entity which presents itself as Jesus Christ Himself.[26] In describing this process, Morton Kelsey reveals the chilling heart of this demonic work:

> 'If one does not shut the door by disbelief, dream images can bring contact *with other realities of psychic power beyond oneself.* E.L. Rossi has described in some detail *the process of encouraging them to speak*... Christ can be approached in the same way... If we can communicate with other elements of the spiritual world through dream images, then we can also interact with the image of Christ and the reality which He incorporates and expresses... In the quiet I say, *'Here I am. Tell me what you wish of me'*... And then something within me clicks. There is a change, and suddenly I know that I am not talking to myself... Often I ask Him why He bothers to come and be with someone like me. Each time He tells me that He is Love and that it is the nature of Love to give of itself, that He cares for every human being and comes whenever we allow Him to enter and share Himself with us'.[27]

From where has Morton Kelsey derived these techniques? Is it from the explicit (or even implicit) teaching of Jesus or His Apostles? Can we find them anywhere in the pages of the Bible? To save us the trouble of searching, he tells us himself that one of his major influences was *'the writings of an Italian psychiatrist, Roberto Assagioli'*, whom we have already mentioned earlier in this chapter. Readers will be interested to know that in 1932 Roberto Assagioli came within the influence of the celebrated occultist, Alice B. Bailey, and assisted her with her renowned ERANOS Conferences.[28] As one authoritative source reveals: *'Over the many years of his career, [Roberto Assagioli] trained many people in the techniques of mediumship, telepathy and clairvoyance'.*[29] In the book, 'The Aquarian Conspiracy', Assagioli is cited as having been one of the main influences on the New Age Movement.[30] As if this cocktail of spiritist influences was not enough, Morton Kelsey further reveals a Neo-Gnostic connection when he states that

> 'it was C.G. Jung who showed me that such practices can work today, and that images not only open one to the depth of oneself, but also *beyond to the world of psychoid realities* where one is able to come into contact with the realm of God Himself'.[31] [emphasis added]

---

[25] Ibid.

[26] Ibid., pp.137-138.

[27] Ibid., pp.232-233.

[28] See the section on Jung in Chapter 7, pp.258-266.

[29] J. Gordon Melton (ed.), *New Age Encyclopedia* (Gale Research, Inc., 1990), p.32.

[30] Marilyn Ferguson, *The Aquarian Conspiracy: Personal and Social Transformation in the 1980s* (Granada-Paladin, 1982), p.463.

[31] Morton Kelsey, *The Other Side of Silence: A Guide to Christian Meditation* (SPCK,

Added to this, in a highly significant statement, Morton Kelsey discloses another of his influences when he claims that

> 'we find that [Jesus's] life and acts, his teaching and practice, are rather akin to a shamanism based on an intimate relationship with a loving father god. In fact, an important study might be made comparing the ministry of Jesus with that of shamanism'.[32]

In his recent book, 'Transcend' (Element Books, 1991) Morton Kelsey asks the highly leading question: *'What is the role of the modern Christian shaman?'*. He answers this by claiming that

> 'Christ was and is the ultimate shaman. He was the god/man who died once and for all, who restored to human beings their connection to the divine, a connection severed by the Fall... And the Christian shaman needs to have an understanding of psychic phenomena and of his or her own unconscious depths... In a real sense, every Christian who allows the Spirit to move in him or her is a shaman'.[33]

So, coupled with spiritism and Neo-Gnosticism, another of Morton Kelsey's influences is Shamanism. His most recent book 'Dreamquest' (Element Books, 1992), is a wholly shamanistic work. According to the biographical information given in this book, Morton Kelsey's family lived on the reservations of the Seneca Tribe of the Iroquois Nation for generations. Having grown up surrounded by the shamanistic tradition of the American Indian, it is perhaps hardly surprising that he should now be advocating Westernised shamanistic practices. Remember that this man is one of the major influences on the professing evangelical Christian, Richard Foster.

Here we have the clue to one of the major problems of the Christian visualisers: they just do not understand the difference between the unique Son of God and the sundry shamans of the world. When did the Lord Jesus ever practise *'group sharing, psychodrama, dream analysis, suggestion, hypnosis, guided imagery, and psychedelic therapy'* — practices which Dr. Fritjof Capra of Berkeley University has demonstrated were the practices of shamans long before modern-day psychotherapists rediscovered them? The likening of Jesus to a Shaman (who operates in the power of Beelzebub) must surely come close to being a blasphemy against the Holy Spirit, of which our Lord accused the Pharisees when they said He was casting out demons by the power of Beelzebub, the prince of demons (Mt.12:23-32).

Morton Kelsey's visualised entities may well soothe his troubled brow, but they have also led to his being an advocate of global interfaithism, 'Christianised' mysticism and Shamanism on a grand scale. In this present age, the demonic realm manifests itself to humanity as angels of light, purveyors of love and peace, promoting a oneness throughout the world, making people feel more positive about

---

1977), pp.138-139.

32 Morton Kelsey, *Healing and Christianity* (Harper & Row, 1976), p.51.

33 Morton Kelsey, *Transcend* (Element Books, 1991), pp.218-220. Readers should note that Element Books is a well-established occult publishing house.

themselves and their sin, while assuaging their guilt. It is particularly significant that these spirit-entities, these 'inner guides', never actually upbraid those who contact them. The whole ambience of their communication is akin to the unbeliever's typically distorted view of the Sermon on the Mount: *'Blessed be...Blessed be...Blessed be... '*, ad nauseam. One would never hear one of these 'inner guides' posing as Christ saying: *'Generation of vipers! Woe to the hypocrites and sorcerers who transgress My commandments!'* In the writings of the Christian visualisers, there is never any reference to the judgement of God; it is always His goodness rather than His severity which is emphasised (cf. Rom.11:22).

All this soothing cotton-wool advice received by the Christian visualisers from the spirit-world is thoroughly in line with the undermining of the holistic biblical message by their secular counterparts in the New Age Movement. David Spangler, the leading medium connected with the Findhorn Foundation in Scotland, has a spirit-guide calling itself *'Limitless Love and Truth'*. This entity, which claims to be God and Christ rolled into one, tells visualisers that

> 'I am the Light within all humanity. I am the Love that has never passed from this world but has walked with Man through darkness... Receive my blessings into me, for we are one, and let it pour into our Body of the earth. I bless you all'.[34]

It is all 'strokes' — as the psychotherapists would say — not a trace of admonition or chastisement. This is the hallmark of all these entities, who proclaim

> 'I have not come to sift the good from the bad. I am not a judge. I simply am what I am. If you are what I am, then you are of me. None are saved. None are lost. If you would build the new as I call upon you to do, then you cannot set yourselves against the old. There can be no separation'.[35]

This may sound very soothing and reassuring, but it is in direct contradiction to such Scriptures as Mt.12:34-36; 13:24-30,36-43,47-50; 25:31-46; Lk.12:51-53. One of the hallmarks of all false prophecies is 'false peace', contentment, and the denial of God's judgement (e.g., Jer.23:16-17). The true Christian should never seek the soothing sounds of such false security (Jer.6:14; 1 Th.5:3), but should rather always be prepared to be **dis**-illusioned — eschewing the cotton-wool fabrication and saccharin comfort of these visualised fairylands.

It is so important, when picking one's way through the 'Christian' books which recommend visualisation, to be able to discern what is a valid spiritual practice and what is simply an ancient deception. Some practices may sound highly attractive to the untaught believer or new convert. Richard Foster, for instance, provides a visualisation exercise which he claims will lead his readers to an actual meeting with the biblical Jesus Christ Himself. In reality, they could well be led into making personal contact with a spirit-guide. You will recall that in our earlier chapter on Mysticism, Richard Foster gave a pre-prayer relaxation exercise

---

[34] David Spangler, *Revelation: The Birth of a New Age* (Findhorn Foundation, 1978), p.50.
[35] Ibid., p.143.

which we showed was virtually identical to that of a Tibetan Buddhist. The same deception holds true for the visualisation exercise he recommends: It could have come straight from the textbook of any occultist or magical practitioner. He presents his version like this:

> 'In your imagination, picture yourself walking along a lovely forest path. Take your time, allowing the blaring noise of our modern metropolis to be overtaken by the sound of rustling leaves and cool forest streams... Try to feel the breeze upon your face as if it were gently blowing away all anxiety... When you are able to experience the scene with all your senses, the path breaks out into a lovely grassy knoll... Lie down on your back looking up at the blue sky and white clouds. Enjoy the sights and the smells'.[36]

So far, this is just the preliminary auto-hypnosis, relaxation, Alpha-wave inducing exercise.[37] After this, he guides his readers through the doorway which leads to a radically altered state of consciousness:

> 'After awhile, there is a deep yearning to go into the upper regions beyond the clouds. In your imagination allow your spiritual body, shining with light, to rise out of your physical body. Look back so that you can see yourself lying in the grass and reassure your body that you will return momentarily. Imagine your spiritual self, alive and vibrant, rising up through the clouds and into the stratosphere. Observe your physical body, the knoll and the forest shrink as you leave the earth. Go deeper and deeper into outer space until there is nothing except the warm presence of the eternal Creator. Rest in His presence. Listen quietly, anticipating the unanticipated. *Note carefully any instruction given...* Do not be surprised if the instruction is terribly practical and not in the least what you thought of as 'spiritual'. Do not be disappointed if no words come; like good friends, you are silently enjoying the company of each other. When it is time for you to leave, audibly thank the Lord for His goodness and return to the meadow. Walk joyfully back along the path until you return home full of new life and energy'.[38] [emphasis added]

Regardless of Richard Foster's hollow denial, in a footnote to later editions, that he is not endorsing 'astral travel' or 'astral projection' in this exercise, there is nothing else that it could possibly be. It certainly cannot be squared up with anything recommended in the Bible, either explicitly or 'by good and necessary consequence'. In fact, this exercise is a classic which can be found in all occult and magical literature, where it is rightfully referred to as 'astral projection'. In these occult exercises, the 'spiritual self' which one imagines to be 'rising up

---

[36] Richard Foster, op. cit., p.27.

[37] Readers will find a discussion on Alpha-type brain-waves in the section on 'Eclectic Mysticism' in Chapter 9, 'The Secret Ladder'.

[38] Ibid., pp.27-28.

through the clouds' is known as the 'astral body'. Let us compare carefully the similarity of language and experience between Richard Foster's account above and the following Cabbalist exercise recommended in a book called *'The Magical Arts'* (originally published as *'The Black Arts'*) by the celebrated occultist (and clergyman's son!) Richard Cavendish:

> 'To explore the world of the Sephiroth [the spiritual spheres], you must disentangle yourself from the world of everyday life. A man cannot wander through the landscape of the spheres until he is free from all the physical sensations, thoughts and worries which keep him tied to his usual surroundings... The cabbalist learns the mastery of both his body and his mind... *Concentration and imagination are vitally important in magic*... He concentrates on imagined sensations — the smell of a rose, the feel of velvet, the ticking of a watch. He must imagine and concentrate with such intensity that the object or sensation is present in his mind to the exclusion of everything else... Eventually, he must be able to put himself into a trance in which he can totally disregard his body, focus his entire being on one thought, or prevent any thought whatsoever from entering his mind.
>
> 'Blind and deaf to anything which might tug him back to the normal world, the cabalist can adventure into the realm of the sephiroth. He imagines his own body as if it was standing in front of him. He must have a clear, vivid mental picture of it. Then he transfers his consciousness to the imaginary body, so that he sees through its eyes and hears through its ears. This body is his astral body, astral double or body of light, a replica of the physical body made of finer material. It is capable of moving freely through space and can pass through apparently solid objects. The world which this body perceives is the astral plane, which includes the ordinary physical plane, but extends beyond it. The threshold of this plane is...the connecting point between the pure spheres of the heavens above it and the corruptible world of earth beneath it.
>
> 'When he is comfortably settled in his astral body, the cabalist makes it rise high in the air. He will become aware of landscapes and figures, apparently human or animal... The cabalist explores the strange country he has entered and speaks to any of the figures which approach him, but he must be cautious. The figures may try to deceive and ensnare him'.[39]

These accounts have been quoted in extended form so that readers will see the clear comparison between the exercise recommended by a professing evangelical and that of a transcendental magician. Ironically, one could say that the occult

[39] Richard Cavendish, *The Magical Arts* (Routledge & Kegan Paul, 1984), pp.95-96. Cabbalism — of which the *'Cabbalah'* represents the teachings — is the Jewish equivalent of Gnosticism. Some readers may recall a monthly magazine published by Richard Cavendish in the U.K. in the early 1970s entitled *Man, Myth and Magic*.

version is preferable because it at least has a cautionary note at the conclusion, whereas Richard Foster's exercise simply makes the assumption that it is God with whom He has been interacting in the course of the exercise. Even occult publications contain plain warnings about the perils of such forms of meditation. For example, the theosophist Alice Bailey speaks urgently of the danger of *'opening doors on the astral plane which the student may have difficulty closing'*.[40] But Richard Foster gives no such warning. No doubt he would answer this by saying that the Lord would not permit any trusting child of God to be approached by a demonic manifestation in a visualisation exercise; but this assumes that the practice of these exercises has a biblical foundation and that they will therefore have Divine approval. The fact that Richard Foster denies in a footnote that he is endorsing astral travel is no consolation to his readers, because he goes on to state that his exercise is instead meant to provide *'an aid for our centering down'*.[41] What exactly is 'centering-down'? As we have shown in an earlier chapter, it is a recognised term used chiefly by Zen Buddhists to refer to the altered state of consciousness which they seek to realize as a preparation for deep meditation. Actually, it is only the first half of his visualisation that would constitute a genuine 'centering-down' exercise; the second half is a full-blown occult meditation!

The word 'occult' is deliberately applied here, as the use of such exercises is basic to good occultic practice. When Richard Foster says that *'the inner world of meditation is most easily entered through the door of the imagination'*,[42] he is echoing to the letter the teachings of all the occultists on the alteration of human consciousness. For example, in a chapter on 'Self-Initiation' into occult science, the German occultist Rudolf Steiner — whom we have already discussed earlier in Chapter 3 — reveals that *'the pupil has to give himself up entirely to certain thought-pictures [which] are of such a kind as to have in them an awakening power'*.[43] It is this *'awakening power'* which forms the secret purpose behind the entire practice of visualisation, and which is designed by the powers of darkness to induce an occult experience deep with the individual human psyche. Steiner calls the use of such visualisation *'Imaginative Cognition'* and it forms a vital part in the attainment of *'a supersensible state of consciousness'*.[44]

Throughout his book, 'Knowledge of the Higher Worlds', Rudolf Steiner gives a number of specific exercises though which one can eventually encounter a spirit-entity which he refers to as *'the Guardian of the Threshold'*.[45] Acknowledging in his book 'Occult Science' that such experiences happen through the *'influence of the Luciferic powers'*,[46] Steiner writes:

---

[40] Alice B. Bailey, *Externalisation of the Hierarchy* (Lucis Press, 1957), p.18.

[41] Richard Foster, op.cit., p.28, footnote.

[42] Richard Foster, op.cit., p.22.

[43] Rudolf Steiner, *Occult Science: An Outline* (Rudolf Steiner Press, 1979), p.229.

[44] Ibid., p.235.

[45] Rudolf Steiner, *Knowledge of the Higher Worlds: How is it Achieved?* (Rudolf Steiner Press, 1969). See also Rudolf Steiner, *Occult Science: An Outline*, op. cit., pp.276-297.

[46] Rudolf Steiner, *Occult Science*, op. cit., p.292.

> 'It will be clear from the above that the "Guardian of the Threshold" is *an astral figure*, revealed to the awakening higher vision of the esoteric pupil... To make the Guardian of the Threshold physically visible also is *an operation connected with lower magic*'.[47] [emphasis added]

It is this 'lower magic' through the 'influence of the Luciferic powers' which provides the impetus to both 'Christian' visualisation and the occult version. Just as in Richard Foster's exercise one can have a meeting with an entity from whom one is to *'note carefully any instruction given'*, so the one meditating through 'imaginative cognition' in Steiner's exercises will also receive extensive direction from *'the Guardian of the Threshold'*,[48] an entity which is *'an astral figure'*.

It is of great concern that throughout Richard Foster's writings, which are very widely read by many gullible believers today, one finds an eclectic assortment of ideas borrowed from many different religious and psychotherapeutic influences. In fact, *'Celebration of Discipline'* is the perfect study manual for any would-be mystics, occultists, transcendental magicians and religious syncretists.

A serious question arises at this point: Are these 'inner guides' — whether Christian or secular — merely the creation of the human imagination, or do they indeed have an objective reality of their own? This last question was the cause of a major sectarian split in the Neo-Gnostic Movement in the 1930s. Alice Bailey and the theosophically-inclined held that their 'Ascended Masters' were actual discarnate beings who dwelt in an etheric retreat called Shambhala, who had been preserved as a 'good' remnant from the lost civilisation of Atlantis, which had fallen into great spiritual evil and therefore been destroyed in a deluge (the theosophists' version of the Flood). The Baileyites claimed that these Super-Beings from Atlantis are now actually manifesting themselves to any visualisers and meditators who call on their name for help and seek them in their visualisations. However, Carl Jung and his followers held that such entities are merely archetypal products of the 'collective unconscious' which are capable of manifesting as 'helpful constructs' in individual consciousness.[49] Alice Bailey and her followers resented this assertion, and this led to her abandonment of the ERANOS Conferences in Switzerland so that they later became dominated by the Jungians.[50]

However, as communication with these entities appears to provoke those contacting them into progressively deeper mystical or occult activity beneficial to the strategy of Satan, we must conclude that they are neither the 'good remnant from Atlantis' nor a variety of benign 'archetypes from the collective unconscious' of a

---

47 Rudolf Steiner, *Knowledge of the Higher Worlds*, op. cit., p.196.

48 Ibid., pp.191-196.

49 Annie Besant's protégé, Jiddu Krishnamurti, when he broke away from the Theosophical camp, had also came to a conclusion similar to the Jungians, that the 'Ascended Masters' were simply *'incidents'* in the mind of man, rather than having an objective reality of their own (Mary Lutyens, *Krishnamurti: The Years of Awakening*, Rider, 1975, p.242).

50 See Chapter 7, p.262 for details of the involvement of Alice Bailey and Carl Jung in the Eranos Conferences.

depraved humanity. Instead, we hold that these entities are of malignant spiritual origin (cf. 1 Tim.4:1; Eph.6:10-12). The fact that they also deceptively purport to be helping their recipients with beneficial advice only serves to highlight the predominant angel-of-light quality of the twentieth century demonic realm. Let us remember the advice of Irenaeus of Lyons, who said

> No false teaching desires to offer itself to our view openly, lest such exposure should lead to conviction; but, craftily putting on a plausible dress, makes itself by its outward form appear to the simpler sort to be truer than Truth itself '.[51]

Whatever these so-called 'inner guides' or 'sub-selves' are, you can be certain they are of demonic origin. This does not necessarily mean that these entities are *actual* demons themselves (albeit under a benevolent disguise). The fact that demons are by nature liars and deceivers *par excellence*, it could well be that an appropriate manifestation is somehow implanted by the powers of darkness into any human consciousness which willingly opens itself up to such an experience.

In this section, we have attempted to demonstrate that Christian visualisers are as adept at leading their students into non-ordinary or altered states of consciousness as their occult counterparts. We shall now examine a further use of visualisation: its use as a method of neutralising behavioural problems which have allegedly come about because of suppressed early-life traumas.

2. Visualisation: An Aid to 'Inner Healing'

The use of a visualised Christ or heavenly landscape in order to enter an altered state of consciousness does not stop merely at receiving flattering encouragement and esoteric messages. There is now a growing advocation of the use of these images as aids in a form of psychotherapy known as 'Inner Healing' or 'Healing of the Memories', in which the image of Jesus (and sometimes His mother Mary) is summoned up as a psychotherapeutic 'inner guide' and brought into deliberately recalled painful memories in a therapy session.

The use of this 'Inner Healing' technique in the churches originated with Agnes Sanford (1897-1982). Heavily influenced by the teachings of Carl Jung, she was the Charismatic wife of an Episcopalian priest. After experiencing healing from a long-standing depression she became involved in the healing movement and, after publication of her book *'The Healing Light'* (1947), her worldwide ministry began — a ministry which was to have an enormous influence on the subsequent development of the use of healing in the Charismatic Movement. She later published *'The Healing Gifts of the Spirit'*, the seventh chapter of which was entitled *'The Healing of the Memories'*.[52] It was this chapter that spawned a wave of literature which drew on its assumptions.

One of the major influences in the use of this visualisation technique in the Christian scene is Ruth Carter Stapleton, the sister of ex-President of the U.S.A.,

---

[51] Irenaeus of Lyons, *Against Heresies* or *A Refutation of Knowledge Falsely So-Called*, Introduction §2.

[52] Agnes Sanford, *The Healing Gifts of the Spirit* (Arthur James, 1966), pp.100-113.

Jimmy Carter. She packages visualisation into a form of therapy which she calls *'faith-imagination'*. In her classic book, *'The Gift of Inner Healing'*, she gives numerous examples which clearly illustrate what this system of belief is all about. On one occasion, she asks a woman who had been sexually abused by her father, to imagine a visualised Jesus forgiving the man for his assault, which then results in a cure of her psychological distress. Mrs. Stapleton specifically denies that she uses hypnotic suggestions and manipulative techniques, but instead she alleges that

> 'The miracle...takes place in the conscious imagination of the person healed. The manipulation, if any, is that of our Lord Jesus — His Holy Spirit — 'manipulating' to heal'.[53]

This confusion of an *imagined* Jesus with the *actual* Person of Christ is the fatal flaw in the entire psychotherapeutic visualisation process, about which we shall say more shortly. How convenient it is to invite the Jesus of your own imaginings into scenes where sins can be forgiven without repentance — not only those of others who have wronged you, but also your own! In another example, Mrs. Stapleton recounts a therapy session she led, in which a man who was a sexual exhibitionist was taken back in his mind to an early experience when he had been caught by his uncle in an act of masturbation. She writes:

> 'Memories of his uncle's roars and cursing rebukes flooded his mind in that moment. I repeated the words continuously, *'Jesus, Jesus, Jesus'*, throughout his story. As Zeb began to regain his composure, he visualized Jesus there in that room blessing him, blessing the room, blessing his life, and most important, blessing the part of his body that Zeb so hated and rejected. This last act, Zeb joining with Jesus in blessing his body, was the act that assured Zeb's healing'.[54]

Mrs. Stapleton states here that throughout Zeb's story she *continuously* repeated the words: *'Jesus, Jesus, Jesus'*, after which a visualised Jesus 'appears' in the therapy session. Think of the effect this would have on any counsellee. No hypnotic powers of suggestion? No manipulative techniques? In another therapy session, Mrs. Stapleton encourages an unbelieving homosexual to embrace a visualised image of Jesus as a substitute for his rejecting father. The scene that she conjures up for this man is simply riddled with a heady cocktail of powerful suggestions and mysticism. She tells him to imagine Jesus kneeling before him and accepting him unconditionally: *'Imagine Jesus saying to you, "Because I love you so much, I want you to love me"'*.[55] She then continues this therapy session by saying to the man:

> 'Put all your weight against [Jesus]. Let every care and burden fall on Jesus. Lean hard against him and feel that firmness. His love pulls you closer. Let go and sense your body moving into his body. Your body

[53] Ruth Carter Stapleton, *The Gift of Inner Healing* (Hodder & Stoughton, 1977), p.82.
[54] Ibid., p.110.
[55] Ibid., p.103.

> merges a little more and suddenly you are standing where he was standing. This oneness is what [Jesus] was longing for. *'I want you to be flesh of my flesh and bone of my bone. Where my heart beats, it is your heart. My mind is within your mind'.* Every part of you has entered into Jesus. Nothing can separate you. You are one body in the Father. He will never leave you or forsake you. In your weakness, let go and his thoughts will come through. Jesus tells you, *'My Spirit will direct your path. If you'll let me, I will speak my words through your mouth. The kingdom of heaven will come on earth because of your willingness to be open to me".*[56]

Bear in mind that all this powerful mystical suggestion is happening to a person who has never repented of his sin, who has never become a Christian in the biblical sense. Moreover, the root cause of our adult relationship problems does not lie merely in any unfulfilled childhood need for a loving earthly parent, for which Christ has to act as a substitute in the imagination. It is an evasion of responsibility to blame others for our ills in this way. As we discussed at length in our first look at the mind-sciences in Chapter 7, it is our alienation from God which gives us a distorted relationship with our parents in the first instance, on whom we subsequently make impossible demands. The Bible teaches believers to focus their minds on Christ and His life experience in times of personal difficulty, rather than on their own early-life traumas (Heb.12:1-4). We will develop this theme in more detail shortly.

In yet another example — this time with the psychotherapeutic manipulation even more highlighted — a woman whose marriage was in decline was told by Mrs. Stapleton to

> 'spend a little time each day visualising Jesus coming in the door from work. Then see yourself walking up to him, embracing him. Say to Jesus, 'Its good to have you home, Nick'. If you do this each day, you will condition yourself to respond to Nick as you would respond to Jesus... *This is the most powerful prayer you can pray for your husband*'.[57] [emphasis in original]

This technique is so obviously using a manufactured image of Jesus as a highly manipulative psychotherapeutic tool: *'You will condition yourself...'*. Yet Mrs. Stapleton can actually make the absurd claim that *'Faith-Imagination creates an objective experience. It does not approximate or simulate one'.*[58] In other words, she is saying that these visualised 'Jesuses' have an objective reality of their own. How can each of these products of a variety of sinful, fallen, human imaginations possibly be an objective experience of the risen Jesus Christ? Surely, this is yet another manifestation of the central claim of the New Gnosticism: that reality is nothing more than whatever each individual makes it out to be.

---

[56] Ibid., pp.103-104.
[57] Ibid., pp.35-36.
[58] Ibid., p.64.

A further question can here be raised: If each of these visualised 'christs' is *not* the objective, risen Christ of Scripture, then who or what are the entities which are conjured up in the imaginations of professing Christians and others who are encouraged to fantasise these images by Christian psychotherapists? The plain truth is that they are little different to those 'inner guides' of the secular visualisers whom we discussed earlier in this chapter. The 'Jesuses' and the 'Marys' of the Christian visualisers are, at best, merely the pathetic products of our impoverished imaginations (how easily we manufacture God in our own image!) or, at worst, they are actually the 'inner guides' of the shamans and occultists dressed up in a clothing which is socially, culturally, and spiritually acceptable to the one doing the 'imagineering'.

It is true that the secular psychotherapists and occultists may not use the specific images of Jesus or Mary for their visualisations, but they **do** involve the corresponding use of an idealised archetypal image which panders to our desires through tranquillising our sinful guilt (and, theoretically, the guilt of others who have wronged us) without any profession of repentance. In other words, they are reforming spirits rather than regenerating ones. They are counterfeiting true spiritual salvation and renewal with an induced psychological *catharsis.* They are taking away people's **feelings** of guilt without the slightest reduction in their **actual** moral guilt and standing before a holy, righteous and just God. This is the natural outcome of the fact that the majority of people on this planet (and a great many professing Christians also) do not recognise the existence of moral guilt as an objective reality which must be dealt with *forensically* before God's bar of justice. Instead, their understanding of guilt is that it is a psychological condition which must be relieved *therapeutically* on the psychiatrist's couch. Such deceptive developments are an intrinsic part of the 'Satanic Initiation' which is now becoming widely available within the institutions of the professing Church throughout the world. Christians have discovered the demonic ways used by the people of the world to make themselves feel good — and then mimicked them!

A particularly dangerous aspect of Inner Healing is the use, by the counsellor, of what purports to be the biblical gift of a 'Word of Knowledge' (cf. 1 Cor.12:8) in order to make suggestions to counsellees about the traumas of their past lives. This puts the counsellee in a very vulnerable position and at the behest of powerful suggestions given by the therapist. When Ruth Stapleton describes the gift of a 'Word of Knowledge' as *'a capacity to tune in on the psychic life of another without conscious communication'*,[59] this sounds far more like ESP than any of the biblical gifts of the Spirit. Indeed, very similar 'Words of Knowledge' are used by the psychic healers of today in the Neo-Gnostic scene.[60]

Another well-known exponent of this form of visualisation therapy is Methodist minister David Seamands. In common with the other Inner Healers, he has latched onto an essential secular psychodynamic principle — that bad early-life

---

[59] Ibid., p.125.

[60] For example, one can visit the 'Centre of Light' in Inverness-shire where it is openly claimed that *'guidance is channelled from the spirit world to help unfold problems'*.

experiences distort later relationships — and then devised a Christianised form of it which he refers to as *'imagineering'*. Explaining the need for this 'Healing of Memories', he writes:

> 'So many pastors and Christian workers...assume if the doctrines and ideas they preach and teach are biblically correct, they will automatically clear up a person's concepts of God and enable him to believe in God and trust Him. They imagine that the Holy Spirit, as it were, somehow drills a hole in the top of the hearer's head and pours the pure truth into him.
>
> 'With many people, nothing could be further from the truth. For although the Holy Spirit is the One who reveals the truth, what the listener hears and pictures and feels still has to be filtered through him. The Holy Spirit Himself does not bypass the personality equipment by which a person perceives things. *And when those perceiving receptors have been severely damaged, the biblical truths get distorted'*.[61] [emphasis in original]

But it is not because of the Holy Spirit's inability to *'bypass the personality equipment'* of the believer that biblical truths get distorted. In fact, the very idea that the Holy Spirit's work can be impeded merely by the 'personality equipment' of a person is itself a distortion of biblical truth! For the Bible teaches that the Word of God is distorted and stolen away by Satan (Mt.13:4,19), who has *'blinded the minds of unbelievers'* (2 Cor.4:4). The Holy Spirit was not too put out by the personality equipment of the Gadarene demoniac (Mk.5:1-15). The 'personality equipment' of a hypocritical tax-collector could not stand in the way of the Spirit of God inducing him to follow Christ (Mk.2:14). Neither was He unable to 'bypass the personality equipment' of a certain Pharisee who was breathing out threatenings and slaughter against the disciples of the Lord (Acts 9:1-9). The primary reason that so many believers who profess to have Jesus Christ as their Saviour do not grow spiritually and emotionally is because of their refusal to really listen to what God's Word is telling them, coupled with a refusal to be led exclusively by the Spirit in matters of sanctification (Gal.5:22-26; 2 Pet.1:3-11). The Bible does not teach that it is our early-life traumas which are the problem-generating factor in the believer's behavioural and emotional life. Instead, it teaches that it is *'the flesh'* — our sins and sinful pattern-making — which is the *real* source of our emotional and behavioural problems.

Let us just examine some of the claims of those who use the occult art of Visualisation as a psychotherapeutic tool.

The Spiritual Way Versus the Psychological Way

When Jesus told His disciples how to overcome worry, anxiety and fear for the future, He did not recommend that they should probe into the past to see if their problems were being caused by early-life deprivation trauma. Instead, He commanded them to *'seek first the kingdom of God and His righteousness'*

[61] David Seamands, *Healing of Memories* (Scripture Press, 1986), p.97.

(Mt.6:25-34). In other words, He dealt with their present reality and the need for them to take radical spiritual action **in the here-and-now**. Many other biblical examples could be given to show conclusively that these therapeutic methods are a recent, worldly invention, rather than a godly spiritual exercise. King David, for example, was a man who had innumerable difficulties, and often wrote about them graphically in the Psalms. But there is never a hint that in order to be free from his fear (Ps.31:13,14ff.), anxiety (Ps.70:5), loneliness (Ps.25:16; 31:11,14-15), depression (Ps.38:1-12), or low self-esteem (Ps.22:6), he had to re-live emotional traumas in his early life. Such obsessive focussing on self would never have occurred to one who could say, *'My eyes are ever **toward the Lord**, for He shall pluck my feet out of the net'* (Ps.25:15). Rather than seeking the offices of a local pagan (or pseudo-Israelite) Shaman, David could boldly declare: *'The Lord is my Shepherd'*.

We should not spend time whining and whingeing about the crazy-paving left by other people's sin upon our lives. That we should be the victims of the sin of others is inevitable; but when one becomes a new creation (2 Cor.5:17), all things are made new in order to display the incandescent glory of the one and only God, whose love brings with it the power to transform far more than simple stones into crude-baked bread. The Lord Jesus said, *'No one, having put his hand to the plough, and **looking back**, is fit for the kingdom of God'* (Lk.9:62); and when the man who Jesus commanded to follow Him asked if he could go and bury his father, Jesus said, *'Let the dead bury their own dead'* (Lk.9:59-60). The Christian disciple is not to dwell on his past. The old hurts and pains which have been induced by others pale into insignificance after conversion, when compared with the life which believers are now called to lead (Rom.8:18; 2 Cor.4:17).

People in biblical times — with their open exposure to death, demon possession, human sacrifice, disease, and other elemental hardships — must have had far more traumatic childhoods that we do today. Yet we never find so much as a hint of a 'Healing of the Memories' therapy in the Bible. Far from inducing Christians to apportion the blame for their personality problems to their parents' failure to nurture them correctly as new-born infants and children, Christian counsellors should be encouraging them to accept the promises of the Holy Spirit and to focus themselves on the Lord Jesus Christ, who endured far more hostility from sinners than any one of us will ever know (Heb.12:3-4). In following this simple pathway, we will discover the wealth of power He gives His people to change *through the use of spiritual rather than psychological means.*

As we have already discussed in Chapter 7, the 'personal growth therapy' recommended in the Bible for the believer is Mortification — the eradication, in the power of the Holy Spirit, of sinful behaviour patterns (Rom.8:13; Col.3:5; Eph.4:22). When Paul tells the Ephesians to shake off any anger they may feel before the day has ended, so that they will not provide a foothold for the devil in their lives (Eph.4:26-27), he is assuming an ability to do so without the aid of any psychotherapeutic techniques. When Paul tells the Philippian church, *'I have learned in whatever state I am, to be content'* (Phil.4:11), was it 'Healing of the

Memories' which had effected that Divine contentment? Had he put 'Faith-Imagination' to work for him in order to attain this mindset? Of course not! Instead, he goes on to reveal the great fact which applies to every child of God: *'I can do all things* ***through Christ*** *who strengthens me'* (Phil.4:13). It is to the *Living Christ* that Paul is referring here — the One who indwells His people through His Spirit — not a counterfeit 'christ' which has been conjured up in the imagination through psychological techniques.

We maintain that where the Word of God is ministered in power, where there is a real belief in the transforming energy of the Spirit, where the truths of the Bible are not just paper-based propositions, where there is a congregational thirst for spiritual (and thereby psychological) growth, then the believer will have all the resources available to cut through any residual problems of the flesh or sinful behaviour patterns, without the need for visualisation therapy as an aid to healing specific individual memories from the past. As the Apostle Peter assures us: *'[the Lord's] divine power has given to us all things that pertain to life and godliness'* (2 Pet.1:3). We pour scorn on this 'divine power' when we use cheap-jack techniques of human devising.

Actually, *genuine* inner-healing is a most vital and relevant part of the life-long transformation of the Christian. However, this does not mean that we have to dismantle our pasts and probe into every bad experience ever undergone. The Bible clearly teaches that Christians should not be obsessed with focussing on themselves; in fact, Jesus explicitly taught that the one who would follow Him must *'deny himself, and take up his cross daily'* (Lk.9:23). The one seeking to save his life will lose it; but the one who seeks to lose his life for Christ's sake shall preserve it (Lk.9:24; 17:33). It is true that the believer may need in-depth spiritual counsel during the course of his or her life; and he or she may even need to have some painful memories and past hurts expunged. For example, some people may need to let go of resentment or bitterness which they have been harbouring against others for many years. But the pastoring required in such cases will not need to rely on secular psychotherapeutic techniques for its effective resolution. Neither should it enlist the assistance of visualised entities. If we have bitterness, resentment or anger at those who in the past have hurt us, then we are guilty of sin; and we can only be healed of that through obedience to Christ rather than by therapy (cf. Mt.6:14-15; 18:21-35; cf. Eph.4:26-27). We should use the Biblico-spiritual way rather than the secular-psychological way for our inner healing.

The reliving of early childhood traumas as a form of therapy goes back to Sigmund Freud (1856-1939). He pioneered this therapeutic approach in conjunction with Josef Breuer (1842-1925).[62] Finding it too intense, Freud panicked as he developed his regression therapy and he later back-tracked to a strictly analytical-couch approach. Thereafter, this 'abreactive' therapy was developed further by Freud's pupil, Wilhelm Reich (1897-1957), who crudely renamed it as 'Vegeto-Therapy'. One of Reich's better known patients was A.S. Neill, headmaster of the

---

[62] See *Studies in Hysteria*, Vol.III, Pelican Freud Library (Penguin, 1973), for details of the work which Freud carried out with Josef Breuer.

liberal school Summerhill, whose philosophy of child-rearing was based on Reich's ideas. After Reich died in 1957, this work was taken further by others whom he had influenced such as Alexander Lowen (Bioenergetics) and Arthur Janov (Primal Therapy) in the U.S., and Frank Lake (Clinical Theology) and William Swartley (Structural Integration Therapy) in the U.K. The therapeutic principles behind Christian 'Inner Healing' and 'Healing of Memories' have simply been lifted from their secular counterparts in the field.

From a biblical standpoint, the sheer redundancy of Healing of the Memories is revealed when David Seamands presents his four biblical foundations for his psychotherapeutic teaching: **1)** The putting away of childish things, as based on 1 Corinthians 13:11; **2)** Accepting Christ as one's *present* Helper, based on such verses as Mt.28:20; Jn.14:23; Heb.13:8; Jn.8:57-58; etc; **3)** The need to pray specifically about sins, failures and needs; **4)** Ministry to one another (body-ministry).[63] But these four foundations cannot possibly provide a solid base on which to ground his teachings on Inner Healing. When Paul speaks of 'putting away childish things', it is a master-feat of *eisegesis* to read into the text that he means being freed from painful childhood memories through cathartic therapy! The context of the passage is actually about the deepening of objective revelation rather than self-centred experience. Similarly, the fact that we have the Holy Spirit as our Helper during this Gospel Age does not provide any justification to conjure up a visualised Jesus in our imaginations. When He is said to come alongside His people in times of need (the word *paraclete*, from the Greek *parakletos*, means 'one who is called alongside'), it is a purely figurative expression, as the Holy Spirit — by definition — cannot have a bodily form (cf. Jn.3:8).

The third 'biblical' foundation given by David Seamands for his therapy is *'the need to pray specifically about sins, failures and needs'*. That we should so pray, we would wholeheartedly support; but, again, this does not justify the use of a visualised image of Christ in our prayers. Every prayer recorded in Scripture is linguistically based. David Seamands' visualisation activities cannot possibly be classed as 'prayers'. His fourth 'biblical' justification for 'imagineering' is the need for ministry to one another — what some call 'body ministry'. Again, we would support the entire concept of saints ministering to one another's needs (cf. Gal.6:2; Rom.15:1; 1 Th.5:14). But what these biblical injunctions have to do with invoking ancient painful memories and conjuring up visualised images of Christ is quite beyond the present writer to ascertain.

Visualisation is Idolatry

What, therefore, should be the response of the Christian to the use of visualisations involving the image of Jesus Christ? Of primary concern should be the fact that this type of activity is specifically forbidden and warned against within the pages of the Bible. It is a solemn fact that every figurative representation of God contradicts His being; and although we do not wish to obscure the fact that Jesus (as God manifested in the flesh) was *a real human being*, the conjuring up of a

---

[63] David Seamands, op. cit., pp.61-78.

visualised image of Christ for the purposes of mental manipulation is surely a gross form of idolatry. The last thing that the Christian should be doing is relying on such images in the imagination for guidance in life or to increase faith.

When Richard Foster makes the statement that *'imagination opens the door to faith'*,[64] this is in direct opposition to the authoritative statement in the Bible that the Christian walks *'by faith, not by sight'* (2 Cor.5:7). The use of the imagination to generate an image of Christ is therefore a sign of a *lack* of faith, and an attempt to walk by sight! In fact, the entire context of this verse of Paul is most instructive concerning visualisations involving the Lord Jesus Christ. The Apostle tells us that *'while we are at home in the body, we are absent from the Lord'* (2 Cor.5:6). In v.8, he says that we would rather be freed from this limitation of earthly life in order to be in the presence of Jesus. In other words, he is saying that being alive ('in the body') involves not having the visible Christ with us: We would have to be freed from the body before we could be in His presence. That must surely make a nonsense of the claim of the Inner Healers that their visualised 'christs' are the *real* Christ! Paul goes on to say that the way we overcome this problem of not having the Lord with us in the flesh is to remember that God has given us the indwelling Holy Spirit as a 'downpayment' on or 'guarantee' of our future heavenly inheritance (2 Cor.5:5). In other words, Jesus is present with us through the invisible, indwelling Holy Spirit. Paul then crowns it all with the grand affirmation that *'we walk by faith, not by sight'*. 'Faith' and 'sight' are mutually exclusive. This includes any 'sightings' of Jesus.

It is completely untrue to say that imagination *'opens the door to faith'*, as Richard Foster claims. In the Christian life, it is faith that opens the door to assurance. The Holy Spirit's own definition of 'faith' is that it is *'the substance of things hoped for, the evidence of things not seen'* (Heb.11:1). *'Things **not** seen'*. Contrary to Richard Foster's claims, faith does not need the human imagination to open the door for it. Faith is self-sufficient — a miraculous provision of God. It is only in those Christian circles which have a defective doctrine of sanctification and assurance that one will find people who need to rely on the use of their imagination to increase their faith. In fact, it is our sincere belief that these visualised images of Christ could well provide an opportunity for demonic deception.

Jesus is not present in bodily manifestation — either on the earth or in people's minds — throughout the entire Gospel Age. It is also true that He has not left us as orphans (Jn.14:18; Mt.28:20b). But from the time of His Ascension until His second coming, the presence of Christ is manifested through His Holy Spirit, who is an indwelling gift to all those who believe in Him. If the bodily form of the Lord Jesus Christ was to be so accessible to anyone who wants to imagine it or conjure it up, regardless of his or her standing before God, then the unmistakable significance and reality of His future return would be lost. This is precisely why Jesus made it clear that the next possible sighting of Him, after His Ascension, would be unique and inimitable:

'Therefore if they say to you, *'Look, He is in the desert!'*, do not go out;

[64] Richard Foster, op. cit., p.36.

> or *'Look, He is in the inner rooms!'*, do not believe it. For as the lightning comes from the east and flashes to the west, so also will the coming of the Son of Man be' (Mt.24:26-27).

The 'christs' which are visualised in the 'inner rooms' of the visualisers' minds are just as much of an abomination before the Lord as those dredged up within secret societies and mystery cults through special gnosis. Again, when John the Apostle refers to Jesus' second coming, he makes it absolutely clear that our Lord's bodily form will be seen *only* when He returns, and not before:

> 'And now, little children, abide in Him, that when He appears, we may have confidence and not be ashamed before Him at His coming... Beloved, now we are children of God; and it has not yet been revealed what we shall be, but we know that when He is revealed, we shall be like Him, for we shall see Him as He is' (1 Jn.2:28 & 3:2).

Do you see the tremendous significance of what the Apostle is saying here? If it was possible for us to see the real Jesus **now**, then this statement of John that *'it has not yet been revealed what we shall be'* would be wrong. For he says that the only way we will be able to determine what we shall be like in eternity is to receive a visible manifestation of Jesus. But, as John says, it is only when Jesus is revealed at the Second Coming that *'we shall see Him as He is'* and thereby have a revelation of what *we* shall be like.[65] In the meantime, it is just as Paul said: *'While we are at home in the body we are absent from the Lord'*. The visible, bodily form of the authentic Jesus Christ is not available 'on tap' to all those who want to receive a psychological 'inner healing' on the cheap. Far from being available to be flashed onto the mind-canvasses of all the recipients of 'Inner Healing', Jesus Christ is the One *'whom **heaven** must receive until the times of restoration of all things'* (Acts 3:21). He is figuratively represented in Scripture as *'sitting at the right hand of God'* throughout the Gospel Age (Col.3:1), and will not be bodily revealed until lawlessness has reached its fullness at the end of the age, when His enemies will be made His footstool (Ps.110:1; Mt.22:41-46).

In the same way that the sign of a true Christian is that he walks by faith and not by sight, so the mark of the true heathen is that he walks by sight rather than by faith. This is why the unbeliever inevitably *'change[s] the glory of the incorruptible God into an image made like corruptible man'*. He walks by sight rather than by faith. He cannot help but exchange the truth of God for the Lie — worshipping and serving the creature rather than the Creator (Rom.1:16-25). The faith of the Children of Israel was so hopelessly lacking that as soon as their divinely-inspired leader went up the mountain and disappeared out of view, they built themselves a golden calf (Exod.32:1-8). They walked by sight rather than by faith. But where true faith in the power of the invisible God is strong and real, there will be no dependence on mere man-made images for our succour. 'Faith-Imagination' is a latter-day golden calf. 'Inner Healing' is actually a New Age

---

[65] Actually, when John did see a vision of the risen Christ in glory by special revelation, it was anything but a psychologically soothing experience (Rev.1:17)!

stand-in for true biblical counselling, and has been designed by Satan as a counterfeit of the sanctifying work of the Holy Spirit in the life of the believer.

Let us also remember our exposé, in Chapter 7, of the fact that *'somnambulistic trance is the rule rather than the exception in people's everyday "waking activity"'*, and that *'most of the techniques in different types of psychotherapy are nothing more than hypnotic phenomena'.*[66] You will recall that these words came from a trainer of psychotherapists during one of his training sessions. What is being carried out by these Christian therapists and visualisers is a form of powerful hypnotic suggestion which has been 'sanitised' by the presence of an alleged vision of Jesus Christ. Inner Healing and Healing of the Memories are a mixture of hypnotherapy and unadulterated idolatry practised on gullible people who are seeking a quick and easy answer to their struggles with sin by any means available. Its origin is not in the Word of God, but in the psychological theories of men who were inspired by the occult tradition. This is frankly admitted in an article on 'Pentecostal and Charismatic Spirituality' in the authoritative 'Dictionary of Pentecostal and Charismatic Movements', which states:

> 'One sector of the Charismatic movement, a sector that could be called "The Jungian School" (Agnes Sanford popularised the approach) takes dreams very seriously and finds in the intricate psychological writings of Carl Jung a theoretical basis (Kelsey, 1964, 1968). *Inner Healing* was an understandable development that emerged out of that school'.[67]

Whether one walks by sight or by faith is determined by whether or not one has received the Spirit who is from God (1 Cor.2:6-16), for faith itself is a gift from the Lord (Eph.2:8). Those who indulge in the 'new idolatry' of a visualised Christ are actually behaving as if they were His enemies. Although they may achieve some measure of renewed psychological healing, this will by no means compensate for the anguish of being left outside the gates of the New Jerusalem when all things are revealed and all will be judged (Mt.13:41-42; Rev.22:15). *'Little children, keep yourselves from idols'* (1 Jn.5:21).

3. Visualisation: Manipulating the Material World

So far in this chapter, we have seen that visualisation can be used as a preparation for occult meditation, as a 'doorway' into altered states of consciousness and as a manipulative technique for psychological 'healing'. We have seen how these techniques — because of their quasi-devotional and cathartic qualities — have been dressed up to look like *bona fide* Christian practices. There is yet another form of visualisation — and probably the most diabolic of all — which involves its use as a technique for **the manipulation of matter and consciousness**.

Let us remind ourselves once more of the occultist's position on this whole process of the magical use of the imagination. Earlier, we learned that Alice

---

[66] Richard Bandler and John Grinder, *Frogs into Princes: Neuro-Linguistic Programming* (Real People Press, 1979), p.100.

[67] Stanley M. Burgess & Gary B. McGee, *Dictionary of Pentecostal and Charismatic Movements* (Zondervan, 1988), p.808.

Bailey's 'inner guide', the Ascended Master Djwal Khul, had written through her: *'The clue to all this esoteric work demanded by Shambhala is to be found in the development of the Art of Visualisation'.*[68] One of the prime reasons why occultists wish to develop the capacity and power of their imaginations is so that they can effect extraordinary changes in their lives, the lives of others and in their circumstantial environments through powerful visualisation of the desired change.

In its Christian expression, this technique has come to be known by a variety of names, including 'Possibility Thinking', 'Praying with the Imagination', or 'Incubating Prayer'. The first of our 'Christian' examples of this technique is the Korean minister, Dr. Paul Yonggi Cho. In his book, *'The Fourth Dimension: The Key to Putting Your Faith to Work for a Successful Life'*, Dr. Cho develops a doctrine of prosperity through the use of 'mind-power' which any occultist would enthusiastically applaud. He is pastor of the Pentecostal Assemblies of God Full Gospel Central Church in Seoul, Korea, which has more than half a million members. Dr. Cho is highly admired by many in the West because of the size of his congregation and most especially because he has come to symbolise the Charismatic Movement's ideal of 'renewal' and revival in the Church. In Pentecostal-Charismatic circles it is anathema to speak badly of this Korean leader, who is held up as the paragon of an 'anointed and Spirit-filled ministry'. However, a simple perusal of his books reveals a theology which has been 'ripped off' from some primary teachings of the New Gnosticism.

Dr. Cho has devised a theory which he calls *'incubation'*. He uses this to refer to a period of development which is needed in the imagination before a desired object can be physically manifested. He argues that because Scripture tells us that faith is the substance of things hoped for (Heb.11:1), this substance must undergo a period of 'incubation' in what he calls the 'Fourth Dimension' *'before its usage can be full and effective'.*[69] His proof text for this occurs in Gen.1:2, where the Hebrew states that the Spirit of God was 'brooding' over the waters. This act of creation can, claims Dr. Cho, be repeated through each Christian believer, who only has to visualise something in his or her mind's eye and it will become a reality, provided it is painted in sufficient detail. He puts it like this: *'What becomes pregnant in your heart and mind is going to come out in your circumstances'.*[70]

In successive extravagant feats of exegetical juggling, Dr. Cho also cites certain portions of Scripture as being examples of this incubated visualisation. Sarah could only conceive Isaac because she visualised him; Jacob's cattle gave birth to speckled and spotted offspring because he visualised them first; Moses could build the tabernacle because he was first given a visualised picture of it by God on Mount Sinai; Peter became the rock on which the Church was built because Jesus visualised it and therefore made it happen. The mind simply boggles at the

---

[68] Sir John Sinclair, *The Alice Bailey Inheritance* (Turnstone Press, 1984), p.154. Shambhala is the name of the 'etheric' headquarters of the so-called 'Ascended Masters'.

[69] Paul Yonggi Cho, *The Fourth Dimension: The Key to Putting Your Faith to Work for a Successful Life* (Logos International/Valley Books Trust, 1979), p.9.

[70] Ibid., p.31.

ingenious way that Dr. Cho manages to bend text after text in support of his warped understanding of Christian prayer.

Dr. Cho claims to have discovered this technique early in his ministry. He was living in some hardship and felt that, as a child of God, he deserved a desk and chair, and a bicycle to ride. After praying for these objects for several months, nothing had happened — at which point he remonstrated with the Lord that He was making a mockery of his ministry, since who would believe in a God who would not answer the prayers of His servant? He then asked God to 'speed things up' and, after some accompanying pleasant physical sensations, he claimed to receive the following reply:

> 'That is the trouble with you, and all my children. They beg me, demanding every kind of request, but they ask in such vague terms that I can't answer. Don't you know that there are dozens of kinds of desks, chairs and bicycles? But you've simply asked me for a desk, chair and bicycle. You never ordered a specific desk, chair or bicycle'.[71]

This alleged statement from God was the turning point in Dr. Cho's life. He 'cancelled' all past prayers and got off to a fresh start. He then 'ordered' from God a Philippine mahogany desk (stating size, etc.), an iron-framed chair with rollers on (*'so that I could push myself around like a big shot'*), and a U.S. made bicycle with gears.[72] He then adds that he ordered them *'in such articulate terms that God could not make a mistake in delivering them'*.[73] Before examining further examples of Dr. Cho's prayer technique, let us mark well the fact that a god who is even *capable* of making a mistake cannot possibly be the Sovereign God of the Bible! One begins to gain a grasp of where Dr. Cho is coming from when, in the commendatory foreword by U.S. minister Robert H. Schuller, we read, *'Thank you, Paul Yonggi Cho, for allowing the Holy Spirit to give this message to us and to the world. God loves you and so do I'*.[74] Yonggi Cho *allows* the Holy Spirit to do things! These people actually believe that they are above the Lord God of creation and that He exists simply to do their bidding. Such 'Aladdin's Lamp' religion is gathering many advocates within the Charismatic-Pentecostal churches today.

A further example of Dr. Cho's prayer technique involved the procurement of a husband for an unmarried woman in a congregation he was visiting. Having been told that she had been praying for a spouse for more than ten years, he asked her what kind of a husband she had been praying for. *'Well'*, she replied, *'that's up to God. God knows all'*. To which Cho retorts: *'That's your mistake. God never works by Himself, but only through you'*.[75] Whereupon, the two of them devise an accurate description of the desired husband, and Cho asks her to close her eyes and visualise this model of a husband, telling her: *'Until you see your husband*

[71] Ibid., p.12.
[72] Ibid., pp.12-13.
[73] Ibid., p.13.
[74] Ibid., p.viii.
[75] Ibid., p.18.

clearly in your imagination, you can't order, because God will never answer'.[76] Then the woman kneels down, Dr. Cho lays hands on her, and prays thus:

> 'Oh, God, now she knows her husband. I see her husband. You know her husband. We order him in the name of Jesus Christ'.[77]

Some questions awould be appropriate here: What sort of a god is it that *'never works by himself but only through you'*? What sort of a Christian pastor is it who can say, *'God is as large as you allow him to be'*? or *'Before you give the word, the Holy Spirit does not have the proper material with which to create'.*[78] This sheer manipulation of God, the forcing of the Lord's hand to get exactly what we want — and the suggestion that God is somehow *dependent* on us to get certain things done — is a growing trend in the Church today. These people need to digest the words of the hymn which says:

> 'Thou wast, O God, and Thou wast blest
> Before the world began.
> Of Thine eternity possessed
> Before time's hour-glass ran.
> Thou neededst none thy praise to sing
> As if Thy joy could fade:
> Shouldst Thou have needed anything
> Thou couldst have nothing made.

Many purportedly Christian gatherings are promoting seminars which encourage such a self-centred mindset by offering believers the tantalising opportunity to

> 'discover how God's Word can explode into powerful demonstration when mixed with faith... Learn how to tap into the powerful resources of God on the inside of you and experience a lifestyle that is marked by the supernatural'.[79]

Such a description is designed to appeal to the sensual rather than the spiritual. Indeed, it all sounds far more like a New Age workshop — where the emphasis is very much on developing extraordinary powers — than a genuine Christian conference gathering. This is the brand of Christianity which is attracting the people *en masse* today. It is what 'Church Growth' in the 1990s is all about.

MY Will be Done

Coupled with this 'power' Christianity, an increasing number of people who profess to be believers have decided that when they pray, there is no need to wait on the will of the Lord for an answer; one simply has to decide what one wants, make it the will of God, and then 'tap into the god within' to obtain it. That is not Christianity; that is occultism purely stated. Richard Foster unfolds his discovery

---

76 Ibid., p.20.

77 Ibid.

78 Ibid., p.75.

79 Covenant Ministries programme, *'Restoration 90: A Holy Convocation'*, Royal Welsh Showground, Wales.

of this startling revelation when he tells us that:

> 'Perhaps the most astonishing characteristic of Jesus' praying is that when He prayed for others He never concluded by saying *'if it be Thy will'*. Nor did the apostles or prophets when they were praying for others. They obviously believed that they knew what the will of God was before they prayed the prayer of faith... I saw that when praying for others there was evidently no room for indecisive, tentative, half-hoping, *'if it be Thy will'* prayers'.[80]

Another well-known Christian counsellor, Selwyn Hughes, makes a very similar statement:

> 'In the whole of the record of the Bible we have only one person who ever came to Jesus with the words, 'IF IT BE THY WILL', and that person was the poor helpless leper who revealed his ignorance of God's will by asking for his healing in this way... If you are not SURE that it is God's will to heal you then your faith is undermined from the start... If you are not sure about it being God's will to heal you then how can you pray the 'prayer of faith'?' [81]

This supplanting of God's will by an act of the human will is a very common occurrence in Neo-Pentecostal circles. The Charismatic teacher, Kenneth Copeland, sums up this philosophy when he endorses the teaching that

> 'Your will determines everything you do. It determines your success or failure. It opens or closes the door to your financial success. It determines everything you are, everything you have been, and everything you ever will be. No one can determine your life and its outcome but you'.[82]

In rejecting a deference to the *inscrutable* will of God in their prayer-life, these men have discovered that most treasured secret of all magic and sorcery: **the primacy of the will of the creature over against the will of the Creator**. This is the primal sin of pride which man learned on Satan's knee in Eden, and which had already led to Satan's downfall prior to that. This supremacy of the human will, when coupled with man-made visualisations, forms the ultimate alliance for occult-magical work. As Macgregor Mathers, one of the founders of the magical 'Order of the Golden Dawn' once stated in a lecture: *'To practise magic, both **the Imagination and the Will** must be called into action'*.[83]

Notice also that both Richard Foster and Selwyn Hughes refer to the 'prayer of faith'. This is a reference to the passage in James's letter, which says, *'And the prayer of faith will save the sick, and the Lord will raise him up'* (Jas.5:15). This

---

[80] Richard Foster, op. cit., p.33.

[81] Selwyn Hughes, *Lord, Heal me Now* (Crusade for World Revival, n.d.), p.13.

[82] Kenneth Copeland, *Walking in the Realm of the Miraculous* (KCP, n.d.), p.101.

[83] Colin Wilson, *Mysteries: An Investigation into the Occult, Paranormal and Supernatural*, op. cit., p.244.

is understood by many to mean that if a person praying for one who is sick has absolute certainty that the invalid will be healed, then it will happen, the Lord will definitely raise him up. This is yet another example of plucking a solitary verse out of its biblical context and forcing it to support a theory. In this instance, the theory is that it is God's will that no one should ever be ill. However, this is a most dangerous theory, for the following reasons. Since it is patently obvious that not every sick person prayed for (even by them) is healed, then for those who hold this theory, this must mean one of two things: either **1)** the person praying did not have enough faith, or **2)** the Lord has been outsmarted by Satan. Whichever one you go for, the precious name of God is besmirched, for the first implies that healing is of human origin, commensurate with the amount of faith exercised by the person praying; while the second implies that God is not the Lord of creation. What these people fail to recognise is that the efficacy of any prayer must always be seen in the light of the 'control text' in John's first letter, which says:

> 'Now this is the confidence that we have in Him, that if we ask anything **according to His will**, He hears us' (1 Jn.5:14).

This does not mean that we can, or must, infallibly know God's will every time we pray for someone or something. Children ask their human parents for all sorts of things that they are unable to have, but they could not have known that before they asked. It is the same with God and His spiritual children. We can pray in total confidence for those things that God has promised to give, which we know from His Word, the Bible. Only then can we invoke the name of Jesus — just as the command, *'Open in the name of the law'* can only be properly said when the law provides a warrant for the demand.

God answers prayer in one of three ways: *'Yes'*, *'No'*, or *'Not yet'*. One of the primary purposes of prayer is to teach us to be dependent on the will of God for all things, not so that we can manipulate God into doing anything we desire. To claim that all we have to do to make a prayer work is to strongly *believe* that it will work is a totally carnal — nay, fundamentally magical — concept. Furthermore, no less an authority than the Lord Jesus taught His disciples to pray to God with the words, *'Thy will be done'* (Mt.6:10). And when He was Himself plunged into anguish in the Garden of Gethsemane, and pleaded with His Father to let this cup pass from Him, He was careful to add those all-important words, *'yet not as I will, but as You will'* (Mt.26:39).

So the 'prayer of faith', for these visualisers, does not mean resting on the Lord to do whatever He sees fit with regard to our humble petitions. Instead, it means making God into a 'Genie of the Lamp' who can be invoked to do our bidding. Thus, the tail is made to wag the dog. We first visualise what we want to happen; then order God to make it work. Because this visualisation occurs in what Dr. Cho calls *'the Fourth Dimension'*, he claims that *'through visualizing and dreaming you can incubate your future and hatch the results'*.[84] And does it work? You bet! His entire writings — if one is willing to believe the train of tall stories —

---

[84] Paul Yonggi Cho, op. cit., p.44.

form one continuous testimony of what it means to live the miraculous, abundant life. Dr. Cho's big discovery, therefore, is that

> 'Men, by exploring their spiritual sphere of the fourth dimension through the development of concentrated visions and dreams in their imaginations, can brood over and incubate the third dimension, influencing and changing it. That is what the Holy Spirit taught me'.[85]

Dr. Cho freely confesses that this same technique of miraculous procurement in the third dimension through 'praying' with the imagination in the fourth dimension is practised, with similar results, by unbelievers — including various religious sects in Korea.[86] He attributes this to the fact that believers and unbelievers alike have the ability to exercise 'fourth dimension power' over third dimension circumstances — the one for good, the other for evil purposes.

The Ways of Witchcraft

Before we identify the true origins of Dr. Cho's religion, let us look at another exponent of the visualisation techniques in this present category. The striking similarities between them will amply prove that Yonggi Cho is not an isolated case. Richard Foster, admired by many Evangelicals, freely acknowledges that his inspiration for practising such techniques was the 'faith healer', Agnes Sanford. Having made that extraordinary claim that *'imagination opens the door to faith'*, he then goes on to give the fundamental teaching on this form of visualisation:

> 'If we can 'see' in our mind's eye a shattered marriage whole or a sick person well, it is only a short step to believing that it will be so'.[87]

As an example of this, he tells of how, with a four year old boy, he 'prayed' for his seriously ill baby sister. After describing the visualisation exercise through which he took the child, during which an image of Jesus lays hands on the baby, he says: *'Together we prayed in this childlike way and then we thanked the Lord that what we 'saw' was the way it was going to be'.*[88] Richard Foster sets up the visualised scene, and then simply assumes that the image *he* has created is how it will really be. As a betrayal of his lack of assurance in his visualised image of Christ, he attributes the child's subsequent healing to either of two causes: *'a posthypnotic suggestion in the child or...divine fiat'*. This is a telling admission. Were *any* of the real-life healings of Jesus ever effected by posthypnotic suggestion? How then is it possible for the healing effected by this visualised Jesus — which Mr. Foster believes to be the real Jesus — to be a posthypnotic suggestion?

As a matter of fact, *all* the faith-healing and visualisation being done today — whether in the Charismatic-Pentecostal Movement or its secular counterpart, the New Age Movement — relies entirely on powerful posthypnotic suggestion. These people are using visualisation techniques as a means of manipulating

---

85 Ibid., pp.39-40.

86 Ibid., pp.37-41.

87 Richard Foster, op. cit., p.36.

88 Ibid., p.37.

external matter and the internal consciousness of both themselves and others. Although 'visualisation' is the specific label by which these methods are euphemistically known in the secular world, from a biblical standpoint they all come under the umbrella heading of **witchcraft**. By deception or design (only the Lord knows which), these people are peddling a 'Christianised' form of what is known in the vocabulary of the New Gnosticism as *'New Thought Teachings'*.

The occult mind-science of 'New Thought' has been defined by one of its leading advocates as the practice of *'spiritual psychology'* and as *'Ancient Wisdom, Westernized, Christianized, and pragmaticized'.*[89] You will recall that a common feature of the New Gnosticism is the concept of a lost primeval wisdom which is now being rediscovered through psychotherapy, mind-expanding drugs, meditation, mysticism, etc. The techniques of the New Gnosticism are an attempt to syncretise these various strands and make them palatable to the Western mind. Christian Science, Attitudinal Healing, Silva Mind Control, Psychosynthesis and Possibility Thinking, are just a few of the modern New Thought manifestations of the so-called 'Ancient Wisdom'. It is also worth noting that the lyrics of the well-known song, *'Imagine'* (1970), a veritable anthem of the New Gnosticism written by the former member of the Beatles pop group, John Lennon, were based on essential New Thought visualisation principles which echo precisely Richard Foster's assertion: *'If we can 'see' [something] in our mind's eye...it is only a short step to believing that it will be so'*. J. Gordon Melton, founder of the Institute for the Study of American Religion, states that

> 'New Thought is a religious movement founded in the United States in the late nineteenth century as a popular religious expression of idealism, a form of philosophical thought that can be traced through Western culture to Plato (428-348 BCE). The movement's institutional roots can perhaps be traced to movements such as ancient Gnosticism and Neoplatonism'.[90]

From the early part of this century, professing Christians have adapted certain aspects of this Gnostic and Neoplatonist movement to the Christian life and message. In recent decades, New Thought principles have become especially attractive to many teachers and evangelists in the Charismatic Movement. When Yonggi Cho says that *'God never works by Himself, but only through you'*,[91] he is mimicking, almost to the letter, the parallel 'New Thought' occult principle which says: *'[God's] Power can work for you only as it works through you'.*[92] When Richard Foster says, *'If we can 'see' in our mind's eye a shattered marriage whole or a sick person well, it is only a short step to believing that it will be so'* (see footnote 86), and after visualising he *'thanked the Lord that what we 'saw' was the way it was going to be'*, he is mimicking a fundamental 'New Thought' occult principle which says:

---

[89] John Randolph Price, *The Planetary Commission* (Quartus Books, 1986), p.164.

[90] J. Gordon Melton, *New Age Encyclopedia* (Gale Research Inc., 1990), p.221.

[91] Paul Yonggi Cho, op. cit., p.18.

[92] John Randolph Price, *The Superbeings* (Quartus Books, 1981), p.xxi.

> 'Make a list of what you want in life, claim it as your own, visualize the experience of having the fulfillment of your desires, affirm that it is done, and give thanks. Then stand by for a miracle'.[93]

In another statement in a classic manual of the 'New Thought' Movement, the true source of the techniques advocated by Richard Foster and Yonggi Cho is again exposed: *'One must...rejoice and give thanks that he has already received... Man can only receive what he* ***sees*** *himself receiving'*.[94] In yet another example, exposing the source of the Christian visualisers, the 'New Thought' Center for Attitudinal Healing sums up its own creed in just the same way, with a quote taken from the 'New Thought' book, *'A Course in Miracles'*:

> 'I am responsible for what I see. I choose the feelings I experience, and **I decide upon the goal I would achieve**. And everything that seems to happen to me I ask for, and receive as I have asked'.[95]

In yet another example proving that Richard Foster's 'prayer' method of visualisation is secular and occult, sample this description from a 'motivational' book published by the Neo-Gnostic publishers Thorsons:

> 'You first create the mental image of what you desire, and then project it upon the inner mental screen through an act of will, letting yourself feel a strong desire for the materialization of this picture in real life, having faith, at the same time, that what you have visualized has already been achieved in mind and is even now on the way to you'.[96]

This conceptual framework behind the 'New Thought' Movement (and the 'Christian' visualisers) is the essential principle of all witchcraft. The practice of making something happen through a concentrated act of the human will — no matter how one may dress it up in terms such as 'Incubation', 'Visualisation', 'Imagineering', 'Faith-Imagination', or 'Possibility Thinking' — is simply the ancient art of casting or weaving a spell. Just as Richard Foster can say that *'if we can 'see' [something] in our mind's eye...it is only a short step to believing that it will be so'*, feminist theologian and witch, Naomi R. Goldenberg, states that *'all witchcraft begins with a psychic picture that a woman works to weave into reality'*.[97] Similarly, leading witch Miriam Simos (Starhawk) writes:

> 'To work magic is to weave the unseen forces into form... Spells are an important aspect of magical training. They require the combined faculties of relaxation, *visualisation*, concentration and projection... *The*

---

[93] Ibid., p.xv.

[94] Florence Scovel-Shinn, *The Game of Life and How to Play it* (Fowler, 1925), pp.18-19.

[95] Gerald G. Jampolsky, *Teach Only Love: The Seven Principles of Attitudinal Healing* (Bantam, 1983), p.25. *A Course in Miracles* (RKP, 1983) was dictated by automatic writing, and is available in most High Street bookshops, and also in some 'Christian' bookshops.

[96] Claud M. Bristol and Harold Sherman, *TNT — The Power Within You: How to Release the Forces Inside You and Get What You Want* (Thorsons, 1992), p.179.

[97] Naomi R. Goldenberg, *Changing of the Gods* (Beacon Books, 1979), p.97.

> *visualisation we create in a spell should be that of the desired end*'.[98] [emphasis added]

In a book for our times, *'Magic for the Aquarian Age'*, the leading British witch, Marion Green, rightly claims that

> 'Creative visualisation...is a method of directing what you see and of creating...a new place or condition. It is the most important key to practical magical work and allows you to direct your will effectively, through the images you create'.[99]

As another echo of Richard Foster's statement that *'if we can 'see' in our mind's eye a shattered marriage whole or a sick person well, it is only a short step to believing that it will be so'*, this witch says

> 'Through experiencing the images creative visualisation can show you, and by learning to see things as they are, you are moving into a greater, virtually infinite world of visions. *By recognising what you see as real now*, you can create a new future for that scene in which things can be changed for the better'.[100] [emphasis added]

Many more examples could be given here to show the true source of the teaching of Richard Foster, Yonggi Cho and all the other 'Christian' visualisers. This does not mean that visualising a future goal is inherently wrong. There are occasions when such determined thinking is necessary; for example, when planning out a strategy for the implementation of ideas. This is why we have the gift of imagination from God. But this practice moves from being positive thinking to being outright occultism when the person begins to think that he is actually *creating the future as it will be*, rather than merely imagining it how he would like it to be. Any form of visualisation which is used as a technique for the alteration of matter and consciousness is pure, unadulterated witchcraft. These 'Christian' visualisers, who have been so adulated in the Christian press, are (presumably unwitting) agents of Satan operating within the Church itself.

In view of all that we have said above, is it not extraordinary that the U.K. 'Christian' magazine 'Today' (which merged with '21st Century Christian' to become the 22,000-circulation magazine 'Alpha') could refer to Richard Foster's book as *'one of the classics of modern devotional writing'*? Likewise, the 'Catholic Herald' proclaims this book as *'a mine of spiritual wisdom, psychological insight, common sense and gentle humour'*, while 'Floodtide' reckons it to be *'beautifully concise and scriptural'*. How can it be that the 'Church Times' should describe it as *'constantly lively and penetrating'*, while the 'Evangelical Quarterly' judged that it *'abounds with concentrated wisdom'*?[101] One can only

---

[98] Starhawk, *The Spiral Dance: The Rebirth of the Ancient Goddess* (Harper & Row, 1979), pp.109-113. Readers will recall from Chapter 10 that the witch, Starhawk, is a frequent conference speaker at the Anglican St. James' Church, Piccadilly, London.

[99] Marion Green, *Magic for the Aquarian Age: A Contemporary Textbook of Practical Magical Techniques* (Aquarian Press, 1983), p.37.

[100] Ibid., p.43.

gasp in amazement at the sheer blindness of so many in the Church today — blinded by the false light emanating from the god of this evil age. And when the blind lead the blind, the ditches just fill up with willing victims. Truly, Satan has produced *'signs and lying wonders'* which are so consummately clever that even the elect can be seduced.

With a little research, one can see how Dr. Cho has been so easily taken in by this satanic doctrine whilst amassing a powerbase for what is now the world's largest church. In Korea, the indigenous religion involves *'the belief in evil spirits peopling air, sea and earth, promoters of evil and authors of disease, and the respect paid to the shamans who control them'*.[102] The chief form of Shaman in Korea is known as the Mudang, who wields considerable power among the people through healing, exorcism and crisis intervention. Dr. Cho has simply stepped into the shoes of the Mudang as the controller of evil spirits, disease, poverty, discomfort and all the other problems of life, whilst presenting himself to the people as being empowered by a 'better' god (something he mistakenly calls 'the Holy Spirit') than those of his compatriots.

We are not claiming that there is no legitimate use for the imagination or, as some have said at earlier periods of the Church, that the human imagination is inherently evil. As one Christian writer has said:

> 'A Biblically Christian conception of imagination will distinguish imagining from perceptual error, from imaging and from being an oracle of truth... Imagining is a gift of God with which humans make-believe things. With imagining ability one pretends and acts "as if" this is that (e.g., God is a rock, Isa.17:10; Christ is a bridegroom, Mt.25:1-13). Human imagination is a source of metaphorical knowledge and the playfulness so important to anyone's style of life. Imagination is meant to be an elementary, important, residual moment in everything God's adopted children do. Imagination becomes a curse only if it becomes an exercise in vanity'.[103]

In spite of this fact, the collective mind and imagination of this fallen world, in these last days, have become the fertile playground of the demonic realm. For these areas provide the ideal interface between the dimension of the spirit world and that of humanity: They are the spheres in which they can best utilise their permitted powers. As we can see from what has been said above, they get all the encouragement they desire.

The Dawning of the Age of Antichrist?

What can account for this burgeoning use of witchcraft in the Church in recent decades? Could it just be that these happenings within the Church are part of what is happening to human consciousness on a wider scale throughout the world — the many phenomena of which we have recorded so far throughout this book?

---

[101] Richard Foster, op. cit., rear cover.

[102] *Chambers's Encyclopaedia* (George Newnes, 1963), Vol.VIII, p.258.

[103] S.B. Ferguson & D.F. Wright (eds.), *New Dictionary of Theology* (I.V.P., 1988), p.331.

There is, in fact, something supremely sinister behind all the goings-on that we have documented so far in this chapter. A clue is given in an article on visualisation in the mainstream women's magazine *'Harper's Bazaar'*. Here, clinical psychologist Robert Gerard, founder of the International Society for the Waking Dream, states that he uses visualisation *'primarily **to advance psychospiritual evolution**, the reason we are on the planet'*, adding the very germane fact that *'in pursuit of higher states of consciousness, imagery is a powerful tool'*.[104]

For years now, the esoteric theosophists have been using diverse techniques to get as many people as possible all over the world to meditate at a certain time in order to force the next 'quantum leap in evolution'. As we have read in earlier chapters, that was the purpose behind all those United Nations Peace Meditation Days which the occultists organised.[105] However, there is a parallel move in esoteric and occult circles to goad as many people as possible to get into visualisation and mental imaging as another way of raising the global level of consciousness. But what exactly is the goal of all this frantic 'consciousness-raising'? We have already spoken of these matters in an earlier chapter; here we see their practical outworking. Although the vast majority of people in the Church are entirely unaware of it, for the past one hundred and twenty years, occult initiates across the globe have been trained up in preparation for two mighty events in world history, the substance of which has now been revealed in esoteric writings. These two events, as we have already shown are

> 'First, the coming of the World Teacher towards the close of this present century, and the other, the founding of the new sixth sub-race in the reconstruction of the present world conditions'.[106]

This can be attested in many examples of the occult literature. We are now living in the midst of one of the greatest deceptions ever to manifest in the world, but through which the vast majority of Christians are sleep-walking. Occult adepts of the higher degrees have known these secrets for decades. As occultist Alice Bailey has told her pupils:

> 'Very definitely may the assurance be given here, that prior to the coming of the [World Teacher], adjustments will be made so that at the head of all great organisations will be found either a Master, or an initiate who has taken the third initiation. At the head of certain of the great occult groups, of the Freemasons of the world, *and of the various great divisions of the Church*, and resident in many of the great nations will be found initiates or masters. This work of the Masters is proceeding now, and all their efforts are being bent towards bringing it to a successful consummation. Everywhere [the Masters] are gathering in *those who in any way show a tendency to respond to high vibration,*

---

[104] *Harper's Bazaar*, April 1988, p.222.

[105] For details of the way the U.N. is being used to further the New Gnosticism, see Chapter 4, pp.175-184, and Chapter 12, pp.548-553.

[106] Alice A. Bailey, *Initiation, Human and Solar* (Lucis Press, 1922), pp.60-61.

> *seeking to force their vibration and to fit them* so that they may be of use at the time of the coming of the [World Teacher]. Great is the day of opportunity, for when that time comes, through the stupendous strength of the vibration then brought to bear upon the sons of men, it will be possible for those who now do the necessary work to take a great step forward, and to pass through the portal of initiation'.[107]

Do you see the significance of this statement to the subject matter of our study? Two things emerge: First, that there are now high-degree occult initiates occupying influential positions in the Church. The second fact to emerge from the above statement is that anyone *'who in any way shows a tendency to respond to high vibration'* (i.e., who attempts to develop their 'mind-powers') will receive every encouragement from the (angel-of-light) powers who are guiding these things in order to fulfil their purpose — all, of course, under the permissive and controlling hand of God. In view of the claims made for this 'World Teacher' by the occultists, it is quite conceivable that he will be none other than the culminatory Man of Sin — the final manifestation of antichristian humanity as revealed in the writings of the Apostle, Paul (2 Th.2:3-11). All this meditation, visualisation and consciousness-raising that is taking place throughout the world would be the perfect preparation for the global conditions necessary for his coming. And masses of professing Christians across the globe are participants in the process! This should give believers great pause for thought before they go rushing off to their next workshop/seminar on 'Inner Healing', or 'Prayer for Power' conference.

All this visualisation is being encouraged for a specific purpose. As Alice Bailey elaborates in her 1944 book entitled 'Discipleship in the New Age':

> 'The secret of all true meditation work in its earlier stages is the power to visualise... In [this process] lies eventually the ability to use the creative powers of the imagination, plus mental energy as a measure to further the ends of the Hierarchy [of Ascended Masters]... All the new processes in meditation techniques (for which the New Age may be responsible) must and will embody visualisation as a primary step... Visualisation is the initial step in the demonstration of the occult law that "energy follows thought"... This visualising process and this use of the imagination form the first two steps in the activity of thought-form building. It is with these self-created forms...that the [Ascended] Masters work and hierarchical purpose takes shape'.[108]

Christian visualisers should be in no doubt about the purpose behind the work in which Satan has encouraged them to be involved — for visualisation is an initiation into the New Age, *'to further the ends of the [occult] Hierarchy'*. There is no fundamental difference between the visualisation taught by the 'evangelical' Quaker Richard Foster, the Pentecostalist Yonggi Cho, and that of the occultists or esotericists. The professing Christians enlist a power within that they

---

[107] Ibid., pp.61-62.

[108] Alice B. Bailey, *Discipleship in the New Age* (Lucis Press, 1944), Vol.I, pp.89-91.

mistakenly call 'the Holy Spirit', while the others tap into a pantheistic force that they refer to as 'the Universal Spirit'. Even the title of Dr. Cho's book, *'The Fourth Dimension'*, has been lifted straight from 'New Thought' writings. One of the pioneers of the 'New Thought Movement' earlier this century has said:

> 'There is a tremendous power alone in the name Jesus Christ... He said, 'Whatsoever ye ask the Father, in my name, he will give it to you'. The power of this name raises the student into *the fourth dimension*, where he is freed from all astral and psychic influences, and he becomes 'unconditioned and absolute, as God Himself is unconditioned and absolute'... The Christ within is his own *fourth dimensional self*, the man made in God's image and likeness'.[109]

We see here that the 'New Thought' practitioner believes in his own divinity — what he calls the Christ within — which can be tapped into at will. And this is the same impression we receive from the writings of the 'Christian' visualisers, is it not, as they place the determination of their own will over and above that of the Lord God of creation? Yonggi Cho's 'Fourth Dimension' idea is also the inspiration of a leading 'New Thought' organisation called the 'Quartus Foundation'. *Quartus*... Get it? *Quartus* is Latin for 'fourth'. As its founder states, this occult organisation is designed specifically for those who are *'seeking the* ***Fourth Dimensional*** *Consciousness'*.[110] As an echo of Yonggi Cho's 'prayer incubation', this occultist states that *'Quartus suggests the bringing of* ***the fourth dimension*** *into man's comprehension'*.[111] Significantly, the 'New Thought' Quartus Foundation was also a major joint organiser of the United Nations Peace Meditation Days designed to inseminate a 'quantum leap' in global human consciousness through collective visualisation and meditation.

All these developments have not been happening of their own volition. There is a pattern to the unfolding religious influences of these present days. As one leading occultist reveals:

> 'The Great Awakening is taking place. In the cities and towns across America, hardly a week goes by without a symposium, seminar or workshop on spiritual healing, extrasensory perception...new age living, *the power within, creative imagination, the dynamics of positive thinking, mind control*, awareness training, higher sense perception, the art of meditation, new dimensions of consciousness, holistic medicine, yoga... This is not by chance. According to one Advanced Soul, through the silent hidden work of the Masters, men and women throughout the world are beginning to intuitively understand the Truth. There is a vibration, call it the Master Vibration, that is flowing through the consciousness of mankind, turning each individual toward the Light within, and it is only a matter of time before the Dawning'.[112]

---

[109] Florence Scovel-Shinn, op. cit., p.92.

[110] John Randolph Price, *The Superbeings*, op. cit., p.xxii.

[111] Ibid., p.xxiii.

The true identity of this imminent *'Dawning'* is a matter of some urgency for discerning Christians today. For it has further been revealed in the secret writings of the occultists that the global development of 'creative visualisation' techniques has actually been taking place under the guiding hand of certain spirit-entities:

> 'The Master P. works under the Master R. in North America. He it is Who has had much to do esoterically with the various mental sciences, such as Christian Science, *and New Thought*, both of which are efforts put forth by the Lodge in an endeavour to teach men *the reality of that which is not seen, and the power of the mind to create*. This Master occupies an Irish body, is on the fourth ray, and the place of his residence may not be revealed'.[113] [emphasis added]

Does all this send a cold chill down your spine? Christian pastors have been working under the direct manipulation of demonic powers and influencing millions of people professing to be Christian believers. Christian churches have discovered the demonic ways that occultists weave their spells — and then imitated them! Think of it: Millions of people the world over, professing to be biblical Christians, claiming to be filled with the Holy Spirit (in some cases, double-filled!), asserting their ability to discern demons at the drop of a hat, yet avidly engaged in learning the ancient satanic art of 'mind-power', and possibly making a grand contribution to the coming earthly kingdom of the ultimate Man of Sin, the fulfillment of Antichrist in world history. How complete has been the devil's deception of the poor sheep who are without true shepherds.

II. OUT OF THE DRAGON'S MOUTH: The Occult Art of Word-Power

Having now demonstrated the first arm of magic and sorcery in action in the churches — 'mind-power' — we now come to examine its co-worker, 'word-power'. In just the same way that 'mind-power' techniques operate to manipulate matter and consciousness through a concentrated use of the imagination, so 'word-power' techniques work for the magician through personal fiats or affirmations, and spoken commands addressed directly to people, diseases or the powers of darkness themselves. Wrapped up in this technique is the use of extremely powerful suggestion and auto-suggestion operating at the level of the hypnotic.

We will now examine briefly the magical practice of 'word-power' under two separate heads. First, its use as a means of the manipulation of matter and consciousness through spoken affirmations; second, its use as a way of attempting to control the forces of darkness through spoken commands or as a way of controlling people through powerful verbal suggestions.

1. The Power of 'Positive Confession'

In this section, we will examine the way that spoken words are used as a form of 'creative power' — the idea that the very words we utter can have a magical

---

[112] John Randolph Price, *The Superbeings*, op. cit., pp.2-3.
[113] Alice A. Bailey, op. cit., p.60.

effect on both living and inanimate objects. Our primary purpose is to show how this idea has been lifted directly from the occult and has rooted in the Church.

A classic example of this technique is given by Christian counselling 'supremo' Selwyn Hughes. When he asks himself the question, *'How can I use my faith to bring healing?'*, he answers *'with the power of our words'*, and advises his readers to *'say what you believe and believe what you say'*.[114] This is what is known in Christian circles as 'Positive Confession', the Christianised version of occult 'word-power' and the verbal equivalent of the occult mind-power technique 'Positive Thinking', as popularised by the 33rd degree Freemason and false teacher Norman Vincent Peale.[115] Some of the prophets of this 'Positive Confession' are the Charismatic teachers Kenneth Hagin, Kenneth Copeland, Charles Capps and Frederick K.C. Price. Many others have been influenced by these men and their teachings. The original 'Christian' advocate of this technique was E.W. Kenyon (1867-1948), who *'went beyond the scientific shamanism of the New Thought movement when he first taught "the positive confession of the Word of God"'*.[116]

'Positive Confession' is rooted in the New Thought practice of 'Decreeing' which was founded by Emma Curtis Hopkins, a Christian Scientist who lived in the 1880s. In many ways, she was the true founder of the New Thought Movement, which we have discussed earlier in this chapter. Hopkins' student, Annie Ritz Militz then founded 'Homes of Truth', a New Thought denomination. From Militz, the torch passed to Guy Warren Ballard, and from there to Mark and Elizabeth Prophet who founded the Summit University and the Church Universal and Triumphant — also known as the 'I AM' movement. The Old Testament proof-text which was speciously claimed for this practice was Job 22:28, which states: *'Thou shalt also decree a thing, and it shall be established unto thee; and the light shall shine upon thy ways'* (A.V.). The New Testament proof-text claimed for 'Positive Confession' is based on a misapplication of Romans 10:8: *'The word is near you, even in your mouth and in your heart' (that is, the word of faith which we preach)'*. One Christian writer states that 'Positive Confession' *'refers quite literally to bringing into existence what we state with our mouth, since faith is a confession'*.[117] Another 'Christian' publication which advocates this blasphemous teaching states: *'He who masters his words will master his works. Say what you want, speak it into existence. The principle of command is a life-changing concept'*.[118] In similar vein, faith-healer Morris Cerullo, in his book 'A Guide to Total Health and Prosperity', maintains that *'If [Christians] will only confess it out of their mouth and claim it'*, they could have anything they want —

---

[114] Selwyn Hughes, *Lord Heal Me Now* (CWR, n.d.), p.31-33.

[115] See the article on Peale in the U.S. Freemasonic 'Scottish Rite Journal', February 1993. Peale was Grand Chaplain of the Grand Lodge of New York, Past Grand Prelate of the Knights Templar and of the Shrine. For details of this and of his modernist theology, see *Christian News Enclyopedia*, Missourian Publishing Co., Vol.IV, pp.2833-2835.

[116] Stanley M. Burgess & Gary B. McGee, *Dictionary of Pentecostal & Charismatic Movements* (Zondervan, 1978), p.719.

[117] Ibid., p.718.

[118] Skip Ross, *Say Yes to your Potential* (Word Books, 1983), p.100.

worldly riches and success, even complete immunity to colds and influenza![119] He presumptuously lists twenty-eight 'Covenant Blessings' which can immediately be 'claimed' by any believer — all of which are related to health and material prosperity. One of these states:

> 'Take your every success right now with this claim: "The Prosperity and success that God has for me is being multiplied even this minute. I receive it and apply it in every area of my life, my whole family, my business, my job"'.[120]

One of the world's most popular 'Christian' teachers, Kenneth Hagin, also advocates this 'Name-it-and-Claim-it', 'Positive Confession' prosperity teaching:

> 'Our confession is the key to receiving God's blessings and it is the key to holding on to God's blessings... The confessions of your faith in God's Word will bring the desired realities into your life'.[121]

According to Kenneth Hagin, the steps involved in this process are as follows: 'First...decide what you want from God and find Scriptures which cover your case...[then] let every thought and desire affirm that you have what you've asked for'.[122] The vast majority of heresies have been caused by this approach to the Bible. First decide what you want to believe — then plunder the Word of God for texts which you imagine to support it. Another fatal flaw in this teaching is that it presumes that worldly prosperity and complete physical comfort in this life should be a primary aim of the believer and a fundamental Christian right. The New Testament, however, teaches that this life is but a brief preparation for the life to come and that everything we do must be planned with that goal in mind (Lk.12:32-34; 2 Cor.4:17-18). Not only that, but the people of God of all eras are also taught in Scripture that they should seek neither prosperity nor poverty, nor the desires of their own heart, but rather they should pray earnestly to the Lord: *'Feed me with the food **You** prescribe for me'* (see Prov.30:7-9; cf. Mt.6:11).

In 1978, Morris Cerullo claimed that *'the world laughs at and ridicules the Church'* because God's people do not claim the healing, prosperity and blessings which are theirs by right.[123] He 'prophesied' that *'those days soon will be over'*, when the Church 'takes the limits off God' and moves into a 'new dimension' or 'Deeper Life' in the power of the Holy Spirit as manifested in the Charismatic Movement. He claimed that God 'showed' him

> 'that there is coming a time when those who want the real moving of His Holy Spirit will be distinguished clearly from anybody else...so that the real and the middle-of-the-road compromisers are easily distinguishable.[124]

---

[119] Morris Cerullo, *A Guide to Total Health and Prosperity: God Wants to Bless You* (World Evangelism Inc., 1978), p.42.

[120] Ibid., p.104.

[121] *Word of Faith Magazine*, Kenneth Hagin Ministries, September 1990, pp.6-7.

[122] *Word of Faith Magazine*, Kenneth Hagin Ministries, January 1990, pp.4-5.

[123] Morris Cerullo, op. cit., p.44.

This is the last refuge of the Gnostic, who claims that his (perverse) brand of Christianity is the genuine, higher, deeper, spiritual article; while those who do not follow this trend are at best, compromisers, at worst, impostors. But how can those who so clearly (and so readily) twist the Scriptures and mimic occultic practices be the 'real', Holy Spirit-inspired Christians? This 'Positive Confession' technique is precisely the same as that practised at the Neo-Gnostic Findhorn Community, where it is known as 'Prosperity Consciousness'. The sad truth is that it is the cultic antics of the Charismatic Movement — in its departure from historic, evangelical Christianity into the realms of Shamanism and the occult — which have brought the Church into ridicule and the Gospel into disrepute.

When Selwyn Hughes gives his biblical justification for Positive Confession theology, we can clearly see that his error lies in imagining that all Christians are endowed with exactly the same power as Jesus. He writes:

> 'Just as Jesus spoke the WORD of rebuke to the fig tree so you as a child of God can speak the withering word of rebuke to that disease or sickness upon your body. When Jesus spoke, His WORD was with power. When you speak, your WORD can have just as much power'.[125]

The present writer has yet to meet a single Charismatic leader who can make a fig-tree immediately wither, let alone effect a genuine Divine healing which has an instantaneous transformative effect on organic matter![126] Yonggi Cho also endorses the same magical principle of word-power when he advises his readers to

> 'Claim and speak the word of assurance, for your word actually goes out and creates. God spoke and the whole world came into being. Your word is the material which the Holy Spirit uses to create. So give the word, for this is very important. The church today has lost the art of giving commands. We Christians are becoming perennial beggars, for we are constantly begging'.[127]

Actually, the real reason that the church has 'lost the art of giving commands' is because it is no longer in God's will for us to practise such an art. The art of 'giving commands' to disease and demons died with the last of the Apostles, as we shall later demonstrate. Moreover, only God has the power to create with a personal fiat. Yet it is clear from the statements above that these people believe that they are God and that they have exactly the same divine power that Jesus exercised during His earthly ministry. Bishop Earl P. Paulk, who has held the office of Bishop in the International Communion of Charismatic Churches since 1982, has written: *'Just as dogs have puppies...so God has little gods. Until we comprehend that we are little gods and we begin to act like little gods, we cannot manifest the Kingdom of God'.*[128] Perhaps it is this arrogant belief that has led to

---

[124] Ibid., pp.6-7.

[125] Selwyn Hughes, op. cit., p.39.

[126] They can certainly grow giant cabbages at the New Age Findhorn Community; but that is not by the power of the Holy Spirit!

[127] Yonggi Cho, op. cit., p.31.

the recent downfall of Bishop Paulk and three of his office-bearing family members in a sex scandal at their 7,700 seat 'neo-Gothic cathedral' in Atlanta. A story in *Christian News* has revealed that women who served in this and a sister church *'charge that the ministers pressed them into having sex, saying they would be serving God'*.[129] Clearly it is very dangerous for a minister of the Gospel to believe that he is God! In similar vein, Methodist faith-healer John G. Lake (1870-1935) said, *'Man is not a separate creation detached from God, he is part of God Himself... God intends us to be gods'*.[130] Kenneth Copeland also supports this view when he says, *'You don't have a God in you. You are one'*.[131] Now, it is true that Christians are described in the Bible as being *'partakers of the divine nature'* (2 Pet.1:4), but this is by virtue of the *imputed* righteousness of Christ and the indwelling Holy Spirit. It does not mean that they are partakers in a divine *essence* which can be plugged into at will, for that is occult-mysticism, as we have clearly shown. This point of distinction is the fundamental difference between the orthodox, Biblico-Christian concept of the spiritual relationship between God and man, and the *'divinisation-of-man'* theory which is at the heart of all the Satan-inspired religions and cults of the world.

This entire technique of 'Positive Confession' is nicely summed up in the words of Selwyn Hughes as, *'Say what you believe and believe what you say'*. But this is just another 'rip-off' from the teachings of Transcendental Magic and Theosophy. One 'New Thought' occultist confirms this fact with the statement: *'Owing to the vibratory power of words, whatever man voices, he begins to attract'*.[132] Another Theosophical publication, in which the words of the 'Ascended Master' Kuthumi are recorded, shows clearly the origin of this doctrine:

> 'When we contemplate methods of *God realization*, we dare not exclude *the power of the spoken Word* [in which] the body of your letter is composed of *statements phrasing your desires*...and the supplications that would be involved even in ordinary prayer. Having released the power of the spoken Word through your outer consciousness, your subconscious mind, and your super-conscious or Higher Self, you can rest assured that *the supreme consciousness of the Ascended Masters whom you have invoked is also concerned with the manifestation of that which you have called forth*'.[133] [emphasis added]

This statement clearly shows that when such word-power is invoked, the 'vibration' is picked up by the demonic realm and answered accordingly. In other words, these techniques actually work. However, it is not 'God's blessing' that is bringing it about, but the kiss of Satan through his demonic lackeys. When you

---

128 S.M. Burgess & G.B. McGee, op. cit., p.719.

129 *Christian News*, Monday, January 25, 1993, Vol.31, No.4., p.3.

130 S.M. Burgess & G.B. McGee, op. cit., p.719.

131 Ibid.

132 Florence Scovel-Shinn, op. cit., p.25.

133 Elizabeth Clare Prophet, *Prayer and Meditation: Jesus and Kuthumi* (Summit University, 1963), pp.138-139.

pray to God in the manner He has prescribed in His Word, He answers that prayer and honours it with His blessings. When you issue commands and decrees through the power of the spoken word, the Lord hands you over to Satan who responds with a Faustian kiss for encouragement. We need not linger long examining this technique. The system that has been advocated by Selwyn Hughes, Morris Cerullo, Kenneth Hagin, Kenneth Copeland and Yonggi Cho for developing a 'Prosperity Consciousness' is the same as that being utilised by the occultists in 'New Thought' and Neo-Gnostic circles (e.g., the Findhorn Community).

In common with the use of mind-power, the employment of word-power is a manifestation of the 'Satanic Initiation' which our first parents received in Eden and which is the hallmark of all occultism (*'You will be like God'*, Gen.3:5). Selwyn Hughes teaches: *'Say what you believe and believe what you say'*. The witch, Starhawk, teaches that *'Magic works on the principle that, 'It is so because I say it is so''*.[134] Just like its big brother mind-power, word-power is the ancient art of witchcraft dressed up in modern clothes. Therefore, when the so-called 'Ascended Master' quoted above says, *'when we contemplate methods of God realization, we dare not exclude the power of the spoken Word'*, we can begin to understand the true occult power which lies behind this increasingly popular practice in Christian circles. It is but one more component in the process leading to 'The Dawning' of the time of great evil on this earth.

2. The Power of Hypnotic Suggestion

Having examined the magical use of the spoken word as an outworking of occult word-power in order to effect change in one's environment, we now turn to the use of verbal suggestion as a powerful method of effecting change in others — a form of Shamanism which has become astonishingly widespread throughout the Christian Church.

As Charismatic teachings have become increasingly popular, there has also been a major growth of interest in demons and demonology. An alarming number of people have developed for themselves what is commonly called a 'deliverance ministry', through which they claim to practise exorcism and other forms of combat with the demonic realm. Coupled with this, there has been a huge upsurge in a variety of animistic and superstitious practices which are used to ward off demons from an particular geographical area or life-situation. There now follows a list of some of the techniques for the attempted neutralisation of demonic activity which we have personally witnessed or which have been brought to our attention during recent years:

- Ritual exorcism of people, pets and personal environments through spoken commands addressed to the demonic realm.
- 'Pleading the blood of Christ' verbally to demons or drawing an imaginary so-called 'bloodline' round an area to ward off demons.
- Audibly praying over every orifice of one's body to prevent the entry of demons through them.

[134] Starhawk, op. cit., p.111.

- The use of ecstatic 'tongues-speaking' as a means of spiritual warfare, based on a misinterpretation of Eph.6:17b-18a.
- Continuous playing of contemporary 'Christian' music on cassette or CD players to deter the presence of demons.
- The visualised adorning of oneself in a suit of armour each morning on rising, and the visualised removal of it last thing at night.
- The conducting of so-called 'Jericho Walks' round a geographical area, uttering incantations and commands 'in the name of Jesus'. The Marches for Jesus are a popularised modification of the Jericho Walk, in which one is said to *'reclaim the territory for Christ'* from the demonic realm.
- The formal invocation of the Holy Spirit, sometimes referred to as 'calling down the Spirit', through continuous repetition of sung choruses, interspersed with spoken commands.

In those circles where such superstitions are common, we will invariably find the inducement of a post-conversion, highly emotive religious experience involving so-called 'Spirit Baptism', tongues-speaking, faith-healing and, very often, the claimed expulsion of demons — all of which are usually generated by the powerful suggestions of an influential teacher. Because of the vast number of evangelical churches which are being seduced into using these deceptive influences, in the belief that such things are valid Christian experiences, there is a great need to show the trie origins of these approaches, while at the same time searching out the biblical data on things demonic.

A great number of the activities of the Charismatic-Pentecostal Movement stem from the ignorance of its adherents concerning the 'not-yetness' of the kingdom, in the sense that they have failed to realise that although the kingdom has come in grace, it has *not yet* come in glory; tears have *not yet* been wiped from every eye; pain has *not yet* been eradicated; suffering has *not yet* been put to one side; death and disease have *not yet* been done away with — even for the Christian. Such things will not happen until the inauguration of the New Heavens and New Earth (see Rev.21:1-5). However, there is a contrasting but parallel ignorance in such circles of the fact that the demonic realm has been far more soundly defeated than they appear to understand. Now, it is true that many Charismatics will *profess* that *'Christ has won the victory'*, but this profession is not matched by the seemingly endless techniques they have to employ against a rampant demonic realm.

All these ritualistic techniques to ward off demons, illness and other afflictions have their roots in Babylon rather than Zion. They were used in ancient Babylonia some five millennia in the past, and they have been used for thousands of years by the heathen religions in their futile attempts to escape from the more immediately unpleasant aspects of being in the clutches of their master, Satan. Now, in the closing stages of the twentieth century after the birth of Christ, thanks to the crusading zeal of the Charismatic-Pentecostal Movement, Roman Catholicism and syncretistic liberalism, these shamanistic, occult practices are being advocated by churches professing the name of Christ. Through the gradual eradication of sound doctrine from the pulpits of the land, a majority of professing Christians have been duped into endorsing practices which are actually outlawed in Scripture (Exod.20:7; Dt.18:9-12).

In fact, the practices mentioned above are not only (as we will show) unnecessary, but they are manifestations of superstition and fear — not the permissible, wholesome and highly desirable fear of the Lord, but the fear of Satan, fear of demons, fear of the unseen and the unknown. Of course, the old serpent already has the unsaved masses riddled with such fear: witness the growing interest in divination, occultism, horror films, 'earth mysteries' and tales of the supernatural. However, he also has a great interest in terrorising the children of God. Lamentably, because of the weak faith and untaught minds of many of the Lord's people, they can easily become ensnared by his undermining wiles. But if we simply rest in the doctrinal truth and bountiful promises of Scripture, we will not be misled by these perversions of biblical spiritual warfare. *'For God has not given us a spirit of fear, but of power and of love and of a sound [Greek 'healthy'] mind'* (2 Tim.1:7). It is a faithful saying for the elect that nothing *'shall be able to separate us from the love of God which is in Christ Jesus our Lord'* (Rom.8:39). *'If God is for us, who can be against us?'* (Rom.8:31).

The Lord uses many means by which to bring His children to a full dependence upon Him. Once in a while He will withdraw the closeness of His comforting presence in order that we will seek His unique counsel all the more diligently (2 Chron.32:31). Often He will raise up oppressive human adversaries to test us and ultimately to drive us to His bosom (Jdg.3:1-4; 2 Sam.16:5-14; Ps.59; 1 Kgs.11:14-25). Sometimes He will plague us with seemingly insurmountable difficulties to wean us from the diverting clutches of earthly pleasures (Ps.39; cf. Ps.131). At other times, He will send us on missions which are arduous to the point of breaking, so that we will learn to rely on Him alone for deliverance (Jer.15:10-21; 17:14-18; 20:7-12; 2 Cor.12:9; Phil.4:12-13). He may even send us disease or other severe affliction to remind us of our ungodly condition, our frailty and His power (Num.12:1-16; Job 2; Jn.9:1-5; 1 Cor.11:30; 2 Cor.12:7-10). Ultimately — and perhaps most difficult for people to accept — our awesome God will take away our loved ones by way of providence, so that we may at last recognise Him as our sole Sovereign over life itself and turn to Him alone for comfort (2 Sam.12:1-23; Ruth 1:1-5; Ezek.24:15-18; Job 1-2; cf. Gen.22:1-9). It is also a solemn fact that the true Christian — even though he has really been taken out of Satan's power into the kingdom of Christ (Col.1:13) — will still sometimes be subjected to affliction at the hand of demonic entities (e.g., 2 Cor.12:7; Rev.2:10).

To respond to any of these situations with pathetic rituals which imply that Satan has got the better of God is so futile. And yet an increasing number of believers today imagine that the onset of a severe headache or a feeling of nausea may be indicative of demon oppression or even possession. For this reason, we need to be as lucid as we can concerning what the Bible says about the present power of Satan and our methods for dealing with it. We are certainly presented with the inescapable fact that Satan goes to and fro on the earth (Job.1:7; 2:2). As the

Apostle Peter puts it: *'Your adversary the devil walks about like a roaring lion, seeking whom he may devour'* (1 Pet.5:8). But because Satan and his demonic followers have been legally ousted from their usurpation of rule over the earth by the victory of the Lord Jesus Christ on the cross, the old serpent's days are numbered (Jn.12:31). However, because his powers are now limited (Rev.20:1-3; Col.2:15; Eph.4:8), his anger knows no bounds and he can still create havoc in the lives of humans. The devil is certainly aware that it has been written that he only has a short time left before he will be cast into the lake of fire (Rev.20:10); and this is the chief reason for his anger (Rev.12:12,17). Therefore, he does all that he can to upset the faith, assurance and spiritual security of those who love the Lord Jesus and wait for His coming.

In spite of all this, the Christian should never be held in fearful bondage to Satan. There is certainly no need to pray demons out of geographical areas in order to 'reclaim the territory for Christ'. It is over unregenerate men and women's hearts that Satan now reigns, not over the plots of land where they live. The greatest weapon by far, in this instance, is the good old-fashioned (but never outdated) Gospel of Jesus Christ. God's children may certainly be afflicted at the lawless hands of demonic discarnates, but their response to such activity is clearly laid out in Scripture — as we shall shortly elaborate. One of the most detailed and rewarding works to be published on the subject of spiritual warfare is *'Precious Remedies Against Satan's Devices'* by the seventeenth century Puritan, Thomas Brooks. Among the demonic devices by which the Christian will be afflicted, he lists:

> 'The drawing of the soul to sin; the keeping of souls from holy duties; the hindering of souls in holy services; and the keeping of saints in a sad, doubting, questioning and uncomfortable condition.[135]

These are the real nuts and bolts of the Christian's personal spiritual warfare. Such warfare does not centre on personal, ritualised, occult combat between the Christian and individual demons; but, rather, it centres on the quality of our relationship and communion with the Lord.

The Charismatic presentation of the Christian needing to battle directly with the powers of darkness in 'hand-to-hand' combat, with exorcistic commands, invocations and rituals, is itself one of the greatest tricks pulled by Satan in these last days. Such spiritual 'star-wars', rather than cleansing people of demonic pollution, actually defiles them still further as they disobey commandments of the Lord which are as valid today as they were three and a half thousand years ago (Dt.18:9-14). This huge upsurge in the Christianised use of the occult techniques of word-power, far from having a biblical basis, has been skilfully designed by the powers of darkness themselves as a way of duping Christians into: **1)** the propagation of 'Christianised' occult practices (Christian Shamanism); **2)** the practical denial of the sovereignty of God over **all** His creation; **3)** the false exaltation of

---

[135] Thomas Brooks, *Precious Remedies Against Satan's Devices* (Banner of Truth, 1984, first published in 1652), pp.29-182.

demonic powers; and **4)** the neglect of their personal responsibility in combating indwelling sin. It is the ultimate form of escapism from the divinely-ordained, difficult and afflicted pathway of progressive sanctification, to go running off to the nearest faith-healer, exorcist or charismatic 'Prayer for Power' seminar at the first sign of affliction in our lives.

This does not at all mean that believers since Apostolic times have no involvement in spiritual warfare. On the contrary, the experience of the Christian involves incessant combat against the powers of darkness on one front or another. But the manner in which believers conduct themselves in relation to the demonic realm is very different from the sensational (and often perilous) methods found on the shelves of so many Christian bookshops today. We will be delving further into the spiritual armoury and weaponry available to the Christian before the close of this chapter.

What many professing Christians do not seem realise is that the widespread practice of ritualistic 'exorcism' is actually a primitive (shamanistic) form of psychotherapy, which works through powerful suggestion and is very different from the way that Jesus Christ cast demons out into the abyss. This fact has even been unwittingly revealed in a Charismatic 'deliverance' handbook. During a section on 'Questions and Answers on Deliverance', the question is asked, *'Is there a relationship between the 'healing of memories' and deliverance?'* The reply states:

> 'Yes there is. The 'healing of memories' is the bringing of deliverance to people in a 'low-key' way. Many who minister 'healing of memories' or 'inner healing' would not realize that they are actually ministering deliverance from demons; yet this is what is happening'.[136]

Although the man who gave this answer certainly did not intend it, he has put his finger on what ritualistic exorcism is all about. Modern exorcism and the 'Healing of the Memories' address the same experiences, invoke the same phenomena, and produce the same result: namely, *catharsis.* In this respect, both Inner Healing and ritual exorcism work on the same level. *They are shamanistic in origin; hypnotherapeutic in practice.* Readers may recall the statement in our earlier chapter on the mind-sciences, by a trainer of psychotherapists that *'most of the techniques in different types of psychotherapy are nothing more than hypnotic phenomena'.*[137] The experience that many people so glibly call 'deliverance' today is 'Mesmerism', pure and simple — the manipulation of minds by people who wield great influence. Consider this description of a session in Mesmer's clinic in the late eighteenth century:

> 'Mesmer marched about majestically...passing his hands over the patients' bodies or touching them with a long iron wand. The results varied. Some patients felt nothing at all, some felt as if insects were crawling over them, others were seized with hysterical laughter,

---

[136] Graham & Shirley Powell, *Christian Set Yourself Free: Proven Guidelines to Self-Deliverance from Demonic Oppression* (New Wine Press, 1983), p.177.

[137] Richard Bandler and John Grinder, op. cit., p.100.

> convulsions or fits of hiccups. Some went into raving delirium, which was called 'The Crisis' and was considered extremely healthful'.[138]

In R.B. Ince's book *Three Famous Occultists* — demonstrating that Mesmer is regarded by experts as an 'occultist' — a contemporary record of Mesmer's clinics by the historian Bailly gives a similar portrayal of his manipulative sessions:

> 'Some are calm, tranquil and experience no effect. Others cough, spit, feel slight pains, local or general heat, and have sweatings. Others, again, are agitated and tormented with convulsions. These convulsions are remarkable in regard to the number affected with them, to their duration and force. They are preceded and followed by a state of languor or reverie... Patients experienced more or less violent perspiration, palpitations, hysterics, catalepsy, and sometimes a condition resembling epilepsy. When the crisis was at its height, the patient was carried by attendants into one of the adjoining "Salles de Crises"; he was there laid on a couch, and usually he subsided gradually into a deep sleep from which he awoke refreshed and benefitted'.[139]

Although its practitioners are ignorant of the fact, variations of this 'Mesmeric Crisis' are being repeated in Pentecostal-Charismatic meetings throughout the world today, where it is often accompanied by a hypnotic 'swoon' known as being 'slain in the spirit'. It is not only ritualistic exorcisms that have similar origins to the 'Mesmeric Crisis'. The ecstatic religious experience known deceptively in Christian circles as a 'Baptism with the Holy Spirit' and its (usually) accompanying experience of babbling 'tongues' are intimately caught up with such hypnotic phenomena. All this highly theatrical curfuffle comes about as the result of powerful suggestion from an influential teacher. It is an 'Initiation' into Mystery Religion — an experience that is available to anyone who is open to receive it, of whatever religious persuasion, and it has as much to do with Christian spirituality as a Dionysian rite.

One of the major concerns about the Charismatic-Pentecostal Movement is that an untold number of people within its ranks who believe that they are Christians may never have experienced a genuine biblical conversion. Very often a person is counted as having been saved if he has merely had hands laid on him by someone praying over him in the ecstatic-babbling style of 'tongues' (often while attempting to 'exorcise' demons from him), which has resulted in certain physical sensations (e.g., heat, tingling flesh, falling down, etc.) followed by a display of the same style of 'tongues-speaking'. That phenomenon can certainly be classified as a 'psycho-mystical' or 'Mesmeric' experience — or even a Neo-Gnostic experience — but it is *not* an evidence of the New Birth in the power of the Holy Spirit.

Way back in 1784 — long before the present-day Charismatic Movement was even a twinkle in Satan's eye — the King of France appointed a Commission to examine the claims of Franz Mesmer, consisting of reports from two reputable

---

[138] Richard Cavendish, *The Magical Arts* (Routledge & Kegan Paul, 1984), p.180.

[139] R.B. Ince, *Three Famous Occultists* (Gilbert Whitehead, 1939), pp.87-88.

medical bodies: the Faculty of Medicine of the Academy of Sciences and the Royal Society of Medicine. How perceptive it was for this Commission to come to the following conclusion,

> 'That man can act upon man at any time, and almost at will by striking his imagination; that the simplest gestures and signs can have the most powerful effects; and that the action of man upon the imagination may be reduced to an art, and conducted with method, upon subjects who have faith'.[140]

This is the essence of the 'Crisis Experience' being generated in Charismatic-Pentecostal circles today, which has nothin whatsoever to do with biblical Christianity but has everything to do with Shamanism, Mesmerism and hypnotic suggestion. When Anton Mesmer discovered, in the late eighteenth century, what shamans have known for thousands of years, the seeds of Western psychotherapy were sown — a fact which is confirmed by the claim of a prominent psychiatrist in a recent issue of the prestigious Journal of the Royal Society of Medicine:

> 'What is important is the impact and influence [Mesmer] had on the subsequent development of psychiatry. It would indeed be no exaggeration to say that he was one of the world's first psychotherapists'.[141]

And it is Mesmer's crude form of manipulative hypnotherapy which is being practised by the 'deliverance ministries' and 'healing' crusades of the Pentecostal-Charismatic Movement, through which the strong suggestions of a powerful teacher can turn the lives of the gullible inside-out. Like the Christian 'visualisers' in the last section of this chapter, the healers and deliverance peddlars have also not understood that there is a vast gulf between work of the Son of God and the sorcery of the sundry shamans of this world.

This is what the Full Gospel Businessmens' Fellowship International (F.G.B.F.I.) has specialised in from its inception: *a dinner-date with Anton Mesmer.* For those not familiar with the F.G.B.F.I., which has branches all over the world, it holds regular evangelistic dinners in a hired hall, to which people invite their neighbours, workmates, friends, etc. After the dinner has been eaten, people give emotive testimonies about what Jesus is alleged to have done for them (usually involving spectacular effects), followed by an invitation to come to the front of the room for 'healing' and 'deliverance ministry'. Those who do so will find themselves in a queue known as a 'prayer-line', waiting for one of the leaders to 'lay hands' on them in order to induce the above-mentioned experience. This is a very common methodology used in the invoking of such mystical experiences and in the inducing of people to speak in the ecstatic-babble style of 'tongues' used today.[142] As an example of the crude technique used to induce this experience in Christian circles, consider the following account in a popular Charismatic book:

---

[140] Ibid., pp.107-108.

[141] Journal of the Royal Society of Medicine, Vol.85, no.7, July 1992, p.383.

[142] For details of a complete F.G.B.F.I. session, read Don Basham, *Spiritual Power: How to Get it – How to Give it!* (Whitaker House, 1976), 89pp.

> 'When people have asked for the Baptism in the Holy Spirit in prayer-lines in many countries of the world, I have simply instructed them to start repeating the word "Blood", and within a matter of seconds they have begun to speak in tongues. Usually I then call over another worker and suggest that he or she praise God with them so that they do not stop speaking in tongues. They are now entering another spiritual dimension, and it is wonderfully strange! It is important that they do not begin to doubt at this point. I then go on to the next one in line and begin all over again'.[143]

In the introduction to Don Basham's book 'Spiritual Power: How To Get It, How To Give It!', we are told that the kernel of his message involves a set of *'simple instructions'* in the fifth chapter which is virtually guaranteed to induce the so-called 'Spirit Baptism' experience. If only spiritual growth was really that easy! What such an experience does is to hoodwink immature believers into a state of perpetual spiritual pride. This is why people who have received this so-called 'Baptism' spend so much of their time going round telling others about it. In this the work of Satan is manifest. For the work of the Holy Spirit is to 'testify of Jesus', not to glorify Himself (Jn.15:26; 16:14-15).

It is quite clear from reading Don Basham's transcript that people are being 'psyched-up' with a heady cocktail of suggestion and a massively exaggerated sense of expectancy and tension-building, to undergo a mighty emotional experience of trance-ecstasy — a letting go of oneself to such an extent that there is a release of powerful forces which can manifest either as a feeling of great euphoria (often accompanied by yelps and laughter) or desperately uncomfortable hysteria (often accompanied by screams and convulsions). These same phenomena are repeated in many Pentecostal-Charismatic situations — all manufactured in the heavy hothouse atmosphere of emotional manipulation.

Such special effects have been generated in pagan religions throughout history through the use of repetitive prayer (mantras), powerful suggestion from a dominant teacher (Shaman), dancing (Dervishism), meditation (especially the Kundalini variety) and hallucinogenic drugs. The present writer has seen the same technique (and the same results) occurring within the context of a meditation session led by the self-styled Indian guru Shree Bhagwan Rajneesh (whose followers were aften known as the 'Orange People'), in which he would touch devotees on the forehead to effect the desired religious experience. In Charismatic-Pentecostal circles, many similar methods to induce such an experience are used, although they are dressed up in Christian clothing, e.g., repetitive chorus-singing, invocation of the Spirit, powerful emotional suggestion from a dominant teacher, the laying on of hands, etc. This is pure Mesmerism — the generation of hypnosis and trance. Nowhere is this deception and manipulation more apparent than in the theatrical ritual performed at Charismatic gatherings which is referred to as being 'slain in the spirit', in which a person will fall backwards to the floor in an induced swoon, often after being 'touched' (some would say pushed) by an

[143] H.A. Maxwell Whyte, *The Power of the Blood* (Whitaker House, 1973), p.83.

influential teacher.[144] But true spirituality is not something which can be sought out by simply going to a meeting and plugging into an experience. It is in this sense that the Charismatic Movement can be said to be very much a part of the New Gnosticism, with its mysticism, superstition, 'higher life' teachings, disdain of the intellect and emphasis on the development of extraordinary mind-powers.

One should not lightly dismiss this connection between the Charismatic-Pentecostal Movement and the New Age. Despite the fact that many Charismatics strenuously oppose the New Age Movement, they have unquestioningly accepted many of its practices — as can be seen from our studies earlier in this chapter. A Christianised form of Shamanism is being pursued today by a number of the well-known teachers in the Charismatic-Pentecostal Movement. Central to all forms of Shamanism are the practices of *'suggestion, hypnosis, [and] guided imagery'*, which were used *'for centuries before they were rediscovered by modern psychologists'*.[145] Parallel to this is the fact that shamanistic religion involves *'the belief in evil spirits peopling air, sea and earth, promoters of evil and authors of disease, and the respect paid to the shamans who control them'*.[146] When we add to this the fact that in all forms of magic *'the methods adopted are usually quite simple and rely mainly on auto-suggestion for their results'*,[147] we begin to piece together a startling explanation for so many developments in the Church today.

Among the leading promoters of the New Gnosticism in the U.S. in recent years is a guru known as Master Da Free John (alias Franklin Albert Jones), a former Lutheran seminarian who heads up a 'spiritual fellowship' known as the 'Johannine Daist Communion'. In his booklet 'A Call for a Radical Reformation of Christianity', Da Free John writes:

> 'John says not only that Jesus taught that God is the Living Spirit...but that he taught that the Way to worship God is to worship in the Spirit. That is, Jesus taught a method of worship that involved ecstatic bodily Communion with the Life-Power via breathing and feeling, based on Truth (or an awakened understanding of the Divine Reality)'.[148]

All this has a great bearing on the experiences being generated in Charismatic-Pentecostal circles today. For the ecstasy induced in these circles is nothing less than an initiation into the New Gnosticism. The guru Da Free John, who received initiation into the 'serpent-power' of Kundalini Yoga from Swami Rudrananda, advocates precisely the same experience for his devotees, claiming that

---

[144] It is worth remembering that in the Bible it is only God's *enemies* who fall backwards when confronted with His naked spiritual power (e.g., Jn.18:6; cf. Isa.28:13); whereas the Lord's *true* people always fall forwards on their faces in awestruck adoration and worship (e.g., Gen.17:3; Jos.5:14; Ezk.1:28; 44:4; Mt.7:5-6; Rev.7:11; 11:16).

[145] Fritjof Capra, *The Turning Point: Science, Society and the Rising Culture* (Flamingo-Collins, 1982), p.337.

[146] *Chambers's Encyclopaedia* (George Newnes, 1963) Vol.VIII, p.258.

[147] Ibid, p.792.

[148] Da Free John, *A Call for a Radical Reformation of Christianity* (Dawn Horse Press, 1982), p.28.

> 'The "Spirit-Power of baptism" is an esoteric process wherein the Life-Current in the body-mind (and principally the central nervous system) of the human individual is stimulated to a point of profound intensity and turned about in its basic polarization or tendency... The effect of Spirit-baptism was an experience of bodily conversion to a subjective movement of Life-Energy away from the "flesh"... As a result of such baptism, the various classical mystical phenomena arose, and this entire procedure was called..."to be born again, via the Spirit"'.[149]

The intense religious experience which is being induced in Charismatic-Pentecostal circles is no different to that being induced in countless world religion circles and New Age Communities. Only the terminology is different. As far as the Yogic practitioner, Tantric Buddhist, Neo-Gnostic, Navajo 'Hand-Trembler' or Asiatic Shaman are concerned, the modern charismatic practices (which are very different to the original New Testament practices laid out in Scripture) are immediately identifiable with their own. Such a 'second blessing' and the attendant supernatural occurrences are not only common in these cultures but are counted as something to be eagerly sought after. In the pathway of the Indian mystic on his way to enlightenment, for instance, such psychic powers are known as 'Siddhis'.[150] He seeks to achieve a state which is known in Sanskrit as 'Nirvana', the literal meaning of which is 'a blowing-out-of-the-mind' — hence the drug-user's phrase which refers to a 'mind-blowing' experience. This blowing out of the mind is precisely what the Charismatic phenomenon is all about. These are the facts which account for the huge success of the Charismatic Movement in the so-called Third World countries, where magic and superstition hold sway.

The true evangelical Christian could so easily fall into despair at this point. Not only has the word 'Christian' long fallen into misuse, but the word 'evangelical' has also been hijacked from its rightful designation. The full significance of this is shown by the fact that a photograph, in a book on world religion, of a group of people with their eyes closed — arms waving ecstatically in the air — has a caption which describes it as *'an evangelical meeting'*.[151] Whatever else that is, such religious behaviour is not representative of true evangelical Christianity. The word 'evangelical' is derived from the Greek words *eu*, 'well' or 'good', and *angellos*, 'message'. An evangelical has an 'excellent message' to proclaim which involves *verbal* propositions. An evangelical engages with people's minds

---

[149] Ibid., p.29.

[150] To gain a sense of the uncanny parallellism between the psychic powers developed within the Charismatic Movement and those 'Siddhis' produced through the practices of Eastern mysticism, compare Ajit Mookerjee, *Kundalini: The Arousal of the Inner Energy* (Thames & Hudson, 1978). The 'serpent power' unleashed through Kundalini Yoga is startlingly similar to the 'power' which is 'hyped-up' in Charismatic meetings. These facts should be opened up when witnessing to Charismatics as they are most afraid of the occult. An undergirding characteristic of the Charismatic Movement is flight from fear through superstitious ritual and the effecting of mass-hypnosis.

[151] Ninian Smart, *The World's Religions: Old Traditions and Modern Transformations* (Cambridge University Press, 1992), p.369.

in the world of ideas. To be 'evangelical' is to hold spiritual concepts that make things happen, rather than to induce religious experiences that stop people thinking. Even secular wordsmiths know what the word 'evangelical' means. Chambers English Dictionary, for example, defines it as:

> 'Of the school that insists especially on the total depravity of unregenerate human nature, the justification of the sinner by faith alone, the free offer of the Gospel to all, and the plenary inspiration and exclusive authority of the Bible'.[152]

But the corruption of Christianity today has reduced all this to a mindless, arm-waving ecstasy. Fallen human beings have always preferred religious experiences to dynamic ideas; and the same tendency has always threatened the Church. There are so many people today who profess to be Christian believers, yet who seem to spend their time *'in nothing else but either to tell or to hear some new thing'* (Acts 17:21). They have become 'seed-pickers' — spiritual dilettantes pecking around in the religious and psychological market-places of the world. All this is not representative of the true Church of Jesus Christ. When we begin to consider the full implications of the words of the Lord Jesus in Matthew 7:14, an awesome truth should impale itself upon our hearts.

Because there has been so much confusion in the Church concerning these matters, let us now embark on an in-depth examination of the four common components of the Shamanic-Mesmeric 'Crisis Experience' which has been induced by powerful suggestion techniques in so many Charismatic-Pentecostal meetings throughout this century: first, 'Spirit Baptism'; second, speaking in 'tongues' or 'languages'; third, faith-healings; fourth, exorcisms.

i. Spirit-Baptism

If we are serious in discovering the true meaning of 'Baptism with the Holy Spirit', what do we find? We discover the remarkable fact that *it is an experience that it is applied to all believers at the time of their regeneration***.** This is the clear and unequivocal teaching of Scripture on the Baptism with the Holy Spirit. Even before the Lord Jesus began His earthly ministry, John the Baptist was preaching:

> 'There comes One after me who is mightier than I, whose sandal strap I am not worthy to stoop down and loose. I indeed baptised you with water, *but He will baptise you with the Holy Spirit*' (Mark 1:7-8; cf. Mt.3:11; Lk.3:16; Jn.1:33). [emphasis added]

Was the Baptist saying here that Jesus would merely baptise a few with the Holy Spirit? Not at all. The Baptism with the Holy Spirit was to be for all those who come to Him in repentance and faith. Even in the Old Testament prophecies of the outpouring of the Spirit on the Church, this Baptism with the Holy Spirit is shown to be for all those who come to Christ. As the Lord prophesied through His servant prophet, Isaiah:

---

[152] *Chambers English Dictionary* (W. & R. Chambers, 1988), p.493.

> 'Hear now, O Jacob My servant, and Israel whom I have chosen... I will pour water *on him who is thirsty*, and floods on the dry ground; I will pour My Spirit *on your descendants*, and My blessing *on your offspring*' (Isa.44:1,3,4). [emphasis added]

Who are the thirsty 'descendants' and 'offspring' of Israel that Isaiah was speaking of in these verses? Are they an elite group who happen to have attended highly-charged, emotional meetings and followed to the letter the instructions and powerful suggestions of their religious leaders? Of course not! The descendants and offspring of ancient Israel referred to in this passage are the spiritual seed of Abraham, the Church, the *children of God* by adoption on whom the Spirit has been poured out in these last days (see Gal.3:14; 4:5-7; Rom.8:9,14-17). The water in these verses of Isaiah is symbolic of Holy Spirit baptism which is said to be for all those who are thirsty, i.e., all those who hunger and thirst after righteousness and are then *filled* with the Holy Spirit (see Mt.5:6; Jn.7:37-39).

There are numerous other Scriptures which make it quite clear that *all* believers receive the fullness of the Holy Spirit from the moment of their new birth in Christ Jesus. Paul the apostle tells *all* the believers at Ephesus that, *'having believed, you were sealed with the Holy Spirit of promise'* (Eph.1:13). To the foolish Galatians who had become fascinated with false teachings, he poses the question, *'Did you receive the Spirit by the works of the law, or by the hearing of faith?'* (Gal.3:2), followed by an assertion *'that the blessing of Abraham might come upon the Gentiles in Christ Jesus, that we might receive the promise of the Spirit through faith'* (v.14). And Jesus Himself said that the Holy Spirit would come and take up residence within the person who has salvation through Jesus Christ (Jn.14:16-17). This receiving of the Holy Spirit at the new birth is the true Baptism with the Holy Spirit. However, Pentecostal-Charismatic teachers claim that there is a difference between *'receiving'* the Holy Spirit at the new birth and subsequently being *'baptised'* with the Holy Spirit. But to teach such a difference is contrary to the evidence of the Scriptures which, instead, show that the two are exactly synonymous. Let us demonstrate this with a real example.

When Peter saw that the Gentile Cornelius and his household had been saved by the power of God, he said: *'Can anyone forbid water, that these should not be baptised who have* ***received the Holy Spirit*** *just as we have?'* (Acts 10:47). Then, a few verses later, when accurately recounting this exact episode to the brethren in Jerusalem, Peter said that he

> 'remembered the word of the Lord, how He said, *'John indeed baptised with water, but you shall be* ***baptised with the Holy Spirit****'*. If therefore God gave them the same gift as He gave us when we believed on the Lord Jesus Christ, who was I that I could withstand God?' (Acts 11:16-17).

It is clear from a comparison of these verses that Peter precisely equated *'receiving'* the Holy Spirit (Acts 10:47) with the *'baptism'* with the Holy Spirit (Acts 11:16). This proves without a doubt that in the apostolic way of thinking, there never was a post-conversion 'Baptism with the Holy Spirit'. Moreover, the Scripture expressly says that Cornelius *'repented'* in response to Peter's evangelism (Acts 11:18b) — a clear reference to his conversion. Spirit-baptism is therefore contemporaneous with regeneration and conversion, rather than being an optional module of progressive sanctification *after* conversion.

At this stage, a cry is usually raised by Pentecostals and Charismatics that we are ignoring the other cases in Acts 2, 8, 10 and 19 which appear to prove conclusively that there is a post-conversion experience of the Holy Spirit which is separate from the receiving of the indwelling Holy Spirit, and which is normative for all Christians. However, if we apply sound rules for biblical interpretation and exercise discernment before immediately rushing into imitating an example given to us in the Book of Acts, we will learn that the support offered by these passages is merely superficial. A deeper examination of their immediate contextual meaning and relevance, coupled with an application of what we are taught elsewhere in Scripture about Holy Spirit Baptism, gives an entirely different understanding, not only of these passages but also of the wonderful ministry of the Holy Spirit in the inauguration of the Church.

It is the complete failure and wilful refusal to enter into a more profound understanding of these passages which has led to the rise of the Pentecostal-Charismatic Movement in recent decades. Indeed, this movement, which has led to so much heartache and division in the Church this century (at a time when unity between Bible-believing Christians against secular humanism and Neo-Gnosticism is absolutely vital) would never have come into being had there been a willingness to get beyond a merely superficial understanding of the history of the Early Church recorded in the Book of Acts.

So, what are we to make of the four passages in Acts which appear to show that one can be 'baptised' with the Holy Spirit as a post-conversion experience? No single event recorded in the Book of Acts can be taken as an isolated event. For this book is tracing the carefully purposed work of the Holy Spirit in the establishment of the Church. Right at the outset, the agenda is set when the Lord Jesus Christ tells His Apostles:

> 'But you shall receive power when the Holy Spirit has come upon you; and you shall be witnesses to Me in Jerusalem, and in all Judea and Samaria, and to the ends of the earth' (Acts 1:8).

In this verse the ministry of the Holy Spirit in the Church recorded in the Book of Acts is compressed into a brief précis: From Jerusalem to Judea and Samaria, and from there to the ends of the earth. Do you see the significance of these words? This is what the Book of Acts encompasses: The Spirit-inspired spread of the Gospel begins in the place that was the heartland of the Old Covenant nation, Israel, and then spreads out through Judea and the land of the Samaritans (despised by the Jews) and thence to the Gentile nations of the world, to places such as Ephesus, Corinth, Macedonia, etc., (also despised by the Jews) — an event which finds its ultimate fulfillment in Paul's arrival in Rome (the very apex of Gentile culture at that time) at the close of the Book of Acts. In other words, in this book, we see the authoritative cataloguing of the historically unique and necessary development from Judaism to Christianity.

Of the four extraordinary occurrences of the Holy Spirit which are cited by Pentecostals and Charismatics as being normative for the Christian, three of these (Acts 2, 8 & 10) occur in places corresponding exactly with these target zones of the Holy Spirit's rapidly spreading Gospel ministry. In Acts 2, we have the initial outpouring of the Spirit on the Church in Jerusalem. In Acts 8, because of the persecution of Christians in Jerusalem, the work of the Spirit moves to Judea and Samaria. In Acts 10, the Gentile centurion, Cornelius of Caesarea (the 'capital' of Judea, according to the Roman historian Tacitus), becomes the focus of the Spirit's attentions. The fourth extraordinary occurrence of the Holy Spirit carried an important message for all remaining disciples of the last of the O.T. prophets, John the Baptist (Acts 19). We shall now examine briefly each of these four events in turn, so that we can appreciate their significance to the movement of the Spirit in and beyond the confines of Jerusalem.

Acts 2:1-21 — 'Beginning at Jerusalem'

This passage is claimed as proof of a post-conversion religious experience because, it is argued, the disciples were already converted when they were *'filled with the Holy Spirit and began to speak with other tongues'* (Acts 2:4). However, the once-for-all-time nature of this event must surely exclude it from being normative for all Christians throughout every era of the Church. The idea that we can reproduce today what was a unique event in Church History is facile, to say the least. Just as Luke had recorded the unique coming of the Holy Spirit upon the Lord Jesus as the beginning of His ministry (His baptism by John in Lk.3:21-22 is followed by the words, *'Now Jesus Himself began [His ministry at] about thirty years of age'*), so the coming of the Holy Spirit on the Church at Pentecost was the beginning of the Gospel ministry of the Church. *'For John truly baptized with water, but you shall be baptized with the Holy Spirit not many days from now'* (Acts 1:5).

One must also bear in mind here that, although there have been believers saved by the power of Christ in all ages (the Cross is *retro*spective in its effects as well as *pro*spective), the Holy Spirit had not yet been given in fullness as a permanently-indwelling reality in the life of the Lord's people as individuals (cf. Jn.7:37-39). So when the Spirit was given to the Church at Pentecost, the disciples were brought into a new relationship with the Lord and were given a new commission. It was the powerful fulfilment of O.T. prophecy.

Furthermore, the tongues which were spoken here, when the gift was given, were *real human languages* rather than the ecstatic babble spoken by believers today (Acts 2:5-11), and they were also functioning as a judicial 'sign' to unbelieving Jews, exactly as Paul had shown was the true purpose of the gift (1 Cor.14:22), as we shall later see. The sign-nature of this happening can be seen in the response of those present. Some were *'amazed and perplexed, saying to one another, "Whatever could this mean?"'*, whereas *'others mocking said, "They are full of new wine"'* (Acts 2:12-13). To some, the fragrance of Christ is the aroma of death to death, to others the aroma of life to life (2 Cor.2:15-16). Those who have ears to hear let them hear. To those who have, more will be given; to those who have not, even what they have will be taken away from them. After the giving of the 'sign' in tongues, the way was then paved for Peter's evangelistic sermon in the native Aramaic which resulted in about three thousand souls being added to the number of the redeemed (Acts 2:41).

All this is a far cry from the ecstatic babbling which is spoken by people in the churches today, which does not function as a sign to anyone, and which is used mainly as a devotional aid to personal prayer or for the effecting of trance-inducement. Similarly, the 'Tarrying Meetings' held in Pentecostal churches while people wait to receive a 'Baptism with the Holy Spirit' are a vain attempt to bring on what people *imagine* to have happened at Pentecost. Anyone who thinks that they can replicate that original Pentecostal phenomenon has misunderstood entirely the unique work of the Holy Spirit in the initiation of the Church.

Acts 8:14-17 — 'In all Samaria'

This event in Samaria is also extraordinary, and was a unique event in God's redemptive timetable. The Samaritans were despised by the Jews and the feeling was mutual — a state of affairs which went back a thousand years to the time when ten of the tribes of Israel had set up their own state, with Samaria as the capital, and practised a syncretised mixture of true religion and heathen idolatry (1 Kgs.16:21-24; 2 Kgs.17:24-41). At one time the Apostles had been forbidden by Jesus to enter any Samaritan city (Mt.10:5), while James and John had once wished to call down fire from heaven on a Samaritan community (Lk.9:54).

The movement of the preaching of the Gospel away from Jerusalem really began when the persecution of the Church by Saul of Tarsus (later Paul the Apostle) providentially scattered converts around the world (Acts 8:1-4). Phillip the evangelist was really very bold in going to Samaria to preach the Gospel, because of the history of hostility. The fact that he was successful should not surprise us too much, as the Samaritans were waiting for the Messiah as much as the Jews (cf. Jn.4:29). But the problem here, at this point in Church history, was the special need to convince the Jewish Christians in Jerusalem that the Samaritans really were being admitted into the household of God. It is no wonder that when the authoritative Apostles who were at Jerusalem heard that Samaria (of all places!) had actually received the word of God, they sent the Apostles Peter and John down to them (Acts 8:14). It was most vital that Apostolic authority should be brought to determine whether or not the reception of the Gospel in these formerly-hated Gentile domains was genuine — not to mention the need for the Jewish Christians in Jerusalem to be convinced that these were indeed movements of God.

It is no coincidence that it was Phillip the Hellenist who had gone to Samaria to evangelise. This was a shrewd move. The Jewish converts from Jerusalem might have resisted carrying out such an action themselves, and the Samaritans would have been far less likely to accept the Gospel if some Apostles of Jewish origin turned up at the outset. So once the job had been successfully done by Phillip, who would be accepted, the way was paved for the Apostles to come to Samaria and authenticate the events of recent days.

The only explanation which can account for what was happening here in Samaria was that it was a 'Mini-Pentecost', in which the giving of the Spirit was delayed until Apostolic authority had ratified that the Gospel had genuinely been received there. Added to this was the necessity for the Samaritans to feel that they had truly been accepted back into the household of God. All this was an act of grace on God's part. For if things had not been done this way, it is possible that the Samaritan reception of the Gospel would never have been accepted in Jerusalem and a split would have befallen the Church at a delicate point in redemptive history.

There is no reason to believe that the coming of the Spirit on the Samaritans was anything other than an isolated event which is not to be imitated by all believers in every era of the Church. It was part of God's singular care and providence in the initial extension of the Great Commission in the Apostolic era, and, as such, was a one-off occasion applicable only to that situation.

Acts 10:1 - 11:18 — 'In all Judea'

The events surrounding the conversion of Cornelius in Acts 10 and 11 are commonly used as a proof text for the post-conversion Baptism with the Holy Spirit. The stress is on the word 'post-conversion' here, because some brethren claim that Cornelius was already converted before he was baptised with the Holy Spirit. However, this could not be the case, for the Scripture observes that the Jewish Christians who were present when Cornelius spoke in tongues said: *'Then God has also granted to the Gentiles* ***repentance to life****'* (Acts 11:18), a clear reference to the fact that what was involved in the scene between Peter and Cornelius was that the latter and his household repented in response to Peter's openly evangelistic sermon in Acts 10:34-43.

A major thread in this event was the necessity to convince the Jewish believers from Jerusalem that the Holy Spirit had been poured out on believing Gentiles as well; and that was the purpose behind this entire episode with Cornelius (see Acts 11:1-18). After thousands of years of God carrying out His redemptive dealings almost exclusively with the single nation, Israel, one can have some sympathy with this. It was necessary that Cornelius and his household should undergo this 'mini-Pentecost' — this replication of the original Pentecost in Jerusalem — in order to authenticate the inclusion of the Gentiles in the new body of the Lord's people. The Lord does not automatically 'zap' information into our brains: He uses means, agents, channels and intermediaries to persuade us of things about which we need convincing (e.g., Jn.2:11). Added to this is the fact that the gift of tongues given to Cornelius and his household was functioning as a true 'sign'. Any unbelieving Jews who heard about this history-making event would be astounded to learn that God had granted repentance to the Gentiles.

There is a further lesson to be gained from the record of this event. Contrary to those who imagine that there were continuous tongue-speakings and post-conversion Holy Spirit baptisms in every corner of the church, Peter tells us that when Cornelius was baptised with the Holy Spirit, it was a carbon copy of the original outpouring of the Spirit at Pentecost (Acts 11:15) — thereby also proving that it was genuine languages which were spoken here rather than ecstatic babbling. How significant it is that the only event used by Peter for comparison with what took place in the household of Cornelius was a unique occasion which had taken place *some eight years earlier*! Such an event was something really special — a rarity — not one that can be worked up at any time by bringing an emotionally-manipulative evangelist into town who can give out some crude instructions on how to plug into a pseudo-spiritual experience. In common with the other Spirit baptisms in the Book of Acts, this conversion of the Gentile Cornelius is a uniquely important milestone in the Holy Spirit's gradually-spreading, post-Pentecost ministry, and is not to be used as a normative example for all Christians in every era.

Acts 19:1-7 — Beyond the Baptism of John

This event in Acts 19 is cited by many Charismatics and Pentecostals as being supportive of a post-conversion Baptism with the Holy Spirit; but this is based on an unclear translation of the original Greek by the authors of the King James Version, which reads, *'Have ye received the Holy Ghost* ***since*** *ye believed?'* (v.2). Instead, the literal translation reads: *'Believing, did you receive the Holy Spirit?'*, or *'Did you receive the Holy Spirit when you believed?'* And this is the translation given by all other versions of the Bible today. As readers will notice, this clearer translation actually works *against* the Pentecostal belief in a *post-conversion* second-blessing baptism with the Holy Spirit, and shows that the normative reception of the Holy Spirit is contemporaneous with believing.

A further consideration hinges on whether or not these disciples of John the Baptist were Christians at the time that Paul came upon them. Surely they were not. It was only when Paul showed them the One to whom John's baptism pointed that they really believed (vv.4-5). Even Anglican Charismatic Michael Green admits that it is *'crystal clear that these disciples were in no sense Christians'*.[153] So this example cannot be used to support the notion of a post-conversion Baptism with the Holy Spirit. It was another 'Mini-Pentecost' designed to bring the blessings of the original Pentecost to yet another special group which had not yet come into the fullness of Christian blessing.

* * * * * * *

Surely, in the light of the above discussion in this section, it is clear that none of these four passages supports a post-conversion Baptism with the Holy Spirit — a mystical experience which is normative for *all* Christians in *every* era of the Church. The laying-on of Apostolic hands, conferring the spiritual gifts of tongues and prophecy, was unique to these few events to show categorically that certain groupings were now incorporated into the body of Christ through the Spirit. *Firstly*, the Holy Spirit does not need to be poured out on the Church a second time — once, at Pentecost was quite enough. *Secondly*, there are no

---

[153] Michael Green, *I Believe in the Holy Spirit* (Hodder & Stoughton, 1985), p.135.

Samaritans left in the world today. *Thirdly*, we do not now need convincing that the Gentiles have been grafted into the people of God. *Fourthly*, there are no disciples of John the Baptist alive today. The above four passages portray extraordinary circumstances which are intimately tied in with the giving of the Spirit to the Church at Pentecost. The original Pentecost comes in Acts 2, while the other three instances were 'mini-Pentecosts', in which the Spirit was poured out on Judea, Samaria and the ends of the earth — the line of progress of the Gospel from its onset in Jerusalem. The laying on of hands by genuine Apostles which led to the receiving of the Holy Spirit, as manifested in tongues-speaking and prophesying, were distinctive to the situations in Samaria and Ephesus, to give a visible demonstration to all sceptics (especially the brethren in Jerusalem) that the Holy Spirit was given to those outside the nation of Israel, as well as fulfilling the function of being a sign to unbelieving Jews. There were many thousands of people added to the Church in Acts, yet there is no mention of them manifesting extraordinary phenomena.

Lest anyone should still be in doubt as to whether or not ***all*** believers are baptised with the Holy Spirit, rather than this being confined to those who have a dramatic post-conversion experience, consider the sheer force of truth in 1 Cor.12:13 which states incontrovertibly:

> 'For by *one* Spirit we were *all* baptised into *one* body — whether Jews or Greeks, whether slaves or free — and have *all* been made to drink into *one* Spirit'. [emphasis added]

This verse turns on its head what is being advocated in highly-charged Pentecostal and Charismatic meetings around the world, where gullible people are told to expect a religious experience called 'Baptism with the Holy Spirit'. The division which this bogus experience brings in the churches is in stark opposition to the statement in 1 Cor.12:13, which asserts the fact that *Baptism with the Holy Spirit is an immediate, conversion-effecting event which brings unity among the brethren rather than division.* It is our sincere belief that the global development of the Charismatic phenomenon in the past two decades has been brought into being primarily through the work of the Vatican as part of its bid to unite all professing Christians under the Pope. And what better vehicle for this than a purported 'Baptism with the Holy Spirit' manifested in the ecstatic 'tongues-speaking' of the Mystery Religions — an experience which can be induced in anyone gullible enough to receive it, Catholic or Protestant, liberal or orthodox, believer or unbeliever. Thus, an international, ecumenical body is built up which rests on mysticism rather than the Gospel — subjective experience rather than objective truth. The hypnotic, compelling power of this 'Baptism in the Holy Spirit' which so many are seeking has an inescapable eschatological dimension. We need great discernment if we are not to be pulled into its powerful wake.

It is certainly true that Christian believers can have an overwhelming spiritual experience in the course of their lives which is a part of genuine Christian experience. However, this should not be confused with the manufactured 'Spirit Baptism' so common in Charismatic-Pentecostal circles. It would be foolish to deny that there *are* real and profound inward spiritual experiences which can happen to any Christian believer. However, these are isolated occurrences — what we can call spiritual peak-experiences — which can happen occasionally (or never at all) at any stage in one's Christian development. And they are marked by certain infallible hallmarks: They do not happen to order, they can never be predicted, and they tend to happen out of the public eye — often in the deep privacy of personal communion with the Lord or while meditating on the wonders of His work in creation and redemption.

When believers do have a brief but overwhelming experience of the ineffability, beauty, majesty and glory of God and all that He has done for us through Jesus Christ, these are precious, faith-enhancing experiences which one should only share with others under extraordinary circumstances. They are certainly not to be sought after; neither are they to be paraded or prostituted before the world — least of all should they be institutionalised into the distinguishing mark of a tendentious 'movement' — a spiritual elite who regard as inferior those who have not yet shared such bounties. The true work of the Spirit is actually very inobtrusive (Eccl.11:5), is usually invisible to the eye (Jn.3:8), and always glorifies Christ rather than Himself (Jn.16:14-15). Paul the apostle had the ultimate Christian interior experience (2 Cor.12:1-6), yet it was not lawful for him even to speak about it — let alone boast about it or encourage others to seek after it. In fact, the Lord Himself ensured that Paul would not turn his experience into an opportunity for pride by using Satan to give him that famous thorn in the flesh (2 Cor.12:7-10).

It is so tragic that the devil has stepped in and has packaged what should be uniquely-lovely spiritual moments into a universal religious experience which one can plug into by following a few clockwork instructions from spiritual con-men who know how to bend gullible people's minds. When one sees a book with a cover which says 'Spiritual Power: How to get it – how to give it!', listing what are claimed to be infallible techniques for the inducement of a mystico-religious experience, one cannot help being overwhelmed by its crass materialism, gross superficiality and sheer lack of biblical support. What is being advocated and practiced in such circles is not the genuine experience of Divine communion — an exclusively Christian experience — but a form of self-hypnosis through powerful suggestion techniques that are far more in the realm of the satanic and demonic than an inner experience of the Holy Spirit.

What needs to be pressed home to Pentecostals and Charismatics is that 'peak-experiences' are not the sole province of the Christian. Unbelievers are also subject to such things — although within the parameters of their own particular belief-system. The capacity for such experience is built into the psycho-physical nature of all human beings. In fact, such experiences are what mysticism and much of pagan religion as a whole are all about. Take this example from the recent experience of a famous psychiatrist:

> 'Then I had one of the strangest and most amazing experiences in my life, an experience which resulted in a radical shift in my belief system. After sitting quietly for five minutes, my body began to quiver and

> shake in an indescribable manner. Beautiful colors appeared all around me, and it seemed as though I had stepped out of my body and was looking down at it... I began to talk in tongues — a phenomenon I had heard about but discredited. A beautiful beam of light came into the room and I decided at that moment to stop evaluating what was happening and simply be one with the experience, to join it completely'.[154]

This experience did not happen during a Charismatic revival meeting or as the result of one of Richard Foster's visualisation exercises, but in the inner rooms of an Indian guru known as Swami Muktananda! This psychiatrist — a friend of Crystal Cathedral founder and 'Possibility Thinking' teacher Robert Schuller — went on to found a Centre which propagates 'New Thought' occult teachings of 'visualisation' and 'affirmation'. It is precisely for this reason that Christians — if they do undergo a 'peak-experience' — must not automatically assume that it is of Divine origin. In fact, Satan is very good at manufacturing such experiences in order to confirm his own teachings, whereas the Lord God would generally use ordinary means to engender assurance in His children.

If you do undergo such an experience, you should ask yourself a number of questions: Does this experience make me believe in Christian truth more fully than before? Do I have a greater desire to read the Bible as God's Word? Is the Lord Jesus Christ more of a focus in my life than before? Do I begin to appreciate His Deity as never before? Am I committed to keeping silent about this experience before others? Do I understand the importance of not attempting to reproduce the experience? Have I grasped the fact that this experience does not make me a better Christian than others who have never been through it? Have I realised that undergoing such an experience is not what biblical Christianity is really all about? Can I accept the fact that it is just a kind of 'icing on the cake', a little gift which was appropriate for that moment but which may never come again? If you cannot answer 'yes' to all these questions, then it is unlikely that the experience was from the Holy Spirit of God. Unfortunately, this is the case with a great many experiences which believers are having today. And 'experience' is the keyword here; for so many believers base their theology almost entirely on their subjective experience rather than on the objective Word of God.

This is precisely what has led to the Charismatic phenomenon today. It is a significant fact that Charismatic-Pentecostal religion has been most successful in certain predictable situations: in countries where there is already a high degree of shamanistic, spiritistic religion; in denominations and churches where there has been little or no expository biblical teaching; in those circles where there is already an avid acceptance of man-centred rather than God-honouring theology; in those churches where the authentication of religious truth is rooted in emotional expression and experience; in highly ecumenical circles where there is a naive desire to base Christianity on some superficial creed; and in those fellowships where dead 'orthodoxy' has prevailed for some decades. The Charismatic Movement

---

[154] Gerald G. Jampolsky, *Teach Only Love: Seven Principles of Attitudinal Healing* (Bantam, 1983), p.12.

pulls all these strands together and creates a hybrid religion which destroys dependence on biblical revelation and grounds the truth in the illusions of sensory experience. And the stark upshot of all this is that you don't have to be a Christian to be a Charismatic. Thus existentialism, mysticism, liberalism and superstition are commingled to form the basic ingredients of one of the most distinguished counterfeits to hit the Church since its Founder walked the earth.

A religion which seeks to 'claim the victory' and wallow in mindless triumphalism is a religion which has forsaken the need to take up its cross daily, and to follow Jesus; such a religion has failed to understand that it is in creature-weakness that Creator-strength is shown. A religion which would rather manufacture false 'miracles' and 'healings' than preach the Gospel of spiritual salvation has far more in common with pagan Shamanism than biblical Christianity. A religion which rests its laurels on the ability to induce 'ecstatic utterances' in its adherents has forfeited the right to the Crown of Life. There is a burning need to demonstrate the startling fact that the Charismatic religion of today is not the Christianity of the Bible. There is an analogy here with Roman Catholicism, in the sense that it has enough in common with true Christianity to render it an air of biblical respectability to the untaught and unstable; but once a little research is carried out into its theology and practice, the differences between it and and the breadth of biblical truth gape like yawning chasms.

ii. Tongues-Speaking

The influence of experience-based religion has been especially prominent in regard to the next aspect of the 'Crisis Experience' induced at Charismatic or Pentecostal gatherings today — the art of speaking in 'tongues'. Indeed, it has almost become the benchmark for genuine Christian experience in these circles. But what does the Bible reveal?

The spiritual gift referred to in the New Testament which people call 'tongues' can be translated literally as *'varieties of languages'*.[155] In the time when the KJV was written, the word 'tongue' — the word which has come most to be associated with this gift — meant an identifiable human language. And an in-depth study of the Greek word *glossa*, translated as 'tongue' in many versions, shows that it must refer to an identifiable human language (see, e.g., Rev.5:9; 9:11). When we look for clear texts elsewhere in the New Testament which will provide us with examples of this gift in action, we see that it indeed functioned as *the supernatural ability to speak in previously unlearned, identifiable human languages*. And in our search for such a text, we find that Acts 2:1-13, for example, gives us a superb

---

[155] As the central purpose of this chapter is to examine the use of the mind-sciences in the churches, we will not be discussing all the spiritual gifts which are mentioned in the New Testament. For a full examination of these and their relevance to today's Church, see J. Edgar, *Miraculous Gifts* (Loizeau Brothers, 1983), 394pp.; Victor Budgen, *The Charismatics and the Word of God: A Biblical & Historical Perspective on the Charismatic Movement* (Evangelical Press, 1985), 281pp.; Richard Heldenbrand, *Christianity and the New Evangelical Philosophies* (Words of Life, 1991), 199pp.; Douglas Judisch, *An Evaluation of Claims to the Charismatic Gifts* (Baker Book House, 1979), 96pp.

practical model of the biblical gift of 'varieties of languages'.

However, there is not a scrap of evidence in Scripture which would support the notion that the biblical gift of tongues involved the commonplace ecstatic babbling which one can witness across the world, in Christian and non-Christian circles alike. Such babbling has been a hallmark of heathen religion from the beginning of time. It is an intrinsic part of human psycho-physiology to be able to enter such a state of mind. Christians, as partakers in the same flesh, are not exempt from the ability to reproduce this experience. It is actually an incipient trance-like condition brought on through powerful suggestion or auto-suggestion, in which there is increased Alpha-Wave activity of the brain (which is why tongues-speakers feel so good), coupled with a stimulation of the part of the brain which governs articulate speech, known as 'Broca's area'. Such an experience has been generated in pagan religions throughout history through the use of repetitive prayer (mantras), powerful suggestion from a dominant teacher (Shamanism), wild dancing (Dervishism), meditation (varieties of Yoga) and drugs (the word 'pharmacology' is actually derived from the Greek word for sorcerer, *pharmakos*). All this is entirely different from the phenomenon described in Acts 2, 8, 10, & 19, and bears no relation to the spiritual gift of *'languages'* mentioned in 1 Cor.12.

Revelation and Sign Gifts

Here it would be relevant to show that the spiritual gift of 'varieties of languages' was given by the Lord in order to function as a 'sign'. The epoch of Church history known as the Apostolic era was an extraordinary time of development. The Mosaic order was giving way to the age of the New Covenant; the God-ordained, theocratic nation-state of Israel was being wound up for the final time; the Gentile nations were being opened up to the Gospel in an unprecedented fashion; and there was a need for fresh revelation after four hundred years of silence in the Inter-Testamental period.

At this point in history, God gave four spiritual gifts which served a unique purpose during a time of great change in the Church. First, there was the gift of prophecy, by which Divine revelation was given 'piecemeal' to the primitive Church at a time when the written New Testament revelation was still incomplete. Then there were 'gifts of healings', 'workings of miracles', and 'varieties of languages' — all of which are said to have functioned as *'signs'*. The word sign in Scripture is a translation of the Greek word *semeion*, from which our English words 'semeiology' (study of symptoms) and semaphore (signalling apparatus) are derived. A 'sign' in Scripture refers to something which is signalling a matter of *sign*ificance to whoever witnesses it. For example, in the course of the Gospel of John, the Apostle presents to his readers seven 'signs' which were performed by Jesus to convince them *'that you may believe that Jesus is the Christ, the Son of God, and that believing you may have life in His name'* (Jn.20:31).

Signs always have a vital function. In the Apostolic era, 'signs' were either for the purposes of *authentication* of the fact that the Messiah had come, or they were *judicial* in character — a fact which we shall shortly develop more fully in relation to 'tongues'. Such 'signs' were predominantly directed at the Jews, whose nation-state, together with its ceremonial and legal system, was about to be wound up — the final hammer-blow being the complete destruction of Jerusalem and the temple in AD.70.

The nature and purpose of the 'sign-gifts' can be gleaned from a few places in Scripture. One such passage is Mk.16:17-18. Some expositors, in a well-meaning bid to negate the common Pentecostal teaching that **all** believers will speak in tongues, cast out demons and practise healing, have held that this final passage of Mark's Gospel (Mk.16:9-20) is not authentic. But there is no need to resort to such radical surgery with God's Word in order to prove this point. Almost every available manuscript contains this passage, whereas it is lacking only in the more suspect codices Vaticanus and Sinaiticus. Furthermore, John Burgon has adequately proven the authenticity of this passage in a work that has never been answered.[156] The main problem with Mk.16:17 has been its consistent mistranslation and the misinterpretation which results from that. When the majority of translations say, *'And these signs will follow those who believe...'* (Mk.16:17), we are led to assume that the verse is referring to all believers of whatever era. But the tense of the verb *'believe'* here is aorist, which indicates that the phrase is really saying, *'these signs will follow those who **have already** believed'* — in this context, the Apostles. This verse looks back to earlier verses, where reference is made to a contrasting **un**belief on the part of the Apostles (see vv.11,13,14). Verses 15 and 16 are a parenthetical statement of the Great Commission. In any case, the signs referred to here cannot possibly be applicable to *every* believer as there is a reference to an immunity from normally-fatal snake bites and the ability to drink poison unharmed — qualities which are hardly universal in their ecclesiastical application! We do know for certain of at least one instance where a genuine Apostle of Christ was unharmed by the bite of a deadly snake (Acts 28:3-6).

Signs of an Apostle

In fact, the signs being referred to in the Marcan passage are some of the *'signs of an Apostle'* to which Paul refers in 2 Cor.12:12. Just as God had set out certain infallible ways in O.T. times for testing whether or not a prophet was true or false (Dt.13:1-3; 18:20-22), so He also declared certain 'signs' which would enable N.T. believers to distinguish between a true and a false apostle. These signs of an Apostle of Christ consisted of those things listed in Mk.3:14-15 and Mk.16:17-18 (healing, tongues-speaking, casting out of demons, etc.), plus the working of miracles (2 Cor.12:12; Rom.15:19), prophecy (Mt.10:40-41; Acts 5:3-9; 13:6-12; 14:8-10), and — most important to our present study — *the unique ability to distribute these revelation and sign gifts to others* (Heb.2:4). The only means that God has used for distributing the 'revelation' or 'sign' gifts to others in the New Testament era is through the mediation of the unique Apostles of Jesus Christ. These gifts and abilities — tongues, prophecy, the casting out of demons, healing

---

[156] Jay P. Green (ed.), *John W. Burgon: The Last Twelve Verses of the Gospel According to Mark*, Vol.I of 'Unholy Hands on the Bible' (Sovereign Grace Trust Fund, 1990; first published in 1871), pp.C1-C177.

and miracle-working — were imparted to believers by the laying on of hands of the Apostles. There is no account in Scripture of anyone receiving a 'revelation' or 'sign' gift other than through the distribution of an Apostle;[157] whereas a number of people are spoken of as having received these gifts through this unique Apostolic ministry. Stephen and Philip had both had Apostolic hands laid on them and thereby were given the gift of miracle-working (Acts 6:5-8; 8:6). Barnabas, who had been renamed by Apostolic decree (Acts 4:36) and probably had Apostolic hands laid on him when he was sent to Antioch (Acts 11:22), was given the gift of prophecy (13:1). Furthermore, Paul spent eighteen months establishing the Corinthian church (Acts 18:11), during which he authenticated his Apostleship with signs and wonders (1 Cor.2:4-5; 2 Cor.12:12), and distributed gifts to others there as part of his Apostolic office (1 Cor.1:6-7). So it is hardly surprising that there was such a broad manifestation of these gifts in Corinth.

There is a particular proof that these gifts could only be received through the agency of an Apostle of Christ. When we are shown that Paul authenticated his Apostleship to the Corinthians by appealing to his *'signs and wonders and mighty deeds'* (2 Cor.12:12), we can also deduce that none of the Corinthian believers could have received any of the revelatory/sign gifts other than by the distribution of an Apostle. For, if they had the ability to prophesy, to execute miracles or healings, or to speak in tongues, without Apostolic mediation, then the performance of such signs and wonders and mighty works would be no proof of Apostleship.

That such gifts were distributed by the exclusive mediation of the Apostles was certainly not lost on Simon the Sorcerer. This was why he preferred to 'buy' the Apostolic ability to impart the revelatory/sign gifts of the Spirit to others rather than the mere capacity to work miracles (Acts 8:17-19). To be a false apostle would amass far more power and authority than merely being a false miracle-worker! It is precisely for this reason that a right understanding of the unique nature of the Apostleship is fundamental to 'getting it right' about the claims of the Pentecostal-Charismatic Movement regarding healings, prophecies, miracle-working and tongues.[158] In view of the fact that the spiritual gift of 'languages' depended so much on Apostolic ministry, let us see how the New Testament identifies apostles. What are the distinguishing marks of an apostle? If we can identify these, then we will see if they can be applied to anyone alive today.

---

[157] The Gentile, Cornelius, was a special case — although an Apostle was certainly present, having been specially sent to preach the Gospel to him. Some cite Timothy as an exception (cf. 1 Tim.4:14). However, this does not refer to Timothy himself receiving the gift of prophecy, but to the office of Pastor being conferred upon him by the laying on of hands of the eldership, as the result of a prophetic revelation.

[158] There is considerable confusion today on this question of the Apostleship. When the present writer's wife asked a young woman what she was hoping to do when she completed her studies at a Bible College, she was told: *'I haven't made up my mind yet whether to be an Apostle or a composer'*. In the face of such ignorance, a right understanding of these matters is of the utmost importance. Many Bible Colleges have much to answer for in terms of the spawning of false doctrine and superficial Christian thought among impressionable young people throughout the evangelical churches.

Qualifications of an Apostle

The word *apostle* comes from the Greek *apostolos*, which means, literally, one who is sent. Our word 'posted' is derived from it. So, loosely speaking, the word apostle can apply to anyone given a special commission or posting in the Church in any era of its existence. Occasionally in the New Testament the word is used in this broader sense to refer to those who have been specially commissioned for missionary work by the churches (e.g., 2 Cor.8:23; Phil.2:25). But such general, church-commissioned, sent-ones were not the same as those entrusted with the unique spiritual gift of Apostleship, who were *'Apostles of Jesus Christ'* (see Gal.1:1) — sent **personally** by Him, and who had unique qualifications for receiving that gift and distributing spiritual gifts to others. The sole qualifications which the Bible gives for being a spiritually-gifted Apostle are as follows:

1. He must have accompanied Jesus during His earthly ministry, which was from His baptism until His Ascension (Acts 1:21-23).
2. He must have been a *personal* witness of the resurrected Lord Jesus (1 Cor.15:7; 1 Cor.9:1; Acts 1:22; 4:33; 10:39-42).
3. He must have received a personal call from Christ to Apostleship and a commission to fulfil its duties (Lk.6:13; Mk.3:14-15).
4. He must have had, as his field of labour, *the whole world*, rather than a local church or group of churches (Mt.28:19; Mk.16:15).

On this basis, and in the power of Jesus Christ (*'in His name'*, Mk.9:38-41), such a one was given a commission (Mt.28:18-20) to herald out the *kerygma* — the essential message of the Gospel on which the Church was founded — the proclamation of the death and resurrection of Jesus Christ. Paul refers directly to this special apostolic commission in Tit.1:1-3. Furthermore, there were distinctive *'signs of an Apostle'* of Jesus Christ. When certain people in the church at Corinth suggested that Paul was not really an Apostle, he answered by referring specifically to these signs as proof of his Apostleship (2 Cor.12:12; cf. Heb.2:3-4).

In carrying out this personal commission from the Lord Jesus Christ, these Apostles (along with the N.T. Prophets) were in the process of *laying the foundations of the Church* — a historical architectural procedure which is a once-for-all exercise and which cannot be repeated throughout every era of Church history (read Eph.2:20; Rev.21:14). This is precisely the context in which the Lord Jesus told the Apostle Peter that he and his testimony to the Messiahship of Christ were **the rock** upon which He would build His Church (Mt.16:18). This is a further confirmation that one of the prime characteristics of genuine Apostles was that they (and their teachings) were the foundations of the Church — the solid bedrock — and we are the building that rests upon that which they established. Once a foundation is laid, the building proper begins. That foundation consisted of the setting up of the primitive Church on a correct doctrinal footing (*'Imitate me, just as I also imitate Christ'... 'Remember me...keep the traditions'*, 1 Cor.11:1-2; cf. 2 Tim.1:13-14; Tit.1:9), authenticating the Messianic coming with miraculous works (Heb.2:3-4; Acts 2:43; 5:12), and writing the Scriptures for a testimony of these things to later generations of Christians (Eph.3:3-5). The gifts are given for the 'edification' of the Church as a whole. Edification means building up. *The Apostles' primary contribution to the building up of the Universal Church was to lay the rock on which it would be built.*

These unique Apostles — God's foundation gift to the church (1 Cor.12:28) — were also *directly* commissioned and *personally* sent by Jesus Christ, the Head of the Church. That is why they are called *'Apostles **of Christ**'* and *'Apostles **of Jesus Christ**'* (see the first verse of 1 Cor., 2 Cor., Eph., Col., 1 Tim., 2 Tim., Tit., 1 Pet., 2 Pet.; and especially Gal.1:1; 1 Th.2:6; Jude 17). This is why false apostles are those *who transform themselves* into the Apostles **of Christ**, (2 Cor.11:13). A further aspect of the foundation-laying of the Apostles of Christ is that they laid down the New Testament Scriptures on which the truth of the Gospel is grounded and authenticated (Jn.17:20; Eph.3:3-5; cf. Jn.20:30-31).

There were just two exceptions to the above qualifications for the Apostleship. One was Matthias, who had not been directly commissioned by Christ but was chosen as a replacement for Judas Iscariot (Acts 1:21ff.). The other was Saul of Tarsus, who became Paul. Although Paul had not been with Jesus during His earthly ministry, he received an extraordinary manifestation of the resurrected Jesus on the road to Damascus and was given a special commission to minister to the Gentiles (1 Cor.9:1; 15:8; Acts 26:15-18). Thus, the hallowed Twelve Apostles became thirteen — one having been *'born out of due time'* (1 Cor.15:8). There is a remarkable touch of typology here in the way that the twelve tribes of Israel (of which the twelve Apostles were a New Testament echo) also became thirteen with the elevation of two of Joseph's sons to the rank of tribal heads (Gen.48:5).

What significance does all this have for us in the twentieth century? Can anyone alive today make the bold claim that they have the spiritual gift of Apostleship — that they are therefore an Apostle of Jesus Christ? A consideration of the above facts must surely necessitate a negative answer, for the following reasons:

- None of us alive today has spent any time with the Lord Jesus during His earthly ministry.
- None of us has ever been *material* witnesses of His Resurrection. In fact, our evidence for the Resurrection rests solely on the foundation which was laid by the true Apostles, who were commissioned to write these things down for us in the Scriptures (1 Cor.15:1-9).
- None of us today has been *personally* commissioned by Christ to be witnesses to the fact of His Resurrection in the way in which the original Apostles were.
- None of us can possibly be called the *founders* of the Church.
- Neither have we ever been *personally* commissioned by Christ to perform those signs which were exclusively those of an Apostle of His (Mt.10:1-4; Mark 3:13-15; 16:17-18; 2 Cor.12:12).

For these compelling reasons, there can be no genuine Apostles of Jesus Christ today. The spiritual gift of Apostleship lasted only for the infancy of the Church, during its foundation-laying period, for the duration of the lives of the Apostles, and has no functional relevance today. Anyone claiming to be an Apostle now is a false apostle — of which there were many even in the early church (Acts 15; Gal.1:7-9; 2 Cor.10 & 11; Col.2), whose end shall be according to their works (2 Cor.11:13-15; cf. Rev.2:2).

It represents an attempt to move the goalposts to say, as many do today, that the Spiritual gift of Apostleship is a secondary form of apostleship, lacking the authority that we see exercised by the Apostles in Scripture. The whole notion of spiritually gifted 'secondary' apostles and prophets has only served to create fear, confusion and false authority in the churches, while giving Satan a supreme foothold in a place where he should really fear to tread.

Since it is plain that there can be no genuine Apostles of Jesus Christ today, therefore there can be no one around to distribute the revelatory/sign-gifts. Not only is there no one to impart them, but they have served their purpose in the development of the Church — a fact which we will now prove in relation to the gift of 'tongues'. Once the N.T. canon was completed and all the Apostles were dead, the gifts which served for a sign and for revelation were finished. There was no further need for *piecemeal* prophetic revelation to be given now that God's Word was *complete*. There was no further need for signs to be given to Israel for authenticating or judicial reasons, as that national state had been wound up by the Lord. Neither was there anyone available to impart or distribute these gifts, because the Apostolate was no longer in existence.

These sign-gifts were specifically intended to aid the establishment of the Church through the ministry of the Apostles. The pattern is clearly shown in Heb.2:3-4. Read it through. First came the word of the Gospel spoken by the Lord Jesus (v.3b), which is then confirmed to *'us'* (believers in general, v.3c) as a result of the special ministry of *'those who heard Him'* (the Apostles, v.3c). This special Apostolic ministry is spoken of as *'God also bearing witness both with signs and wonders, with various miracles and distributions of the Holy Spirit'* (i.e., spiritual gifts, v.4). This use of the word *'distributions'* is especially significant, because it shows that the gifts of the Spirit which were the special province of Apostolic ministry — i.e., those which involved revelation (prophecy) and authentication (signs) — were distributed by the Apostles. The need for such revelation and authentication was a hallmark of the foundation-laying period of Church History; but, as we shall see, there was no further need for such 'signs' after the conclusion of the Apostolic era. In fact, the Scriptures give a clear indication that as the Gospel Age progresses there will be an increasing manifestation of 'revelation' and 'signs' which are the special work of false christs and false prophets (Mt.24:24; Mk.13:22). The biblical teaching on 'signs and wonders' is that the beginning of this Age was characterised by the signs of the Apostles of Christ and genuine wonders worked by those empowered by them; whereas the end of the Age will be characterised by the signs of Antichrist and *'lying wonders'* worked by those empowered by him (2 Th.2:9; Rev.13:13-14; cf. 1 Tim.4:1).

Having now established the true identity of an Apostle of Jesus Christ and ascertained the nature of those gifts which were given to the Church for a sign and for revelation, let us return to consider the true purpose of the gift of 'tongues'.

The Undergirding Purpose of 'Tongues'

A primary hallmark of the biblical gift of tongues is that it was practised either spontaneously by the Apostles of Christ, or by those who had received the gift through the laying on of hands by these self-same Apostles (e.g., Acts 19:6). As with the other revelatory/sign-gifts, it is impossible for anyone to exhibit the genuine version of this gift unless they have had Apostolic hands laid on them. The only exception to this was the 'mini-Pentecost' at Caesarea, when Cornelius and his household were empowered by God to demonstrate definitely to the Jewish believers present that the Gentiles had been grafted into the Church (Acts 10). Here, the gift of tongues was being used in its biblical manifestation; for when the Gentiles were admitted into the People of God, this would truly be a 'sign' to unbelieving Jews that the judgement of the Lord was falling on Israel. And this brings us to the real purpose of the gift of tongues.

There is an undergirding purpose for the biblical gift of tongues which seems to have escaped the attention of many believers today: namely, its function as a 'sign'. There were two kinds of 'signs' in Early Church phenomena: *authenticating signs* and *judicial signs*. Miracles, healings, the casting out of demons, and prophecy all fall into the former category. Their purpose was to be a witness to the presence of the promised Messiah. This can be proven from the fact that, when John the Baptist sent some of his disciples to Jesus to ask the question: *'Are You the Coming One, or do we look for another?'*, the Scripture explicitly states:

> 'At that very hour He cured many people of their infirmities, afflictions, and evil spirits; and to many who were blind He gave sight. Then Jesus answered and said to them: "Go and tell John the things you have seen and heard: that the blind see, the lame walk, the lepers are cleansed, the deaf hear, the dead are raised, the poor have the gospel preached to them"' (Lk.7:20-22).

All this was a clear reference back to the prophecy given in Isa.35:5-6, so that they would see the authenticity of the 'signs' being performed. However, the gift of tongues is unique among the gifts in that it was given primarily as a *judicial* sign. Let us expand this concept, which is vital to our understanding of the use of this gift, and whether or not its alleged manifestations today are compatible with Holy Scripture.

From the beginning of Jehovah's relationship with the children of Israel, His primary way of judgement was to bring a foreign language-speaking nation down upon them. This was the ultimate penalty for breaking the Covenant with Him. This was clearly spelled out to them, along with other curses, in Dt.28:33,36. Here, God told them that if they break the Covenant:

> 'The LORD will bring a nation against you from afar, from the end of the earth, as swift as the eagle flies, a nation *whose language you will*

> *not understand*' (Dt.28:49). [emphasis added]

The essential element of this Covenant curse is that it comes *through a Gentile nation speaking in a language which is not understood* by the People of God. This is one of the curses which would ensue if they broke the covenant, and is specifically referred to as a *'sign'* of God's judgement in the passage concerned (see Dt.28:46). Further on in time, this judgemental 'sign' did indeed fall upon the rebellious nation of Israel under their idolatrous (but later repentant) king, Manasseh (2 Chr.33:10-13). The prophet Isaiah predicted this with the words: *'For with unintelligible speech and another tongue He will speak to this people... yet they would not hear'* (Isa.28:11-12). That was the 'sign' of God's judgement: An invading Gentile nation (in this case, the Assyrians) speaking in a foreign language. The same incident is referred to by Isaiah elsewhere, when he describes these Assyrians as *'a fierce people, a people of obscure speech, beyond perception, of unintelligible speech that you cannot understand'* (Isa.33:19). The prophet Jeremiah also shows that same 'sign' of the covenantal curse on rebellious Israel as being fulfilled in the fact that the Babylonians would destroy Jerusalem and carry away its people:

> '"Behold, I will bring a nation against you from afar, O house of Israel," says the LORD. "It is a mighty nation, it is an ancient nation, a nation *whose language you do not know, nor can you understand what they say*"' (Jer.5:15). [emphasis added]

And when we come to Paul speaking about the gift of tongues to the Church in his first Letter to the Corinthians, he quotes a couple of the verses from Isaiah that we have given above (1 Cor.14:21; cf. Isa.28:11-12) and then concludes: *'Therefore [the gift of varieties of] languages are for a sign, not to those who believe but to unbelievers'* (1 Cor.14:22). Here he shows the Corinthians (and us) the undergirding purpose of the gift of tongues. It was given to the Church by God in order to function primarily as a 'sign' to unbelievers — but not just any unbelievers: for the context plainly shows that Paul meant unbelieving Jews.

A number of elements can be shown from this sequence of passages. First, it shows that *the gift of what people call 'tongues' consisted of real human languages* — the languages of the Gentile nations — rather than the ecstatic babble that is spoken by believers and unbelievers alike today. Second, it shows that the gift of tongues discussed in 1 Cor.12-14 was given primarily to act as a 'sign' to unbelieving Jews that, because of their rejection of the Messiah who had been sent to them by God, they would shortly be coming under the Covenant curse, through which a Gentile nation who spoke a foreign language (the Romans) would destroy Jerusalem and the Temple — an event which actually came to pass in A.D.70. Therefore, no matter how the miraculous ability to speak in foreign languages manifested itself — whether as revelation, teaching, or just simply praising and glorifying God — *its underlying purpose was to function as the final manifestation of the original Covenant curse on the people of Israel.* That being the case, there can no longer be any purpose in the practice of the gift of tongues since the

Fall of Jerusalem in A.D.70. Any alleged manifestations of the gift since that time are entirely spurious. This does not 'limit God in His works', as some would claim. Of course, God can do whatever He wants to do whenever He chooses to do it. But that is hardly the point in the case of this gift. When God has clearly stated the purpose of something, if that purpose no longer exists, then we must count it as finished.

There are actually a great many similarities between the function of tongues and that of the parables of Jesus (read Mt.13:9-17; Mk.4:9-13, 33-34). It is in this respect that we can speak of tongues as being a *judicial* rather than an authenticating sign. *'Those who have ears to hear, let them hear'.* Just as it was with the Parables of Jesus, the specific purpose of the Holy Spirit gifting Christians to speaking in unlearned languages was to 'signal' God's alienation from Israel. Every occurrence of tongues recorded in Acts was clearly acting in this way as a 'signal' to the Jews that, as a nation, they would be coming under the judgement of God. Acts 2:4-11 corroborates this fact, where they are shown to function as a *sign*, which could then be followed by successful evangelism in a language they *could* understand! The other examples also show the gift of tongues functioning as a 'sign' to Israel (Acts 8:14-17; 10:44-47; 19:1-6). These have already been discussed in the previous section entitled 'Spirit Baptism'.

Abuses of the Gift of Tongues by the Corinthians

A common assertion in Christian literature about the spiritual gift of tongues is that it is given to be used for personal communication with God and is for the benefit of the individual rather than the whole church.[159] This has led many believers into the false notion that this gift is for devotional prayer or for the purposes of engaging in spiritual warfare. But these notions are based on a misinterpretation of Paul's words in 1 Cor.14:1-5. In these few verses, Paul is not delivering a lecture on 'how-to-speak-in-tongues'. In common with the rest of this letter, he is addressing severe pastoral problems which needed the input of Apostolic authority.

In chapters 12–14, Paul is actually chiding the Corinthians for the way that they were misusing spiritual gifts — especially the gift of tongues, which they performed in their own strength when the Holy Spirit had not given the gift of interpretation to the hearers. The pivotal verse concerning tongues is when the Apostle makes the statement, *'he who speaks in a tongue edifies himself, but he who prophesies edifies the church'* (1 Cor.14:4). That is not a statement about the *true* nature of tongues; it is Paul's criticism of the Corinthians for the way that they used the gift. Paul cannot be saying that the *normative* use of tongues is for personal edification, for that would be to contradict his statements in this letter regarding the general purpose of all the gifts — which is for the enhancement of the whole Church (1 Cor.12:7,24-25; 14:4-5,12) — and the specific purpose of the gift of tongues (1 Cor.14:22). It seems highly likely that Paul is using the word

---

[159] See, for example, *The Zondervan Pictorial Encyclopedia of the Bible* (Zondervan, 1975-6), Vol.V, p.508.

'edify' in 1 Cor.14:4 in a derogatory sense. For there is not a single instance elsewhere of Paul using the term to refer to somebody edifying *themselves*. The whole concept of 'edification' in Scripture refers to something one does *for others*. When he says: *'Knowledge puffs up, but love edifies'* (1 Cor.8:1), he does not mean that love edifies the one doing the loving! It edifies others. In 1 Cor.14, it is as if Paul was saying:

> 'When you speak in tongues as you do, without anyone knowing what you are saying, you are simply making yourself feel good; whereas prophecy can never be used in this way because others benefit from it'.

All the gifts are for service and ministry to others, therefore there can be no purpose whatsoever in speaking gobbledegook, other than the enhancement of oneself.

Furthermore, 1 Cor.13:1 completely confounds the idea of devotional tongues. First, if I speak in tongues outside of the context of love (Greek, *agape*, caring for others), I am merely making a worthless noise. Second, if tongues are to be exercised in the context of such love for others, then they cannot be for personal use. This is why Paul says that there must be a purpose to tongues-speaking which brings it into the realm of service to others (1 Cor.14:5-6). It is more than likely that the Corinthians were speaking tongues in the same manner as that of the heathen religions — ecstatic babbling without interpretation — for that certainly appears to fit the information we can glean from Paul's criticisms (1 Cor.14:2,4,12-19). Such 'tongues-speaking' was the norm among the mystery-cults which thrived in the Mediterranean countries at this time, and it accounts for all the babbling tongues-speaking of today, which may give people a nice 'buzz' and generate a sense of piety, but it is not the biblical gift of tongues.

This entire section of the letter is actually a very complex passage, and we cannot fully understand all that Paul is saying to the Corinthians here. This is why we must be so careful in our analysis of what he is saying. For instance, a number of misunderstandings have arisen because many believers overlook the fact that every time the word *'spirit'* is used in 1 Cor.14 (vv.2,14-16), it is not referring to the Holy Spirit but to the person's own spirit (as in Jn.4:24). It is not our purpose to give a detailed exegesis of this passage, but once it is realised that Paul is not writing a 'How-To' manual on tongues-speaking, but is very graciously criticising the Corinthians for their misuse of this gift as a means of self-edification, then things will begin to fall into place.

The sole purpose of brothers and sisters in Christ receiving the spiritual gifts is for the building up of the church in history. Tongues were never given as a 'private prayer language'. Since we can easily deduce from Scripture that *not all* believers would have the gift of tongues (1 Cor.12:10,28-31), then if this gift was to provide a special devotional 'hotline' to God solely for a limited, privileged élite, it would go entirely against the many places where we are told that *all* believers have a full personal channel of direct communication which is ever open (e.g., Heb.4:14-16; Jas.5:16b). True prayer is discursive and is based on intelligent and intelligible two-way communication between God and His people. The idea of 'tuning-in' to the Divine Being through ecstatic babbling which is not understood by the one praying, belongs instead to the realms of mysticism and occult meditation.

Yet another misunderstanding about the gift of Languages is that it was given as an aid to Christians in their mission work to foreign-language speaking cultures. But there is no biblical justification for this either. At Pentecost, in the best biblical example of the gift in action, the actual evangelising was done in the native Aramaic (Acts 2:14-39), whereas the tongues-speaking functioned as a preliminary 'sign' to the unbelieving Jews, exactly as described in 1 Cor.14:22.

Having established that the 'tongues' that people are speaking today cannot be squared with the biblical gift of tongues, the discussion should surely be lifted entirely out of the area of 'the gifts' and taken into the realm of the Bible's own testimony concerning how God desires to be worshipped. It should give all would-be tongues-speakers today pause for thought to know that Jesus specifically forbade using unintelligible speech in one's prayers to God. He told His disciples: *'When you pray, do not use vain repetitions as the heathen do'* (Mt.6:7). The Greek verb translated here as 'use vain repetitions' (*battalogeo*) means literally to 'babble' or to 'speak without thinking', and this is the only occasion that it is used in the New Testament.[160] So it is doubly significant that the Lord went on to recommend the ultimate in intelligible speech — the Lord's Prayer — in opposition to the meaningless babble of heathen devotions. The gift that so many people claim is 'tongues' today is precisely the same phenomenon which one can find in many other religious and non-religious groups in the world. It is really a work of the mind-sciences — having far more in common with hypnosis and mysticism than with biblical Christianity.

iii. Faith-Healings

Another component in the suggestion-based 'Crisis Experience' induced in Charismatic-Pentecostal meetings is that of faith-healing. One famous practitioner of this activity is Morris Cerullo, whose claims for healing were held up to scrutiny by a BBC television documentary entitled 'The Heart of the Matter' after his 'Mission to London' at Earls Court in 1992. Of the 2,250 claimed healings, nine 'best cases' were submitted for investigation but none was found to bear out the truth of the claims.[161] Such mendacious claims are typical of Charismatic faith-healing — all of which is in stark contrast to the healings of Jesus, which were 100% successful every time, involving genuine organic change in body structure, and about which there could be no controversy.[162]

So what does the Bible say on the matter of divine healing. It is of great significance that the 'gifts of healings' and 'workings of miracles' are referred to in the plural in the Greek texts (1 Cor.12:9-10,28). This is because all occurrences

---

[160] W. Bauer, W.F. Arndt & F.W. Gingrich, *A Greek-English Lexicon of the New Testament* (University of Chicago, 1979), p.137.

[161] For full details of this, see *Sword and Trowel*, No.3, 1993, pp.2-4.

[162] It is worth noting the extraordinary fact that Morris Cerullo's 'Mission to London' faith-healing circus is an accredited member of the Evangelical Alliance in the U.K.

of healings and miracles were separate gift-events which took place through the immediate impetus of the Holy Spirit. A person did not receive 'the gift of healing' on a permanent basis, so that he became a professional 'healer' and could heal at will, as it were. Every time a healing or a miracle took place, the one through whom the healing or miracle was performed received a *specific* prompting from the Holy Spirit to carry out the act. That person might never receive such a prompting again; or, on the other hand, he might receive many.

Some especially notable examples of this process in action are recorded in the New Testament. First, the healing of the lame man at the temple-gate called Beautiful (Acts 3:1-10). Peter and John must have gone up to the temple at the ninth hour by this route on many occasions; but it was only on this one occasion that the Holy Spirit prompted them to perform this healing. It was a classic example of the use of a 'sign', after which evangelism could follow, as it did (Acts 3:11–4:4). Second, the deliverance of the slave girl possessed with a spirit of divination (Acts 16:16-19). She harassed Paul for many days, but was ignored by him. Suddenly, on one particular moment of one particular day, Paul wheeled round and commanded the demon to come out. One must assume that this was the time chosen by the Holy Spirit for Paul to be empowered to do this. Without such prompting of the Spirit and the accompanying gift, even the Apostles did not attempt to work a miracle or perform a healing. This is presumably the reason why, when Peter was given the gift of working a miracle to bring Dorcas back to life, instead of simply uttering a command, he prayed to the Lord to discern whether or not it was the Spirit's intention to do this (Acts 9:40). Understanding all this is most important today, because there are a great many people who set themselves up with what they call 'a healing ministry'. However, not only are they attempting to use a spiritual gift which is no longer extant (as we shall shortly show), but they are usurping what is the sole prerogative of the Holy Spirit in distributing 'gifts of healings' *according to His own will* (Heb.2:4). There were no Christians who set themselves up as professional, full-time, Spirit-empowered healers in the New Testament. To set oneself up in this way would be pure Shamanism — and indeed that is the way that the 'Christian' faith-healers function.

The gifts of healings referred to in 1 Cor.12:9 were an extension of the Apostolic sign-ministry of healing set out in Mk.16:18, as these sign-gifts could only be received through the personal distribution of one of the Apostles. The healings of Christ and His Apostles were never intended to be an end in themselves, to make people feel better. Neither were they given in order that we may have an example to mimic. They were instead carried out as a sign that the promised Messiah had truly and finally arrived. In other words, *they were performed both as fulfillment of O.T. prophecy and as practical parables of the spiritual healing that a person receives when he or she comes to Christ.* Let us expand on this concept.

It is of signal importance that the Lord Jesus, at the beginning of His public ministry, identified the nature of His messianic work by quoting Isaiah 61:1-2a in the synagogue in Nazareth, which has been recorded in Lk.4:16-30: *'He has sent Me to heal the brokenhearted, to preach deliverance to the captives and recovery of sight to the blind'*. The healing miracles and deliverance ministry which He subsequently carried out were in fulfillment of this and other Old Testament prophecies (e.g., Isaiah 35:5-6; 42:6-7) and served to identify Jesus Christ to Israel as the long-awaited Messiah. When John the Baptist sent men to Jesus to ask if He was the Coming One, Jesus then authenticated His Messiahship to this last of the Old Testament prophets by presenting a detailed catalogue of His healing ministry (see Mt.11:2-5). Why did He do this? Precisely because it was these things which represented the infallible 'signs' that He had come. Moreover, these healing 'signs' provided vital spiritual lessons about His redemptive mission as the Saviour of the world (e.g., Jn.9:39).

It cannot be over-emphasised that Jesus did not practice healing, or empower His Apostles to do so, in order to provide us with a nice example to imitate. Mark discloses the *real* reason why Jesus healed when he records Him as saying to the Scribes and Pharisees, *'Those who are well have no need of a physician, but those who are sick. I did not come to call the righteous, but sinners to repentance'* (Mk.2:17). Here we are shown by the Lord Himself that the true healing which is at the heart of the revelation of God in Jesus Christ is the forgiveness of sins. The *real* sickness of humanity is sin. All Jesus' healings were an illustration of this. Nowhere is this brought out more powerfully than in the healing of the paralytic who was lowered through the roof:

> ''Which is easier, to say to the paralytic, 'Your sins are forgiven you', or to say, 'Arise, take up your bed and walk'? But *that you may know that the Son of Man has power on earth to forgive sins* — He said to the paralytic, "'I say to you, arise, take up your bed, and go your way to your house"' (Mark 2:9-11). [emphasis added]

The Scribes knew full well that only God can forgive sins (Mk.2:7), and that Jesus was here ascribing Divine status to Himself. That is precisely why He performed healings and miracles: to give unassailable proof of His Deity (cf. Jn.20:30-31) — a fact which would eventually lead to His being executed by the religious authorities (Mt.26:63-65; Jn.19:7). He authorised only His Apostles to continue that sign-ministry (Mk.3:15; 16:17-18). To imitate Christ by attempting to enact such miraculous healings, as many do today, is to deny the uniqueness of His sign-ministry and that of the Apostles sent personally by Him to establish the *solid foundations* of His Church (2 Cor.12:12; Mark 16:17-18; Heb.2:4).

Another facet of gifts of healings is that they occurred exclusively *by direct command* of the Apostles or those empowered by them (e.g., Lk.4:39; Acts 3:6; 9:34; 9:40). God still heals today, if it is His will to do so — not through direct command, but by means of prayer — not through apostles or other gifted people with a sign ministry, but through the pastoral ministry of the elders of the local churches (James 5:14-16). It is impossible to reconcile this passage in James with the Charismatic 'faith-healing' of today. The way is clearly set out for the Christian who is sick: There is no advice to seek out a 'gifted' healer. Just a simple exhortation to *'call for the elders of the church, and let them pray over him, anointing him with oil in the name of the Lord'*. This conveys some significant information: for, either the spiritual gifts of healings were no longer in existence by the time that James's letter was written (*c.* A.D.60), or the original Charismatic gifts of healings were solely for the authentication of the Gospel rather than as a form of medical treatment. Whichever of these is the case, the present practice of faith-healing is not in the least consistent with the explicit teaching on healing in James 5, which must surely be the 'control text' to which we must turn for instruction in this pressing pastoral area.

Because the gifts of healings were given for a sign that the promised Messiah had come and that He was God manifested in the flesh who had power to forgive sins, they were only applicable to the church in the Apostolic era. But the sign-healings of Jesus, the Apostles, and those empowered by them are just as much for our benefit as they were for the people alive at the time. So, when the N.T. canon was complete, all the 'signs' necessary for the authentication of the Messiah throughout the remainder of the Age had been recorded in the Scriptures. Once the churches had been established throughout the world, they provided the proper place for an ongoing healing ministry through the eldership.

A Challenge to all 'Healers'

How vastly different are the immediate, instantaneous, organic healings of the Lord Jesus and His Apostles, compared with the shoddy, psychosomatic, shamanistic, suggestion-based 'healings' being practised by so many in the Charismatic and Pentecostal churches today. *Here is a challenge to any readers who may imagine that they can lay claim to a personal ongoing 'healing ministry' today:* Don't just minister in your tent meeting, conference or prayer seminar, waiting for all those misled people to line up in front of you. Instead, go out into the casualty departments of your local hospitals on a Saturday night and bring *instantaneous organic healing* to the battered and broken victims of the brawls and accidents that present themselves there for treatment. Then nip up to the surgical wards and lay your hands on the amputees, everything-ectomies and hopeless cases, so that their limbs and entrails will be restored to them whole. When those places have been emptied, find your local 'Institute for the Blind' and bring some colour into their lives for the first time with your remarkable 'healing' powers. Then buzz over to the offices of one of societies for the handicapped and get them to take you out to their many training centres, where you can restore those withered and calipered limbs *on the spot.* If you still want to show you have a 'proven anointed' ministry, find some local authority Special Schools and make that Down's Syndrome melt away from those pleading little faces. And if you still have any energy left, take a taxi across to the local mortuary and bring some of its frigid occupants out with you for a breath of fresh air and a good meal.

If you lay claim to a 'healing ministry', the Word of God challenges you to do all these things today. Why wait? For those are the kinds of healings which the Lord Jesus and the Apostles carried out in the course of their ministry (e.g., Lk.22:50-51; Mk.3:1-5; Lk.8:43-44; Jn.9:1-11; 11:43-44). Not only did they have a 100% success-rate, but nothing was too difficult for them to tackle. If you believe you should be healing just like Jesus, then anything less than the same success-rate and instantaneity of His healing is a complete sham. By all means, call yourself a 'faith healer' or even a Shaman, but do not make the false claim that you are doing the works of Jesus. It is a sobering thought that there will be *many* in the Day of Judgement who will 'knock on the door of heaven' and say to Jesus: *'Lord, Lord, have we not...done many wonders in Your name?'* But He will declare to them, *'I never knew you; depart from Me, you who practice lawlessness!'* (Mt.7:21-23).

iv. Ritualistic Exorcism

So far, we have looked at three of the central components of the suggestion-based Mesmeric 'Crisis Experience' induced within Charismatic-Pentecostal circles: so-called 'Spirit-Baptism', tongues and faith-healing. When we come to examine the practice of ritualistic exorcism, we find that it is also a major hallmark of Charismatic-Pentecostal practice and is intimately tied up with the 'Crisis Experience' induced by powerful suggestion techniques. One of the major centres for this type of practice is the 'healing centre' at Ellel Grange in Lancaster.[163] In one newspaper report, the wife of the centre's director, Peter Horrobin, described Ellel Grange as *'a dangerous place'*, claiming that *'what he is doing is as dangerous as the occult practices he preaches against'*.[164] She reported how people going there for help and prayer would be *'told they were possessed'*. She said:

> 'My husband prayed over them in tongues and I've seen them go into trances and need physical restraining. They would be screaming and spitting. Often they needed psychiatric help afterwards'.[165]

The activities of this centre are typical of many so-called 'deliverance ministries' being set up today by people who are obsessed with things demonic and who practice ritual exorcism in a highly cavalier fashion, based on techniques derived from Anton Mesmer. It would take an entire book to show the vast amount of literature available on this subject today — some of which make the most outlandish claims, one of the more popular being the notion that *'evil spirits are frequently transferred from parents to child even before the child is born'*.[166]

A great deal of hysteria has been generated in this area today. On one occasion, the present writer gave a lecture on the New Age Movement to a Christian women's organisation which was largely made up of Charismatics and Pentecostals, during which he claimed that a good deal of Charismatic-Pentecostal practice is based on pagan sorcery. At the conclusion of the meeting, he was inundated with queries from many tearful and confused women who had been suspicious about the practices in their churches but were too fearful to question them openly.

So, let us see what the Bible has to say on this issue. For we have here yet another example of people mistakenly believing that just because something is practised in Scripture, then it is for all of us to practise in exact imitation. Herein lies

---

[163] This centre has justly acquired the nickname 'Hell-Hole Grange'.

[164] *The Mail on Sunday*, March 8th 1992.

[165] Ibid. Peter Horrobin is one of the compilers of the hymnbook 'Mission Praise'.

[166] Graham & Shirley Powell, op. cit., p.51.

the fundamental error at the heart of the Charismatic-Pentecostal ritual of exorcism. It is the belief that *'In His commission, Jesus said that His followers would cast out devils in His name'*.[167] This interpretation of Mk.16:17-18 as being applicable to *all* Jesus's disciples highlights a common misunderstanding. The 'signs' mentioned in these verses are said by Jesus to follow those *'who **have** believed'* (the aorist tense is mistranslated in most versions as *'those who believe'*) — a clear reference to the Apostles whose temporary unbelief is recorded in Mk.16:14. In any case, the signs in these verses cannot possibly refer to **all** believers of every era, as there is no record of anyone taking up serpents and drinking poison with impunity other than that of an Apostle (e.g. Acts 28:3-5).

Not all those who follow Jesus are empowered to cast out demons into the abyss. Only our Lord and His Apostles (Mk.3:13-15) had the power personally to cast them out, or to give that power to others (e.g., Philip, who was empowered through the laying-on of Apostolic hands, Acts 6:5-6; 8:6-7). Even Simon the Sorcerer knew that such power could only be passed on through the hands of the Apostles (Acts 8:18-19). Exorcism was widely practised by the Jews (and the heathen) in biblical times (e.g., Acts 19:13-14), but Jesus and the Apostles did not practise exorcism: they actually *'cast out'* demons **into the abyss**, where they are reserved for judgement until the end of the age (Lk.8:31; 2 Pet.2:4; Jude 6). This was a divinely sovereign, punitive action which had never before been carried out by any of the Jewish or heathen exorcists. This was very obvious to the people who observed Jesus casting out demons. They could immediately see that His expulsion of these entities was entirely different from the technique practised by their own religious leaders (read Mk.1:27,34). This was a 'sign' that the powers of darkness had met their match. The strong man was being ousted by One stronger — a fact prophesied by Zechariah some five hundred years earlier, when God said that He would *'cause...the unclean spirit to depart from the land'* with the advent of the Messianic age (Zec.13:2). This was fulfilled when Jesus forecast that His victory on the Cross would *'cast out'* the *'ruler of this world'*, as Satan indeed then was (Jn.12:31). Satan's power has been broken by One who did *'the works which no one else did'* (Jn.15:24), either before or since the Apostolic era.

It is also common in the 'deliverance' circles of today to use the name of Jesus as a kind of talisman — as if the name itself held some hidden power. But casting out demons *'in His name'* had nothing to do with the literal incantation of the name of Jesus at supposed demons, in the manner in which a person is said to wave a cross or piece of garlic in the face of a vampire. The biblical phrase *'in the name of'* simply refers to the act of doing something *by the authority of* another. However, only the Apostles of Christ had His authority to cast out demons or to give that power to another (Mk.3:13-15). To think that the phrase, *'in the name of Jesus'*, has a magical power in the face of demons is pure superstition, and constitutes the use of 'name-magic' — a practice which was specifically outlawed in the Third Commandment of the Decalogue.[168]

---

[167] S.M. Burgess & G.B. McGee, op. cit., p.293.

[168] see Geerhardus Vos, *Biblical Theology* (Banner of Truth, 1975), pp.137-138.

If all Christians, from the Apostles onward, were expected to be involved in the ritualistic exorcism of the powers of darkness, is it not a serious oversight that there are no instructions to believers in the Word of God on how to carry this out? One would at least have expected there to be specific instruction concerning such a procedure in the Pastoral Epistles in connection with the duties of elders, or even in the final chapter of Ephesians, where there is some solid counsel concerning spirit-entities, rulers of darkness, spiritual hosts of wickedness in the heavenlies. But there is nothing. Why? Because the use of commands spoken directly to diseases and demons was the province of Apostolic power, and ended when all the Apostles and those empowered by them had died. It is surely significant that even the archangel Michael, when contending with the devil, did not dare to deliver a direct command at him, but instead said, *'The Lord rebuke you'* (Jude 9).

If this ritualistic exorcism practised by so many today is not the biblical way to handle the devil and his cohorts in spiritual warfare, then what are we to do? It is as plain as a pikestaff that the devil still wanders around like a roaring lion, and that he can cause great misery in both the world and in the Church. What action, therefore, is a Christian to take in the event of his being confronted with one who he believes may be demon-possessed? Does the Bible present us with explicit instructions on how we are to respond to such things? The Charismatic answer to this is known as *'Power Evangelism'* — in which one dives in with both guns firing from the hip, uttering purportedly authoritative commands, exorcising any number of demons which may allegedly indwell the person; and, according to many Charismatic sources, there may be dozens — even in a Christian — and they may take days of sweaty ritual to dislodge![169]

So how are people to respond to the activity of the demonic realm? First, let it be clear that it is only unbelievers who are under the complete dominion of Satan. It is a fact that every single human being who has not been converted by the power of God in Christ is under the authority and dominion of Satan. This applies equally to the most rabid murderer and to the most polite, law abiding citizen. A person cannot serve two masters; if he is not Christ's, he is Satan's. This is a fact. He is of his father the devil (Jn.8:44; Acts 13:10; 1 Jn.3:10); the whole unbelieving world lies under the power of the wicked one (1 Jn.5:19). Now, how that authority of Satan manifests itself will vary from one person to another, according to his or her circumstances, personality, opportunity for sin, etc. The more deliberately sinful a life a person leads (sexual immorality, occult practices, criminal behaviour, drug abuse, etc.), the more he will be given over to Satan's destructive power. This can culminate in what we would call actual 'possession', when the individual human will has become well-nigh obliterated and utterly subservient to the will of the demon (e.g. Mk.5:2-5). This extreme is relatively rare — especially in those countries which have had a history of Christianity as the established religion — although the Bible shows that such demonisation will considerably worsen as the end of the Age draws near.

[169] There are numerous examples of this fiction of the demon-possession of believers, e.g., Graham & Shirley Powell, op. cit., pp.180ff.

So far as the unbeliever is concerned, there can be no lasting solace for him through any mere ritual exorcism, whatever effects it may have produced. Instead, there must be an inward renewal from the Holy Spirit, otherwise the post-exorcism state of the person will be even worse that his pre-exorcistic condition (Lk.11:24-26). The only way for the unbeliever to obtain real 'deliverance' is to obey the Gospel: to repent and believe in Jesus Christ. Regeneration — the new birth effected by the Holy Spirit — casts the devil out of the heart of the unbeliever once-and-for-all. The Bible clearly states that it is only through this experience that an afflicted person obtains complete 'deliverance' from the dominion of Satan, (whether one is a gross sinner or a 'well-behaved' citizen), thereby becoming a new creation in Christ. In other words, we practise deliverance on unbelievers — no matter how much they have been pulverized by Satan — by preaching the Gospel to them with love and ministering in the power of prayer.

Every regenerated believer can say, with the Apostle Paul

> 'He has delivered us from the power of darkness and transferred us into the kingdom of the Son of His love, in whom we have redemption through His blood, the forgiveness of sins' (Col.1:13-14).

That is *real* deliverance. When Paul was preaching to King Agrippa, he said that Christ had sent him to the Gentiles

> 'to open their eyes in order to turn them from darkness to light, and from the power of Satan to God, that they may receive forgiveness of sins and an inheritance among those who are sanctified by faith in [Christ]' (Acts 26:18).

It is clear from these texts alone that repentance and conversion are sufficient for full deliverance from the power and clutches of Satan. However, we must recognise that there are some people whose lives before their conversion have been so messed-up with gross sin and evil that they may well need special ministry during, and even after, their conversion to Christ. Some brethren mistakenly hide their heads in the sand from this solemn fact. We do not refer here to 'exorcism' in its ritualistic sense; but, rather, to the application of the Word of God which is the sword of the Spirit (Eph.6:17), to the offering up of powerful prayer to the Lord, coupled with support from strong Christians who can get alongside the afflicted one. We can call powerfully on the Lord to rebuke Satan, believing wholly in His authority over Satan, and that He will answer that prayer with deliverance. It seems today that all kinds of people (professing Christians and non-Christians alike) practise an exorcism which is little more than magic and sacerdotalist ritual. But we repeat again that Jesus was NOT an exorcist: He actually *cast out demons into the abyss* (Luke 8:31); He is the eternal, divine Strong One who is stronger than the strong man (i.e., Satan) who is fully armed in his own palace (cf. Luke 11:21-22). Your average common or garden exorcist can never cleanse a person in the way that Christ can and does. That was precisely the point of the Lord Jesus in Luke 11:24-26. It is not enough to have your house swept and put in good order; it must actually be indwelt and sanctified by the Holy Spirit in order to be impervious to the authority or possession of Satan, the ruler of the demons. Only Christ can apportion the indwelling Holy Spirit to a person (Jn.14:14-24). The Holy Spirit comes through repentance and conversion, not via ritualistic exorcism. Salvation is of the Lord, not by the machinations of men. We repeat that sometimes, when there is clear evidence of demonic affliction or, in comparatively rare cases, of demon possession, very sustained and powerful prayer on the part of others will be necessary to provide support during and after a person's conversion. But the person so afflicted must *already* be willing to come to Christ. *Exorcism of any kind can never make a person into a Christian; and becoming a Christian is the only true deliverance.*

The Christian Believer and Demon Possession

Regarding the question of whether or not a Christian can be 'possessed' by a demon, the biblical answer must surely be a resounding 'No!' Some samples of the evidence from the Scriptures are as follows:

- The Christian is *'a new creation; old things have passed away; behold, all things have become new'* (2 Cor.5:17).
- The Christian has been *'sealed with the Holy Spirit of promise'* (Eph.1:13).
- The Christian has been fully delivered from the authority of darkness and therefore from the power of Satan (Col.1:13; cf. Acts 26:17-18).
- The Christian has not received *'the spirit of bondage again to fear'*, but he has *'received the Spirit of adoption by whom we cry out, "Abba, Father"'* (Rom.8:15).
- The Christian is one of a company of whom the Apostle can say: *'For God has not given us a spirit of fear, but of power and of love and of a sound mind'* (2 Tim.1:7). The Greek word translated here as 'a sound mind' literally means 'self-controlled' (as opposed to demon-controlled).
- The Christian has *'the mind of Christ'* (1 Cor.2:16), not the mind of Satan.
- The Christian is not his own person, but belongs to Christ, in both body and soul (1 Cor.6:19-20; 2 Cor.10:7; Gal.3:29). It is no longer the 'I' who lives but Christ in the believer (Gal.2:20).
- When John tells his flock to *'test the spirits'*, he can then go on to say: *'You are of God, little children, and have overcome them, because He [the Spirit of Christ] who is in you is greater than he [Satan/spirit of antichrist] who is in the world'* (1 Jn.4:1-5). How can a demon possibly possess a person who is already indwelt by the infinitely superior Holy Spirit? Surely there can be no house-room!
- The Christian is clothed with the whole armour of God, which is Christ (Eph.6:10-18). This armour — truth, righteousness, the gospel of peace, faith, salvation, the sword of the Spirit — is a panoply of gifts which every Christian has received from God through Christ. They cannot be cultivated by human endeavour. When you put on Christ (Gal.3:27; Rom.13:14), you put on HIS truth, HIS righteousness, etc. Christ is all in all.

- The Christian is *'the temple of God'* and the Spirit of God dwells in him (Jn.14:23; 1 Cor.3:16). As Paul then says: *'If anyone defiles the temple of God, God will destroy him. For the temple of God is holy, which temple you are'* (1 Cor.3:17).
- The Christian is one who has received the greatest freedom possible; *'If the Son makes you free, you shall be free indeed'* (Jn.8:36). No more bondage for the Christian — to sin, to Satan, or to anyone.
- The Christian is part of the Body of Christ — the Church — against which the gates of hell can never prevail (Mt.16:18).
- Jesus said that no one can snatch His sheep out of His hand. *'My Father, who has given them to Me, is greater than all; and no-one is able to snatch them out of my Father's hand. I and My Father are one'* (Jn.10:28-30).
- The Christian is the one who has only to *'Resist the devil'*, (steadfast in the faith, 1 Pet.5:9) *'and he will flee from you'* (Jas.4:7). This simple antidote is overlooked by many brethren today.
- The Christian is the one who can never be separated by anything (even evil angels and dark powers) from the love of God which is in Christ Jesus our Lord (Rom.8:38-39). As Paul puts it: *'If God is for us, who can be against us?'* (Rom.8:31).
- This, above all: *'We know that* ***all things*** *work together for good to those who love God, to those who are the called according to His purpose'* (Rom.8:28).

These are but a few of the realities of our life in Christ. Surely this must drive us to the conclusion that it is a most serious blasphemy to assert, as many do today (even among evangelicals) that the Christian can actually be possessed by an evil spirit. When the Pharisees dared to suggest that Christ cast out demons by the power of the devil (they had also claimed that He had a demon Himself), He implicitly accused them of blasphemy against the Holy Spirit (Mt.12:24-32). Surely when it is claimed that the person indwelt by the Holy Spirit is also possessed by a demon, this must constitute a very similar blasphemy.

However, the fact that a Christian cannot be 'possessed' by demons does not mean that he is impervious to being 'pestered' by them. This should not surprise us, given that Satan and his cohorts go about like a roaring lion, seeking whom they may devour (1 Pet.5:8). The adversary makes constant war against those who keep the commandments of God and have the testimony of Jesus Christ (Rev.12:17). Even Paul the Apostle had a thorn in his flesh, a messenger of Satan (2 Cor.12:7-10). But this was designed by God for a specific gracious purpose: namely, the restraining of Paul from pride and vainglory. So although Satan could rub his hands together with glee about this thorn in Paul's flesh (whatever it may have been: illness, false teachers, etc.), the fact is that it was happening under the sovereignty of God and for His glory alone (He always gets the glory in our weakness). William Green throws much light on the relationship between Satan and the believer, when he writes:

> 'If you steadfastly resist the devil, confiding in the grace of God and the salvation of Jesus, he cannot touch a hair of your head. Temptation and sin, if you bravely resist them, will react to your everlasting welfare: your position is impregnable, the protection is ample, the armament is invincible, the supplies abundant, and the fortress can never be entered by the enemy, unless betrayed into his power by your own treacherous hands'.[170]

Professor Green here asserts that great biblical truth of deliverance: *'Submit to God. Resist the devil and he will flee from you'* (Jas.4:7). It is that simple. No complex exorcisms for the Christian are set forth in Scripture. No need for reliance on medicine-men, witch-doctors and shamans to incant *'abracadabra'* and other strange commands. Instead, we have the simplicity which is in Christ and the strength which is guaranteed us by the Spirit. It is so very challenging of Professor Green to say that Satan has no power over us as Christians, unless we give it to him. This must be understood properly. He is not suggesting that the Christian can be actually demon-possessed, but, rather, that he can certainly be demon-*pestered* if he does not oversee his spiritual life with care. And as Christians, who are heirs of God through Christ, we exercise a good measure of personal responsibility under the leading and guidance of the Holy Spirit (cf. Phil.2:12-13). It is precisely for this reason that the Apostle Paul tells us not to *'give a foothold to the devil'* in our lives, through falling into flagrant sin (Eph.4:25-32).

However, if the Christian *is* hampered and pestered by the forces of darkness, one can be sure that there is a good reason for it, in the providence of God. For everything that happens to the one who is Christ's — even the pesterings of demons — happens under God's sovereignty. Satan is *not* a free agent. To quote again Prof. Green's excellent treatise:

> 'With all Satan's hatred of God and spite against His people, he cannot emancipate himself from that sovereign control which binds him to God's service. In all his blasphemous designs he is, in spite of himself, doing the work of God. In his efforts to dethrone the Most High, he is actually paying Him submissive homage. In moving heaven and earth to accomplish the perdition of those whom Christ has ransomed, he is actually fitting them for glory. Fiend as he is, full of bitterness and malignity and intent on every form of mischief, he is constrained to be that which he most abhors, and is furthest from his intentions and desires: to be helpful and auxiliary to the designs of grace!'[171]

This is the great secret which every Christian has had revealed to him. The reason that there is so much superstition among Christians today is that they have failed to grasp the fact that Satan is viewed in Scripture as ultimately *'helpful and auxiliary to the designs of grace'* — although it is rarely clear that this is the case. This is well brought out in the Book of Job. In the opening chapters, we see that it

---

[170] W.H. Green, *The Argument of Job Unfolded* (Klock & Klock, 1978), pp.68-69.
[171] Ibid., pp.63-64.

was Jehovah Himself who brought Job to the attention of Satan, *'Have you considered My servant Job...?'* (Job 1:8,12; 2:3,6). Think through the precious information that this gives us. It shows two things: **First**, that Satan must have permission from God before he is able to inflict suffering and evil in the world (Job.1:6; 2:1). Anything that Satan does is absolutely subordinate to the will of God. The **second** element that is revealed in this Book of Job is that in all that Satan does, he can only go as far as he is permitted by the Lord (Job.1:12; 2:6). In fact, the devil, no matter how devilish he may become, is, in a very real sense — like his non-fallen angelic counterparts — a *'ministering spirit sent forth to minister for those who will inherit salvation'* (Heb.1:14). This is an astonishing point, but it is true. In spite of all the superstition and incantations that are mustered against Satan in many professing Christian circles today, he is completely under the control of his Creator, and no matter what evil and havoc he may make in the world, he can never do any more than will ultimately be necessary towards the furthering and fruition of God's final purpose in Christ (cf. Eph.3:8-11). Christians can take real comfort in that.

There is yet another classic biblical example which shows that Satan is an unwitting servant of God in all that he does. We are referring here to the Apostle Paul's famous *'thorn in the flesh'* (2 Cor.12:1-10). The Apostle spoke of how he had received *'visions and revelations of the Lord'* (2 Cor.12:1), of how he was *'caught up into Paradise and heard inexpressible words, which it is not lawful for a man to utter'* (2 Cor.12:4). Such privileges could easily render a person prone to boast or to develop ideas that he had become a super-spiritual person, as many do today. But the Lord had taken certain necessary measures to ensure that this would not happen to His servant. Paul recognised this and disclosed the following information:

> 'Lest I should be exalted above measure by the abundance of the revelations, a thorn in the flesh was given to me, a messenger of Satan to buffet me, lest I be exalted above measure' (2 Cor.12:7).

The actual identity of the 'thorn' is not important, but its function as an affliction certainly is. For we see here that although the 'thorn' was administered by Satan, it had been *prescribed* by the Lord. Just as He had done with Job, the Lord used the unwitting services of Satan to afflict one of His servants and bring about the greater good. But whereas Job was afflicted by God to eradicate any pride which was already present, Paul was given his affliction to prevent him from the possibility of falling into any future pride as a result of his high spiritual calling. Just as Jacob had to live with a permanent limp after winning a blessing from the Lord (Gen.32:24-32), so the believer who enjoys the benefits of a closeness with God will often have to bear a burdensome cross to keep him from being 'exalted above measure'.

That Paul was wholly aware of this subordinate use of Satan is shown by his advice to the Church at Corinth, when discussing the case of a member who had committed incest, that they should *'deliver such a one to Satan for the destruction of the flesh, that his spirit may be saved in the day of the Lord Jesus'* (1 Cor.5:5).

Later, the church was urged *'to forgive and comfort him, lest perhaps such a one be swallowed up with too much sorrow'* (2 Cor.2:7). Satan is shown here to be used by the Church as an agent in the encouragement of repentance for sin — another example of which is given by Paul in 1 Tim.1:19-20:

> 'Some have rejected [faith and a good conscience] and so have shipwrecked their faith. Among them are Hymenaeus and Alexander, whom I have handed over to Satan to be taught not to blaspheme'.

The fallen angel is entirely subordinate to the will and uses of the Sovereign Lord. We must never forget this mighty fact. So if a Christian believer **is** suffering at the hands of the demonic realm, it is in the Lord's chastening purposes, for his instruction and learning (see Heb.12:3-11). If Christ was continually subject to the testings of Satan, you can be sure that His disciples will be also. But when the Christian is attacked in this way, he does not need to go running off to the Shaman, priest or exorcist; but he must first of all say: 'Why is this happening to me? Why is God permitting it to be so? What lessons does He want me to learn?' All the while, remembering that any strength to resist comes from Christ (Eph.6:10). It is in our weakness that His strength is made perfect.

If you are Christ's, then everything about your life is unfolding under His jurisdiction. Every facet of the life of the Christian is in His hand (Mt.10:30-31). If He protects us absolutely from our human enemies, how much more does He protect us from those principalities and powers of darkness which He may permit to scourge us from time to time (Lk.21:12-19)? In one sense, it is something of a comfort for the Christian to be buffeted by Satan, because it proves that the old serpent has something against you (you are, after all, a Christian who has wholly escaped from his dominion), and this gives the Lord yet another opportunity to show His superiority and build your strength. If you were a child of Satan rather than a child of God, the devil would give you very little trouble. But nothing can separate you from the love of God which is in Christ Jesus our Lord — neither angels (fallen or otherwise) nor principalities nor powers of darkness. Nothing! (Rom.8:28-39). They may try; but they can never harm you on a lasting basis.

The Bible actually gives a lovely parallel between the two Testaments concerning the battle between the Lord's elect and their spiritual opponents. The O.T. historical record of the Children of Israel's experiences in the wilderness and subsequent conquest of the Canaanite territory under their leader, Joshua,[172] provides us with a number of eternal truths about our spiritual warfare as believers in Christ. It is a fact that many of the earthly principles in the Old Covenant were types and shadows of spiritual realities in the New. Just as the nation Israel is rescued from bondage to Pharaoh in Egypt and brought into the promised territory of Canaan — a land flowing with milk and honey — so the Body of Christ is rescued from bondage to Satan in this present world and brought into the promised reality of eternal life in the New Heavens and the New Earth: a spiritual state of

---

[172] The name 'Joshua' is based on the Hebrew word for *'Jehovah is Salvation'*, of which the name Jesus is the Greek form.

illumination by God in the light of the Lamb rather than earthly milk and honey (Rev.21:23). Whereas the members of the nation, Israel, did battle with *material* weapons against the surrounding nations, in the strength of the Lord, to maintain national purity, the member of the Body of Christ wars with *spiritual* weapons against discarnate enemies, in the strength of the Lord, as part of a lifelong personal sanctification process (2 Cor.10:4-6; Eph.6:10ff.). It is highly significant that the Lord saw fit to leave some of the surrounding nations untamed, *'that He might test Israel by them'*, even after they had been brought into the promised land (Jdg.3:1). It just the same manner, he has left a large part of the demonic realm with a measure of power to test the Church — even in the wake of Christ's victory on the Cross.

So let us cast aside the vast majority of books on 'deliverance' which litter the shelves of most Christian bookshops today. So many of them are downright dangerous, irresponsible and based on both fundamental misunderstandings of the Scriptures and a rejection of the Bible as the fount of Divine revelation today. Instead, let us turn to the Spirit-inspired writings of the Apostles of Jesus Christ for our instructions on how to overcome Satan and handle the deceits of the demonic realm. Concerning any possible demonic interference in the life of the Christian, there are four places where we are given express light in this area, and a clear pattern of behaviour to follow. It is significant that they come from the pens of the three most prominent Apostles in the early church — Peter, John and Paul.. To conclude this chapter, we shall now examine these precious teachings.

The Teaching of the Apostle Peter on Spiritual Warfare

The only direct reference to Satan in Peter's writings occurs in his first letter, when he reminds believers of the necessity of vigilance and a humble heart:

> 'Therefore humble yourselves under the mighty hand of God, that He may exalt you in due time, casting all your care upon Him, for He cares for you. Be sober, be vigilant; because your adversary the devil walks about like a roaring lion, seeking whom he may devour. Resist him, steadfast in the faith' (1 Pet.5:6-9).

The teaching of the Apostle here is this: even though the devil walks about like a roaring lion, seeking whom he may devour, all that is necessary to combat this is to resist him, remaining steadfast in the faith. This approach is very similar to that recommended by the Jerusalem church leader, James, who, after reminding us that *'God resists the proud, but gives grace to the humble'*, concludes: *'Therefore submit to God. Resist the devil and he will flee from you'* (Jas.4:6-7). The thinking behind these two texts is so similar that it was surely *axiomatic* in terms of the teaching of the early church on the subject of spiritual warfare. An undergirding element of this exhortation is the need for sobriety. No need for hysteria, superstition or ecclesiastical ritual when considering these matters.

Notice also how resistance to the devil is intimately tied up with 'steadfastness in the faith', which involves assurance and the foundations of solid Bible teaching — qualities which are sadly lacking in so many churches today. But above all, the greatest panacea for demonic oppression is to *'draw near to God and He will draw near to you'* (Jas.4:8). Submission in prayer to God is the central key to overcoming Satan. When a child was possessed by a particularly malign spirit (Mk.9:14-29), Jesus emphasised the profound importance of *prayer* and the *personal spiritual life* of the disciples as the key to the boy's deliverance, rather than adherence to any ritual form of exorcism. Indeed, the very reason that the disciples had not been able to exercise their God-given gift for casting out demons into the Abyss was because they had neglected their spiritual exercises and simply assumed a magical reliance on exorcistic commands.

The one who exercises humility, faith and a prayerful mind-set — who resists Satan in this Divinely-appointed way — will discover that the devil will always turn tail and run. Guaranteed.

The Teaching of the Apostle John on Spiritual Warfare

Although John said a great deal about Satan and his overthrow by the Lord Jesus Christ (e.g., 1 Jn.3:8), in terms of the personal spiritual warfare of the believer, his greatest statement by far occurs in the Book of Revelation:

> 'And they overcame [the devil] by the blood of the Lamb and by the word of their testimony, and they did not love their lives to the death' (Rev.12:11).

This verse has been seized on by ritualistic Christians in their vain attempts at 'deliverance' from Satan. But there is no reference here to the superstitious, ritual 'pleading of Christ's blood' to the demonic powers in order to frighten them off, as many are teaching today. Engaging with demons in this way is pure Shamanism. One self-styled exorcist, giving an account of an alleged ritual exorcism, writes:

> 'Prayerfully, I then sealed off the area of her soul, i.e. mind, heart, will, conscience and memory with the Blood of the Lamb... The Blood as the holy deterrent to evil is the Divinely imposed and impressed means of prohibition'.[173]

Another 'Bible teacher' writes about this same phenomenon, claiming that *'he who scoffs at this teaching is in a pathetic plight... up the creek, without a paddle'*.[174] He sums up his teaching in this way:

> 'As the priests offered up daily blood sacrifices on behalf of the Israelites, so today in New Testament times, we **by faith** offer the Blood of Jesus Christ to God, as our plea on behalf of ourselves, our children and our loved ones. This ritual only comes to LIFE when we individually put it personally to the test'.[175] [emphasis in original]

According to this writer, anyone (including Christians) not indulging in the

---

[173] See, for example, Arthur Neil, *Aid us in Our Strife* (Heath Christian Trust, 1985), p.340.

[174] *Bible News Review*, No. 191, February 1987.

[175] Ibid.

shamanist ritual of 'Pleading the Blood':

> 'leaves himself without protection (a covering), without healing (except conventional medicine), and with no defence against demonic attack upon his person or property — thus exposing himself and his loved ones to just any devilish onslaught in this dangerous, demon-infested world'.[176] [parentheses in original]

However, in spite of this menacing threat, the truth is that the believer's ability to stand before Satan does not rest in anything which *he* can perform, but rather on what *the Lamb* did on the Cross for him or her almost two thousand years ago. That is what 'overcoming Satan by the blood of the Lamb' really means. When you are a beneficiary of Christ's atonement, you are naturally *'delivered...from the power of darkness and transferred..into the kingdom of the Son of [God's] love'* (Col.1:13). Believers do not need to 'plead the Blood of Christ' to Satan (or any-one else) as if we were occultists waving crosses at Dracula. We should simply rest in the finished work of Christ through His gracious atonement.

Similarly, the use of the phrase, *'by the word of their testimony'*, in connection with the overcoming of Satan, is not a reference to any mystical *'power of the spoken word'*, as many Charismatics are teaching today. This text simply refers to faithfulness to the Truth which is in Christ and the fearless preaching of it in the world (see Rev.6:9; 11:7; 12:17). It was for just such faithfulness and preaching that John was exiled on the Isle of Patmos in the first place — *'for the word of God and for the testimony of Jesus Christ'* (Rev.1:9). Preaching the Gospel provides deliverance for the Lord's people and confirms the mighty fact that the devil has *already* been overthrown.

A third element of deliverance in this verse is that *'they did not love their lives to the death'*. Is it not astonishing how so many believers have actually got their feet comfortably under the table in this world? Do they not know that because Satan is the power behind the world-system (1 Jn.5:19), therefore friendship with the world is enmity with God (Jas.4:4)? John here teaches us that a prime factor in overcoming Satan is to have a 'loose' hold on this world — more, to hate our lives in the world to such an extent that we are willing to sacrifice them for the sake of the Gospel (Lk.14:26; Jn.12:25). It is to such self-sacrifice that John is referring in Rev.12:11, as in his first letter when he said *'we also ought to lay down our lives for the brethren'* just as the Lord Jesus *'laid down His life for us'* (1 Jn.3:16; cf. Jn.15:12-13).

The Teaching of the Apostle Paul on Spiritual Warfare

Although Paul alluded to spiritual warfare in his other letters, in his letter to the Ephesians, we discover a complete manual on spiritual warfare — on how to cope with living in a totally dark society where the powers of darkness are revered and even worshipped. The teaching here must be fundamental to our understanding of this subject, as this entire letter concerns the cosmic relationship between the Church and the powers of darkness. All this would be especially relevant to

[176] Ibid.

those living in Ephesus, which was the centre of the cult of the goddess Diana and a major focal point for occultism and magic in the first century (cf. Acts 19). It is equally as relevant in our own day, as we have learned throughout this present book.

In the first chapter of Ephesians, we learn how believers have been chosen for salvation and holiness by the Lord and Creator of the universe even before it was ever created (Eph.1:1-12). Then we learn how the recipients of this salvation have been sealed with the Holy Spirit until the return of the Lord Jesus (Eph.1:13-14). He also tells us of *'the exceeding greatness of His power toward us who believe, according to the working of His mighty power'* and how He has been seated at God's right hand in the heavenlies, *'far above all principality and power and might and dominion'* (Eph.1:19-21). In the second chapter, Paul reminds believers what they have been saved from, contrasting the power of Jesus Christ with *'the prince of the power of the air, the spirit who now works in the sons of disobedience'* (Eph.2:2). In the third chapter, he reveals a great mystery, *'that the Gentiles should be fellow-heirs, of the same body, and partakers of His promise in Christ through the Gospel'* (Eph.3:6). This is the realisation of Jesus' promise that He would 'plunder' Satan's goods — the nations over which that wicked one had held sway for so many millennia. Then, after showing that God's eternal purpose in Christ Jesus was that the *'multi-faceted wisdom of God might be made known by the church to the principalities and powers in the heavenlies'* (Eph.3:10-11), he speaks of *'the power that works in us'* which comes through being filled with all the fullness of God and having Christ dwelling in our hearts through faith (Eph.3:16-21).

Then, in the fourth chapter, he begins a careful exposition of the practical application which arises naturally out of the teaching given in the previous three chapters, that there is a 'power' (Greek, *dunamis,* from which our word 'dynamite' is derived) in the believer which far surpasses any authority or power to which Satan may aspire. Here we discover that there is a twofold strategy in spiritual warfare with Satan — the one involving our works, the other involving our weaponry. The first involves the necessity for believers to *'have a walk worthy of the calling'* with which they are called and that they should *'no longer walk as the rest of the Gentiles walk'* (Eph.4:1, 17ff.). The second involves being *'able to stand against the wiles of the devil'* through being equipped with the *'whole armour of God'* (Eph.6:11).

When Paul says: *'Do not give a foothold to the devil'* (Eph.4:27), the footholds he envisages are the various sins and sinful situations into which we can so easily fall, such as lying (4:25,15a), sinful anger and contentious behaviour (4:3-6,26,31), corrupt communications (4:29; 5:4), a lack of kindness, compassion and forgiveness (4:32), the merest hint of sexual immorality, uncleanness or covetousness (5:3,5), drunkenness (5:18), the wrong choice of associates (5:6ff.), failure to discern false doctrine (4:14), a lack of humility and submission (4:2; 5:21), and the fostering of sectarianism or divisiveness (4:3-6).

The greatest weapon in our spiritual warfare against Satan is to *'put off, concerning your former conduct, the old man which grows corrupt according to the deceitful lusts'* (Eph.4:22) and to *'put on the new man which was created according to God, in righteousness and true holiness'* (Eph.4:24). After all, the very reason that Christ *'bore our sins in His own body on the tree'* was in order *'that we, having died to sins, might live for righteousness'* (1 Pet.2:24). The Christian who takes his need to root out sin seriously and live an upright and righteous life will receive the most cast-iron protection against all the onslaughts of the devil because he does not provide any footholds for him. As the Apostle John puts it:

> 'We know that whoever is born of God does not sin; but he who has been born of God guards himself, and the wicked one does not touch him' (1 Jn.5:18).

However, working alongside this incessant mortification of sin and zeal for an upright life, there is also a need to ensure that one is making full use of the spiritual armoury provided by the Lord to every believer (Eph.6:11-18). This putting-on of Divine armoury is not to be taken literally, as a number of superstitious Christians do today with a ritual exercise in which, upon rising in the morning, one visualises oneself being kitted out with a real suit of armour, and then divesting oneself of it at night.[177] Instead, Paul reminds us that each piece of the armoury mentioned in Eph.6:13ff. symbolises a 'grace-gift' from God which is given to **every** believer and of which we are to make full us. Paul lists seven items in this *'armour of God'*, which we shall examine briefly as we bring this chapter to a close.

1. The Belt of Truth

First, we are told to gird our waists with truth. Girding up one's waist or loins in Scripture means to be in a state of sober readiness and repose (cf. Lk.12:35; 1 Pet.1:13). It is only through a sober knowledge of the truth that we can hope to stand against all evil. But, to quote a well-known but confused first-century Roman official, *'What is truth?'* God Himself is described as the God of truth (Dt.32:4), while Jesus Christ *is* the truth (Jn.1:14; 14:6; Eph.4:20-21), and the Holy Spirit is known as the Spirit of Truth (Jn.14:16-17; 15:26; 16:13). The Lord Jesus came to tell His disciples the truth:

> 'Then Jesus said to those Jews who believed Him, "If you abide in My word, you are My disciples indeed. And you shall know the truth, and the truth shall make you free"' (Jn.8:31-32).

The Church itself is described as *'The pillar and ground of the truth'* (1 Tim.3:15). So it is hardly surprising to find the Apostle John saying: *'I have not written to you because you do not know the truth, but because you know it'* (1 Jn.2:21). We have already seen the way in which Satan, the father of lies, has

---

[177] The present writer has come across a small booklet, put out by a teacher and counsellor in the Church of England, which advocates this visualisation exercise for protection against the demonic.

always sought to foster the notion that there is no Absolute Truth.[178] If you gird yourself about with this truth, you will hold the whole suit of armour together. It is the absolute Truth of a personal Transcendent God:

> 'God was manifested in the flesh, justified in the Spirit, seen by angels, preached among the Gentiles, believed on in the world, received up in glory' (1 Tim.3:16).

Without the inner knowledge of these things (i.e., if one is not girded about with the belt of truth) a person is in a dismal position indeed. In the run-up to the revealing of the Man of Sin at the end of this evil Age, Paul tells us that people will perish

> 'because they refused to love the truth and so be saved. For this reason God sends them a powerful delusion so that they will believe the lie and so that all will be condemned who have not believed the truth but have delighted in wickedness' (2 Th.2:10-12).

2. The Breastplate of Righteousness

The second piece of armour in the Christian's spiritual warfare is the breastplate of righteousness (v.14). This righteousness is not simply our own personal righteous behaviour, for that could never enable us to stand completely against all the wiles of the devil. In his letter to the Philippians, Paul explicitly says that he has no desire for his own righteousness but, instead, *'that which is through faith in Christ, the righteousness which is from God by faith'* (Phil.3:9). This is none other than the righteousness of Christ which is imputed to every regenerated believer (Rom.3:21-22; 5:17-21), who is *'filled with the fruits of righteousness which are by Jesus Christ, to the glory and praise of God'* (Phil.1:10-11).

3. The Preparedness of the Gospel of Peace

Again, this refers to something which is a gift from God to the believer. If we have a firm and solid footing based on the peace which lies in the true Gospel — the Good News which comes from the finished work of Christ — we will then be well equipped to do battle with Satan.

True peace can only come through having been forgiven by God and reconciled to Him. As Paul says elsewhere: *'Therefore, having been justified by faith, we have peace with God through our Lord Jesus Christ'* (Rom.5:1). This is a great comfort. If we have this 'peace with God' — which can come only through being justified by faith in Christ — then we will be all the better equipped to deal with the wiles of the devil. For, as the Lord Himself said, *'Peace I leave with you, My peace I give to you; not as the world gives do I give to you. Let not your heart be troubled, neither let it be afraid'* (Jn.14:27).

4. The Shield of Faith

The shield which Paul would have been taking as his symbol here is the standard shield of the Roman soldier: four feet by two feet six inches of protection for

---

[178] See Chapter 5, pp.185-194.

the entire body, interlocking with those adjacent to it — a beautiful illustration of the building-up of the Body of Christ through faithful believers who have strengthening fellowship with one another.

What is this faith which is like a shield against *'all the fiery darts of the wicked one'*? Again, it is another gift from God: *'For by grace you have been saved through faith, and that not of yourselves; it is the gift of God'* (Eph.2:8). And how does this faith work? The answer is in the Letter to the Hebrews: *'Now faith is the substance of things hoped for, the evidence of things not seen'* (Heb.11:1). What this means is that faith actually makes things substantial which do not yet have a present full reality or which appear from a human standpoint to be impossible. Thus, although believers are prone to the temptations of the flesh and subject to disease and infirmities, they can have every assurance that He who has begun a good work in them will complete it until the day of Jesus Christ (Phil.1:6). Faith tells them that the Holy Spirit who indwells them is a guarantee of the resurrection to come (Rom.8:11; 2 Cor.5:5; Eph.1:13-14). Faith makes things substantial which do not yet have a present full reality.

It is for this reason that the believer must walk by faith and not by sight.

5. The Helmet of Salvation

Another gift from God to the believer is the helmet of salvation, the intellectual comprehension that God has saved him through Jesus Christ from certain death and hell. The true believer knows whom he has believed (2 Tim.1:12). The true believer knows that his Redeemer lives (Job 19:25). The true believer *knows* that once he was blind but now he can see (Jn.9:25). The true believer knows that he has passed from death to life (1 Jn.3:14).

This is head knowledge that leads to the inner confidence of supernatural faith and a sure protection against all the fiery darts of the wicked one.

6. Sword of the Spirit which is the Word of God

Here we have an actual weapon rather than a mere piece of protective clothing, *'the sword of the Spirit, which is the word of God'* (v.17). But this is no common weapon of human vengeance or wanton combat. It refers to the sayings of God which have come to us in the Scriptures. The 'word' here is not the Greek *logos*, i.e., verbal thought or concept, but is *rhema*, an actual saying. We must not read too much into this differentiation as both words are used in the Bible to refer to the Scriptures as God's Word (e.g., 1 Pet.1:25; 1 Cor.14:36). There are some who interpret this verse as if it means that we are to use Spirit-inspired verbal commands as a formula for exorcism; but there are no biblical grounds for believing this.

The sword of the Spirit is not referring so much to the Bible as a book, but to the Word of God as spoken in it — God-breathed. Jesus Himself used this very weapon in His temptation by Satan in the wilderness, as He quoted Scripture, rather than any other formula, to ward off Satan. Three times He was tempted. Three times He replied by quoting the Bible (Dt.8:3; 6:13,16). When He said: *'It is written, "Man shall not live by bread alone, but by every word of God"'*

(Lk.4:8), the Greek word for 'word' of God here is the same as in the description of the sword of the Spirit in Eph.6:17. It is the Word of God spoken in the hearing of Satan — the same Word of God which is described as being

> 'living and powerful, and sharper than any two-edged sword, piercing even to the division of soul and spirit, and of joints and marrow, and is a discerner of the thoughts and intents of the heart' (Heb.4:12).

When we preach the Gospel, read the Scriptures aloud or expound them before an assembly, we cut through and prick the hearts of the people, winning souls for Christ, thus doing irreparable damage to the aims of the satanic realm. In this way, we pull down strongholds and cast down arguments which set themselves up against God. Our Redeemer Himself is portrayed as having a *'mouth like a sharp sword'* (Isa.49:2; cf. Rev.1:16; 2:12). *'"Is not My word like a fire?", says the* L*ORD*, *"and like a hammer that breaks the rock in pieces?"'* (Jer.23:29). We have to carry this Word of God in our very hearts (Dt.6:6; 11:18), not merely to assist us in direct confrontations with the demonic realm, but to avert us from sin (Ps.119:9-11), to admonish us (1 Cor.10:11), to give us faith (Rom.10:17), to teach (Col.3:16), to preach the Gospel (1 Pet.1:22-25; 1 Cor.1:17-25) and to save souls (Jam.1:21). All this causes real damage to the aims and strategy of Satan within the Church. Moreover, it is through the proclamation of His Word that

> 'the manifold wisdom of God might be made known by the church to the principalities and powers in the heavenly places, according to the eternal purpose which He accomplished in Christ Jesus our Lord' (Eph.3:10-11).

This was well understood by John when he told some of the recipients of his first letter: *'I have written to you, young men, because you are strong, and the word of God abides in you, and you have overcome the wicked one'* (1 Jn.2:14). This is the real secret of being able to take a stand against the demonic realm. Do you now see why it is so necessary to have a great armoury of Scriptures at one's disposal? How else are we going to take on the cultists, heretics, false teachers and angels of light in the Church, if not from Scripture? This weapon is *'the word of [our] testimony'* (Rev.12:11) — not our own personal testimony, but the testimony of Jesus Christ (Rev.12:17), our Risen Saviour.

'The word of our God stands forever' (Isa.40:8; cf. 1 Pet.1:22-25; Mt.24:35).

7. Prayer in the Spirit

The final piece in the Christian's spiritual armoury is prayer which is 'in the spirit' (v.18). This is a most important part of the armoury. In a sense, it is such prayer which holds it all together. When Paul speaks about praying in the spirit, he is not referring to praying in ecstatic 'tongues', as many in the Pentecostal-Charismatic Movement appear to believe today. Because of their tendentious approach to the Holy Spirit, the phrase 'in the spirit' can only be interpreted by them as referring to some ecstatic spiritual state; but that is mysticism rather than biblical prayer. But the word 'spirit' here does not primarily refer to the Holy Spirit.

The use of the term 'in the spirit' here means prayer which is genuine, from the heart, arising out of a dynamic personal relationship with God. It is 'in the spirit' — that is, not just an external ritual but a vital activity, coming from a person's spirit rather than from his lips only. Paul stressed the same importance of the 'interiority' of the spiritual life when he spoke of serving God 'with his spirit' (Rom.1:9), of praying and singing 'with his spirit' (1 Cor.14:14-15), and of worshipping God 'in the spirit' (Phil.3:3) — that is, in just the manner that the Lord Jesus said He must be worshipped: *'in spirit and in truth'* (Jn.4:23-24). Although it is perfectly true that a Christian cannot pray fervently in his own spirit unless he has first been inspired by the Holy Spirit, the phrase 'praying in the spirit' refers principally to the attitude of heart of the one so praying — a person who is 'in tune with' the Spirit of God. On this phrase, William Gurnall writes:

> 'We pray in the spirit when these three are found in the duty:—FIRST, when we pray *with knowledge*. SECOND, when we pray *in fervency*. THIRD, when we pray *in sincerity*. These three exercise the three powers of the soul and spirit. By knowledge the understanding is set on work; by fervency the affections; and by sincerity the will. All these are required in conjunction to "praying in the spirit"'.[179]

The Lord Jesus scolded the Pharisees for *not* worshipping *'in spirit and in truth'* when he said to them:

> '"Hypocrites! Well did Isaiah prophesy about you, saying: "These people draw near to Me with their mouth, and honour Me with their lips, but their heart is far from Me"' (Mt.15:7-8).

Unless our prayers are 'in the spirit' of fervency and from the heart, they will have little effect on Satan in terms of spiritual warfare. But the effective, fervent prayer of a righteous person bears much fruit. Without it, the armour we wear will be far less effective against the onslaughts of a devil who is very angry because he knows he only has a short time. And if we really think about this divine armoury — taking into account its symbology, and considering all that it does — what does it *really* represent? What is the sum of all its parts? It is nothing other than Christ Himself! As Paul reveals: *'For as many of you as were baptised into Christ have put on Christ'* (Gal.3:27). Elsewhere, he says:

> 'The night is far spent, the day is at hand. Therefore let us cast off the works of darkness, and let us *put on the armour of light*. Let us walk properly, as in the day, not in revelry and drunkenness, not in licentiousness and lewdness, not in strife and envy. But *put on the Lord Jesus Christ*, and make no provision for the flesh, to fulfil its lusts' (Rom.13:12-14). [emphasis added]

The Greek words translated as 'put on Christ' in these verses mean, literally, 'clothe yourself with Christ'. So, in Rom.13:12-14, we have an exact replica of

---

[179] William Gurnall, *The Christian in Complete Armour: A Treatise of the Saints' War Against the Devil* (Banner of Truth Trust, 1964), Vol.II, p.468.

Paul's twofold strategy for effective spiritual warfare against the powers of darkness: first, the necessity for believers to *'have a walk worthy of the calling'* with which they are called and that they should *'no longer walk as the rest of the Gentiles walk'*; second, the need to be *'able to stand against the wiles of the devil'* through being equipped with the *'whole armour of God'* (Eph.6:11). In Ephesians 4:22-24, it is expressed as 'put off the old man, put on the new'; in Romans 13:12-13, it is 'cast off the works of darkness and put on the armour of light'. The 'new man', 'armour of light', and 'whole armour of God' which the Christian puts on refer to the same thing: Jesus Christ as the image of God created in righteousness and true holiness. To be clothed with Christ means to become a partaker in the divine nature (2 Pet.1:4). Such is the intimacy of our union with Christ as believers, that every true Christian can say:

> '"I have been crucified with Christ; it is no longer I who live, but Christ lives in me; and the life which I now live in the flesh I live by faith in the Son of God, who loved me and gave Himself for me"' (Gal.2:20).

That is what true deliverance is all about. There can be no rescue from being enslaved to the powers of darkness until a person is no longer 'in Adam' but 'in Christ'. And to be 'in Christ' means to eschew anything which may provide a foothold for the devil in our lives. Deliverance from enslavement to the demonic comes only through regeneration, which brings with it the whole armour of God. From the moment you are saved by Christ you are outside of Satan's authority (Col.1:13). But it doesn't stop there. For, although believers cease to be enslaved to sin and Satan, they have still to contend with the *'lust of the flesh'* (Gal.5:16-21) and *'the wiles of the devil'* (Eph.6:11; cf. 2 Cor.2:11b; 1 Pet.5:8). So, while the *unbeliever's* deliverance from *enslavement* to the demonic comes through *regeneration*, the *believer's* deliverance from *harassment* by the demonic comes through *sanctification*. Christians who purify themselves, just as the Lord Jesus is pure (1 Jn.3:3), who work out their own salvation with fear and trembling (Phil.2:13), who diligently *'cast off the works of darkness'* (Rom.13:12), who *'no longer walk as the rest of the Gentiles walk'* (Eph.4:17), who *'have a walk worthy of the calling with which [they] were called'* (Eph.4:1), who *'walk as children of light...and have no fellowship with the unfruitful works of darkness'* (Eph.5:11), who consistently refuse to *'give a foothold to the devil'* (Eph.4:24) — these will be the ones who *'shall abide under the shadow of the Almighty'* and be delivered *'from the snare of the fowler'* (Ps.91:1-3). The clear promise to the believer is:

> 'Because you have made the LORD...even the Most High, your habitation, no evil shall befall you...for He shall give His angels charge over you, to keep you in all your ways' (Ps.91:9-11).

The Lord Himself says of such a one:

> 'Because he has set his love upon Me, therefore I will deliver him; I will exalt him, because he has known My name. He shall call upon Me, and I will answer him; I will be with him in trouble; I will deliver him and honour him' (Ps.91:14-15).

That is deliverance; true deliverance — which does not come through superstitious rituals but by divine rescue followed by prudent Christian living.

CONCLUSION

Here we believe that we have given the complete biblical strategy for dealing with any demonic influence in the life of the Christian. If you follow these principles you will be fully protected under the healing wings of the Lord. What a far cry this is from the superstition, bondage and lack of assurance which is generated within so many Charismatic-Pentecostal groups today! How right the Apostle was when he showed that instability and an untaught mind go hand-in-hand with a lack of true Christian doctrine (2 Pet.3:16). And how sad it is that this instability is rocking the Church and wrecking the fragile hearts of so many believers today. The main reason that so many believers are in error today is because they do not know the Scriptures or the real power of God.

If we have gone to great lengths in this chapter, it is because of our strong conviction that we need discernment more than ever in these present times, as Satan and his henchmen assault the Lord's people with teachings which bring them into spiritual bondage and inspire them to practise religious techniques and systems which are far removed from the ways of God in Scripture. In the following chapter — the last of our explorations into religious corruption — we will learn that the encouragement of professing Christians to indulge in the practices of world religions (which all have their roots in the ancient religion of Babel) is a most advantageous strategy in the current satanic bid to eradicate the gulf between Christianity and the religious beliefs of the world.

Chapter Twelve

NOT PILGRIMS, BUT STRANGERS

Christianity and World Religions

'Assemble yourselves and come; draw near together, you who have escaped from the nations. They have no knowledge, who carry the wood of their carved image, and pray to a god that cannot save... Look to Me, and be saved, all you ends of the earth! For I am God, and there is no other' (Isa.45:20,22).

'For there is one God and one Mediator between God and men, the Man Christ Jesus' (1 Tim.2:5).

'Nor is there salvation in any other, for there is no other name under heaven given among men by which we must be saved' (Acts 4:12).

In recent years, many Christians have expressed disquiet with what is popularly known as the Ecumenical Movement. In response to biblical calls for Christian unity, this movement — operating at both formal and informal levels — seeks to bring all Christian denominations and organisations into a universal conglomerate. If the prime objective of those behind this movement was to unite all believers in the cause of God's truth and to preach the fullness of the Gospel with love and power to a spiritually corrupt and needy world, we would be the first to gather with them. We would not want to oppose our Lord's prayer, in His last great discourse, for believers to manifest their unity as a means of evangelism to unbelievers (Jn.17:20-23). We can fully identify with those in the Ecumenical Movement who have a heartfelt desire to see an end to sectarianism and unbiblical divisiveness. But the knowledge that there is a *hidden agenda* of global proportions behind the work of the modern Ecumenical Movement has motivated this exposé of its historical and developmental roots.

Among the more prominent characteristics of the many deceptions which have plagued the Church from its beginnings are the subtlety of their origin and the stealth of their development. Never has there been such a need for believers to discern that when Satan-inspired movements are at work in the Church, they never appear to be malevolent but, rather, present themselves as being highly desirable and so filled with spiritual integrity, that they are capable of deceiving the Lord's own people, if such a thing is possible (cf. Mt.24:24). The Lord Jesus was referring to this mode of deception when he described false prophets as 'wolves in sheep's clothing' (Mt.7:15). Similarly, Paul the Apostle warned that Satan cleverly disguises himself as an 'angel of light' in order to conceal his darkness (2 Cor.11:14). As that discerning early Church Father, Irenaeus of Lyons (*c.* A.D. 130-200), has put it:

> 'No false teaching desires to offer itself to our view openly, lest such exposure should lead to conviction; but, craftily putting on a plausible dress, makes itself by its outward form appear to the simpler sort to be truer than Truth itself '.[1]

It is our considered belief that the Ecumenical Movement, in spite of its professed aspirations, falls into just such a category. We acknowledge that there are a great many sincere and well-meaning believers who support this movement, and it is chiefly for their benefit that this chapter has been included. But once we have obtained a full grasp of the vast network of intrigues to which the Ecumenical Movement belongs, this will remove all remaining vestiges of the sheep's clothing and will reveal it for what it is: A Trojan Horse within the temple of the Lord.

PROLOGUE: The True Ground of Church Unity

Although the Christian can speak in terms of the bare letter as being 'dead' when compared with the bounties of the Spirit (2 Corinthians 3:6), it cannot be denied that words themselves carry a powerful charge which will often determine our responses to them, for better or for worse. Sometimes words are 'hijacked' from their biblical roots in the name of a particular cause. A classic modern example is the word *charismatic* which, considered simply from Scripture, means *divinely gifted* — a term which really applies to every true believer rather than the limited sense in which it has come to be used in some Christian circles today.

Another such 'hijacked' word is *ecumenical*. Although this word has come to have a tendentious association, it has an innocent biblical pedigree. The words 'ecumenism' and 'ecumenical' come to us from a Greek word *oikoumene*, meaning 'the whole inhabited earth' or simply 'the world'. In a primary Scriptural example, we are told that *'this gospel of the kingdom will be preached in **all the world** as a witness to all the nations, and then the end will come'* (Mt.24:14). This meant that all the nations were to be evangelised by the Gospel, which the Lord Jesus Christ announced when He said: *'The time is fulfilled, and the kingdom of God is at hand. Repent, and believe in the gospel'* (Mk.1:15). No longer were God's people to be primarily confined to the Old Covenant nation of Israel. A remnant of that people would constitute the firstfruits of the New Covenant people, the Church; but the nations of the whole inhabited world would thereafter be brought within the sphere of the preaching of the Gospel — exactly as forecast by the Old Testament prophets (e.g., Isa.11:10; 66:19; Mal.1:11). This does not mean that everyone from those nations will be saved. Only those who obey the Gospel, repent of their sin and have faith in Christ for salvation will be grafted

---

[1] Irenæus of Lyons, *Against Heresies* or *A Refutation of Knowledge Falsely So-Called*, Intro. §2. This is a great rebuttal of the second-century heresy of Gnosticism.

into the true Church and receive the gift of eternal life (Rom.11:16-17; 2 Th.1:7-8; Jn.3:36).

This Church is revealed by Paul the Apostle as the 'body of Christ' in which all the parts have been *'made to drink into one Spirit'*, the Holy Spirit of God, and in which there should be no schism but only love and care for one another (1 Cor.12:12-27). In the midst of a fallen world, the Church is exhorted to function as 'the salt of the earth' and the 'light of the world', in order to fulfil a vital evangelistic purpose (Mt.5:13-16). Jesus echoed this when He gave a new commandment, that believers are to love one another as He has loved them, so that they will be recognised as His disciples (Jn.13:34-35). Shortly after this, He prayed that there would be a oneness among believers which would be so manifested to the unbelievers of the world that they would know without a doubt that Christ has been sent by the Father (Jn.17:21-23). It is clear from this prayer that the unity within the Church which is referred to by Jesus is intimately linked to the unity which exists within the Triune Godhead. *True ecumenism, therefore, lies in the spiritual unity which exists on the basis of the mutual indwelling of the Holy Spirit in all genuine believers throughout the world.* This is a far cry indeed from the prevailing *false* ecumenism, which is founded instead on a very limited and compromised 'confession of faith'. Those advocating such false ecumenism have failed to recognise that the Church is not as all-inclusive as they would imagine. For the same Apostle who recorded the mighty intercessory prayer of the Lord Jesus in Jn.17:21-23 also wrote the following words to some fellow-believers to warn them about false teachers:

> 'Whoever transgresses and does not abide in the doctrine of Christ does not have God. He who abides in the doctrine of Christ has both the Father and the Son. If anyone comes to you and does not bring this doctrine, do not receive him into your house nor greet him; for he who greets him shares in his evil deeds' (2 Jn.9-11).

This highlights the exclusive aspect of the true Church founded by Jesus Christ — a fact which was emphatically endorsed by the Lord Himself (Mt.7:13-14; Luke 13:24). The unity of the Church depicted in the Bible embodies a spiritual *organism* which is gathered out of the world by the grace of God through Jesus Christ, in the power of the Holy Spirit (Jn.10:4,14-16,26-27; Titus 3:4-6). It does not consist of an earthly *organisational* alliance of professing believers which is rooted in the politics of human effort. Such pseudo-ecumenism began to pervade the Church almost a century ago, and has today caused much confusion among believers.

The Three Phases of Ecumenical Development

We fully appreciate that there are many well-meaning people who support the Ecumenical Movement because it is their heart's desire to see an end to sectarianism. But their efforts are based on a profound ignorance of the global influences which have sought to take things far beyond the original intentions of those who first advocated ecumenism among the churches. One of the primary reasons for the confusion in the Church today is the fact that the word 'ecumenism' has come to possess a very different meaning from that with which it is associated in the Bible. In the historical growth of the Ecumenical Movement we can trace a three-phase development in ecumenical thinking. In the **first** phase, the emphasis was on creating some genuine unity among all those throughout the world who professed faith in Jesus Christ. In the **second** phase the emphasis shifted to include all those who were members of any denomination or religion. In the **third** and most recent phase, the concept of 'ecumenism' is being widened to its ultimate possibility — that every human creature should be included in the idea of the Church: the whole inhabited world in its *absolute* universal sense.

In other words, phase one of the Ecumenical Movement epitomised the Church in terms of a *universal brotherhood of Christian faith*; phase two stylised it as a *universal brotherhood of religious faith*; while phase three — of which the majority of Christians are entirely unaware — is emphasising the *universal brotherhood of mankind* as a whole, regardless of religious affiliations. Thus, religious syncretism and humanistic universalism are realised within a movement which professes to represent solely the Christian Church and the interests of Jesus Christ.

We shall now examine the development of these three phases in greater detail, so that we can gain an understanding of the power which lies behind it.

I. FROM REFORMATION TO ECUMENISM: The Origins of the Ecumenical Movement

Although others had previously talked about Christian Unity, the earthly fountain-head of the modern Ecumenical Movement springs out of soil which was nurtured during the European Reformation. For it comes from the Protestant churches, as the result of a single event in history and the subsequent determined actions of a relatively small number of misguided men who were among its participants. Initially, false ecumenism developed out of a sincere desire to fulfil the prayers of the Lord Jesus Christ for Christian unity in Jn.17:20-23. At the turn of the century, a group of Christians looked at the vast number of interests competing in the mission field, and came to the understandable conclusion that a sectarian spirit was detrimental to the witness of the faith to the world. The net result of this was a gathering of 1,355 delegates in Edinburgh at the World Missionary Conference on June 14th, 1910. This was the true beginning of what we today call the 'Ecumenical Movement'.

This conference was a cosmopolitan gathering, designed to discuss a wide range of issues related to *'the evangelisation of the world in this generation'*. The World Missionary Conference of 1910 was the culmination of seven previous international meetings of missionary organisations held in various parts of the world. However, the gathering in Edinburgh was the first wholly inter-denominational conference ever to be held. Interestingly, it had originally been designated as 'The Third Ecumenical Missionary Conference'; but the word 'ecumenical' was eventually dropped from the title in the interests of evangelical unity![2]

The venue for this conference was the General Assembly Hall of the United Free Church of Scotland — now the Assembly Hall of the current Church of Scotland. As an example of the ever-shifting denominational scene in nineteenth century Scotland, the United Free Church was itself a denomination resulting from the union of the majority of the then Free Church of Scotland and the United Presbyterian Church. The key organiser of the World Missionary Conference in 1910 was the American Methodist layman, John R. Mott (1865-1955), whose simple desire was to

> 'bring Christ within the reach of every person in the world, so that he may have the opportunity of intelligently accepting Him as personal Saviour... It is our duty to evangelise the world, because Christ has commanded it'.[3]

Although many who are opposed to the Ecumenical Movement have sneered at the naïvety of these early ecumenists, this simple desire for evangelism represented a genuine Scriptural purpose. Unfortunately, the nobility of such an aim was to be buried under a welter of developments which moved away from the original design.

The World Missionary Conference had come about as a result of concern over competitive denominationalism on the mission field and a desire to unify the Christian mission of world evangelisation. John Mott had been organiser of the Student Volunteer Movement for Foreign Missions — an interdenominational outcome of the mission work of Dwight L. Moody (1837-1899). This student-oriented background is significant. As one impartial observer of the history of ecumenism has stated:

> 'It was in the student world that ecumenical collaboration developed most fully in the twentieth century, through two movements that are still active today: the Young Men's Christian Association...and the Student Christian Movement'.[4]

At the World Missionary Conference in 1910, Anglo-Catholics and evangelicals came together for the first time (albeit warily) through this very factor. As Bishop Talbot of Winchester put it in his speech to the conference: *'We would not have been here had it not been for the Student Christian Movement'*.[5] Many years later, William Temple, as Archbishop of Canterbury, would write:

> 'Members of the [Student Christian] Movement ought to know that

---

2 William Richey Hogg, 'Edinburgh 1910: Ecumenical Keystone', article in *Religion and Life: A Christian Quarterly of Opinion and Discussion*, Vol. XXIX, No.3, Summer 1960, p.344.

3 C.H. Hopkins, *John R. Mott: A Biography*, Eerdmans, 1980, p.232.

4 Lorna J.M. Brockett, *The Development of the Ecumenical Movement* (the Christian Education Movement in collaboration with Roehampton Institute of Higher Education, 1981), p.5.

5 Hugh Martin, *Beginning at Edinburgh: A Jubilee Assessment of the World Missionary Conference, 1910*, (Edinburgh House Press, 1960), p.5.

without their movement there could never have been held the Edinburgh Conference, which was the greatest event in the life of the Church for a generation'.[6]

It is a singular fact that the young and idealistic have always been the target for humanistic movements which seek, with great zeal, to revolutionise social and cultural developments in the world-system. We need to appreciate the implications of this for the evolution of ecumenism. A perusal of the published list of names and addresses of the World Missionary Conference delegates makes interesting reading, and it is certainly no coincidence that many of the

> 'ubiquitous, youthful stewards [of the World Missionary Conference] who had been chosen by the Student Christian Movement from among its leaders in the Universities became, in later years, outstanding leaders in the ecumenical movement'.[7]

Moreover, many of these young men went on to make lasting contributions to the new 'orthodox liberalism' and the 'Social Gospel' approach to Christianity — both being twin pillars of ecumenism. Men such as Neville Talbot (1879-1943), Walter Moberly (1881-1974), John Baillie (1886-1960) and William Temple (1881-1944) are but a few of the better-known names who involved themselves in Ecumenism and the 'Social Gospel' throughout their lives.

Although the only resolution of the World Missionary Conference in 1910 was the establishment of a full-time 'continuation committee', it was to have far-reaching consequences in the history of the professing Church. For this 'continuation committee' constituted

> 'the first-ever representative, inter-denominational organisation to be formed and, with its originating committee, is regarded as the beginning of the modern ecumenical movement'.[8]

Perhaps the most important ecumenical enthusiast to emerge from the World Missionary Conference was William Temple. He was a lifelong socialist and champion of the 'Social Gospel' — the idea that the preaching of the Gospel can be best fulfilled through social activism and the promotion of societal change. Significantly, William Temple's theological position has been described by one reputable source as *'Hegelian Idealism'*.[9] He was rector of St. James' Church, Piccadilly, London from 1914 to 1917. This so-called 'church' was to become — and is still to this day — the principal centre for syncretism, occultism and libertarian politics in the Church of England.

Eventually, William Temple became Archbishop of Canterbury — although Winston Churchill had delayed the appointment because of Temple's left-wing views and membership of the Labour Party. He pioneered the now common

---

6 Ibid.

7 Ibid., p.8.

8 J.D. Douglas (ed.), *The New International Dictionary of the Christian Church* (Zondervan, 1974), p.329.

9 *Encyclopaedia Britannica*, 15th edition, 1985, Vol.XI, p.625.

tradition of bishops criticising governmental policy, and was president of the Workers' Educational Association from 1908-1924. Most important of all, it was largely through the initiatives of William Temple that the World Council of Churches (W.C.C.) and the British Council of Churches were to come into being. As the first president of the World Council 'in process of formation' in 1938, and first president of the British Council in 1943, he was to make the ominous, prophetic statement about the new Ecumenical Movement which he helped to develop: *'Almost incidentally the great world-fellowship has arisen; it is the great new fact of our era'*.[10]

Although many others nurtured at the World Missionary Conference also made major contributions to the progression of the Ecumenical Movement, the conference itself gave birth to three major developments:

- The International Missionary Council in 1921.
- The World Conference of Faith and Order (convened in Lausanne 1925, Edinburgh 1937), designed to sort out doctrinal questions which divided churches.
- The Universal Christian Conference on Life and Work (convened in Stockholm 1925, Oxford 1937). This was designed to deal with 'the relationship between Christ and economics, industry, social and moral problems, international relations and education'.

It is interesting to note that the slogan of the Life and Work Conference was 'Doctrine Divides; Service Unites'. The significance of applying this slogan to bodies of Christian believers should not be overlooked; for it undermines the unique foundations of the faith which was originally delivered to the Church by Christ through the Apostles (2 Tim.1:13; Jude 3), and for which the Fathers of that Church had contended against all heresy and denial in order to preserve its integrity for future generations. It is true that Christianity creates division in the world — between believers and unbelievers; but that has been decreed by the Lord Jesus Christ Himself (Luke 12:51; Jn.15:19-21) and is a natural outcome of the Gospel (e.g., Jn.7:43; cf. Gen.3:15). Insofar as true believers are concerned however, it would be far more biblical to affirm that 'True Doctrine Unites; Service Sanctifies'. The sum of Christian Truth, of which the Church is the *'pillar and ground'* (1 Tim.3:15), can never truly divide the faithful, even though there may be superficial differences of opinion.

In 1948, the Life and Work Conferences united with those on Faith and Order to form the World Council of Churches. Thirteen years later the International Missionary Council merged with the W.C.C. to become the section of 'World Mission and Evangelism' within the World Council. This was a watershed development. As one objective observer so succinctly puts it:

> 'Thus the world mission of the Church was brought into the very centre of the Ecumenical Movement'.[11]

---

[10] Carl McIntire, *Servants of Apostasy* (Christian Beacon Press, 1955), p.229.

[11] *Encyclopaedia Britannica*, Vol.XVI, 15th edition, 1985, p.297.

The organiser of the World Missionary Conference in 1910, John R. Mott, had gone on to become chairman of the International Missionary Council in 1921 and, in 1948, he became co-president of the World Council of Churches, which came into being largely as a result of his work.

Political-Utopianism

One of the most controversial aspects of the World Council of Churches — and one which has caused many people to question its credibility as a custodian of the Christian Gospel — is the fact that it has shown a consistently 'political-utopian' line through giving support to a wide variety of left-wing revolutionary causes.[12] Although within the W.C.C. there has always been a professed concern for human rights, this was rarely made on behalf of those violated by the Soviet Union when it held its reign of terror over Eastern Europe. This state of affairs had been encouraged by the fact that in 1961 the Orthodox Churches of Russia, Bulgaria, Romania and Poland were accepted into the World Council.

One gets the distinct impression that the World Council of Churches is a globally-based 'ecclesio-political' organisation rather than a genuine expression of *spiritual* Christian unity throughout the world. Although it is fronted with a Christian confession (albeit a very limited one), it is in reality a syncretistic organisation promoting 'Liberation theology' — the inevitable outcome of its structure and its doctrinal position, having been thoroughly infiltrated by antichristian forces. In the words of one discerning reviewer, the World Council of Churches is *'an example par excellence of situation ethics and the double standard'.*[13]

In many ways, the W.C.C. represents the fulfilment of the preoccupation of many portions of the Church with the establishment of 'Political-Utopianism' — in which the attempted building of the kingdom of God on Earth takes precedence over the preaching of the biblical Gospel. This deception can take a number of forms. One such form is Liberation Theology — the reformation of the world through revolutionary politics.[14] Although Roman Catholics have been spearheading this movement, many Protestant organisations have also been propagating and supporting the use of revolutionary protest and even uprisings against the authority of the state in the cause of social change. The World Council has played its own role in this respect. When its Central Committee Meeting was held in Moscow in July 1989, a grand reception was provided in the St. George's Hall of the Great Kremlin Palace. In a major speech, the then General Secretary of the

---

[12] For further information on this, see **1.** *The World Council of Churches: A Soviet-Communist Catspaw in Africa* (Canadian League of Rights, 1976); **2.** Bernard Smith, *The Fraudulent Gospel: Politics and the World Council of Churches* (Canadian Intelligence Publications, 1978); **3.** *Readers' Digest*, August 1982, January 1993. Canadian Intelligence Publications' address is Box 130, Flesherton, Ontario, Canada, NOC 1EO.

[13] John Cotter, *A Study in Syncretism: the Background and Apparatus of the Emerging One-World Church* (C.I.P., 1979), p.61. This book is highly recommended.

[14] For an excellent basic overview of Liberation Theology, read *Family Protection Scoreboard: Liberation Theology Special Edition*, available from P.O. Box 10459, Costa Mesa, CA 92627, U.S.A.

W.C.C., Dr. Emilio Castro, referred to the writings of Karl Marx as including *'hopes and dreams about a new humanity and a future transformed for the better'.*[15] He then went on to state that *'Marxists and Christians in significant measure share a common source for such longings, which makes it possible for them to do much together'.*[16] Although Marxism appears to be a spent force in the world today (with the exception of Nelson Mandela's African National Congress), this statement demonstrates the true leanings of the W.C.C. and the willingness of its leaders to bend the Scriptures to suit their aims. In fact, the activities of the W.C.C. represent the realisation of the perennial Communist dreams. In the U.S. Congressional Record of January 10th 1963, forty-five worldwide goals of Communism were listed, many of which are now being fulfilled. Goal No.27 reads:

> 'Infiltrate the churches and replace revealed religion with "social" religion. Discredit the Bible and emphasise the need for intellectual maturity which does not need a "religious crutch"'.

This is surely being fulfilled through the World Council of Churches today, a 'united nations' of churches preaching liberal theology and the social gospel — a mixture of leftish politics and social action programmes, masquerading as a Gospel-inspired, Christ-promoting endeavour. What becomes of the real Gospel when it is submerged under such quasi-political aims and manoeuverings? What will be the attitude to the unique claim of salvation through the atoning blood of Christ? Will this biblical claim be suppressed in the interests of 'unity'?

Many people, of course, claim that being attentive to human rights, feeding and clothing the poor, helping 'Liberation' groups and guerillas is the work of the true Gospel, and that preaching the Word may be offensive to people from different faiths. There is a well-known story related to this which tells of an occasion when Francis of Assisi was confronted by his brothers after a long day which they had spent tending to the sick and the poor. They remonstrated with him for not preaching the Gospel, which he countered by telling them that this was precisely what they had been doing through their work. But to use such a tale in support of the social gospel is highly disingenuous. Of course Christians should be in the forefront of work which cares and nurtures and loves — for the Church first and then for those outside where appropriate and possible (Gal.6:10). But what is the point of 'liberating' people from 'structural oppression', starvation and poverty if we do not give them the **real** *'bread of life'* (Jn.6:27,35; cf. Mk.6:34)? When Jesus performed the miraculous feedings of the five thousand and four thousand, he was providing a living parable about what He does for human souls — the eternal condition of which is more important than the temporal state of their bodies.

Throughout Jesus' earthly ministry, He preached the Word night and day, obediently submitted to the civil authorities (e.g., Mt.17:24ff.) and never criticised the Roman colonialist oppressors of Israel (Mt.8:5ff.; 22:21). In contrast to the 'Liberation theologians' and 'Social Gospellers' of our own day, Jesus' prime concern

---

[15] *Christian News*, September 25th 1989, p.13.

[16] Ibid.

was not about changing the secular affairs of a morally, politically and spiritually corrupt humanity. When He performed a miracle, He was not simply doing folk a 'good turn' — He was signalling to the (especially Jewish) world that the Messiah had arrived. He performed these 'signs' as a proof of His Divine authority and majesty, not to create a more healthy, peaceful and just society or to found a universalist, multi-faith earthly brotherhood (cf. Mt.10:34-35; Lk.12:51-53).

As an example of the cock-eyed thinking in these ecumenical circles, let us briefly examine a couple of statements in a nationwide study course organised jointly by the British Council of Churches and the Catholic Truth Society. This was entitled 'What on Earth is the Church For?' and was part of the Lent 1986 ecumenical activities 'Not Strangers but Pilgrims'. In the course's study book — prefaced with a commendation from the liberal Archbishop of York, John Habgood — the theme of ecumenism was constantly stressed, while the familiar call for the creation of a 'New Church' which would be more relevant to the modern world, formed the backbone of its philosophy.

After claiming that *'Christians need a threefold conversion — to Christ, to the church and to the world'* (cf. Rom.12:1-2), we find the following statement:

> 'Different churches and different groups have different understandings of the world and of the church's mission in it. To caricature the extreme viewpoints: some churches believe that the world is in the power of the devil and is doomed to destruction, and that the church's task is to bring Christ's salvation to as many individual people as possible by bringing them into a personal knowledge of Jesus Christ and into the holy community of the church, the saints who are being prepared for heaven in the next world'.[17]

This is not, as the study guide claims, *'an extreme viewpoint'*. It is a close enough approximation to the biblical view (1 Jn.5:19-21; Gal.1:3-4; 6:14; Phil.3:17-21; Rom.8:5; 2 Cor.4:16-18; 5:1-4; Col.1:13; 2:8-10,20; 3:1-4; 2 Pet.3:10; Rev.21:1). It is certainly far closer to the overall message of the Bible than the social gospel. Nevertheless, the above section of the Lenten ecumenical Study Guide concludes: *'What happens in the next world is God's concern. Our best preparation for it is our work on behalf of the poor and oppressed in the world'*.[18] This could not be more clearly contrasted with the words of Paul the Apostle, when he tells us that *'our citizenship is in heaven, from which we also eagerly wait for the Saviour, the Lord Jesus Christ'* (Phil.3:20; see also 2 Cor.4:16 – 5:5).

In contrast to the politicking ecumenists of today, the Lord Jesus Christ said that the poor *'have the gospel preached to them'* as a priority over mere material sustenance (Mt.6:19-21; 11:5; 26:11). The spiritual work of the Church (especially feeding on the Word) should always take priority over feeding people with mere manna (Dt.8:3; Job.23:12; Ps.119:103; Isa.55:1-2; Jn.6:27,49-50), while its

---

[17] Martin Reardon, *What on Earth is the Church For?* (BCC/CTS, 1985), p.8.

[18] Ibid.

material work should be a natural outgrowth of this movement of the Spirit. But when the Scriptures are persistently interpreted through the eyes of liberation theology, the fundamental doctrines of the Christian faith drop out of view.

An illustration of this occurred a few years ago when the Labour-controlled council in Manchester proposed sending out Christmas cards which featured a picture of the South African Marxist, Nelson Mandela. The Anglican Bishop of Manchester, socialist Stanley Booth-Clibborn, rushed to the council's defence when it was criticised for attempting to carry out a cheap publicity stunt. Kenneth Leech, the Church of England's 'senior race relations adviser' also added:

> 'The gospel of incarnation is all about God taking human flesh and entering into human lives, and if that is the case, which is what Christians believe and what Christmas is about, something which draws attention to injustice and oppression in South Africa would be highly suitable'.[19]

Leaving aside the salient fact that Mandela was in jail for terrorist crimes, in one sentence this bishop reduces the miraculous incarnation of God to a justification for Liberation Theology. The belief that Christians should become involved in the revolutionary movements of the world in order to straighten out the planet is based on a huge misunderstanding of the Gospel and of what it means to build the kingdom of God, which the Lord Jesus said *'does not come with observation'* (Luke 17:20) and therefore cannot be set up on earth. The kingdom of God is, rather, a spiritual edifice made up of individuals who respond positively to the Gospel of Christ and who will therefore inherit eternal life in the age to come. Although Christians are certainly called on to *'do good to all'* (Gal.6:10), history shows that wherever there is an emphasis on *social* rather than *spiritual* change in the outreach ministry of the churches, the former eventually comes to eclipse the latter. In the modern Ecumenical Movement — and especially in the World Council of Churches — we can observe the consummation of a 'social gospel', the advocates of which, even sixty years ago, could make the bold assertion that they

> 'must construct new models, new pageantry, new hymns, new forms of prayer, new anthems of praise, new dramatizations in which, for example, the Labour Movement may be caught up in the embrace of religion, and the scientific movement, and the peace movement, and the civic conscience, and the community spirit, and the family life, and every great human aspiration of our time'.[20]

It is no coincidence that 'political-utopianism' is becoming the norm in many evangelical circles today, in which it is increasingly common to find support for such concerns as Third World liberation movements, Feminism, the Peace Movement, 'Gay' Liberation, etc. Thus, in one evangelical publication, we find the ambiguous assertion that *'We must engage in a double listening, both to the voice of*

---

[19] *The Guardian*, October 15th 1986.

[20] Charles Clayton Morrison, *The Social Gospel and the Christian Cultus* (Harper & Bros., 1933), pp.67-68.

feminists and to the voice of God'.[21] Of course, we must be sensitive to others in terms of our evangelism; but this does not mean that the Christian who is rooted in the fullness of Scripture can have anything to learn from the secular ideology of Feminism. It is certainly true (and very sad) that the special gifts of women have often been ignored, and even suppressed, within many churches, due to the paranoia of certain men in authority. But the antidote to this dilemma lies in obedience to the overall position of the Bible on the work of women in the Church, rather than in being deferential to the philosophy of women's liberation (feminist-utopianism), behind which lies the increasingly popular religious expression of goddess-worship and witchcraft.[22]

Once one gains a true understanding of, and a deeper insight into, the real origins and aims of the political-utopianism (whether Christian or otherwise) which is now such a radical part of the Ecumenical-Interfaith Movement, it can easily be recognised as yet another device of Satan to distract the Church from its necessary *spiritual* Gospel mission and service, while at the same time allowing opportunity for the intrusion into the Church of ideologies which are completely opposed to the Word of God and the cause of Christ. As Anglican minister Philip Blair puts it, in a recent book which superbly exposes the folly of the social gospel,

> 'Let the Church remain true to her task, to her single abiding mission, that of sharing with all men — whatever their race, background, outlook, politics, social or moral standing — a transcendent message of unparalleled hope... We live today in a world which, racked by doubt and disaster, cries out for a hope beyond itself. Let the Church offer to such a world what she has it in her power to offer. Let her not, for the living bread, offer a stone'.[23]

All the socio-political activity which we see today in the Church is the lamentable end-product of the World Missionary Conference in Edinburgh in 1910 — a meeting originally intended to improve the mission-work of the Gospel of Jesus Christ. Through these naïve attempts to take the Church into the world, the world has been brought into the Church, and as a result the latter has become increasingly corrupted and subject to apostasy. Unfortunately, the organisers of that original World Missionary Conference had failed to reckon with the denominational liberalism, politicisation of mission, religious corruption and other forces which would mould their work into a very different creature. This brings us to the second phase of ecumenical development.

---

21 Kathy Keay (ed.), *Men, Women and God* (Marshall Pickering, 1987), p.vii.

22 For full details of the origins and true direction of Feminism, see Chapter 8, 'Daughters of Babylon'.

23 Philip Blair, *What on Earth? — The Church in the World and the Call of Christ* (Lutterworth Press, 1993), p.83. For a revealing analysis of the antichristian historical background to Socialism and Political-Utopianism see, for example, Nesta Webster, *The Socialist Network* (London, 1926), and *Secret Societies and Subversive Movements* (London, 1924). Available from Bloomfield Books, 26, Meadow Lane, Sudbury, Suffolk, CO10 6TD, U.K.

II. FROM ECUMENISM TO SYNCRETISM
Christianity and the Interfaith Movement

Many Christians do not realise that in the World Council of Churches there has been, over the years, a subtle shift from exclusively inter-denominational ecumenism to syncretistic multi-faithism. This extension of ecumenical fellowship began in earnest with the retirement in 1966 of the first General Secretary of the W.C.C., Dr. Willem Visser 't Hooft. He was an ardent lifelong *opposer* of syncretism and, ironically, wrote a passionate book outlining its dangers. In this work, he was at pains to point out that syncretism poses *'a far more dangerous challenge to the Christian Church than full-fledged atheism is ever likely to be'*.[24] Shortly before his retirement, Dr. Visser 't Hooft had expressed his firm conviction that the Gospel *'is to be given in its purest form... in accordance with the biblical witness and unmixed with extraneous or cultural elements'*.[25] However, once he had left office in 1966, the way was opened to all those within the W.C.C. who wished to see the word *ecumenical* used more broadly, so that it would embrace all people of any religion rather than the narrower world of the Christian believer.

This was first apparent at the Fifth Assembly of the World Council of Churches in Nairobi in November 1975, when representatives from non-Christian religions — Judaism, Islam, Hinduism, Buddhism and Sikhism — were for the first time invited to present papers. After hearing the plea from the new Secretary of the World Council of Churches for *'a dialogue with people of other faiths, people of other ideologies or of none'*, a handful of members walked out (including the Bishop of London, Graham Leonard), protesting their impotence to change the syncretist direction in which the World Council of Churches was heading.

The New Babel

To aid us in our understanding of the occult connections in these events, let us open up a most revealing association here. The Hindu representative who was invited to present a paper at this 1975 World Council of Churches Assembly was Professor K.L. Seshagiri Rao, the editor of a magazine called *Insight*, published by a syncretist organisation known as the 'Temple of Understanding'. This was in stark contrast to the situation thirteen years earlier when the World Council of Churches had refused a request to sponsor this 'Temple of Understanding' on the basis that it was *'dangerously syncretic'*.[26] This global multifaith group, branded by its founders as the *'Spiritual United Nations'*, was set up in the U.S.A. in 1960 to represent all the religions of the world and to promote interfaith dialogue and education. Many well-known celebrities have given their public blessing to this syncretist 'Temple', including Eleanor Roosevelt, the Dalai Lama, Nehru, Anwar Sadat, Mother Teresa and the former Secretary-General of the United Nations, U Thant. At the time that it was founded, Dr. Albert Schweitzer said, *'My hopes*

---

[24] Willem Adolf Visser 't Hooft, *No Other Name: The Choice Between Syncretism and Christian Universalism* (SCM Press, 1963), p.10.

[25] An interview in *Christianity Today*, quoted in J.D. Douglas (ed.), op. cit., p.1021.

[26] From an article on the 'Temple of Understanding' in *Life Magazine*, Dec. 1964.

and prayers are with you in the realization of this great Temple of Understanding, which has a profound significance... The Spirit burns in many flames',[27] a reference to the idea that all religions — which, as far as interfaithists are concerned, includes Christianity — are diverse expressions of the same essential deity.

The 'Temple of Understanding' was the brainchild of a wealthy American woman who had studied comparative religion at Union Theological Seminary in New York. By 1963, it had been sponsored by six thousand politicians, occultists, celebrities, one-world religion advocates and multinational companies, including Robert McNamara (then U.S. Secretary of Defence; later head of the World Bank), financier John D. Rockefeller IV, Dr. Henry A. Smith (President, Theosophical Society of America), Walter N. Thayer (President, New York Herald Tribune), James Linen (President, Time-Life Inc.), Milton Mumford (President, Lever Bros.), Barney Balaban (President, Paramount Pictures), Thomas B. Watson Jnr. (President, IBM), Richard Salant (President, CBS News), Cary Grant (Hollywood actor), Dr. Martin Israel (now an Anglican vicar and renowned teacher in the Church of England); the Presidents of Egypt, India and Israel; representatives of Methodist, Unitarian, Episcopalian, 'Spiritualist', Lutheran and Presbyterian churches; various U.N. officials; and many others.

Since its inception thirty years ago, this 'Temple of Understanding' has organised a highly influential series of 'World Spiritual Summits' in Calcutta (1968), Geneva (1970), Harvard University (1971), Princeton University (1971), Cornell University (1974), and the Episcopalian Cathedral of St. John the Divine in New York (1984). More recently, the Temple of Understanding was a major sponsor of the 'Parliament of the World's Religions' in Chicago in August 1993. It is also an official Non-Governmental Organisation within the United Nations, through which it has done much to promote interfaith dialogue, as we shall later show.

Some readers may wonder what this 'New Babel' could have to do with the World Council of Churches and Christian Ecumenism. One minute we are reporting on a gathering of Christians in Edinburgh with a global missionary interest, the next minute we are speaking of strange temples, spiritualists, film stars and international financiers! Just how did we move from one to the other? We made this leap simply by looking at the sphere of influence of one man who was a key speaker at the Fifth World Council of Churches Assembly: Professor K.L. Seshagiri Rao, editor of the 'Temple of Understanding' magazine, *Insight*. Although it is true that many modern Christian ecumenists have no interest whatsoever in multifaith syncretism, they have failed to grasp the historical fact that once the World Council of Churches had been established by well-meaning (but naïve) Christians, it became the concentrated focus of all those who saw in it the potential for a global body which could be the harbinger of *world religion* rather than the ecumenical Christianity envisioned by its original founders.

East Comes West

It is important for us to realise that the process leading from the World

---

27 From the current official leaflet of the 'Temple of Understanding'.

Missionary Conference in 1910 to the formation of the World Council of Churches and its offspring did not take place in a vacuum. In September 1893, only seventeen years before the World Missionary Conference in Edinburgh, the first 'Parliament of the World's Religions' was held in Chicago. Virtually every religion in the world was represented there. To demonstrate the 'ecumenical' nature of this gathering, John Henry Barrow, pastor of the First Presbyterian Church in Chicago, was head of the organising committee, while the proceedings were opened with the Lord's Prayer by the Roman Catholic Cardinal Gibbons. For seventeen days the Parliament continued, as 140,000 visitors were exposed for the first time to the teachings of Eastern religion. The importance of this event for the development of syncretism can be seen in the fact that one occultist organisation, the Theosophical Society, rejoiced in this Parliament as being a fulfilment of its aims and *'distinctly a Theosophical step'*.[28] During this gathering, there can be no doubt that the star of the show was the Hindu mystic, Swami Vivekananda (1862-1902), who came over from India with a deliberate missionary objective. His influence on the subsequent development of interfaith dialogue cannot be over-estimated. As one writer has put it:

> 'It is true that Emerson and others had paved the way towards "transcendental religion", but it was left to Vivekananda to give this idea a practical application for people of widely divergent opinions and temperaments'.[29]

In his blasphemous book, 'The Sea of Faith', the Anglican priest Don Cupitt writes approvingly of Vivekananda, while informing us of the significant fact that

> 'Two of his doctrines became part of the consciousness of the West. He spread the idea that all religions are one, treading different paths to the same goal... the union and indeed the identity of the soul with God. Secondly, he rejected the Christian idea of sin, and taught that by living a virtuous life you can realise God in yourself'.[30]

In the same section of his book, Cupitt had also spoken approvingly of theosophist Annie Besant and her Society's *'dreams of founding a universal Church of Man that would draw together socialists, radical Christians and freethinkers'*.[31] Is it conceivable that Christians — who have a commission from Christ to evangelise the unbelieving nations (Mt.28:19), and who know that salvation cannot be attained through personal endeavour (Eph.2:8-10) — could have a genuine 'dialogue' with those who hold such antichristian beliefs, whether it be Don Cupitt,

---

[28] Carl T. Jackson, *The Oriental Religions and American Thought: Nineteenth Century Explorations* (Greenwood, 1981), p.252. This book, by the Professor of History at the University of Texas (who is also a Zen Buddhist), gives a clear and scholarly account of the penetration of Western culture by Eastern Mysticism in the previous century.

[29] Marcus Toyne, *Involved in Mankind: The Life and Message of Vivekananda* (Ramakrishna Vedanta Centre, 1983), p.61.

[30] Don Cuppitt, *The Sea of Faith: Christianity in Change* (BBC, 1984), p.175.

[31] Ibid., pp. 173-174.

Annie Besant or Swami Vivekananda? Vivekananda, who went on to found the influential Vedanta Society in the U.S. and Europe, was a disciple of the Indian mystic Ramakrishna Paramahamsa (1834-1886), whose meditations were

> 'directed indifferently to the revelation of God in divine and prophetic figures of many religions, whether the Great Mother or Krishna or Jesus or Mohammed; he taught therefore the essential unity of all religions'.[32]

The influence of such thinking on Vivekananda's work at the 'First Parliament of the World's Religions' represented a watershed in the movement of Eastern mysticism to the West. As his official biographer has noted:

> 'Swami Vivekananda foresaw the great interchange between East and West that is taking place at the present time. This interchange would lead to a complete world civilisation'.[33]

These developments had also been foreseen many years beforehand by another advocate of the blending of East and West. In 1851, the philosopher and mystic Arthur Schopenhauer, made an extraordinarily prophetic statement:

> 'At present we may perceive shining through in the writings of the learned, the nature pantheism of India, which is destined sooner or later to become the faith of the people. *Ex oriente lux* [from the East comes light]... In India, [Christianity] will now and never strike root: the primitive wisdom of the human race will never be pushed aside by the events of Galilee. On the contrary, Indian wisdom will flow back upon Europe, and produce a thorough change in our knowing and thinking'.[34]

This mystical philosopher was here predicting the phenomenon which would fulfil every ambition of the religious syncretists in these last days. The hidden agenda behind all interfaith gatherings is not the encouragement of friendly dialogue but the deliberate infiltration of Eastern mysticism into the heartlands of Christianity. Forty years after the writings of Schopenhauer, during the 'Parliament of the World's Religions' in 1893, Vivekananda had also made it clear that his aim was nothing less than the creation of *'a society compounded of Western Science and Socialism and Indian Spirituality'*.[35] It does not involve much research to discover the extraordinary degree to which this aim has now been fulfilled. We have already shown the extent to which the New Physics, Socio-Political Utopianism and Eastern Mysticism have become united in their neo-Gnostic approach to the questions of human existence, spirituality and the future course of planetary development.

---

[32] John Ferguson, *Illustrated Encyclopaedia of Mysticism and the Mystery Religions* (Thames & Hudson, 1976), p.207.

[33] *The Story of Vivekananda* (Advaita Ashrama, 1970), p.71.

[34] Quoted in F. Max Müller (Trans. & Ed.), *The Sacred Books of the East: Vol.XV* (OUP, 1900), 'The Upanishads', Vol.I, pp.lxi-lxii, lxiv.

[35] John Ferguson, op. cit., p.207.

A Canterbury Tale

Three thousand people attended the 1893 Parliament, including representatives of Deism, Judaism, Islam, Hinduism, Buddhism, Jainism, Taoism, Confucianism, Shintoism, and the *'three largest branches of Christianity'*. Significantly, the then Archbishop of Canterbury, Edward White Benson, declined an invitation to attend the Parliament. Responding to a request for support, he wrote:

> 'I am afraid that I cannot write the letter which... you wish me to write, expressing a sense of the importance of the proposed conference, without its appearing to be an approval of the scheme. The difficulties which I myself feel are not questions of distance or convenience, but rest on the fact that the Christian religion is the one religion'.[36]

How times have changed! Today, it is impossible to coax an Archbishop to say, without any qualification, that Christianity *'is the one religion'*. Less than one hundred years later, Edward Benson's successor at the See of Canterbury, Dr. Robert Runcie, has eagerly attended numerous multifaith gatherings. Among these was a syncretistic international convergence of 150 religious leaders of the world at Assisi in 1986, all in the name of 'peace'. This gathering was also attended by the Roman Pope, the General Secretary of the World Council of Churches, together with Baptist and Methodist world leaders. The rest of the entourage included Shinto priests, Buddhists, North American 'medicine men', and other ethnic shamans. It was remarkable to see these professing ambassadors for Christ praying for the peace of the world along with a number of modern-day religious leaders whose beliefs and practices include idolatry, sorcery and pantheism. Actually, one can only find true peace — that is, inner peace — through faith in Jesus Christ (Jn.14:27; Rom.5:1). Jesus did not come the first time in order to bring world peace (Mt.10:34). For the peace of the nations, we must wait for His second coming (Rev.21:1-4; cf. Isa.2:1-4; 11:1-10). In spite of their gropings after worldly peace, the only element which really binds these people together is their erroneous mutual belief that there is a single river which runs through all religions, a mystical stream, travelling under a variety of different names: God, the goddess, Universal Spirit, Great Mother, the Life Force, the Tao, Ch'i, Ki, Brahman, Atman, Allah, Kami — call it whatever you will.

During Dr. Robert Runcie's time of office as Archbishop of Canterbury, the Church of England was led promiscuously into the seductions of syncretism. His attendance at Assisi is entirely in harmony with his multifaith convictions. It is interesting to note that on November 21st 1983, Dr. Runcie's wife, Rosalind, gave a piano concert in Lambeth Palace in aid of the World Congress of Faiths — one of the big four international organisations devoted to global interfaithism.[37] This was surely a portent of an ever-deepening involvement with the Interfaith Movement. On 28th May 1986, Dr. Runcie gave the 'Sir Francis Younghusband Memorial Lecture' at Lambeth Palace to mark the fiftieth anniversary of the World

---

[36] Quoted in James Webb, *The Occult Underground*, (Open Court, 1974), pp.67-68.

[37] Advertised in *Interfaith News*, No.3, Autumn 1983, p.2.

Congress of Faiths. In this role, Dr. Runcie followed an eminent line of previous 'Younghusband' lecturers, such as Dr. Ursula King (Lecturer in Theology at Leeds University, founder of the 'Teilhard de Chardin Centre' in London, and author of 'The New Mysticism'), Sir George Trevelyan ('guru' of the New Age Findhorn Community in Scotland), and Professor K.L. Seshagiri Rao ('Temple of Understanding' journal editor). One becomes accustomed to finding the same names recurring in every area of syncretistic activity. The one situation intertwines with the other in this developing web of intrigue.

The contents of Dr. Runcie's 'Younghusband Memorial Lecture' make most interesting reading. In view of its syncretist leanings, it is hardly surprising that it has never been placed among his officially published sermons. After praising various heathen idols and deities for their relevance and beauty, venerating 'Christian' ashrams in India (ecumeno-speak for syncretist Hindu-Catholic shrines) and commending Eastern 'spirituality', Dr. Runcie affirmed the Hegelian notion that *'all religions possess a provisional, interim character as ways and signs to help us in our pilgrimage to Ultimate Truth and Perfection'*.[38] As if this was not enough of a compromise on the uniqueness of Christian truth, the Archbishop finally confessed that his chosen pathway of dialogue with other religions *'will mean that some claims about the exclusiveness of the Church will have to be renounced'*.[39] Although it is true that in fine ecclesio-political fashion he professed a disinterest in *'a single-minded and synthetic model of world religion'*,[40] he concluded apocalyptically by quoting with approval what he described as *'a remarkable prophecy'* of Arnold Toynbee which claimed that

> 'the present century would be chiefly celebrated by historians hundreds of years hence as the time when the first sign became visible of that great interpenetration of eastern religions and Christianity which gave rise to the great universal religion of the third millenium AD'.[41]

Robert Runcie's successor at Canterbury, Dr. George Carey, appears to be equally ambivalent towards the uniqueness of the Gospel with which he has been entrusted to evangelise the nations. In March 1992, he broke a 150-year-old tradition by turning down an invitation to become patron of the Anglican 'Church's Ministry Among the Jews', declaring that it would be unhelpful in his efforts to *'encourage trust and friendship between different faith communities in our land'*.[42] Later, we will see that the Archbishop's understanding of a 'faith community' is considerably broader than that of the Apostolic fathers of the Church he claims to represent.

The syncretist, compromised example of these men has not been lost on those serving in the Anglican Church ministry. So widespread is the notion that Christianity is just one option out of a number of religious choices, one is hard-pressed

[38] Robert Runcie, *Christianity & World Religions* (World Congress of Faiths), p.10.
[39] Ibid., p.13.
[40] Ibid., p.14.
[41] Ibid.
[42] Reported in *Christian News*, Vol.30, No.44, November 30, 1992, p.6.

to discover many clergy who will assert that there is no other name apart from Jesus Christ through whom people can be saved. As one of many examples of such syncretism today, when the 'Religious Leaders Association' in Salem, Massachusetts, officially welcomed a high priest witch into its ranks, the local Anglican-Episcopalian priest, Randal Wilkinson, said that *'nobody in the interfaith clergy support group could think of any compelling reason to forbid the witch from joining'.*[43] When asked about the presence of this leader of a Wiccan coven — the Temple of the Black Rose, which *'gathers to worship the raw forces of nature'* — in the interfaith clergy group, Wilkinson said: *'We needed to make a positive statement about including people of different religions. These witches don't mean any harm. We don't discriminate based on creed'.*[44] This is a dark day for God's people. When so many professing Christian shepherds openly declare that the disciples of Christ and the witches of the devil walk down the same spiritual road, surely Satan's *'little season'* must almost be upon us.

The Fall of the House of Windsor

At this point, having considered the contributions of Anglican Archbishops, one may wonder what the Queen — as Governor of the Church of England and alleged 'Defender of the Faith' (*Fidei Defensor*)[45] — would make of all this interfaith activity in the the denomination under her 'Governorship'. Perhaps we have a hint in the fact that her husband, the Duke of Edinburgh, in his capacity as President of the Worldwide Fund for Nature (W.W.F.) officiated at its 25th Anniversary gathering in Assisi in September 1986. The main theme was the connection between nature conservation and the religions of the world, during which the Duke gave a speech exhorting what he called 'the five great faiths of the world'

> 'to come together to listen and to share perspectives derived from spiritual experience and from the stores of wisdom and understanding which the great religions have gained over the centuries'.[46]

It is clear the the Royal Family in Britain is wholeheartedly behind the moves towards syncretism today. In 1989, three years after the fiasco in Assisi, a UPI despatch from the United Nations claimed that Britain's Prince Philip had

> 'launched a global interfaith organisation that will translate into English key texts of world religions. Prince Philip said the publishing venture will involve texts of the Baha'i sect, Buddhism, Islam, Christianity, Hinduism, Judaism, Sikhism and Taoism'.[47]

That the Worldwide Fund for Nature should have climbed on the ecumenical,

---

[43] *Christianity Today*, September 13th 1993, p.58.

[44] Ibid. It is interesting to recall here that the Church of England minister William Perkins (1558-1602), when comparing black and white magic in his 'Discourse on the Damned Art of Witchcraft', wisely said that the white variety *'is the worser of the two'.*

[45] This can still be seen on every U.K. coin, next to the date, as 'D.G. Reg. F.D.'.

[46] From the Duke of Edinburgh's speech during the WWF church service at Assisi, September 29th 1986. Recorded live on BBC Radio 4.

[47] *Toronto Sun*, May 23rd, 1989.

multi-faith bandwagon is hardly surprising. First, the W.W.F. is one of a number of front organisations for the Bilderberg Group — a shadowy organisation with a hand behind the formation of a secret world government — with which Prince Charles, the Duke of Edinburgh and Prince Bernhard of the Netherlands have been closely associated. Second, the connection between the earth and human 'spirituality' has been the anti-monotheistic province of paganism for millennia. The fertility cults which were in constant conflict with the nation of Israel were a classic expression of this. Today, the 'Greens' and ecologists have revived these pantheistic concepts and practices, referring to the planet as *'Gaia'* — the Greek goddess and name for Mother Earth,[48] often referred to by polytheists as *'the oldest of divinities'*.[49] Although a healthy concern for the earth's environment and its wildlife is thoroughly biblical (Gen.1:26-31; 2:15; Pro.12:10; Dt.25:4), some simple research into the many branches of 'green politics' and ecology today shows that there has been a grand revival of the ancient, pagan, pantheist, fertility-cult approach to nature.[50] Parallel to this development, people with 'one-world', syncretist ambitions have been steadily infiltrating environmental groups and other organisations with an international influence, in order to achieve their aims. The global outworking of these activities will become increasingly clear during the remainder of this watershed decade of Church history.

The Coming Confederation of Religions

The information which we have given so far denotes, in no uncertain terms, the pattern of all current international ecclesiastical developments. We are witnessing in our time the culmination of the progressive gathering, throughout this century, of all the religions, philosophies and faiths of the world into one ecumenical confederation. Many Christians would reject this as pessimistic speculation; but they do so either in ignorance or in the spirit of the ostrich.

We are not referring specifically to a monolithic one-world religion, for that would be virtually impossible, in view of the underlying separatism and discordant dogmas involved. But we are envisaging a future coming together of denominations, cults, sects and religions of the world in such a way that they cooperate as a common body, along similar lines to the United Nations — professing to share a common goal, yet still retaining their individual identities. However, despite their differences, this league of religions will be most united in three particular areas:

- To foster the view that *all* religions (in which they mistakenly include Christianity) share the same God and are one in their ultimate ambitions.
- To create permanent world peace and justice through cooperation with a similarly-confederated form of world government (e.g., the United Nations).

---

[48] See, for example, J.E. Lovelock, *Gaia* (Oxford University Press, 1979).

[49] Barbara G. Walker (ed.), *The Woman's Encyclopedia of Myths and Secrets* (Harper & Row, 1983), p.332.

[50] This is apparent from the content of such journals as those of the Wicca-based *Women for Life on Earth* (who also started the Greenham Common Peacecamp), *The Sacred Trees Trust Newsletter*, and *Resurgence* (edited by Satish Kumar).

- To propagate the concept that biblical, evangelical Christianity is a hindrance to 'evolutionary' progress and spiritual growth on this planet.

It is these areas of united purpose which represent the 'hidden agenda' of the Ecumenical and Interfaith Movements now at work across the globe. What does the Bible reveal regarding this agenda? A parallel is surely to be found in the 'Mystery of Lawlessness', which had already begun in the time of Paul the Apostle and which is leading to the greatest deception ever to engulf the Church (2 Th.2:1-12). It involves an apostasy from the faith and the building of a global confederation which goes far beyond the confines of the Church as manifested in the world. It is the culmination and fulfilment of that political and religious conglomerate which Satan has contrived to build on Earth, through the schemings of sinful men, ever since his tyrannous ambitions were first confounded by the Triune God at Babel, in the land of Shinar (Gen.11:1-9; cf. Rev.13:1-18; 17:7-18).

Extremely rapid changes have been taking place throughout this century in the circles of the world's religions, and in the way they are seeking to work together. As soon as the bid for an ecumenical unity in Protestantism had started in Edinburgh in 1910, the forces working towards the development of the Interfaith Movement — which had emerged as a result of the 'Parliament of the World's Religions' in 1893 and the ensuing widespread enthusiasm for comparative religion — began to worm their way into the resulting organisations. Immediately after the 'Universal Conference on Life and Work' in Stockholm in 1925, an openly interfaith gathering was held: the 'Universal Religious Peace Conference'. As a result, even Dr. Visser 't Hooft, the first General Secretary of the World Council of Churches, was forced to confess that

> 'Some Stockholm leaders confused the picture by organising immediately after the Stockholm Conference a movement called the *'Universal Religious Peace Conference'* which stated that it did not want to mix the religions, but did in fact move towards syncretism by publishing a book of devotions taken from the Scriptures of all religions'.[51]

By 1930, when the 'Laymen's Foreign Missions Inquiry' was held, one of the main conclusions of this influential report was that the Christian *'should regard himself as a co-worker with the forces within each such religious system which is making for righteousness'*.[52] The necessary contrast between the Church and the antichristian forces of the world then became subject to unprecedented erosion. But the influences generating this movement towards an interfaith ideology were not confined to apostate ecclesiastical circles. In another revealing link, the World Council of Churches 'Ecumenical Institute' at Boissy, near Geneva, was financed with a $1,000,000 grant from John D. Rockefeller, the international financier and owner of the prestigious Chase-Manhattan Bank.[53] Later in this chapter, we will come to understand why there should be a connection between the forces

---

[51] W.A. Visser 't Hooft, op. cit., pp.108-109.

[52] W.E. Hocking, *Rethinking Missions*, Harper, 1932, pp.326-327.

[53] *Time Magazine*, December 8th 1961.

of international finance and those of global ecumenism.

Significantly, towards the end of his life, the original 1910 World Missionary Conference organiser, John Mott, began to have *'grave reservations about a world body not motivated by missions, and [to have] fears that the World Council [of Churches] might swallow the International Missionary Council'*.[54] Such fears were well-founded; for the second deviation from 'first-phase ecumenism' came with the removal of independent missionary concern from the International Missionary Council when, in 1961, that organisation was absorbed into a World Council of Churches which would become increasingly syncretistic. Thus the W.C.C. had successfully brought a major arm of international Christian mission work within the domain of an Ecumenical Movement which was in the process of compromising with the world. The stage was now set for the third and final phase in ecumenical development.

III. FROM SYNCRETISM TO UNIVERSALISM: All One in Adam

A major shift in ecumenical thinking occurred when there was a subtle but far-reaching change in the way that the word *Ecumenism* is defined. In his second BBC Reith Lecture in 1978, Dr. Edward Norman, Dean of Peterhouse College, Cambridge, rightly noted the fact that

> 'The word **ecumenical** itself has changed its meaning, and is now used by the World Council of Churches to mean, not just fellowship within the different Christian bodies, but within the entire human race'.

In the wake of this shift, what we call *Ecumenism* has now come to involve the concept spoken of as *'the integrity and unity of all creation'*. These are the new 'buzz-words' in ecumenically-minded churches, which, along with the utopian-idealist phrase *peace and justice*, forms part of the slogan of the current 'Decade of Evangelism' in the U.K. This concept of 'the integrity of all creation' in ecumenical affairs stresses not so much the common ground of all Christian denominations, or even of all religious faiths but, rather, the idea of the mutual essence of all *creaturehood*. In other words, for the new breed of ecumenist, Christian Unity has come to have its significance in the *Brotherhood of Man* rather than in the *Children of God* — in the earthly bonds of the first Adam rather than in the mystical Body of Christ.

This is surely a most pernicious development, of which many believers may be entirely unaware. There had been a portent of this at the Fifth Assembly of the World Council of Churches in Nairobi in 1975, when there had not only been a plea for *'a dialogue with people of other faiths, people of other ideologies or of none'*, but also a call for *'a radical transformation of civilisation'*.[55] The fact that the Church should suddenly concern itself with the radical transformation of the structures of this present fallen world (rather than the spiritual heart of humanity) is entirely in harmony with the twentieth century upsurge of Neo-Gnosticism —

---

[54] C. Howard Hopkins, op. cit., p.689.

[55] Bernard Grun, *The Timetables of History* (Simon & Schuster, 1991), p.580.

the religious impulse of which centres on the 'transformation of matter', as we have often recorded throughout the pages of this book. As an example of the pervasiveness of this new ecumenical idea of 'the radical transformation of civilisation', we discover this same tendency in the writings of the ecumenical leader, the Roman Catholic Archbishop of Westminster, Cardinal Basil Hume, from whom there is the strange claim that

> 'Christians recognise the unity of all things and their inherent goodness despite the effects of human waywardness and sin. They also see God's presence everywhere, manifesting itself even in unlikely places and people. The Church is not a lone force in the building of God's kingdom on earth but makes a unique contribution to a world where many forces operate for the education, healing and developing of the world's peoples'.[56]

In this statement, Cardinal Hume was echoing Pope John XXIII when he said that *'the Church today is faced with an immense task: to humanise and to Christianise this modern civilisation of ours'*.[57] According to the Cardinal, the Church is just a transitory development until the moment that the entire world is made one in Christ — an event which is allegedly being brought about through many different organisations cooperating with the Church in the building of the kingdom of God on earth. As Cardinal Hume puts it: *'When the whole of creation is caught up into a single symphony of love, the kingdom of God will have reached fulfilment and God will be all in all'*.[58] Rejecting the biblical data on eternal life and endless punishment (2 Th.1:7-9), the spiritual battle between the forces of light and the powers of darkness (Eph.6:10-13), and all the implications of the imputation of Adam's sin (Rom.5:12ff.), Cardinal Hume believes that those of us who *'fail to recognise the inherent goodness of all created things'* have much in common with the third century dualist gnostic heresy known as Manichaeanism; and he blames Augustine of Hippo (A.D.354-430) for bringing such 'heretical' notions into the Church.[59] Not only is that a complete misreading of the great North African theologian, but it also denies the Spirit-inspired teachings of the Apostle Paul, who had little regard for any *'inherent goodness of all created things'* when he uttered the anathematizing words in Rom.1:18-32 and 3:10-18, and who could only say of himself: *'For I know that in me (that is, in my flesh) nothing good dwells'* (Rom.7:18). What is more, the Apostle clearly stated that for unbelievers

> 'nothing is pure; but even their mind and conscience are defiled. They profess to know God, but in works they deny Him, being abominable, disobedient, and disqualified for every good work' (Tit.1:15-16).

One may also wonder what Cardinal Hume would do with the statements of the

---

[56] Cardinal Basil Hume, *Towards a Civilisation of Love: Being Church in Today's World* (Hodder & Stoughton, 1988), p.175.

[57] *Mater et Magistra*, May 15th, 1961.

[58] Cardinal Basil Hume, op. cit., p.171.

[59] Ibid., p.168.

Lord Jesus which clearly show that the One through whom all things were created (Col.1:16) did not at all regard fallen creatures as being 'inherently good' (e.g., Jn.2:24-25; Mk.7:18-23; Mt.7:11; 12:34; Lk.11:13). But this is the heterodox message of religious universalism being propagated by Cardinal Hume and the other leaders of the modern Ecumenical Movement. Although Jesus Christ, the Head of the Church, clearly proclaimed otherwise (Mt.7:13-14), the modern Ecumenical Movement has not only decided that the road that leads to eternal life is *broad* but also that, ultimately, *everyone* will inherit it as of their birthright. In this, it has aligned itself with the false doctrine of the religions of the world.[60]

Today, instead of holding that Christians are to take the exclusive message of the Gospel into the whole inhabited world, and then endure the difficulties and antagonism which will naturally arise (and which the Lord Jesus Himself forecast in Mt.10:32-42 and Jn.15:19), the modern Ecumenical-Interfaith Movement teaches that a spark of God indwells *every* person unconditionally, which can be kindled into flame through practising the various mystical techniques which can be found in all the religious systems of the world. In this way, true spirituality is presented as any means by which a person can realise personal 'Christ-consciousness', according to whatever tradition and culture in which one happens to be living. It is, after all, only a short phonetic step from Christ to Krishna!

When one understands the true nature of the spiritual battle today, the reasons behind all this ecumenical activity become clear. Because the new Ecumenical Movement no longer confines itself to the simple desire to propagate the Gospel throughout the whole inhabited world, it has failed to retain the distinctiveness which is necessary for the spreading of the Truth which sets men and women free. This is often referred to in theological literature as the 'Antithesis' — that God-ordained contrast between God's people and the children of the world (Gen.3:15; cf. Luke 12:51; Jn.7:43). When this necessary Antithesis is removed, the work of the Church becomes indistinguishable from the progressive humanistic ambitions of the nations and the spiritual aims of the New Age Movement, as they seek to build a global consciousness — a universal brotherhood fabricated on the pattern of humanity, with the religions of the world as the tapestry on which it is woven. *For this reason, religious syncretism and universalism must surely be the greatest threats to the Christian witness of the Church since it was almost destroyed by Arianism in the fourth century.* One of the major proponents of such influences is the United Nations, the religionist work of which we will now examine.

United Nations 'Oneness' Religion

We have already seen, in the previous section of this chapter, that a real acceleration in interfaith affairs occurred in 1975 at the Fifth Assembly of the World Council of Churches in Nairobi. It was in this same year that the United Nations became seriously involved in promoting interfaith activities by playing host to a so-called 'Spiritual Summit' which heralded a movement from syncretism to full-blown universalism. This conference, the first international religious meeting at

---

[60] For more on this, see ¶2, p.390 in Chapter 9.

the U.N. in its thirty-year history, had the highly significant title 'One is the Human Spirit'. Organised in celebration of the 30th Anniversary of the U.N. by the 'Temple of Understanding', it was held first at the Episcopal Cathedral Church of St. John the Divine in New York, culminating in a final meeting at the United Nations headquarters. After opening meditations by official U.N. meditation instructor Sri Chinmoy and an official welcome by the U.N. Secretary-General Kurt Waldheim, there were addresses by representatives of the 'five major faiths', with Mother Teresa supposedly representing Christianity. Shortly before the conference, the head of the Sufi Order triumphantly revealed to the press that

> 'Political leaders feel a kind of bankruptcy and despair and have become aware of the need for spiritual unity... That's why they're opening their doors to us'.[61]

We have here a perfect illustration of the mutual work of the two beasts portrayed in chapter 13 of the Book of Revelation. Through the auspices of bodies such as the United Nations and its 'Temple of Understanding', global religion and world government have become irreversibly intertwined. Shortly before its occurrence, the Chairman of this U.N. 'Spiritual Summit', Jean Houston (President of the New-Age-promoting 'Foundation for Mind Research' and co-author of the book 'Varieties of Psychedelic Experience') also made a revealing press statement claiming that

> 'We need to renew our rootage *in the deeper spiritual realities*, in the image and *oneness of humanity*, and *do it from within*. We need to draw on the fundamental resources of the human race, on the *taproots of existence*'.[62] [emphasis added]

The italicised Neo-Gnostic 'buzz-words' contained in this statement are a sure giveaway concerning the spiritual thrust of this 'Summit'. A variety of rituals (including a 'Cosmic Mass'), dances and discussions were held throughout this week-long event. The host at the New York Cathedral of St. John was its syncretist dean, the Very Rev. James P. Morton. In his opening speech, he recalled with admiration some words of Thomas Merton's closing speech at the Temple of Understanding's First World 'Spiritual Summit' in India in 1968, in which the priest had spoken of an essential unity between all people as he addressed the assembled delegates from every religion under the sun with the following words:

> 'Not that we discover a new unity. We discover an older unity. My dear brothers, we are already one. But we imagine that we are not. And what we have to recover is our *original unity*. What we have to be is what we already are'.[63]

Here we can see that the modern Ecumenical-Interfaith Movement grounds itself in the fallen race of Adam rather than in the regenerated people of Christ.

---

[61] *The Inquirer*, Vernon, Connecticut, October 18th 1975.

[62] Ibid.

[63] *The New York Times*, Tuesday, October 21st 1975.

But this is in contradiction to the Bible, which teaches that in Adamic unity there is only sin, endless death and enslavement to Satan; whereas in true Christian unity there is spiritual healing, eternal life and release from bondage to the devil (Rom.5:12ff.; 1 Cor.15:20-23,45-50; Col.1:13; Jn.6:47-58; Acts 26:17-18).

We have already catalogued the involvement of the United Nations as a major harbinger of the New Gnosticism in an earlier chapter. But let us just remind ourselves of the *spiritual* dimension of U.N. activity which has provided great support for ecumenical and syncretistic developments. Historically, the seduction of the United Nations into religious syncretism has been initiated primarily through the offices of three men. Two were Secretary-General of the U.N., Dag Hammarskjöld (1905-1961 – held office, 1953-1961) and U Thant (1909-1974 – held office, 1962-1971), and one was an Assistant Secretary-General, Dr. Robert Muller. In a book written to celebrate the philosophy of Pierre Teilhard de Chardin (and edited by Dr. Muller, a disciple of Teilhard), it was stated that

> 'Dag Hammarskjöld, the rational Nordic economist, had ended up as a mystic. He too held at the end of his life that spirituality was the ultimate key to our earthly fate in time and space'.[64]

If readers are wondering what kind of 'spirituality' Dag Hammarskjöld advocated, a leaflet about the United Nations Meditation Room written under his direction stated that its eerie lodestone altar *'is dedicated to the God whom man worships under many names and in many forms'*.[65] In 1973, the U.N. Secretary-General U Thant — who was also a Thai Buddhist mystic — formed the organisation 'Planetary Citizens' with Donald Keys, an international New Age activist who has close links with the Neo-Gnostic Findhorn Community. 'Planetary Citizens' is an influential Non-Governmental Organisation within the U.N., and is described as being *'devoted to preparing people for the coming of the new culture'*.[66] In other words, it is a harbinger of the Neo-Gnostic New World Order.

Another major player in the increasing commitment of the United Nations to interfaith universalism is Dr. Robert Muller. He first came to the U.N. in 1948, and was an Assistant Secretary-General there for many years. Today he is the influential Chancellor of the United Nations Peace University. As the editor and co-author of a book in honour of Teilhard de Chardin, who had apparently *'always viewed the United Nations as the institutional embodiment of his philosophy'*,[67] Dr. Muller has stated:

> 'I believe that humanity on this miraculous, wondrous, life-teeming planet has a tremendous destiny to fulfil and that a major transformation is about to take place in our evolution'.[68]

---

[64] Robert Muller (ed.), *The Desire to be Human: A Global Reconnaissance of Human Perspectives in an Age of Transformation* (Miranana, 1983), p.304.
[65] Quoted in R.K. Spenser, *The Cult of the All-Seeing Eye* (C.B.C.A., 1962), p.9.
[66] J. Gordon Melton (ed.), *New Age Encyclopedia* (Gale Research Inc., 1990), p.357.
[67] Robert Muller (ed.), op. cit., p.304.
[68] Ibid., p.17.

This is a pure statement of the 'Hundredth Monkey Theory' which we discussed in an earlier chapter.[69] In the context of this present chapter, it is interesting to note that Dr. Muller has also written a book entitled 'Shaping a Global Spirituality' (Doubleday, 1978/82). In another of Dr. Muller's books, 'Decide to Be', we are given a glimpse into the 'spirituality' that the Interfaith Movement is building through the offices of the United Nations. One passage reads:

> 'Decide to open yourself to God, to the Universe, to all your brethren and sisters, to your inner self... to the potential of the human race, to the infinity of your inner self, and you will become the universe... you will become infinity, and you will be at long last your real, divine, stupendous self '.[70]

As a further recent indicator of the depth of the involvement of the United Nations in the interfaith movement from syncretism to religious universalism, a meeting was held at the U.N. on April 15th 1992 in which the Roman Catholic theologian, Professor Hans Küng, Director of the Institute for Ecumenical Research at the University of Tübingen, Germany, gave a talk entitled 'Global Responsibility: A New World Ethic in a New World Order'. Organised jointly by the 'Temple of Understanding' and the 'Pacem in Terris' [Peace on Earth] Society and attended by two hundred guests in the Dag Hammarskjöld Auditorium, the conclusion of this meeting was that

> 'the United Nations has the potential for leading the way in global ethical considerations. The Golden Rule offers the nucleus of what could be a declaration of world ethics. UNESCO is focusing on these ideas... The topic will also be explored at the Parliament of the World's Religions to be held in Chicago in 1993'.[71]

The so-called 'Golden Rule' — that we should behave toward others as we would have them behave toward us — has been used by many in the Interfaith Movement as a starting point for a 'Confession of Faith' which will foster syncretic universalism. Because variations on such a saying can be found in all the world's religions, as well as in the Bible, it is concluded that both they and Christianity have the same underlying goals. However, there are some profound misunderstandings in the notion that the saying of the Lord Jesus in Mt.7:12 proves that all religions have a common foundation.

In the first place, the context of this saying — the Sermon on the Mount — was addressed primarily to Jesus' disciples rather than to the whole world (cf. Mt.5:1-2). It was referring primarily to *spiritually regenerated people* — to those *'chosen out of the world'* by Jesus Christ (Jn.15:16-19). This teaching of Jesus was revealed to the world in the Word of God to make us aware of our complete

---

[69] See Chapter 4, §2.

[70] R. Muller, *Decide to Be*, p.2. Published by the U.K. New Age Journal, *Link-Up* (now called *Planetary Link-Up*) in 1986.

[71] From the article 'Dr Hans Küng at the United Nations', in *The Temple of Understanding Newsletter*, Summer 1992, p.1.

spiritual inadequacy without a Divine Mediator. It should convict us of sin, showing us that only through God's appointed Saviour can we hope to *'do'* the Sermon on the Mount as well as merely aspire to it (cf. Mt.7:24). As Professor Gresham Machen lucidly highlighted, as early as 1923, in his comparison of true Christianity and theological liberalism:

> 'Strange indeed is the complacency with which modern men say that the Golden Rule and the high ethical principles of Jesus are all that they need. In reality, if the requirements for entrance into the kingdom of God are what Jesus declares them to be, we are all undone; we have not even attained to the external righteousness of the Scribes and Pharisees, and how shall we attain to that righteousness of the heart which Jesus demands? The Sermon on the Mount, rightly interpreted, then, makes a man a seeker after some divine means of salvation by which entrance into the Kingdom can be obtained... The Sermon on the Mount, like all the rest of the New Testament, really leads a man straight to the foot of the Cross'.[72]

The real reason that the so-called Golden Rule is such a favourite with ecumenists, interfaithists and universalists is because it means that a reductionist religious ideal can be formed which denies the fullness and necessary divisiveness of the Gospel of Jesus Christ. Removed from its context, it can be made to conform to the ethical, philosophical and religious doctrines of the world. So let us beware of those who wish to wrest this teaching from its context and make it into a neat universalist 'soundbite' on salvation by works, while linking up nicely behind the New Age teachings of the 'Universal Fatherhood of God' and comfortable programmes promoting global 'love and peace'. A religious ideal which is built on the delusion that we can attain to the high spirituality of the Sermon on the Mount without a true faith in **all** the unique Messianic claims of Jesus Christ — and the new life which He alone brings — has its foundations in sinking sand rather than on the Rock of Ages. What must be faced is that the creation of a 'Declaration of World Ethics', a common global religious norm based on the so-called 'Golden Rule', would have serious implications for the international spread of the Christian Gospel if it ever becomes enforceable by international law — which, as we shall see, is not beyond the bounds of possibility.

When the second 'Parliament of the World's Religions' was held in Chicago in 1993, a 'declaration of world ethics' formulated by Dr. Hans Küng and rooted in the so-called 'Golden Rule' — which would later be ratified by the United Nations — formed a major part of its considerations. Entitled 'A Declaration of a Global Ethic', the motivation behind it is clearly shown in Dr. Küng's statement to his U.N. audience in the Dag Hammarskjöld Auditorium on April 15th 1992: *'If we want to overcome fundamentalism we have to do it in a constructive way'.*[73] Let it

---

[72] J. Gresham Machen, *Christianity and Liberalism* (Eerdmans, 1985), p.38.

[73] From the article 'Dr Hans Küng at the United Nations', in *The Temple of Understanding Newsletter*, Summer 1992, p.1.

not be forgotten that for the Interfaith advocate, 'fundamentalism' is not confined to certain forms of Islam but is also identified with Evangelical Christianity. This 'Declaration' will, in effect, constitute the 'basis of faith' or 'collective creed' of the confederated religions of the New World Order, by which the strongly missionary and evangelistic foundation of Christianity will be made out to be 'divisive to the human family' and will become increasingly subjected to the forces of suppression. If we wish to identify a likely spiritual vehicle for a gathering Armageddon, we need look no further than the 'oneness' religion being manufactured through the auspices of the United Nations.

The Parliament of the World's Religions

It would be revealing for us here to explore the context and outworking of the second Parliament of the World's Religions which considered this 'Declaration', as it represents a 'quantum leap' in Ecumenical-Interfaith activity.

The year of 1993 was designated as 'The Year of Inter-Religious Understanding and Cooperation', and numerous 'Interfaith Summits' were held throughout that year as part of the centenary celebrations of the first 'Parliament of the World's Religions' a century beforehand in Chicago. The centre-piece of the 1993 celebrations was the week-long second 'Parliament of the World's Religions' in the same location. From August 28th – September 5th, 1993, the ballroom of the exclusive Palmer House Hilton Hotel in Chicago, U.S.A. was given over to the second Parliament of the World's Religions, which was sponsored by 125 religious interests, including 'Christian' ecumenical bodies such as the 'National Council of Churches', the 'National Conference of Christians and Jews' and the 'World Alliance of Reformed Churches'. Also sponsoring the Parliament was the 'Covenant of the Goddess', a witchcraft-based pagan cult popularised by the feminist witch Starhawk.[74]

Over 4,500 delegates from all over the world attended, including representatives of Orthodox, Protestant and Roman Catholic 'Christianity', and those of Baha'ism, Buddhism, Confucianism, Hinduism, Jainism, Judaism, Islam, Native American Shamanism, Wicca (witchcraft), Shintoism, Neo-Paganism, the polytheistic Native African Yoruba cult, Sikhism, Taoism, Unitarianism, Zoroastrianism, etc. The Parliament, chaired by Dr. David Ramage, President of McCormick Theological Seminary in Chicago, was opened with a silent meditation led by Sri Chinmoy, official spiritual guru to the United Nations (and also to world government puppet Mikhail Gorbachev!), followed by some 'blessings' from a variety of religious influences. One of these was brought by a High Priestess of the pagan Temple of Isis, whose devotions were given *'in the name of the 10,000 names, the spirits, the birds, reptiles and trees'*.[75]

For almost $1000 per head (including hotel accommodation), those attending

[74] Readers will recall that Starhawk (alias Miriam Simos) is a much-favoured guest at the Anglican St. James' Church, Piccadilly in London. She is also the author of *The Spiral Dance: The Rebirth of the Ancient Goddess* (Harper & Row, New York, 1979), in which details are given of how to 'hex' a person through inserting pins in a small doll.

[75] BBC Sunday Programme, August 28th 1993, 0750 hrs. BST

could indulge in a great many activities and experiences. There were keynote presentations from a number of well-known religious personalities, such as Roman Catholic Cardinal Joseph Bernardin, United Nations Peace University Chancellor Dr. Robert Muller, Dr. Hans Küng, Mother Teresa (who was unable to attend through illness), comparative religionist Diana Eck, Harvard Divinity School liberal theologian Harvey Cox, and the ubiquitous Dalai Lama. More than 500 seminars were held, with such titles as 'The Role of the High Priestess in the Temple of Isis', 'Euthanasia', 'Human Abduction by UFOs – Its Significance for the Future', 'Humanism – The Modern Alternative to Traditional Religion', 'The Return of the Goddess', 'AIDS as Social Symbol', 'Christian Reflections on the Bhagavad Gita', and 'Spiritometry – the Scientific Step Towards God'. There was a variety of 'interfaith celebrations, meditations and contemplative vigils', coupled with 'sacred art, music, dance, poetry and theatre'. There were 'Neo-Pagan' concerts, Theravada Buddhist group chantings and other exotic entertainments. Ta'i Ch'i and Hindu meditations were held before breakfast each morning; and in every nook and cranny of the hotel during that week, characters could be found posing in meditational *asanas* from every tradition imaginable!

In spite of all these syncretistic activities, the Parliament has received the official sanction of many professing Christian leaders, including the Archbishop of Canterbury, Dr. George Carey, who said in a statement of support: *'Few things are more important to our world today than the growth of mutual respect and understanding between different faith communities'*.[76] One has to stretch the term 'faith communities' some considerable way in order to make it embrace Neo-Paganism, Theosophy, Shamanism, witchcraft and polytheism — all of which figured so prominently at this Parliament.

Ironically for a conference which was supposedly dedicated to *'promote understanding and cooperation among religious communities'*, it was dogged by its own disputes and factionalism. Four Jewish organisations withdrew from sponsorship after a few days when Louis Farrakhan of the controversial 'Nation of Islam' was allowed to participate. The Greek Orthodox Diocese of Chicago also withdrew on August 30th because *'it would be inconceivable for Orthodox Christianity to establish a perceived relationship with groups which possess no belief in God or a supreme being'*.[77] One proposal put forward by the American Indian Committee requested that New Agers, neo-pagans and those practising *wicca* (witchcraft) should stop using Native American sacred rites just to make money out of Shamanism[78] — a request which was highlighted by the fact that one of the sponsoring religions, the witchcraft-based Covenant of the Goddess, successfully applied to the Parliament's organising committee to hold a *wiccan* Full-Moon Ritual in Chicago's Grant Park during the conference. As a further example of the 'promotion' of religious understanding and cooperation at the Parliament (and providing an invaluable glimpse into the hidden agenda of the Ecumenical-Interfaith

---

[76] *English Churchman*, No.7357, August 20th-27th, 1993, p.1.

[77] *Christianity Today*, October 4th, 1993, p.43.

[78] *Christian News*, September 20th, 1993, p.15.

Movement), a priest from the Orthodox Church, in a seminar on the subject of 'Satanism in West Texas', said that *'it is good to study the Fundies [Fundamentalists] so that you will know your enemy'*.[79]

The formulation of a successful 'Global Ethic' document has also highlighted the shortcomings of this Parliament. Because such a document had to be rendered as acceptable to witches and neo-pagans as to dedicated Roman Catholics and Baptists, it had to speak extremely vaguely and avoid all reference to such modern ethical minefields as abortion and euthanasia. The ethics in these areas of those influencing interfaith developments are by no means beyond reproach. When the Dalai Lama, in his closing speech to the Parliament, said that when a human sperm and an egg join *'it creates a precious life'*, he immediately joked: *'But now we have too much precious life!'*.[80] What price is abortion and euthanasia for the 'Holy Ones' of the East?

All this shows just how difficult it would be to create a single one-world religion which would be satisfying to all the various religious strands in the world. For this reason, the most likely scenario in the years following this Parliament will be the gradual formation of a 'World Council of Religion' which will function in a way similar to that of the present World Council of Churches or the United Nations. Indeed, one of the main lectures at the Parliament was entitled 'A Proposal To Evolve the Parliament Toward a United Nations of Religions'. In his keynote speech, United Nations executive Dr. Robert Muller called for the establishment of a permanent World Council of Religion by 1995, along the lines of the United Nations. Although a number of delegates were sceptical about the setting up of an actual World Council of Religion, it was generally felt that this Parliament brought the global interfaith movement one step nearer to much closer collaboration. Dr. David Ramage, who chaired the Parliament, saw the next step as one of setting up centres of interfaithism in various key regions of the world and then networking relationships between them.[81] However, others saw the setting up of a global religious council as a very real possibility during the next few years.

It is interesting to note that an article in 'Sunrise' — the official journal of the Theosophical Society, a co-sponsor of the Parliament — spoke of the upcoming event as seeding the climate of world thought *'so that those having leadership responsibilities in the 21st century will banish intolerance from every phase of human experience'*.[82] When one recognises that Evangelical Christianity is regarded as part of the 'intolerance' which they wish to banish, then the hidden agenda behind the Interfaith Movement and this Parliament becomes easy to comprehend. Indeed, as one perceptive observer has noted:

> 'At the 1893 Parliament, the theme was the "Fatherhood of God". [But in the 1993 Parliament] this theme seemed to be missing, leaving only the "Brotherhood of Man" as a theme. By ignoring mutually exclusive

[79] Ibid.

[80] Ibid.

[81] BBC World Service *Focus on Faith* programme, Thursday, Sept. 2nd, 1815 hrs GMT.

[82] *Sunrise: Theosophic Perspectives*, Vol.42, No.1, October/November 1992.

> truth claims about a personal God and stressing [instead] good works by issuing the Global Ethic document, the Parliament may have unwittingly set up a litmus test for the validity of religion — a sort of "religious correctness"'.[83]

How would evangelical Christianity fare if it had to face such a 'litmus test'? If the new 'Global Ethic' which 'banishes intolerance' was to be made international law and policed by the United Nations or a future World Council of Religion, we can easily imagine what fate would befall the mission of the Christian Gospel. It will be interesting to discover the worldwide developments which take place in the wake of this 1993 Parliament. In many ways, the first such Parliament in 1893 was an event before its time. The world was still dominated by a nominal Christian Commonwealth, and the then Archbishop of Canterbury, Edward White Benson, refused to attend or give his support, declaring that Christianity was *'the one religion'*. Today we live in a very different world which is clamouring for peace, unity and stability **at any cost**. For this reason, 1993 constitutes a watershed year in Church history, compounding an international religious movement which is fervently opposed to biblical, Apostolic Christianity.

Enfleshing the Teachings of Jesus

A great many other groups and conferences — far too numerous to mention — have contributed to this new, universalist phase of interfaith activity. One U.K. organisation which has been in the forefront of the creation of this new universalism is the National Association of Christian Communities and Networks, which has been based in the Selly Oak Colleges complex in Birmingham since 1981. Now known as the National Centre for Christian Communities and Networks (NACCCAN), this organisation claims to be *'the most diverse yet ecumenical body of Christian groups linked together in the United Kingdom'*.[84] In a report for the 'Lent '86 Inter-Church Process' sponsored by the British Council of Churches in 1986 (known as 'Not Strangers, but Pilgrims'), NACCCAN offered replies to the question 'What on Earth is the Church For?' The conclusions provide us with a classic depiction of the new universalist ecumenism. In a section significantly headed 'NACCCAN Groups Believe that the Church Exists For the Transformation of the World into the Kingdom of God', one answer claimed that *'the church is about enfleshing the teachings of Jesus'*. Among the many ways suggested for this enhancement of Christ's teachings were *'the development and preservation of our planet'*, and *'the growth and development of one human family on earth'*.[85]

One intelligence document shows that there are over four hundred political and religious organisations which were loosely connected with NACCCAN, including one hundred Roman Catholic ecumenical groupings. Although the development

---

[83] Keith Edward Tolbert, Director of the American Religions Center in Trenton, Missouri, U.S.A., writing in *Christian News*, September 20th, 1993, p.15.

[84] *Towards a New Vision of Church* (NACCCAN, September 1986).

[85] Ibid., pp.3-5.

of NACCCAN was distinctly amorphous, it had definite roots in, and connections with, such organisations as 'ONE for Christian Renewal', a radical political grouping of Baptists, Methodists and Roman Catholics set up in 1970, and the 'Christian Peace Conference', a former Soviet front-organisation set up in Prague in 1958 which operated worldwide within Christian churches and was controlled by the International Division of the Communist Party.

The NACCCAN report, 'Towards a New Vision of Church', also stated its commitment to the establishment of what it called 'A New Form of Church' working through small quasi-autonomous groups and networks — the detailed description of which bears an uncanny likeness to the New Age Movement concept of 'networking'. Among the groups contributing to this conference and report were the Christian Campaign for Nuclear Disarmament (CCND), the Anglican New-Age-promoting St. James' Church, Piccadilly, the Christian Ecology Group, the Roman Catholic pacifist group Pax Christi, and the syncretist Teilhard de Chardin Centre in London. Readers who may be wondering what this 'New Form of Church' will be like, will be interested to know that the founder of the Teilhard de Chardin Centre and lecturer in Theology at Leeds University, Dr. Ursula King, has said that *'we are in need of a global, worldwide ecumenism which goes beyond the ecumenism of the Christian churches by being truly universal'.*[86] In her book, 'Towards a New Mysticism', Dr. King calls for a religious confederation of world faiths, with the following remarks:

> 'Taking full cognisance of the religious experience of mankind may produce what has been called a "global religious consciousness". It may bring with it a profound transformation, a mutation in religious awareness and a new awakening to what is most central to all faith and genuine spirituality... The experience of an emerging global society has brought with it the idea that we must develop a new consciousness and identity as world citizens'.[87]

In all these developments, we can see the prolific planting of seeds which would spawn the new universalist approach to Christian ecumenism, with its confusion between the kingdom of God and the kingdoms of the world, the Christian people of God and the Adamic family of man. However, it will not suffice for discerning and concerned Christians to shout empty rhetoric about these matters. We must strive to develop a real understanding of all the forces which have led to this phenomenon which has deceived so many within the churches today: things such as national sin and unbelief, an underestimation (or even negation) of the power of Satan, ignorance concerning the diabolic origin of the world's religions, and so on. And when we do strive for an understanding of these phenomena, we will come to see the special place which the Vatican has played in this evolving process. To this we will now turn.

---

[86] Ursula King, *Towards a New Mysticism: Teilhard de Chardin and Eastern Religions* (Collins, 1980), p.226.

[87] Ibid., pp.229-230.

IV. THE VATICAN CONNECTION

So far, in these pages, we have examined the links between Christian Ecumenism and religious syncretism primarily so far as bodies within Protestantism are concerned. However, this process is also being nurtured through the ambassadorship of the Church of Rome. The World Council of Churches does not 'contain' the Roman Catholic Church. This is because the Vatican still regards itself as the only true Church with a genuine 'apostolic succession', as well as having the supreme primacy and *ex cathedra* infallibility of the Pope as head of the Church, and therefore as its sole representative throughout the world. However, the monolithic Church of Rome has activated its own massive, international ecumenical programme, with considerable effectiveness, at both denominational and multi-faith levels.

The increasing global power of the W.C.C. in the 1950s must have been both a daunting and a mouth-watering prospect to the Roman Church: daunting, because of the possibility of being upstaged by the 'opposition'; mouth-watering, because of the potential of sweeping a vast range of ecumenical Protestant groupings under its wing. Bearing in mind the Roman belief that *'the Catholic apostolic work is based on a certainty that we are members of Christ's single and visibly united Church'*,[88] one can imagine the mixed response in the Vatican to the Study Guide for the Second Ecumenical Conference of the W.C.C. in 1954, which stated:

> 'Our first resolve must be to apprehend the meaning of the statement...that oneness in Christ is the sure mark of the Christian Church. Do we believe this? Are we ready to consider the consequences of such a belief ? Let us understand at once that this means that there is no Church at all apart from Christ... It is forever true that Christ and his Church are one and indivisible... There can no more be a number of Churches than there can be a number of Christs, of incarnations, crucifixions or Holy Spirits. The Church is one as Christ is one'.[89]

Through statements such as these, the Vatican came to realise that a powerful, globally-active, Protestant Ecumenical Movement had been well-established through the World Council of Churches. How would the church aspiring to global Christian dominion manage to capitalise on this? In the Second Vatican Council's 'Decree on Ecumenism' (1964), Pope Paul VI announced a major change in the official Catholic attitude towards those of other denominations and of other religions. Although maintaining its historical assertion that *'only through the Catholic Church of Christ, the universal aid to salvation, can the means of salvation be reached in all their fullness'*, for the first time in its history it was willing to admit that there were genuine Christians — 'separated brethren', as it called

---

[88] John M. Todd, *Catholicism and the Ecumenical Movement* (Longmans, Green & Co., 1956), p.95. John Todd went on to co-create the Roman Catholic, ecumenical publishing house Darton, Longman & Todd (D.L.T.).

[89] Ibid., p.65.

them — outside the Roman fold.[90] The Vatican was now anxious to recall these 'separated brethren' back to their 'rightful home'. Rome had not failed to observe that, prior to the Second Vatican Council's 1964 Decree, there was a return in other denominations *'to the norm of central Catholic tradition'*.[91] At that time, there was a growing Roman Catholic awareness that in other denominations,

> 'the trend is undeniable. Many of the doctrines which were once anathema are gradually creeping back into acceptance. And with them come the Catholic practices... It is not for Catholics to look scornfully on these developments, but to be thankful for the steps which are being taken slowly but surely back to the norm, and to see in them the preparation of these bodies by God for their eventual return to full communion'.[92]

However, lest we forget what *'full communion'* means to the Roman Church, behind this awareness lies the ever-present assumption that

> 'Any return, corporate or individual, *must involve recognition of the Pope as the vice-regent of Christ.* Once an individual has reached the point of recognising this truth, he cannot stay outside Catholic unity, since he would in that case be refusing obedience to Christ in the person of his earthly vicar'.[93] [emphasis added]

The enticement to return to Rome was put into practice through the auspices of a permanent 'Secretariat for the Promotion of Christian Unity' (1960). The severance from Rome in the sixteenth century, which the Anglican vicar David Watson had once naïvely depicted as *'one of the greatest tragedies since Pentecost'*,[94] was about to be reversed. The twentieth century Counter-Reformation wooing-process had set out in earnest to bring all aspiring ecumenists back to Rome. In 1968, a Joint Working Group was initiated between the Vatican and the World Council of Churches known as the Committee on Society, Development and Peace (SODEPAX), and on a visit to the World Council of Churches Headquarters in Geneva, Pope Paul VI described the people there as *'a marvellous movement of Christians, of children of God scattered abroad'*.[95] The Italian weekly, *Il Borghese*, drily described the visit as

> 'a further step toward the creation of a sort of ecclesiastical United Nations where the Roman Catholic Apostolic Church will sit as equal among equals with a microscopic group of Anabaptists'.[96]

Today, a great many Protestant Evangelicals are avidly seeking to engage in

---

[90] Walter A. Elwell (ed.), *Evangelical Dictionary of Theology* (Baker Book House, 1984), p.341. Article on 'Ecumenism'.

[91] John M. Todd, op. cit., p.23.

[92] Ibid., p.23.

[93] Ibid., pp.xii-xiii.

[94] Quoted in *Peace and Truth*, 1979, no.1, p.9.

[95] John Cotter, op. cit., p.62.

[96] Ibid.

ecumenical activities with the Roman Catholic denomination and are eagerly responding to requests to join in events designed by the Vatican to encourage 'Church Unity'. Perhaps if they familiarised themselves with what the Roman Catholic religion involves, their zeal for such fellowship would be considerably reduced. Let us now reveal the religion propagated by the Vatican and that with which it seeks to involve the entire Christian Church.

Romanism is Syncretism

It will help our understanding considerably if we realise that when we are dealing with the Vatican, we are not dealing merely with one of many manifestations of professing Christianity; we are dealing with syncretism, pure and simple. This syncretism works on two levels, diffusive and infusive. On the *diffusive* level it has compromised with indigenous heathen religions everywhere it has taken its mission in the world. Among the more notable examples are in Latin America, where Romanism has easily blended itself with indigenous sorcery into occult religions such as *Umbanda.* In a recent BBC World Service report, journalist Ben Bradshaw spoke in some detail about the Brazilian Catholic Church's admission of local mysticism and spiritism into conventional Roman Catholic beliefs and practice.[97] In Guatemala, too, there has been an open blending of Romanism with the predominant indigenous *Mayan* religion, which can be observed in the major cathedrals. Over in India, we find the cult of 'Hindu-Catholicism' propagated by the monk Abhishiktananda (alias Dom Henri le Saux O.S.B.).[98] Jesuit missionaries in the lands of the East are renowned for being ready to *'soften the transition from oriental modes of thought to Christianity'*,[99] a tendency which has persisted to this present day. We should not be surprised, therefore, when a Jesuit theologian in India is reported as saying: *'The fact that members of the higher religions, such as Hindus and Buddhists, do not convert may be a sign that they are not meant to convert'.*[100] It is through means such as these that the diffusion of syncretism has been taking place through the auspices of Rome.

On the *infusive* level, many aspects of the religion of the Church of Rome are themselves a blend of the ancient satanic religion, as well as other derivative forms of paganism disguised with the trappings of Christianity. There must be many genuine believers within the Roman Catholic churches, but the false religion which the Vatican has been building for centuries, in common with other world religious powers, is not Bible-based Christianity. Nor is it a church a Bible-believer could approve of in any sense. With a little research, one can easily discover that Roman Catholicism is far more rooted in the cultic heritage of the nations than in the doctrines of the Bible. Because the leaders of the mystical-occult world religions of today recognise this fact, they are happy to forge links with the Pope as the 'vicegerent' of the 'Christianised' version of ancient pagan mythology, in the belief that the various mythologies of all faiths can be demonstrated to

[97] BBC World Service report on 20th August 1993 at 1345 GMT.

[98] See Abhishiktananda, *Hindu-Christian Meeting Point* (ISPCK, 1976).

[99] *Chambers's Encyclopaedia* (Newnes, 1963), Vol.VIII, p.81.

[100] From an article in the Jesuit magazine *America*, August 25, 1979, p.75.

be compatible with those of the false church, as a fitting preparation for the future political and religious climax of all time (cf. Rev.17:1-18; 20:7-10).

It requires only a modicum of intelligence to discern that the allegedly 'infallible' Popes, when acting *ex cathedra*, have given out a great many erroneous dogmas. Some of these dogmas centre on the person of Mary, the mother of Jesus, who they claim to have been free from all original sin from conception (1854) — in spite of her assertion, in the Bible, that she needed a Saviour (Luke 1:47) — and to have been *'raised body and soul to the glory of heaven'*, assuming the position of 'Queen of Heaven' at the right hand of her Son (1950, 1965). As far as the Bible is concerned, the only 'Queen of Heaven' is that mentioned in the book of Jeremiah (7:18; 44:15-30), which refers to the Babylonian goddess Ishtar, who assumed a variety of names throughout the Near East such as Astarte, Ashtoreth, Dea Syria, Venus, Aphrodite, etc. She was the goddess of sexual mysticism and was worshipped through sex-rites with temple prostitutes in a similar way to the sex-rites of the Far Eastern Tantric cult of Buddhism, from which the Lamaism of the Dalai Lama is partially derived. In this respect, it is interesting to note that the renowned Neo-Gnostic psychologist and occultist, Carl Jung, said that *'the most significant religious event since the Reformation was the Papal pronouncement in 1950 of the dogma of the Assumption of the Blessed Virgin'*,[101] on the basis that it represented the resurgence of the 'feminine principle' in religion which, according to many interfaithists, has been suppressed by the concept of the Jehovah of Judaeo-Christianity for far too long.

Many Protestants have also been seduced by this seductive worship of Mary. For example, in one Anglican journal an article claims that *'the Virgin Mary, full of grace, should be a focus of unity among Christians'*, as well as being worthy of the worship and praise *'due to His handmaid without whom the Word of God could not have been made flesh and dwelt among us'*.[102] Nowhere in the Bible is there the remotest notion that disciples of Jesus Christ should worship and praise His mother Mary. She was simply a humble woman who was blessed by God to be the divinely-ordained bearer of the Messiah on earth. She takes her place alongside countless other biblical servants who were chosen by God to play a human role in sewing the tapestry of redemption.

The advance of 'Mariolatry' (the worship of Mary) in denominations outside Rome is no chance happening. For there has been a deliberate evangelisation of the cult of Mary through the ecumenical movement. This was highlighted by Cardinal Suenens in his Malines Document 2:

> 'It is interesting to note the existence and success of the 'Ecumenical Society of the Blessed Virgin Mary'. Founded in London in 1970 by Martin Gillett, this international group aims to foster brotherly discussions on the subject of Mary among Christians of various traditions. These discussions are held in the friendly atmosphere of a spiritual gathering. The Society's specific charism is to transform a stumbling-

---

[101] Vincent Brome, *Jung: Man and Myth* (Paladin, 1978), p.254.

[102] *Anglicans for Renewal*, no.26, Summer/Autumn 1986, pp.13-14.

block — Mary — into a welcoming haven of reconciliation'.[103]

The occultists and Neo-Gnostics of today are well aware that the worship of Mary by the Roman Catholic Church is historically linked with the goddess cult of the ancient Babylonians and their successors, themselves believing that Mary serves only as a mythological consummation of all the goddesses of every pre-Christian culture.[104] One of the principal objections of the goddess-worshipping feminists of today is that Christianity in general is exclusively 'male-oriented and patriarchal'. However, the Mary-goddess of the Roman Church is seen to counterbalance this alleged deficiency, thus bringing it more into line with other world religions, with their bevy of goddesses and associated cultic practices. It is interesting to note here that in the development of the Greek Orthodox Church, the ancient shrines to Aphrodite (the Greek version of the Babylonian Ishtar) were simply transformed into shrines to the Virgin Mary when their particular mode of mystical Christianity moved into the ascendancy.

In the first few centuries A.D., the city of Rome had become a syncretistic dustbin for every cult in the empire, and when the Emperor Constantine professed the Christian faith, many of these traditions were gathered into the Church of Rome which he founded. This pagan link is unashamedly admitted by Roman Catholic leaders themselves. For example, in spite of his omission of the fact that Mariolatry is derived from pagan goddess worship, and that the Madonna and Child concept has been lifted from a number of comparable ancient cults, Cardinal John Henry Newman unashamedly confirms that

> 'The use of temples... incense, lamps and candles... the tonsure... turning to the East... perhaps the ecclesiastical chant and the Kyrie Eleison, are all of pagan origin, and sanctified by their adoption in the Church'.[105]

This lack of *biblical* support for Roman Catholic doctrine is brazenly admitted even by Cardinal Joseph Ratzinger, the chief enforcer of dogma in the Vatican and head of the 'Congregation for the Doctrine of the Faith'. In an article in *Time* magazine, the Cardinal explained his faith through the story of one of his theology professors, *'a man who questioned the thinking behind the church's 1950 declaration that the Assumption of the Virgin Mary into Heaven was an infallible tenet'.*[106] Apparently, this theology professor had concluded, regarding this doctrine: *'No, this is not possible — we don't have a foundation in Scripture. It is impossible to give this as a dogma'.*[107] The *Time* article then continues:

> 'This led the professor's Protestant friends to hope they had a potential

---

[103] Léon Joseph Cardinal Suenens, *Ecumenism and the Charismatic Renewal* (Darton, Longman & Todd, 1978), p.80.

[104] See Barbara G. Walker, op. cit., p.602.

[105] John Henry Cardinal Newman, *An Essay on the Development of Christian Doctrine* (Penguin Books, 1974), p.369.

[106] *Time*, December 6th, 1993, p.56.

[107] Ibid.

> convert. But the professor immediately reaffirmed his abiding Catholicism. "No, at this moment I will be convinced that the church is wiser than I"'.[108]

Ratzinger greatly admired this man's stance in upholding the dogma of the church over and against the witness of the Bible. Here we can see that the Roman Catholic church confessedly creates its own dogma without any reference to Scripture whatsoever. In other words, there is no final divine revelation by which to determine Christian doctrine. Thus, in common with a fundamental tenet of the New Gnosticism — that there is no objective reality — Roman Catholicism can be whatever anyone wants it to be. As the Neo-Gnostic scientist Lyall Watson has said: *'When a myth is shared by large numbers of people, it becomes a reality'.*[109] Although mingled with just enough truth to make it acceptable to the ignorant and undiscerning, the greater part of the Roman Catholic religion is based on myths (cf. 2 Tim.4:4), and is about as far removed from biblical, Apostolic Christianity as one can get.

Furthermore, in spite of its outward adherence to the name of Christ, the Church of Rome has provided more syncretists than any other branch of the professing Christian church. Indeed its entire mission hinges on a syncretistic pivot which is rooted in its Pelagian concept of salvation.[110] And the persistent Roman Catholic involvement in interfaith gatherings has lent a great deal of support to this notion.

When the Pope attended the pioneering interfaith gathering at Assisi in 1986, one lone voice protested on that syncretic occasion. A Roman Catholic follower of the traditionalist Archbishop Marcel Lefèbre braved the inevitable accusation of 'being negative' by handing out leaflets in the main square, telling reporters that *'the Pope is trying to make a super-religion with himself at the head'.*[111] This was an astute observation. He is not alone in his concern about the ecumenical, interfaith activities of the Vatican. Prof. Peter Beyerhaus, President of the International Conference of Confessing Fellowships — an umbrella organisation of conservative evangelicals — wrote to the Pope after the Assisi event telling him of his fear that such meetings could trigger off a *'crevasse of syncretism'* in many Christian churches.[112] In the course of his letter, Prof. Beyerhaus asked the rhetorical question: *'Is it now official Catholic teaching that the adherents of all religions worship the same God?'*.[113] Let us here go ahead and provide an answer to his question. It will not prove difficult. For example, the Roman church, in an

---

[108] Ibid.

[109] Lyall Watson, *Lifetide* (Hodder & Stoughton, 1979), p.158.

[110] Pelagius was a 4th century British monk who taught *'the heresy that man can take the initial and fundamental steps towards salvation by his own efforts, apart from Divine Grace'*, F.L. Cross & E.A. Livingstone (Eds.), *Oxford Dictionary of the Christian Church*, OUP, 1983, p.1058.

[111] *The Independent*, October 20th 1986, p.1.

[112] *The Christian Herald*, November 11th 1986, p.1.

[113] Ibid.

official publication, can brazenly make the following assertion:

> 'Even a person who does not explicitly know the Gospel may be saved by a positive response to the grace of God, expressed in a life motivated by true love and charity'.[114]

This statement is completely at variance with fundamental biblical teaching on the subject of salvation (see e.g., Job 25:4; Jn.10:1-2,9; 14:6; Acts 4:11-12; Romans 3:20,27-28; Galatians 2:16; 5:4; Eph.2:8-10; 2 Th.1:7-8; Tit.3:4-5), and instead promotes the notion that salvation comes through good works. The biblical view is that salvation comes by the grace of God to those who believe in the Lord Jesus Christ, with good works following. Salvation first, then good works. But Satan turns this right around (he inverts everything good) and makes the salvation follow the good works. This, in spite of the fact that the Scripture says: *'Without faith it is impossible to please [God]'* (Heb.11:6) and *'Whatever is not from faith is sin'* (Rom.14:23; cf. Tit.1:15). In point of fact, the Roman Catholic church is now in the forefront of a syncretic preparationism which completely denies the biblical understanding of salvation. A brief survey of the authoritative statements of the Vatican demonstrates, without a doubt, its commitment to the Hindu concept of religions which claims that *'all paths lead to the top of the mountain'*. A few sample quotations will illustrate:

- 'The Fathers of the Church rightly saw in the various religions... so many reflections of the one truth, "seeds of the Word", attesting that, though the routes taken may be different, there is but a single goal to which is directed the deepest aspiration of the human spirit as expressed in its quest for God'.[115]
- 'Since Christ died for all men, and since the ultimate vocation of man is in fact one, and divine, we ought to believe that the Holy Spirit in a manner known only to God offers to every man the possibility of being associated with this paschal mystery'.[116]
- 'Different religions have tried to respond to mankind's search for the ultimate explanation of creation and the meaning of man's journey through life. The Catholic Church accepts the truth and goodness found in these religions and she sees reflections there of the truth of Christ, whom she proclaims as *'the Way, the Truth and the Life'*. She wishes to do everything possible to cooperate with other believers in preserving all that is good in their religions and cultures'.[117]

We can easily see these principles worked out in the syncretistic writings and activities of such people as Pierre Teilhard de Chardin, the well-known Jesuit and Marxist who has had a great influence on the New Age Movement and the people

---

[114] Gavin DaCosta, *Is One Religion as Good as Another?* (Catholic Truth Society, 1985), p.7. This book has the official *Imprimatur* of the Vatican.

[115] Pope John Paul II, *Redemptor Hominis*, n.11.

[116] Vatican II, *Gaudium in Spes*, n.22.

[117] Vatican II, *Nostra Aetate*, nn.1-3.

behind the recent development of the United Nations.[118] Other Roman Catholics who have also been prominent in this respect are Thomas Merton, champion of the amalgamation of Zen Buddhism and Christianity,[119] Fr. Bede Griffiths,[120] and Dom Aelred Graham.[121] Bede Griffiths sums up their philosophy that all people of all religions are really believers, when he writes:

> 'No one can say in the proper sense that the Hindu, the Buddhist or the Muslim is an "unbeliever". I would say rather that we have to recognize him as our brother in Christ'.[122]

Between them, these three monks have done much to promote the interfaith gospel, utilising such vogue concepts as 'cosmic spiritual evolution', the 'Omega Point', and Hindu or Zen Catholicism.[123]

Mother Teresa and the Spirit of Peace

Another important cog in this syncretistic process is the renowned Mother Teresa of Calcutta. Who is this mysterious lady whose good works are paraded before the world in celebrity fashion? Mother Teresa, in spite of her charitable works, is involved in making a major contribution to the religious development of the rising interfaith universalism.

In July 1981, Mother Teresa gave the first public pronouncement of what is known as the 'Universal Prayer for Peace'. This took place at the Anglican St. James' Church, Piccadilly in London.[124] This well-known 'Prayer', with its white lettering on a pale blue background, was designed to be truly international — a prayer which would be capable of transcription into any language and in supplication to any god. The prayer, in full, reads:

> 'Lead me from death to life, from falsehood to truth. Lead me from despair to hope, from fear to trust. Lead me from hate to love, from war

---

[118] See, for example, his works: **1.** *The Phenomenon of Man* (Collins, 1959); **2.** *The Future of Man* (Fontana, 1969); **3.** *Hymn of the Universe* (Fontana, 1970); **4.** *Christianity and Evolution* (Collins, 1971). Interestingly, Teilhard was also a great admirer of the Communist system in China.

[119] See his works: **1.** *Zen, Tao et Nirvana* (Paris, 1970); **2.** *The Zen Revival* (Buddhist Society of London, 1971); **3.** *Thomas Merton on Zen* (Sheldon Press, 1976).

[120] Bede Griffiths lives on an ashram in India, of which he is the director. He has written a number of books outlining his syncretist philosophy: **1.** *Essays Towards a Hindu-Christian Dialogue* (London, 1966); **2.** *The Marriage of East and West* (Collins, 1982); **3.** *Cosmic Revelation: The Hindu Way to God* (Collins, 1983).

[121] See, e.g., his *Zen Catholicism* (Harcourt, Brace & World Inc., 1963).

[122] Bede Griffiths, *Christ in India* (Charles Scribner, 1966), p.196.

[123] For a good overall understanding of the New Gnosticism in relation to syncretism, the diligent enquirer could do no better than to read Ursula King, *Towards a New Mysticism: Teilhard de Chardin and Eastern Religions* (Collins, 1980). Dr. King, a Senior Lecturer in Theology at Leeds University and founder of the Teilhard de Chardin Centre in London, is a leading promoter of religious syncretism.

[124] This Anglican church, having been heavily influenced by Findhorn teachings, is at the forefront of promoting New Age philosophy in Christian circles today.

> to peace. Let peace fill our heart, our world, our universe. Peace. Peace. Peace'.

The publicity leaflet to which this 'prayer' is attached makes the significant claim that it is *'not confined to members of religions, but equally to humanists and agnostics and generally to those who believe in the power of positive thought'*.[125] The leaflet also makes the claim that the original source of the 'Prayer for Peace' *'is not clearly known, and it has no ties with any single denomination or faith'*.[126] This must surely be a deliberate deception. A little research reveals that this 'prayer' was originally adapted by the former Jain monk and environmentalist, Satish Kumar, from a *mantra* in the Indian Hindu Upanishads.[127] The Upanishads are essentially monistic treatises, secret Hindu doctrines, written from 800-400 B.C. They are much loved by occultists, esotericists and syncretists. Although, as in much occult literature, there is reference to a 'Universal Spirit' or 'Supreme Being', this is overlaid with the polluted stream of pantheism, monism and the quest for personal divinity. The 'god' of the Upanishads is not the transcendent God of the Bible. A typical example of the mystical twaddle at the heart of this work is encapsulated in the following lines referring to the Hindu idea of the 'Self' (i.e., God) in all things:

> 'It is conceived by him whom it is not conceived of; he by whom It is conceived of does not know It. It is not understood by those who understand It; It is understood by those who do not understand It'.[128]

How very different this is from the revelation which has been given to the Christian disciple, to whom it is said without equivocation: *'You shall know the truth, and the truth shall make you free'* (Jn.8:32). The true believer and follower of Jesus Christ has the words ringing in his heart:

> If you had known Me, you would have known my Father also; and from now on you know Him and have seen Him... He who has seen Me has seen the Father' (Jn.14:7-9).

In the Upanishads there is no real place for a personal God. Instead, one finds such abstruse monistic claims as: *'Like butter or cream is the Self in everything'*. Bear in mind that 'Self' is the equivalent of God in Upanishadic terminology. Yet many professing Christians and all interfaithists claim that these Hindu scriptures are as valid as the Bible! And presumably this is what led Satish Kumar to lift an

---

125 Taken from the official *Prayer for Peace* leaflet. This was available from the Peace Prayer Centre, which was set up by an ecumenically-minded minister and his wife, c/o Seniors Farmhouse, Semley, Shaftesbury, Dorset, SP7 9AX.

126 Ibid.

127 This origin was clearly laid out in Merfyn Temple, *Angelus for Peace in the South Atlantic* (Self-published, 1982), p.1. This weird autobiographical document, written by a Methodist minister who became obsessed by the 'Prayer for Peace', was available from the author at 103, Appleford Drive, Abingdon, OXON, U.K., OX14 2AQ.

128 Quoted in John Ferguson, *Illustrated Encyclopaedia of Mysticism and Mystery Religions* (Thames & Hudson, 1976), p.202.

Upanishadic mantra from its context and exalt it as a prayer suitable for Christian believers: a 'Prayer for Peace' which can be intoned by Mother Teresa from an Anglican pulpit.

The original mantra reads: *'Lead me from the unreal to the real! Lead me from darkness to light! Lead me from death to immortality!'* [129] The commentary given by the Upanishads on this *mantra* shows that each of the three lines is really saying, *'Make me immortal!'*,[130] revealing that the words *'unreal'* and *'darkness'* carry an esoteric reference to death,[131] which, like life in the Hindu cosmology, is considered to be an illusion. In fact, this *mantra* forms part of a special ceremony known as the Abhyaroha (the Ascension), *'a ceremony by which the performer reaches the gods, or becomes a god'*, through which he may *'obtain whatever desire he may desire'* and become *'the conqueror of the worlds'*.[132] In this prayer-*mantra*, we have the major thrust behind all world religions: that we can have unconditional eternal life, boundless wisdom, and the realisation of personal 'divinity'. All this is the natural legacy of Satan's threefold lie in Eden (Gen.3:4-6), a lie which eventually became enshrined in the doctrine and practice of all the corrupt, false religions of the world, about which we shall have more to say shortly.

The true purpose of the creation of the 'Prayer for Peace', now naïvely used by many ecumenically-minded churches, is to introduce into Christian worship a subtle adaptation of a Hindu scripture with idolatrous, self-deifying ceremonial associations, and thereby to substitute syncretistic religious thought for Christocentric spirituality. Actually, it is not a prayer at all; it is an *invocation* — a kind of plea to the 'Higher Self' used by occultists and others who believe in 'the power of the spoken word' exemplified in the mantric cults of the Orient. Those who have a living faith in the true Jesus Christ have no need to make hollow invocations to an unknown god for a false peace!

As to Satish Kumar himself, the designer of the 'Universal Prayer for Peace', he was the founder and editor of the New Age 'green' magazine 'Resurgence' — a medley of one-world politics, esotericism, ecology, mysticism, psychobabble, eco-feminism, holistic health and occult healing. Not long after the first reading of his 'Prayer for Peace', he was residing, along with a variety of psychotherapists, occult healers and Shamans, in the New Age Spanish holistic health centre, 'Cortijo Romero', running a course entitled 'Finding the Spirit Within', which involved the techniques of *'group meditation, yoga and chanting'*.[133] At a cost of £150 per person, receiving the 'spirit' of Neo-Gnosticism does not come cheap (cf. Isa.55:1-2; 1 Pet.5:2)!

---

[129] F. Max Müller (ed.), *The Sacred Books of the East* (OUP, 1900), Vol.XV, the Upanishads, pp.83-84.

[130] Ibid., p.84.

[131] Ibid.

[132] Ibid., p.83n. This information is given in a footnote by the editor of the Upanishads and early propagandist for Eastern religion in the West, Professor Max Müller of Oxford University.

[133] The postal address of Cortijo Romero was c/o Nigel Shamash, Aptdo, De Correos 31, Orgiva, Granada, Spain.

Mother Teresa's history of support for syncretistic people and events is a sad commentary on the error which lies at the heart of Roman Catholic religion. One report by a missionary to India, detailing the practice at one of Mother Teresa's hospices in Nepal, states:

> 'In 1984, my wife and I had a recorded interview with a nun who works with Mother Teresa's organization in Nepal. Seated in a small, dirty room by Nepal's 'holiest river', surrounded by Hindu temples and idols — and sick, and elderly, waiting to die in this 'holy place', in hope of escaping the life-cycles of reincarnation — we asked questions. Sister Ann had spent three years in Calcutta in training and service at Mother Teresa's main centre. Now she was in Nepal, and one of her duties was daily to visit these sick and aged people, to do what she could to help alleviate their pain and their need... I queried: "These people are waiting to die. What are you telling them to prepare them for death and for eternity?" She replied candidly, "We tell them to pray to their Bhagwan, to their gods".[134]

What a wealth of lost opportunities for straight Gospel-sharing! The missionary then concludes:

> 'Those who are familiar with the beliefs of Mother Teresa and Pope John Paul II will not be surprised at this, as they are both universalists who believe that all who sincerely follow their own religions or beliefs will be saved'.[135]

It is perhaps not wholly insignificant to discover that Mother Teresa's hospice in Calcutta is built on temple property dedicated to *Kali*, the Hindu goddess of destruction, who is propitiated by the nocturnal sacrifice of animals. The entire pantheon of Hindu gods lies in stark contrast to the first two commandments of the Decalogue (Ex.20:3-6) and the commands of Christ's Apostles (1 Cor.10:14; 2 Cor.6:16-17; 1 Jn.5:21) in the Bible which Mother Teresa purports to represent.

In a film entitled 'Mother Teresa', which was originally given its world première at the United Nations 40th Anniversary celebration in 1985, she plugs her familiar message of universalism: *'No colour, no religion, no nationality, should come between us. We are all children of God'*. However, only those who have the Spirit of Christ are the true children of God (Rom.8:14-16). That is why the Holy Spirit is known as the *'Spirit of adoption [or sonship]'* (Rom.8:15). Everyone is born a *'child of wrath'* by nature; the only way to become a child of God is through adoption into His family (Gal.4:4-7) by faith in Jesus Christ. It is Christ not Krishna who saves. That is why the Apostle can say: *'If anyone does not have the Spirit of Christ, he is not His'* (Rom.8:9). Those who have the Spirit of Christ are God's children. Those who do not have the Spirit of Christ are not God's children. Therefore, we are not all children of God. Therefore, Mother Teresa's theology does not come from the Christian Bible.

---

[134] *Christian News Encyclopedia* (Missouri Publishing, 1992), Vol.V, p.3920.
[135] Ibid.

In March 1985, Mother Teresa was honorary guest at an 'intercultural, interfaith gathering' in Malta called 'Spirit of Peace: Culture, Science and Religion at a Turning Point',[136] a title taken from the name of a book by Neo-Gnostic physicist, Fritjof Capra. This was organised by the United Nations University for Peace to *'celebrate 40 years of the United Nations'*, and to bring together delegates from a variety of influences such as Kabbalism, Shamanism, Sufism, the peace movement, the Ecumenical Movement, plus New Age sociologist Marilyn Ferguson (author of the acclaimed book, 'The Aquarian Conspiracy'), the then Assistant Secretary-General of the U.N., Dr. Robert Muller, and the exiled Tibetan Buddhist leader, the Dalai Lama.

The description on the advertising leaflet of the 'Faculty' teaching at this U.N. conference is a masterpiece of Neo-Gnostic deception. For example, Joan Halifax, who is blandly billed as *'a teacher of religion and medical anthropologist'*, is actually a well-known doyenne of the New Age Movement and an ardent advocate of Shamanism, having written one of the most thorough modern books on the subject.[137] She has also co-authored a book with the psychiatrist Stanislaf Grof entitled 'Human Encounter with Death', which catalogues their work in the use of the drug LSD on dying people. On the U.N. leaflet, 'Faculty' member Philip Deere is described as *'the spiritual adviser to the American Indian Movement'* — in other words, he is a teacher of Shamanism. And when Rabbi Zalman Schacter is respectably referred to as *'a professor of religion in Jewish Mysticism and psychology'*, it was presumably judged preferable to a frank admission of his expertise in the tradition of the Kabbala — a Jewish occult heresy. Likewise, when we are told that Faculty member, Dr. Huston Smith is merely a *'professor of religion and philosophy searching for spiritual truth'*, it might help us to understand just exactly what kind of 'spiritual truth' he is searching for. In fact, as early as 1962, Dr. Smith (then the Professor of Philosophy at Syracuse University, New York), having already become a sponsor of the above-mentioned 'Temple of Understanding' in the same year, gave a lecture in Sydney, Australia on *'Is a New World Religion Coming?'* at the Theosophical Society's 'Blavatsky Lodge'.[138]

Such is the background to the teaching 'Faculty' at the United Nations 40th Anniversary celebrations. The euphemistic descriptions of this 'Faculty' — graced by Mother Teresa of Calcutta — belie an established network of people who are highly efficient proponents of the New Gnosticism, the New World Order and global religionism. The sad truth is that Mother Teresa has allowed herself to become a mere symbol of good works religion — the epitome of the universal Golden Rule — a 'respectable' figurine who can be wheeled out to front utopian gatherings as a supposed representative of Christianity. Her social work may be impeccable, but she is no friend of the true Church of Jesus Christ. Her support for causes which destroy the unique foundations of Christianity has seen to that.

---

[136] The information on this and other such U.N. fiascos was freely available from the publicists at AGAPE, Gerberau 14, D-7800, Freiburg, Germany.

[137] Joan Halifax, *Shaman: Wounded Healer* (Thames & Hudson, 1982).

[138] Recorded in Robert Keith Spenser, *The Cult of the All-Seeing Eye* (CBCA, 1964), p.49.

The Heart of World Religion Revealed

As we have frequently mentioned the Dalai Lama of Tibet — another regular face alongside Mother Teresa at these gatherings — let us pause at this point to carry out some research into his background which will bring us face-to-face with the illusory nature of the spiritual goodness purported to be at the heart of all religions.

This religious leader engenders some sympathy in the West because of the treatment of his countrymen at the hands of the Chinese Communist army in 1959. To the world, he seems to be a respectable religious and patriotic leader with a gentle disposition. In these non-judgemental, multi-cultural, pluralistic times it would appear that there is a general reluctance to raise a question about the spiritual credentials of such a man. We do not seek to make *ad hominem* statements against the Dalai Lama here; we are merely attempting to expose a fundamental spiritual deception — to take issue with the destructive illusion that at the heart of all the world's religions lies a kernel of truth which is indistinguishable from that of Christianity. This we must deny emphatically, if we are to be faithful to the Bible. Even in Evangelical circles today, it is becoming increasingly common to disclaim the fact that eternal salvation is withheld from those who embrace religions other than Christianity. But this denial is in direct contradiction to the Word of God, which makes clear references to the conditions necessary for the avoidance of eternal punishment and for the attainment of eternal life (Jn.14:6; 3:14-16; 5:24; 2 Th.1:7-9).

The Dalai Lama's religion is known as 'Lamaism'. So we ask: what exactly is Lamaism? The answer will surprise many. Lamaism is a politico-religious derivative of the Tibetan version of Buddhism, which was first introduced into Tibet twelve hundred years ago by one Padma-Sambhava, who brought with him a mixture of

> 'the Madhyamika system of Nagarjuna modified by the alaya-doctrine of the Yoga-cara school, and in association with the magical and occult practices of the Tantrayana (mystical formularies)'.[139]

This, in itself, represents a heavy blend of demonic influences. But the development of Lamaism in Tibet comes through a further amalgamation of the above three Buddhist schools with the indigenous Tibetan shamanism.[140] In the thirteenth century, an actual Lama hierarchy was set up, and the theory was later put forward that the Dalai Lama (English meaning: *Ocean-Like Supreme One*) was

> 'a reincarnation of the god of mercy, Avalokiteshvara, whose famous spell [i.e., *mantra*] *'Aum-Mani-Padme-Hum'* is inscribed on prayer-wheels throughout Tibet'.[141]

---

[139] *Chambers's Encyclopaedia*, Vol.II (George Newnes, 1963), p.645.

[140] Ibid. Shamanism can be defined as *'the religion of N. Asia based essentially on magic and sorcery'* (Chambers's English Dictionary), although the term has come to be used to describe any religious system involving these two elements.

[141] Ibid. A *mantra* is a verbal formula with breathing techniques which is chanted repeti-

Each successive Dalai Lama is alleged to be a reincarnation of his predecessor, and the 'Vice-Regent' on earth of the Buddha. He is also regarded by his followers as 'infallible'. When a Dalai Lama dies, his successor is chosen by prophetic revelation from the male infants of the country born shortly after his death. The present incumbent, Dalai Lama Tenzin Gyamtsho, received the following selection of names at his initiation ceremony: 'The Holy One, the Tender Glory, Mighty in Speech, of Excellent Intellect, of Absolute Wisdom, Holding the Doctrine, the Ocean'.[142] By biblical standards, this must be a demonically-inspired claim for any human being to make concerning himself, and must surely give credence to the fact that the Dalai Lama has received an *initiation* far beyond his mere installation as the Dalai Lama.

Ever since his exile from Tibet, the Dalai Lama has been travelling around the world to gather support for his interfaith syncretistic dream. In terms of the development of interfaithism within the Ecumenical Movement, one of his foremost triumphs was a high-profile meeting with the World Council of Churches in Geneva in July 1985.[143] Readers will remember our testimony from an earlier chapter that Tibetan Buddhists are awaiting a World Teacher called *Bodhisattva Maitreya* to come to establish 'a reign of peace and justice' on the earth — a name which corresponds precisely with that of the World Teacher and 'Ascended Master' expected by the New Age Movement of today.

Here we can mention the relationship between the Pope of Rome and the Dalai Lama, who are often featured together in the press, having private talks in the Vatican.[144] On one occasion, the caption to a photograph of the two men said:

> 'The Pope greets the Dalai Lama, spiritual leader of Tibet, for private talks at the Vatican yesterday. The Vatican, sensitive about its strained relations with China, stressed that the talks were religious, not political'.[145]

What could possibly lie behind the private 'religious' meetings between these two men? This relationship is one of the more revealing elements in the syncretic goals of the Vatican. For it is with the occultic, mystical religions of the East that the Pope of Rome seeks to link Roman Catholicism and, ultimately, the entire visible Christian Church. The ecumenical-interfaith thrust of these private meetings is wholly consistent with the Pope's syncretistic attitude to Eastern religions, whose goal — as any student of the Orient will confirm — is *self-deification*. During his well-publicised visit to India in 1986, the Pope's spokesman, Joaquin Navarro, stated that inter-denominational ecumenism is not enough. *'What is needed now'*, he said, *'is a profound dialogue with all the faiths of the world, so that we can agree on the main issues of man and mankind'*.[146] Throughout this

---

tively during Eastern meditation to release latent forces which will allegedly induce a mystical experience of the divine. This has been discussed earlier in Chapters 9 and 10.

142 *Chambers's Encyclopaedia*, op. cit., Vol.XIII, p.621.

143 *The Times*, July 12th 1985.

144 Two examples of this took place in February 1986 and on June 15th 1988.

145 *The Daily Telegraph*, June 9th 1990.

Indian visit, the Pope did not preach the biblical Gospel but, instead,

> 'He preached a gospel of peace and reconciliation, of respect for India's cultural heritage and religious diversity. He sought the common ground of all faiths, buttressing his message with well-researched quotations from Mahatma Ghandi, Pandit Nehru and the national poet. Rabindranath Tagore'.[147]

The sad truth is that many of the people of India are in an abject state of spiritual bondage to idolatry, cruel caste-systems, astrology, yoga, mysticism, magic, a multitude of religious charlatans, cults and gurus, which polluted river has been gradually flooding the Western world throughout this century.[148] This is the true nature of the *'cultural heritage and religious diversity'* of India, for which the Pope could offer only compliments and compromise, diplomacy and dialogue. In a most revealing statement on his approach to Eastern religion, the same Pope, speaking in Manila on 21st February 1981, had made the assertion that

> 'Ways must be developed to make this dialogue [with the believers of all religions] become a reality everywhere, but especially in Asia, the continent that is the cradle of ancient cultures and religions'.[149]

This utterance brings us to a most important phenomenon concerning the religions of the world. A repeated claim of those who support interfaith activity is that there is an essential unity of all religions: that behind all the world's faiths there is a *common* 'ancient wisdom-tradition'; that they all worship the same God and that the aim of all religions is one. However, there is, indeed, a common source of all the religions of the world (Christianity not included), but it is not at all the pure fountain of wisdom which their adherents would have us believe. Let us expand this concept a little.

The Fall of Man in Eden did not merely involve disobedience to the Creator; it actually embodied a total seduction — spiritual, moral and ethical — into the ways of Satan. All false religion, occultism, sorcery and magic have their source in the relationship which our first parents contracted with the devil, in which he promised unconditional eternal life (*'You will not surely die'*), the experience of personal 'divinity' (*'You will be like God'*), and fulfilment of the desire for wisdom beyond that which God had originally bestowed on them (read Gen.3:1-6). This was the historical source of what we have often referred to as the 'Satanic Initiation'; and it is in *this* experience that we find the *real* common 'ancient wisdom-tradition' of all the religions of the world.

In the wake of the Fall, human beings still retained a strong religious impulse,

---

[146] *The Times*, February 7th 1986.

[147] *The Guardian*, February 3rd 1986.

[148] For a good secular exposition of this phenomenon, read *Karma-Cola* (Penguin, 1974). For the testimony of an Indian Hindu converted to Christianity, read Rabindranath R. Maharaj, *Death of a Guru* (Hodder & Stoughton, 1978).

[149] *Roman Catholic Committee for Other Faiths: What does the Church Teach?* (Catholic Truth Society, 1986), p.26.

an intrinsic urge to find answers to the riddle of life — what Benjamin Warfield calls a *notitia Dei insita* (a natural knowledge of God) and what John Calvin refers to as a *Divinitatis sensum* (awareness of divinity) and a *semen religionis* (seed of religion). But their gropings after the God from Whom they had been alienated would become horribly corrupted and distorted. Justly described as *'having no hope and without God in the world'* (Eph.2:12), unregenerated fallen humans can only engage in religious practices which will further estrange them from their Maker. And if we look closely at the practices of the world's religions, we will find the essential hallmarks of all false 'spirituality' and provide ourselves with a great deal of insight into heathen consciousness, as well as the revealing of important biblical truths.

First, we will discover that there is a doctrine of the 'God within' or 'inner light', an alleged 'spark of divinity' in all people which can be 'tapped' through certain techniques which have very often been preserved in secret 'wisdom' teachings handed down through centuries. However, contrary to these claims of a 'universal God within', the Bible shows that, in the wake of the Fall, human beings no longer had the indwelling Holy Spirit originally received by Adam at his creation,[150] but became spiritually dead (Eph.2:1-2), consisting merely of *'flesh'* (Gen.6:3), *'not having the Spirit'* (Jude 19; cf. Rom.8:9), and remaining in that condition unless they are saved by grace through faith in Jesus Christ (Jn.3:3-5; 7:37-39) — and even then, they become partakers of the divine *nature* (2 Peter 1:4), **not** the divine essence. Secondly, in the world's religions one will invariably find the substitution of a created thing (either an external object, or even oneself) for the true Creator as the object of worship and the focus of spiritual power (cf. Rom.1:25). Such idolatry is expressly condemned in the Bible (e.g., Isa.45:5-9,20-22; 1 Jn.5:21; cf. Mk.8:34). Thirdly, we also find teachings which support the notion of universal, unconditional eternal life, e.g., reincarnation, spiritualism, out-of-the-body experiences, etc. But the Scriptures show that humans have but one life, in which their response to the Gospel of Christ will lead to either eternal salvation or everlasting punishment (Heb.9:27; Ps.78:39; 2 Th.1:7-9; Mt.25:31-46).

Now, if we add to all this the formalistic ritualism, divination, spiritism, sorcery and the endless placatory sacrifices to an infinite number of gods — all of which are present to a greater or lesser degree — then we have the ingredients of the religions of the world and the false spirituality which is so roundly condemned in the Bible (e.g., Lev.19:26; Dt.18:10-14; Ps.51:16-17; Acts 16:16-18).

After the Fall, the ungodly descendants fathered by Cain had carried the 'Satanic Initiation', and the ensuing wickedness became so great that the Lord intervened with a universal Flood which wiped out all but eight people (Gen.6:5-7). During the following period of renewed human development in the postdiluvian world, the 'Satanic Initiation' worked especially through the line of Ham (Gen.10:6-10), culminating in the episode at Babel in Sumero-Mesopotamia, which is the very *'cradle of ancient cultures and religions'* referred to by the Pope

[150] See Chapter 5, §8, 'The God Within', for the background to this.

of Rome. On that plain in the land of Shinar, there had been a mustering of 'socio-spiritual people-power' which found its expression in the use of towers or 'ziggurats' as a way of 'reaching up to the gods' (Gen.11:1-4). Magic, fertility cults and idolatry all played their part in this expression of ancient 'spirituality'. And when the divinely-appointed judgemental scattering took place (Gen.11:5-9), these people took their religion with them across the globe, which surely goes some way to explaining the remarkable similarity of myths, sorceries, gods and goddesses in all the religions of the world — each one developing idiosyncratically according to the culture in which it was to unfold.[151] In other words, the 'ancient wisdom-tradition' which is purported to be common to all the world's religions, and so beloved by the Pope of Rome, does not have its historical roots in the redemptive plan of God but in the corrupting work of Satan.

An Unholy Alliance

It was out of just such a polluted religious background in Chaldea that Abraham, the father of the faithful, was called by the one, true God for spiritual separation from the world and its corrupt religions (Acts 7:2-4; cf. Josh.24:2-4). Thereafter, the Lord's people in both Testament eras have been in constant conflict with these Satan-inspired religions, with their varying combinations of mysticism, idolatry, asceticism, sorcery and superstition.

Today, the so-called *Vicar of Christ* on earth, the Pope, exhorts the universal Christian to throw in his lot with this syncretistic cocktail. However, as Paul the inspired Apostle affirmed (Acts 26:16-18) and Ignatius of Antioch (died *c.* A.D.100) highlights in his Letter to the Ephesians,[152] the Lord Jesus Christ came to sweep away these pagan religions and break their power. It is for this reason (amongst others) that the Holy Scriptures have so touchingly recorded the homage paid by the Magi from the East to the newly-born Christ-child in Bethlehem. Who were these mysterious Magi? What were their religious interests? In his enlightening book 'Earth's Earliest Ages', G.H. Pember writes:

> 'Originally the Magi were a Persian religious caste [*c.* 7th Century B.C.]; but their influence was subsequently extended to many countries. They acted as priests, prescribed sacrifices, were soothsayers, and interpreted dreams and omens. Origen (3rd cent. A.D.) [*Contra Celsum*, I. 60] affirms that they were in communication with evil spirits, and could consequently do whatever lay within the power of their invisible allies. Certainly...they were well acquainted with Mesmerism and every practice of modern Spiritualism'.[153]

In support of this, an authoritative Bible encyclopedia states that among the Magi *'there was a strong tradition which favoured the exercise of sacerdotal and occult powers'*.[154] In other words, the Magi were pagan sorcerers. So when

[151] See Chapter 1, §4, 'The Satanic Roots of World Religion' — especially footnote 20.

[152] Ignatius of Antioch, *The Epistle to the Ephesians*, §19.

[153] G.H. Pember, *Earth's Earliest Ages and their Connection with Modern Spiritualism, Theosophy, and Buddhism* (G.H. Lang, n.d., first published in 1876), p.162.

representatives of this cult came to bring gifts to Christ and pay homage to Him, they were signalling the spiritual change which was to be effected in the world through the bodily manifestation of the Son of God — the end of demonic religious enterprise among the nations (Gentiles). The birth of Jesus Christ rang loudly the death knell of the devil and all his evil works (1 Jn.3:8; Heb.2:14).

Small wonder, then, that Satan, the vanquished prince, should expend so much energy, throughout these last days, in an attempt to destroy that which the Lord has initiated: the building of His spiritual kingdom through the true Church. Satan's objective has always been to undermine the Lord's work through His people, from the very moment that God declared that there would be a state of warfare, throughout the rest of history, between the offspring of the woman (the Lord Christ and His people) and the seed of the serpent (Satan and his children), which would culminate in the victory over the devil by the Lord Jesus Christ on the cross of Calvary (Gen.3:15; cf. Jn.12:31; 1 Jn.3:8; Col.2:15). One of the most efficient methods of undermining the Church is to deny its *exclusive* nature while, at the same time, fostering the notion that all religions are one and the same in object and essence. It is a stark fact that the primary thrust behind all syncretism is the destruction of the Church of Christ. Our knowledge of this reality will enable us to grasp the significance of the many ecumenical and interfaith activities which have so bewitched the Christian Church throughout this century.

These will not be welcome facts for those professing Christians who have both feet comfortably planted in a pluralist world in which global, humanistic values are the predominant yardstick. But the faithful ones who live their lives in conformity to the Word of God will, as Jesus reminds us, be hated by the unbelieving world because they have been chosen for separation by the Lord from everything which is an abomination and a lie (Jn.15:18-21; Rev.21:27; 22:15). Such separation in our pilgrimage through the wilderness of this world is an integral part of the discomfort of the Cross (Lk.6:22; 2 Cor.6:17; Rev.18:4). As a wise pastor from an earlier age has said: *'The Gospel is a rose that cannot be plucked without prickles'* (Thomas Watson, died 1689). But those who seek to forge a link between the Christian Church and the religions of the world are building a church of universal appeal; a false church without a Cross which will be hated by none and loved by the very world out of which it should be drawn. All this is far removed from the Christianity of the Bible, which Jesus clearly showed would be genuinely followed by comparatively few people and rejected by the majority (Mt.7:13-14).

What can be the purpose of attempting, in the words of Cardinal Suenens, *'to restore the visible unity of the Church of Jesus Christ'*,[155] when that unity is based on doctrinal shallowness and the acclaim of the unbelieving world? In what way is Christ being honoured when such 'unity' is forged with people whose religious beliefs — behind their angel-of-light disguise — are, at best, theologically liberal, at worst, preposterously deluded and blasphemous? Here we have a classic

[154] Merrill C. Tenney, *The Zondervan Pictorial Encyclopedia of the Bible* (Zondervan, 1975), Vol.IV, p.31.

[155] Leon J.C. Suenens, *Ecumenism and Charismatic Renewal* (D.L.T., 1978), p.viii.

illustration of the way that differing ideologies will forge a superficial unity in order to overcome a common enemy. This is the true meaning of the word 'syncretism', which does not at all imply the creation of a single, monolithic world religion, as many believe today. The word is derived from the Greek *sunkretismos*, which originally referred to a saying about the Cretans, and how they were *'very much disposed to wage war against each other, but immediately made peace and joined hands when attacked by foreigners'*.[156] The word 'syncretism', therefore, refers to a broad confederation which is formed in the pursuit of mutual interests among those of disparate beliefs — an unholy alliance.

Here we have the key to the Interfaith and Ecumenical Movements: the suppression of all differences in order to further the destruction of a common enemy. In this case, that enemy is none other than the biblical Gospel of Jesus Christ, the exclusiveness of which is despised by the world (Jn.15:18-21). One is reminded of such events as the non-aggression treaty between Hitler and Stalin in the 1930s. Two men with opposing ideologies and smiling masks, sitting on opposite sides of a table, yet resolutely linked by their corrupt mutual interests and common thirst for power. There are also two notorious biblical precedents for such a dishonest liaison, highlighting the perils of humanistic ecumenism. The Pharisees and Sadducees had very different worldviews and theologies, yet their common antagonism towards the Lord Jesus Christ was a most unifying and destructive force (Mt.16:6,11; cf. Mk.3:6). Similarly, in one of the more chilling verses of the Bible, Luke records the subversive accord which ensues when unregenerate men drink from the same poisoned chalice (Luke 23:12; cf. Acts 4:27). The stark question hovers unanswered above them: *'Can two walk together, unless they are agreed?'* (Amos 3:3).

If the truth be known, the Church of Rome is not really ecumenising at all. Under the guises of 'visible unity' and 'maintained denominational independence', it is carrying out its own evangelising mission to unite all professing Christendom under the universal leadership of the Pope — a role to which this office has always aspired. Let us note well that the Roman Catholic Bishop, Joseph McKinney, advised fellow Catholics that when they are involved in ecumenical activity, *'the Catholic teaching that within this Church there is a certain fullness of the Christian tradition which can be found in no other denomination is to be maintained'*.[157] It is interesting to note that a former Roman Catholic nun has written:

> 'Today a wind of change has blown over the surface of the Church of Rome which makes many people think that it is part of the Bible-believing church. After all, Roman Catholics believe in the Three-in-One God, the death and Resurrection of the Lord Jesus Christ, and in the Virgin Birth, unlike many Protestants today.
>
> 'But in spite of changes on the surface, at heart the Church of Rome is

[156] Philip Schaff (ed.), *Schaff-Herzog Encyclopaedia of Religious Knowledge* (Funk & Wagnalls, 1891), Vol.4, p.2278.

[157] *New Covenant: The Magazine of the Catholic Charismatic Renewal*, Vol.I, No.12, June 1972, p.10.

the same as ever. Her objective is a one-world church, but her methods of achieving it have changed'.[158]

In order to gain a real grasp of what lies behind the current world-wide Ecumenical Movement under the auspices of the Church of Rome, one must understand not only the view which this Church has of its Pontiff, but also the way that he is regarded by the leaders of world religions. Let us now examine this revealing information.

The Roman Church believes that the Pope, as Bishop of Rome, is the sole successor to Peter the Apostle and (drawing on Mt.16:15-20) that he is the earthly head of the Church by appointment of Christ.[159] However, it is not only Rome which holds this spiritually-elevated view of the Papal office; it is also the view taken by representatives of the Satan-inspired religions of the world. This is clearly stated by B.K.S. Iyengar in the explanatory preface to his renowned, classic work on Yoga:

> 'The Western reader may be surprised at the recurring reference [in the book] to the Universal Spirit, to mythology and even to philosophical and moral principles. He must not forget that in ancient times all the higher achievements of man, in knowledge, art and power, were part of religion and were assumed to belong to God and to His priestly servants on earth. The Catholic Pope is the last such embodiment of divine knowledge and power in the West'.[160]

This is a very significant statement for our consideration of syncretism in the Ecumenical Movement. It shows the true status of the Pope as seen through the eyes of world religious leaders: *'an embodiment of divine knowledge and power'*. Because of this, we should not be surprised that there is a special relationship between the Dalai Lama of Tibet and the Pope of Rome. In the same way that the Dalai Lama is regarded as the 'Vice-Regent of the Buddha', the Pope is also known by his Church as the 'Vicar of Christ'. Therefore, the papal office in the West is regarded by Eastern religious leaders, such as the Dalai Lama, as having a similar kind of esoteric power to their own. In fact, Tibetan Buddhism (from which the Dalai Lama derives his religion) regards Christ as having been one of the greatest of the *Bodhisattvas*, 'Enlightened Ones' dedicated to serving humanity, which are equivalent to the 'Ascended Masters' which occultists and New Age advocates claim are influencing human affairs and religious leaders on the planet.[161] The other world religions are also happy to regard Jesus as just one of many great prophets. It is precisely for these reasons that the leaders of the world's religions — who cannot tolerate a biblical Christianity which upholds that

---

158 *Evangelical Times*, Vol.XXI, no.1, p.12.

159 In fact, it was Peter's pioneering Apostolic confession of Christ as the Messianic Son of God (Mt.16:16-18) that formed the foundation on which the Church was based — **not** the man himself as a leader in the future church in Rome.

160 B.K.S. Iyengar, *The Concise Light on Yoga* (George Allen & Unwin, 1980), pp.xi-xii.

161 See Chapter 4, §4 for details of the 'Ascended Masters'.

Jesus Christ holds forth the only way to God — can so easily have fellowship, dialogue and even unity with the liberal, universalist, professing Christians who also believe that Jesus is merely another great world teacher.

Mysticism and the Ancient Gnosis

Some people may still wonder why the Pope, who professes a belief in some orthodox biblical doctrines, should be held in such great esteem by the leaders of religions and ideologies which can never accept those doctrines as true. There is a sound reason for this strange paradox. All occultists and world-religionists advocate that esoteric, heretical form of a second-century Christianity known as 'Gnosticism', which they regard as being the *true* religion and thoroughly in conformity with their own systems of belief. But they also believe that another expression of this Gnosticism is the Mysticism which plays such a great part within traditional Roman Catholicism — having been 'Christianised' in order to render it more acceptable within the Church. It is worth our while examining this situation.

Roman Catholic mysticism has its origins in a treatise called the *Mystica Theologia,* which was written by a fifth century Syrian Neoplatonist monk who mischievously pretended it was penned to Timothy by the Pauline convert to Christianity, Dionysius the Areopagite mentioned in Acts 17:34. We have already examined this phenomenon in some detail in an earlier chapter.[162] Because of this absorption of syncretic Neoplatonism into the Church via Roman Catholic mystical theology, and its intimate relation to the Gnosticism which infiltrated the Church in the first three centuries, it is hardly surprising to discover that occultists, Eastern mystics, esotericists and world religionists believe that true Christianity can be confidently identified with the *gnosis.* Thus, theosophist Annie Besant, after examining Roman Catholicism (which, like all unbelievers, she mistakenly identifies with true Christianity) observes that

> 'two streams may nevertheless be tracked through Christendom, streams which had as their source the vanished mysteries. One was the stream of mystic learning, flowing from the Wisdom, the Gnosis, imparted in the Mysteries; the other was the stream of mystic contemplation, equally part of the Gnosis, leading to the ecstasy, to spiritual vision'.[163]

Because of this, all occultists and world religionists hold the understanding that the Vatican's professions of biblical doctrine are only 'transitional' until their desired world religious confederation comes to pass. For it is at the level of this mysticism that the 'grassroots' blending of Christianity and world religion can take place. The modern interfaith advocate is therefore able to say, with the occultists and theosophists,

> 'You must not limit your thought on religion to the few hundred years since the Reformation, to the minority of Christians that you find in the

---

[162] See the section entitled 'The Dionysian Deception' in Chapter 9.

[163] Annie Besant, *Esoteric Christianity* (Theosophical Publishing House, 1901), p.80.

so-called Protestant communities. You must take a larger view than that: go back over the whole of Christian antiquity and further back still over the ancient religions of the East, and then you will find that identity of knowledge which is the mark of reality, which is the keynote of Mysticism.

'And so you find the existence of a Path and a method declared by which the supreme knowledge may be gained. The Roman Catholic has always kept a knowledge of that Path and he calls the end of it by a startling name. Generally the word Union is used, but take up some great book of Roman Catholic theology and you will find the startling word which I have in mind; they call it 'Deification', the deification of man, man become God, for nothing less is meant by 'Deification'. And the Hindu and the Buddhist call it 'Liberation', the setting free of the human Spirit from the bonds which have tied him down, from the matter which has blinded him. The meaning is the same, the method the same, the thing the same.

'And so we realise that in the realm of the Spirit there are none of those divisions that mark off one religion from another in the separative plane of earth, and we realise that the Spirit is united where the earth holds diversity, and that where knowledge [*gnosis*] takes the place of faith, there controversies sink into silence and the certainty of truth is known'.[164]

Now we can begin to understand where the Roman Catholic religion really fits into the Ecumenical-Interfaith Movement. It is, in truth, a transitional force, professing an outward adherence to some orthodox biblical doctrines (enough to maintain a semblance of respectability in many Christian circles); yet — through its mysticism which is derived from Neoplatonist syncretism — it is a secret holder of the same 'Satanic Initiation' (into *gnosis*) which is the hallmark of all occultism and the religions of the world.

The Vatican has a great many ancient manuscripts containing Gnostic and esoteric doctrine within its vaults. Occultists and world religionists (such as the *Ocean-like Supreme One*, the Dalai Lama) are only too well aware of this fact. They must surely be marking time until such a day that the hidden 'truths' in the Vatican will be revealed as the 'real' Christianity. In their way of thinking, the present outward doctrine is merely transitory, awaiting the time when the 'oneness' will come. On this note, the Theosophical Society founder and former Anglican clergyman (and paederast), C.W. Leadbeater, reminds his readers

'that the Roman Catholic Church possesses what is called the doctrine of development, and also that it has proclaimed the Pope to be the infallible exponent of divine doctrine, the viceregent of God upon earth'.[165]

---

[164] Annie Besant, *Mysticism* (Theosophical Publishing House, 1914), pp.15-16.

[165] C.W. Leadbeater, *The Inner Life*, Vol.I, (Theosophical Press, Wheaton, Illinois, 1949), p.122.

Then, speaking on behalf of every other occultist, syncretist and world-religionist, he dreams of the day when the Pope will freely confess to them the following words:

> 'Certainly this which you bring forward is the true meaning of Christian doctrine. We have always known this, and we have plenty of manuscripts in the Vatican Library to prove it. We did not tell you this before, because all through the ages until now men have not been fit for such a revelation. They have been too crude, too rough, too undeveloped to understand a philosophical and mystical interpretation. The outer husk of the religion has been all that could be usefully offered to them. Now one stage more has been attained and the world is ready for this further revelation'.[166]

We cannot now be far from that stage of which the theosophist Leadbeater dreamed in his occult talks at Adyar in India in 1910. The only component necessary is a new, more openly-liberal and syncretist Pope as successor to John Paul II, who would then be able to capitalise on all the preparations which have been put in place by his predecessors. Indeed, this is what the 'new super-spirituality' is really all about: the modern manifestation of ancient Gnosticism and the provision of a vehicle for the mounting of a massive global deception. The world is now poised on the brink of the most phenomenal subterfuge yet to be staged by Satan and his disciples on this earth. If we grasp this fact, we will appreciate the role of the Vatican in the building of the coming conglomerate 'spirituality'. Now, perhaps, we can understand the significance of the frequent and secret 'religious talks' held in the Vatican between the Pope and such men as the Dalai Lama.

Because the offence and foolishness of the Cross of the true Gospel have been eclipsed by the carnal power of the Vatican (a power the world so loves), the Pope is perceived by those of other faiths as a potential leader to bring the Christian Church into that religious confederation which Satan is now fabricating through the Ecumenical and Interfaith Movements. They see in the Vatican, not a 'Defender of the biblical faith' — as it is deceptively presented to the Church — but a force which can unite a great mass of humanity in the converging of the conglomerate 'spirituality', which ungodly people are surreptitiously using to pave the way for a parallel form of world government to serve their own interests and those of Antichrist.

Although we are only touching the tip of the iceberg in this brief study, perhaps we can now understand why international financiers are so willing to provide millions of dollars to promote the ecumenical, interfaith cause, as they build the new Babel of global consciousness. As one example of many which could be given, the same family money (Rockefeller) which fuels the internationally influential Chase-Manhattan Bank not only gave $1,000,000 to the World Council of Churches Institute near Geneva, but also provided $8,500,000 for the purchase of land for the United Nations Headquarters in New York.[167] It is equally revealing

---

[166] Ibid.

to learn that this same family money was a major sponsor of the syncretist 'Temple of Understanding', and also of the idolatrous, multi-faith United Nations Meditation Room in New York, prompting one occult organisation to say:

> 'Whatever interpretations one may attribute to the United Nations Meditation Room, it can be said with certainty that the words and the repercussions have only just begun'.[168]

We can see here that the corrupt institutions of the world are riding on the back of the interfaith-ecumenical activities of the apostate Church in order to fulfil their own despotic purposes. Why should this be? Once one understands the nature of the *'Mystery of Iniquity'* (2 Th.2:3-12) and the true direction of *'this evil age'* (Gal.1:4), such a question becomes unnecessary.

We recognise that there are many sincere, ecumenically-minded Christians who would claim to have no desire to become involved in interfaith activities, and would be repulsed by the corrupt capers of the world political and banking systems. Yet they seem to have no qualms about ecumenising with a Vatican which is officially committed to such interfaith goals, and whose financial and political activities are far from spotless. This seduction of well-meaning believers by the worldly power of Rome is not a new phenomenon. As the perceptive Otto Borchert has pointed out:

> 'Many an evangelical among our own people looks enviously towards Rome, and many a Protestant government sees something very imposing in the Pope's position'.[169]

As early as the 1930s, Borchert saw clearly that even the militant atheists of the world have a certain respect for the despotic global pervasiveness of the Papal See:

> 'Even Nietzsche, who concludes his [book] "Anti-Christ" with the words, "I call Christianity the one great curse... I call it the undying blot of shame on humanity", even he cannot help feeling something like sympathy with the Roman Church. For in it he finds his ideal of the absolute ruler realized, and the contrast between master and slave carried out to his heart's content. But what a judgement on Rome Nietzsche's approval is!'[170]

The hyped-up world image of the Pope as a global powermonger has been greatly assisted by such events as his tour of Australia in November 1986, which one commentator likened to *'a mega-star rock marathon'*.[171] In fact, the commercial arrangements for this tour were organised by a specialist rock-music merchandiser who had an exclusive licence to sell more than a hundred endorsed

---

[167] Robert W. Lee, *The United Nations Conspiracy* (Western Islands Press, 1981), p.181.

[168] From 'Lodestone' in the *World Goodwill Bulletin*, Lucis Trust, July, 1957. The Lucis (formerly Lucifer) Trust was founded in 1922 by the occultist Alice B. Bailey.

[169] Otto Borchert, *The Original Jesus [Der Goldgrund des Lebensbildes Jesu]* (Lutterworth Press, 1933), pp.113-114).

[170] Ibid., p.114.

[171] *Daily Telegraph*, November 24th 1986, p.8.

products, including tee-shirts, for which a factory was on a 24-hr standby to top up the stock. The entourage consisted of two assassin-proof 'popemobiles', complete with outriders and sniffer dogs. Two doctors constantly accompanied him, and hospital operating rooms with teams of top surgeons were on standby along the entire route of the tour. A fleet of huge pantechnicons full of papal souvenirs also followed him around the country. The mass which was held in Sydney was attended by over a quarter of a million people, and the Pope, together with eight hundred concelebrating priests dressed in specially-designed matching vestments, ministered from a podium costing A$350,000 to build. How does all this square up to biblical examples of Church leadership? As one astute secular commentator shrewdly observed at the time: *'In more simple days, Jesus entered Jerusalem riding on a donkey'.*[172]

In many ways, it is impossible to identify, in the wake of the Second Vatican Council, what the Roman Catholic religion actually consists of. It appears to be all things to all people, depending on what they want to believe and practise. It can be supportive of gun-toting guerilla warfare, arm-waving Charismatic ecstasy, or incense-burning, goddess-worshipping high priesthood! Cardinal Danneels of Brussels reports with embarrassment the extraordinary phenomenon that *'twenty-three per cent of Catholics in Western countries and up to thirty-one per cent of practising Catholics believe in reincarnation'.*[173] Yet, there must be an untold number of true (although ignorant) believers who have taken refuge in this denomination because of its appearance of biblical orthodoxy over against the overt liberalism of other denominations, but who have little or no idea of the extent of the corruption and syncretism of their Vatican masters. There are also many sincere folk in the Protestant denominations who have been seduced into believing that ecumenical involvement with Roman Catholicism is to be greatly desired. But the power of Rome, with which so many well-meaning ecumenists desire to link themselves today, is nothing more than the power of the world and of Satan.

In the coming years, the true direction of the Vatican and its relationship with the Ecumenical-Interfaith Movement will become clear for all to see. For behind all the idealistic talk of ecumenical unity lies the dark reality of another universal movement — a mighty alliance of demonic power in the form of the many occult and secular organisations of 'world brotherhood', posing as angels of light and servants of righteousness, which has made the political work of the United Nations and the ecumenical activity of the worldwide professing Church the major focus of its secret endeavour.

V. APOLOGIA AND EPILOGUE

Before we bring this chapter (and book) to a close, there are a few loose ends which need tying up. Firstly, many people may wonder what could possibly be wrong with the creation of a better world through ecumenical and interfaith

---

[172] Ibid.

[173] Godfried Cardinal Danneels, *Christ or Aquarius* (Veritas, 1992), p.28. This is an excellent little booklet showing the antichristian nature of the New Age Movement.

cooperation. This is an understandable question in a world which is fumbling after solutions to its evils. Secondly, alongside this question — and perhaps even because of it — a number of believers may be genuinely perplexed about how to respond biblically to ecumenism and interfaithism. To provide answers in these areas we will first show that there are some fundamental flaws in the ambitions of the institutions and organisations which make up the Ecumenical-Interfaith Movement, followed by a few brief thoughts to assist those who feel unable to withstand the pressure to capitulate to the new ecumenism and interfaith demands.

1. The Fatal Flaws of Interfaithism

i. Rejection of the Bible as the Authoritative Word of God

The primary flaw in the aims and ambitions of the Ecumenical-Interfaith Movement is its deliberate denial of the authority of Scripture in all matters of faith and practice. This is the primary flaw because all the other flaws have their roots in this one. Indeed, every problem in the universe stems from that original questioning of the authority of God's words at the outset of human history (Gen.3:1). The situation ethics, theological reductionism, undiscriminating inclusivism and attempts at false peace and unity which pervade the many organisations which make up the Ecumenical-Interfaith Movement could only come about among those who have wilfully set their minds against the unique revelation which has been breathed into the world through His chosen agents (2 Tim.3:15-17; Mt.24:35).

ii. Rejection of the Corruption of Human Nature

The second flaw in the aims and ambitions of the Ecumenical-Interfaith Movement involves the mistaken belief in the innate goodness of humanity — a belief which is expressly refuted in the Bible, e.g., Gen.8:21; Jer.17:9; Rom.3:10-18; Mt.7:11a; Jn.2:25 — together with the failure to take into account the fact that we live in a world which has been ravaged by a Fall. The movement toward world ecumenism has ignored the biblical data which proves that there is a vast horde of evil spiritual beings which operates under the tyranny of a malevolent angel, and who are continually working in opposition to their Creator (Eph.2:2; 6:11-12; cf. Mt.12:22-29) — a situation which Jesus Christ has uniquely come to remedy (Jn.12:31; 1 Jn.3:8; cf. Isa.27:1).

iii. Rejection of the Judgement to Come

The third flaw in the aims and ambitions of the Ecumenical-Interfaith Movement involves its wilful rejection of the testimony of the Bible that the world is now awaiting the full enforcement, on Christ's return, of the devastating and renewing judgement from God for rejecting His Son when He came two thousand years ago to herald a *spiritual* kingdom (Jn.12:31; 5:22-24; 3:35-36). It appears to have escaped these people that the gentle Jesus, meek and mild who they so love will one day return as the One who 'Himself treads the winepress of the fierceness and wrath of Almighty God' (Rev.19:15; cf. 14:19-20). Meanwhile, the leaders and luminaries of the nations are under obligation to pay homage to Jesus Christ (Psalm 2:10-12) and to give up the idolatry and sorcery of their religions — all of which they persistently refuse to do. The fact is that the Bible does not depict the progress of history as leading to the founding of a kingdom of 'peace and justice' in this world as it is presently constituted. Of course, Christians everywhere should peacefully cooperate in promoting order and harmony in the world, but not at the expense of the unique Truth which can only be found in Jesus. It is only in submission to Christ and His law that true peace can be found (Isa.66:12; Jn.14:27; Acts 10:36; Rom.5:1).

iv. Rejection of the Uniqueness of Christianity

The fourth flaw in the aims and ambitions of the Ecumenical-Interfaith Movement involves its notion that Christianity is just another religion which arose in response to certain cultural and historical circumstances in Palestine two thousand years ago. Such a concept may be acceptable in the comparative religion courses of the universities and theological seminaries of the world today, but it cannot be reconciled with God's own revelation in the Bible. For Jesus Christ did not come to start a temporal world religion, but to establish an eternal spiritual kingdom (Jn.18:36; Daniel 7:15-27). Contrary to what the idolatrous, self-deifying faiths of the world believe, Christianity is *not* a religion — it is **the** Truth (Isa.45:18-22; 1 Timothy 2:5; Acts 4:12; Jn.14:6).

2. Answering the Interfaithists

What should be the response of the believer to these things? How should he or she respond to the overtures of the Ecumenical-Interfaith Movement? There is an interesting precedent in the Bible. Over 2,500 years ago, the religious syncretists of the time offered to help the descendants of the Babylonian captivity in their rebuilding of the temple. Their offer was wisely rejected by the leaders of Israel (Ezra 4:1-5). In view of the fact that all the major deceptions with which the Church has been plagued have emerged from such seemingly innocuous beginnings, should we not also exercise the same discernment when faced with the missionary zeal of the ecumenists of today who wish to seduce the Church into ever-deepening compromise? Therefore, to be equal to this task, we must develop a biblical apologetic — a response which we know will be honouring to God and faithful to His Word.

Our apology to world-religionists is no new thing. The Christian Church, from its earliest days, has been continually confronted with the spectre of syncretism. We explored this in relation to Gnosticism in an earlier chapter. Even as early as A.D.134, the Roman emperor Hadrian, in a letter to Servianus states that in Alexandria, *'there is no ruler of a synagogue there, no Samaritan, no Christian presbyter, who is not an astrologer, a soothsayer, a quack'*.[174] Even if such a remark is only partially true, it shows the depths to which the early Church had been corrupted by false doctrine. So how are we to respond to the flood of false doctrine which has engulfed the churches today and the syncretistic practices which such

---

[174] J.H. Srawley (trans.), *The Epistles of St. Ignatius* (S.P.C.K., 1900), p.51n.

corruption breeds?

Three biblical texts provide us with a model of how to respond to these things — of how to function effectively as a Christian in a pluralist culture. The first of these can be found in 2 Cor.10:3-5; the second in 1 Pet.3:15; the third in Acts 17:16-34. The first shows us what should be our first concern in any area of our lives; the second shows us what should lie at the back of any interaction we have with ecumenists and interfaithists; the third gives us a model of how to conduct ourselves when we are functioning as apologists. Let us look at a few of the hints these texts give to us. First, Paul's advice:

> 'For though we walk in the flesh, we do not war according to the flesh. For the weapons of our warfare are not carnal but mighty in God for pulling down strongholds, casting down arguments and every high thing that exalts itself against the knowledge of God, bringing every thought into captivity to the obedience of Christ' (2 Cor.10:3-5).

Here we are shown that it is our duty to be apologists in the face of any ideology which dares to set itself against the knowledge of God and the obedience of Christ. However, the resources we have been given to handle these things are *spiritual.* The Christian standing in the face of the philosophical and ideological genius of the world is like David standing before Goliath. By himself, he was powerless: *'There was no sword in the hand of David'* (1 Sam.17:50). He relied on God's power to destroy the giant. Indeed, the very reason he went into battle against Goliath was so that *'all this assembly shall know that the LORD does not save with sword and spear; for the battle is the LORD's'* (1 Sam.17:47). That is why Paul tells us to *'be strong in the Lord and in the power of His might'* (Eph.6:10), rather than to imagine that we can engage in spiritual warfare (for that is what we are speaking of) in our own strength.

Then, we have Peter's advice:

> 'But sanctify the Lord God in your hearts, and always be ready to give a defence to everyone who asks you a reason for the hope that is in you, with meekness and fear' (1 Pet.3:15).

The context of this passage involves the response of believers to persecution for the sake of the Gospel. Peter's advice is clearly designed to eliminate any thoughts of fear and to encourage us to view such a situation as an opportunity for evangelism. This tallies with the advice given by the Lord Jesus in relation to similar circumstances (see Luke 21:12-15). We must always be ready to confess Christ before people and to give a defence (Greek, *apologia*) for the hope which is in us — that is, eternal life. But notice that Peter gives an important rider to his counsel: he says our 'apology' must be given *'with meekness and fear'.* Although we are encouraged to be eager to demolish every pretension that sets itself up against the knowledge of God (2 Cor.10:4-5), this must be tempered by the knowledge that we should conduct ourselves in a way which is fitting to our calling. We tread firmly but delicately, knowing that we too have lived in darkness, and must approach other creatures in a spirit of compassion, speaking the truth in love, rather than generating caustic enmity towards the Ecumenical Movement or the adherents of world religions. The Christian who confronts the world with a carping, finger-pointing, siege-mentality will never achieve much in the way of evangelism.

In the third of our texts which has a bearing on responding to those caught up in world faiths, Acts 17:16-34, we discover Paul's missionary Gospel preaching in Athens. This passage is often put forward by ecumenically-minded people to show that because Paul spoke courteously to polytheists, therefore Christians should never say anything which may be spiritually offensive to non-Christians. But Paul's sermon was not a bashful or tentative reference to his faith. Let us not forget that he preached in the first place because *'his spirit was provoked within him when he saw that the city was given over to idols'* (Acts 17:16). Unlike the Pope of Rome, Paul did not attempt to ingratiate himself to the sophisticated Athenians by telling them about their wonderful *'cultural heritage and religious diversity'*. Unlike the Archbishop of Canterbury, Paul did not waffle about the necessity for *'mutual respect and understanding between different faith communities'*. Instead, he recognised the spiritual poverty of the Greeks and preached *'Jesus and the resurrection'* (Acts 17:18). He *'reasoned in the synagogue with the Jews and with the Gentile worshippers, and in the marketplace daily with those who happened to be there'* (Acts 17:17). Finally, he stood up in the heartlands of Greek philosophy and told them something which the world finds a foolish joke but which the Spirit reveals to be the truth.

And we should do likewise. There is no need for us to be equivocal when we are presenting Gospel truth to those enslaved to world religion. When Jesus said *'Go into all the world and preach the gospel to every creature'* (Mk.16:15), He knew that the vast majority of those creatures would have world-views ranging from the outright weird to the hardened worldly-wise. We do not need to feel intimidated by the weapons of so-called 'scholarship' ranged against the Church and its unique teachings. Our only concern should be to plant and to water; for it is God who gives the increase (1 Cor.3:6-7). Let us remember that some of the greatest scholars have had their eyes opened by the Lord to the fullness of His simple truth. One of those scholars, the Oxford Professor of Sanskrit, Sir M. Monier-Williams (1819-1899), in an address at the Annual Meeting of the Bible Society in 1886, brings out the essential difference between Christian spirituality and the religions of the world:

> 'In the discharge of my duties for forty years as professor of Sanskrit in the University of Oxford, I have devoted as much time as any man living to the study of the Sacred Books of the East, and I have found the one keynote, the one diapason, so to speak, of all these so-called sacred books, whether it be the Veda of the Brahmans, the Zend-Avesta of the Parsees, the Tripitaka of the Buddhists — *the one refrain through all — salvation by works*. They all say that salvation must be purchased, must be bought with a price, and that the sole price, the sole purchase money, must be our own works and deservings.

> 'Our own holy Bible, our sacred Book of the East, *is from beginning to end a protest against that doctrine.* Good works are, indeed, enjoined upon us in that sacred Book of the East; far more strongly than any other sacred book of the East; but they are only the outcome of a grateful heart — they are only a thank offering, the fruits of our faith. They are never the ransom money of the true disciples of Christ. Let us not shut our eyes to what is excellent and true and of good report in these sacred books, but let us teach Hindus, Buddhists, Mohammedans, that there is only one sacred Book of the East that can be their mainstay in that awful hour when they pass all alone into the unseen world. It is the sacred Book which contains that faithful saying, worthy to be received of all men, women, and children, and not merely of us Christians — that Christ Jesus came into the world to save sinners'.[175]
>
> [emphasis in original]

So let us not lose heart or confidence in the Bible, imagining (as Satan desires) that the ground on which we stand has been muddied into quicksand by higher criticism, comparative religion or scientific theories of various kinds.

We are now living in an extraordinary period of Church history and standing on the threshold of what will surely prove to be a testing time for all Christian believers. In this chapter, we have only skimmed the surface of the syncretistic developments within and without the professing Church today. The hidden agenda of the Ecumenical-Interfaith Movement will one day be exposed for what it is — a movement which plays a major role in the satanic strategy designed to destroy the unique witness of the Christian Gospel. For with their global 'superchurch', the interfaithists are bringing in the earthly kingdom of Antichrist, in an attempted opposition to the building of the spiritual temple of God, the Body of Christ, which is the real Church.

While the Gospel of Christ, under increasing tribulation and ridicule, gradually calls in the true Church — scattered throughout all nations — the universal Satanic appeal to 'oneness' floats enticingly on a global tide of false peace and unity (1 Th.5:3), progressively building the confederation of world religions in preparation for the ultimate Man of Sin (2 Th.2:3-12). In this way, the spiritual, political and economic bodies of the world will become united as *'a habitation of demons, a prison for every foul spirit, and a cage for every unclean and hated bird'* (Rev.18:2). The (almost) perfect work of the devil is being brought to fruition within this present generation.

In spite of all that has been said in this book, the true believer has nothing to fear from these things and must hold onto the reality of the victory of Christ over all those who oppose the establishing of His kingdom (Ps.2:4-6; Dan.2:44; Mt.21:42-44; 2 Th.2:8; Rev.11:15; 13:10: 14:12; 17:17). But neither must the child of God be ignorant of Satan's devices, lest the adversary seize the advantage

---

[175] Bible Society Monthly Reporter, June 1986, pp.91-95. Quoted in *Christian News*, September 6th, 1993, p.14, coupled with a reference in *Christian News Encyclopedia* (Missourian Publishing Co., n.d.), Vol.IV, p.2528.

(2 Cor.2:11). The existence of these developments demonstrates the necessary culmination of the ugly anomaly of sin in this universe, which must always come to its fullness to be ripe for divine judgement (e.g., Gen.15:16; Dan.8:23; Mt.23:32; 1 Th.2:16). Whenever we think of the forces of evil in this world, let us remember that it is *'God [who] has put it into their hearts to accomplish his purpose by agreeing to give the beast their power to rule, until God's words are fulfilled'* (Rev.17:17). We should rejoice in the omnipotence of our God in overruling the humanistic systems of man, in spite of all temporary appearances to the contrary. As G.K. Chesterton has so lucidly expressed it: *'The Church has gone to the dogs at least five times — but each time it was the dog that died!'*[176]

The present days are times in which the people of God need patience and faith as they await the joyful moment when the King of Kings and Lord of Lords shall return in avenging wrath and judgement (Rev.19:15) to establish the 'New Heavens and a New Earth' (Isa.65:17; 2 Pet.3:11-13), in which righteousness dwells and in which there shall by no means be:

> 'anything that defiles, or causes an abomination or a lie, but only those who are written in the Lamb's Book of Life' (Rev.21:27).

When that time comes, the 'great' city of Babylon — that spiritual portrayal of everything in history which is opposed to Jehovah — shall be *'thrown down [with violence], and shall not be found anymore'* (Rev.18:21). The 'spiritual summits', the 'Parliaments', the World Councils, workshops, rituals, meetings, meditations and dreams will be seen in their true perspective: the impotent product of human wisdom, destined to destruction (1 Th.5:3). That will be the Lord's verdict on the satanic deception of syncretism — the lie that puts the temporal 'brotherhood of man' above the eternal judgement of God.

Thus, the entire history of religious corruption will be brought to an abrupt and violent end, while the voice of God resounds across the universe:

> 'I am the LORD, and there is no other; there is no God besides Me...I am the LORD, and there is no other; I form the light and create darkness, I make peace and create calamity; I, the LORD, do all these things'.
>
> (Isa.45:5-7)

---

[176] G.K. Chesterton, *The Everlasting Man* (Hodder & Stoughton, 1924), pp.294-295.

POSTSCRIPT

Our explorations into the origins and extent of religious corruption in this evil age have now come to a close. But before we take leave of one another, let us share some concluding thoughts which will put these matters in their true spiritual perspective.

First, let us remember that the churches have *always* been ravaged by schism and false teaching: the fact itself has not changed, merely the intensity. There has never been a moment in which the Church of Jesus Christ on earth has been free from the doctrinal and divisive assaults of Satan. One has only to read through the extensive polemical writings of the early Church Fathers to realise this.

Second, remember that Jesus said that His disciples would have *'tribulation'* as long as they remained in the world (Jn.16:33). The Spirit-indwelt believer is an anomaly in the midst of an evil age. He or she is a *'stranger and pilgrim'* on this planet and cannot hope to find abiding comfort or fulfilment here (Heb.11:13-16; 2 Cor.5:4). This earthly pilgrimage was never supposed to be easy for those who tread the narrow and afflicted way that leads to life (Mt.7:13-14), and who wish to follow in the footsteps of their Master (Mt.10:37-39; Mk.8:34). Although we may sometimes come upon what Bunyan calls *'a delicate plain called Ease'* in isolated moments, we will also, as that author says, be *'quickly got over it'*.

Third, let us not forget that alongside this inevitable 'tribulation' of the saints is the firm assurance that this selfsame world is in total subjection to the risen, ascended Christ (Jn.16:33). All authority in heaven and on earth has been given to Him, and it is on that foundation that the Great Commission rests (Mt.28:18-20). It is especially important to understand this in the light of the many phenomena that we have recorded in this book. No matter how desperately wicked world developments and church affairs appear to become, we should not be cast down, for everything is unfolding under Divine scrutiny (cf. Acts 4:24-31).

Around the time that the Lord Jesus will return, world conditions will be very similar to how they were in the time of Noah: widespread wickedness, atheism, debauchery, false religion, lawlessness, and a complete absence of concern that these things should be so (Mt.24:37-39; cf. Gen.6:1-2,5-7,11-13). But all this mayhem did not deter Noah from being a faithful *'preacher of righteousness'* until the moment that the Lord shut him in the ark, rescuing him with his family from the judgement of the flood (2 Pet.2:5). Neither should we be deterred from heralding the same Gospel until that moment when the Lord comes to take His own into glory and His sickle of judgement is thrust into the world for the final time (Rev.14:17-20). According to Apostolic counsel, even when people no longer endure sound doctrine, and have heaped up for themselves false teachers, the faithful pastor must continue to be *'watchful in all things'*, and *'endure afflictions'* as a fulfilment of evangelistic ministry (2 Tim.4:5). Preaching the Word continues unruffled both in season *and* out of season (2 Tim.4:2).

The information given in this book should motivate believers to realise that the professing Church has, in many ways, failed to stand mightily against the dark principalities and powers which are having such a field-day in the world at present. The bewitching teachings of Gnosticism have stepped in where the visible church has feared to tread in its Divinely-appointed duty throughout the present Age. Stultifying legalism, cultish extremism, magisterial enforcement of Christianity through barbaric forms of persecution, incessant sectarianism and in-fighting, dependence on outward ritual and manmade ceremonies, the lack of a true spirituality of the heart — all these have driven people to conclude that a more genuine Christianity is to be found in the siren tones of Gnosticism and a more fulfilling faith in the world religions devised by Satan. It is high time that we set about reversing this trend. The role of the believer in every era is to pull down these heathen strongholds and to busy himself in

> 'casting down arguments and every high thing that exalts itself against the knowledge of God, bringing every thought into captivity to the obedience of Christ' (2 Cor.10:4-5).

Let us also remember that this present universe was never designed to be the final product of God's creative activity. As the Scriptures clearly show, the ultimate purpose in the mind of God has always been a completely reconstituted universe in which suffering and evil will have no place (Isa.65:17; 66:22; Acts 3:20-21; Mt.19:28; 2 Pet.3:13; Rev.21:1-5). Therefore the universe, as it is currently constituted, is but a vast stepping stone on the pathway to a new heaven and a new earth. In this way, we can see that everything that happens within it is in some sense, in the inscrutable will of God, making a contribution to that ultimate purpose. As a servant of the Lord from an earlier age has put it: *'Whatever poison Satan produces, God turns it into medicine for His children'*. Understanding this fact will bring a new perspective to our knowledge of the many forces of this evil age, which must always be seen as provisional, transient, and under the controlling hand of God.

It is widely believed today that the world is now moving into a Post-Christian Era, and that this will be an age of 'peace, justice and human brotherhood'. But this is not at all the 'age of enlightenment' that the world imagines; for in claiming to be in such an epoch, the world has pronounced upon itself the curse of darkness. For the only post-Christian era revealed in the Bible is that known as Satan's *'little season'* (Rev.20:3, A.V.) — that brief period of tribulation prior to the return of the Lord Jesus Christ, in which the people of God become subject to the full wrath of a devil who knows he has been defeated and that he has only a very short time in which to vent his spleen. Having considered all the detail that is in this book, and pondered the religious and political developments of the past one and a half centuries, one may well wonder if that time is coming upon us now.

However, even if this should be so, we have no need to despair. The assaults of Satan on the Church — however intense they may become — should never give us cause for pessimism or depression, for three good reasons: First, Satan's assaults on the Church give believers great assurance that every word of the Bible is true and that the Lord's people do indeed belong to the one true God and Creator of the universe. You can be sure that if Christianity was just a myth, the academics, media pundits and philosophers of the world would not take the great interest they do in destroying it. Second, rather than plunging us into pessimism, Satan's assaults should give us even greater impetus to become able apologists and proclaim the glorious Gospel to a needy world. Third, the more intense Satan's assaults become, the more likely it is that the return of the Lord Jesus Christ is fast approaching; and that is hardly a reason for pessimism or depression. As we are told by Jesus Himself: *'Now when these things begin to happen, look up and lift up your heads, because your redemption draws near'* (Luke 21:28).

When that fullness of redemption comes, then the true 'New Age' can begin. There will then be a transformation of every constituent of the universe, in which no place will be found for the devil, his fellow fallen angels, and all those who have helped him unrepentingly. In that glorious moment, *'the creation itself also will be delivered from the bondage of corruption into the glorious liberty of the children of God'* (Rom.8:21). The only recipients of this inheritance will be those who have faithfully followed Jesus Christ rather than grasped at forbidden *gnosis.* If all this could be fathomed for but a moment, there would be silence on the earth for half an hour.

Even so, come, Lord Jesus! The grace of our Lord Jesus Christ be with all the saints. Amen.

BIBLIOGRAPHY

Listed below are the works which have either been directly quoted in the main text or which have provided foundational background information.

General Works of Reference

ATTWATER, Donald (ed.), *Penguin Dictionary of Saints*, Penguin, 1982.

BAUER, W., ARNDT, W.F. & GINGRICH, F.W., *A Greek-English Lexicon of the New Testament*, University of Chicago, 1979.

BIEDERMANN, Hans, *Dictionary of Symbolism: Cultural Icons and the Meanings Behind Them*, Facts on File, 1992.

Chambers's Encyclopaedia, 14 Vols., George Newnes, 1963 edition.

CHETWYND, Tom, *A Dictionary of Symbols, Granada, 1982.*

ELIADE, Mircea , (ed.), *Encyclopedia of Religion*, Macmillan, 1987.

Encyclopaedia Britannica, 15th edition.

GRUN, Bernard, *The Timetables of History*, Simon & Schuster, 1991.

HASTINGS, J., (ed.), *Encyclopaedia of Religion and Ethics*, 12 Vols., T.& T. Clark, 1920.

HINNELLS, J. R., (ed.), *The Penguin Dictionary of Religions*, Penguin, 1984.

——— (ed.), *The Handbook of Living Religions*, Pelican, 1985.

Hutchinson Encyclopedia, 1992.

MAGNUSSON, M., *Chambers Biographical Dictionary*, Chambers, 1990.

ONIONS, C.T., (ed.), *The Oxford Dictionary of English Etymology*, Oxford University Press, 1966.

SCHAFF, Philip, (ed.), *Schaff-Herzog Encyclopaedia of Religious Knowledge*, 4 Vols., Funk & Wagnalls, 1891.

The Macmillan Encyclopedia, 1986.

WHISTON, W. (trans.), Flavius Josephus: *Antiquities*, Hendrickson, 1985.

ZAEHNER, R.C. (ed.), *Hutchinson Encyclopedia of Living Faiths*, 1988.

Christian Works of Reference

ATTWATER, Donald, *The Penguin Dictionary of Saints*, Penguin, 1983.

BLUNT, John Henry (ed.), *Dictionary of Sects, Heresies, Ecclesiastical Parties and Schools of Religious Thought*, Rivingtons, 1874.

BROMILEY, G.W., (ed.), *The International Standard Bible Encyclopedia*, 4 Vols., Eerdmans, 1982.

BURGESS, S.M. & MCGEE, G.B., *Dictionary of Pentecostal and Charismatic Movements*, Zondervan, 1988.

Christian News Encyclopedia, 5 Vols., Missouri Publishing, 1992.

CROSS, F.L. & LIVINGSTONE, E.A., (eds.), *The Oxford Dictionary of the*

Christian Church, O.U.P., 1983.
DOUGLAS, J.D., (ed.), *New International Dictionary of the Christian Church*, Zondervan, 1974.
ELWELL, Walter A., (ed.), *Evangelical Dictionary of Theology*, Marshall Pickering, 1984.
FERGUSON, S., WRIGHT, D.F., & PACKER J.I. (eds.), *The New Dictionary of Theology*, IVP, 1988.
GREEN, J.P. (ed.), *The Encyclopedia of Christianity*, 4 Vols., N.F.C.E., 1964-1968.
HARRIS, R.L., ARCHER, G.L. Jr., & WALTKE, B.K. (eds.), *The Theological Wordbook of the Old Testament*, 2 Vols., Moody Press. 1980.
HASTINGS, J., (ed.), *Dictionary of the Apostolic Church*, 2 Vols., T. & T. Clark, 1915.
HASTINGS, J., (ed.), *Dictionary of the Bible*, 2 Vols., T. & T. Clark, 1898.
KELLY, J.N.D., *The Oxford Dictionary of Popes*, O.U.P., 1986.
MOYER, Elgin S., *The Wycliffe Biographical Dictionary of the Church*, Moody Press, 1982.
PAYNE, J. Barton, *Encyclopedia of Biblical Prophecy: The Complete Guide to Scriptural Predictions and their Fulfillment*, Baker Book House, 1980.
TENNEY, M.F., (ed.), *The Zondervan Pictorial Encyclopedia of the Bible*, 5 Vols., 1975.

Anthropology, Evolution, Ecology

BOWDEN, M., *Ape Man: Fact or Fallacy*, Sovereign Publications, 1977.
DEELY, John N. and NOGAR, Raymond J., (eds.), *The Problem of Evolution: A Study of the Philosophical. Repercussions of Evolutionary Science*, Appleton-Century-Crofts, 1973.
DESMOND, A. & Moore, J., *Darwin*, Michael Joseph, 1991.
IRVINE W., *Apes, Angels and Victorians*, Weidenfeld & Nicholson, 1956.
JOHNSON, Wallace, *Evolution?*, TAN Books, 1992.
LOVELOCK, J. E., *Gaia*, Oxford University Press, 1979.
MORRIS, Henry M., *The Long War Against God*, Baker Book House, 1989.
RUSSELL, Peter, *The Awakening Earth: The Next Evolutionary Leap*, Routledge & Kegan Paul, 1982.
———, *The White Hole in Time: Our Future Evolution and the Meaning of Now*, Aquarian Press, 1992.
SHELDRAKE, Rupert, *A New Science of Life: Hypothesis of Formative Causation*, Blond, 1981.
SMITH, Wolfgang, *Teilhardism and the New Religion: A Thorough Analysis of the Teachings of Pierre Teilhard de Chardin*, Tan Books, 1988.

TAYLOR, Ian T., *In the Minds of Men: Darwin and the New World Order*, T.F.E. Publishing, 1987.

TEILHARD DE CHARDIN, Pierre, *Christianity and Evolution*, Collins, 1971.

———, Pierre, *The Heart of the Matter*, Collins, 1978.

Charismatic Movement & Pentecostalism

BABCOX, Neil, *A Search for Charismatic Reality: One Man's Pilgrimage*, Multnomah Press, 1985.

BASHAM, Don, *Spiritual Power: How to Get it – How to Give it!*, Whitaker House, 1976.

BUDGEN, Victor, *The Charismatics and the Word of God: A Biblical & Historical Perspective on the Charismatic Movement*, Evangelical Press, 1985.

CHANTRY, Walter J. *Signs of the Apostles: Observations on Pentecostalism Old and New*, Banner of Truth, 1976.

COPELAND, Kenneth, *Walking in the Realm of the Miraculous*, KCP, n.d.

EDGAR, J., *Miraculous Gifts*, Loizeau Brothers, 1983.

GAFFIN, Richard B., *Perspectives on Pentecost*, Presbyterian & Reformed, 1978.

GREEN, Michael, *I Believe in the Holy Spirit*, Hodder & Stoughton, 1985.

GROMACKI, Robert G., *The Modern Tongues Movement*, P. & R., 1972.

HUGHES, Selwyn, *Lord, Heal me Now*, Crusade for World Revival, n.d.

JUDISCH, Douglas, *An Evaluation of Claims to the Charismatic Gifts*, Baker Book House, 1979.

KELSEY, Morton, *Healing and Christianity*, Harper & Row, 1973.

MacARTHUR, John F., *Charismatic Chaos*, Zondervan, 1992.

MARSTON, George, *Tongues Then and Now*, Presbyterian & Reformed, 1983.

MASTERS, Peter, *The Healing Epidemic*, Wakeman Trust, 1988.

MATZAT, Don, *Inner Healing: Deliverance or Deception?*, Harvest House, 1987.

NEIL, Arthur, *Aid us in Our Strife*, Heath Christian Trust, 1985.

O'CONNOR, Edward D., *The Pentecostal Movement in the Catholic Church*, Ave Maria Press, 1973.

POWELL, Graham & Shirley , *Christian Set Yourself Free: Proven Guidelines to Self-Deliverance from Demonic. Oppression*, New Wine Press, 1983.

ROBERTS, Phil, *The Gift of Tongues: An Evaluation*, Interdisciplinary Bible Research Institute, 1991.

SANFORD, Agnes, *The Healing Gifts of the Spirit*, Arthur James, 1966.

SEAMANDS, David, *Healing of Memories*, Scripture Press, 1986.

STAPLETON, Ruth Carter, *The Gift of Inner Healing*, Hodder & Stoughton, 1977.

SUENENS, Léon Joseph Cardinal, *Ecumenism and the Charismatic Renewal*, Darton, Longman & Todd, 1978.

WARFIELD, Benjamin, *Counterfeit Miracles*, Banner of Truth, 1972.

WHYTE, H.A. Maxwell, *The Power of the Blood*, Whitaker House, 1973.

WIMBER, John, *Power Evangelism*, Hodder & Stoughton, 1985.

———, with SPRINGER, K., *Power Healing*, Hodder & Stoughton, 1986.

Christian Works (general)

ANCIENT AND MODERN Library of Theological Literature, *The Apostolic Fathers, Part II*, 'The Epistles of St. Ignatius and St. Polycarp', Griffith, Farran, Okeden & Welsh, 1889.

ARNOLD, Clinton E., *Powers of Darkness*, I.V.P., 1992.

BATTLES, F.L. (trans.), *John Calvin: Institutes of the Christian Religion*, Westminster Press, 1960.

BORCHERT, Otto, *The Original Jesus [Der Goldgrund des Lebensbildes Jesu]*, Lutterworth Press, 1933.

BROOKS, Thomas, *Precious Remedies Against Satan's Devices*, Banner of Truth, 1984, f.p. 1652.

BROWN, Harold O.J., *Heresies: The Image of Christ in the Mirror of Heresy and Orthodoxy from the Apostles to the Present*, Baker, 1984.

BURGON, John W., (ed. J.P. Green), *The Last Twelve Verses of the Gospel According to Mark*, Vol.I of 'Unholy Hands on the Bible', Sovereign Grace Trust Fund, 1990, f.p.1871.

COLE, Henry (trans.), *Calvin's Calvinism*, Reformed Free Publishing Association, n.d.

CHESTERTON, Gilbert K., *Orthodoxy*, John Lane, The Bodley Head, 1908.

DABNEY, Robert L., *Systematic Theology*, Banner of Truth, 1985, first published in 1871.

GOOLD, W.H., (ed.), *John Owen: Works*, 6 Vols., Banner of Truth, 1967,

GREEN, W.H., *The Argument of Job Unfolded*, Klock & Klock, 1978.

GRENZ, Stanley J., & OLSON, Roger E., *20th Century Theology: God and the World in a Transitional Age*, I.V.P., 1992.

GURNALL, William, *The Christian in Complete Armour: A Treatise of the Saints' War Against the Devil*, Banner of Truth Trust, 1964.

GWATKIN, H.M., *Early Church History*, Macmillan, 1909.

HELDENBRAND, Richard, *Christianity and the New Evangelical Philosophies*, Words of Life, 1991.

HISLOP, Alexander, *The Two Babylons*, S.W. Partridge, 1916.

HODGE, Archibald A., *Outlines of Theology*, Thomas Nelson, 1879.

HORTON, Michael Scott, *Made in America: The Shaping of Modern American*

Evangelism, Baker Book House, 1991.

ICE, Thomas, & DEAN, Robert, *Overrun by Demons: The Church's New Preoccupation with the Demonic*, Harvest House, 1990.

JOHN, Bishop of Bristol, *The Ecclesiastical History of the Second and Third Centuries*, Griffith, Farran, Okeden & Welsh, 1825.

KEBLE, John, (trans.), *The Five Books of St. Irenaeus Against Heresies*, A.D. Innes, 1893.

LAW, Robert, *The Tests of Life: A Study of the First Epistle of St. John*, T. & T. Clark, 1909.

LEAHY, F.S., *Satan Cast Out: A Study in Biblical Demonology*, Banner of Truth, 1975.

MACHEN, J. Gresham , *Christianity and Liberalism*, Eerdmans, 1985.

MAURO, Philip, *The Number of Man: The Climax of Civilisation*, Morgan & Scott, 1910.

MacARTHUR, John F., *Ashamed of the Gospel: When the Church Becomes Like the World*, Crossway Books, 1993.

McILHENNY, Chuck & Donna, with YORK, Frank, *When the Wicked Seize the City*, Huntington House, 1993.

MOSHEIM, John L., *An Ecclesiastical History, Ancient and Modern, from the Birth of Christ to the Beginning of the Eighteenth Century*, Two Vols., Blackie, Fullarton & Co., 1827.

PASCAL, Blaise, *Pensées*, Penguin, 1966.

PEMBER, G.H., *Earth's Earliest Ages and their Connection with Modern Spiritualism, Theosophy, and Buddhism*, G.H. Lang, no date, first published by Pickering & Inglis, 1876.

PERKINS, William, *Workes*, Cambridge, 1604, 1611, 1616.

RYLE, J.C., *Expository Thoughts on the Gospels*, 3 Vols., James Clarke, 1985.

SCHAFF, Philip, *History of the Christian Church*, 8 Vols., Scribner's, 1910.

SHAEFFER, Francis, *Genesis in Space and Time*, Inter Varsity Press, 1972.

———, et al, *Whatever Happened to the Human Race? — Study Guide*, Marshall, Morgan & Scott. 1980.

SIRE, James W., *The Universe Next Door*, I.V.P., 1988.

SMEATON, George, *The Doctrine of the Holy Spirit*, Banner of Truth, 1974.

SRAWLEY, J.H., (trans.), *The Epistles of St. Ignatius*, S.P.C.K., 1900.

STAFFORD WRIGHT, J., *What is Man: A Christian Assessment of the Powers and functions of Human Personality*, Paternoster Press, 1955.

STRONG, Augustus H., *Systematic Theology*, Pickering & Inglis, 1981.

VOS, Geerhardus, *Biblical Theology*, Banner of Truth, 1975.

WARFIELD, Benjamin B., *Biblical and Theological Studies*, P. & R., 1968.

WATSON, Thomas, *A Body of Divinity*, Banner of Truth, 1968.

Ecumenical Movement, Interfaithism, Social Gospel, Syncretism

ABHISHIKTANANDA, *Hindu-Christian Meeting Point*, ISPCK, 1976.

BAHA'I WORLD CENTRE, *Haifa, The Promise of World Peace: A Statement by the Universal House of Justice*, October, 1985.

BLAIR, Philip, *What on Earth? — The Church in the World and the Call of Christ*, Lutterworth Press, 1993.

COTTER, John, *A Study in Syncretism: The Background and Apparatus of the Emerging One-World Church*, Canadian Intelligence Publications, 1979.

Council for a Parliament of World Religions Newsletter, Vol.4, No.1, June 1992.

CUPITT, Don, *The Sea of Faith: Christianity in Change*, BBC, 1984.

DACOSTA, Gavin, *Is One Religion as Good as Another?*, Catholic Truth Society, 1985.

FERRÉ, Nels, *The Universal Word: A Theology for a Universal Faith*, Collins, 1970.

GRAHAM, Dom Aelred, *Zen Catholicism*, Harcourt, Brace & World Inc., 1963.

GRIFFITHS, Bede, *Towards a Hindu-Christian Dialogue*, London, 1966.

———, *The Marriage of East and West*, Collins, 1982.

———, *Cosmic Revelation: The Hindu Way To God*, Collins, 1983.

———, *Christ in India*, Charles Scribner, 1966.

HOCKING, W.E., *Rethinking Missions*, Harper, 1932.

HOGG, William Richey, 'Edinburgh 1910: Ecumenical Keystone', article in *Religion and Life: A Christian Quarterly of Opinion and Discussion*, Vol. XXIX, No.3, Summer 1960.

HOPKINS, C.H., *John R. Mott: A Biography*, Eerdmans, 1980.

INTERFAITH NEWS, No.3, Autumn 1983.

JACKSON, Carl T., *The Oriental Religions and American Thought: Nineteenth Century Explorations*, Greenwood, 1981.

KING, Ursula, *Towards a New Mysticism: Teilhard de Chardin and Eastern Religions*, Collins, 1980.

Life Magazine, December, 1964. Article on the origin of the Temple of Understanding entitled 'Judith Hollister and her Wonderful Obsession'.

MACGREGOR, G., *The Christening of Karma*, Theosophical Pub., 1984.

MARTIN, Hugh, *Beginning at Edinburgh: A Jubilee Assessment of the World Missionary Conference, 1910*, Edinburgh House Press, 1960.

MCINTIRE, Carl, *Servants of Apostasy*, Christian Beacon Press, 1955.

MERTON, Thomas, *The Zen Revival*, Buddhist Society of London, 1971.

———, *Thomas Merton on Zen*, Sheldon Press, 1976.

MORRISON, Charles Clayton, *The Social Gospel and the Christian Cultus*, Harper & Bros., 1933.

NATIONAL CENTRE FOR CHRISTIAN COMMUNITIES & NETWORKS, *Towards a New Vision of Church: A Report to the Interchurch Process*, NACCCAN, 1986.

REARDON, Martin, *What on Earth is the Church for? — A Study Course for Lent 1986 prepared for the Inter-Church Process*, British Council of Churches & the Catholic Truth Society, 1986.

REDFORD, John, *What Catholics Believe: in Twenty Lessons*, Catholic Truth Society, 1981.

ROMAN CATHOLIC COMMITTEE FOR OTHER FAITHS, *What does the Church Teach?*, Catholic Truth Society, 1986.

RUNCIE, Robert, *Christianity and World Religions*, Sir Francis Younghusband Lecture, World Congress of Faiths, n.d.

SMITH, Bernard, *The Fraudulent Gospel: Politics and the W.C.C.*, Canadian Intelligence Publications, 1978.

STRYK, Lucien, (ed.), *World of the Buddha: An Introduction to Buddhist Literature*, Grove Press, 1982.

SUENENS, Leon Joseph Cardinal, *Ecumenism and Charismatic Renewal*, Darton, Longman & Todd, 1978.

TEMPLE, Merfyn, *Angelus for Peace in the South Atlantic*, 1982.

TEMPLE OF UNDERSTANDING NEWSLETTER, Summer, 1992.

TODD, John M., *Catholicism and the Ecumenical Movement*, Longmans, Green & Co., 1956.

TOYNE, Marcus, *Involved in Mankind: The Life and Message of Vivekananda*, Ramakrishna Vedanta Centre, 1983.

VISSER 'T HOOFT, William, No Other Name: The Choice Between Syncretism and Christian Universalism, SCM Press, 1963.

———, (ed.), *The First Assembly of the World Council of Churches: The Official Report*, SCM, 1949.

Feminism, Witchcraft, Cult of the Goddess, Women's Studies

BEGG, Ean, *The Cult of the Black Virgin*, Routledge & Kegan Paul, 1985.

BUDAPEST, Zusanna, *The Holy Book of Women's Mysteries, Part II*, Susan B. Anthony Coven No. 1, 1980.

COOK, A. & KIRK, G., *Greenham Woman Everywhere: Dreams, Ideas and Actions form the Women's Peace Movement*, Pluto, 1983.

FREER, Jean, *Raging Womyn*, Amazon Press, 1984.

FRYE, Roland M., *Language for God and Feminist Language: Problems and Principles*, The Handsel Press, no. date.

GOLDENBERG, Naomi R., *Changing of the Gods: Feminism and the End of Traditional Religions*, Beacon Books, Boston, 1979.

GRIFFIN, Susan, *Woman and Nature: The Roaring Inside Her*, Women's Press, 1984.

HEINE, Susanne, *Christianity and the Goddesses: Systematic Criticism of a Feminist Theology*, SCM Press. 1988.

———, *Women and Early Christianity: Are the Feminist Scholars Right?*, SCM Press, 1987.

KEAY, Kathy, (ed.), *Men, Women and God*, Marshall Pickering, 1987.

MONAGHAN, Patricia, *Women in Myth and Legend*, Junction Books, 1981.

PARVATI, Jeannine, *Hygieia: A Woman's Herbal*, Wildwood House, London, 1979.

PHILLIPS, A. & RAKUSEN, J., *Our Bodies Ourselves*, Penguin Books, 1978.

PRIME, Derek, *Women in the Church: A Pastoral Approach*, Crossway, 1992.

SJÖÖ, M, & MOR, B., *The Ancient Religion of the Great Cosmic Mother of All*, Rainbow Press, 1981.

STARHAWK, *The Spiral Dance: A Rebirth of the Ancient Religion of the Great Goddess*, Harper & Row, 1979.

WALKER, Barbara G., (ed.), *The Woman's Encyclopedia of Myths and Secrets*, Harper & Row, 1983.

Futurism, UFOs

HUXLEY, ALDOUS, *Brave New World*, Panther, 1977.

———, *Island*, Penguin, 1964.

KINSMAN, Francis, *Millennium: Towards Tomorrow's Society*, Penguin, 1990.

MULLER, Robert, (ed.), *The Desire to be Human: A Global Reconnaissance of Human Perspectives in an Age of Transformation*, Miranana, 1983.

ORWELL, George, *Nineteen Eighty-Four*, Penguin, 1984.

TAYLOR, John, *The Shape of Minds to Come*, Michael Joseph, 1971.

TEILHARD de Chardin, Pierre, *The Future of Man*, Harper & Row, 1955.

WILSON, Clifford and WELDON, John, *Close Encounters: A Better Explanation*, Master Books/CLP, 1978.

Holistic Health & Healing

BAUMAN, Edward, et al, *Holistic Health Handbook*, And/Or, 1978.

BAYLY, Doreen E., *Reflexology Today*, Thorsons, 1978.

GORDON, Richard, *Your Healing Hands: The Polarity Experience*, Unity Press, 1978.

MARQUARDT, Hanne, *Reflex Zone Therapy of the Feet*, Thorsons, 1983.

OHASHI, W., *D-I-Y Shiatsu*, Unwin, 1977.

REISSER, P., REISSER, T. & WELDON, J., *New Age Medicine*, I.V.P., 1987.

RIEHL-SISCA, J., (ed.), *Conceptual Models for Nursing Practice*, Appleton & Lange, 3rd. ed., 1989.

St. PIERRE, G., & BOATER, D., *The Metamorphic Technique: Principles and Practice*, Element Books, 1982.

STALKER, Douglas & GLYMOUR, Clark , (eds.), *Examining Holistic Medicine*, Prometheus Books, 1985.

WIMBER, John, *Practical Healing: A Practical Guide to Power Healing*, Hodder & Stoughton, 1987.

Theosophy, Gnosticism, New Age & Esotericism

ANNETT, Stephen (ed.), *The Many Ways of Being: A guide to Spiritual Groups and Growth Centres in Britain*, Abacus, 1976.

ARGUELLES, José, *The Transformative Vision: Reflections on the Nature and History of Human Expression*, Shambhala, 1975.

ANON, *A Course in Miracles*, Arkana/Routledge & Kegan Paul, 1974.

BAIGENT, M. & LEIGH, R., *The Temple and the Lodge*, Jonathan Cape, 1989.

BAILEY, Alice B., *Discipleship in the New Age*, 2 Vols., Lucis Press, 1944 & 1955.

———, *Externalisation of the Hierarchy*, Lucis Press, 1957.

———, *Initiation: Human and Solar*, Lucis Press, 1922.

———, *The Reappearance of the Christ*, Lucis Press, 1922.

BARTHOLOMEW, Alick (ed.), *Crop Circles: Harbingers of World Change*, Gateway, 1991.

BESANT, Annie, *Mysticism*, Theosophical Publishing House, 1914.

———, *Esoteric Christianity: The Lesser Mysteries*, Theosophical Pub., 1901.

BLAVATSKY, H.P., *The Secret Doctrine*, Quest Books, 1966.

BOYD, Donald M., *New Age Nursing in the Highlands*, Free Presbyterian Religion and Morals Committee, 1993.

BROOKE, Tal, *The Other Side of Death: Does Death Seal your Destiny?*, Tyndale Press, 1979.

BRUNTON, Paul, *The Secret Path: A Technique of Spiritual Self-Discovery for the Modern World*, Rider, 1934.

CAPRA, Fritjof, *The Turning Point: Science, Society and the Rising Culture*, Flamingo, 1982.

CAREY, Ken, *Starseed: The Third Millennium: Living in the Post-Historic World*, Harper, 1991.

———, *The Starseed Transmissions*, Harper, 1982.

CHURTON, Tobias, *The Gnostics*, Channel 4 with Weidenfeld & Nicholson, 1990.

DA FREE JOHN, *A Call for the Radical Reformation of Christianity*, Dawn Horse Press, 1982.

DANNEELS, Godfried Cardinal, *Christ or Aquarius*, Veritas, Dublin, 1992.

EDMUNDS, Frances, *Anthroposophy: A Way of Life*, Carnant Books, 1982.

ENGLAND, Randy, *The Unicorn in the Sanctuary: The Impact of the New Age on the Catholic Church*, TAN Books, 1991.

ESSENE, Virginia, *New Teachings for an Awakened Humanity*, Spiritual Education Endeavours Publishing, 1986.

FERGUSON, Marilyn, *The Aquarian Conspiracy: Personal and Social Transformation in the 1980s*, Granada, 1982.

GOODRICK-CLARKE, Nicolas, *The Occult Roots of Nazism: The Ariosophists of Austria and Germany, 1890-1935*, Aquarian Press, 1985.

GRANT, R.M. & FREEDMAN, D.N., (trans. & eds.), *The Secret Sayings of Jesus: According to the Gospel of Thomas*, Fontana, 1960.

HIEBEL, Frederick, *Treasures of Biblical Research and the Conscience of the Times*, Anthroposophic Press, 1970.

HOELLER, Stephan A., *The Gnostic Jung and the Seven Sermons to the Dead*, Quest Books, 1982.

HUMPHREYS, Christmas, et al (eds.), *Helena Blavatsky: The Secret Doctrine*, abridged, Theosophical Publishing House, 1966.

ISRAEL, Martin, *Coming in Glory: Christ's Presence in the World Today*, Darton, Longman & Todd, 1986.

JONAS, Hans, *The Gnostic Religion*, Beacon Press, 1963.

JUNG, C.G., *Psychology and Alchemy*, Routledge & Kegan Paul, 1957.

KEYES, Ken, *Handbook to Higher Consciousness*, Living Love Publications, 1975.

KOLISKO, Eugen, *Zoology for Everybody*, Kolisko Archive Publication, 1978.

———, *The Twelve Groups of Animals*, Kolisko Archive Publications, 1978.

KRISHNAMURTI, Jiddu, *Freedom from the Known*, Harper & Row, 1969.

———, *The Impossible Question*, Penguin, 1978.

KÜBLER-ROSS, Elizabeth, *Death: The Final State of Growth*, Prentice-Hall, 1975.

KUTHUMI, *Studies of the Human Aura*, Summit University Press, 1971.

LEADBEATER, C.W., *The Inner Life: Philosophical Talks at Adyar*, Vol.I, Theosophical Press, 1949.

LEMESURIER, Peter, *This New Age Business: The Story of the Ancient and Continuing Quest to Bring Down Heaven to Earth*, Findhorn Press, 1990.

LÉVI, *The Aquarian Gospel of Jesus Christ: The Philosophic and Practical*

Basis of the Religion of the Aquarian Age of the World, L.N. Fowler, 1964.

LIEVEGOED, Bernhard J., *Man on the Threshold: The Challenge of Inner Development*, Hawthorn Press, 1985.

———, *Towards the 21st Century*, Steiner Book Centre, 1979.

LINDEN, Jan van der, *The Inner Life of the United Nations*, School for Esoteric Studies Inc., n.d.

LOOMIS, Evarts G., *Amy: The Search for the Treasure Within*, DeVorss & Co., 1986.

LUTYENS, Mary, *Krishnamurti: The Years of Awakening*, Rider, 1984.

———, *Krishnamurti: The Years of Fulfilment*, John Murray, 1983.

McDERMOTT, Robert A. (ed.), *The Essential Steiner*, Harper & Row, 1984.

MCINTOSH, Christopher, *The Rosecross and the Age of Reason: 18th century Rosicrucianism in Central Europe and its Relationship to the Enlightenment*, E.J. Brill, 1992.

———, *The Rosicrucians*, Thorsons, 1987.

———, *The Rosicrucians: The History, Mythology and Rituals of an Occult Order*, Crucible, 1987.

MELTON, J. Gordon, *New Age Almanac*, Visible Ink, 1991.

———, *New Age Encyclopedia*, Gale Research, 1990.

MOODY, Raymond A., *Life After Life*, Mockingbird Books, 1975.

MURCHIE, Guy, *Music of the Spheres: The Material Universe from Atom to Quasar Simply Explained*, Rider Hutchinson, 1979.

NORTHCOTT, Michael S., *The New Age and Pastoral Theology: Towards the Resurgence of the Sacred*, Pastoral Monograph No.2, Contact, 1992.

PAGELS, Elaine, *The Gnostic Gospels*, Weidenfeld & Nicholson, 1979.

PENNICK, Nigel, *Hitler's Secret Sciences: His Quest for the Hidden Knowledge of the Ancients*, Neville Spearman, 1981.

POPPELBAUM, Hermann, *New Light on Heredity and Evolution*, St. George Pubs., 1977.

PRICE, John Randolph, *The Planetary Commission*, Quartus Books, 1986.

———, *The Superbeings*, Quartus Books, 1981.

PROPHET, Elizabeth Clare, *Prayer and Meditation: Jesus and Kuthumi*, Summit Press, 1963.

———, *The Lost Years of Jesus*, Summit University Press, 1984.

ROBERTS, Jane, *The Seth Material*, Bantam Books, 1970.

ROSSNER, John, *Toward Recovery of the Primordial Tradition*, 'The Psychic Roots of Ancient Wisdom and Primitive Christian Gnosis', University Press of America, 1983, 3 Vols.

RUDOLPH, Kurt, Gnosis: *The Nature and History of Gnosticism*, Harper & Row, 1987.

SHEPARD, Leslie A., (ed.), *Encyclopedia of Occultism and Parapsychology*, Gale Research Co., 1979.

SINCLAIR, Sir John, *The Alice Bailey Inheritance*, Turnstone Press, 1984.

SPANGLER, David, *Reflections on the Christ*, Findhorn, 1978.

———, *Revelation: The Birth of a New Age*, Findhorn Press, 1971.

———, *Towards a Planetary Vision*, Findhorn, 1977.

———, *Vision of Findhorn: Anthology*, Findhorn Foundation, 1976.

SPENSER, R.K., *The Cult of the All-Seeing Eye*, Christian Book Club of America, 1962.

STEINER, Rudolf, *Christianity as Mystical Fact and the Mysteries of Antiquity*, Rudolf Steiner Press, 1972.

———, *Evolution of Consciousness*, Rudolf Steiner Press, 1979.

———, *From Buddha to Christ*, Anthroposophical Press, 1978.

———, *Knowledge of the Higher Worlds: How is it Achieved?*, Rudolf Steiner Press, 1969.

———, *Occult Science: An Outline*, Rudolf Steiner Press, 1979.

———, *Study of Man*, Rudolf Steiner Press, 1966.

STOCKMEYER, E.A. Karl, *Rudolf Steiner's Curriculum for Waldorf Schools*, Steiner Schools Fellowship, 1969.

STREIKER, Lowell D., *New Age Comes to Main Street*, Abingdon, 1990.

SZEKELY, Edmund Bordeaux, *The Teachings of the Essenes from Enoch to the Dead Sea Scrolls*, C.W. Daniel, 1978.

TANSLEY, David, *Raiment of Light: A Study of the Human Aura*, RKP, 1984.

TILLETT, Gregory, *The Elder Brother: A Biography of Charles Webster Leadbeater*, Routledge & Kegan Paul, 1982.

TIPPETT, Michael, *Moving into Aquarius*, Granada, 1974.

TREVELYAN, Sir George, (ed.), *A World Within a World: X7 Reporting — Transmissions from Russia on the Theory and Practice of Solar Light Radiations*, Neville Spearman/Findhorn, 1981.

KNIGHT, Stephen, *The Brotherhood: The Secret World of the Freemasons*, Granada, 1985.

VERNEY, Stephen, *Into the New Age*, Collins, 1976.

WEBB, James, *The Flight from Reason*, Macdonald, 1971.

———, *The Occult Establishment*, Open Court, 1976.

———, *The Occult Underground*, Open Court, 1974.

WERBECK-SVÄRDSTRÖM, Valborg, *Uncovering the Voice: A Path Towards Catharsis in the Art of Singing*, Rudolf Steiner Press, 1980.

WILMHURST, W.L., *The Meaning of Masonry*, Bell Publishing, 1980.

WILSON, Colin, *Rudolf Steiner: The Man and his Vision*, Aquarian Press, 1985.

WILSON, R.McL., (ed.), *The Gospel of Philip*, Mowbrays, 1962.
YATES, Frances A., *The Rosicrucian Enlightenment*, R.K.P., 1972.

Magic, Spiritism & Divination

CAVENDISH, Richard, *The Magical Arts*, Routledge & Kegan Paul, 1967.
FINDLAY, Arthur, *On the Edge of the Etheric: or Survival After Death Scientifically Explained*, Psychic Press, 1931.
GREAVES, Helen, *Testimony of Light*, Neville Spearman, 1969.
———, *The Challenging Light*, Neville Spearman, 1984.
GREEN, Marian, *Magic for the Aquarian Age: A Contemporary Textbook of Practical Magical Techniques*, Aquarian Press, 1983.
GAUQUELIN, Michel, *The Truth About Astrology*, Hutchinson, 1984.
HAWKEN, Paul, *The Magic of Findhorn*, Fontana, 1975.
HITCHING, Francis, *Earth Magic*, Cassell, 1976.
INCE, R.B., *Three Famous Occultists*, Gilbert Whitehead, 1939.
KILEY, S. & GORDON, R., *Your Name is your Destiny*, Pan, 1984.
LÉVI, Eliphas, *Transcendental Magic: Its Doctrine and Ritual*, Rider, 1968.
LIONEL, Frédéric, *The Magic Tarot: Vehicle of Eternal Wisdom*, RKP, 1980.
MALINOWSKI, Bronislaw, *Magic, Science and Religion*, Doubleday, 1954.
MOREY, Robert A., *Horoscopes and the Christian*, Bethany House, 1981.
PERRY, Michael, *Psychic Studies*, Aquarian Press, 1985.
SELIGMANN, Kurt, *Magic, Supernaturalism and Religion*, Granada, 1975.
STEWART, R.J., *Advanced Magical Arts: Visualisation, Meditation and Ritual in the Western Magical Tradition*, Element Books, 1988.
TAYLOR, Mike, *The Tarot: Your Questions Answered*, Diasozo Trust, 1983.
WATSON, Lyall, *Gifts of Unknown Things*, Sceptre, 1987.
WELDON, J. & LEVITT, Z., *Psychic Healing: An Exposé of an Occult Phenomenon*, Moody Press, 1982.
WILSON, Colin, *Mysteries: Investigation into the Occult, Paranormal and Supernatural*, Hodder & Stoughton, 1978.
———, *The Occult: A Study of the Latent Power that Human Beings Possess to Reach Beyond the Present*, Hodder & Stoughton, 1971.
———, with GRANT. J., (eds.), *The Directory of Possibilities*, Webb & Bower, 1981.

Mind-Sciences: Psychology, Parapsychology, Psychotherapy

ADAMS, Jay E., *The Biblical View of Self-Esteem, Self-Love & Self Image*, Harvest House, 1986.
ALBERTI, R.E., & EMMONS, M.L., *Your Perfect Right: A Guide to Assertive Living*, Impact, 1985.

BAKER, Elsworth F., *Man in the Trap: The Causes of Blocked Sexual Energy*, Collier Macmillan, 1967.

BALINT, Michael, *The Basic Fault: Therapeutic Aspects of Regression*, Routledge & Kegan Paul, 1973.

BANDLER, R. & GRINDER, J., *Frogs into Princes: Neuro-Linguistic Programming*, Real People Press, 1979.

BOADELLA, David, (ed.), *In the Wake of Reich*, Coventure, 1976.

BOBGAN, Martin & Deidre, *How to Counsel from Scripture*, Moody Press, 1985.

———, *Psycho Heresy: The Psychological Seduction of Christianity*, Eastgate, 1987.

———, *The Psychological Way: The Spiritual Way*, Harvest House, 1979.

BROME, Vincent, *Jung: Man and Myth*, Granada, 1978.

BROWN, J.A.C, *Freud and the Post-Freudians*, Penguin, 1964.

COLLIER, Andrew, *R.D. Laing: The Philosophy and Politics of Psychotherapy*, Harvester Press, 1977.

CONSTABLE, Trevor James, *The Cosmic Pulse of Life: The Biological Power Behind UFOs*, Neville Spearman, 1976.

DRYDEN, Windy, (ed.), *Individual Therapy in Britain*, Harper & Row, 1984.

DYCHTWALD, Ken, *Bodymind: A Synthesis of Eastern and Western Ways to Self-Awareness, Health and Personal Growth*, Wildwood House, 1979.

EYSENCK, Hans & Michael, *Mind-Watching*, Multimedia Publications, 1981.

FERGUSON, Marilyn, *The Brain Revolution: Frontiers of Mind Research*, Davis-Poynter, 1974.

GAGE, Barbara, *Channels*, Journal of the North of England Christian Healing Trust, September 1985.

GRIS, Henry, & DICK, William, *The New Soviet Psychic Discoveries: A First-Hand Report*, Souvenir, 1979.

GROF, Stanislaf, *Beyond the Brain: Birth, Death, and Transcendence in Psychotherapy*, University of New York. 1985

———, *The Realms of the Human Unconscious: Observations from LSD Research*, Souvenir Press, 1975.

HUNT, Morton, *The Universe Within: A New Science Explores the Human Mind*, Corgi, 1982.

INGLIS, Brian, *Natural and Supernatural: A History of the Paranormal*, Prism, 1992.

JAMES, Jenny, *Room to Breathe: An Ongoing Life-Therapy*, Coventure, 1975.

JANOV, Arthur, *The Anatomy of Mental Illness: The Scientific Basis of Primal Therapy*, Abacus, 1978.

———, *The Feeling Child*, Abacus, 1977.

———, *The Primal Revolution*, Abacus, 1975.

JAYNES, Julian, *The Origin of Consciousness in the Breakdown of the Bicameral Mind*, Penguin, 1982.

JUNG, C.G., *Aion: Researches into the Phenomenology of Self*, Routledge & Kegan Paul, 1981.

———, *Memories, Dreams and Reflections*, Routledge & Kegan Paul, 1968.

KELEMAN, Stanley, *Your Body Speaks its Mind*, Center Press, 1981.

KILDAHL, John P., *The Psychology of Speaking in Tongues*, Hodder & Stoughton, 1972.

KILPATRICK, William Kirk, *Psychological Seduction: The Failure of Modern Psychology*, Arthur James, 1983.

KOVEL, Joel, *A Complete Guide to Therapy: From Psychoanalysis to Behaviour Modification*, Penguin, 1983.

LAKE, Frank, *Clinical Theology*, Darton, Longman and Todd, 1986.

LEWIS, B.A. & PUCELIK, R.F., *Magic Demystified: A Pragmatic Guide to Communication and Change*, Metamorphous Press, 1982.

LOWEN, Alexander, *Fear of Life*, Collier, 1981.

MOSS, Thelma, *The Body Electric: A Personal Journey into the Mysteries of Parapsychology and Kirlian Photography*, Granada, 1979.

REICH, Wilhelm, *Character Analysis*, Farrar, Straus & Giroux, 1945.

———, *The Function of the Orgasm*, Farrar, Straus & Giroux, 1973.

———, *The Murder of Christ*, Farrar, Straus & Giroux, 1953.

ROAZEN, Paul, *Freud and his Followers*, Penguin, 1979.

ROGERS, Carl, *Encounter Groups*, Penguin, 1975.

ROWAN, John, *Ordinary Ecstasy: Humanistic Psychology in Action*, Routlege & Kegan Paul, 1980.

STEVENS, J.O., *Gestalt is*, Real People Press, 1975.

STRACHEY, James & RICHARDS, Angela, (eds.), *The Pelican Freud Library*, Vol.IV, 'The Interpretation of Dreams'. Penguin, 1976.

———, *The Pelican Freud Library*, Vol.I, 'Introductory Lectures on Psychoanalysis', Penguin, 1975.

TARG, Russell, & HARARY, Keith, *The Mind Race: Understanding and Using Psychic Abilities*, New English Library, 1985.

VITZ, Paul C., *Psychology as Religion: The Cult of Self Worship*, Lion Publishing, 1979.

WILSON, Colin, *Frankenstein's Castle — The Double Brain: Door to Wisdom*, Ashgrove Press, 1980.

———, *The Quest for Wilhelm Reich*, Granada, 1982.

Mysticism, East and West, Yoga, Meditation

ABHISHIKTANANDA, *Prayer*, SPCK, 1967.

ABHISHIKTANANDA, *Hindu-Christian Meeting Point*, ISPCK, 1969.

BALU, Shakuntala, *Living Divinity*, Sawbridge Enterprises, 1981.

BOLEN, Jean, *The Tao of Psychology: Synchronicity and the Self*, Wildwood House, 1980.

CHANG, Jolan, *The Tau of Love and Sex: The Ancient Chinese Way to Ecstasy*, Wildwood House, 1977.

COHEN, J.M., *The Rider Book of Mystical Verse*, Rider, 1983.

DODSON, Peter, *Towards Contemplation*, S.L.G. Press, 1977.

———, *Contemplating the Word: A Practical Handbook*, S.P.C.K., 1987.

DUNN, Jean, *Seeds of Consciousness: The Wisdom of Sri Nisargadatta Maharaj*, Grove Press, 1982.

FERGUSON, John, *An Illustrated Encyclopaedia of Mysticism and the Mystery Religions*, Thames & Hudson, 1976.

FOSTER, Richard, *Celebration of Discipline: The Path to Spiritual Growth*, Hodder and Stoughton, 1980.

FRANCK, Frederick, (trans. & ed.), *The Book of Angelus Silesius*, Vintage-Random, 1976.

FRYDMAN, Maurice, *I Am That: Talks with Sri Nisargadatta Maharaj*, Chetana, Bombay, 1973.

GALANTE, Lawrence, *Tai Chi: The Supreme Ultimate*, Samuel Weiser, 1981.

GRAHAM, Aelred, *Zen Catholicism*, Harcourt, Brace & World Inc., 1963.

GYATSO, Geshe Kelsang, *Meaningful to Behold*, Wisdom Publications, 1980.

HILTON, Walter, *Eight Chapters on Perfection & The Angel's Song*, Sisters of the Love of God, 1983.

HUGHES, S., *Catherine of Genoa: Purgation and Purgatory*, S.P.C.K., 1979.

IGNATIUS LOYOLA, *The Spiritual Exercises*, Burns & Oates, 1900.

ISRAEL, Martin, *Gethsemene*, Collins, 1987.

———, *Summons to Life*, Mowbrays, 1974.

IYENGAR, B.K.S., *The Concise Light on Yoga: Yoga Dipika*, George Allen & Unwin, 1980.

JOHNSTON, William, *The Inner Eye of Love: Mysticism and Religion*, Collins, 1978.

———, *Silent Music: The Science of Meditation*, Collins, 1983.

KANU, Victor, *Sai Baba: God Incarnate*, Sawbridge Enterprises, 1981.

KAVANAUGH, K. & RODRIGUEZ, O. (trans.), *Teresa of Avila: The Interior Castle*, SPCK, 1979.

KELSEY, Morton H., *The Other Side of Silence: A Guide to Christian*

Meditation, SPCK, 1977.

———, *Transcend*, Element Books, 1991.

LAMBA, Bhag Singh, *God Realisation*, Stirling, 1981.

LAU, D.C., (trans.), *Lao Tzu: Tao Te Ching*, Penguin, 1963.

MAHARAJ, Rabindranath R., *Death of a Guru: A Hindu Comes to Christ*, Hodder & Stoughton, 1977.

MATTHEW, Father, *Contemplative Meditation for All: How to do it*, Catholic Truth Society, 1979.

MERTON, Thomas, *Seeds of Contemplation*, Hollis & Carter, 1949.

———, *Contemplation in a World of Action*, Mandala/Unwin, 1980.

MOOKERJEE, Ajit, *Kundalini: The Arousal of the Inner Energy*, Thames & Hudson, 1982.

MÜLLER, F. Max, (ed.), *The Sacred Books of the East*, Oxford University Press, 1900.

PARRINDER, Geoffrey, *Mysticism in the World's Religions*, Sheldon Press, 1976.

PEERS, E. Allison (trans. & ed.), *St. John of the Cross: Ascent of Mount Carmel*, Burns & Oates, 1935.

PRABAVANDA, S. & MANCHESTER, F., (trans. & eds.), *The Upanishads*, Mentor, 1957.

RAMON, Brother, *A Hidden Fire: Exploring the Deeper Reaches of Prayer*, Marshall Pickering, 1985.

ROBBINS, J. & FISHER, D., *Tranquillity Without Pills: All About Transcendental Meditation*, Souvenir. Press, 1973.

RUSSELL, Peter, *The TM Technique: An Introduction to Transcendental Meditation and the Teachings of Maharishi Mahesh Yogi*, Routledge & Kegan Paul, 1977.

SEKIDA, Katsuki, (trans. & ed.), *Mumonkan and Hekiganroku: Two Zen Classics*, Weatherhill, 1977.

STACE, W.T., *Mysticism and Philosophy*, Collins, 1960.

VAN OVER, Raymond, *Total Meditation: Mind Control Techniques for a Small Planet in Space*, Collier Macmillan, 1978.

——— (ed.), *I Ching: The Definitive Rendering of the Ancient Chinese Book of Divination*, Mentor, 1971.

VIVEKANANDA, Nikhilananda, *The Yogas and Other Works*, Ramakrishna-Vivekananda Center, 1953.

WILHELM, Richard (ed.), *I Ching*, Routledge & Kegan Paul, 1970.

WOLTERS, Clifton (trans.), *The Cloud of Unknowing and Other Works*, Penguin, 1961.

———, *Julian of Norwich: Revelations of Divine Love*, Penguin, 1966.

YOGI, Maharishi Mahesh, *On the Bhagavad Gita: A New Translation and Commentary*, Penguin, 1969.

ZIMMERMAN, Benedict, (trans. & ed.), *St. John of the Cross: The Dark Night of the Soul*, James Clarke, 1973.

Science, New Physics

BARROW, John D. & TIPPLER, Frank J., *The Anthropic Cosmological Principle*, OUP, 1988.

CAPRA, Fritjof, *The Tao of Physics*, Flamingo, 1988.

———, *The Turning Point: Science, Society and the Rising Culture*, Fontana, 1982.

DAVIES, Paul, *God and the New Physics*, Penguin, 1983.

———, *Superforce*, George Allen & Unwin, 1986.

HABGOOD, John, *A Working Faith: Essays and Addresses on Science, Medicine and Ethics*, Darton, Longman & Todd, 1980.

HAWKING, Stephen W., *A Brief History of Time*, Bantam, 1988.

HELLEMANS, A. & BUNCH, B., *The Timetables of Science*, Simon & Schuster, 1988.

JACOBS, Michael, *Living Illusions*, SPCK, 1993.

KUHN, Thomas, *The Structure of Scientific Revolutions*, University of Chicago, 1970.

NEWMAN, W., R., (ed.), *What is Science?*, Simon & Schuster, 1955.

SMITH, Wolfgang, *Cosmos and Transcendence: Breaking Through the Barrier of Scientistic Belief*, Open Court. 1984.

TEILHARD DE CHARDIN, Pierre, *Science and Christ*, Collins, 1968.

WATSON, Lyall, *Lifetide*, Hodder & Stoughton, 1979.

Visualisation, New Thought, Possibility Thinking

BRISTOL, C.M. & SHERMAN, H., *TNT — The Power Within You: How to Release the Forces Inside You and Get What You Want*, Thorsons, 1992.

CERULLO, Morris, *A Guide to Total Health and Prosperity: God Wants to Bless You*, World Evangelism Inc., 1978.

CHO, P. YONGGI, *The Fourth Dimension: The Key to Putting your Faith to Work for a Successful Life*, Logos, 1979.

COPELAND, Kenneth, *Walking in the Realm of the Miraculous*, KCP, 1979.

GAWAIN, Shakti, *Creative Visualisation: Use the Power of your Imagination to Create what you want in your Life*, Whatever Publishing, 1978.

HAANEL, Charles F., *The Master Key*, Psychology Publishing, n.d.

JAMPOLSKY, Gerald G., *Teach Only Love: The Seven Principles of Attitudinal Healing*, Bantam Books, 1983.

ROSS, Skip, *Say Yes to your Potential*, Word Books, 1983.

SCOVEL-SHINN, F., *The Game of Life and How to Play it*, Fowler, 1925.

SHONE, Ronald, *Creative Visualisation: How to Use Imagery and Imagination for Self-Improvement*, Thorsons, 1984.

World Government, New World Order

BENTWICH, N. & MARTIN, A., *A Commentary on the Charter of the United Nations*, Routledge & Kegan Paul, 1950.

COOPER, M. William, *Behold a Pale Horse*, Light Technology Pub., 1991.

EPPERSON, A. Ralph , *The New World Order*, Publius Press, 1992.

———, *The Unseen Hand: An Introduction to the Conspiratorial View of History*, Publius Press, 1985.

LEE, Robert W., *The United Nations Conspiracy*, Western Islands Press, 1981.

ROBISON, John, *Proofs of a Conspiracy Against all the Religions and Governments of Europe Carried on in the Secret Meetings of Freemasons, Illuminati and Reading Societies*, 3rd Edition, 1798.

SPENSER, R.K., *The Cult of the All-Seeing Eye*, The Christian Book Club of America, 1964.

WEBSTER, Nesta H., *Secret Societies and Subservsive Movements*, Christian Book Club of America, first published in 1924.

———, *The Socialist Network*, Christian Book Club of America, first published in 1926.

World Religions, Comparative Religion, Shamanism

ALLAN, J., BUTTERWORTH, J., & LANGLEY, M., *A Book of Beliefs: Religions, New Faiths, the Paranormal*, Lion Publishing, 1981.

BECKWITH, Francis, *Baha'i: A Christian Response to Baha'ism, the Religion which Aims Towards One World Government and One Common Faith*, Bethany House, 1985.

BLOFELD, John, *Taoism: The Quest for Immortality*, Mandala/Unwin, 1979.

BOYD, James W., *Satan and Mara: Christian and Buddhist Symbols of Evil*, Lieden, 1975.

CASTANEDA, Carlos, *The Teachings of Don Juan: A Yaqui Way of Knowledge*, Penguin, 1968.

DOORE, Gary (ed.), *Shaman's Path: Healing, Personal Growth and Empowerment*, Shambhala Publications, 1988.

FRAZER, J.G., *The Golden Bough: A Study in Magic and Religion*, Macmillan, 1922.

GYATSO, Geshe Kelksang, *Meaningful to Behold: View, Meditation and Action in Mahayana Buddhism*, Wisdom, 1980.

HALIFAX, Joan, *Shaman: The Wounded Healer*, Thames & Hudson, 1982.
KELSEY, Morton, *Dreamquest*, Element Books, 1992.
———, *Transcend*, Element Books, 1991.
MASCARÓ, Juan, (trans.), *The Dhammapada: The Path of Perfection*, Penguin, 1973.
MULLER, Robert, *Shaping a Global Spirituality*, Doubleday, 1982.
REPS, Paul, *Zen Flesh, Zen Bones*, Penguin, 1957.
PARRINDER, Geoffrey, *Worship in the World's Religions*, Association Press, 1961
SMART, Ninian, *The World's Religions: Old Traditions and Modern Transformations*, Cambridge University Press, 1992.
SOO, Chee, *Taoist Yoga: The Chinese Art of K'ai Men*, Aquarian Press, 1977.
TAYLOR, Rogan P., *The Death and Resurrection Show: From Shaman to Superstar*, Anthony Blond, 1985.
TZU, Lao, *Tao te Ching*, Penguin, 1963.
WATTS, Alan W., *Tao: The Watercourse Way*, Penguin, 1975.
———, *The Way of Zen*, Pelican, 1957.

Miscellaneous

BURCKHARDT, Jacob, *The Age of Constantine the Great*, Routledge & Kegan Paul, 1949.
HUME, Cardinal Basil, *Towards a Civilisation of Love: Being Church in Today's World*, Hodder & Stoughton. 1988.
JONES, Kathleen, (ed.), *Living the Faith: A Call to the Church*, OUP, 1980.
LENNON, John, *Skywriting by Word of Mouth*, Harper & Row, 1986.
POSTMAN, Neil, *Amusing Ourselves to Death*, Methuen, 1987.
VERMES, G., *The Dead Sea Scrolls in English*, Penguin Books, 1975.
WILLEY, Basil, *The Seventeenth Century Background: Studies in the Thought of the Age in Relation to Poetry and Religion*, Ark/Routledge & Kegan Paul, 1986.
YALLOP, David, *In God's Name,* Corgi, 1987.

INDEX OF AUTHORS AND NAMES

Page numbers of occurrences found in the footnotes are italicised

D

E

F

J

K

L

M

N

O

P

Q

R

S

T

V

W

Y

Z

INDEX OF SUBJECTS

Titles of books, journals, magazines, films, plays, talks, foreign words, and page numbers of occurrences found in the footnotes are italicised. Names of organisations appear in inverted commas. See also the expanded table of contents at front of book.

A

B

C

D

E

F

G

H

I

J

K

N

O

P

T

U

X

Y

Z